June 20–21, 2013
Seattle, Washington, USA

**Association for
Computing Machinery**

Advancing Computing as a Science & Profession

LCTES'13

Proceedings of the 2013 ACM SIGPLAN/SIGBED Conference on

Languages, Compilers and Tools
for Embedded Systems

Sponsored by:

ACM SIGPLAN and ACM SIGBED

The Association for Computing Machinery
2 Penn Plaza, Suite 701
New York, New York 10121-0701

Notice to Past Authors of ACM-Published Articles

ISBN: 978-1-4503-2085-6

Additional copies may be ordered prepaid from:

ACM Order Department
PO Box 30777
New York, NY 10087-0777, USA

Phone: 1-800-342-6626 (USA and Canada)
+1-212-626-0500 (Global)
Fax: +1-212-944-1318
E-mail: acmhelp@acm.org
Hours of Operation: 8:30 am – 4:30 pm ET

ACM Order Number: 533130

Printed in the USA

Foreword

Welcome to the 14th ACM SIGPLAN/SIGBED Conference on Languages, Compilers, Tools and Theory for Embedded Systems – LCTES'13. This year's symposium continues its tradition of being the premier forum for presentation of research results on leading-edge issues in embedded systems.

The call for papers attracted 60 submissions from Asia-Pacific, Europe, North and South America. Each submission was reviewed by at least four Program Committee members. An online Program Committee meeting was held over a week (25 – 31 March) using the START Conference Manager Infrastructure. During the meeting, all Program Committee members could read, review and discuss all papers with which they had no conflicts of interest. The Program Committee considered all submissions carefully, taking into account the reviewers' assessments and external reviews solicited when necessary, and accepted 16 papers for presentation and publication at LCTES'13. The accepted papers cover a variety of topics, including safety and reliability, code optimization, performance prediction and testing, new storage technologies, programming language implementation, scheduling and design space exploration.

We are honored to have two keynote talks. The first one is given by Dr Youfeng Wu of Intel on *HW/SW Co-designed Acceleration of Dynamic Languages*. The second one is given by Dr Marcel Beemster of ACE on *The Role of C in the Dark Ages of Multi-Core*.

We would like to express our sincere gratitude to the members of the Program Committee and external reviewers, who contributed their expertise and time from their busy schedules to ensure the quality of the reviewing and shepherding processes. We would like to thank the Chair of the LCTES Steering Committee - Bruce Childers - for his excellent advice and support. We would also like to thank all other members of the organizing committee, Jeremy Singer (publicity chair) and Yulei Sui (web chair), for keeping the conference running smoothly. The help of Rich Gerber in customizing the START reviewing software to fit the specific needs of our online Program Committee meeting is greatly appreciated. Last, but not least, we would like to thank all the authors who submitted papers to LCTES'13 and the conference participants.

We hope you enjoy the conference!

Björn Franke
LCTES'13 General Chair
University of Edinburgh, UK

Jingling Xue
LCTES'13 Program Chair
UNSW, Australia

Table of Contents

Session 1: Keynote Talk 1

Session 2: Safety and Reliability
Session Chair: Marcel Beemster *(ACE Associated Compiler Experts bv)*

Session 3: Optimization
Session Chair: Youfeng Wu *(Intel)*

Session 4: Performance Prediction and Testing
Session Chair: Bruce Childers *(University of Pittsburgh)*

Session 5: Keynote Talk 2

Session 6: New Storage Technologies
Session Chair: Björn Franke *(University of Edinburgh)*

Session 7: Scheduling and Design Space Exploration
Session Chair: Zili Shao *(The Hong Kong Polytechnic University)*

Session 8: Programming Language and Implementation
Session Chair: Jingling Xue *(University of New South Wales)*

LCTES 2013 Conference Organization

General Chairs: Björn Franke *(University of Edinburgh, UK)*

Program Chair: Jingling Xue *(University of New South Wales, Australia)*

Publicity Chair: Jeremy Singer *(University of Glasgow, UK)*

Web Chair: Yulei Sui *(University of New South Wales, Australia)*

Steering Committee Chair: Bruce Childers *(University of Pittsburgh, USA)*

Steering Committee: Heiko Falk *(Ulm University, Germany)*
Krisztián Flautner *(ARM Limited, UK)*
Mahmut Kandemir *(Penn State University, USA)*
Christoph Kirsch *(University of Salzburg, Austria)*
Jaejin Lee *(Seoul National University, Korea)*
John Regehr *(University of Utah, USA)*
Reinhard Wilhelm *(Saarland University, Germany)*
Wang Yi *(Uppsala University, Sweden)*

Program Committee: Philip Brisk *(University of California, Riverside, USA)*
John Cavazos *(University of Delaware, USA)*
Wenguan Chen *(Tsinghua University, China)*
Albert Cohen *(INRIA, France)*
Heiko Falk *(Ulm University, Germany)*
Sebastian Fischmeister *(University of Waterloo, Canada)*
Rajiv Gupta *(University of California, Riverside, USA)*
Sebastian Hack *(Saarland University, Germany)*
Mahmut Kandemir *(Penn State University, USA)*
Jörg Henkel *(Karlsruhe University, Germany)*
Andreas Krall *(Vienna University of Technology, Austria)*
Jaejin Lee *(Seoul National University, Korea)*
Lian Li *(Oracle Labs, Australia)*
Scott Mahlke *(University of Michigan, USA)*
Florence Maraninchi *(Grenoble INP / VERIMAG, France)*
Tulika Mitra *(National University of Singapore, Singapore)*
Frank Mueller *(North Carolina University, USA)*
Sanjay Rajopadhye *(Colorado State University, USA)*
Aviral Shrivastava *(Arizona State University, USA)*
Zili Shao *(Hongkong Polytechnic University, HongKong)*
Weng-Fai Wong *(National University of Singapore, Singapore)*
Youtao Zhang *(University of Pittsburgh, USA)*
Yi Wang *(Uppsala University, Sweden)*

Additional reviewers:
Pansy Arafa
Akramul Azim
Ke Bai
Gergö Barany

Lars Bauer
Jian Cai
Gonzalo Carjaval
Gaurav Chadha

Additional reviewers *(continued)*:

Sudipta Chattopadhyay	Jeffrey McDaniel
Sandeep Chaudhary	Ramy Medhat
Jian-Jia Chen	Yehdhih Moctar
Liang Chen	Laurent Mounier
Renhai Chen	Matthieu Moy
Hyoun Kyu Cho	Thannirmalai Somu Muthukaruppan
Brian Crites	Guan Nan
Alexander Dean	Samaneh Navabpour
Huping Ding	Augusto Oliveira
Wei Ding	Kenneth O'Neal
James Elliott	Zhong Liang Ong
David Fiala	Shruti Padmanabha
Jonas Flodin	Shrinivas Panchamukhi
Giovani Gracioli	Jason Park
Scott Grauer-Gray	Jungho Park
Daniel Grissom	Shri Hari Rajendran Radhika
Artjom Grudnitsky	Tushar Rawat
Clemens Hammacher	Jan Reineke
Bryce Holton	Arahs Rezaei
Min Hung	Abhishek Rhisheekesan
Janmartin Jahn	Pooja Roy
Reiley Jeyapaul	Dipal Saluja
Alexander Jordan	Mehrzad Samadi
Sandeep Kandula	Benjamin Sanders
Ralf Karrenberg	Dietmar Schreiner
Hany Kashi	Sangmin Seo
Daya Khudia	Ankit Sethia
William Killian	Muhammad Shafique
Hongjune Kim	Martin Stigge
Junghyun Kim	Kevin Streit
Jungwon Kim	Pavele Subotic
Yooseong Kim	Aditya Tammewar
Sai Charan Koduru	Wen-Jun Tan
Pavel Krcal	Wai Teng Tang
Sameer Kulkarni	Joseph Tarango
Deepak Kumar	Tristan Vanderbruggen
Kai Lampka	Wei Wang
Janghaeng Lee	Yi Wang
Jun Lee	Bryan Ward
Roland Leißa	Yiwen Wong
Changhui Li	Lifan Xu
Jonatan Liden	Jun Yang
Jun Liu	Aleksandar Zeljic
Jing Lu	Yulin Zhang
Andrew Lukefahr	Christopher Zimmer

LCTES 2013 Sponsors

Sponsors:  **SIGPLAN**

SIGBED

HW/SW Co-designed Acceleration of Dynamic Languages

Youfeng Wu

Intel Labs
Programming Systems Lab
youfeng.wu@intel.com

Abstract

Dynamic Programming Languages, such as Java, JavaScr ipt, PHP, Perl, Python, Ruby, etc., are dominating languages for programming the web. HW/SW co-designed virtual machine can significantly accelerate their executions by transparently leveraging internal HW features via an internal compiler. We also argue for a com mon API to interfa ce dynamic languages with th e HW/SW co-designed vir tual machine, so that a si ngle internal compiler can accelerate all major dynamic languages.

Categories and Subject Descriptors   D.3.4 [**Processors**]: Compilers, Optimization, Run-time Environments

General Terms   Languages, Measurement, Performance.

Keywords   Dynamic languages;   Just-in-time Compilation; HW/SW Co-designed Virtual Machine; Acceleration

1.   Introduction

Dynamic Languages are designed for productivity, portability, and secure web programming. Many of their featur es, such as dynamic type checks, bound/null checks, just-in-time compilation (JIT), etc., hinder their execution efficiency. Accelerating dynamic languages not only improves performance and power efficiency, but also significantly enhances the end-user experience.

A JIT compiler needs two kinds of information to generate efficient code for programs written in d ynamic languages. First, high level lang uage information, such as type, aliasing, control flows, is necessar y for compiler to perform agg ressive optimizations. Second , detailed micro architectural information would allow compiler to generate the most efficient code.

Computer architectures (e.g . x86) are evolvin g slowly although microarchitectures ar e changing dramatically in every generation. Existing JIT compiler has access to high level language information but has to g enerate code using architectural Instruction Set Architecture (ISA), without much knowledge o f microarchitectural features.

Hardware/Software (HW/SW) co-designed virtual machines [2] allow micr oarchitecture innovations while preserving ISA backward compatibility. An int ernal compiler can m orph programs written in legac y ISA to an interna l ISA and full y take advantage of the microarchitectural innovations. Many of the microarchitecture-level features can benefit dynamic languages.

The internal compiler in the H W/SW co-designed virtual machines can also access high level information in programs written in dynamic languages. One wa y to achieve this is to pass the information through a virtual device driver to the internal compiler. Our experience with Dalvik b ytecode [1] shows that the inter-nal compiler equipped with both high level lan guage information and microarchitecture knowledge can speed up dynamic language programs significantly.

We argue for a common app lication programming interface (API) for all major d ynamic languages. The common API should carry high level langu age information, through which a single internal compiler can accelerate all major dynamic language programs expressed in the API   by leveraging both high level language knowledge and internal HW features. This framewor k can achieve low-cost, transparent, and power-efficient acceleration of dynamic languages.

2.   Example: Acceleration of Java on Andriod

We identified a few ke y HW features to acc elerate dynamic languages, such as:

1) Branch linkage to reduce indirect branch overhead
2) Conditional rollback for runtime specialization
3) Native method invocation and return, and
4) Large number of internal registers, etc.

These features are not supporte d in the ar chitectural ISA of popular processors, such as X8 6, and would require signif icant effort to extend any architectural ISA to support them.

However, these features can be easily implemented at microchitecture level. For example, they are supported in Transmeta Efficeon systems without exposing them to the X86 ISA.

For accelerating Java programs on Andriod s ystems [3], we can leverage the virtual device driver techniqu e in [1] to pass Dalvik bytecode to the internal compiler inside the co-designed processor without requiring any ISA extensions. Th e internal compiler directly generates efficient Efficeon code for th e bytecode. F igure 1 s hows that the acceleration technique can reduce execution time of the Caffein eMark by 44% and energ y consumption by 40% when running it in Android Dalv ik virtual machine on an Efficeon system.

3.   Acceleration Opportunities

As illustrated by the example, HW/SW co-designed vir tual machines can easily add new ha rdware features or remove obso-lete ones transparently according to m arket requirements and the latest technology development. The interna l compiler may also evolve, and when new optimizations are develop ed, they can be deployed quickly by updating the virtual device driver to b enefit

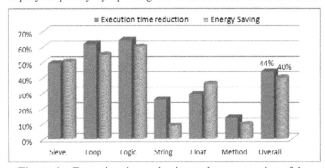

Figure 1.   Execution time reduction and energy saving of the CaffeineMark on an Efficeon Machine.

LCTES'13, June 20–21, 2013, Seattle, Washington, USA.
ACM 978-1-4503-2085-6/13/06.

all dynamic languages. We e nvision that, beside the example usage, many more opportunities for HW/SW co-designed accelerations can b e explored, such as parallelization, vectorization, specialized accelerators, and so on.

3.1 Parallelization

Native support for threading at the HW level can significan tly reduce the overheads involved, as demonstrated b y the lightweight hardware threading on today's GPUs. Unfortunately, using the latter requires significant changes to the SW, hindering adoption or leaving valuable hardware resources unused.

Dynamic languages in combination with high level concurrency abstractions, like Para llel JavaScript [5], offer rich run time information, from properties of data (e.g. array sizes) to semantic of operations (e.g. primitives like map or reduce). A JIT may pass this information to the in ternal compiler, which may choose the best implementation of the parallel primitives or accelerators.

Alternatively, the internal compiler can perform parallelization that has been s hown promising for X86 binary programs with special HW support [6]. Parallelizing bytecode by the intern al compiler should be easier than parallelizing X86 binary programs, as there is high level program information available in bytecode.

3.2 Vectorization

Processor architectures have b een experiencing continuous improvement in SIMD supports (e.g. MMX, SSE, and AVX o n X86 processors). Every new SIMD extension requires significant enabling efforts in SW a nd also presents performance scalability issues for existing programs.

With HW/SW co-designed acceleration, the bytecode can express vectorization opportunities in terms of variable length vector operations, and the internal compiler can tailor the programs to the latest SIMD support in microarchitecture at runtime.

3.3 Special Accelerators

Special accelerators in AS IC and FPGA have been us ed successfully to im prove the p erformance and en ergy efficiency of modern workloads [4]. Th e programmer or t he compiler can identify units of code tha t benefit from special acceleration, and annotate the desire patterns in b ytecode. The internal compiler can map the pa tterns to int ernal accelerators (if available). Th e internal compiler may also discover special acceleration patterns by itself.

4. A Case for a Common API

Similar to the Universal Computer Oriented Language (UN-COL) proposal for a universal in termediate language for compilers [8], we argue for a common acceleration API between dynamic languages and the int ernal ISA on HW /SW co-designed systems. The JIT compiler only needs to generate code using th e common acceleration API and passes the API code to the int ernal compiler via th e virtual dev ice driver. The i nternal compiler translates the AP I to internal IS A to accel erate the exe cution of programs written in d ynamic languages. A single int ernal compiler also allows intimate co-design of the compiler optimizations and the in ternal innovative hardware features. The acceleration API should be able to carry enough high level information so that the underlying hardware features can be fully utilized. Figure 2 shows the general acceleration framework with the common API.

5. Related Work

HW support for Java has been mostly focused in the ISA level, such as Jazelle Direct Bytecode eXecution (DBX) and Runt ime

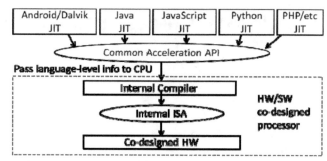

Figure 2. Common API for Dynamic Language Acceleration.

Compiler Target (RCT) [7]. S ince language and optimization techniques change over time, th e ISA level support is not eas y to be standardized and deployed in general purpose processors.

GreenDroid [4] provides specialized pro cessors targeting k ey portions of Goo gle's Android s martphone platforms. It redu ces energy consumption significantly. These specialized accelerators could be easily deployed by the internal compiler in HW/SW co-designed systems.

There have been early attempts to have com mon API for dy namic languages. D ynamic Language Runtime (DLR) [9] , an environment from Microsoft, b rings support f or dynamic languages to the .NET Framework and can support P ython, Ruby, Jscript, and others. Da Vinci Mach ine is an extension of the Java Virtual Machine to add support for d ynamically typed languages (e.g. JRuby). None of th ese APIs targets H W/SW co-designed acceleration and won't be able t o take full adv antage of microarchitecture innovations.

There are many potable IRs, such as Java bytecode, Dalvik bytecode, LLVM/SPIR, and others . An y of th em would benefit from acceleration on a HW/SW co-designed virtual machine by extending the internal compiler to optimize for it (as we did wi th Dalvik bytecode). It would be in teresting to extend some of them to be the common acceleration API for dynamic languages.

Acknowledgments

I would like to thank our colleagues at Programming Systems Lab for contributions to the dynamic language acceleration research.

References

[1] C. Wang, Y. Wu, M. Cintra, "AccelDroid: Co-designed Acceleration of Android Bytecode", CGO-2013

[2] J. E. Smith, R. Nair, "Virtual Machines: Versatile Platforms For Systems And Processes", Morgan Kaufmann, May 2005

[3] E. Burnette, "Hello, Android: Introducing Google's Mobile Development Platform", Pragmatic Bookshelf, Aug. 2010.

[4] N. Goulding, et. al, "The GreenDroid Mobile Application Processor: An Architecture for Silicon's Dark Future", IEEE Micro, Mar - Apr, 2011

[5] S. Herhut, et al, "Parallel Programming for the Web", Hotpar'12

[6] C. Wang, et al, "Dynamic parallelization of single-threaded binary programs using speculative slicing". ICS 2009.

[7] Microprocessor Report, "ARM Strengthens Java Compilers", Jul 11, 2005

[8] M. E. Conway, "Proposal for an UNCOL", Communications of the ACM 1:3:5 (1958)

[9] B. Chiles, "CLR Inside Out: IronPython and the Dynamic Language Runtime". MSDN Magazine. October 2007

Low Cost Control Flow Protection Using Abstract Control Signatures

Daya Shanker Khudia and Scott Mahlke

Advanced Computer Architecture Laboratory
The University of Michigan
{dskhudia, mahlke}@umich.edu

Abstract

The continual trend of shrinking feature sizes and reducing voltage levels makes transistors faster and more efficient. However, it also makes them more susceptible to transient hardware faults. Transient faults due to high energy particle strikes or circuit crosstalk can corrupt the output of a program or cause it to crash. Previous studies have reported that as much as 70% of the transient faults disturb program control flow, making it critical to protect control flow. Traditional approaches employ signatures to check that every control flow transfer in a program is valid. While having high fault coverage, large performance overheads are introduced by such detailed checking. We propose a coarse-grain control flow checking method to detect transient faults in a cost effective way. Our software-only approach is centered on the principle of abstraction: control flow that exhibits simple run-time properties (e.g., proper path length) is almost always completely correct. Our solution targets off-the-shelf commodity embedded systems to provide a low cost protection against transient faults. The proposed technique achieves its efficiency by simplifying signature calculations in each basic block and by performing checking at a coarse-grain level. The coarse-grain signature comparison points are obtained by the use of a region based analysis. In addition, we propose a technique to protect control flow transfers via call and return instructions to ensure all control flow is covered by our technique. Overall, our proposed technique has an average of 11% performance overhead in comparison to 75% performance overhead of previously proposed signature based techniques while maintaining approximately the same degree of fault coverage.

Categories and Subject Descriptors B.8.1 [*Performance and Reliability*]: Reliability, Testing, and Fault Tolerance

General Terms Experimentation; Reliability

Keywords Soft Errors; Control Flow Checking; Fault Injection

1. Introduction

In the quest to make chips faster, cheaper and energy efficient, transistors are being scaled down in size. As silicon technology is moving deeper down into the nanometer regime, reliability of microprocessors is emerging as a critical concern for manufacturers. Factors such as increasingly smaller devices, reduced voltage levels, and increasing operating temperatures exacerbate the problem of reliability of these components. Furthermore, billions of transistors are packed into modern microprocessors, and a fault in even a single transistor has the ability to corrupt the output of the application or crash the entire system.

In this work, we focus on the reliability concerns caused by soft errors. **Soft errors**, also referred to as Single Event Upsets (SEUs) or **transient faults**, are caused by high energy particle strikes from space or circuit crosstalk in an electronic circuit. A high energy particle such as a neutron from cosmic rays or an alpha particle from packaging material impurities releases charge in the circuit that in turn can disturb the functionality or the charge stored at a semiconductor device. As the name suggests, transients faults do not cause permanent damage to the chip and devices work correctly once the effect of the fault is over.

The semiconductor industry has reported many instances of the problems caused by soft errors over the last few decades. In 1978, one of the first soft error instances occurred when the packaging material used in the chip produced by Intel became contaminated with uranium from a nearby mine [23]. In another instance of soft errors, Cypress semiconductor reported that a single soft error caused a billion-dollar automotive industry to halt every month [40]. In 2005, HP also reported [27] that cosmic rays were the cause of frequent crashes of its 2048-CPU system installed at the Los Alamos National Laboratory. These studies illustrate the issues caused by soft errors and necessitate the need for reliability solutions at all levels (e.g., circuit, architecture or application level) of the system stack.

Traditionally, memory cells have been more vulnerable to transient faults and are usually protected by mechanisms such as parity checks or Error Correcting Codes (ECC). The use of smaller transistors to implement logic circuits in microprocessors increases susceptibility of logic circuits to transient faults. Shivakumar et al. [35] reported that Soft Error Rate (SER) for the logic on chip is steadily rising with technology scaling while SER for memory is expected to remain stable. SER is the rate at which a component encounters soft errors. Also, SER scales with number of transistors and level of integration [12]. Without actively addressing these issues, SER is expected to rise significantly in new products. Moreover, Venkatasubramanian et al. [37] reported that more than 70% of the transient faults lead to disturbance in control flow and are the cause of control flow errors. Control flow errors are defined as the incorrect change in the sequence of instructions executed by processors under the influence of external events such as soft errors.

Traditional solutions in server space for reliability have provided fault tolerance via DMR (dual-modular redundancy) and TMR (triple-modular redundancy). IBM Z-Series [5] servers and HP NonStop [6] systems are two pioneers of such schemes. These solutions incur a large energy and/or performance overhead and are not directly applicable in the embedded design space. Signature based solutions [29] employ signature updates in every basic block and check that all control flow transfers lead to a correct target address. This checking results in high instruction overheads due to the combination of computing, updating, and checking the unique control signatures of each potential control flow edge. Typical performance overheads of prior work are on the order of 75% (Section 2.3 describes such techniques in detail).

In this work, we propose Abstract Control Signatures (ACS) to provide a practical low cost solution for Commercial Off-the-Shelf (COTS) embedded microprocessors to protect against control flow target (i.e., the branch destination address) errors. These errors are usually not covered by redundancy-based data protection techniques [10, 15], yet they lead to a disproportionately high number of incorrect executions. ACS is a software-only solution and does not require any modifications in the hardware. Our solution

LCTES 2013, June 20–21, 2013, Seattle, Washington, USA.
Copyright © 2013 ACM 978-1-4503-2085-6/13/06... $10.00

is based on the principle of abstraction and the insight that control flow that exhibits simple but repeated properties of correctness is almost always entirely correct. ACS achieves abstraction by checking simpler properties (e.g., path length) and promoting control flow signature checking from individual basic blocks to group of blocks.

ACS is targeted for COTS commodity systems. In the commodity embedded market, achieving performance targets in a cost-effective manner is of paramount importance. Due to the associated cost of providing high reliability, commodity systems typically cannot target 100% protection against faults. Our solution is designed considering these requirements of embedded market space. The proposed solution provides opportunistic fault coverage but does not guarantee 100% fault coverage and hence is not applicable to mission critical systems. The contributions of this work are as follows:

- A novel abstraction based technique to insert simplified signatures. Under the proposed scheme, more complex signatures can be used to explore trade-offs in performance overhead and fault coverage.

- A novel region based method to insert checking at a coarse granularity abstracting away the details of fine-grain control flow.

- A global signature based method for protecting control flow transfers through *call* and *return* instructions.

- Microarchitectural fault injection experiments to validate ACS.

2. Background and Motivation

In this section, we present background details that are necessary to understand ACS and discuss the motivation behind the approach.

2.1 Fault Detection

In order to protect against transient faults, detection of these faults is a necessary first step. Fault detection can be achieved by introducing some form of redundancy. For example, time redundancy involves executing the same instructions twice on the same hardware, space redundancy involves executing the same instructions on duplicate hardware and information redundancy involves usage of parity, ECC etc. High reliability systems typically use a mixture of fault detection techniques such as DMR/TMR and/or ECC for protection against soft errors. These solutions are too expensive in terms of energy/performance/area overheads (~100%) to be used in the embedded market. A relatively inexpensive class of solutions for commercial market use time redundancy based software-only techniques. *Data flow* and *control flow* checking are usually employed in software-based techniques [8, 10, 29, 30, 37] against soft errors. Data flow checking ensures that computation (e.g., addition) is correct. Software-based data flow checking techniques work by replicating instructions. Control flow protection techniques usually employ signatures to ensure correct control flow [29, 37]. A brief

Table 1: Brief comparison of ACS with other techniques.

	Data flow	Control flow	
		Branch	calls/rets
High overhead	DMR, TMR SWIFT [29] EDDI [30]	DMR, TMR SWIFT EDDI ALLBB [8] ACFC [37]	DMR, TMR ALLBB (ret only)
Low overhead	Shoestring [10] ProfileBased [15] ACS+ProfileBased	ACS	ACS

comparison of related technique to ACS is shown in Table 1. The techniques are classified based on their relative performance overhead and whether they handle data flow errors, control flow errors or both. Control flow protection techniques are further classified into two categories based on whether they protect branches and call/ret

instructions. The techniques are also classified based on their relative performance overheads. Techniques having overhead ~70% or more are in high overhead row and those with ~40% or less in low overhead row. Typically low overhead techniques reduce overhead by sacrificing on fault coverage. A more detailed description of related work is presented in Section 6.

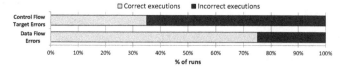

Figure 1: Control flow target errors are ~2.5x as likely to cause incorrect executions.

Figure 1 shows the number of incorrect executions resulting from errors in register files (corrupting the data) and branch targets for SPECINT2000 benchmarks. A high masking rate (~75%) for data errors is consistent with the reported masking data in previous works [10, 39]. On average, errors in the branch targets are ~2.5x more likely to result in incorrect executions. Hence, in this paper, we focus on efficient detection of control flow errors, in branches as well as call/ret instructions, and our technique can be combined with previously proposed [10, 15, 29] code duplication based solutions for a complete solution (see Section 5.3 for a combined solution).

2.2 Control Flow Errors

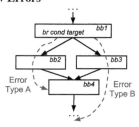

Figure 2: Control Flow Target Errors: Corruption of branch target can result in nearby (Type A) or far away (Type B) displacement of control flow.

To better understand control flow protection techniques, we need to comprehend the various cause of control flow errors. A control flow error can occur in a non-control flow (e.g., *add*) or in a control flow (e.g., *branch*) instruction. A non-control flow instruction of the application can be converted into a control flow instruction by a soft error thus erroneously affecting control transfers. Errors occurring in control flow instructions can be divided into two categories: Firstly, **control flow condition errors** are caused by the errors in the direction of a conditional branch. Secondly, **control flow target errors** are caused by the errors in the destination of a branch. Branch conditions are usually protected by data flow protection schemes by duplicating the computation leading to a condition. As shown later in Figure 10 (Section 4.3), the errors in branch targets result in disproportionately high number of incorrect executions. Hence, we focus on the control flow disturbances caused by the errors in branch targets. From here onwards, unless otherwise specified, the use of control flow errors with respect to ACS refers to the errors in branch targets. Figure 2 shows a part of a Control Flow Graph (CFG) containing 4 Basic Blocks (BBs). Two types of errors that affect branch target are also shown in the Figure. Type A errors cause the erroneous jump to nearby locations and Type B errors direct the control flow to far away locations. Type A errors cause the program to skip a few instructions and are more likely to result in masking or program output corruptions. In contrast, Type B errors are more likely to crash the program either by directing the control flow to out of program scope or to a different function in the same program. In Section 3, we describe how our proposed method handles these control flow errors.

2.3 Signature Based Techniques and Associated Overheads

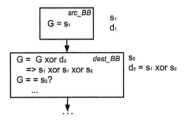

Figure 3: Basic signature scheme: If the correct control flow transfer takes place, G at $dest\_BB$ would be equal to s_2 otherwise not.

Many of the previously proposed software-only techniques for control flow protection embed signatures or assertions into BBs at compile time [3, 13, 29]. This section briefly describes the fundamentals of these signature based techniques, especially CFCSS [29]. CFCSS assigns a unique signature S_i to each BB in the program. A general purpose register (G) is used to hold the signature of the currently executing BB. G is initialized to the signature of first BB when a program starts. Subsequently, whenever a transition is made from src_BB to $dest\_BBs$ the value of G is updated with the newly computed value. This new value is calculated by taking the xor of G and the static signature difference (xor) of src_BB and $dest\_BB$. After this, G should be equal to the unique signature assigned to $dest\_BB$. A comparison of G with unique value of $dest\_BB$ is inserted in $dest\_BB$ to make sure that control flow is correct. If this comparison fails, an incorrect control flow transfer has taken place. A simple case of this scheme is shown in Figure 3. For a complex case of branch-fan-in nodes, extra dynamic adjusting signatures must be inserted to avoid aliasing [29]. This necessitates the need for multiple signature updates in branch-fan-in nodes and dynamic signature computation in predecessors BBs of the branch-fan-in nodes. These extra updates contribute to the overhead of such a scheme.

Essentially, every BB in the application contains signature computation or update instructions as well as comparison instructions for ensuring correct control flow. The cost of embedded signature checking at runtime in every BB can be prohibitive, making these techniques impractical. We have implemented CFCSS and in our experiments on small benchmarks (the same ones used in CFCSS [29]) we observe, on average, a performance overhead of 68%. Though, for *Insertsort* benchmark from the set of benchmarks, it is as high as 222%. For real representative benchmarks from SPECINT2000, we observe up to a 144% overhead (75% on average) for the CFCSS technique. The opportunity to reduce this huge overhead is one of the motivations behind proposing ACS.

3. Abstract Control Signatures

Fundamentally, there are two critical aspects of any signature based control flow protection scheme. The first is signature computations (or updates) in each BB and the second is signature comparisons (or checking) to check for erroneous control flow. These two computations are the main contributors to the performance overhead of signature-based control flow checking schemes. To reduce performance overhead, we propose raising the level of abstraction of signature checking and simplifying signature updates in every BB. The abstraction level is raised by working at the levels of **regions***. The whole program is divided into regions that are larger than just a BB. These regions are more than just a collection of BBs and ideally should possess certain properties that help in minimizing the number of signature comparisons and signature updates. Each region has a signature variable associated with it. For example, one

---

*In this paper, **region** is used to refer to a single entry multiple exit code section that satisfies the following property among others: loop back edges are only allowed to the entry node (see Section 3.1).

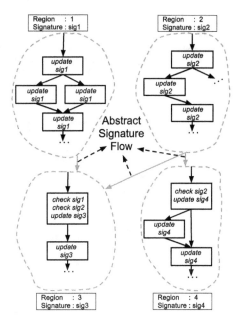

Figure 4: Abstract signatures: The whole program is divided into regions at a higher abstraction level. Such regions are enclosed by dashed light blue (grey) lines in this Figure. Every region is assigned a signature. Every abstract region updates its signature based on the control transfers among the BBs inside it. These signatures are only checked in other abstract regions.

desirable property of regions is to have a single entry point so that the associated signature variable need not be initialized at every entry point. As shown later (Section 3.2), this reduces the number of required signature comparisons. The signature variable associated with a region is checked in other regions that are the target of the control flow edges from the region under consideration. Essentially, signature information flows between these abstract regions. The signature associated with each region represents the correctness of control flow internal to that region. In this sense, checking control flow outside regions abstracts away the details about control flow inside a region, hence the name ACS (Abstract Control Signatures). A high level diagram for ACS concept is shown in Figure 4. In Figure 4 the signature *sig1* is associated with region 1 and is updated inside the BBs of region 1. Assuming a BB in region 1 has a control flow edge to a BB in region 3, *sig1* would only be checked in that BB in region 3.

3.1 Design of ACS

The idea of ACS is very generic and can be realized in various ways. ACS can be implemented by forming regions at various granularity levels and different signature updates according to the required trade-offs in performance overhead and fault coverage. The signature update inside each BB can also be tuned. For example, the signature update inside each BB can be as simple as having a parity bit set/reset and the corresponding check would be to check against 0 if even number of blocks were traversed and against 1 if odd number of blocks were traversed. These updates can be more complex such as usage of hash functions or *xors*. Similarly, the region formation can also be customized. For example, if the region is a single BB then this scheme is the same as regular signature checking in each BB.

For ACS implemented as a part of this work, we have made following choices for signature updates and regions. We use a simple counter variable as the signature. For signature updates, we increment the signature by 1 in the beginning of every BB. The intuition behind using increment by 1 is as follows: Consider 2 points in a

5

program, X is a region entry and Y is the corresponding region exit. If control reaches X, we expect it to reach Y. If in going from X to Y, a valid number of BBs are traversed and the first instruction in each of those BBs is executed, we hypothesize that control flow is likely correct. Obviously, this is not always true, but our experiments have confirmed that small disruptions (fault in the lower bits of the branch target) in the control flow will result in changes to the path length due to positioning of counter updates at the beginning of BBs and large disruptions (fault in upper bits) will result in Y never being reached. Thus, if the hypothesis is statistically true, individual control transitions need not be checked with minimal loss in fault coverage. This allows only the higher level information to need checking. To see the usefulness of such counters, let us consider the control flow errors shown in Figure 2. On one hand, Type B errors (far away erroneous jumps) that would transfer control from one region to another, are easily caught. On the other hand, Type A errors (nearby erroneous jumps) are likely to skip the signature updates, so they are also caught. We use intervals [2] as regions because of the desirable properties they possess.

Intervals: An interval is a set of BBs such that every BB except the header BB in the interval has its predecessors in the interval. An interval satisfies the following, and many other, properties.

1. The header block of an interval dominates all the BBs in that interval. Basically, this implies that control can only enter at the header node of an interval.

2. If a loop is part of an interval then the loop header and interval header are the same. The header BB of a loop is the target BB of back edges in that loop.

Figure 5 shows an example of intervals for a CFG that has nested loops. Interval 1 contains only *bb1* and its header is also *bb1*. Interval 2 contains all the remaining blocks shown in the Figure. Interval 2 contains a loop and note that loop header *bb2* is also the header node of the interval 2. Another interesting observation is that the outer loop is never contained in a single interval. We use intervals formed according to the maximal interval definition [26]. A **latch BB** of a loop is defined as the block that has a branch to the header of the loop. For example, *bb_latch1* is the latch block for the inner loop starting at *bb2*.

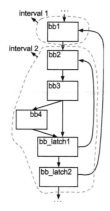

Figure 5: Intervals in the Figure are shown by enclosed dashed light blue (gray) lines. This Figure shows two intervals for a control flow graph that has a nested loop.

A basic overview of the implemented scheme is shown in Figure 6. The counter C_1 (signature for the shown region) is incremented by 1 in each BB, and in the successor BB of *bb4*, a check would be inserted to make sure that the value of C_1 is 3. In the presence of a control flow error, assume that the transition happens such that after *bb1*, either signature updates of *bb2* or *bb3* is skipped or *bb4* is executed. The signature value would not be 3 in the successor BB of *bb4* and this would be detected. We put the increment as the first instruction in the BBs so that the signature won't get updated in case of small erroneous jumps. Thus, very small changes to

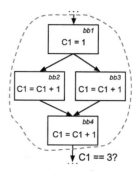

Figure 6: Every interval is associated with a signature. In our scheme, signature are simple counters. The signature is initialized in the header and incremented by 1 in other blocks. The signature checks are made in the BBs that are destination BBs of exits out of an interval.

the branch target are caught because of this positioning of signature updates.

However, if we naively insert the increments in each BB of the program, the counter value at the exit points of the interval will depend on 1) the path taken during runtime 2) the particular exit taken. For example, consider the CFG shown in Figure 7. If at runtime, edge *bb1* → *bb2* is traversed, the signature value at the exit out of *bb3* would be 3 since each BB increments signature by 1. However, if the edge *bb1* → *bb3* is traversed signature value at the same point would be 2. Another similar problem exists if there are multiple exit points from an interval. The signature values at the exit points of an interval would be different if the exits originate from different BBs. Different signature values from an interval exit would imply that checks would need to be inserted with different values. To solve this problem, we make sure that from every exit out of an interval, the same signature value needs to be checked no matter which exit is taken. To tackle the aforementioned problems, we have developed a method to calculate extra balancing increments required along edges. The details of this method are described in the next subsection.

3.2 Calculating Balancing Increments

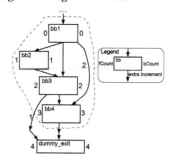

Figure 7: The extra increments required to be inserted along control flow edges is shown. This balances out signature values at the exits out of an interval.

The goal is to calculate the extra balancing increment required to be inserted along the imbalanced edges in the CFG. Figure 7 shows an imbalanced CFG. An imbalanced CFG implies that at every exit there could be multiple signature values depending on the path traversed during runtime. If the CFG is not balanced, we will need to check against multiple values at exit points. Checking against multiple values will require multiple comparison instructions.

We solve these problems by using a technique of slack distribution, a modified version of the algorithm used by Chu et al. [9] for optimal work partitioning. Our adapted version of the technique works as follows: First, every exit out of an interval is connected to a dummy exit node. All BBs in the interval are assigned a *fCount* of 0. All *edgeWeights* are initialized to 1 and represent an initial increment along the associated edge. *fCount* is a number associated with each **BB** that represents the path length from the header of an interval to the **BB** under consideration. The algorithm starts from the header **BB** of the interval. By iterating over predecessors, the sum of *edgeWeight* and *fCount* for each predecessor is calculated. *fCount* for the current block is then maximum value over all predecessors. This can be written as follows: $fCount(bb) = \max_{x \in predecessors(bb)}(fCount(x) + edgeWeight(x \to bb))$. For every interval, this calculation is repeated until there is no change in *fCount* value of any **BB**. The pseudo code of the algorithm is described in Algorithm 1. Every **BB** is also associated with a number called *bCount*. *bCount* is the number calculated starting from dummy exit nodes and traversing the predecessors. *bCount* are initialized to *fCount* for each **BB**. Using an algorithm similar to the one shown in Algorithm 1, *bCount* is calculated for every **BB** in the interval. The update equation of *bCount* is as follows: $bCount(bb) = \min_{x \in successors(bb)}(bCount(x) - edgeWeight(x \to bb))$. Note that during the calculation of *fCount* and *bCount* only the successors and predecessors that are in the interval are considered. The dummy_exit block is considered a part of the interval during analysis. Once the *fCount* and *bCount* calculation is completed for every **BB** in the interval, the amount of extra balancing increment to be inserted along an edge between *srcBB* and *destBB* can be calculated as follows: $extraIncrement[srcBB \to destBB] = fCount[destBB] - edgeWeight[srcBB \to destBB] - bCount[srcBB]$.

Figure 7 shows an example of extra increment calculation for a CFG. Numbers on the left side of blocks represent *fCount* and numbers on right side of the **BB** represent *bCount*. Numbers on the edges are the extra increments required to be inserted along that edge. e.g., based on the algorithm described above edge *bb1 → bb3* edge gets an increment of 1 and edge *bb1 → bb4* gets an increment of 2. Once this step is executed, all the required increments are inserted along all edges of an interval.

```
Create dummy_exit block and connect all exit edges to this block;
Initialize all edgeWeight to one;
Initialize all fCount to zero;
change = 1;
while change do
    change = 0;
    for each bb in Interval do
        maximum = max(fCount(x) + edgeWeight(x → bb)) for x in
        predecessors[bb] and x → bb is not a backEdge;
        if fCount[bb] < maximum then
            change = 1;
            fCount[bb] = maximum;
        end
    end
end
```

Algorithm 1: Algorithm for calculating *fCount* for every **BB** in an interval.

3.3 Error Detection Analysis

Let C_i be the counter associated with an interval. Every block inside that interval updates the counter by 1 and at every exit out of the interval the counter value should be the maximum path length (since we insert balancing increments) through that interval. Let that max value for an interval be *CMax*. If C_i is not equal to *CMax* when control exits out of the interval then the control flow inside the program got disturbed. For all the intra-interval control flow errors, if any update to the path length counter is skipped, the path length calculation would be wrong and hence the control flow error will get caught. Erroneous jumps to other intervals are detected as the path length is not correct at the entry point of those intervals. However, there could be multiple paths of same length inside the interval. In the presence of single errors, the probability of traversing a different path of the same length path and still having the same *CMax* at exits is very low as explained below. We refer to this probability as

aliasing probability. Consider two BBs BB_i and BB_j and assume that an error occurs while executing the branch in BB_i transferring control to BB_j. In such a case and under single bit errors, aliasing occurs if all of the following three conditions are satisfied:

$$\begin{cases} pathLength(BB_j) == pathLength(BB_i) + 1 \\ BB_j \notin successors(BB_i) \\ BB_i \text{ jumps to the first instruction of } BB_j \end{cases}$$

$pathLength(BB_i)$ is the length of the path (number of BBs required to be traversed) from the interval header to BB_i. The first condition implies that the path length at erroneous destination block should be 1 more than source block. The second condition requires that BB_j is not a valid successor of BB_i according to the CFG and the third condition requires the jump to be at the beginning of the BB. If the jump is not at the beginning of the BB_j, the counter update would be skipped and the error would be caught. Fortunately, this a very specific case, so the aliasing probability is very low, dependent on the structure of the CFG. For SPECINT2000 benchmarks, the probability of such an aliasing is on the order of 10^{-5}. This is calculated by analyzing the CFG for such a case. This probability encompasses the aliasing probability between predecessor blocks (an erroneous jump between two predecessors) of a common successor BB in the same interval. An erroneous change in branch condition can transfer control to a statically valid target in the CFG and is another case of aliasing. We assume that such a case can be handled by data flow protection methods.

3.4 Insertion of Checking Instructions

An important part of the technique is to find the BBs where the comparison instructions should be inserted. Each interval has a unique signature variable. We compare this variable with the statically known *CMax* to test that the proper number of increments occurred. For our initial implementation, we chose to insert checks at all the exit points of an interval and in the latch block of loops. However, this is suboptimal and in the next section we show that how this can be further optimized.

3.5 Optimization for Loops

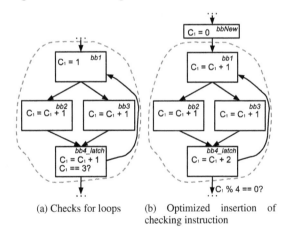

(a) Checks for loops   (b) Optimized insertion of checking instruction

Figure 8: Optimizing signature checking for loops: The checks on signatures are moved out of loops to exit blocks so that they are not executed in each iteration.

A naive way to insert a checking instruction for a loop is as shown in Figure 8(a). The latch block contains the checking instruction (the instruction that compares C_1 to 3). However, in this situation, the check is executed once every loop iteration. This can be optimized as shown in Figure 8(b). In the optimized case, the checking instruction is moved out of the loop and check is now made against a remainder. Essentially, a multiple of loop path length gets tested by the remainder. Remainders are a costly operation and one important issue to consider here is the fact that loop increments are inserted in such a way that the remainder is always taken by a power of two. This is shown in Figure 8(b), in *bb4* counter C_1 is incremented by 2 instead of 1 to make sure that remainder by 4 is taken. If this is the case the remainder instruction can simply be converted to a bitwise *and* instruction (e.g., remainder by 4 can be computed as bitwise *and* with 3).

3.6 Call and Return Instructions

A source of control flow transfers are *call* and *return* instructions. In this work, we propose a new technique to protect the control flow from caller to callee header and the return from callee to caller. The idea is akin to the path length approach used for branches except each function call has a unique path length (a unique number) that is checked upon entry of the callee and upon return to the caller to ensure call/returns go to and return from proper targets. We make the path length unique for each function to ensure that there is no aliasing among calls to different functions. The technique works as follows: Let F be the set of all the functions in an application. Every $f_i \in F$ is assigned a unique code such a way that the following is true.

$$HammingDistance(ACode(f_i),\ ACode(f_j)) > 1$$
$$\forall f_i,\ f_j \in F \ and\ i \neq j$$

For binary numbers a and b, Hamming distance is equal to the number of positions at which the corresponding bits in a and b are different. Simply put, Hamming distance is the number of errors required to transform a to b, and vice versa. $HammingDistance(a, b)$ is the Hamming distance between a and b. $ACode(f_i)$ represents the code assigned to f_i. Every function in the application is assigned a unique code in a way such that the Hamming distance between any two codes is greater than 1. This ensures that there is no aliasing among calls because of erroneous transition from one function to another function in presence of single bit errors. Figure 9 shows an exam-

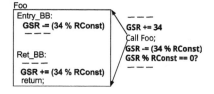

Figure 9: Handling call and return instructions. Instructions in bold represent the inserted instructions.

ple of instrumented code. The Global Signature Register (GSR) is updated before and after the call as shown. RConst is a convenient constant (power of 2) chosen in a way such that the costly remainder operation can be converted to simple bit shift operation. 34 is the Hamming code assigned to the function Foo. Inside the callee, the GSR is updated in the entry BB of the callee and return BB of the callee. This ensures that other calls inside Foo can use the same type of instrumentation. If source code of a call (e.g., library calls) is not available then the increments inside the callee cannot be inserted and only the increments around the call are inserted. In such a case, the transition to the beginning of the callee cannot be checked but the instrumented code ensures the return from callee should be right after the call instruction. Calls through pointers and compiler built-ins (i.e., compiler intrinsics) are treated in the same way as library calls.

4. Experimental Setup

A common practice in the literature to evaluate transient fault detection solutions is to use Statistical Fault Injections (SFIs) into a microarchitectural model of a processor. We believe that SFI provides the opportunity to inject faults into various hardware structures and hence are close to real transient fault scenarios. SFI has been previously [10, 32] used in validating the solutions proposed to protect against soft errors.

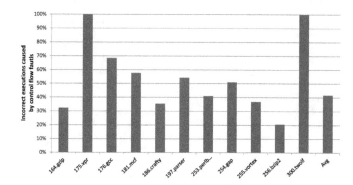

Figure 10: The incorrect executions as a percentage of unmasked faults caused by disturbance in control flow targets. Faults are injected in register file as well as branch targets.

4.1 Compiler Transformations

We have used the LLVM [16] compiler infrastructure to insert ACS into an application's code. Firstly, application source code is converted into LLVM's internal representation called LLVM IR (Intermediate Representation). ACS is implemented as a pass over LLVM IR. ACS insertion pass should be run after all the optimization passes on IR so that these passes do not interfere with ACS code. Our ACS insertion pass takes IR as input and as output it generates IR with signature computations and checks embedded into it. An LLVM interval formation pass is internally run and the information is used to insert control flow checking signatures. Some optimization passes such as constant propagation in code generation phase can propagate the constant initialization of signatures into the next BB. This can effectively remove the effect of inserted signature from the BB where the signature was initialized to its successors BBs. We have disabled such optimizations during the phase when LLVM prepares the IR for code generation.

4.2 Benchmarks

We have used 11 benchmarks from the SPECINT2000 benchmark suite (*gzip, vpr, gcc, mcf, crafty, perlbmk, parser, gap, vortex, bzip2, twolf*) as representative workloads in experiments. All these benchmarks were compiled with -O3 option of gcc frontend for LLVM. SPECINT2000 benchmarks. In the context of embedded systems, if the change in execution time affects program output, these programs might not run correctly after control flow protection. We do not consider multithreaded benchmarks in this work. However, we do not foresee any problems of using ACS with multithreaded programs.

4.3 Fault Injection Campaign

To evaluate the proposed approach, we ran an extensive fault injection campaign. An acceptable way in literature to model transient faults is using single bit-flips. These faults are inserted by flipping a random bit at a random cycle during the course of the application run. We injected faults in the register file (a large part of the processor's architectural state) and branch targets. A fault in a register used as branch target or in the computation of branch targets for indirect branches can disturb the control flow. Figure 10 shows the results of this experiment and Y-axis in the Figure is incorrect executions caused by control flow target errors as a percentage of the unmasked faults. The results show that a large percentage (on average 42%) of the unmasked faults result in incorrect executions and are caused by control flow faults. *175.vpr* and *300.twolf* (100% bars in the Figure 10) have high masking rate and all the remaining incorrect executions for these two benchmarks are caused by control flow faults. Even though the size of branch target (32 bit) is smaller than register file (16 registers of size 32 each), the contribution of branch target errors to incorrect executions is disproportionately high. Hence, control flow faults are an important category of faults to consider. Therefore, for the rest of the experiments, we chose to inject faults in branch targets only. Injecting faults in branch targets represents stress testing (a pessimistic case) control flow protection schemes since all the injected faults are guaranteed to disturb the control flow and subsequently do not inflate coverage numbers as they result in less masking compared to data errors as shown in Figure 1. The same method of fault injection is used for the baseline (CFCSS). To inject a fault, the program runs normally until it encounters the first control flow instruction after the selected random point is encountered. Once the control flow instruction is selected, a random bit is selected from the target address of the control flow instruction. This selected random bit is flipped to complete the injection of fault. Faults in PC (Program Counter) and other address circuitry are expected to disturb the control flow in a similar manner. Our technique is also capable of detecting faults injected into other microarchitectural units that affect the program control flow.

We used the GEM5 [7] simulator to simulate the workloads and implemented fault injection infrastructure into this simulator. The simulator was run in ARM syscall emulation mode and modeled the ARMv7-a profile of ARM architecture. To obtain performance overhead, workloads are simulated in an out-of-order model of the target processor. We use atomic model for processor configuration to inject control flow faults. The details of the processor configuration for out-of-order model used for the experiments are in Table 2.

Table 2: GEM5 Simulator parameters (models an ARMv7-a profile of ARM architecture).

Processor core @ 2GHz	
Simulation configuration	out-of-order core
Simulation mode	Syscall emulation
Physical integer register file size	256 entries
Reorder Buffer Size	192 entries
Issue width	2
Memory	
L1-D cache	64KB, 2-way
L1-I cache	32KB, 2-way
DTLB/ITLB	64 entries (each)

We have chosen to inject 1100 faults per technique to evaluate the solution. The statistical significance of these faults can be calculated by leveraging the work done by Leveugle et al. [17]. The calculation for our experimental setup shows that we need 96 fault injection trials for each benchmark to have a 10% margin of error and confidence level of 95%. Note that the margin of error only applies to fault coverage data. The performance overhead shows the exact simulation cycles consumed by the simulator. Therefore, we chose 100 fault injection trials for each benchmark to yield results with reasonable accuracy in a timely manner. After the fault injection, the program runs until completion. The result of each simulation trial is classified into one of the following five categories:

- **Masked**: The injected fault did not corrupt the program output. Application-level or architecture-level masking occurred in this case.

- **HWDetect**: The injected fault produces a symptom such as a page fault so that a recovery can be triggered. A fault is considered under this category only if the symptom is produced within a number of cycles (2000 for our experiments) after the fault was injected.

- **CFDetect**: The injected fault was detected by the control flow checking instructions inserted at the time of compiler transformation.

- **Failure**: The injected fault resulted in out-of-bound address access and resulted in simulation termination. Also, faults causing infinite loops in the program are classified under this category.

- **SDC**: Faults that corrupt the program output are classified into this category. These are Silent Data Corruptions.

Traditionally, the fault tolerance research community considers a program to be correct if the architectural state is correct at every cycle. Li et al. [20] showed that 17.6% of the multimedia and AI applications showed correct results even though they had architecturally incorrect states. We believe that user-visible program output corruptions truly matter to end users and cycle-by-cycle correct architectural state is not important to them. So in the context of evaluating this work, a program is considered to have executed correctly if the final output of the program matches. The result classifications of the injection experiments in this work are based on the fact that only program output corruptions really matter. Therefore, for this work we do not regard the number of faults that propagate to the microarchitectural state as a metric of importance. The percentage of faults that actually do corrupt program output are considered harmful because these faults corrupt program output without any hint of failure and represent the worse case scenario.

4.4 Recovery Support

ACS, like CFCSS, is a detection-only solution for control flow errors. Once a control flow error is detected, we rely on a recovery mechanism to recover from the detected error. A software-only recovery scheme such as Encore [11] or checkpointing-based recovery schemes can be used in conjunction with our solution. Feng et al. [10] and Wang et al. [38] proposed that future microprocessors with aggressive performance speculation will need recovery support. If available, the same scheme can be used by our solution. However, the cost of checkpointing-based and software-only schemes increases with respect to the number of instructions executed from recovery point. So, one important target for our scheme is to keep a bound on fault detection latency.

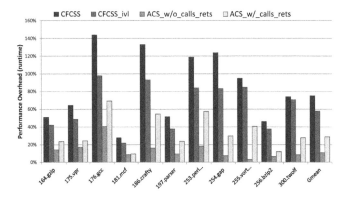

Figure 11: The performance (Runtime on simulated core) overhead for all techniques.

5. Experimental Evaluation and Analysis

Using the experimental setup described in Section 4, we obtain performance overhead and fault coverage results. Figure 11 shows the performance overhead measured in terms of runtime. These overheads are in comparison to unmodified applications compiled at -O3 optimization level. CFCSS shows the runtime overhead for the CFCSS scheme [29] and CFCSS_ivl bar shows the instruction overhead if the interval information is used in conjunction with CFCSS to insert checking at a coarser granularity. CFCSS_ivl has the *xor* (same as CFCSS) signature update inside every BB and in contrast to CFCSS only signature checking is moved at a coarser granularity. Also, CFCSS_ivl does not have any loop optimizations (Section 3.5). The third and fourth bar for each benchmarks shows the runtime overhead when we use ACS. ACS_w/o_calls_rets bar in this Figure shows the overhead without the protection for calls and returns (Section 3.6) and ACS_w/_calls_rets the overhead if protection for calls and rets is included. Overall, the performance overhead is 75%, 57.8%, 11% and 28.8% for CFCSS, CFCSS_ivl, ACS_w/o_calls_rets and ACS_w/_calls_rets, respectively. We have

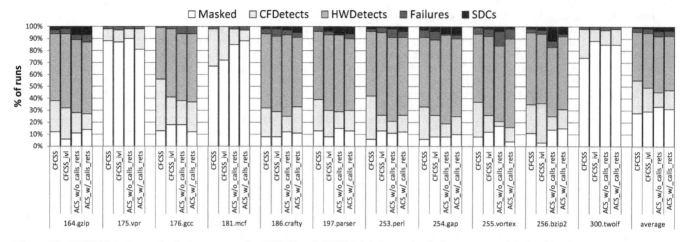

Figure 12: CFCSS bar shows the fault coverage for CFCSS and CFCSS_ivl shows the fault coverage with checking inserted using interval information. ACS_w/o_calls_rets shows the fault coverage without protection for calls/returns and ACS_w/o_calls_rets shows the fault coverage if calls/returns are also protected.

also measured the impact of code size expansion on application binaries and on average code size overhead is 22% with ACS. The code size overhead is largest for *176.gcc* showing largest performance overhead. To give more insight on the reduction in overhead, we measured the number of intervals and basic blocks in benchmarks. On average, there are 13302 basic blocks and 1993 intervals across the evaluated benchmarks and the number of checks required to be inserted are 2461. This represents a 5.4x decrease in the number of checks by abstracting from BBs to intervals.

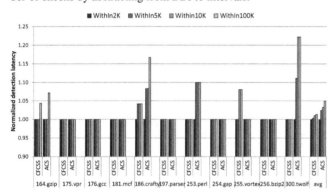

Figure 13: Comparison of fault detection latency with CFCSS. The fault detection latency is not adversely affected.

In the next experiment, we explore the fault coverage provided by these techniques. We define fault coverage as the percentage of faults out of total injected faults that do not result in Silent Data Corruptions (SDCs). SDCs are the most harmful errors because the program silently corrupts data while the user thinks that application worked as expected. The faults classified in *HWDetects* imply that these symptoms can be used to trigger recovery [10, 38]. Each bar in Figure 12 shows the distribution of faults among different categories when the instrumented application runs with fault injections. The four bars are the fault distribution for CFCSS, CFCSS_ivl, ACS_w/o_calls_rets and ACS_w/_calls_rets and the average fault coverage for these techniques is 98.8%, 98.4%, 96.6% and 96.3%, respectively. All these techniques reduce the number of SDCs in comparison to unprotected application, but ACS without calls/rets protection has only 11% performance overhead in comparison to 75% performance overhead of CFCSS.

5.1 Fault Detection Latency

Another important metric with regard to fault detection techniques is the detection latency. Fault detection latency is directly related

to the overhead of a recovery scheme. A longer latency implies that either the fault cannot be recovered or the recovery overhead would be high. Figure 13 shows the latency of ACS with respect to CFCSS. *WithIn2K* represents the number of faults detected in less than 2000 (2K) cycles of injections. Similarly, *WithIn5K*, *WithIn10K* and *WithIn100K* represents the number of fault detected within 5000, 10000 and 100000 cycles of injection, respectively. These categories are cumulative and faults classified under *WithIn5K* include all the faults detected with in 5K cycles, i.e., it subsumes the faults classified under *WithIn2K*. Similar rules apply for faults detected with in 10K and 100K cycles. The bars in the figure are normalized with respect to the number of faults detected in *WithIn2K*. For example, the *WithIn5K* bars represent the ratio of the number of faults detected with in 5K cycles and number of faults detected with in 2K cycles. In case of ACS, on average, *WithIn5K* contains 2% more than *WithIn2K*. Similarly, *WithIn10K* and *WithIn100K* contain only 3% and 5% more faults than *WithIn2K*. The same numbers for CFCSS are 0%, 1% and 1% for 5K, 10K and 100K cycles, respectively. Overall, ACS only increases the detection latency for at most 5% of the faults detected within 2K cycles.

5.2 Analysis of SDCs

In this subsection, we discuss some of the cases that escape the detection by CFCSS and ACS control flow methods and eventually result in silent data corruptions. LLVM IR supports the *switch* statements as the terminating instruction of BBs. When the code generation phase converts this switch statement to machine instructions, it is converted into multiple branches. Since these branches were not visible to our code instrumentation pass, these do not get protected by ACS or CFCSS. Some of the faults that affect such unprotected branches eventually cause SDCs. One way to handle these *switch* statements is to convert all the *switch* statements to *if-else* in the LLVM IR itself before running our code instrumentation pass. Another frequent case of SDCs is the faults that displace target address (i.e., faults in low order bits) only by few instructions usually result in SDCs. For example, we noticed that a fault in second bit of target address of a back edge caused only two extra instructions to be executed. Those two extra instructions happened to be immediate *mov* instructions and they just disturbed the value of two registers. Affected registers were written to memory and hence caused SDC. A similar problem also exists with CFCSS.

5.3 Data and Control Flow Protection

In this subsection, we present the results for combining a profile-based data flow [15] and our proposed control flow solution. Figure 14 shows the performance overhead on the primary vertical axis and fault coverage on the secondary vertical axis when a combination of ACS and profile based data flow protection is used. SWDetects category in the fault outcome classification represents the number of faults detected by software (both data and control flow) and other category are same as previously mentioned. Control flow condition errors are handled by duplicating the computations for branch conditions. A combined solution incurs an average performance overhead of 47.4% and provides 96.5% fault coverage. The binary is 35% larger and overhead on dynamic instructions is 55.4%. SWIFT [32] is another solution that used data duplication.

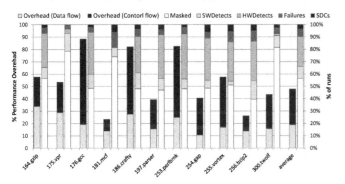

Figure 14: Performance overhead and fault coverage for complete data and control flow protection.

By leveraging the ideas from CFCSS, SWIFT also enhances control flow protection. In comparison to ACS with data duplication, SWIFT incurs an increase of: 2.3x for dynamic instructions, 2.3x for binary size and 1.53x for execution time over the same set of benchmarks as used in this work even though the performance overhead of SWIFT was measured on a aggressive server class workstation targeting a different ISA (IA64) than our evaluations (ARM). An IA64 system can take better advantage of instruction level parallelism introduced by duplication of instructions.

5.4 Discussion and Limitations

Similar to other signature based schemes [3, 29], ACS cannot detect faults in branch conditions. Though other schemes [13, 36] can detect errors in a branch condition if the error occurs after the branch condition is evaluated. This still misses the errors happening before condition evaluation and in variables used in evaluation of that condition. Corrupt branch conditions or other variables used to compute branch conditions can cause control flow condition errors. These errors in branch conditions can be handled by combining ACS with data flow protection based methods as described in Section 5.3. In this paper, we focus on the faults in branch targets and other variables used in computing branch targets.

In the presence of an error in the inserted checking code, the following scenarios can occur: 1) If the check evaluates to True, then the error in signature comparison branch will result in skipping the signature updates of next basic block, hence the error will be caught at the next check. 2) If the check is wrong (i.e., an error has already occurred), then considering that a transient fault is a rare event, a second error in this short span of time in signature comparison is probabilistically unlikely to occur.

In LLVM, the CFG is the basis of data flow analysis and many optimizations. To facilitate this data flow analysis, LLVM doesn't allow the address of a BB to be taken and then jump to it. Jumps to a location specified in a variable can only exist in the form of call instructions and for other control flow instructions target BBs are known at LLVM IR level. So at LLVM IR level, there is no special handling for *indirect branches* is required.

6. Related Work

Control flow protection is becoming an increasingly important concern for reliability researchers. Two particularly noteworthy pieces

of software-only work in this area are CFCSS [29] and ECCA (Enhanced Control Flow Checking using Assertions) [3]. In our experimental results, we have compared our work with CFCSS in detail. ECCA assigns a unique prime identifier to each BB in the program and checks prime identifier at runtime using an assertion in every BB. The authors of [37] reported that ECCA incurs 150% memory overhead. Venkatasubramanian et.al [37] use parity in each BB to check for correct control flow. Control flow is checked by special variables inserted in each routine. The main difference with respect to these techniques and ACS lies in the fact that we raise the level of abstraction for checking and the signature update is simplified in each BB. Borin et al. [8] presented a control flow error detection technique where the signature checks are made in 1) every BB, 2) only in the BBs with back edges and BBs with return instructions, 3) only in BBs with return instructions and 4) only at the end of the application. This previous work reports 77% overhead for the case 1 and 37% for the case 3, in comparison to 11% overhead of ACS. Fault coverage data or detection latency for these different checking granularity is not reported in the paper. It is expected that delaying the checking to loop end points (blocks with back edges) and function ends (return blocks) will result in relatively more failures and program corruptions or will affect detection time. CEDA [36] is an assertion based scheme that assigns static signatures while minimize aliasing. The overhead of CEDA for common benchmarks is 27.1% in comparison to 11% of ACS. CEDA work also presents comparison with CFCSS and YACCA [13]. The performance overhead of CEDA reported in that paper is comparable to CFCSS for the chosen five benchmarks with a slightly better fault coverage. Since ACS has lower overhead than CFCSS, it will also have lower overhead than CEDA. The paper reports YACCA's overhead even larger than that of CFCSS and CEDA.

A comparison with SWIFT [32] is already described in Section 5.3. Other works such as CRAFT and PROFIT [33] improve upon the SWIFT solution by using additional hardware structures and architectural vulnerability factor (AVF) analysis [28]. Our goal in this work is to make the control flow protection practical for commodity embedded systems by reducing the performance overhead. Our experimental results demonstrate that this can be achieved at significantly less performance overhead than these previously proposed techniques.

Symptom detection based solutions rely on anomalous microarchitectural behavior to detect soft errors. A light-weight approach for detecting soft errors, ReStore [38], analyzes symptoms including memory exceptions, branch mispredicts, and cache misses. mSWAT [18] presented a solution which detects anomalous software behavior to provide a reliable system. It requires special simple hardware detectors to detect faults. These techniques are orthogonal to ACS, as they rely on specialized hardware. If available, they can be leveraged along with ACS to increase the number of faults detected under HWDetects category.

A category of previous works related to control flow protection are watchdog processor based solutions [22]. The general idea of these techniques is to have a watchdog processor, along side the main processor, that monitors and checks the program executing on the main processor. These solutions rely on the availability of watchdog processor and in some cases even propose specific changes to the watchdog processors. A variety of watchdog based solutions [21, 25, 36] are proposed in literature by modifying some aspect (e.g., changing the type of signatures) of the technique. Some recent solutions also suggest the idea of distributed checking in the core for various components. Argus [24], for example, relies on a series of hardware checker units to perform online invariant checking to ensure correct application execution (data flow as well as control flow). Argus achieves very low overhead by adding extra hardware. In comparison to these techniques, ACS targets COTS components and does not require any hardware changes.

An interesting approach to soft error reliability is using Redundant Multithreading (RMT). AR-SMT [34] introduced the idea of RMT on SMT cores; The work is done by a leading thread, and the trailing thread checks for the correctness. Subsequent works [14, 31] in this category have tried to reduce the overhead due to RMT. All these techniques come with the overhead of running an extra thread which executes a skeleton of the original program.

Another compiler assisted solution for control flow checking uses extra hardware to minimize the overhead [19]. It requires compiler, as well as hardware changes. Ours is a software-only approach to produce protected programs.

There is a large body of related work in Control Flow Integrity (CFI) [1] for computer security against external software attacks. CFI works by making sure that all the control transfer occur as determined by the static CFG. The failure model targeted by CFI schemes is very different from soft errors failure mode. In CFI, constant destinations (direct branches) are statically verified and while computed (dynamic branches) are verified for correct destination by instrumenting the code. Soft errors can affect the direct as well as indirect branches and hence CFI, as is, is not directly applicable for soft errors. Though direct branches can also be protected in a manner similar to dynamic branches, but the already high overhead (20%-60% for dynamic branches only) would become prohibitive.

Path profiling [4] finds the execution count of a path in a Directed Acyclic Graph (DAG). It is a related problem to our work and gives an unique number for each path in a DAG. However, we want to have a balanced path length along with information about edges in the path to insert balancing increments. This can not be obtained with path profiling. Moreover, usually profiling is created with training inputs but later the program might be executed with a different set of inputs. In ACS, we need the correct path length with the current inputs a program is executing. Therefore, the data produced by off-line profiling can not be used in ACS.

7. Conclusions

The ever increasing desire to create powerful and efficient microprocessors, with each successive new generation, has led to the use of increasingly smaller transistors into these devices. Aggressive scaling makes transistor devices more susceptible to transient faults. To tackle the problem of control flow protection at minimal performance overhead, we have proposed Abstract Control flow Signatures (ACS). ACS achieves its efficiency by working at a coarse-grain level than the previously proposed signature based techniques and also by simplifying signature updates in each basic block. ACS reduces performance overhead, on average, from 75% down to 11% while maintaining the similar level of fault coverage in comparison to a previously proposed approach (CFCSS [29]).

8. Acknowledgements

The authors would like to thank the shepherd and the anonymous reviewers for their constructive comments and suggestions for improving this work. This research is supported by the National Science Foundation under grant CCF-0916689 and STARnet, a Semiconductor Research Corporation program sponsored by MARCO and DARPA.

References

[1] M. Abadi, M. Budiu, U. Erlingsson, and J. Ligatti. Control-flow integrity principles, implementations, and applications. *ACM Trans. Inf. Syst. Secur.*, 13(1): 4:1–4:40, Nov. 2009. ISSN 1094-9224.

[2] A. Aho, M. Lam, R. Sethi, and J. Ullman. *Compilers: principles, techniques, and tools*, volume 1009. Pearson/Addison Wesley, 2007.

[3] Z. Alkhalifa, V. Nair, N. Krishnamurthy, and J. Abraham. Design and evaluation of system-level checks for on-line control flow error detection. *TDPS*, jun 1999.

[4] T. Ball and J. R. Larus. Efficient path profiling. In *ACM/IEEE Micro*, 1996.

[5] W. Bartlett and L. Spainhower. Commercial fault tolerance: A tale of two systems. *In TDSC*, pages 87–96, 2004.

[6] D. Bernick, B. Bruckert, P. D. Vigna, D. Garcia, R. Jardine, J. Klecka, and J. Smullen. Nonstop advanced architecture. In *DSN*, pages 12–21, June 2005.

[7] N. Binkert et al. The gem5 simulator. *SIGARCH Comput. Archit. News*, 39(2), Aug. 2011.

[8] E. Borin, C. Wang, Y. Wu, and G. Araujo. Software-based transparent and comprehensive control-flow error detection. In *CGO*, 2006.

[9] M. Chu, K. Fan, and S. Mahlke. Region-based hierarchical operation partitioning for multicluster processors. In *PLDI*, pages 300–311, June 2003.

[10] S. Feng, S. Gupta, A. Ansari, and S. Mahlke. Shoestring: Probabilistic soft-error reliability on the cheap. In *ASPLOS*, Mar. 2010.

[11] S. Feng, S. Gupta, A. Ansari, S. A. Mahlke, and D. I. August. Encore: low-cost, fine-grained transient fault recovery. In *MICRO*, pages 398–409, 2011.

[12] B. T. Gold, J. C. Smolens, B. Falsafi, and J. C. Hoe. The granularity of soft-error containment in shared memory multiprocessors. *IEEE Workshop on SELSE*, 2006.

[13] O. Goloubeva, M. Rebaudengo, M. Sonza Reorda, and M. Violante. Soft-error detection using control flow assertions. In *DFT*, pages 581 – 588, nov. 2003.

[14] M. Gomaa and T. Vijaykumar. Opportunistic transient-fault detection. In *ISCA*, pages 172–183, June 2005.

[15] D. S. Khudia, G. Wright, and S. Mahlke. Efficient soft error protection for commodity embedded microprocessors using profile information. In *LCTES*, pages 99–108, New York, NY, USA, 2012. ACM.

[16] C. Lattner and V. Adve. LLVM: A compilation framework for lifelong program analysis & transformation. In *CGO*, pages 75–86, 2004.

[17] R. Leveugle, A. Calvez, P. Maistri, and P. Vanhauwaert. Statistical fault injection: quantified error and confidence. In *DATE*, pages 502–506, 2009.

[18] M. Li, M. Pradeep, R. S. Sahoo, S. Adve, V. Adve, and Y. Y. Zhou. Swat: An error resilient system. In *IEEE Workshop on SELSE*, pages 8–13, 2008.

[19] X. Li and J.-L. Gaudiot. A compiler-assisted on-chip assigned-signature control flow checking. In *Advances in Computer Systems Architecture*, volume 3189 of *LNCS*, pages 554–567. Springer Berlin, 2004.

[20] X. Li and D. Yeung. Application-level correctness and its impact on fault tolerance. In *HPCA*, pages 181–192, Feb. 2007.

[21] D. Lu. Watchdog processors and structural integrity checking. *IEEE Transactions on Computers*, C-31(7):681 –685, july 1982.

[22] A. Mahmood and E. J. McCluskey. Concurrent error detection using watchdog processors-a survey. *IEEE Trans. Comput.*, 37(2):160–174, Feb. 1988.

[23] T. May and M. Woods. Alpha-particle-induced soft errors in dynamic memories. *IEEE Transactions on Electron Devices*, 26(1):2–9, Jan. 1979.

[24] A. Meixner, M. Bauer, and D. Sorin. Argus: Low-cost, comprehensive error detection in simple cores. *IEEE Micro*, 28(1):52–59, 2008.

[25] T. Michel, R. Leveugle, and G. Saucier. A new approach to control flow checking without program modification. In *FTC*, pages 334 –341, jun 1991.

[26] S. Muchnick. *Advanced Compiler Design Implementation*. Morgan Kaufmann Publishers, 1997.

[27] S. Mukherjee. *Architecture Design for Soft Errors*. Morgan Kaufmann, 2008.

[28] S. S. Mukherjee, C. Weaver, J. Emer, S. Reinhardt, and T. Austin. A systematic methodology to compute the architectural vulnerability factors for a high performance microprocessor. In *MICRO*, pages 29–42, Dec. 2003.

[29] N. Oh, P. Shirvani, and E. McCluskey. Control-flow checking by software signatures. *IEEE Transactions on Reliability*, 51(1):111 –122, mar 2002.

[30] N. Oh, P. Shirvani, and E. McCluskey. Error detection by duplicated instructions in super-scalar processors. *Reliability, IEEE Transactions on*, 51(1):63–75, 2002.

[31] S. K. Reinhardt and S. S. Mukherjee. Transient fault detection via simulataneous multithreading. In *Proc. of the 27th ISCA*, pages 25–36, June 2000.

[32] G. Reis, J. Chang, N. Vachharajani, R. Rangan, and D. I. August. SWIFT: Software implemented fault tolerance. In *CGO*, pages 243–254, 2005.

[33] G. A. Reis, J. Chang, N. Vachharajani, R. Rangan, D. I. August, and S. S. Mukherjee. Software-controlled fault tolerance. *ACM TACO*, 2(4):366–396, 2005.

[34] E. Rotenberg. AR-SMT: A microarchitectural approach to fault tolerance in microprocessors. In *International Symposium on Fault Tolerant Computing*, 1999.

[35] P. Shivakumar, M. Kistler, S. Keckler, D. Burger, and L. Alvisi. Modeling the effect of technology trends on the soft error rate of combinational logic. In *DSN*, pages 389–398, June 2002.

[36] R. Vemu and J. Abraham. Ceda: Control-flow error detection using assertions. *IEEE Transactions on Computers*, 60(9):1233 –1245, sept. 2011.

[37] R. Venkatasubramanian, J. Hayes, and B. Murray. Low-cost on-line fault detection using control flow assertions. In *IOLTS 2003.*, july 2003.

[38] N. J. Wang and S. J. Patel. ReStore: Symptom-based soft error detection in microprocessors. *In TDSC*, 3(3):188–201, June 2006.

[39] N. J. Wang, J. Quek, T. M. Rafacz, and S. J. Patel. Characterizing the Effects of Transient Faults on a High-Performance Processor Pipeline. In *DSN*, June 2004.

[40] J. F. Ziegler and H. Puchner. *SER-History, Trends, and Challenges: A Guide for Designing with Memory ICs*. Cypress Semiconductor Corp., 2004.

Boosting Efficiency of Fault Detection and Recovery through Application-Specific Comparison and Checkpointing

Hao Chen and Chengmo Yang

Department of Electrical and Computer Engineering
University of Delaware
140 Evans Hall, Newark, DE 19716
email:{hchen, chengmo}@udel.edu

Abstract

While the unending technology scaling has brought reliability to the forefront of concerns of semiconductor industry, fault tolerance techniques are still rarely incorporated into existing designs due to their high overhead. One fault tolerance scheme that receives a lot of research attention is duplication and checkpointing. However, most of the techniques in the category employ a blind strategy to compare instruction results, therefore not only generating large overhead in buffering and verifying these values, but also inducing unnecessary rollbacks to recover faults that will never influence subsequent execution. To tackle these issues, we introduce in this paper an approach that identifies the minimum set of instruction results for fault detection and checkpointing. For a given application, the proposed technique first identifies the control and data flow information of each execution hotspot, and then selects only the instruction results that either influence the final program results or are needed during re-execution as the comparison set. Our experimental studies demonstrate that the proposed hotspot-targeting technique is able to reduce nearly 88% of the comparison overhead and mask over 38% of the total injected faults of all the injected faults while at the same time delivering full fault coverage.

Categories and Subject Descriptors C.4 [*Performance of Systems*]: Fault-tolerance

General Terms Performance, Reliability

Keywords Reliability; Fault detection & recovery; Checkpointing; Application-Specific optimization

1. Introduction

As device feature sizes scale towards nanoscale, future computer systems are destined to suffer from various types of device failures that may occur during execution. Researchers have shown that the fault rate has increased by three orders of magnitude (from 10^{-7} to 10^{-4}) [1, 2] as technology advanced from 180nm to 45nm. Along with the projected high fault rate, we also expect a significant variance in fault duration. In addition to *transient* faults, typically caused by particle strikes, and *permanent* faults,

that occur repeatedly after a device sustains irreversible damage, *intermittent* faults may occur frequently and irregularly for a period of time, commonly due to process variation or in-progress wear-out combined with voltage and temperature fluctuations.

In the past, the tradeoffs between system size and complexity have dictated that the cheaper option is to create a compact, non-robust implementation and then replace it when it fails. However, in more and more cases, it is either too expensive to access the system, or too expensive to remotely diagnose its failure state and repair it. Therefore, it is more and more preferable to develop designs that consume non-traditionally large areas, but are highly resilient to internal failures.

To tolerate faults, existing solutions either use different techniques (such as error coding, signature monitoring [3, 4]) to protect individual components of a processing core, or redundantly execute a unit of computation two (or more) times and then compare their results. Compared to error coding techniques, redundant execution techniques offer greater fault coverage across the entire system against arbitrary faults. However, their high overhead limit their applicability to embedded systems that usually have tight power and resource constraints. As these techniques usually employ a blind strategy to compare instruction results, they not only need to buffer and verify all these values, but also induce unnecessary rollbacks to recover faults that will never influence subsequent execution.

A widely-recognized program characteristic is locality: 90% of the execution time is spent on loops that constitute only 10% of the code size. This high regularity has been intensively exploited, primarily in application-specific embedded systems [5, 6], to achieve performance and power optimizations. In this paper, we will exploit this high regularity to boost the efficiency of redundant execution. We introduce a technique which, through analyzing the control and data flow of the hottest loops of a given application, is able to identify the minimum set of register values for comparison and checkpointing. Register values are verified and checkpointed only if they impact program final results, or they are needed to recover a detected fault. In this way, the fault detection and checkpointing overhead is minimized, the probability of *false errors* (i.e., faults that do not impact program results) is maximally reduced, while high fault coverage is still guaranteed. These advantages will broaden the applicability of redundant execution to embedded systems of tight power and resource constraints.

The rest of this paper is organized as follows. Section 2 briefly reviews current fault tolerance techniques and their limitations, while Section 3 outlines the technical motivation. Section 4 presents the proposed loop-based fault detection and checkpointing framework. Section 5 experimentally verifies the efficacy of the technique, while Section 6 summarizes and concludes the paper.

LCTES'13, June 20–21, 2013, Seattle, Washington, USA.
Copyright © 2013 ACM 978-1-4503-2085-6/13/06...$15.00

2. Background and Related Work

The elevation in fault rates has caused increasing research attention to be paid to the incorporation of fault resilience techniques into computation systems. For embedded systems with tight power and resource constraints, the need for highly efficient fault resilience methods becomes increasingly critical and urgent. It is thus necessary to evaluate a technique not only by its *effectiveness* in detecting faults and recovering the affected computation, but more importantly by its *efficiency* in terms of the associated performance, energy and hardware overhead.

2.1 Fault Detection

The detection of faults requires redundancy. The degree of the required redundancy increases for components that lack a regular structure. For storage components and communication channels with regular structures, data can be protected by Error Correcting Codes (ECC) and parity bits. In contrast, logic and computation blocks, which typically have irregular structures, require greater redundancy so *redundant execution* is usually considered the best approach for detecting arbitrary faults.

Researchers have performed intensive studies on redundant execution. AR-SMT [7] adopted simultaneous multithreading (SMT) to redundantly execute two threads. It compares all the instructions, and prevents instructions from committing their results until these results have been verified. SRT [8] reduced overhead of AR-SMT by maintaining a constant slack between the two redundant threads to reduce branch misprediction and cache misses, and only comparing store instructions. The same idea was later applied to chip multiprocessors (CMPs) in [9].

To further reduce the overhead of redundant execution, a set of techniques that selectively avoid executing certain regions of the program were developed. These techniques either reuse the results of previously executed instructions [10], or avoid the execution of dynamically dead instructions [11], or turn off one thread in high performance regions [12, 13]. They sizably reduce duplication overhead, however, at the cost of significantly increased rates of undetectable faults.

2.2 Error Recovery

Recovering from a detected fault can be achieved either by preventing it from modifying system states, or by rolling the computation back to a previously saved clean state – a *checkpoint*.

Systems that prevent faults from modifying computation states can recover from a fault in the same way as they recover from incorrect execution speculation. Techniques of this category include SRTR [14] for SMT processors and CRTR [15] for CMPs. However, these techniques need to buffer and check each instruction result. To reduce comparison overhead, dependence-based checking elision (DBCE) [14] was proposed to dynamically construct dependence chains of instructions and only check the last instruction in each chain. As DBCE can only identify dependence chains that are simple (single parent and single child) and short (not across branch instructions), only 35% reduction in the comparison overhead was achieved [14]. More crucially, these techniques still suffer from large probability of false errors, as they always re-execute a faulty instruction even if the instruction has no impact on program final results.

Alternatively, a system can allow unconfirmed results to be written into the registers, and only compares store values and addresses for fault detection. Techniques of this category include the RVQ-free recovery (RVQ_f) [16] and the cache-based checkpointing [17]. To ensure the existence of a clean state upon a detected

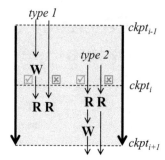

Figure 1. Minimum checkpoint requirements

fault, these techniques need to periodically save the processor states (including program counter, register file, and other hardware registers) and verify its correctness to ensure that a newly created checkpoint is fault-free. The higher the fault rate, the more frequently the processor states need to be saved.

3. Technical Motivation

The brief review in the last section shows that existing redundant execution techniques were developed under the assumption that the fault rate is low and hence the recovery cost will not be a critical concern. These techniques either solely focus on fault detection, or sometimes even increase recovery cost or sacrifice fault coverage to reduce fault detection overhead.

In contrast, the goal of the proposed technique is to simultaneously minimize the fault detection and recovery overhead in redundant execution without sacrificing fault coverage. To reduce fault detection overhead, the technique compares only the store values and addresses and periodically checkpoints the register file. The challenge, however, is to identify the minimum set of registers for comparing and checkpointing, so that the benefit obtained through selectively comparing instruction results will not be overwhelmed by the overhead in checking register values.

At minimum, a checkpoint needs to ensure that upon a failure all the values needed to restart the computation from that exact point can be recovered. From this perspective, it seems that all the register values that are live[1] at the checkpoint needed to be compared. However, our detailed analysis shows that this is not necessarily the case. Figure 1 shows a generic case of execution with three consecutive checkpoints (i-1, i, and i+1). It includes two pairs of register access patterns showing that for register values that are live at checkpoint i, comparison is needed only in two conditions.

- The *type 1* patterns show that only the live variables that are updated during the the [i-1, i] region need to be checked at checkpoint i, since the ones never updated during this region have already been checked at checkpoint i-1.

- The *type 2* patterns show that only the live variables that are updated during the the [i, i+1] region need to be checked at checkpoint i, sine the ones never updated during this region will not be polluted by faults generated in the execution pipeline.

Using R_{live} and R_{write} to respectively denote the live and the written registers, the analysis above indicates that, at minimum, the set of registers for comparing and checkpointing should be:

---

[1] At a given time point, a register is *live* if the very first subsequent access to that register is a read operation.

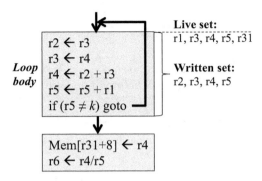

Figure 2. Loop example

Table 1. Register classification of the loop example

Type	In Figure 2	In R_{live}	In R_{write}
Read then Write	r3, r4, r5	Yes	Yes
Read only	r1	Yes	No
Write (then Read)	r2	No	Yes
Not accessed, live	r31	Yes	No
Not accessed, dead	r6	No	No

$$R_{ckpt}(i) = R_{live}(i) \cap (R_{write}[i-1,i] \cup R_{write}[i,i+1]) \quad (1)$$

This equation provides a tight bound for the minimum set of register values to be checked. Yet it also shows that the minimum checking requirements for checkpoint i is determined not only by its own position, but furthermore by the positions of checkpoints i-1 and i+1. Application-specific optimizations are needed to select best checkpointing positions in advance. The challenge is to not only statically analyze the application and extract checkpoint information, but furthermore to efficiently embed such information into the platform to guide the runtime fault detection, checkpointing, and recovery process. To minimize the overhead of static analysis while at the same time maximizing the benefit attainable dynamically, we therefore propose a *loop-based* comparison and checkpointing scheme targeting application hotspots that account for 90% of the execution time and only 10% of the code size.

4. Proposed Technique

In this section we present the proposed loop-based fault resilience technique. In line with other redundant execution-based fault tolerance schemes, we assume that an application is duplicated into two threads for execution. The technique targets arbitrary faults that may occur in the execution pipeline, while storage structures such as caches, register files, and the main memory are protected using ECC.

As mentioned before, for a given application the proposed technique compares only the values and addresses of store instructions and checkpoints only a minimum set of registers at pre-selected checkpoint positions. To maintain high fault coverage, the proposed technique also guarantees that if a fault occurs in a register that is not selected for comparing and checkpointing, the fault will always be masked during subsequent execution and hence will never impact program final results.

4.1 Minimum Comparison and Checkpointing Set

Most execution hotspots have highly regular control and data flows and generate regular access patterns to registers. The proposed technique inserts *a single checkpoint* within the loop body, resulting in checkpoints being taken at the same position across various loop iterations. This guarantees that during the steady state of loop execution, the set of registers updated between two consecutive checkpoints is identical. In other words, the two terms $R_{write}[i-1,i]$ and $R_{write}[i,i+1]$ in Equation (1) will be equal to $R_{write}(\text{loop body})$, which represents the set of registers updated during loop execution. Equation (1) therefore can be re-written as follows:

$$R_{ckpt}(i) = R_{live}(i) \cap R_{write}(\text{loop body}) \quad (2)$$

Equation (2) indicates that the **minimum set of registers to be compared** at checkpoint i consists of the registers that are updated during loop execution and are live at the selected checkpoint position.

One noteworthy aspect is that Equation (2) does not require a checkpoint to be taken per loop iteration. As both $R_{live}(i)$ and $R_{write}(\text{loop body})$ do not vary across loop iterations, checkpointing frequency can be arbitrarily selected. Specifically, if one wants to take a checkpoint per M instructions, the loop-based approach can be tuned to take a checkpoint per $\lceil M/(loop\ size) \rceil$ iterations. The value of M can be selected according to the fault rate. A larger value of M reduces fault detection overhead, yet requires more instructions to be rolled back upon a detected fault.

Comparing and checkpointing the selected set of registers is sufficient to deliver full fault coverage during loop execution. To illustrate this property, let us consider the loop example presented in Figure 2. Assume that the checkpoint position is right before the first instruction of the loop. A quick examination shows that registers r_1, r_6, and r_{31} do not serve as destination registers within the loop body. These three registers therefore do not need to be checked since their values will never change during loop execution. Moreover, register r_2, although it is updated during loop execution, also needs no comparing or checkpointing. Even if there may exist a fault in r_2, the fault will always be masked since the first access to r_2 starting from the checkpoint is a write operation. Overall, the exclusion of these four registers results in the final comparing and checkpointing set consisting of registers r_3, r_4, and r_5. It can be easily verified that all the three registers are live at the checkpoint and have been updated within the loop body. Detailed register classification of this example is shown in Table 1.

4.2 Best Comparison and Checkpoint Position

While the proposed technique inserts a single checkpoint within the loop body, this checkpoint does not always need to be placed at the beginning of a loop. Instead, there may exist multiple possible checkpoint positions. While the set of the updated registers (R_{write} in Equation (2)) is fixed for a give loop, the set of the live registers (R_{live}) may vary across these different positions. Therefore, it is necessary to develop an approach that first identifies all the possible checkpoint positions within a loop body and then compares these positions to select the best one.

4.2.1 Identify possible checkpoint positions

An application execution hotspot may contain multiple basic blocks[2]. Among these blocks, some may be conditionally executed (e.g., on a "if" branch). If a checkpoint is placed in such blocks, in

---

[2] A basic block is a linear sequence of instructions with single entry and single exit points.

an extreme case it may never be reached during loop execution. To avoid this undesirable situation, the proposed technique only considers, as possible checkpoint positions, the basic blocks that are *unconditionally* executed during a loop iteration. A quick examination shows that these blocks are the ones that dominate[3] the tail block of the loop. Through control flow analysis, the domination set of the tail block can be easily identified.

4.2.2   Select best checkpoint positions

Once the possible checkpoint positions are identified, the next step is to compare these positions and select the one that (1) imposes minimum fault detection and checkpointing overhead, and (2) minimizes the amount of computation to be rolled back during the recovery process.

The fault detection and checkpointing overhead is proportional to the number of registers selected for comparing and checkpointing. For each of the identified possible checkpoint positions, Equation (2) can be used to determine the minimum set of registers needed for checking. Both the R_{write} and the R_{live} sets of registers can be obtained through data flow analysis [18]. Subsequently, among these possible positions, the one with the smallest set of registers can be selected as the best position.

If more than one checkpoint position has the smallest comparison and checkpointing set, the one that has the shortest overall distance to store instructions will be selected as the best position. As mentioned before, the proposed fault resilience scheme compares the values and addresses of store instructions for fault detection, and rolls the computation back to the most recent checkpoint if a fault is detected. Accordingly, by selecting the checkpoint position with the shortest overall distance to store instructions, the amount of computation to be rolled back during the recovery process can be minimized.

4.3   Runtime Coordination

With the information of the best checkpoint position and the selected registers extracted through static control and data flow analysis, at runtime the fault detection, checkpointing, and recovery process can be coordinated as follows:

- Fault detection is performed by checking store instructions and the selected registers. The checking of store values and addresses is performed before committing the store operation to memory, while the checking of the selected registers is performed when the computation reaches a new checkpoint.

- To detect faults in the control flow, the branch outcomes of one thread will be buffered and delivered to the other thread for comparison. Any mismatch in the branch outcomes of the two threads indicates a fault in the control flow.

- Through static analysis, a "write disable" signature will be extracted to mark all the registers that are never updated within the loop body (i.e., the complement set of R_{write}(loop body)). At runtime, write operations to these registers will be disabled, thus protecting them from being polluted by undesired writes.

- Once a fault is detected in a store instruction or in a selected register or in the control flow, the computation will be rolled back to the last saved checkpoint and the clean values of the pre-selected set of registers will be restored.

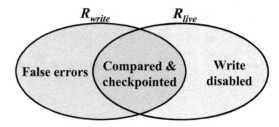

Figure 3. Resilience solutions for various register classes

- When reaching a pre-selected checkpoint position, the selected registers will be checked. If no fault is detected, these registers will be saved to form a new checkpoint.

One significant advantage of the proposed technique is its ability to deliver full fault coverage while sizably reducing the probability of false errors. Full fault coverage is guaranteed by precluding faults to propagate across any checkpoint. As shown in Figure 3, all the registers that are live at the checkpoint are either disabled from being overwritten or compared for fault detection, thus ensuring the absence of undetected faults in these registers. Meanwhile, the proposed technique reduces false errors by masking two types of faults that never affect program final results. The first type are the faults that never propagate to a store instruction or to a register at the checkpoint. Typically these faults are the ones occurring in *dynamically dead* instructions[4]. The second type of masked faults are the ones that propagate to registers that are not selected for comparison and checkpointing. The proposed register selection approach guarantees that starting from the checkpoint position, a non-selected register will never be used by any instruction until being overwritten, thus precluding faults in these registers from being propagated to subsequent computation.

4.4   Software and Hardware Support for Scheme Setup

The proposed technique can be incorporated into any redundant execution scheme based on verifying store instructions to detect and recover transient, intermittent, or permanent errors in execution pipeline. Outside the execution hotspots, the application can be protected using the traditional approach. Within a hotspot, the proposed technique can be applied to reduce the overhead in comparing and checkpointing the register file. Additionally, the register file is checkpointed when switching between the two mechanisms, that is, right before entering a hotspot and right after exiting it.

Like existing optimization techniques [19] targeting application hotspots, the statically extracted information will be embedded into the application at the end of the static analysis phase. For each hotspot, three pieces of information will be delivered to the runtime system: the selected checkpoint position (the address), a "checkpoint enable" bit vector with each bit indicating whether a register is selected for comparison and checkpointing, as well as a "write disable" bit vector with each bit indicating whether a register is disabled from being overwritten.

A special setup code is inserted prior to the entrance to the application hotspots. The purpose of this code is to set up the hardware support for enabling selective register comparison and checkpointing and disabling undesired overwriting of registers. This can be accomplished by using two store instructions to respectively program two hardware registers, specialized to perform "checkpoint

---

[3] Given two basic blocks B_p and B_q, B_p is said to *dominate* B_q if B_p is on all the possible execution paths that go to B_q.

[4] Dynamically dead instructions are those whose values are either not used by any instruction or only used by other dynamically dead instructions.

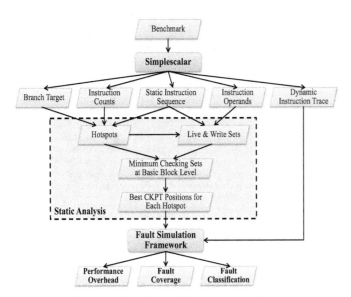

Figure 4. Experimental framework and flow

Table 2. Application hotspot statistics

benchmarks	hotspots	BBs	registers selected
adpcm	1	18	8
crc	1	4	1
epic	1	4	3
g721	2	2	2
		7	2
gsm	1	9	4
mpeg2	3	3	3
		3	2
		13	2
stringsearch	1	1	2
susan	1	8	2

enable" and "write disable". Similarly, two store instructions can be executed when exiting the hotspot in order to bring fault tolerance back into the normal mode. In this case, all the bits in the "checkpoint enable" will be set to 1, while all the bits in the "write disable" will be set to 0.

To support the arbitrary selection of checkpointing frequency, a saturating hardware counter can be used to record the desired frequency, e.g., one checkpoint per M instructions. During application execution, the counter value is set to M in three conditions: 1) at the beginning of execution, 2) upon entering a hotspot, and 3) upon exiting a hotspot. The counter value decrements upon completing an instruction. Outside execution hotspots, a new checkpoint is taken when the counter value reaches 0. Yet within a hotspot, a new checkpoint is taken when the counter is 0 AND the PC reaches the pre-selected checkpoint position. After taking a checkpoint, the counter will be reset to M.

5. Experimental Evaluation

5.1 Methodology

To evaluate the effectiveness of the proposed technique in reducing comparison and checkpointing overhead and in providing high fault coverage, we have conducted a set of experimental studies on Mediabench [20] and Mibench [21] programs. The flow of the evaluation framework is shown in Figure 4.

We first extend the Simplescalar toolset [22] to extract useful program information, including instruction execution counts, branch targets, destination and source registers of each instruction, and instruction execution sequence. Then hotspots for each application are selected based on the instruction execution counts.

Subsequently, static control and data flow analysis is performed for each identified hotspot. We apply the dominator-based approach [23] to identify loops and the possible checkpointing positions for each loop. Subsequently, we perform live variable analysis [23] to identify the written set, as well as the live variables at the entry of each basic block. Based on these values, the best checkpoint positions are selected for each hotspot using the approach outlined in Section 4.

Finally, dynamic fault simulation is performed to evaluate the fault coverage and the overhead of the proposed technique. We ex-

tend the Simplescalar toolset [22] to implement the functions of fault injection and propagation. During execution, each instruction in the selected hotspots is allowed to produce a fault at a certain probability. We have varied the fault rate from 10^{-7} to 10^{-3} in our studies. To eliminate the impact of randomness, Every benchmark is repetitively tested for 10 times under each fault rate configuration. To track fault propagation, a set of poison bits [24] are used in the register file. For store instructions, both their values and addresses are compared for fault detection. When reaching a new checkpoint, only the selected set of registers will be compared, and only the faults in these registers will be recovered. In other words, a fault is allowed to stay in a register that is not in the selected set and to propagate to subsequent computation. In this way, we can evaluate the fault coverage of the proposed technique by capturing any fault that is neither detected nor masked during execution.

5.2 Results

5.2.1 Application Characteristics

Table 2 reports the collected profiling results. For each benchmark, the number of hotspots, the number of basic blocks in each hotspot, as well as the minimum number of registers to be checkpointed are reported. These benchmarks constitute our study set as their hotspots occupy the largest fraction of the total execution time among all the programs we have tested.

5.2.2 Fault detection overhead

To evaluate the ability of the proposed technique in reducing fault detection overhead, we compare it against two existing approaches.

- The first is *SRTR* [14] which conservatively compares the result of each instruction, and only commits an instruction if it is fault free. This approach does not need to maintain any checkpoint.

- The second is *RVQ_f* [16] which only compares the store values and addresses in the same way as the proposed schem. However, when reaching a checkpoint, this approach compares and checkpoints the entire register file to ensure its absolute cleanness at that point. To ensure fairness in comparison, both RVQ_f and the proposed scheme adopt the same checkpoint frequency, that is, whenever the execution reaches the pre-selected checkpoint position.

Figure 5 shows the ratio of the number of total comparison operations over the instruction counts in the fault-free case. On average, the proposed scheme only performs 0.24 comparisons per instruction, while the SRTR and the RVQ_f schemes need to perform 0.74

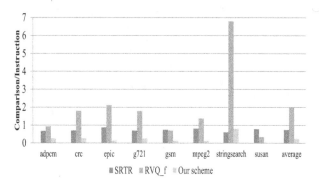

Figure 5. Fault detection overhead evaluation

Table 3. Ratio of various types of faults

	RVQ_f			Our scheme		
	Detect	Mask	Miss	Detect	Mask	Miss
adpcm	0.835	0.165	0	0.749	0.251	0
crc	0.800	0.200	0	0.799	0.201	0
epic	0.897	0.103	0	0.794	0.206	0
g721	0.855	0.145	0	0.588	0.412	0
gsm	0.676	0.324	0	0.645	0.355	0
mpeg2	0.796	0.204	0	0.769	0.231	0
stringsearch	0.786	0.214	0	0.600	0.400	0
susan	0.572	0.428	0	0.115	0.885	0
average	0.777	0.223	0	0.632	0.368	0

and 1.98 comparisons, respectively. Furthermore, a detailed examination of the results illustrates the following properties:

- The proposed scheme significantly outperforms the SRTR scheme except for the *stringsearch* benchmark. This is because the hotspot size in stringsearch is very small. Therefore, the number of instructions compared in the SRTR scheme is comparable to the number of registers compared in the proposed scheme.

- The proposed scheme strictly outperforms the RVQ_f scheme, as both of them check store instructions and adopt the same checkpointing frequency, while the proposed scheme always checkpoints fewer number of registers than the RVQ_f scheme.

- The comparison overhead of the RVQ_f scheme exhibits significant variations, as a result of the large variations of hotspot size across these benchmarks. Since RVQ_f needs to compare the entire register file at each checkpoint, it imposes high comparison overhead on the benchmarks of tiny hotspot size (such as *stringsearch*, *epic*) and low overhead on the benchmarks of large hotspot size (such as *gsm*) or the ones whose checkpoints are taken at outer loops(such as susan).

5.2.3 Fault coverage

To characterize the fault coverage of the proposed technique, we have performed a set of fault injection studies. The faults are classified into three groups: *detected*, *masked*, and *missed*. Detected faults are the ones captured through comparing store instructions and the selected register values. For the faults that never propagate to store instructions or the selected registers, they are considered either as "masked" if they never propagate across a checkpoint, or as "missed" if they propagate across a checkpoint. The ratio of these three types of faults is reported in Table 3. These values are the average of the three fault rates: 10^{-3}, 10^{-4}, and 10^{-5}.

Table 3 confirms that the RVQ_f and out scheme are able to deliver full fault coverage even when the fault rate is extremely high (1 per 1000 instructions). The SRTR scheme compares the result of each instruction, thus all the injected faults will be categorized into detected faults. We don't list the data of SRTR 3for simplify. The RVQ_f scheme masks 22% of all the injected faults, while the proposed scheme masks 37%. The 15% more masked faults are the ones that propagate to the registers that are not selected for comparison by the proposed scheme. Clearly, excluding these registers from the comparison set does not impact the attainable fault coverage.These results confirm that the proposed scheme is able to sizably reduce false errors.

5.2.4 Recovery overhead

The ability to mask more faults in turn allows the proposed scheme to reduce the number of unnecessary rollbacks caused by false errors. Table 4 shows the percentage of instructions re-executed to recover a detected fault for the RVQ_f scheme and the proposed scheme. The SRTR scheme is not included in this study since it precludes unconfirmed instructions from altering processor states and hence does not need to rollback the execution upon a detected fault.

As the overall recovery overhead is determined by the number of faults that have occurred during execution, we report three cases of fault rates: 10^{-3}, 10^{-4}, and 10^{-5}. It can be clearly seen that the recovery overhead is proportional to fault rate. A 10X increase in the fault rate roughly causes a 10X increase in the recovery overhead. More importantly, the proposed scheme strictly outperforms the RVQ_f scheme as it is able to mask more false errors. This is consistent with the results shown in Table 3. For the benchmarks which the proposed scheme is able to mask more faults (e.g., *susan*), larger reduction in recover overhead is achieved.

By comparing Table 4 to Figure 5, it can be observed that recovery overhead is inversely proportional to fault detection overhead, especially for the RVQ_f scheme. The underlying reason is that both types of overhead are determined by checkpointing frequency. When checkpoints are taken frequently, fault detection is costly (e.g., *stringsearch*) while the amount of computation to be rolled back is small. In contrast, when checkpoints are taken infrequently, fault detection overhead is low (e.g., *susan*, *epic*, and *mpeg2*) but a large amount of computation needs to be rolled back upon a detected fault. Therefore, in order to balance fault detection and recovery overhead of an application, the best checkpointing frequency should be determined according to the fault rate in the underlying embedded system.

Table 4. Percentage of re-executed instructions (%) at various fault rates

	1/1000		1/10000		1/100000	
	RVQ_f	Our	RVQ_f	Our	RVQ_f	Our
adpcm	2.732	2.419	0.268	0.238	0.027	0.024
crc	1.264	1.265	1.125	1.126	0.013	0.013
epic	6.188	5.892	0.598	0.560	0.059	0.055
g721	0.579	0.391	0.058	0.039	0.006	0.004
gsm	2.838	2.646	0.283	0.265	0.027	0.026
mpeg2	5.327	5.134	0.517	0.498	0.052	0.050
stringsearch	0.401	0.298	0.040	0.029	0.004	0.003
susan	10.91	1.338	1.046	0.131	0.104	0.012
average	3.780	2.423	0.367	0.236	0.036	0.023

6. Conclusions

In this paper, we have presented a fault resilience scheme, capable of minimizing the fault detection, checkpointing and recovery overhead without sacrificing the fault coverage property. Through performing in-depth control and data flow analysis on the execution hotspots of an application, the proposed technique is able to identify the most efficient checkpoint position for each hotspot. Utilizing the extracted checkpointing information, the runtime fault tolerance scheme can be organized in a way that only the minimum set of registers needs to be compared and checkpointed in conjunction with the store instructions. This sizably reduced comparison and checkpointing set not only lowers the associated fault detection and checkpointing overhead, but furthermore allows more false errors to be masked during execution, thus completely eliminating the overhead in recovering these false errors. The experimental studies on static profiling and dynamic fault simulation confirm that the proposed technique is able to deliver full fault coverage while at the same time reducing nearly 88% of the comparison overhead and masking over 38% of the total injected faults. Such high efficiency in fault detection, checkpointing and recovery will broaden the applicability of redundant execution to systems of tight power and resource constraints.

References

[1] P. Shivakumar, S. W. Keckler, D. Burger, M. Kistler, and L. Alvisi, "Modeling the effect of technology trends on the soft error rate of combinational logic," in *Intl. Conf. Dependable Syst. & Netw. (DSN)*, June 2002, pp. 389–398.

[2] J. Srinivasan, S. V. Adve, P. Bose, and J. A. Rivers, "The impact of technology scaling on lifetime reliability," in *Intl. Conf. Dependable Syst. & Netw. (DSN)*, June 2004, pp. 177–186.

[3] N. Oh, P. P. Shirvani, and E. J. McCluskey, "Control-flow checking by software signatures," *IEEE Trans. Rel.*, vol. 51, no. 1, pp. 111–122, Mar. 2002.

[4] G. A. Reis, J. Chang, N. Vachharajani, R. Rangan, and D. I. August, "SWIFT: software implemented fault tolerance," in *3rd Intl. Symp. Code Gener. & Optim. (CGO)*, Mar. 2005, pp. 243–254.

[5] T. Liu, A. Orailoglu, C. Xue, and M. Li, "Register allocation for simultaneous reduction of energy and peak temperature on registers," in *Design Autom. & Test in Europe (DATE)*, Mar. 2011, pp. 1–6.

[6] C. Xue, E.-M. Sha, and M. Qiu, "Effective loop partitioning and scheduling under memory and register dual constraints," in *Design Autom. & Test in Europe (DATE)*, Mar. 2011, pp. 1202–1207.

[7] E. Rotenberg, "AR-SMT: a microarchitectural approach to fault tolerance in microprocessorse," in *29th Intl. Symp. Fault-Tolerant Computing (FTCS)*, Jun. 1999, pp. 84–91.

[8] S. K. Reinhardt and S. S. Mukherjee, "Transient-fault detection via simultaneous multithreading," in *27th Intl. Symp. Comput. Archit. (ISCA)*, June 2000, pp. 25–36.

[9] S. S. Mukherjee, M. Kontz, and S. K. Reinhardt, "Detailed design and evaluation of redundant multithreading alternatives," in *29th Intl. Symp. Comput. Archit. (ISCA)*, May 2002, pp. 99–110.

[10] A. Parashar, S. Gurumurthi, and A. Sivasubramaniam, "SlicK: Slice-based locality exploitation for efficient redundant multithreading," in *12th Intl. Conf. Archit. Support for Program. Lang. & OSs (ASPLOS)*, Oct. 2006, pp. 95–105.

[11] A. Sodani and G. S. Sohi, "Dynamic instruction reuse," in *24th Intl. Symp. Comput. Archit. (ISCA)*, June 1997, pp. 194–205.

[12] M. A. Gomaa and T. N. Vijaykumar, "Opportunistic transient-fault detection," in *32th Intl. Symp. Comput. Archit. (ISCA)*, June 2005, pp. 172–183.

[13] V. K. Reddy, S. Parthasarathy, and E. Rotenberg, "Understanding prediction-based partial redundant threading for low-overhead, high-coverage fault tolerance," in *12th Intl. Conf. Archit. Support for Program. Lang. & OSs (ASPLOS)*, Mar. 2006, pp. 83–94.

[14] T. Vijaykumar, I. Pomeranz, and K. Cheng, "Transient-fault recovery using simultaneous multithreading," in *29th Intl. Symp. Comput. Archit. (ISCA)*, May 2002, pp. 87–98.

[15] M. A. Gomaa, C. Scarbrough, T. N. Vijaykumar, and I. Pomeranz, "Transient-fault recovery for chip multiprocessors," *IEEE Micro*, vol. 23, no. 6, pp. 76–83, Nov. 2003.

[16] J. Sharkey, N. Abu-Ghazeleh, and D. Ponomarev, "Trades-offs in transient fault recovery schemes for redundant multithreaded processors," in *13th Intl. Conf. High Perform. Computing (HiPC)*, Dec. 2006, pp. 135–147.

[17] C. Yang and A. Orailoglu, "A light-weight cache-based fault detection and checkpointing scheme for MPSoCs enabling relaxed execution synchronization," in *Intl. Conf. Compilers, Archit. & Synthesis for Embedded Syst. (CASES)*, Oct. 2008, pp. 11–20.

[18] G. A. Kildall, "A unified approach to global program optimization," in *1st Symp. Principles of Programming Languages*, 1973, pp. 194–206.

[19] P. Petrov and A. Orailoglu, "Customizable embedded processor architectures," in *Symp. Digital System Design*, 2003, pp. 468–475.

[20] C. Lee, M. Potkonjak, and W. H. Mangione-Smith, "Mediabench: A tool for evaluating and synthesizing multimedia and communications systems," in *30th Intl. Symp. Microarchitecture (MICRO)*, Dec. 1997, pp. 330–335.

[21] J. S. Ringenberg, D. Ernst, T. M. Austin, T. Mudge, and R. B. Brown, "MiBench: A free, commercially representative embedded benchmark suite," in *4th Workshop on Workload Characterization*, Dec. 2001, pp. 3–14.

[22] T. Austin, E. Larson, and D.Ernst, "Simplescalar: an infrastructure for computer system modeling," *IEEE Computer*, vol. 35, no. 2, pp. 59–67, Feb. 2002.

[23] S. S. Muchnick, *Advanced Compiler Design and Implementation*. Morgan Kaufmann Publishers, 1997.

[24] C. Weaver, J. Emer, S. S. Mukherjee, and S. K. Reinhardt, "Techniques to reduce the soft error rate of a high-performance microprocessor," in *31th Intl. Symp. Comput. Archit. (ISCA)*, June 2004, pp. 264–275.

A JVM for Soft-Error-Prone Embedded Systems

Isabella Stilkerich   Michael Strotz   Christoph Erhardt   Martin Hoffmann   Daniel Lohmann
Fabian Scheler   Wolfgang Schröder-Preikschat

Friedrich-Alexander University Erlangen-Nuremberg
{istilkerich, strotz, erhardt, hoffmann, lohmann, scheler, wosch}@cs.fau.de

Abstract

The reduction of structure sizes in microcontollers, environmental conditions or low supply voltages increase the susceptibility of embedded systems to soft errors. As a result, the employment of fault-detection and fault-tolerance measures is becoming a mandatory task even for moderately critical applications. Accordingly, software-based techniques have recently gained in popularity, and a multitude of approaches that differ in the number and frequency of tolerated errors as well as their associated overhead have been proposed. Using type-safe programming languages to isolate critical software components is very popular among those techniques. An automated application of fault-detection and fault-tolerance measures based on the type system of the programming language and static code analyses is possible. It facilitates an easy evaluation of the protection characteristics and costs as well as the migration of software to new hardware platforms with different failure rates. Transient faults, however, are not bound to the application code secured by the type system, but can also affect the correctness of the type system itself. Thereby, the type system might lose its ability to isolate critical components. As a consequence, it is essential to also protect the type system itself against soft errors. In this paper, we show how soft errors can affect the integrity of the type system. Furthermore, we provide means to secure it against these faults, thus preserving its isolating character. These measures can be applied selectively to achieve a suitable tradeoff between level of protection and resource consumption. [1]

Categories and Subject Descriptors   D.3.4 [*Programming Languages*]: Processors—Compilers;   D.3.3 [*Programming Languages*]: Language Constructs and Features—Classes and Objects;   D.4.5 [*Operating Systems*]: Reliability—Fault-tolerance;   D.4.7 [*Operating Systems*]: Organization and Design—Real-time Systems and Embedded Systems

General Terms   Reliability, Design, Languages

Keywords   KESO; Java; RTSJ; Embedded Systems; Real-Time Systems; Reliability

[1] This work was partly supported by the German Research Foundation (DFG) under grants no. LO 1719/1-1 and SCHR 603/9-1

1.   Introduction

A lot of embedded systems have particular safety requirements regarding hardware and software components to avoid or mitigate malign errors. Functional safety standards such as the IEC 61508 and ISO 26262 address this issue and categorize such errors into so-called *systematic* and *random* errors. *Systematic* errors can occur in hardware and software components and are the result of design and implementation defects. Engineering processes and methods exist to avoid and mitigate systematic defects. On the contrary, *random* errors do not reside in the system in the first place and only occur in hardware. They are referred to as permanent (hard) and transient (soft) errors, where soft errors have – in contrast to hard errors – only a temporary effect on the logical circuits or memory. Soft errors manifesting themselves as bit flips are a result of hardware failures that are becoming more likely to happen as a consequence of shrinking structure sizes [7], extreme environmental conditions such as radiation [25], or voltage-supply problems.

Usually, functional-safety standards outline hardware-based redundancy and the employment of specialized error-correcting hardware components – such as ECC for memory devices or hardware watchdogs to recognize bogus behavior of components – as a possible solution. As these solutions entail additional or more expensive hardware components, this approach is often not feasible due to an immense cost pressure in many industrial domains. Products in such domains often are mass products, where cost differences of few cents on the single device can amount to huge values considering the whole of the produced devices. The tolerance towards added cost is particularly limited when caused by features that do not directly pose an added value visible to the customer, which is the case for robustness regarding soft errors. Besides the cost factor, hardware redundancy is often impractical due to physical size, weight and power constraints, which are an essential requirement in embedded systems.

Software-based fault-tolerance techniques such as spatially and temporally replicated execution of code or monitoring software components go without extra hardware and pose a cheaper alternative for increasing system dependability. A combination of both approaches may also be worthwhile in certain scenarios. In the absence of transient errors, a type-safe software system, for instance, could already provide constructively ensured spatial isolation of software components. However, soft errors can break the soundness of the type system and thus an integral part of software-based replication. For this reason, a memory-protection unit (MPU), for example, is necessary to maintain spatial isolation and to avoid error spreading [19, 26]. Hence, such software-based replication techniques usually cannot be applied at all to embedded systems where such an MPU does not exist. If an MPU is present, transient errors are recognized that cause an address to be out of preconfigured memory bounds. However, software-based fault detection at the granularity of objects – in contrast to region-based mechanisms, as for example provided by an MPU – has some advantages. The error-detection time is lower and effects of errors can strongly be localized, thus allowing for fine-grained reliability measures that scale with the imposed costs and which are not confined by the limited number of address regions provided by an MPU. In this paper, we show how software-based isolation building on the type safety of a programming language can be preserved in the presence of transient errors, which allows for an early detection of bit flips and facilitates the application of software-based redundancy techniques without the need for an MPU. However, a combination of both software- and hardware-based memory protection is still possible to additionally harden the system.

As software-based fault tolerance does not come for free in terms of runtime overhead and different hardware also differs in the failure rates, it is necessary to tune the fault-detection or -toleration technique towards the safety requirements and also the hardware features. Therefore, a separation of the functional code and the non-functional property fault-tolerance is desired. For this, we use KESO [23] – a Multi-JVM for deeply embedded systems. KESO already allows for the automated application of fault-detection/tolerance measures using the results of comprehensive static analyses enabled by the type-safe programming language Java. In summary, the dimension of the fault-detection/tolerance measures could be adapted without touching the functional application code.

At first, a look at our fault hypothesis is taken in Section 2. Afterwards, the targeted domain and surrounding conditions are discussed in Section 3. Sections 4 and 5 describe the characteristics of a protected runtime system as well as the measures taken to ensure software-based memory protection in the context of KESO. In Section 6 we evaluate our approach using the Collision Detector (CD$_x$) benchmark [16]. Section 7 covers work that is related to ours before Section 8 concludes this paper.

2. Fault Hypothesis

As spatial isolation among the different replicas is an indispensable property of replication, we aim at improving the robustness of software-implemented spatial isolation by exploiting a type-safe programming language. Such programming languages can safely isolate different software objects as long as the integrity of the type system can be maintained. This naturally also has an impact on the fault hypothesis our work bases upon.

Firstly, we only consider soft errors that become visible at the programming interface of the processor, as we propose a software-based solution. This comprises bit flips in arbitrary memory locations and registers. It does not matter in which part of the processor these bit flips actually occur – in the memory or the register itself or while data is transferred from memory to a register on the bus – but it is important that software-based checks covering such errors are possible. Thus, we cannot detect errors when data is corrupted after we have checked for its integrity while it is copied from e.g. a register to memory or an output location.

Secondly, we strive for the protection of the type system but not the application itself. That is, we only protect those items which are necessary to preserve spatial isolation provided by a type-safe programming language. Mainly, such items comprise object references, pointers to virtual function tables or type information in object headers. We will explain how a corrupt type system could affect isolation and the measures to harden the type system later on in Section 4. Our intention is to improve the robustness of these elements in the presence of one soft error at a time so we can provide a reliable foundation to implement software-based spatial isolation. Thus, we do not guard application-specific data like computation results. This has to be accomplished on a higher level by means of e.g. replication as presented in a previous paper [26].

Thirdly, there are some elements that have the potential to compromise spatial isolation when affected by transient faults that are

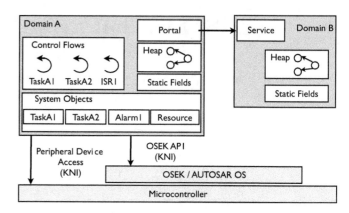

Figure 1: KESO's architecture

not safeguarded by our approach. In particular, these are the program-counter register (PC) and the operating system (OS). Additional measures are necessary to take care of these weak spots. A possible solution to detect the corruption of the PC is e.g. control-flow monitoring [15]. The OS, on the other hand, could be hardened by additional algorithmic measures [20] or – at best – the OS is implemented in the same type-safe programming language [14] that is used to achieve spatial isolation among different replicated components.

Fourthly, we assume that program code and data that is located in non-volatile read-only memory like flash does not suffer from transient faults, as these memory areas normally are more robust than e.g. SRAM or registers [8]. So, we do not make any effort to protect executable code and constant data stored there.

In summary, we certainly cannot tolerate arbitrary transient faults affecting the type system. But we try to reduce the probability that a corrupted type system breaks the isolating property of a type-safe programming language as far as reasonably possible.

3. The KESO JVM

We selected KESO [23] to evaluate the impact of soft errors to a type-safe runtime system, as it targets applications for statically configured embedded systems. In the following section, we introduce the key features of KESO as far as they are relevant for this paper.

3.1 Maxim and Concept

In statically configured embedded systems, all relevant entities of the application itself and the underlying system software are known at compile time. These entities comprise the complete code of the application and also operating-system-level objects (threads, interrupt service routines, synchronization locks, etc.) influencing the runtime behavior of the system. This type of application covers many, if not most, traditional embedded applications, from control units providing safety-critical functions such as the electronic stability program (ESP) and many other electronic functions found in nowaday's railway systems, airplanes or medical devices.

This scheme imposes some restrictions on applications building on top of KESO: It is not possible to dynamically load new code or create new threads at runtime. On the other hand, it allows to create a comprehensively tailored and efficient runtime environment for Java applications – even for small, deeply embedded systems.

3.2 KESO Architecture

The architecture of the KESO Java runtime environment is depicted in Figure 1. KESO provides the control-flow abstractions typical for this domain (i.e. threads called *Tasks* and interrupt service routines (ISRs)) and means to activate (e.g. alarms) and synchronize them properly (e.g. via synchronization locks called *Resources*). Furthermore, KESO applications benefit from Java features like type safety, dynamic memory management and optionally a garbage collector. KESO even allows access to raw memory through Java objects. Thus, it is possible to implement complete embedded applications including device drivers (as long as these devices are interfaced via memory-mapped registers) in Java.

The ahead-of-time compiler *jino*, which is an integral part of the KESO toolchain, generates ANSI C code from the application's Java bytecode. During code generation *jino* also generates a runtime environment specific for that application. Additionally, *jino* can integrate e.g. reliability measures and software-based memory protection. While most of the code directly translates to plain C code, the Java thread API is mapped onto the thread abstraction layer of an underlying OS. In the case of KESO, that abstraction layer is normally provided by AUTOSAR OS.

Like KESO, AUTOSAR OS is configured completely statically, i.e. all relevant system objects (threads, ISRs, locks, etc.) and their properties (task and interrupt entries, runtime priority, interrupt source, etc.) have to be determined ahead of runtime and cannot be altered while the system is running. Thus, an application could not create threads dynamically or attach a different ISR to an interrupt source. Besides the application code itself, an AUTOSAR application needs to provide a system-description file that defines the instances of these OS objects and their attributes. The system-description file is used by the AUTOSAR OS implementation to create an OS variant containing statically allocated instances of the defined OS objects. In the context of KESO, this file is provided by *jino*. Furthermore, many AUTOSAR OS implementations ship with a code generator that outputs an OS implementation that is specifically tailored for the application in order to avoid unnecessary overhead.

3.3 Tailoring KESO

The KESO JVM adopts the idea of creating a tailored version of the infrastructure software that provides only the features required by the application. KESO's compiler *jino* uses a system-configuration file and the entire source code of the application as input to determine these features.

The system-configuration file contains all the information that is needed to generate an instance of AUTOSAR OS plus some KESO-specific extensions such as fault-detection and fault-tolerance options. The configuration file also explictly controls coarse-grained features such as the existence of a garbage collector (GC) or the replication of certain parts of the application.

The JVM features demanded by the application are implicitly extracted from the application code via static analyses. Features like floating-point support, 64-bit integers or virtual methods are detected by the post-reachability analysis. Some of those are not mere boolean features but are tuned on a more fine-grained level. For example, the dispatch tables needed for virtual method binding are only generated if *jino* failed to provide a full static binding.

3.4 Memory Protection in KESO

Being a Multi-JVM, KESO allows tasks to be spatially isolated in different protection domains, each of which appears as a JVM of its own from the application's point of view. If soft errors are not an issue, Java's type safety guarantees that an application can only access memory to which it has been given an explicit reference, and the type of the reference determines how an application can access the memory area pointed to by the reference. Type-safe programs are therefore also memory-safe [2]. In order to enforce type safety, the compiler inserts runtime checks into the code:

- For all invocations of non-static methods and accesses to object fields and arrays, the associated object reference must be valid, that is, non-`null`. A `null`-check is inserted before these operations.

- All array accesses must be within the array's bounds, so the index of the accessed element is checked against the array size.

Since the entire application is known ahead of time, *jino* can perform whole-program analyses and aggressively eliminate unnecessary checks by statically proving accesses to a reference or array to be correct.

Spatial isolation is established based on the logical separation of the object heaps and by maintaining a separate set of the static fields in each domain. Each control flow (i.e. task or ISR) and all other system objects are statically assigned to a domain. A system object can only be accessed from other domains if explicitly permitted by the KESO system configuration.

In order to allow control flows from different domains to exchange data with each other, domains may export a functional interface, a so-called *Service*, that can be invoked from other domains by using a proxy object, a so-called *Portal*, that represents the service in the foreign domain. Deep copying is used for parameters and return values in portal calls in order to retain the heap separation. As a copy-free alternative to the portal mechanism, KESO also provides shared-memory areas that can be accessed by a controllable set of domains using the same programmatic interfaces that are available for accessing raw-memory areas. To maintain isolation, all inter-domain communication mechanisms (IDC – i.e. portals and shared memory) must ensure that no reference values can be propagated to another domain.

In addition to the software-based spatial isolation, KESO can actively support an OS to provide hardware-based memory protection using an MPU. KESO supports the OS by physically grouping the domain data (i.e. the physically separated heaps and static fields) in separate memory regions to recognize addressing errors and so to additionally harden the system.

3.5 Fault Detection and Tolerance in KESO

KESO already supports the creation of dependable embedded systems by mechanisms for fault detection and tolerance such as software-based replication of critical application parts. This feature is smoothly integrated into the *jino* compiler and can be controlled through the system-configuration file. At this point, the developer can specify the number of bit flips that have to be tolerated by an application. KESO then instantiates the needed number of replicas, isolates them from each other spatially, either on the level of the programming language or by means of an MPU, and finally integrates them into the application. Moreover, *jino* is able to generate a majority voter to identify the faulty replica, and code to restore its state with the aid of the remaining intact replicas after a fault has been recognized. Either is only possible thanks to the type safety provided by Java: References can easily be distinguished from primitive data and both are strongly typed, enabling the automated generation of a majority voter and the recovery code.

As spatial isolation is the main prerequisite to build dependable systems based on replication, it is not sufficient in the presence of soft errors to rely only on software-based memory protection as it is implemented in KESO. Bit flips can corrupt references and thus break spatial isolation. This problem could be solved by using an MPU to separate the different replicas of a replicated dependable embedded system. However, many low-end microcontrollers do not offer an MPU and the protection offered by an MPU is rather coarsed-grained.

Instead of relying on an MPU, we examined how spatial isolation via software-based memory protection can be preserved in the presence of soft errors by systematically protecting references and type information. Utilizing the static nature of the system and respective compiler-based techniques makes an efficient implemen-

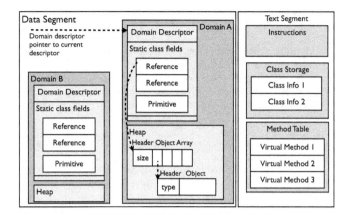

Figure 2: Relations between domain descriptor and object references: The domain descriptor is used by the application through the domain-descriptor pointer. A static reference (accessed through a constant offset) is employed to access an array object that contains references to plain objects. A virtual method is invoked on the first element in the array after type-checking that object. The method table located in the text segment is accessed at a constant offset.

tation of reference checking (RC) possible. This advance can further be assisted by accounting for microcontroller specifics – such as failure rates, special instructions and address layout.

As software-based memory-protection techniques apply on a very fine-grained level, they also call for a fine-grained application of reliability measures and thus a low error-detection time in contrast to MPU-based systems. Furthermore, the application developer can continue to rely on the benefits of a type-safe programming language even in a fault-prone hardware environment.

4. Runtime-System Integrity

The scope of this paper is a reliable type-safe middleware for embedded applications that retains software-based isolation also in the presence of soft errors. Therefore, we focus on the protection of the runtime system itself and not of the application data.

With regard to the fault hypothesis stated in Section 2, we identified the following critical spots which influence the integrity of the runtime system in the context of KESO:

- The type system ensuring memory safety. Here, e.g. **references**, **class identifiers** and **virtual method tables** could be corrupted.

- Per-**protection-domain data** mainly comprising static fields and heaps for each domain. Regarding the memory-management system, data elements used by **memory allocators** and the **garbage collection** for book-keeping purposes could be corrupted, compromising the software-based spatial isolation.

In this paper we only consider the protection of the type system as we want to evaluate its cost and effectiveness in isolation. Thus, we spare complex memory-management strategies using garbage collection and leave this topic as future work. This is not a real drawback as garbage collection is not necessary for many embedded applications [23, 27]. The Java language does, however, not allow a static allocation of objects. For such applications, KESO provides a simple heap strategy that does not provide garbage collection at all. The advantage of this heap implementation (bump-pointer or pseudo-static allocation) is the short, constant and thus easily predictable time required for the allocation of an object. Since there is no way of releasing the memory of objects that are not required any more, the application should only allocate memory objects during the initialization phase.

4.1 Effects of Soft Errors on the Runtime System

In Java, type safety ensures that programs can only access memory regions to which they were given an explicit reference; the type of the reference also determines in which way a program can access the memory region pointed to by the reference. This is utilized by KESO to establish spatial isolation by preventing any shared data between protection domains. For this purpose, heap objects and static class fields of the different protection domains are logically separated as mentioned earlier.

Preserving software-based memory protection in the presence of transient errors is two-fold: Firstly, global book-keeping information of the type system must not be corrupted. Secondly, protection-domain data has to be handled in a correct way, so that each domain only gets access to its private data. Thirdly, it has to be ensured that wild references and faulty type-system information caused by bit flips are recognized in order to maintain type safety and thus, preventing faulty accesses to other memory locations.

In the following, an overview is given how bit flips in book-keeping information of the runtime system and in references can influence the runtime environment. The relationships between the data structures and references are illustrated in Figure 2.

4.1.1 Global Information of the Type System

KESO incorporates a set of runtime-system-internal data structures relevant to enforce the type system. The *method table* is used in conjunction with virtual method invocations, whereas the *class storage* holds essential data about the individual classes such as the size of an object instantiated from a class. Bit flips in the class storage would invalidate static assumptions on the object's type and dynamic type checks.

The virtual method table as well as the class storage are computed statically and are constant, allowing for locating these data structures in robust ROM. Accesses to the structures are performed with constant indices, which is the reason why those accesses can be regarded to be safe (see Section 2).

The remaining part of type-system information is incorporated in each object (in plain objects and the derived array objects).

4.1.2 Global Information of each Protection Domain

For every domain, there exists a descriptor which holds the static class fields (containing both primitive data and references) and a pointer to the domain's heap. Both the descriptor and the heap are non-constant and therefore reside in RAM, which is subject to transient errors. While primitive data is considered as part of the application, a static reference must be secured just like any other reference.

In addition, there is one global pointer which references the descriptor of the protection domain in whose context the current thread of control is running. Context changes are performed by setting the pointer to another domain descriptor. This global pointer is of particular interest and must be explicitly secured. As the static fields and the heap of a protection domain are accessed by dereferencing this global pointer, its corruption could have severe consequences. A domain could get access to the static fields and the heap of another domain and thereby break spatial isolation.

Heaps and management strategies are available on a per-domain basis. In the context of KESO, we consider *pseudo-static* allocation, where the heap can instantly be corrupted due to a bogus bump pointer. This pointer is part of the domain descriptor. In case of garbage collection, bit flips in references in the scan-and-mark phase as well as in the sweep phase cause inconsistencies in the object graph, leading to wild references.

4.1.3 Local Information inside Objects and Arrays

The remaining part of the type system is directly embedded into the objects created and manipulated by the application. Although this information is local to these objects, it has the potential to compromise the complete type system if it is corrupt. In any of the cases explained below, spatial isolation provided through the type system could not be guaranteed any more.

Object and Array References: Bit flips in object references may produce wild object references with devastating impact. Primitive values could be read and interpreted as a reference values, for example. Also, data could be stored to illegal locations so that runtime information of other objects is corrupted. Existing null-checks inserted by the runtime system are invalidated – as they are checking a corrupted reference – and thus faulty dereferencing is not detected any more.

Object-Header Information: In KESO, each object has a header block holding meta-information such as the type of the object, which is represented by a class identifier (ID), and thus determines in which way the memory the reference points to can be used. The class ID is used as an index for lookups in the method table and the class storage. Using a wrong type – because the class ID is affected by a transient fault – breaks the soundness of the type system. If a method not suiting the type of the object is invoked, this may entail memory accesses outside the scope of the particular object and also outside of the protection domain.

Array Header Information: In case of the specialized object variant *array*, there is an additional size parameter that defines the length of an array, and it has to be ensured that any array access is within bounds. The size parameter can be affected by soft errors: In the best case, it has changed to a smaller value. This may cause additional array-bounds exceptions in some cases. If the flipped array size is greater than the actual one, an array bounds check is not able to detect an illegal array access any more. At array locations where the index and array size are both known to be constant, bit flips in the array size information do not affect type safety.

4.2 Protection of Type Safety

Having identified these critical location, we now take a closer look into how isolation and type safety can be preserved in the presence of soft errors. First of all, the protection-domain descriptor and references to it have to be correct. Secondly, an object reference has to refer to the correct memory location and an object which is placed at that location must only be accessed by operations that suit the type of that object to preserve memory and type safety. Both characteristics are needed to establish software isolation.

4.2.1 Protection Techniques

Before we examine these issues in detail, we discuss possible concepts to harden the type system against soft errors.

Attack-Surface Reduction Many transient errors occur directly in RAM or when data is transferred on the bus, that is, on load and store accesses to memory. A reduction of such accesses leads to fewer memory-protection errors [11]. Validating that a reference read into a register is correct reduces illegal addressing, thus error spreading, and can maintain type safety. Bit flips that might occur in registers are currently not in the focus of our approach, but may at least be recognized if a register value is checked whenever it is stored to memory. Such errors are also likely to be detected on the next load of a reference in case of a corrupted address or by an additional protection of application data.

Soft errors which occur on the bus when the data is stored are also outside the scope of our experiments in this paper. If the micro-controller has an MPU that is situated on memory, it can complement reference checking to detect bus store errors, however if the MPU is located on the processor, such errors cannot be detected at the time of the store instruction.

Checking References An RC can be performed in many different ways such as, for example, replication and voting or via a checksum. There is no focus on a specific technique, as it should be adjustable as demanded by the system configuration with regards to runtime overhead, memory consumption and safety requirements. Due to the static nature of the system, all reference accesses can be determined ahead of time and reference checks can be automatically inserted by *jino*. At runtime, these checks ensure the integrity of the respective memory accesses. As an initial technique, we instrumented *jino* to enrich references with parity information. This technique has some advantages over reference replication [6], as it does not inflate the reference size and so the attack surface of the program, which is the reason why we have selected this approach.

We now briefly describe three possible variants of reference checking and in which way this leads to an improvement of protection in the context of the effects of illegal references, which were mentioned in Section 4.1.

Dereference Check (DRC): In this variant, references stay encoded all the time. They are tested and decoded every time they are dereferenced, thus the probability of detecting an illegal reference is very high. Dereferencing takes place when one of the following bytecode instructions is executed: putfield, getfield, *aload, *astore, arraylength, instanceof, checkcast, invokevirtual, invokeinterface, and invokespecial.

A drawback is the possibility that the check will be executed more often than actually necessary – for instance, if the reference in question is used several times in succession but is kept within a processor register between the uses, the first check would suffice[2]. Also, corruption of a reference will not be detected until the reference is actually used. Reference comparisons in the application code may result in a wrong branch being taken.

Load Reference Check (LRC): In this variant, references are checked as soon as they are loaded from memory – that is, from a static field (bytecode instruction getstatic), an object field (getfield) or an object array (aload). They are encoded when being stored and decoded upon being loaded.

This approach offers an early error detection and needs fewer checks than the DRC variant. The disadvantage is that it has a higher false-negative probability, since local variables may be spilled to the stack in case of high register pressure or across the boundaries of method invocations.

Header-Only Check (HOC): A third conceivable possibility is to not check the reference itself, but instead only test upon dereferencing if the reference points to a valid object header containing a certain bit pattern. For efficiency, it can be combined with the class-ID check described in Section 4.2.4. In case of a corrupted reference, it is likely that the target is not an object header but a random piece of data, given that object headers are relatively small (usually four bytes).

This approach is less safe than the LRC and DRC variants. Firstly, the check can result in false negatives if the data pointed to by the faulty reference happens to look like a legal object header. Secondly, the reference may be corrupted in a way that it points to another valid object, which may have a different type than the intended object. In both cases, type and memory safety

---

[2] Of course, the register may be temporarily spilled to the stack at any point in time by an interrupt service routine. Even so, it will stay in memory only for a very short time.

can no longer be maintained. It is even possible that the reference points into the memory belonging to a different protection domain. To prevent breaching the isolation, the runtime system would have to catch such cases by checking the reference against the domain's memory bounds or by using an MPU as a safety net. In theory, the chance of false negatives could be reduced by arranging the heap layout in a way that all valid references have a Hamming distance of at least two from each other. This approach would cause a higher memory clipping and raises the need to adapt garbage collection techniques, where fragmented allocation can be a possible solution. This may be a subject of further research, but will not further be examined here. In the remainder of this paper, we will focus on DRC and LRC rather than the HOC variant.

Choosing a variant for a concrete application scenario involves a tradeoff between protection level and costs. Various combinations of DRC and LRC are thinkable – among others:

- both DRC and LRC (slowest, but highest level of protection and early error detection)

- DRC only (faster, but no early error detection)

- LRC within leaf methods, DRC within other methods (even faster and only slightly less protection)

- LRC only (fastest, but lowest protection)

The reference checks are performed before any existing null- and array bounds checks so that the latter are executed on valid references.

4.2.2 Protecting the Current-Domain Pointer

As described above, the protection domain in which the current control flow is running is determined by a global pointer that points to the descriptor of the domain. To maintain type safety, that pointer must be checked whenever it is dereferenced. Such events include accesses to static fields and memory-management operations. To implement the verification of the pointer, one of the techniques for references to user objects described above is used analogously.

4.2.3 Memory Management

Memory managment by means of pseudo-static allocation is safeguarded by protecting the bump-pointer on access. Dependable GCs are part of our future work.

4.2.4 Protecting Object Headers

By encoding and checking object references, we are able to test the correctness of the memory pointers and preserve the validity of null-pointer checks. In case of bump-pointer allocation, references to deallocated memory are also prevented. However, memory safety is still not attained: Some operations which rely on meta-information stored within the object header definition affect type safety if that information is incorrect. For instance, they may cause writes beyond the object's boundaries. With the employment of more eloborate GCs, bogus object information may cause dangling references. Consequently, the integrity of the object headers must also be encoded and checked.

Each object header contains a class ID. In addition, array objects hold a field containing the array length. Optionally, management data used by the garbage collection is also present. Only if the meta-information is verified can type and memory safety be preserved.

As we do not make use of garbage collection in the scope of this paper, but rely on simple bump-pointer allocation, we do not need to secure any GC information. Thus, a header check is only necessary in the following scenarios:

Access to Type Information   The class ID in the object header is used by `instanceof` and `checkcast` to determine if a given object is of a specific type. Illegally downcasting an object to a bigger type and then writing to one of the instance fields added by the subclass is guaranteed to write beyond the bounds of the object. Under normal conditions, such behavior is the result of a programming error, but it can also occur if a soft error affects the control flow. Consequently, to preserve type safety, such illegal downcasts have to be caught reliably. This requires checking the class ID before performing the actual type check.

Virtual Method Invocations   The target for virtual method invocations is determined by performing a lookup in the global method table. While the table itself is constant and resides in ROM, the index for the lookup is computed using the class ID of the `this`-object. In case the class ID in the object header is affected by a transient error, the CPU will jump to an arbitrary wrong address. To prevent this, the runtime system must again make sure that the class ID is untouched.

Devirtualization, as described in Section 5.1, can help mitigating the costs of such checks.

Array Accesses   An access to an array element always has to be within the array's bounds to guarantee memory safety. If soft errors are not an issue, this property can partially be verified by the compiler, or array bounds checks are necessary at runtime. Taking bit flips into consideration is two-fold:

On the one side, a soft error can affect the index and cause it to become too large or negative. This can be caught by a regular bounds check.

On the other side, the length information of the array can be corrupted, which invalidates any conventional array bounds check. In order to handle this issue, the existing array bounds check is extended to verify the validity of the array size before determining if a given index is within the array's bounds. Thus, this check incorporates an array-header check. It is referred to as *extended array bounds check* in the remainder of this paper. As a consequence, the compiler must be especially careful when deciding whether an array access can be left unchecked or not. The criteria for this optimization are presented in Section 5.1.

5.   Efficient Implementation

Since our approach targets embedded systems, it is crucial to consider factors such as memory consumption, footprint and performance of the application while providing suitable protection for the application and runtime system. KESO's compiler optimizations facilitate creating a tailored runtime environment that suits the safety requirements to balance protection and cost. Less code and less memory usage also leads to a lower susceptability to soft errors, since the probability for a transient error to affect the application decreases with the memory usage. Static type-safe programs show a very good analyzability that allows for optimizations which are not possible if that type information is missing. KESO uses this information for its analyses and optimizations. Further optimizations through the C compiler also have a positive effect on the soft-error susceptability due to [11].

The reference runtime checks are inserted by KESO's backend, when optimization passes have already been run. We used and extended several analyses to gather the information necessary to eliminate, to simplify or to emit RCs. Characteristics of the hardware platform, e.g. if ROM is available, are also included in our analyses. In the following, an explanation on which checks have to be inserted and which can be erased is given.

5.1   High-Level Compiler Optimizations

KESO's static programming and system model enables the compiler to perform aggressive whole-program optimizations that would be far less effective without a closed-world assumption. The optimizations are not only able to increase the application's runtime performance and reduce its memory footprint in general, but also have two additional effects that suit our purposes:

1. They reduce the attack surface for soft errors by decreasing the number of potentially error-prone operations such as memory accesses. The more information can be computed statically ahead of time by the compiler, the fewer operations have to be executed at runtime on the target system.

2. They mitigate the overhead introduced by the integrity checks discussed above.

In the following, we present selected compiler optimizations we implemented in *jino* that serve these purposes. Although modern C/C++ compilers offer comparable optimizations and we rely on such a C compiler as the final stage of our tool chain, the optimizations in *jino* make specific use of the high-level application knowledge available at the early compilation stages – for example, information about the system's designated entry points, about the assignment of tasks to protection domains, or about the target platform. Moreover, most of these whole-program transformations influence each other. Hence, we implement our own high-level transformations in *jino* while at the same time benefiting from the C compiler's low-level optimizations.

Constant Propagation: The constant-propagation algorithm in the KESO compiler is based on Wegman and Zadeck's interprocedural *Sparse Conditional Constant Propagation* [28]. Uses of variables which would normally reside in registers or on the stack are replaced with immediate values that are embedded directly in the code, reducing the number of potentially error-prone variable accesses. In addition, the register pressure is lowered, thereby reducing the need to spill registers to the (vulnerable) stack.

Copy Propagation and Variable Coalescing: Converting the intermediate representation back from SSA form is done using the algorithm proposed by Sreedhar [22], which coalesces variables and eliminates redundant copy instructions in the process. This, too, reduces register pressure and stack usage.

Dead-Code Elimination: Among other things, the *Sparse Conditional Constant Propagation* algorithm can fold conditional branches into unconditional jumps, and it can be used as a reachability analysis: Any basic block or entire method that was never visited is dead and can be safely eliminated. While this optimization itself does not directly contribute to better code performance, the other analyses and optimizations – for instance, method inlining or the rapid type analysis described below – benefit from its results.

Method Devirtualization: The principle of polymorphism in Java requires dynamic dispatch – that is, a method invocation whose target is not known at compile time is dispatched at runtime. As described earlier, this involves a lookup in the global dispatch table, plus an object-header check to enforce type safety in the face of soft errors. When translating the source code into bytecode, the Java compiler by default generates such `invokevirtual` instructions for all calls to an instance method of an object. The programmer could avoid this performance bottleneck by abstaining from the features of polymorphism, writing only static class methods. However, this would not suit the Java programming model very well.

To overcome this, the KESO compiler performs devirtualizations [1, 24] where possible. Since no additional classes can be loaded at runtime, the complete set of callee candidates for each call site is known ahead of time. Invocations whose candidate set contains a single element are converted into `invokespecial` instructions, which are bound statically and require neither a dispatch-table lookup nor an associated integrity check of the object header.

Whole-program analyses allow to further shrink the candidate sets, possibly yielding more single-element sets and thus increasing the effectiveness of the devirtualization optimization. In KESO, we apply a combination of class-hierarchy analysis (CHA) [12] and rapid type analysis (RTA) [3]. CHA analyzes the data flow of reference variables and tries to determine the dynamic types of the referenced objects at call sites as specifically as possible, whereas RTA purges all candidate sets of methods whose class is never instantiated – profiting from the elimination of dead object-allocation sites.

Method Inlining: For method invocations that can be bound statically, the compiler can choose to embed the body of the callee at the call site, eliminating the overhead of the function call. After inlining, it is worthwhile to re-run the constant-folding and -propagation pass because it is now possible to specialize the embedded method body according to the concrete arguments passed at the original call. At the same time, the arguments passed by that call no longer have to be considered when re-analyzing the callee method, which may in turn be further optimized.

Runtime-Check Elision: As the consistency checks are often coupled with regular runtime checks, the efficiency of the compiled code profits from the regular check-elision optimizations performed by the compiler. `checkcast` instructions are eliminated if the data-flow and type analysis proves the respective reference to always be of the correct type – for example, if it follows an `instanceof` case differentiation. In this case, the object-header check preceding the `checkcast` is unnecessary as well.

For array accesses, the following cases have to be differentiated:

1. Both the index and the array size are constant (possibly thanks to constant propagation) and the index is within bounds. Consequently, no bounds check is needed.

2. The array size is constant, but the index is variable. A simple bounds check is sufficient since the size is not read from the array header.

3. The data-flow analysis proves that the access will always be within bounds, but one of the two values is not constant. This can be the case when iterating over an array in a canonical `for`-loop, for instance. In a scenario without fault-detection/tolerance requirements, the bounds check could be elided. In our case, however, the access index may have been corrupted or the array may have been created with a wrong, possibly too small size. Hence, an extended array bounds check must be emitted.

4. None of the above conditions is met. An extended array bounds check has to be inserted.

If it is sufficient to maintain spatial isolation, the restrictions can be somewhat loosened: It can be argued that extended array bounds checking is not necessarily required if reading from an array that contains primitive data. Reading a wrong value would lead to wrong application data, but such data errors could be caught using additional application-specific safety measures. Other protection domains would not be affected. However, if the array contains object references, reading from it must be protected with an extended bounds check, since reading from an invalid position might return a reference pointing into the heap of another protection domain.

ROM Allocation: One of the major drawbacks of Java as a programming language for embedded systems is its insufficient handling of constant data. While there is the keyword `final` to mark variables of primitive type or references themselves as immutable, there is no equivalent concept for the contents of an object. This is especially cumbersome for arrays containing primitive constant values: Such arrays are allocated on the heap and initialized at the time the class is loaded – one element at a time. This scheme induces a number of disadvantages:

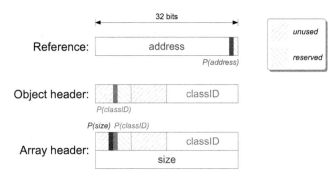

Figure 3: Encoding of parity information on a 32-bit platform

- The explicit initialization code – especially for arrays – needlessly inflates the text segment.

- On small embedded devices, RAM is scarce. Placing constant array data in the ROM instead could save precious memory.

- According to our fault hypothesis, integrity checks (object/array header) for ROM-allocated objects could be elided.

- Protection redundancy techniques for application data can profit from a reduced replication set.

A static analysis could find objects and arrays with immutable contents and mark them as ROM-allocatable, provided this is supported by the target platform. This currently being implemented in KESO and promises to be a worthwhile optimization.

5.2 Incorporation of Platform-Specific Features

Tailoring the KESO runtime environment to a concrete application scenario also involves awareness of the underlying hardware platform. Thus it is possible to adapt the runtime system to the conditions of the target platform and to make use of specific hardware features where available.

Alignment and Address Layout: For 1-bit error detection using parity information, one additional bit is needed for every word that is to be protected. Since every object on the heap is aligned at a minimum of four bytes, each valid pointer always has its two least-significant bits set to zero. In KESO, if a garbage collector is present, it reserves the lowest address bit for its purposes, leaving the second-lowest bit free for storing the parity information. This allows parity-encoded references to be represented as regular pointer variables that can be loaded and stored with a single memory access.

Given certain platform characteristics, the implementation of other, more complex fault-tolerance mechanisms such as ECC (which uses more than one redundancy bit) would not necessarily require inflating the reference size either. For example, the TriCore TC1796 platform has a 32-bit address space but only 1 MiB of physical RAM. Depending on the concrete memory mapping, this would allow up to 12 additional bits in each 32-bit pointer variable to be used by the runtime system.

For the headers of regular objects and of arrays, the parity information can be stored in unused bits of the header as depicted in Figure 3. Consequently, enabling parity-based error detection in KESO does not increase the memory footprint of the application.

Processor Instruction Set: Many processor architectures have special instructions for efficiently computing the parity of a data word. If such instructions are available on the target platform, KESO makes use of them by generating calls to the GCC built-in function `__builtin_parity()`. For instance, on the TriCore platform the parity computation itself amounts to a mere four CPU instructions as can be seen in Listing 1.

```
keso_check_and_decode_reference:
    mov.d   %d4,    %a4
    mov.d   %d15,   %a4
    parity  %d2,    %d4          ; Compute parity
    bsplit  %e2,    %d2
    bsplit  %e2,    %d2
    parity  %d2,    %d2
    jz      %d2,    .Lsuccess ; Catch parity error
    nop
    call    keso_throw_error
.Lsuccess:
    andn    %d15,   %d15,   2   ; Decode address
    mov.a   %a2,    %d15        ; Return it
    ret
```

Listing 1: Reference checking and decoding on the TriCore MCU

Memory-Protection Unit: If an MPU is available, KESO and the underlying AUTOSAR OS can be configured to use it as an additional safety net. If a severe error were to cause the type system to become corrupted and memory safety could no longer be guaranteed, the MPU could maintain the isolation of the protection domains. To achieve this, KESO physically groups the memory portions belonging to a domain (heap, stacks, etc.) in memory and provides the OS with the start and end addresses of these regions.

6. Evaluation

In this section, we evaluate the costs imposed by our reference-checking approach (Section 6.2) and the protection provided by it using the Fail* fault-injection framework, which is explained in Section 6.3. As an exemplary application, the Collision Detector (CD_x) benchmark is employed and a brief introduction to it is presented in Section 6.1.

6.1 The CD_x Benchmark

For our fault-injection and performance evaluation, we use the *Collision Detector (CD_x)* [16] – an open-source benchmark that is available in a C (CD_c) and a Java (CD_j) version with almost equivalent algorithmic behavior – as a representative Java application for embedded systems. KESO bundled with CD_j has already been evaluated against CD_c and results can be found in [23].

The core of the CD_x benchmark is a periodic task that detects potential aircraft collisions from simulated radar frames. A collision is assumed whenever the distance between two aircraft is below a configured proximity radius. The detection is performed in two stages: In the first stage (reducer phase), suspected collisions are identified in the 2D space ignoring the z-coordinate (altitude) to reduce the complexity for the second stage (detector phase), in which a full 3D collision detection is performed (detected collisions). A detailed description of the benchmark is available in a separate paper [16]. Since CD_j allocates temporary objects and uses collection classes of the Java library, it normally requires the use of dynamic memory management. Since protected garbage collection in KESO is currently a work in progress, we use pseudo-static allocation instead.

6.2 Overhead to Unprotected KESO

To determine the overhead imposed by a secured type system, we use CD_x in the *onthegoFrame* variant configured processing 24 frames (it would run out of memory after that), which is suitable to be deployed on the Infineon TriCore TC1796 device (150 MHz CPU clock, 75 MHz system clock, 1 MiB SRAM). The application is compiled with GCC (version 4.5.2) and bundled with KESO and an AUTOSAR OS implementation. Our experiments cover the LRC reference-checking variant. Checks were statically inlined.

	NoChk	SafeChk	AddrChk	HdrChk	LRC
text	45246	49044	59634	61810	64310
data	4005	4005	4109	4109	4109
bss	836138	836138	836138	836138	836138
text ov	-7.74%	0.0%	17.76%	4.60%	24.33%
data/bss ov	-2.53 %	0.0%	0.0%	0.0%	0.0%

(a) Memory footprint

	SafeChk	LRC
NullChecksEmitted	153	153
BoundsCheck	91	0
BoundsCheckElided	15	0
BoundsCheckKnownIndex	12	0
BoundsCheckFullExtended	0	91
BoundsCheckKnownSizeExtended	0	27
ReferenceCheckEmitted	0	301
HeaderCheckEmitted	0	97

(b) Runtime-check emission

	NoChk	SafeChk	AddrChk	HdrChk	LRC
Overhead	-11.84%	0%	18.42%	8.33%	30.71%
# Checks	0	0	225715	69936	417069

(c) Runtime overhead and number of LRC executions

Figure 4: Overhead induced by LRC

Footprint. Figure 4a shows the footprint of various KESO checking variants. NoChk denotes that runtime safety checks, i.e. null and array bounds checks are disabled. However, the memory allocator still checks the bump pointer against the heap bounds to prevent a heap overflow. The generated code is not memory-safe at those locations where *jino* was not able to statically prove the validity of those accesses. This CD_x variant is comparable to a version directly implemented in unsafe C.

The SafeChk variant follows the Java specification and is memory-safe in the absence of soft errors, wherefore it is selected as the baseline variant. AddrChk (address checks), HdrChk (header checks) and LRC are built on top of SafeChk (combined address, null, header and extended array bounds checking). Extended array bounds checks are applied to all array types (not just reference arrays) at necessary locations.

Class-storage information and the method table are located in the text segment in all variants. Although the parity information itself does not increase the memory footprint of the application, the data segment grows by 104 bytes when type-system protection is enabled. This is caused by a missed optimization: Two constant strings in the application are actually dead, but their headers and/or references are encoded at startup, respectively. Hence, the linker regards them as used and is unable to discard them. As expected, the bss segments, containing the heaps and stacks, are of equal size in case of LRC and *unprotected* configurations (safety checks enabled only, no protection against soft errors).

The text segment is inflated by 7.74% due to safety checks. Supplementarily, LRC causes an increase by a total of 24.33%, where 17.76% are caused by address checks and an additional 2.90% by combining them with object-header checks. Extended array bounds checks enlarge the the text segment by 3.67%.

The header checks reuse code from address checks, hence the aggregated code-size increase (20.65%) is smaller than that of the individual parts (17.76% for address and 4.60% for header checks).

KESO performed devirtualizations on 343 method invocations, omitting the header and address checks while retaining type safety, whereas 22 non-static method invocations remained. Seven instanceof occurrences were statically dissolved, which allowed to omit header-check insertion at those locations.

Figure 4b lists the emitted runtime checks. The number of null-checks is unchanged. In the protected variant, 118 *extended* array bounds checks were emitted: 91 of those array bounds checks include the size-integrity check, whereas the remaining 27 array checks are performed on arrays with constantly known size, but varying indices.

Unprotected KESO includes 91 *normal* array checks whereas 15 checks could statically be computed to always succeed. Assuming soft errors, these 15 array bounds checks have to be inserted as extended array bounds check (discussed in Section 5.1). In addition, 301 reference checks and 97 object-header checks (76 on non-static method invocations, 21 on instanceof and checkcast) were emitted in protected KESO.

Runtime. The runtime overhead of LRC is listed in Figure 4c: 18.42% of the increased demand were contributed by address checks and 8.33% by object-header checks. The additional runtime of 3.96% was caused by extended array bounds checks (including 121838 size-integrity checks), which are needed to accomplish full LRC.

Most of the bounds checks that contribute to the increased runtime reside within loops iterating over arrays. In a scenario without soft errors, these checks could be easily elided, but in our fault-detection scenario they have to be kept because the loop index could be corrupted. *jino* is able to statically determine the array size in some cases, which results in a light-weight array bounds check with constant and known size. This check detects corrupted indices. If this optimization is not possible, a full extended array bounds check is emitted.

As a possible future optimization, sufficiently small loops that iterate over an array of known size could be unrolled by the compiler. Since both index and size would be constant, the extended array bounds checks could then be omitted.

6.3 The Fail* Fault-Injection Framework

In order to get an insight into the effects on the protection level provided by the reference-checking extension, the fault-injection (FI) framework Fail* [21] is used. It is currently available for the Bochs simulator [17] on the x86 platform and ARM simulators. The selected AUTOSAR OS is available for x86 and TriCore platforms. Therefore, we built a variant of the CD_x benchmark that runs on top of the x86 port of the AUTOSAR OS. Even though the x86 platform is not a deeply embedded platform, we argue that FI experiments on that platform can be used to evaluate the functional effects of bit flips on the application and software-based isolation.

For the FI campaign, garbage collection is disabled and pseudo-static allocation is used to exclude effects of bit flips that occur during the unprotected GC phase. Faults that occur during the selected pseudo-static allocation strategy are, however, considered in our experiment. Hardware-based memory protection is also disabled, but we use *jino*'s reachability analysis to physically group application data as input for Fail* to determine illegal memory accesses. The heap size is set to 256 KiB, which is enough to compute a set of 5 frames in CD_x before it runs out of memory.

We injected single bit flips into each bit position of each word of the allocated heap space. To reduce the resulting huge fault space, we made use of the fault-space pruning methods of the Fail* framework to concentrate on memory locations that are actually read according to a golden run. This allows to filter out all injections that are known to be ineffective, e.g. bit flips that are overwritten before they are actually read. The campaign was applied to three variants of the system: No runtime checks at all (NoChk, program is not type-safe), SafeChk (type-safe, unprotected against soft errors), and a full LRC-hardened variant, resulting in a total fault space of approximately 4,341,038 experiments.

Table 1 shows the overall results of the FI campaigns grouped by the reachable destination points. In the NoChk variant, approximately 64% of the injections resulted in *No Effect* and 56% for

Result	NoChk	SafeChk	LRC
No Effect	809,918	820,835	867,205
Error Exception	39,655	109,312	37,747
Null-Pointer	0	116,245	43,287
Out-of-Bounds	0	62,926	29,992
Illegal Memory Access	289,159	246,981	17,286
Trap	72,816	56,824	6,084
Timeout	44,762	43,453	37,916
Parity Exception	0	0	588,635
Total	1,256,310	1,456,576	1,628,152

Table 1: Fault-injection results

SafeChk and 53% for LRC, respectively. Here the faults were either masked or silently corrupted the application's data. The LRC variant caused CD_x to pass through without triggering exceptions or traps in some cases: As a result, effects of bit flips could be mitigated on the application layer, where additional application-protection mechanisms can recognize faulty data or control-flow errors (e.g. through replication or control-flow monitoring). Assuming a redundancy and recovery approach as presented in [26], the recovery mechanism is able to restore both application data and respective valid references, as spatial isolation between replicas is maintained.

Comparing the type-safe system (SafeChk) against the plain memory-unsafe version (NoChk), it can be concluded that safety checks in form of null-pointer and array bounds checks already detect some corrupted data and references and reduce illegal memory accesses and traps. However, the triggering of these exceptions is more an effect of the executions of safety checks on invalid application data and references. Regarding these inherent fault-detection mechanisms of the KESO runtime system, the LRC variant reveals an overall decrease of these exceptions, since LRC found corrupted references that illegally triggered those exceptions in many cases. Others were still raised due to, for example, corrupted application data causing to select another control-flow path.

The portion of *Null Pointer*, *Out of Bounds* and *Error* exceptions (caused by failed checkcast or heap-memory bounds errors) and hardware *Traps* is considerably higher in the unprotected system, as depicted in Figure 5. Here, the parity check can detect the injected fault before the error can propagate and result in a hardware trap or error exception.

The extended array bounds check detected 29,992 errors, whereas 588,635 errors were found by additional parity checks. A certain amount of bit flips resulted in a *Timeout* behaviour. These errors influenced a loop-controlling variable residing in the unprotected application data. The *Traps* occurring in the LRC variant were division-by-zero exceptions, which are also caused by the application's computation with faulty operands. Such errors can be handled by fault-tolerance measures at the application level. *Traps* in the unsafe NoChk variant were mainly induced by dereferencing null-pointers (address 0), which leads to a trap on the x86 architecture.

The FI experiments also caught any *Illegal Memory Access*, that is, any access beyond the defined sections and writing accesses into the text section. With LRC, these illegal memory accesses can be traced back to failed executions of instanceof. Some bit flips were injected after the reference check and cause the reference to point to a valid object. The probability of that happening increases with the heap size and the number of objects located there. The object-header check is therefore unable to detect an error, thus producing a wrong outcome of instanceof. A wrong object type is assumed and type safety is corrupted, which leads to the illegal memory usages. This drawback of LRC in contrast to DRC was discussed in Section 4.1.3. Nevertheless, LRC decreased memory isolation violation by 94% (-271,873) compared to NoChk and 93% (-229,695) compared to SafeChk. Based on LRC, application replication as provided by

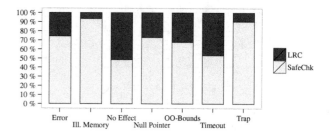

Figure 5: Proportional distribution of the fault-injection results

KESO to protect the application data can be applied on top of our approach. As LRC retains software-based memory protection to a certain degree, hardware-based isolation is not necessary, but can complement LRC if required.

7. Related Work

Reliability in JVMs has been addressed in a few existing projects. Friedman and Napper [13, 18] have their focus on the replication of the entire JVM to tolerate fail-stop errors in distributed systems. In [9] the susceptability of application data in JVMs and their protection was analyzed, targeting JVMs for workstations.

Chen [10] proposed to detect and recover from transient errors by adding a dual-execution and check-pointing extension to KVM. The heaps of both instances are compared against each other. To keep the overhead low, the heaps are divided into subheaps which contain the latest changes and those which have not changed. Unchanged heap parts and moving new heap data is protected by a memory management unit (MMU), however, type safety is not retained. Errors that trigger a trap can be corrected by copying the state from the sane instance to the corrupted one. The focus is on 1-bit error detection and state recovery of heap objects.

We are not aware any research of type-system protection. Besides reduced illegal memory accesses, our approach was able to detect and signal some bogus behavior in the application. Additional application-specific fault-tolerance measures based on static analyses on static type-safe programs can be employed on top of our approach. In [5], it was quantitatively analyzed how an exemplary piece of software reacts to corrupted virtual function calls in the context of C++ and the authors propose to protect the virtual function pointer by a dependability aspect that is applied by the AspectC++ weaver. In their experiments, 75% of all bit flips in virtual function pointers led to an application crash. In contrast to this approach, safeguarding of virtual function calls is included by protecting the type system itself. Thanks to static application knowlegde and type information, an efficient protection of method calls is possible.

8. Conclusion and Future Work

We presented a possible solution to protect the type system of a strongly typed programming languange in the presence of soft errors. The approach targets embedded systems and allows to continue relying on the benefits of Java to the extent discussed in the evaluation section. The effects of soft errors on the type system and software-based memory protection built on top of the type system have been analyzed exemplarily in the context of the KESO JVM. By means of LRC, it is more likely to retain software-based spatial isolation needed for many fault-tolerance techniques such as replication without the need for an MPU. Moreover, LRC can retain type safety and allows for an early error detection at the granularity of objects. The overhead imposed by our solution is dependent on the application itself (e.g. frequent array usage). Also, it is bound to the effectiveness of compiler optimizations, that is, the extent to which they are able to elide dynamic program information that can be corrupted during execution. To the best of our knowledge, we presented and evaluated the first implementation of type safety and software-based memory protection in the presence of soft errors.

There are several aspects which we would like to cover in our future work. At first, there is the evaluation of the more expensive DRC variant, which is able to detect more illegal memory accesses. Our RC variants are easily adaptable to detecting and tolerating more bit flips at a time, so an evaluation of these scenarios is also in progress. Secondly, KESO's optimizations will be extended: The handling of `checkcast`, for example, will be improved. Also, we plan to implement the idea of possible loop unrolling allowing for the elision of expensive extended array bounds checks. Error-detection support for the program counter by means of automated use of control-flow information available in KESO will be examined.

Up to now, we have had to use the protected pseudo-static memory allocation technique. The available GCs are currently extended to detect and tolerate soft errors. We are interested in the overhead imposed by dependable garbage collection, which also facilitates to significantly reduce the heap size and thus the attack surface of the heap. A ROM allocation analysis is currently being developed to be able to place more constant data in ROM to decrease RAM usage. Also, the effects of an *extended escape analysis* – which allows for stack allocation and moreover an automated application of RTSJ's [4] `ScopedMemory` – will be taken into consideration.

References

[1] G. Aigner and U. Hölzle. Eliminating virtual function calls in C++ programs. In *10th Eur. Conf. on OOP (ECOOP '96)*, pages 142–166, London, UK, 1996. Springer. ISBN 3-540-61439-7.

[2] M. Aiken, M. Fähndrich, C. Hawblitzel, G. Hunt, and J. Larus. Deconstructing process isolation. In *MSPC '06: Proceedings of the 2006 Workshop on Memory System Performance and Correctness*, pages 1–10, New York, NY, USA, 2006. ACM. ISBN 1-59593-578-9. doi: 10.1145/1178597.1178599.

[3] D. F. Bacon and P. F. Sweeney. Fast static analysis of C++ virtual function calls. *SIGPLAN Not.*, 31(10):324–341, 1996. ISSN 0362-1340. doi: 10.1145/236338.236371.

[4] G. Bollella, B. Brosgol, J. Gosling, P. Dibble, S. Furr, and M. Turnbull. *The Real-Time Specification for Java.* AW, 1st edition, Jan. 2000.

[5] C. Borchert, H. Schirmeier, and O. Spinczyk. Protecting the dynamic dispatch in C++ by dependability aspects. In *Proceedings of the 1st GI Workshop on Software-Based Methods for Robust Embedded Systems (SOBRES '12)*, Lecture Notes in Informatics, pages 521–535. German Society of Informatics, Sept. 2012.

[6] C. Borchert, H. Schirmeier, and O. Spinczyk. Generative software-based memory error detection and correction for operating system data structures. In *Proceedings of the 43nd IEEE/IFIP International Conference on Dependable Systems and Networks (DSN '13)*. IEEE Computer Society Press, June 2013.

[7] S. Borkar. Designing reliable systems from unreliable components: the challenges of transistor variability and degradation. *IEEE Micro*, 25(6):10–16, November 2005. ISSN 0272-1732. doi: 10.1109/MM.2005.110.

[8] G. Cellere, S. Gerardin, M. Bagatin, A. Paccagnella, A. Visconti, M. Bonanomi, S. Beltrami, P. Roche, G. Gasiot, R. H. Sorensen, A. Virtanen, C. Frost, P. Fuochi, C. Andreani, G. Gorini, A. Pietropaolo, and S. Platt1. Neutron-induced soft errors in advanced flash memories. In *IEDM 2008*. IEEE, Feb. 2009. ISBN 978-1-4244-2378-1.

[9] D. Chen, A. Messer, P. Bernadat, G. Fu, Z. Dimitrijevic, D. J. F. Lie, D. Mannaru, A. Riska, and D. Milojicic. JVM susceptibility to memory errors. In *Java Virtual Machine Research and Technology Symposium*, pages 67–78, Berkeley, CA, USA, Apr. 2001. USENIX. ISBN 1-880446-11-1.

[10] G. Chen and M. Kandemir. Improving java virtual machine reliability for memory-constrained embedded systems. In *Proceedings of the 42nd annual Design Automation Conference*, DAC '05, pages 690–

695, New York, NY, USA, 2005. ACM. ISBN 1-59593-058-2. doi: 10.1145/1065579.1065761.

[11] J. J. Cook and C. B. Zilles. A characterization of instruction-level error derating and its implications for error detection. In *DSN*, pages 482–491. IEEE, 2008. doi: h10.1109/DSN.2008.4630119.

[12] J. Dean, D. Grove, and C. Chambers. Optimization of object-oriented programs using static class hierarchy analysis. *LNCS*, 952:77–101, 1995.

[13] R. Friedman and A. Kama. Transparent fault-tolerant java virtual machine, 2003.

[14] M. Golm, M. Felser, C. Wawersich, and J. Kleinöder. The JX operating system. In *2002 USENIX ATC*, pages 45–58, Berkeley, CA, USA, June 2002. USENIX. ISBN 1-880446-00-6.

[15] O. Goloubeva, M. Rebaudengo, M. S. Reorda, and M. Violante. *Software-Implemented Hardware Fault Tolerance.* Springer, Heidelberg, Germany, 2006. ISBN 0-387-26060-9.

[16] T. Kalibera, J. Hagelberg, F. Pizlo, A. Plsek, B. Titzer, and J. Vitek. CD_x: A family of real-time java benchmarks. In *JTRES '09: 7th Int. W'shop on Java Technologies for real-time & embedded Systems*, pages 41–50, New York, NY, USA, 2009. ACM. ISBN 978-1-60558-732-5. doi: 10.1145/1620405.1620412.

[17] K. P. Lawton. Bochs: A portable pc emulator for unix/x. *Linux Journal*, 1996(29es):7, 1996.

[18] J. Napper, L. Alvisi, and H. Vin. A fault-tolerant java virtual machine. In *In Proceedings of the International Conference on Dependable Systems and Networks (DSN 2003), DCC Symposium*, pages 425–434, 2002.

[19] S. Poledna, A. Burns, A. Wellings, and P. Barrett. Replica determinism and flexible scheduling in hard real-time dependable systems. *IEEE TC*, 49(2):100–111, 2000. ISSN 0018-9340. doi: 10.1109/12.833107.

[20] H. Schirmeier, R. Kapitza, D. Lohmann, and O. Spinczyk. DanceOS: Towards dependability aspects in configurable embedded operating systems. In A. Orailoglu, editor, *3rd HiPEAC W'shop on Des. f. Reliability (DFR '11)*, pages 21–26, Heraklion, Greece, Jan. 2011.

[21] H. Schirmeier, M. Hoffmann, R. Kapitza, D. Lohmann, and O. Spinczyk. FAIL*: Towards a versatile fault-injection experiment framework. In G. Mühl, J. Richling, and A. Herkersdorf, editors, *25th Int. Conf. on Architecture of Computing Systems (ARCS '12), Workshop Proceedings*, volume 200 of *Lecture Notes in Informatics*, pages 201–210. Gesellschaft für Informatik, Mar. 2012. ISBN 978-3-88579-294-9.

[22] V. C. Sreedhar, R. D.-C. Ju, D. M. Gillies, and V. Santhanam. Translating out of static single assignment form. In *Proceedings of the 6th International Symposium on Static Analysis*, SAS '99, pages 194–210, Heidelberg, Germany, 1999. Springer. ISBN 3-540-66459-9.

[23] M. Stilkerich, I. Thomm, C. Wawersich, and W. Schröder-Preikschat. Tailor-made JVMs for statically configured embedded systems. *Concurrency and Computation: Practice and Experience*, 24(8):789–812, 2012. ISSN 1532-0634. doi: 10.1002/cpe.1755.

[24] V. Sundaresan, L. Hendren, C. Razafimahefa, R. Vallée-Rai, P. Lam, E. Gagnon, and C. Godin. Practical virtual method call resolution for Java. *SIGPLAN Not.*, 35(10):264–280, 2000.

[25] A. Taber and E. Normand. Single event upset in avionics. *IEEE Transactions on Nuclear Science*, 40(2):120–126, Apr. 1993. ISSN 0018-9499. doi: 10.1109/23.212327.

[26] I. Thomm, M. Stilkerich, R. Kapitza, D. Lohmann, and W. Schröder-Preikschat. Automated application of fault tolerance mechanisms in a component-based system. In *JTRES '11: 9th Int. W'shop on Java Technologies for real-time & embedded Systems*, pages 87–95, New York, NY, USA, 2011. ACM. ISBN 978-1-4503-0731-4. doi: 10.1145/2043910.2043925.

[27] P. Ulbrich, R. Kapitza, C. Harkort, R. Schmid, and W. Schröder-Preikschat. I4Copter: An adaptable and modular quadrotor platform. In *26th ACM Symp. on Applied Computing (SAC '11)*, pages 380–396, New York, NY, USA, 2011. ACM. ISBN 978-1-4503-0113-8.

[28] M. N. Wegman and F. K. Zadeck. Constant propagation with conditional branches. *ACM Trans. Program. Lang. Syst.*, 13:181–210, Apr. 1991. ISSN 0164-0925. doi: 10.1145/103135.103136.

Improving Processor Efficiency by Statically Pipelining Instructions

Ian Finlayson

University of Mary Washington
Fredericksburg
Virginia, USA
finlayson@umw.edu

Brandon Davis   Peter Gavin

Florida State University
Tallahassee
Florida, USA
{bdavis,gavin}@cs.fsu.edu

Gang-Ryung Uh

Boise State University
Boise
Idaho, USA
uh@cs.boisestate.edu

David Whalley   Magnus Själander   Gary Tyson

Florida State University
Tallahassee
Florida, USA
{whalley,sjalande,tyson}@cs.fsu.edu

Abstract

A new generation of applications requires reduced power consumption without sacrificing performance. Instruction pipelining is commonly used to meet application performance requirements, but some implementation aspects of pipelining are inefficient with respect to energy usage. We propose static pipelining as a new instruction set architecture to enable more efficient instruction flow through the pipeline, which is accomplished by exposing the pipeline structure to the compiler. While this approach simplifies hardware pipeline requirements, significant modifications to the compiler are required. This paper describes the code generation and compiler optimizations we implemented to exploit the features of this architecture. We show that we can achieve performance and code size improvements despite a very low-level instruction representation. We also demonstrate that static pipelining of instructions reduces energy usage by simplifying hardware, avoiding many unnecessary operations, and allowing the compiler to perform optimizations that are not possible on traditional architectures.

Categories and Subject Descriptors   C.1.3 [*PROCESSOR ARCHITECTURES*]: Other Architecture Styles—Pipeline processors

Keywords   compiler optimizations, energy efficiency, static pipeline

1. Introduction

Energy expenditure is clearly a primary design constraint, especially for embedded processors where battery life is directly related to the usefulness of the product. As these devices become more sophisticated, the execution performance requirements increase. This trend has led to new generations of efficient processors that seek the best solution to the often conflicting requirements of low-energy design and high-performance execution. Many of the micro-architectural techniques to improve performance were developed when efficiency was not as important. For instance, speculation is a direct tradeoff between power and performance, but many other techniques are assumed to be efficient.

Instruction pipelining is one of the most common techniques for improving performance of general-purpose processors. Pipelining is generally considered very efficient when speculation costs and scheduling complexity are minimized. While it is true that speculation, dynamic scheduling policies, and superscalar execution have the largest impact on efficiency, even simple, in-order, scalar pipelined architectures have inefficiencies that lead to less optimal implementations of the processor architecture. For instance, hazard detection and data forwarding not only require evaluation of register dependencies each cycle of execution, but successful forwarding does not prevent register file accesses to stale values, nor does it eliminate unnecessary pipeline register writes of those stale values, which are propagated for all instructions.

The goal of this paper is to restructure the organization of a pipelined processor implementation in order to remove as many redundant or unnecessary operations as possible. This goal is achieved by making the pipelined structures architecturally visible and relying on the compiler to optimize resource usage. While techniques like VLIW [8] have concentrated on compile time instruction scheduling and hazard avoidance, we seek to bring pipeline control further into the realm of compiler optimization. When pipeline registers become architecturally visible, the compiler can directly manage tasks like forwarding, branch prediction, and register access. This mitigates some of the inefficiencies found in more conventional designs, and provides new optimization opportunities to improve the efficiency of the pipeline.

Figure 1 illustrates the basic idea of the static pipeline (SP) approach. With traditional pipelining, each instruction spends several cycles in the pipeline. For example, the `load` instruction in Figure 1(b) requires one cycle for each stage and remains in the pipeline from cycles five through eight. Each instruction is fetched and decoded and information about the instruction flows through the pipeline, via pipeline registers, to control each portion of the

LCTES'13,   June 20–21, 2013, Seattle, Washington, USA.

clock cycle (Traditional Pipelining) / **clock cycle** (Static Pipelining)

	1	2	3	4	5	6	7	8	9		1	2	3	4	5	6	7	8	9
add	IF	RF	EX	MEM	WB						IF	RF	EX	MEM	WB				
store		IF	RF	EX	MEM	WB						IF	RF	EX	MEM	WB			
sub			IF	RF	EX	MEM	WB						IF	RF	EX	MEM	WB		
load				IF	RF	EX	MEM	WB						IF	RF	EX	MEM	WB	
or					IF	RF	EX	MEM	WB						IF	RF	EX	MEM	WB
(a) Traditional Insts			**(b) Traditional Pipelining**										**(c) Static Pipelining**						

Figure 1. Traditionally Pipelined vs. Statically Pipelined Instructions

processor that takes a specific action during each cycle. The `load` instruction shares the pipelined datapath with other instructions that are placed into the pipeline in adjacent cycles.

Figure 1(c) illustrates how an SP processor operates. Operations associated with conventional instructions still require multiple cycles to complete execution; however, the method used to encode how the operation is processed while executing differs. In SP scheduled code, the execution of the `load` operation is not specified by a single instruction. Instead each SP instruction specifies how all portions of the processor are controlled during the cycle it is executed. Initially encoding any conventional instruction may take as many SP instructions as the number of pipeline stages in a conventional processor. While this approach may seem inefficient in specifying the functionality of any single conventional instruction, the cost is offset by the fact that multiple SP effects can be scheduled for the same SP instruction. The SP instruction set architecture (ISA) results in more control given to the compiler to optimize instruction flow through the processor, while simplifying the hardware required to support hazard detection, data forwarding, and control flow. By relying on the compiler to do low-level processor resource scheduling, it is possible to eliminate some structures (e.g., the branch target buffer), avoid some repetitive computation (e.g., sign extensions and branch target address calculations), and greatly reduce accesses to both the register file and internal registers. This strategy results in improved energy efficiency through simpler hardware, while providing new code optimization opportunities for achieving performance improvement. The cost of this approach is the additional complexity of code generation and compiler optimizations targeting an SP architecture. The novelty of this paper is not strictly in the SP architectural features or compiler optimizations when either is viewed in isolation, but also in the SP ISA that enables the compiler to more finely control the processor to produce a more energy efficient system.

This paper makes the following contributions. (1) We show that the use of static pipelining can expose many new opportunities for compiler optimizations to avoid redundant or unnecessary operations performed in conventional pipelines. (2) We establish that a very low-level ISA can be used and still achieve performance and code size improvements. (3) We demonstrate that static pipelining can reduce energy usage by significantly decreasing the number of register file accesses, internal register writes, branch predictions, and branch target address calculations, as well as completely eliminating the need for a branch target buffer. In summary, we provide a novel method for pipelining that exposes more control of processor resources to the compiler to significantly improve energy efficiency while obtaining counter-intuitive improvements in performance and code size.

2. Architecture

In this section we discuss the SP architecture design including both the micro-architecture and the instruction set. While static pipelining refers to a class of architectures, we describe one design in detail that is used as the basis for the remainder of this paper.

2.1 Micro-Architecture

The SP micro-architecture evaluated in this paper is designed to be similar to a classical five-stage pipeline in terms of available hardware and operation. The motivation for this design is to minimize the required hardware resource differences between the classical baseline design and our SP design in order to evaluate the benefits of the SP technique.

Figure 2 depicts a classical five-stage pipeline. Instructions spend one cycle in each stage of the pipeline, which are separated by pipeline registers. Along with increased performance, pipelining introduces a few inefficiencies into a processor. First of all is the need to latch information between pipeline stages. All of the possible control signals and data values needed for an instruction are passed through the pipeline registers to the stage that uses them. For many instructions, much of this information is not used. For example, the program counter (PC) is typically passed through the pipeline for all instructions, but is only used for branches.

Pipelining also introduces branch and data hazards. Branch hazards occur because the branch target address is unknown for multiple cycles after fetching a branch. These hazards result in either a pipeline flush for every taken branch, or the need for a branch prediction buffer (BPB), branch target buffer (BTB), and delays when branches are mis-predicted. Data hazards occur when the value produced by an earlier instruction is required before the pipeline has written it back to the register file. Data hazards can be eliminated in most cases with forwarding logic, which contributes to the energy usage of the pipeline. In addition, if the value is only ever consumed by instructions via forwarding paths, the value will be unnecessarily written to the register file at the commit stage, wasting energy. We performed preliminary experiments with SimpleScalar [1] running the MiBench benchmark suite [10] that indicate that 27.9% of register file reads are unnecessary because the values will be replaced from forwarding. Additionally 11.1% of register file writes are not needed due to their only consumer instructions getting the values from forwarding instead. Additional inefficiencies found in traditional pipelines include repeatedly calculating invariant branch target addresses and adding an offset to a register to form a memory address even when that offset is zero.

Figure 3 depicts one possible datapath of an SP processor. The fetch portion of the processor is mostly unchanged from the conventional processor. Instructions are fetched from the instruction cache and branches are predicted by a BPB. One difference is that there is no longer any need for a BTB. This structure is used to store the target addresses of branches in conventional pipelines, avoiding the need to wait for the target address calculation to begin fetching the next instruction when that branch is predicted to be taken. In SP, the branch target address calculation is decoupled from the transfer of control (ToC), which eliminates the need for a BTB since the address is available when the branch target is fetched. In addition, the instruction prior to a ToC sets the PTB (prepare-to-branch) status register to provide information about the ToC, which enables the BPB to be only accessed for conditional branches.

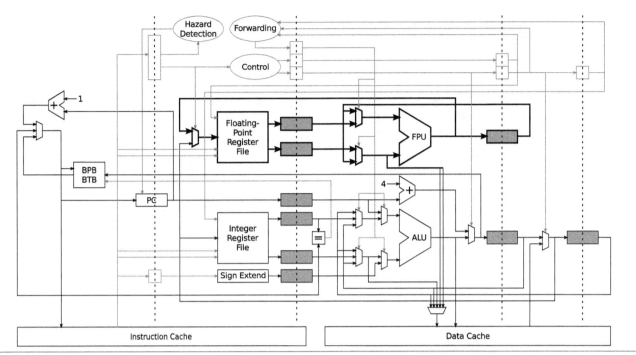

Figure 2. Classical Five-Stage Pipeline

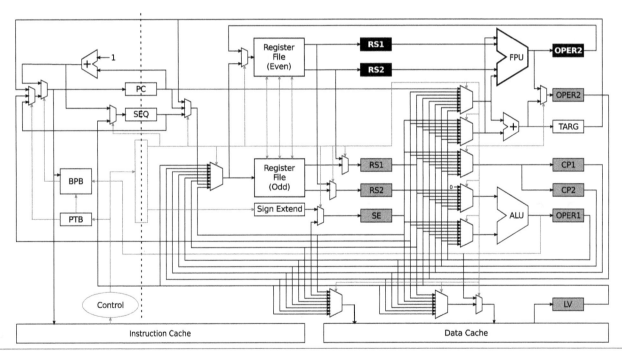

Figure 3. Datapath of a Statically Pipelined Processor

There are more substantial differences in the processor after instructions are fetched. There is no need for pipeline registers because SP processors do not need to break instructions into multiple stages. In their place are a number of architecturally visible internal registers. Unlike pipeline registers, these internal registers are explicitly read and written by the instructions, and can hold their values across multiple cycles.

There are ten internal registers in our SP design. The RS1 and RS2 (register source) registers contain values read from the register file. The LV (load value) register is assigned a value loaded from the data cache. The SE (sign extend) register receives a sign-extended immediate value. The OPER1 (ALU result) register is updated with values calculated in the ALU. The OPER2 (FPU result) register acquires results calculated in the FPU, which is used for multi-cycle operations, and integer addition results. The TARG (target address) register takes the result of adding the program counter (PC) and the SE. The SEQ (sequential address) register gets the address of the next sequential instruction at the time it is written. The CP1 and CP2 (copy) registers hold values copied from one of the other internal registers.

Since these internal registers are small, can be placed near the portion of the processor that accesses them, and are explicitly accessed, each internal register is accessible at a lower energy cost than the centralized register file. Note that while the pipeline registers of the baseline processor are read and written every cycle, the SP internal registers are only updated when needed. Because these internal registers are exposed at the architectural level, a new level of compiler optimizations can be exploited as we will demonstrate in Section 3.

All of the internal registers are caller save (*scratch*) registers, except for SEQ, CP1 and CP2. These three internal registers are callee save because our optimizing compiler primarily uses them to perform aggressive loop optimizations. If a loop has a function call in it, the compiler would disallow the use of these registers for this optimization were they caller save.

Because the internal registers are part of the machine state, they must be saved and restored together with the register file upon context switches and interrupts to allow for precise exceptions. Thus, each internal register must be able to be stored to, and loaded from, memory. Some of these registers have a direct path to/from memory, while others must first be moved through a copy register or the register file.

The integer and floating-point register files are merged into a single 32 entry register file for the SP datapath as the ALU operations are decoupled from accessing the register file. In the SP datapath explicit support is shown for dealing with double-precision values, which requires having extra components shown in black for the RS1, RS2, and OPER2 internal registers.

Data hazards due to multi-cycle operations can easily be detected without special logic to compare register numbers obtained from instructions. If during a given cycle the OPER2 register is to be used as a source and the FPU has not completed a multi-cycle operation, then the current instruction is aborted and the instruction will be reattempted on the next cycle. This process continues until the FPU has completed the operation. Data cache misses can be handled in a similar fashion for LV register reads.

An SP can be viewed as a two-stage processor with the two stages being fetch and everything after fetch. As discussed in the next subsection, SP instructions are already partially decoded as compared to traditional instructions.

2.2 Instruction Set Architecture

The instruction set architecture (ISA) for an SP architecture is quite different than the ISA for a conventional processor. Each instruction consists of a set of effects, each of which updates some portion of the processor. The effects mostly correspond to what the baseline classical five-stage pipeline can do in one cycle, which includes one ALU operation, one FPU operation, one data cache access, two register reads, one register write, and one sign extension. In addition, one copy can be made from an internal register to one of the two copy registers and the next sequential instruction address can be saved in the SEQ register. Lastly, the PTB status register can be set to indicate that the next instruction is a ToC.

All of the effects specified in a single instruction are independent and are performed in parallel. The values in the internal registers are read at the beginning of the cycle and written at the end of the cycle. Note that except for the effects that solely read or write a register file or data cache value, all of the effects operate solely on the internal registers. This is analogous to how RISC architectures only allow load or store instructions to reference memory locations.

Including all possible instruction-effect fields in an instruction would require 77 bits for our design. More than doubling the size of each instruction would have a very negative effect on code size, as well as increasing the power to access the instruction cache, which would negate much of the power benefit static pipelining would otherwise achieve. Therefore we developed a compact, 32-bit encoding for the instructions, which is shown in Figure 4.

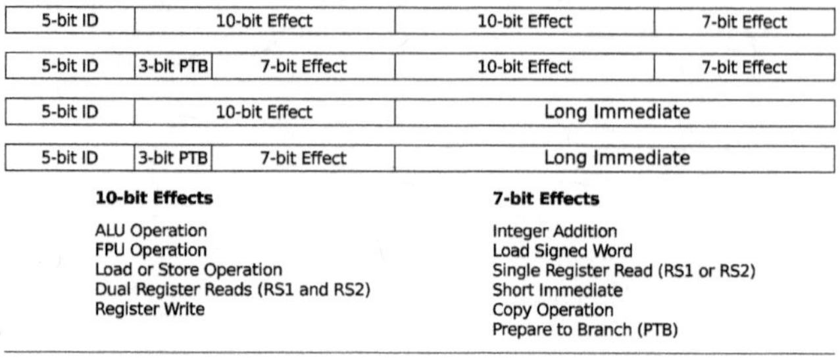

5-bit ID	10-bit Effect		10-bit Effect	7-bit Effect
5-bit ID	3-bit PTB	7-bit Effect	10-bit Effect	7-bit Effect
5-bit ID	10-bit Effect		Long Immediate	
5-bit ID	3-bit PTB	7-bit Effect	Long Immediate	

10-bit Effects	**7-bit Effects**
ALU Operation	Integer Addition
FPU Operation	Load Signed Word
Load or Store Operation	Single Register Read (RS1 or RS2)
Dual Register Reads (RS1 and RS2)	Short Immediate
Register Write	Copy Operation
	Prepare to Branch (PTB)

Figure 4. Static Pipeline Instruction Formats

The encoding scheme is similar to that used by many VLIW processors that use longer instruction formats. Each instruction is capable of encoding a number of fields, with each field corresponding to one SP effect. The *5-bit ID* field is the template identifier, which specifies how the remaining fields should be interpreted. The size of this identifier dictates how many combinations of fields the encoding supports. With a larger number of combinations, there is more flexibility in scheduling, but the template identifier would require more space and the decoding logic would be more complicated. Frequently used effects, such as an ALU operation, should be present in more combinations than less frequently used effects, such as copying an internal register to a copy register. Each type of field has to be present in at least one combination, or it would be impossible to use it. Figure 4 also shows which types of fields can be represented in the different size effects. Most of these fields also have a representation to indicate that no effect associated with that field is to be performed.

The templates are constructed such that each type of effect only appears in at most two distinct places across all instructions, which greatly simplifies the decoding logic. Depending on the timing breakdown of the fetch and execute cycles, this logic can either be at the end of fetch or split between the fetch and execute stage. If necessary, then we can add a stage for decoding instructions, which is discussed in more detail in Section 6. Note that, unlike a conventional five-stage RISC architecture, register file reads occur during the execute stage, so there is no need for a decode stage to fetch values from the register file.

There are many possible ways to combine the available instruction effects into a set of templates for the encoding. In order to choose a good set of templates, we compiled and simulated the MiBench benchmark suite [10] with the ability to use any combination of effects whether it could fit in 32 bits or not in order to determine which combinations of instruction effects were commonly used together. We used this information to guide our choosing of the templates. The 32 templates chosen are able to cover over 81.7% of the combinations used when no restrictions are in place. The compiler makes use of the set of selected templates in order to schedule legal combinations of effects in instructions.

3. Compilation

In this section, we will describe the compilation process in more detail and show how example code can be compiled efficiently for an SP processor. For an SP architecture, the compiler is responsible for controlling each part of the datapath for every cycle, so effective compilation optimizations are necessary to achieve acceptable performance and code size goals. Because the instruction set architecture for an SP processor is quite different from that of a RISC architecture, many compilation strategies and optimizations have to be reconsidered when applied to an SP.

3.1 Overview of the Compilation Process

We have ported the VPO compiler [2] to the SP processor. We believe the selection of the VPO compiler was a good choice as it uses Register Transfer Lists (RTLs) for its intermediate representation, which is at the level of machine instructions. A low level representation is needed for performing code improving transformations on SP generated code.

Figure 5 shows the steps of our compilation process. First, C code is input to the frontend, which consists of the LCC compiler [9] frontend combined with a *middleware* process that converts LCC's output format into the RTL format used by VPO.

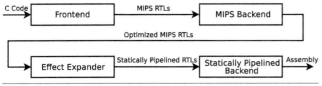

Figure 5. Compilation Process

These RTLs are then input into a modified VPO MIPS backend, which performs many compiler optimizations including control flow optimizations, loop invariant code motion, register allocation, and data flow optimizations. These optimizations are performed before converting the instructions to those for the SP architecture because some of these optimizations are more difficult to apply on the lower level instruction-pipeline representation, which breaks many assumptions in a compiler backend. For instance, register allocation is difficult to perform directly on SP instructions due to the need to have either RS1 or RS2 available to load any registers and that the address specifications and memory references are decoupled. Additionally this strategy allows us to concentrate on optimizations specific to the SP as all higher level (conventional) optimizations are already performed. Additional changes to the MIPS backend include using a single register file for general-purpose and floating-point values and changing some of the calling conventions. A single register file is used since the SP instructions separate accessing the register file from the ALU and FPU operations.

The instructions are next broken down into SP instruction effects by the *effect expander*, which breaks the MIPS instructions into instructions that are legal for the SP. This process works by expanding each MIPS RTL into a sequence of SP RTLs with a single effect per RTL that together perform the same computation.

Lastly, these instructions are fed into the SP compiler backend, also based on VPO. This backend applies additional optimizations and produces the final assembly code.

3.2 Example and More Detailed Discussion

In this section we describe an actual example of how code is translated to SP instructions and more thoroughly optimized by our compiler. This example illustrates that the role of the compiler is greater for an SP architecture.

Figure 6(a) shows the C source code of a simple loop kernel to add a value to every element of an array. The first step in compiling this code for the SP is to generate the optimized MIPS code which can be seen in Figure 6(b). Here r[9] is used as a pointer to the current element of the array, r[6] holds the value of the loop-invariant m variable, and r[5] has had the value a + 400 loaded into it which will equal the last value assigned to r[9] in the loop. There are no other obvious optimizations to this MIPS code that can be applied without increasing the code size. Figure 6(c) shows

the requirements for processing each element of the array when compiled for this MIPS code.

Figures 6(d) through 6(k) depict the actual compiler optimizations that are performed on the SP instructions for this example. To better illustrate the changes associated with each optimization, effects that are to be updated are shown in italics, effects that are to be removed are displayed with lines through them, and effects that were updated are shown in bold.

Effect Expansion The next step in the compilation process is to expand the MIPS instructions into SP instructions. The result of this step can be seen in Figure 6(d). Dashed lines separate instruction effects corresponding to each of the MIPS instructions in Figure 6(b). These instruction effects correspond to the pipeline stages performed by a five-stage MIPS processor when executing the given instruction. For example, for the add instruction, the MIPS processor will first load the registers into internal registers, next perform the addition, and then write the value back to the register file. This expansion increases the loop from five MIPS instructions to nineteen SP instructions. Note the PC is implicitly incremented after each individual SP instruction, just as the PC is incremented in a classical architecture. The offset to the branch target (L2) represents a symbolic offset from the TARG assignment and the exact offset is determined by the assembler.

Copy Propagation The first optimization is copy propagation, which is an optimization that takes into account instruction effects that copy a source to a destination and creates equivalence classes among elements that have the same value. It then replaces uses of any member of the equivalence class with the oldest member of the class with the same or cheaper access cost where possible. This optimization is applied three times. The values to be replaced are depicted in italics in Figure 6(d) and the replaced values are shown in bold in Figure 6(e). For instance, the use of RS1 is replaced with a use of LV in the sixth instruction of the loop. Likewise, OPER2 replaces uses of RS1 and RS2.

Dead and Redundant Assignment Elimination The copy propagation optimization is not useful on its own, but it is helpful in that it enables other data flow optimizations, such as dead assignment elimination. Dead assignments are those that write a value into a register or memory location that is never used before being overwritten. The instructions with solid lines through them in Figure 6(e) are assignments that are now dead. In the example, the dead assignments to RS1 and RS2 are removed first, which causes the two writes to the register file to become dead. The redundant assignment elimination optimization is also shown in the same figure. Redundant assignments are those that assign a value to a register that already has that value. Because the MIPS code reads a value from a register every time it needs it, it is common to repeatedly load the same value. When generating SP code, however, the compiler can simply retain a value in one of the internal registers. The value of r[9] is assigned to RS1 three times without the values changing in between in Figure 6(e), so the compiler removes the last two of these assignments to RS1, which are shown with dashed lines through them.

The resulting code after removing these dead and redundant assignments is displayed in Figure 6(f). Besides representing the SP effects and their costs in the compiler, no other changes were required to perform copy propagation and dead and redundant assignment elimination, or common subexpression elimination on SP instructions. In addition to removing seven instructions in the loop, the compiler has completely eliminated the use of two registers (r[2] and r[3]) to hold intermediary values. In a traditional pipeline, all data values circulate through the centralized register file. By giving the compiler access to internal registers, static pipelining can avoid accessing the register file in many cases.

Figure 6. Compilation Example

`for (i=0; i<100; i++)`
`    a[i] += m;`
(a) Source Code
	`  r[6]=LV;`
	`  r[9]=OPER2;`
	`L2:`
	`  RS1=r[9];`
	`  LV=M[RS1];`
	`  r[3]=LV;`
	`  RS1=r[3];`
	`  RS2=r[6];`
	`  OPER2=RS1+RS2;`
	`  r[2]=OPER2;`
	`  RS1=r[9];`
	`  RS2=r[2];`
	`  M[RS1]=RS2;`
	`  SE=4;`
	`  RS1=r[9];`
	`  OPER2=RS1+SE;`
	`  r[9]=OPER2;`
	`  SE=offset(L2);`
	`  TARG=PC+SE;`
	`  RS1=r[9];`
	`  RS2=r[5];`
	`  PC=RS1!RS2,TARG(L2);`
		`  r[6]=LV;`
		`  r[9]=OPER2;`
		`L2:`
		`  RS1=r[9];`
		`  LV=M[RS1];`
		`  r[3]=LV;`
		`  RS1=r[3];`
		`  RS2=r[6];`
		`  OPER2=LV+RS2;`
		`  r[2]=OPER2;`
		`  RS1=r[9];`
		`  RS2=r[2];`
		`  M[RS1]=OPER2;`
		`  SE=4;`
		`  RS1=r[9];`
		`  OPER2=RS1+SE;`
		`  r[9]=OPER2;`
		`  SE=offset(L2);`
		`  TARG=PC+SE;`
		`  RS1=r[9];`
		`  RS2=r[5];`
		`  PC=OPER2!RS2,TARG(L2);`
			`  r[6]=LV;`
			`  r[9]=OPER2;`
			`L2:`
			`  RS1=r[9];`
			`  LV=M[RS1];`
			`  RS2=r[6];`
			`  OPER2=LV+RS2;`
			`  M[RS1]=OPER2;`
			`  SE=4;`
			`  OPER2=RS1+SE;`
			`  r[9]=OPER2;`
			`  SE=offset(L2);`
			`  TARG=PC+SE;`
			`  RS2=r[5];`
			`  PC=OPER2!RS2,TARG(L2);`

`r[6]=<value m>;`
`r[9]=<address a>;`
`L2:`
`  r[3]=M[r[9]+0];`
`  r[2]=r[3]+r[6];`
`  M[r[9]+0]=r[2];`
`  r[9]=r[9]+4;`
`  PC=r[9]!r[5],L2;`
(b) MIPS Code			

5 instructions 5 ALU opers 1 DC load 1 DC store 8 RF reads 3 RF writes 1 targ calc 2 sign extends **(c) MIPS Requirements for Processing Each Array Element**	**(d) Expanded Statically Pipelined Instructions**	**(e) After Copy Propagation**	**(f) After Dead and Redundant Assignment Elimination**

`r[6]=LV;`
`r[9]=OPER2;`
`SE=offset(L2);`
`TARG=PC+SE;`
`SE=4;`
`L2:`
`  RS1=r[9];`
`  LV=M[RS1];`
`  RS2=r[6];`
`  OPER2=LV+RS2;`
`  M[RS1]=OPER2;`
`  OPER2=RS1+SE;`
`  r[9]=OPER2;`
`  RS2=r[5];`
`  PC=OPER2!RS2,TARG(L2);`
(g) After Loop–Invariant Code Motion
	`CP1=LV;`
	`CP2=OPER2;`
	`SE=offset(L2);`
	`TARG=PC+SE;`
	`SE=4;`
	`L2:`
	`  RS1=r[9];`
	`  LV=M[CP2];`
	`  RS2=r[6];`
	`  OPER2=LV+CP1;`
	`  M[CP2]=OPER2;`
	`  OPER2=CP2+SE;`
	`  CP2=OPER2;`
	`  RS2=r[5];`
	`  PC=OPER2!RS2,TARG(L2);`
	(h) After CP Register Allocation
		`CP1=LV;`
		`CP2=OPER2;`
		`SE=offset(L2);`
		`TARG=PC+SE;`
		`SE=4;`
		`RS2=r[5];`
		`L2:`
		`  LV=M[CP2];`
		`  OPER2=LV+CP1;`
		`  M[CP2]=OPER2;`
		`  OPER2=CP2+SE;`
		`  CP2=OPER2;`
		`  PC=OPER2!RS2,TARG(L2);`
		(i) After Dead Asg Elimination and Loop–Invariant Code Motion
			`CP1=LV;`
			`CP2=OPER2;`
			`SE=offset(L2);`
			`TARG=PC+SE;`
			`SE=4;`
			`RS2=r[5];`
			`SEQ=PC+1;`
			`L2:`
			`  LV=M[CP2];`
			`  OPER2=LV+CP1;`
			`  M[CP2]=OPER2;`
			`  OPER2=CP2+SE;`
			`  CP2=OPER2;`
			`  PC=OPER2!RS2,SEQ(L2);`
			(j) After Using SEQ Register

`CP1=LV;`
`CP2=OPER2;`
`L2:`
`  LV=M[CP2];`
`  OPER1=LV+CP1;`
`  M[CP2]=OPER1;`
	`SE=4;`
	`SEQ=PC+1;`
	
	`OPER2=CP2+SE;`
	`PTB=b:SEQ(L2);`
	`CP2=OPER2;`
		`RS2=r[5];`
		
		`PC=OPER2!RS2,SEQ(L2);`

(k) After Dead Assignment Elimination and Effect Scheduling		

3 instructions   3 ALU opers 1 DC load   1 DC store 0 RF reads   0 RF writes 0 targ calc   0 sign extends **(l) SP Requirements for Processing Each Array Element**

Loop-Invariant Code Motion The next optimization shown is loop-invariant code motion, which moves loop-invariant values to the preheader block preceding of the loop. The italic instructions in Figure 6(f) are loop invariant and are hoisted out of the loop by our compiler. Because the branch target address does not change, the two instructions that calculate the address are first moved out of the loop. Hoisting branch target address calculations out of a loop required a new machine-specific optimization since the two effects have to update the SE and TARG registers. At this point there is only one remaining assignment to SE, so this sign extension is also moved out of the loop. Figure 6(g) shows the result of hoisting these instructions out of the loop, which improves both performance and energy usage. With traditional architectures, these computations are loop invariant, but cannot be moved out with compiler optimizations due to the fact that these computations cannot be decoupled from the instructions that use them.

CP Register Allocation Similar to allocating live ranges of scalar variable references to registers, our SP backend assigns live ranges of register file references to CP registers. In Figure 6(g) there are live ranges of r[6] and r[9] that span both the preheader and the loop. The compiler connects each live range of a register with the live range of the RS register into which its value is loaded. The compiler assigns an available CP register if the CP register is not live in the connected live range. Figure 6(h) shows the assignments to r[6] and r[9] replaced with CP1 and CP2, respectively. Likewise, the uses of RS1 and RS2 loaded from these registers are also replaced. Note that internal register accesses, such as CP1, require less energy than a register file access. At this point the loads from r[6] and r[9] are dead assignments and are eliminated, as shown in Figure 6(i). Thus, CP register allocation not only replaces register file references with internal register references, but also reduces the number of effects. Figures 6(h) and 6(i) also show that there is only one remaining assignment to RS2 and the compiler hoists it out of the loop by applying loop-invariant code motion.

The CP register allocation optimization requires careful heuristics as there are only two CP registers available in our design. We not only have to estimate the number of register load effects that would be eliminated by allocating a live range, but also the number of effects that cannot be eliminated in conflicting live ranges due to allocating the current live range. In addition, there is a definitive cost of using CP registers due to the need to save and restore these callee-save registers and eliminating a register load effect does not necessarily decrease the number of instructions after instruction scheduling. Note that we initially implemented optimizations to hoist register file references out of only the innermost loops of a function by using CP registers. However, we found that we not only missed opportunities for eliminating register file references outside of these loops, but also did not make the best use of CP registers within these loops by not using live range analysis.

SEQ Register   The next optimization shown is using the SEQ register to store the target address of the loop branch to eliminate the calculation of the address. The instruction that saves the next sequential address at the start of the loop is inserted, and the loop branch is modified to jump to SEQ instead of TARG. The result after this machine-dependent transformation can be seen in Figure 6(j). The two instructions that calculate the value of TARG are then removed by the dead assignment elimination optimization. The SEQ optimization also allows a second branch target address calculation to be hoisted out of a loop. Note that TARG(L2) or SEQ(L2) simply indicate that the target address comes from the internal register and the label in parentheses depicts that the target address is known to the compiler.

Effect Scheduling   The optimizations to this point have reduced the original 19 instructions in the loop to only six. In order to further reduce the number of instructions, we schedule multiple instruction effects together in parallel. Figure 6(k) shows the code after scheduling is applied. The SP instruction scheduler must respect structural hazards as well as dependencies between instructions. Because of the fact that the internal registers are used so frequently, and each has a prescribed purpose, code compiled for the SP architecture typically has far more anti-dependencies than code for other machines. As a part of scheduling, we attempt to rename some internal registers to avoid these anti-dependences. In the figure the compiler renames the result of the first addition in Figure 6(j) to use OPER1 instead of OPER2, as both registers can be assigned an integer addition result.

Although not shown in this example, our scheduler also moves instruction effects across basic blocks to obtain greater performance improvements and code size reductions. We attempt to move instruction effects into each of its predecessor blocks if there is an available slot in an instruction and moving the effect does not violate any data dependencies, the effect cannot cause a fault (e.g., load or store), and the effect is not considered too expensive (e.g., multiply or divide).

Handling Branches   The compiler also splits the branch effect into two effects in Figure 6(k). First, the PTB status register is set to specify the type and where the branch target address is to be obtained. In the next instruction, the comparison is then performed and the actual transfer of control takes place. As discussed in Section 2, the presence of a branch is specified one instruction ahead of time to avoid performing branch predictions on every instruction. This strategy also completely eliminates the need for a BTB as target addresses are calculated before transfers of control, which are explicitly identified in the preceding instruction.

Resource Utilization   Figure 6(l) shows the pipeline requirements for each element of the array in the code produced by our SP com-

piler. The SP code has three instructions in the loop as compared to five for the MIPS code. All accesses to the register file inside the loop for the SP code have been eliminated. The SP code also reduced the number of ALU operations by not adding zero when calculating a memory address, and eliminated sign extensions and branch target address calculations.

Immediate Transformation   There are other optimizations that our compiler performs that are not illustrated in Figure 6. One such optimization is to transform large constants (immediates) to small constants when possible. As shown in Figure 4, large constants require 17 bits in our encoding and are used to load a 16-bit value into the low or high portion of the SE register. If a small constant that fits in our 7-bit field can instead be used, then additional effects may be placed in the instruction. Figure 7(a) shows a transformation that can sometimes accomplish this goal. Assume that *const1* and *const2* both require a large immediate field, but the difference between the two constants can fit in the small immediate field. Likewise, assume that OPER2 and RS1 are not updated between the two pairs of instructions shown in the figure. The compiler changes the second pair of instructions to use the difference between the two constants and replaces RS1 with OPER2. Figures 7(b) and 7(c) show instructions in the prologue of a function to save register values after scheduling without and with applying this transformation. The number of instructions is reduced from 11 to eight and four assignments to SE are also eliminated due to the remaining differences being identical.

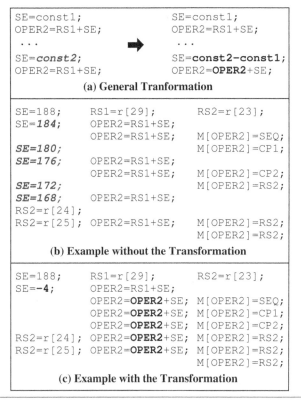

Figure 7. Avoiding the Use of Large Constants

The compiler also encodes branch displacements as constants assigned to the SE register. These displacements can decrease during the scheduling of effects. The compiler marks each branch displacement effect that was initially scheduled into large immediate fields and reschedules a basic block if it later finds that the effect can be represented using a small immediate field. This process is iteratively performed until no such occurrences are found.

Summary of Compiler Modifications The modifications to the compiler were extensive and included expanding MIPS instructions to SP instructions, representing SP instructions in the compiler backend, loop-invariant code motion of register file reads using a CP register, loop-invariant code motion of branch target address calculations, use of the SEQ register to hold a branch target address, allocating live ranges of register file references to CP registers, transforming large immediates to small immediates, an internal register renaming pass to eliminate false dependences, placement of the PTB effect, scheduling of SP effects both within and across basic blocks. Several of these optimizations had to ensure that each transformation was legal before it could be committed due to the restricted SP datapath.

4. Evaluation

This section presents an experimental evaluation of the SP architecture including a description of the experimental setup and results for performance, code size, and an estimation of the energy savings achieved by static pipelining.

4.1 Experimental Setup

We use 17 benchmarks shown in Table 1 from the MiBench benchmark suite [10], which is a representative set of embedded applications. We extended the GNU assembler to assemble SP instructions and implemented a simulator based on the SimpleScalar in-order MIPS [1]. In order to avoid having to compile all of the standard C library and system code, we allow SP code to call functions compiled for the MIPS. A status bit is used to indicate whether it is a MIPS or SP instruction. After fetching an instruction, the simulator checks this bit and handles the instruction accordingly. On a mode change, the simulator will also drain the pipeline.

Category	Benchmarks
automotive	bitcount, qsort, susan
consumer	jpeg, tiff
network	dijkstra, patricia
office	ispell, stringsearch
security	blowfish, rijndael, pgp, sha
telecom	adpcm, CRC32, FFT, GSM

Table 1. Benchmarks Used

For all benchmarks, when compiled for the SP, over 90% of the instructions executed are SP instructions, with the remaining MIPS instructions coming from calls to standard library routines such as *printf*. All cycles and register accesses are counted towards the results whether they come from the MIPS library code or the SP code. Were all the library code compiled for the SP as well, the results would likely improve as we would not need to flush on a mode change, and we would also have the energy saving benefits applied to more of the code.

For the MIPS baseline, the programs were compiled with the original VPO MIPS port with all optimizations enabled and run through the same simulator, as it is also capable of simulating MIPS code. We extended the simulator to include branch prediction with a simple bimodal branch predictor with 256 two-bit saturating counters, and a 256-entry branch target buffer. The branch target buffer (BTB) is only used for MIPS code as it is not needed for the SP. The simulator was also extended to include level one data and instruction caches, which were configured to have 256 lines of 32 bytes each and are direct-mapped.

Each of the graphs in the following sections represent the ratio between SP code to MIPS code. A ratio less than 1.0 means that the SP has reduced the value, while a ratio over 1.0 means that the SP has increased the value.

Each bar represents a different benchmark except for the averages. The ratios are averaged rather than the raw numbers to weight each benchmark evenly rather than giving greater weight to those that run longer. When a given benchmark had more than one simulation associated with it (e.g., jpeg has both encode and decode), we averaged the figures for all of its simulations and then used that figure for the benchmark to avoid weighing benchmarks with multiple runs more heavily.

4.2 Results

Figure 8 shows the ratios for simulated execution cycles. Many of the benchmarks in MiBench are dominated by fairly tight loops. This means that the performance difference is largely determined by how well the SP compiler does on these kernel loops. That is the primary reason for the relatively large deviation among benchmarks. For example, our compiler does quite well with the kernel loops in *dijkstra*, *qsort*, *sha*, and *stringsearch* which leads to the substantial speedups. On the other hand, *adpcm*, *bitcount*, and *ispell* have more control flow in their kernel loops, leading to execution time increases due to the previously mentioned restrictions of scheduling effects across basic blocks. On average, the SP code performed 7.9% better than the MIPS code. This figure also shows that not enforcing the 32-bit instruction size restriction results in 6.5% fewer cycles as compared to using templates, as described in Section 2.2. We describe in Section 6 how we may be able to avoid some of this performance degradation from using templates without significant increases in code size.

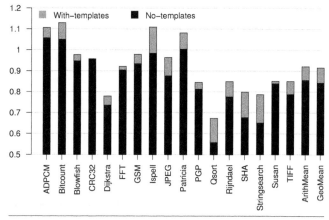

Figure 8. Execution Cycles

Figure 9 shows the compiled code size ratios for the benchmarks. The SP compiler produces code size that is 8.3% smaller than the MIPS compiler on average. These performance and code size improvements are counter-intuitive given that a lower level instruction format is used, but is due to eliminating many SP effects.

Table 2 summarizes the average (arithmetic mean) results from the simulations. Because the SP is able to use values in internal registers directly, it is often able to bypass the centralized register file as discussed in Section 3. For this reason, we are able to remove 74% of the register file reads. For the MIPS baseline pipeline, we only count register reads when the instruction actually references the register file, which is not the case for some pipeline implementations. Like register reads, the compiler is able to remove a substantial number of register file writes, 67% on average. As depicted in the example in Section 3.2, some loops had nearly all of the register accesses removed, such as *rijndael* and *CRC32*. Because the register file is a fairly large structure that is frequently accessed, these register access reductions should result in substantial energy savings. For the MIPS programs, *internal writes* are the number of

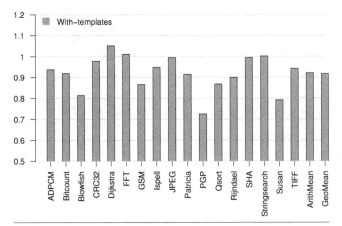

Figure 9. Code Size

Metric	Average SP to MIPS Ratio
Execution Cycles	0.92
Code Size	0.92
Register File Reads	0.26
Register File Writes	0.33
Internal Writes	0.39
Branch Predictions	0.13
Target Calculations	0.59
BTB Accesses	0.00

Table 2. Summary of Results

writes to the pipeline registers. We evaluate each pipeline register as a single element, even though the components of these registers can be viewed separately, as shown in Figure 2. Because there are four such registers, and they are written every cycle, this figure is simply the number of cycles multiplied by four. For the SP, the *internal writes* refer to writes to the internal registers. Because the SP code explicitly instructs the architecture when to write an internal register, we are able to remove 61% of these writes, on average. The SP specifies when a conditional branch will occur one cycle ahead of time, which eliminates the need to predict branches except when the instruction actually is a conditional branch. This results in an 87% average decrease in the number of branch prediction buffer accesses. Because the SP has the ability to avoid calculating branch targets for innermost loops by saving the next sequential address at the top of the loop, and by hoisting these invariant branch target address calculations out of loops, we are able to substantially reduce the number of branch target calculations by 39%. In summary, we have significantly reduced the number of register file accesses, internal register accesses, branch predictions, and branch target address calculations and have completely eliminated the BTB. At the same time, we have also decreased both the number of execution cycles and code size.

4.3 Processor Energy Estimation

This section presents an estimate of the processor energy savings achieved by the SP approach. This estimate uses the simulated counts of events such as register file accesses, branch predictions and ALU operations along with estimates of how much power is consumed by each event.

The SRAMs within the pipeline have been modelled using CACTI [17]. Other components have been synthesized for a 65nm process, then simulated at the netlist level to determine average case activation power. We have normalized the power per component to a 32-entry dual-ported register file read, because the power

per component are dependent on process technology and other implementation dependent issues. The ratios between component power are also somewhat dependent on process technology, however these differences should not have a qualitative impact on the final estimates. The resulting total energy estimate is a linear combination of the number of activations and the power attributions per component. The relative power per activation we attribute to each component is given in Table 3.

Component	Relative Access Power
Level 1 Caches (8kB)	5.10
Branch Prediction Buffer	0.65
Branch Target Buffer	2.86
Register File Access	1.00
Arithmetic Logic Unit	4.11
Floating Point Unit	12.60
Internal Register Writes	0.10

Table 3. Pipeline Component Relative Power

Figure 10 shows the results of this analysis. On average, the SP reduces energy usage by 27%. These savings comes primarily from the reduction in register file accesses, branch prediction table accesses, and the fact that we do not need a branch target buffer. Of course these results are also affected by the relative running time of the benchmark as that has a direct effect on instruction cache usage and static power consumption.

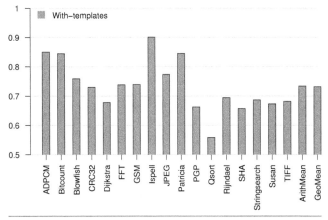

Figure 10. Estimated Energy Usage

While these estimates take into account the number of accesses to the larger structures of the two pipelines the difference in control logic and interconnect routing is not taken into account. The interconnect of the SP has more links than that of a classical five-stage pipeline, which could negatively effect the power and performance. The interconnect shown in Figure 3 has 69 links. Out of these, 16 links are used less than 1% of the time and could be removed with low impact to the SP's performance [12]. As discussed in Section 6, we intend to more accurately estimate energy benefits by doing full pipeline netlist simulations for both the MIPS and SP.

5. Related Work

This paper builds on previous work [6, 7] where the majority of the presented optimizations had not been implemented and only a couple of toy examples were evaluated by hand. We now have implemented all of the presented optimizations and have automatically evaluated the results on a large set of benchmark applications. Our current paper also has a number of new compiler optimizations, an updated architecture, and a completely new instruction set encoding, as described in Section 2.2.

SP instructions are most similar to horizontal microinstructions [20], however, there are significant differences. Firstly, the effects in SP instructions specify how to pipeline traditional operations across multiple cycles. While horizontal micro-instructions also specify computation at a low level, they do not expose pipelining at the architectural level. Also, in a micro-programmed processor, each machine instruction causes the execution of micro-instructions within a micro-routine stored in ROM. Furthermore, compiler optimizations cannot be performed across these micro-routines since this level is not generally exposed to the compiler. It has been proposed to break floating-point operations into micro-operations and optimize the resulting code [5]. However, this approach can result in a significant increase in code size. Static pipelining also bears some resemblance to VLIW [8] in that the compiler determines which operations are independent. However, most VLIW instructions represent multiple RISC operations that can be performed in parallel. In contrast, the SP approach encodes individual instruction effects that can be issued in parallel, where most of these effects correspond to an action taken by a single pipeline stage of a traditional RISC instruction.

A prepare-to-branch (PTB) instruction has been previously proposed [3]. However, the use of this feature has previously required an entire instruction and thus may impact code size and performance. In contrast, our PTB field only requires 3 bits as the target address calculation is decoupled from both the PTB field and the point of the transfer of control.

There have been other proposed architectures that also expose much of the datapath to a compiler. One architecture that gives the compiler direct control of the micro-architecture is the No Instruction Set Computer (NISC) [14]. Unlike other architectures, there is no fixed ISA that bridges the compiler with the hardware. Instead, the compiler generates control signals for the datapath directly. The FlexCore processor [18] also exposes datapath elements at the architectural level. The design features a flexible datapath with an instruction decoder that is reconfigured dynamically at runtime. The Transport-Triggered Architectures (TTAs) [4] are similar to VLIWs in that there are a large number of parallel computations specified in each instruction. TTAs, however, can move values directly to and from functional unit ports, to avoid the need for large, multi-ported register files. Likewise, the TTA compiler was able to perform copy propagation and dead assignment elimination on register references. Thus, both the TTA and the SP avoid many unnecessary register file accesses. However, the SP backend performs many other optimizations that are not performed for the TTA (and the NISC and FlexCore), while using fewer internal registers. These additional optimizations include performing loop-invariant code motion of register file accesses and target address calculations, allocating live ranges of registers to internal registers, using a SEQ register to avoid target address calculations at the top of a loop, and transforming large immediates to small immediates. The NISC, FlexCore, and the initial TTA studies improve performance at the expense of a significant increase in code size and were evaluated using tiny benchmarks. In contrast, static pipelining focuses on improving energy usage while still obtaining performance and code size improvements on the MiBench benchmark suite. An alternative TTA design did achieve comparable code size and performance compared to a RISC baseline, but required an intermixture of 16-bit and 32-bit instructions and the use of internal register queues, which increase the hardware complexity [11]. In addition, the NISC, FlexCore, and TTA rely on delayed branches, where the SP decouples the branch target address calculation from the branch and uses a PTB field, completely eliminating the need for a BTB, which is the most expensive part of branch prediction.

There have also been many studies that focused on increasing the energy-efficiency of pipelines by avoiding unnecessary computations. One study presents many methods for reducing the power consumption of register file accesses [19]. One method, bypass skip, avoids reading operands from the register file when the result would come from forwarding anyway. Another method is read caching, which is based on the observation that subsequent instructions will often read the same registers. Another technique that avoids unnecessary register accesses is static strands [15], where a strand is a sequence of instructions that has some number of inputs and only one output. The key idea is that if a strand is treated as one instruction, then the intermediate results do not need to be written to the register file. Strands are dispatched as a single instruction where they are executed on a multi-cycle ALU that cycles its outputs back to its inputs. All of these techniques attempt to make processors using traditional instruction sets more efficient. An SP processor avoids all of these unnecessary register file accesses without the need for special hardware logic to detect these opportunities, which can negate some of the energy savings.

6. Future Work

As discussed in Section 4, our current energy savings results are only estimates. While our results were estimated conservatively, and are still significant, it would increase the strength of this work to have more accurate results. Our current estimates are based on counting the number of times different events happen in the micro-architecture and estimating the energy costs of each event. This method does not allow us to take into account other changes in energy usage such as the fact that we no longer need to do forwarding and that hazard detection is much simpler. The SP design also includes a number of multiplexers not found in the traditional pipeline. In order to evaluate the changes in energy usage and timing of these components, we plan to construct a netlist implementation using VHDL. Because each portion of the datapath is explicitly controlled, there is less complexity in the operation of the micro-architecture. The logic for checking for hazards is much simpler, forwarding does not take place, and values are not implicitly copied through pipeline registers each cycle. Due to these factors, SP hardware should have decreased area and cost compared to equivalent traditionally pipelined hardware.

The software pipelining compiler optimization could be applied to further improve the performance of SP code. This optimization is a technique used to exploit instruction-level parallelism in loops [16]. Loops whose iterations operate on independent values, typically in arrays, provide opportunities for increased parallelism. Software pipelining overlaps the execution of multiple iterations and schedules instructions in order to allow the micro-architecture to take advantage of this parallelism. Software pipelining would have little benefit for the baseline MIPS, except when long latency operations, such as multiply and divide, are used. However, for an SP machine, software pipelining could be applied in order to schedule many innermost loops more efficiently. Software pipelining, however, can also have a negative effect on code size.

We encode SP instructions in order to attain reasonable code size, however this does have a negative impact on performance as compared to using a larger instruction format. In order to address these conflicting requirements, we could allow both 32-bit and 64-bit instructions in different situations. Like the *Thumb2* instruction set that supports intermixing 16-bit and 32-bit instructions [13], we could use 64-bit instructions where a higher number of effects can be scheduled and 32-bit instructions elsewhere to retain most of the code size benefits of the smaller instructions.

The design of a high performance, SP processor would likely include more internal registers, along with more functional units, and possibly more ports to the register file. This would mean that the instructions would have additional different types of effects, possibly leading to an issue with code size, though larger code sizes are generally less of an issue with general-purpose processors than with embedded ones.

7. Conclusions

Static pipelining is designed to explore the extreme of energy efficient architectural design. It utilizes a fairly radical and counterintuitive approach for representing instructions to provide greater control of pipeline operation. The primary question about this design is if a compiler can generate code that is competitive with a more conventional representation. The challenges in this research included using a low-level representation that violated many assumptions in a conventional compiler, ensuring that transformations resulted in legal instructions given the restricted datapath, and in applying instruction scheduling to such a different target architecture. It was initially unclear how efficiently we could populate pipeline resources around control-flow instructions and if it would be possible to utilize a 32-bit format for SP instructions. Both of these challenges were resolved in our compiler.

Our SP target architecture achieves on average better performance and code size as compared to optimized code generated for the analogous conventional (MIPS) processor architecture. In quite a few cases, we were able to significantly improve performance, and the overall performance was limited by slowdowns in some benchmarks caused by idiosyncratic behavior that can be addressed with future optimizations specific to SP code. Static pipelining clearly provides a benefit from an energy perspective. By reducing accesses to pipeline (internal) registers, and eliminating unnecessary accesses to architectural and micro-architectural resources, an average energy savings of 27% is achieved. The obtained results show that it is useful to re-examine the boundary between hardware and software to improve processor energy efficiency.

8. Acknowledegements

We thank the anonymous reviewers for their constructive comments and suggestions. This research was supported in part by NSF grants CNS-0964413 and CNS-0915926, a Google Faculty Research Award, Korea SMBA grant 0004537, and KEIT grant 10041725.

References

[1] T. Austin, E. Larson, and D. Ernst. SimpleScalar: An Infrastructure for Computer System Modeling. *Computer*, 35(2):59–67, 2002.

[2] M. Benitez and J. Davidson. A Portable Global Optimizer and Linker. *ACM SIGPLAN Notices*, 23(7):329–338, 1988.

[3] A. Bright, J. Fritts, and M. Gschwind. Decoupled fetch-execute engine with static branch prediction support. Technical report, IBM Research Report RC23261, IBM Research Division, 1999.

[4] H. Corporaal and M. Arnold. Using Transport Triggered Architectures for Embedded Processor Design. *Integrated Computer-Aided Engineering*, 5(1):19–38, 1998.

[5] W. Dally. Micro-optimization of floating-point operations. In *Proceedings of the Conference on Architectural Support for Programming Languages and Operating Systems*, pages 283–289, 1989.

[6] I. Finlayson, G. Uh, D. Whalley, and G. Tyson. An Overview of Static Pipelining. *Computer Architecture Letters*, 11(1):17–20, 2012.

[7] Finlayson, I. and Uh, G. and Whalley, D. and Tyson, G. Improving Low Power Processor Efficiency with Static Pipelining. In *Proceedings of the 15th Workshop on Interaction between Compilers and Computer Architectures*, 2011.

[8] J. Fisher. VLIW Machine: A Multiprocessor for Compiling Scientific Code. *Computer*, 17(7):45–53, 1984.

[9] C. Fraser. A retargetable compiler for ansi c. *ACM Sigplan Notices*, 26(10):29–43, 1991.

[10] M. Guthaus, J. Ringenberg, D. Ernst, T. Austin, T. Mudge, and R. Brown. MiBench: A Free, Commercially Representative Embedded Benchmark Suite. In *Workload Characterization, 2001. WWC-4. 2001 IEEE International Workshop on*, pages 3–14. IEEE, 2002.

[11] Y. He, D. She, B. Mesman, and H. Corporaal. Move-pro: A low power and high code density TTA architecture. In *International Conference on Embedded Computer Systems*, pages 294–301, July 2011.

[12] T. Hoang-Thanh, U. Jälmbrant, E. Hagopian, K. P. Subramaniyan, M. Själander, and P. Larsson-Edefors. Design Space Exploration for an Embedded Processor with Flexible Datapath Interconnect. In *Proceedings of IEEE International Conference on Application-Specific Systems, Architectures and Processors*, pages 55–62, July 2010.

[13] A. Ltd. Arm thumb-2 core technology. *http://infocenter.arm.com /help/index.jsp?topic= /com.arm.doc.dui0471c /CHDFEDDB.html*, June 2012.

[14] M. Reshadi, B. Gorjiara, and D. Gajski. Utilizing horizontal and vertical parallelism with a no-instruction-set compiler for custom datapaths. In *ICCD '05: Proceedings of the 2005 International Conference on Computer Design*, pages 69–76, Washington, DC, USA, 2005. IEEE Computer Society.

[15] P. Sassone, D. Wills, and G. Loh. Static Strands: Safely Collapsing Dependence Chains for Increasing Embedded Power Efficiency. In *Proceedings of the 2005 ACM SIGPLAN/SIGBED conference on Languages, compilers, and tools for embedded systems*, pages 127–136. ACM, 2005.

[16] A. Sethi and J. Ullman. Compilers: Principles Techniques and Tools. *Addision Wesley Longman*, 2000.

[17] S. Thoziyoor, N. Muralimanohar, J. Ahn, and N. Jouppi. Cacti 5.1. Technical report, HP Laboratories, Palo Alto, Apr. 2008.

[18] M. Thuresson, M. Själander, M. Björk, L. Svensson, P. Larsson-Edefors, and P. Stenstrom. Flexcore: Utilizing exposed datapath control for efficient computing. *Journal of Signal Processing Systems*, 57(1):5–19, 2009.

[19] J. H. Tseng and K. Asanovic. Energy-efficient register access. In *SBCCI '00: Proceedings of the 13th symposium on Integrated circuits and systems design*, page 377, Washington, DC, USA, 2000. IEEE Computer Society.

[20] M. Wilkes and J. Stringer. Micro-Programming and the Design of the Control Circuits in an Electronic Digital Computer. In *Mathematical Proceedings of the Cambridge Philosophical Society*, volume 49, pages 230–238. Cambridge Univ Press, 1953.

LUCAS: Latency-adaptive Unified Cluster Assignment and instruction Scheduling *

Vasileios Porpodas, and Marcelo Cintra [†]

School of Informatics, University of Edinburgh
{v.porpodas@, mc@staffmail.}ed.ac.uk

ABSTRACT

Clustered VLIW architectures are statically scheduled wide-issue architectures that combine the advantages of wide-issue processors along with the power and frequency scalability of clustered designs. Being statically scheduled, they require that the decision of mapping instructions to clusters be done by the compiler. State-of-the-art code generation for such architectures combines cluster-assignment and instruction scheduling in a single unified pass. The performance of the generated code, however, is very susceptible to the inter-cluster communication latency. This is due to the nature of the two clustering heuristics used. One is aggressive and works well for low inter-cluster latencies, while the other is more conservative and works well only for high latencies.

In this paper we propose LUCAS, a novel unified cluster-assignment and instruction-scheduling algorithm that adapts to the inter-cluster latency better than the existing state-of-the-art schemes. LUCAS is a hybrid scheme that performs fine-grain switching between the two state-of-the-art clustering heuristics, leading to better scheduling than either of them. It generates better performing code for a wide range of inter-cluster latency values.

Categories and Subject Descriptors D.3.4 [*Programming Languages*]: Processors; C.1.1 [*Processor Architectures*]: Single Data Stream Architectures

General Terms Algorithms, Experimentation, Performance

Keywords Cluster Assignment, Instruction Scheduling, Clustered VLIW

1. INTRODUCTION

Clustered designs were introduced as a solution to the poor scalability of wide-issue processors. This is done by partitioning the design into smaller sections called clusters. Within the cluster, data transfers are fast and energy efficient, while across clusters there is a performance and energy penalty. On the contrary, monolithic (non-clustered) architectures have some bulky resources (such as the register file) that are shared across many functional units and

---

* This work was supported in part by the EC under grant ERA 249059 (FP7).

[†] Marcelo Cintra is currently on sabbatical leave at Intel Labs.

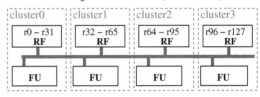

a. A high–level view of a generic Clustered VLIW Architecture with 32 registers and 4 clusters (4 issue in total)

b. A sample schedule on the clustered architecture

Figure 1. A 4-cluster, 4-issue architecture with 32 registers per cluster (a). An example instruction schedule on the architecture (b).

therefore they do not exploit the opportunity to improve performance or to save energy whenever global communication is not required. A clustered design, on the other hand, does exactly that as its resources are partitioned into smaller, locally accessible sections. Each cluster usually contains a portion of the register file tightly connected to a small number of other resources (e.g. functional units). In this way any local communication within the cluster is fast and efficient while any inter-cluster communication comes at extra cost, often higher than that of a monolithic design. It is this partitioning of the global resources and their localization within a cluster that gives the clustered design an advantage in both energy and frequency scaling [26].

The clustering approach has been applied to both statically (e.g., [9, 23, 25]) and dynamically (e.g., [15, 22]) scheduled processors. Statically scheduled processors are based on simpler, smaller and more efficient hardware designs than their dynamically scheduled counterparts. VLIW processors, which are both statically scheduled and wide-issue ILP processors, combine the hardware simplicity and energy advantage of statically scheduled processors with the performance of wide-ILP processors, thus operating at a good energy-performance point. Since they are statically scheduled, VLIWs rely on the compiler to generate high performance code. Compared to dynamically scheduled processors, VLIW processors require that instruction scheduling be done in the compiler.

A clustered VLIW processor (as in Figure 1a) has an additional performance and energy advantage compared to its non-clustered counterpart due to the scalability of the design. In this case though, the compiler has to perform yet another task, that of cluster assignment, deciding the cluster where each instruction should be executed at (as shown in the code example of Figure 1b).

1.1 Code Generation

Originally, cluster assignment was done just before instruction scheduling, in a separate pass [8]. The clustering algorithm traverses the data-flow graph and assigns the instructions to clusters in a greedy manner. The cluster selected is the one suggested by the clustering heuristic. The two state-of-the-art clustering heuristics (Start-Cycle and Completion-Cycle) differ in their aggressiveness. The first one will eagerly spread instructions across clusters as long as the one-way latency cost is covered, hoping for good performance, whereas the latter will only do so if the round-trip cost is covered. The clustering scheme has a major impact on performance and is strongly affected by the inter-cluster latency.

More recent work has combined the instruction scheduling pass with the cluster assignment pass in an attempt to remove some phase-ordering issues between the two [14, 21]. This is done by modifying the instruction scheduler so that upon scheduling an instruction, it also decides on the cluster where it should be assigned to based on the value of the clustering heuristic.

1.2 Contributions

In this paper we identify a fundamental weakness of the existing state-of-the-art heuristics for combined instruction scheduling and cluster assignment. The code generated by these algorithms performs well under very limited conditions. Depending on the heuristic used, they work well under either: i) low inter-cluster latencies, or ii) high instruction latencies. To make matters worse, the intersection point, where one heuristic overtakes the other, varies significantly and is benchmark specific.

In short in this paper:

1. We present a detailed comparison of the best state-of-the-art clustering heuristics (built inside an instruction scheduler) on a range of inter-cluster delays.

2. We propose a novel clustering heuristic that **i)** adapts to the inter-cluster latency and performs best across a wide range of inter-cluster latencies and **ii)** often outperforms both existing heuristics

In the rest of the paper we start by describing some of the fundamental concepts involved (Section 2). Afterwards we motivate the proposed work by identifying the weaknesses of the state-of-the art (Section 3), then we discuss the proposed work in full detail (Section 4) and the experimental setup (Section 5) used to get the results shown in Section 6. Finally we present an overview of the related work (Section 7) and we conclude in Section 8.

2. BACKGROUND

Our work is based on two fundamental concepts. The first one is the clustering heuristics and the second one is instruction scheduling.

2.1 Clustering heuristics

In this section we present the state-of-the-art clustering heuristics which are implemented in several algorithms.

Start-Cycle (SC): Existing combined cluster-assignment and instruction scheduling schemes [14, 21] make use of the same clustering heuristic, which according to [21] proves to be the highest performing one when compared to other greedy heuristics. It is the resource-constrained earliest schedule cycle heuristic, also known as the Start-Cycle. In more detail, it returns the earliest cycle that an instruction can be scheduled at on any given cluster, taking into account not only the dependence constraints of the predecessors but also the inter-cluster latency and the issue-slot occupancy (resource) constraint (Algorithm 1). An example that visualizes how the heuristic works is in Figure 2b,c in red color. The two Start-Cycle values (for (B,CL0) and (B,CL1)) show the value returned by the heuristic for cluster 0 and 1 respectively.

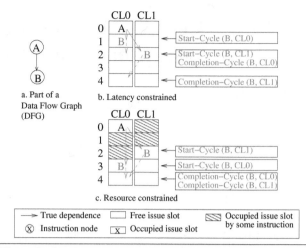

a. Part of a Data Flow Graph (DFG) b. Latency constrained

c. Resource constrained

→ True dependence ☐ Free issue slot ▨ Occupied issue slot by some instruction
Ⓧ Instruction node ☒ Occupied issue slot

Figure 2. The internal workings of Start-Cycle and Completion-Cycle clustering heuristics. Heuristic(N, CLx) signifies the value of the Heuristic when node N is placed on cluster X.

The Start-Cycle heuristic spreads the instructions across the clusters in an aggressive and greedy manner. Each and every instruction gets scheduled on the cluster where it will execute the earliest. As shown in Section 3, this strategy proves to work best on low inter-cluster communication latencies, but the performance degradation on high latencies is unbounded.

Algorithm 1. Start-Cycle heuristic.

```
1  /* Start-Cycle Heuristic */
2  start_cycle (insn, cluster)
3  {
4    i = 0
5    for pred in insn's predecessors:
6      dst = Distance (pred.cluster, cluster)
7      latency_aware_sc = pred.cycle +pred.latency +dst
8      /* Increase cycle until we get a free resource*/
9      cycle = latency_aware_sc
10     while reservation_table_not_free(cluster,cycle):
11       cycle ++
12     resource_and_latencyaware_sc = cycle
13     sc [i++] = resource_and_latency_aware_sc
14   return MAX of all sc[ ]
15 }
```

Completion-Cycle (CC): The problem of Start-Cycle's unbounded performance degradation is addressed in other clustering works (e.g., [8, 17]), which are based on the Completion-Cycle heuristic. This is a conservative clustering heuristic that distributes the instructions only if it is guaranteed that they will not cause a slow-down at that scheduling point.

It works by calculating the Start-Cycle and adds to it the latency of the instruction and the latency until this instruction's data is sent over to its earliest successor (Algorithm 2). Since the cluster number of the successors is only known for the instructions just before the end of a region, the cluster number of the successors is zero for the majority of cases. This case is shown in Figure 2b,c in green color.

Critical-Successor (CS): A more recently introduced clustering algorithm was presented in [28]. The clustering heuristic introduced by it is based on the observation that when a sibling instruction node has been already assigned to a cluster, then it is highly probable that there exists an immediate successor of it that is also a highly critical immediate successor of the current instruction node. In this case the clustering heuristic should select the cluster that achieves the best start-cycle, not of the current instruction but of the critical-successor node instead. To be more precise, the critical-successor start-cycle is selected only if it can pinpoint a single clear winner out of all clusters. The heuristic defaults to standard start-cycle if the code does not meet any of these constraints. The CS heuristic exhibits similar behavior to SC with respect to the increasing inter-cluster delay, mostly due to the fact that it is built upon the start-cycle heuristic. We will therefore focus on the other two heuristics for the following sections.

All heuristics are greedy and are calculated once on a single top-down walk of the DFG with no backtracking. Thus they cannot guarantee a globally optimal solution.

Algorithm 2. Completion-Cycle heuristic.

```
1  /* Completion-Cycle Heuristic */}
2  completion_cycle (insn, cluster)
3  {
4     i = 0
5     start_c = start_cycle (insn, cluster)
6     for succ in insn's successors:
7        dist = distance (succ.cluster, cluster)
8        cc [i++] = start_c + dist
9     return MIN of all cc[ ]
10  }
11 }
```

2.2 Instruction Scheduling

Instruction scheduling is traditionally done by a list scheduler. The list scheduling algorithm works as shown in Algorithm 3. Its input is a Data Dependence Graph (DDG) and its output is the instruction schedule. In short it follows the following steps:

1. Walk the dependence graph and prioritize the nodes (usually based on their height from the bottom of the DDG) (Algorithm 3 line 4).

2. While there are unscheduled nodes, form a list of ready instructions (instructions with scheduled predecessors or with no predecessors at all) (Algorithm 3 lines 6 - 7).

3. Sort the ready list based on the priority of each instruction (Algorithm 3 line 8).

4. Start from the instruction with the highest priority and try to issue it on the current cycle (Algorithm 3 lines 9-11). If this is not possible then skip it (line 13) and try the next instruction in the ready list. In any case remove the current instruction from the ready list (line 14).

5. Once tried all the instructions in the ready list have been considered then increase the current cycle by 1 (Algorithm 3 line 15).

Algorithm 3. Simplified List Scheduling.

```
1  /* List Scheduling: Input DDG, Output: Schedule */
2  list_schedule (ddg)
3  {
4    walk down the ddg and prioritize the nodes
5    cycle = 0
6    while (exist unscheduled nodes):
7       ready_list = list of ready nodes
8       sort ready_list based on priority
9       for node in prioritized ready_list:
10         if (can issue node.instruction on cycle):
11            Issue (node.instr, cycle)
12         else
13            Skip node
14         Remove node from ready_list
15      cycle ++
16  }
```

---

3. MOTIVATION

The major weakness of the state-of-the-art cluster-assignment and instruction-scheduling algorithms is that their clustering heuris-

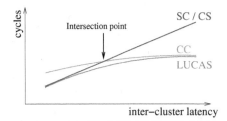

Figure 3. Qualitative performance comparison of clustering heuristics under increasing inter-cluster latency: Start-Cycle (SC), Critical-Successor (CS), Completion-Cycle (CC) and the proposed heuristic used in LUCAS.

tics perform well on a limited range of inter-cluster communication latencies. Figure 3 points out this fact. The Start-Cycle (SC) (and Critical-Successor (CS)) heuristics perform well only on low-latency configurations. The Completion-Cycle (CC), on the other hand performs well only on high-latency configurations. Moreover the intersection point is highly specific to the benchmark and varies unpredictably.

The proposed scheme (LUCAS) addresses the shortcomings of both heuristics by adapting to the inter-cluster latency. LUCAS switches between the aggressive (SC) and conservative (CC) heuristic on a per-instruction basis. As shown in Figure 3 the goal of the proposed approach is to provide the best performance across the whole range of inter-cluster latencies.

3.1 Clustering Heuristics

The reason why the state-of-the-art heuristics perform in general as in Figure 3 and why our heuristic performs the way it does, can be explained by the motivating examples of Figures 4 and 5. The LUCAS heuristic uses two sub-heuristics: i) the cycle-congestion (Figure 4) and ii) the instruction mobility (Figure 5), to guide the decision on when to use the start-cycle or the completion-cycle heuristic. This will be explained in more detail later on. The examples of Figures 4 and 5 show the schedules acquired after scheduling the nodes of the Data Flow Graph (DFG) (Figure 4a and 5a) using the clustering heuristics (vertical axis) for inter-cluster latencies of 1 to 3 cycles (horizontal axis).

The Start-Cycle heuristic (Figures 4 and 5 b-d) performs well on low latencies but the schedule length increases almost linearly to the inter-cluster latency. This is because the heuristic is very aggressive at dispersing the instructions across distant clusters.

On the contrary, the Completion-Cycle heuristic (in both Figures 4 and 5 e-g) performs best under high inter-cluster communication latencies. The schedule length remains unchanged no matter the inter-cluster latency. The reason for this is that an instruction will only be scheduled on a distant cluster if its descendants are not slowed down. This conservative policy bounds the schedule length for high latencies but proves not as effective for low latencies.

LUCAS adjusts better to the inter-cluster latency. We show how it does so by demonstrating how each of the sub-heuristics works in each example (Figures 4 and 5). The Cycle-Congestion sub-heuristic (Figure 4) measures the congestion on each scheduling cycle. If there are too many ready instructions to fit in a single cluster, then it chooses to follow the aggressive Start-Cycle heuristic. This happens in cycles 0 and 1 in Figure 4.h and i (latency 1 and 2). On later cycles however, there is no congestion and therefore instruction 'E' is scheduled based on the conservative Completion-Cycle heuristic.

The instruction Mobility sub-heuristic is shown in Figure 5. The concept is that if an instruction has a high enough mobility, then its slack is high and thus there is little chance that it can degrade the schedule if assigned to a distant cluster (the mobility is calculated as ALAP-ASAP as in [16]). Therefore high-mobility instructions are scheduled with the Start-Cycle heuristic. The mobility numbers

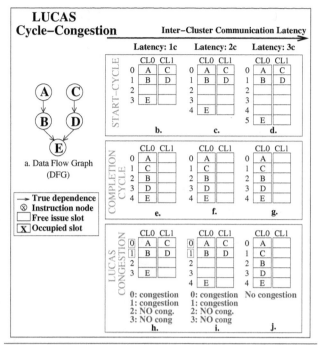

Figure 4. Motivating example 1. Schedules for the instructions in the Data Flow Graph (DFG) (a) on a 2-cluster 2-issue clustered architecture, for the Start-Cycle, Completion-Cycle and LUCAS-Cycle-Congestion clustering heuristics. The inter-cluster delay ranges from 1 to 3 cycles.

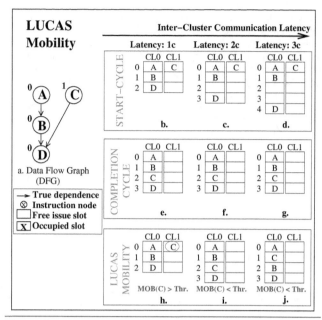

Figure 5. Motivating example 2. Schedules for the instructions in the Data Flow Graph (DFG) (a) on a 2-cluster 2-issue clustered architecture, for the Start-Cycle, Completion-Cycle and LUCAS-Mobility clustering heuristics. The inter-cluster delay ranges from 1 to 3 cycles. Each node in the DFG is tagged with its mobility number.

are shown in the DFG of Figure 5 on the left side of each instruction. Instruction 'C' has mobility 1 which is higher than the threshold for Latency 1. Therefore in that case 'C' is scheduled in Cluster 1, as dictated by the Start-Cycle heuristic.

As shown in the motivating examples, LUCAS is capable of adapting to the best clustering heuristic, for the whole range of inter-cluster communication latencies. The detailed description of the LUCAS algorithm and the sub-heuristics used is presented later in Section 4.

3.2 Scheduling

While both UAS and CARS [14, 21] make use of a list scheduler, they have embedded the clustering decision inside the instruction scheduler in a different way.

CARS [1] always honors the clustering decision and schedules only on the cluster chosen by it (see Figure 6a). The clustering heuristic tags each cluster with a score and next the cluster with the best score wins (Figure 6.a.2 BEST CLUSTER).

On the contrary UAS [21] is more aggressive. It tries to honor the clustering decision only at the first attempt, but if it fails to issue the instruction on the specified cluster, it will try other clusters as well (Figure 6.b). Therefore the cluster with the best score does not always win (Figure 6.b.3). This is an aggressive technique that might work on low inter-cluster latencies but it performs poorly on higher latencies. As shown in Section 6, this method has no major impact on performance even for low inter-cluster latencies when combined with the Start-Cycle heuristic of Algorithm 1 as its aggressiveness is overshadowed by that of the Start-Cycle heuristic.

LUCAS aims at performing best on the whole range of inter-cluster latencies. Therefore it honors the clustering decision made by the heuristic (similarly to CARS) as in Figure 6a.

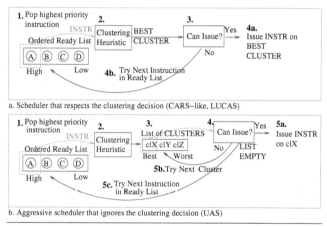

a. Scheduler that respects the clustering decision (CARS-like, LUCAS)

b. Aggressive scheduler that ignores the clustering decision (UAS)

Figure 6. The two variants of embedding the clustering heuristic into the instruction scheduler. The numbers denote the order of execution of each step.

4. LUCAS

The proposed Latency-aware Unified Cluster-Assignment and instruction Scheduling algorithm addresses the shortcomings of the existing algorithms (discussed in Section 3).

LUCAS is a list-scheduling-based algorithm that performs cluster assignment and instruction scheduling simultaneously. The novelty lies in the clustering heuristic. The algorithm is listed in Algorithm 4. A high-level view of the structure of the algorithm is shown in Figure 6a.

In detail, LUCAS performs the following actions:

1. It assigns a priority number to all instruction nodes of the DFG (Algorithm 4 line 6) using a priority function (for example the instruction height in the DFG).

---

[1] CARS also performs register allocation, which is not shown.

2. It updates the ready list with instructions ready to be issued on the current cycle (line 9).

3. It sorts the ready list based on the node priorities of step 1 (line 10).

4. Before scheduling the instruction under consideration, the algorithm determines the *best_cl* (best cluster) by evaluating the heuristic for each candidate cluster and choosing the best among those (Algorithm 4 line 23). The "get_best_cluster()" function incorporates the adaptive heuristic.

5. Then the algorithm tries to schedule the instruction only if it meets the Start-Cycle constraint (which includes both dependence and clustering-related structural constraints) (Algorithm 4 line 13).

6. If all processor structural constraints allow scheduling the instruction at the current cycle on *best_cl* (Algorithm 4 line 14), then we can proceed.

7. If the required Inter-Cluster Copies (ICCs) can be emitted on the inter-cluster network (that is if the network is not fully occupied) (line 15), then it emits the ICCs and register renames the instructions that use the register brought in by the ICCs (line 16) and it finally cluster-assigns and issues the instruction on *best_cl* (lines 17,18).

8. If the instruction has been placed on a distant cluster, then update its mobility metric (decrement it by the inter-cluster delay (ICD)) to reflect this change (line 19). The intuition behind this is that the ICD consumes some of the ability of the instruction to move freely.

9. Repeat steps 5-9, by selecting the highest priority node until the ready list is empty (line 11).

10. Finally repeat steps 2-10 until all instructions are scheduled (Algorithm 4 line 8).

The LUCAS heuristic is a hybrid Start-Cycle / Completion-Cycle heuristic. It decides per instruction which of the two to use based on two metrics:

1. The **cycle congestion** (Algorithm 4 line 38). This is a binary metric. It returns true if there are too many instructions to schedule on the current cycle. That is if the number of instructions that are ready on the current cycle are greater than the congestion threshold. The threshold reflects both the issue resources of a cluster and the inter-cluster penalty. It is computed as the product: Issue-Width Per Cluster (IWPC) times the Inter-Cluster Delay (ICD).

2. The **mobility** of the instruction (Algorithm 4 line 39). The mobility is calculated as ALAP-ASAP values in the Data-Flow-Graph [16]. A high mobility value suggests that there is enough slack in the schedule for the instruction to be executed later with no guaranteed side-effects in the schedule. The mobility threshold corresponds to the inter-cluster round-trip time.

The actual algorithm for the lucas heuristic is listed in Algorithm 4 in *get_best_cluster()* function. It works as follows:

- At first each candidate cluster is tagged with the heuristic value (Algorithm 4 line 25). This uses the *lucas()* function (Algorithm 4 line 36).

- The LUCAS heuristic checks the two metrics (cycle congestion and instruction mobility sub-heuristics) (lines 38-39) for the instruction to be scheduled and decides on the heuristic to be used for the clustering decision (line 40). This is the core of the LUCAS heuristic. The metrics decide whether the aggressive Start-Cycle heuristic (line 41) or the more conservative Completion-Cycle heuristic is used (line 43).

Algorithm 4. LUCAS: Latency-adaptive Clustering and Scheduling.

```
1  /* LUCAS Scheduling and clustering.
2      Input:  DFG
3      Output: Clustered Schedule  */
4  lucas_schedule_and_cluster (DFG)
5  {
6   walk down the DFG and prioritize the nodes
7   cycle = 0
8   while (exist unscheduled nodes)
9     Fill in ready_list
10    sort ready_list based on priority
11    for node in prioritized ready_list
12      best_cl = get_best_cluster(node.instr, cycle)
13      if (start_cycle (node.instr, cluster)<=cycle)
14        if (can issue node.instr on cycle)
15          if (can schedule Inter-Cluster Copies)
16            Emit ICCs and reg. rename node.instr
17            node.cluster = best_cl
18            Issue (node.instr, cycle, best_cl)
19            Update MOBILITY(node.instr) if it gets
                 ↪data from a distant cluster
20    cycle ++
21  }
22
23  get_best_cluster (insn, cycle)
24  {
25   for cluster in all clusters
26     heuristic[cluster] = lucas(insn,cluster)
27   /* Find best cluster: MIN_CL */
28   min_cl = 0
29   for cli in clusters
30     if (heuristic[cli] < heuristic[min_cl])
31       min_cl = cli
32   return min_cl
33  }
34
35  /* Return the score of CLUSTER */
36  lucas (insn, cluster)
37  {
38   high_congestion = (#Ready-instr. > IWPC × ICD)
39   high_mobility = (MOBILITY(insn) > IWPC×2×(ICD-1))
40   if (high_congestion OR high_mobility)
41     return start_cycle (insn, cluster)
42   else
43     return completion_cycle (insn, cluster)
44  }
```

Figure 7. The fully-connected point-to-point interconnect.

- Finally, the algorithm does a linear search over all clusters to find the cluster with the minimum heuristic value (line 29) (as shown in Figure 6.a.2). Once found, the cluster that corresponds to the minimum value of the heuristic is returned as the best cluster (line 32).

5. EXPERIMENTAL SETUP

5.1 Architecture

The target architecture is an IA64 (Itanium2) ISA based statically scheduled clustered VLIW architecture. The architecture is configured to have 4 clusters with an issue-width of 4 or 8 (1 or 2 issue per cluster).

Processor: IA64 based clustered VLIW	
Issue Width:	4 or 8
Clusters:	4
Instruction Latencies:	Same as Itanium2 [19]
Register File:	(32GP, 32FL, 16PR) per cluster
Inter-Cluster Delay:	1 - 4 cycles
Inter-Cluster Bus Bandwidth:	∞
Branch Prediction:	Perfect

Cache: Levels 3 (same as Itanium2 [19])				
Levels :	L1	L2	L3	Main Mem.
Size (Bytes):	16K	256K	3M	∞
Block size (Bytes):	64	128	128	-
Associativity:	4-Way	8-way	12-way	-
Latency (cycles):	1	5	12	150

Table 1. Processor configuration.

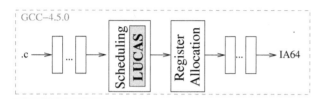

Figure 8. Overview of the GCC compilation pipeline.

The inter-cluster communication bandwidth is infinite [2], meaning that there is no limit in the count of the simultaneous inter-cluster communications. Thus our results have no noise from any inter-cluster bandwidth effects.

The clusters communicate through a fully-connected point-to-point interconnect as shown in Figure 7. All clusters communicate with each other with equal latencies. The latency is adjustable and in our experiments it ranges from 1 to 4 cycles.

The architecture configuration is summarized in Table 1.

5.2 Compiler

We implemented both UAS [21] and the proposed (LUCAS) unified clustering and scheduling algorithms along with all clustering heuristics (see below) in the instruction scheduling pass of GCC-4.5.0 [1] cross compiler with Itanium ([24]) as the target ISA (IA64). As shown in Figure 8 the instruction scheduler (with the clustering built-in) runs before register allocation.

The implementation of the scheduler enables us to easily swap the clustering heuristics while the rest of the instruction scheduling pass remains unchanged. The heuristic is one of the following: i) Start-Cycle ([21]), ii) Completion-Cycle ([8]), iii) Critical-Successor ([28]) or iv) LUCAS (the proposed one).

5.3 Evaluation

We evaluated LUCAS on the 4-cluster architecture described in Section 5.1 configured as a 4-issue and an 8-issue machine. We compare the LUCAS heuristic against the state-of-the-art Start-Cycle (SC) and Completion-Cycle (CC) as well as the recently proposed Critical-Successor (CS) clustering heuristic. In addition we compared all these against an accurate implementation of the UAS algorithm. The algorithms and heuristics compared are summarized in Table.2.

We evaluated LUCAS against the existing state-of-the-art heuristics on 6 of the Mediabench II video [11] benchmarks. All benchmarks were compiled with -O2 optimizations enabled. Each benchmark is compiled several times, once with each clustering heuristic enabled, and each binary is then executed on our modified ski simulator [2], configured as discussed in Section 5.1.

---
[2] This means that the condition in Algorithm 4 line 15 is always true.

	Algorithm	Heuristic		
	Obeys Heuristic	Start Cycle	Completion Cycle	Critical Successor
UAS	×	√	×	×
SC	√	√	×	×
CC	√	×	√	×
CS	√	√	×	√
LUCAS	√	√(Hybrid)	√(Hybrid)	×

Table 2. Evaluated schemes.

6. RESULTS AND ANALYSIS

We have two kind of results: i) the performance results (normalized to the Start-Cycle for delay 1), shown in Figures 9 and 10, which show that LUCAS meets its performance goals and ii) the instruction distribution measurements (Figures 11 and 12) that provide important insights into the workings of the heuristics. Both of these results show two LUCAS heuristics: LUCAS-C which is based only on the Congestion sub-heuristic and LUCAS-C-M which is the full version with both Congestion and Mobility enabled. This is a useful breakdown that lets us better understand the effects of each part individually.

6.1 Performance

The first thing that stands out is the non-scalability of the UAS[21], the Start-Cycle (SC) ([8], Algorithm 1) and the Critical-Successor (CS) ([28]) heuristics. The performance degradation increases almost linearly with the delay as seen in Figure 9. This is caused by the aggressiveness of the Start-Cycle heuristic, which spreads instructions on distant clusters, disregarding the cost of communicating the results back after they have been computed. The Critical-Successor heuristic is partly based on the Start-Cycle, which contributes to its non-scalability.

The performance of **UAS** is very close to that of the Start-Cycle heuristic. As already explained in Section 3.2, the UAS scheduler uses a variation of the Start-Cycle clustering heuristic (which in [21] it is referred to as CWP), but the scheduling algorithm follows a different approach in selecting a cluster. UAS may ignore the decision of the clustering heuristic if it cannot schedule on the chosen cluster due to resource constraints (see Figure 6a). This is a greedy gamble as the scheduler tries to assign an instruction to any cluster possible, even if this means ignoring the primary decision of the clustering heuristic. This does not happen in the unified clustering and scheduling algorithm that we propose (Figure 6.b). In our approach, the primary decision of the clustering heuristic is honored by the scheduler. The CC, SC, CS and LUCAS heuristics follow this second approach. As shown in the results, UAS performs on average very similarly to the Start-Cycle heuristic of our algorithm. The reason is that the Start-Cycle heuristic is aggressive enough and usually overshadows the aggressiveness of the UAS algorithm.

The **Completion-Cycle** heuristic (Algorithm 2) keeps performance at a reasonable level. The reason is that the heuristic is conservative. It only issues an instruction on a distant cluster if it can prove that it is beneficial even in case it needs to send the data back. Therefore if the inter-cluster latency is high, usually the round-trip latency is too expensive and the Completion-Cycle heuristic will keep the instructions on the same cluster. This however proves to be inadequate for low inter-cluster latencies (e.g. Figure 9 mpeg2dec). In the worst case the Start-Cycle heuristic outperforms the Completion-Cycle by over 40% (Figure 9 mpeg2dec).

The measurements of Figure 9 show that while the Completion-Cycle heuristic is better at high inter-cluster delays (e.g. Figure 9 djpeg latency 2 or more), the Start-Cycle heuristic usually works best at low inter-cluster delays. That is when being aggressive at spreading the instructions across clusters as much as possible proves a better choice than being conservative. This is the main motivation behind LUCAS. If both of these approaches are com-

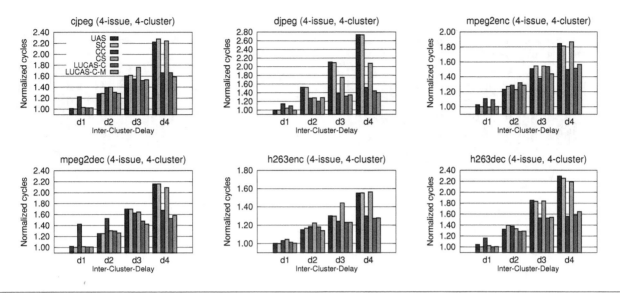

Figure 9. Cycles of the 4-issue,4-cluster configuration for inter-cluster delay 1 to 4, normalized to Start-Cycle (SC), delay 1.

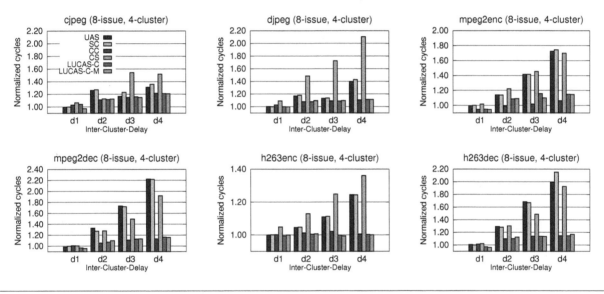

Figure 10. Cycles of the 8-issue,4-cluster configuration for inter-cluster delay 1 to 4, normalized to Start-Cycle (SC), delay 1.

bined together, then we can get a clustering heuristic that performs well across all inter-cluster delays. This assumption is confirmed by the LUCAS results of Figure 9.

The **intersection point** where the Start-Cycle heuristic overtakes the Completion-Cycle heuristic is not fixed. It is can be between delay 1 and 2 (Figure 9 djpeg) or between delay 2 and 3 (e.g. Figure 9 cjpeg). Therefore selecting the right heuristic cannot be based on some fixed magic number. LUCAS performs an effective switching between Start-Cycle and Completion-Cycle with the help of two metrics: the cycle congestion and the instruction mobility.

LUCAS does not only adapt to the best heuristic, but it quite often outperforms both heuristics (e.g. Figure 9 mpeg2dec d3,d4, h263enc d2,d3,d4 and Figure 10 mpeg2dec d1, h263dec d1). This is intuitive because LUCAS performs a **fine-grain switching** between the Start-Cycle and Completion-Cycle heuristic at the instruction level. This can select the best heuristic at a fine granular-

ity, when it is needed, which is better in the long run than selecting one of the two for the duration of the whole program.

The two **sub-heuristics** that form LUCAS, Congestion (C) and Mobility (M), do work together and when combined (logical OR) usually lead to better overall performance. The gains from applying the Mobility heuristic on top of the Congestion one are up to 9% (Figure 9 mpeg2enc d3). In a few cases however, performance decreases (3.5% in the worst case). The reason behind the behavior is that under high inter-cluster delays, any further aggressiveness (introduced by the logical OR-ing of the heuristics), is usually for the worse.

Overall, in most cases LUCAS performs very closely to the best heuristic or better than it (e.g. cjpeg). There are some outliers though. The mpeg2enc stands out from the rest, as for both the 4-issue and 8-issue setups LUCAS cannot keep up with the best for high inter-cluster delays, although it is still much better than UAS, SC and CS. In case of the 4-issue machine, the differences are great,

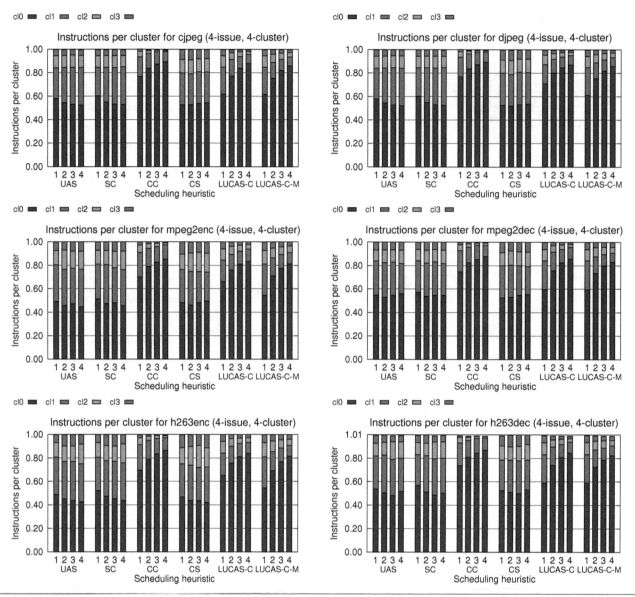

Figure 11. Distribution of instructions on each cluster, for all clustering heuristics and for delays ranging from 1 to 4. This is for the 4-issue 4-cluster machine.

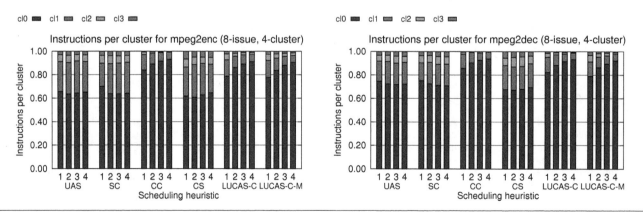

Figure 12. Distribution of instructions on each cluster, for all clustering heuristics and for delay ranging from 1 to 4. This is for the 8-issue 4-cluster machine and just for the mpeg2 benchmarks.

however on the 8-issue machine, where the performance penalties get amplified, this effect is more evident. The mpeg2enc, 8-issue case is a special case as it is the only one that is strongly biased against the Start-Cycle heuristic even for delay 1. Therefore any attempt to spread the instructions to distant clusters will lead to a slowdown. In most other cases if LUCAS performs worse than the best performing heuristic it performs marginally worse (e.g. Figure 10 djpeg d2,d3).

6.2 Instruction Distribution

To provide more insights into the internals all clustering heuristics, including LUCAS, we show the distribution of the program instructions across clusters for all heuristics and for both machine types (Figures 11 and 12). Each of the stacked bar shows the breakdown of the instructions on each cluster (each cluster is represented by a color). Each heuristic corresponds to 4 stacked bars, one for each inter-cluster delay (ranging from 1 to 4). We observe that:

1. First of all, some of the graphs look strikingly similar. For example the breakdowns for Figure 11 cjpeg and djpeg look very similar. This is due to the fact that these benchmarks share a lot of common source files. Since the instruction counts are statically computed, the differences between the benchmarks are minimized.

2. On the 4-issue machine (Figure 11), about 60% of the code is executed on the first cluster, and the rest of it is spread across the rest for inter-cluster delay of 1. The further away from cluster 0, the fewer the instructions. The second cluster (cl1) usually contains about 25% of the instructions, the third cluster (cl2) about 10% and the last one contains about 5%. This behavior is intuitive as any inter-cluster communication has an extra overhead, forcing the scheduler to be reluctant on spreading the instructions across clusters, doing so only when absolutely necessary. This effect gets amplified on the 8-issue machine (Figure 12), where there is usually little need for extra issue slots on other clusters. This is why, on this configuration there are even more instructions ($>$ 80% in some cases) in cluster 0 and fewer in the rest. It is worth noting that the first cluster (cl0) is of no particular significance as the architecture is a symmetric one, as shown in Figure 7.

3. The fundamental difference of the heuristics can be observed as we increase the inter-cluster delay. The aggressive heuristics (UAS, SC and CS) do not seem to adjust to the increase in the inter-cluster delay. Instead of being more conservative in scheduling across clusters, they seem to become even more aggressive (the instructions on cl0 decrease as the delay increases). On the other hand the conservative CC heuristic behaves in the opposite way. As the inter-cluster delay increases, it tries to keep more instructions within cl0. The LUCAS heuristic (LUCAS-C-M in particular), bridges the gap between these two opposite strategies. For small inter-cluster delays it behaves almost like the aggressive heuristics, but as the inter-cluster delay increases, it behaves as the conservative one.

6.3 Algorithmic Complexity

This section calculates the algorithmic complexity of LUCAS. We do that by examining the algorithm (Algorithms 4, 1 and 2). Let's consider an input DFG of N nodes. The LUCAS Scheduling algorithm has 2 visible levels of nested loops (the 3rd is in the Start-Cycle calculation):

1. The outer loop iterates until all instructions in the DFG are scheduled. In each iteration a single cycle gets scheduled. If on average S (with $S \leq issuewidth$) instructions get scheduled, then this loop iterates N/s times. On each iteration of this loop, the ready list is sorted using quick sort. Given an average ready

list size of R, this usually costs $R \times logR$ and R^2 in the worst case.

2. The middle loop iterates until all instructions in the ready list are examined for scheduling. Therefore it iterates R times. The best cluster is found by get_best_cluster(). This iterates once over all clusters and sets the Start-Cycles. The Start-Cycle heuristic iterates over all flow predecessors of the instruction to be scheduled and gets calculated once for each cluster. If P is the number of flow predecessors and C is the number of clusters, then this costs RCP.

The complexity of LUCAS Scheduling is computed as:

- $N/S \times R \times (logR + CP)$ in the usual case
- $N/S \times R \times (R + CP)$ in the worst case

In all practical cases all S, R, P are small constants with typical values: $S \leq 3, R \leq 10, P \leq 10$. This is an $O(N)$ complexity. The worst-case scenario involves $S = 1$ and $R = N, P = N$ which leads to complexity $O(N^3)$.

UAS has a similar 3-nested loop structure and exhibits similar complexity. For all practical cases, the UAS is $O(N)$ and in the worst-case it is $O(N^3)$. Therefore both schedulers have similar complexity.

7. RELATED WORK

This section discusses the previous work on cluster assignment and instruction scheduling for clustered VLIW architectures, that is closely related to our work.

7.1 Combined Cluster Assignment & Instruction Scheduling

The first work that proposes a combined instruction scheduling and clustering pass is Unified Assignment and Scheduling (UAS) [21]. The scheduling algorithm is a modified list scheduler. In this work cluster assignment is aggressive in two ways:

i) This work uses the aggressive Start-Cycle (SC) heuristic for the clustering part (in the terminology of [8]) (or CWP in the terminology of [21]) which is shown to be the best performing one over several others on the architecture that was evaluated. The inter-cluster delay is fixed to 1 cycle, which explains why the Start-Cycle heuristic was found to be the best performing of the heuristics tried out. In our work we show that the Start-Cycle causes an unbounded performance degradation as the inter-cluster latency is increased.

ii) The scheduling algorithm is such that will try to schedule an instruction on the current cycle even if this cluster is not the first choice of the clustering heuristic.

Compared to UAS, LUCAS will always obey the decision of the clustering heuristic. In LUCAS, the heuristic is a hybrid one that switches between the aggressive Start-Cycle and the more conservative Completion-Cycle (CC).

CARS ([14]) is a combined scheduling, clustering, and register allocation code generation framework based on list-scheduling. Similarly to UAS, the Start-Cycle is the heuristic that steers the clustering decisions.

Recently, a new clustering heuristic was introduced by [28]. This differs from the previously mentioned ones in that, under certain conditions, the clustering decision is based on earliest schedule cycle of the most critical successor of the current instruction. Similarly to the Start-Cycle (SC) and Completion-Cycle (CC) heuristics, it is not meant to operate across a wide range of inter-cluster delays. This heuristic quite often defaults to the Start-Cycle, which is why its performance is also unbounded as the inter-cluster delay increases. In our evaluation we name this heuristic as Critical-Successor (CS).

Finally there are several combined loop-scheduling and clustering algorithms [3, 6, 27]. These are based on the software-pipeline scheduling technique of modulo-scheduling. These techniques are only applicable on innermost loops under very specific and strict conditions.

7.2 Clustering on a separate pass

Pioneering work on code generation for clustered architectures was introduced in [8], with the Bottom-Up-Greedy (BUG) cluster-assignment algorithm. This work differs from later cluster assignment algorithms in the order the instructions are considered for clustering, which in this case is a critical-path based ordering. The main heuristic used is the Completion-Cycle, which is more conservative than the Start-Cycle, since it will select a distant cluster only if the instruction's consumers can still get their input data in time.

[5] partitions the register file so as to have more register files with fewer ports each. Cluster assignment takes place after scheduling the code since the input of this code generator is the output of a compiler that targets an ideal VLIW core. This, however, is sub-optimal since the inter-cluster latencies can not be hidden effectively. The clustering heuristic used tries to minimize the inter-cluster communication. This however is a poor clustering heuristic as it is not guided by the schedule length.

[7] is one of the first iterative solutions to clustering. Each iteration of the algorithm measures the schedule length by performing instruction scheduling and doing a fast register pressure and ICC count estimation. This being an iterative algorithm, it has a long run-time and its use is not practical in compilers.

7.3 Clustered Architectures

A comprehensive taxonomy of inter-cluster communication implementations on VLIW architectures is presented in [26]. The design features (such as operating frequency, performance, energy consumption, etc.) of each implementation are quantified and discussed.

Clustered super-scalars, such as [22],[15], use simpler clustering algorithms. A review of the state-of-the-art heuristics are presented in [4]. Such heuristics make use of the register dependence graph and steer instructions based on the cluster where their operands where steered to. Being dynamic approaches, they also try to balance the run-time load of the clusters.

7.4 Instruction Scheduling for VLIW processors

Instruction Scheduling for VLIWs was pioneered by [10] with the Trace-scheduling algorithm. This algorithm expands the scheduling region beyond basic blocks to larger profiling-guided regions called traces. These large regions provide enough instructions for the scheduler to re-order effectively. A less complicated but highly effective alternative to traces are the superblocks [13]. These regions simplify the scheduler's work by only allowing for outgoing control edges from within a region. VLIW architectures with support for predicated execution can benefit from hyperblock scheduling [18]. Extended Basic Blocks (EBB) [20] form tree-like regions which are then scheduled by a normal list scheduler. Treegions [12] are also tree-shaped, and are similar to EBBs. They are shown to outperform superblock scheduling. LUCAS is implemented on top of GCC's [1] Haifa Scheduler which operates on EBBs.

8. CONCLUSION

This paper proposes LUCAS, a new unified cluster assignment and instruction scheduling algorithm for clustered VLIW processors, that is powered by a novel hybrid clustering heuristic. LUCAS outperforms the state-of-the-art as it is capable of switching between two heuristics at a very fine granularity. The switching is controlled by two metrics, the cycle congestion and the instruction mobility. The end result is a scheduler that generates code that performs best across a wide range of inter-cluster latencies.

References

[1] Gcc: Gnu compiler collection. *http://gcc.gnu.org*.

[2] ski ia64 simulator. *http://ski.sourceforge.net*.

[3] A. Aletà, J. Codina, J. Sánchez, A. González, and D. Kaeli. Agamos: A graph-based approach to modulo scheduling for clustered microarchitectures. *IEEE Transactions on Computers*, 2009.

[4] R. Canal, J. M. Parcerisa, A. Gonzlez, D. D. D. Computadors, and J. Girona. Dynamic cluster assignment mechanisms. In *HPCA*, 2000.

[5] A. Capitanio, N. Dutt, and A. Nicolau. Partitioned register files for vliws: A preliminary analysis of tradeoffs. In *MICRO*, 1992.

[6] J. Codina, J. Sanchez, and A. Gonzalez. A unified modulo scheduling and register allocation technique for clustered processors. In *PACT* 2001.

[7] G. Desoli. Instruction assignment for clustered vliw dsp compilers: A new approach. *HP Laboratories Technical Report HPL*, 1998.

[8] J. Ellis. Bulldog: A compiler for vliw architectures. Technical report, Yale Univ., 1985.

[9] P. Faraboschi, G. Brown et al. Lx: a technology platform for customizable vliw embedded processing. In *ISCA*, 2000.

[10] J. Fisher. Trace scheduling: A technique for global microcode compaction. *IEEE Transactions on Computers*, 1981.

[11] J. Fritts, F. Steiling, and J. Tucek. Mediabench II video: expediting the next generation of video systems research. In *SPIE*, 2005.

[12] W. Havanki, S. Banerjia, and T. Conte. Treegion scheduling for wide issue processors. In *HPCA*, 1998.

[13] W.-M. W. Hwu, S. A. Mahlke, W. Y. Chen, P. P. Chang, N. J. Warter, R. A. Bringmann, R. G. Ouellette, R. E. Hank, T. Kiyohara, G. E. Haab, J. G. Holm, and D. M. Lavery. The superblock: An effective technique for vliw and superscalar compilation. *The Journal of Supercomputing*, 1993.

[14] K. Kailas, K. Ebcioglu, and A. Agrawala. CARS: a new code generation framework for clustered ilp processors. In *HPCA*, 2001.

[15] R. Kessler. The Alpha 21264 microprocessor. *IEEE Micro*, 1999.

[16] V. Lapinskii, M. Jacome, and G. De Veciana. Cluster assignment for high-performance embedded vliw processors. *ACM TODAES*, 2002.

[17] P. G. Lowney, S. M. Freudenberger, T. J. Karzes, W. D. Lichtenstein, R. P. Nix, J. S. Odonnell, and J. C. Ruttenberg. The multiflow trace scheduling compiler. *Journal of Supercomputing*, 1993.

[18] S. A. Mahlke, D. C. Lin, W. Y. Chen, R. E. Hank, and R. A. Bringmann. Effective compiler support for predicated execution using the hyperblock. In *MICRO*, 1992.

[19] C. McNairy and D. Soltis. Itanium 2 processor microarchitecture. *IEEE Micro*, 2003.

[20] S. S. Muchnick. *Advanced compiler design and implementation*. Morgan Kaufmann, 1997.

[21] E. Ozer, S. Banerjia, and T. Conte. Unified assign and schedule: a new approach to scheduling for clustered register file microarchitectures. In *MICRO*, 1998.

[22] S. Palacharla, N. Jouppi, and J. Smith. Complexity-effective superscalar processors. In *ISCA*, 1997.

[23] K. Sankaralingam, R. Nagarajan, H. Liu, C. Kim, J. Huh, D. Burger, S. Keckler, and C. Moore. Exploiting ILP, TLP, and DLP with the polymorphous TRIPS architecture. In *ISCA*, 2003.

[24] H. Sharangpani and H. Arora. Itanium processor microarchitecture. *IEEE Micro*, 2000.

[25] M. Taylor, J. Kim, J. Miller, D. Wentzlaff, F. Ghodrat, B. Greenwald, H. Hoffman, P. Johnson, J. Lee, W. Lee, et al. The Raw microprocessor: A computational fabric for software circuits and general-purpose programs. In *IEEE Micro*, 2002.

[26] A. Terechko and H. Corporaal. Inter-cluster communication in vliw architectures. *ACM TACO*, 2007.

[27] J. Zalamea, J. Llosa, E. Ayguade, and M. Valero. Modulo scheduling with integrated register spilling for clustered vliw architectures. In *MICRO*, 2001.

[28] X. Zhang, H. Wu, and J. Xue. An efficient heuristic for instruction scheduling on clustered vliw processors. In *CASES*, 2011.

Practical Speculative Parallelization of Variable-Length Decompression Algorithms

Hakbeom Jang   Channoh Kim   Jae W. Lee

Sungkyunkwan University
Suwon, Korea
{hakbeom, channoh, jaewlee}@skku.edu

Abstract

Variable-length coding is widely used for efficient data compression. Typically, the compressor splits the original data into blocks and compresses each block with variable-length codes, hence producing variable-length compressed blocks. Although the compressor can easily exploit ample block-level parallelism, it is much more difficult to extract such coarse-grain parallelism from the decompressor because a block boundary cannot be located until decompression of the previous block is completed. This paper presents novel algorithms to efficiently predict block boundaries and a runtime system that enables efficient block-level parallel decompression, called *SDM*. The SDM execution model features speculative pipelining with three stages: **S**canner, **D**ecompressor, and **M**erger. The scanner stage employs a high-confidence prediction algorithm that finds compressed block boundaries without fully decompressing individual blocks. This information is communicated to the parallel decompressor stage in which multiple blocks are decompressed in parallel. The decompressed blocks are merged in order by the merger stage to produce the final output. The SDM runtime is specialized to execute this pipeline correctly and efficiently on resource-constrained embedded platforms. With SDM we effectively parallelize three production-grade variable-length *decompression* algorithms—zlib, bzip2, and H.264—with maximum speedups of 2.50× and 8.53× (and geometric mean speedups of 1.96× and 4.04×) on 4-core and 36-core embedded platforms, respectively.

Categories and Subject Descriptors   D.1.3 [*Software*]: Concurrent Programming—Parallel programming; D.3.4 [*Programming Languages*]: Processors—Run-time environments

General Terms   Design, Performance

Keywords   Parallelization, runtime, speculation, compression, multicores, embedded systems

1. Introduction

Compression algorithms are widely used for efficient communication and storage of data. Their application domains include image and video processing, audio processing, networking, and data backups. Regardless of the target domain, *variable-length coding* is commonly employed to maximize compression ratio. Typically, variable-length compression algorithms split the original, uncompressed data into fixed- or variable-length *blocks* and compress each block using variable-length codes, hence producing variable-length compressed blocks.

With adoption of multicores in all scales of system, significant effort has been made to parallelize and accelerate these algorithms. For example, both gzip [2] and bzip2 [1], two popular general-purpose compression utilities, have parallelized versions such as pigz [8] and pbzip2 [7]. Both pigz and pbzip2 demonstrate near-linear speedups to core count when *compressing* a file, but execute sequentially when *decompressing* it.

Although compression (encoding) generally takes more computation than decompression (decoding), [1] parallelizing the decompressor is very important since it often constitutes the critical path of a user application, hence making a perceivable difference in response time. This is particularly true for embedded platforms which cannot afford high-frequency cores due to cost and power constraints. Unfortunately, the decompressor is much harder to parallelize than the compressor because a block boundary cannot be located until decompression of the previous block is completed. Therefore, the main challenge in parallelizing variable-length decompression algorithms is to efficiently identify the boundaries of compressed blocks that can be independently decompressed.

Some parallel decompressors address this challenge by specializing compressors. Examples include insertion of padding bits at the end of each compressed block to effectively equalize the block length [8] and inclusion of hints from which block boundaries can be readily calculated [18]. Obviously, such decompressors have limited applicability only to compressed input streams that were created by the modified compressors. Overcoming this limitation, there are other decompressors that do not require any compressor-side support. For example, Klein and Wiseman exploit the *self-synchronizing* property of Huffman coding [19] to identify the boundaries of compressed blocks. However, this method can only be applied to *static Huffman coding*, which uses a fixed Huffman table, but not to more popular *dynamic Huffman coding*. Also, block boundary locations have nearly zero correlations through an

---
[1] Throughout this paper "compress" and "encode" are used interchangeably. So are "decompress" and "decode".

Algorithm	Domain	Lossless?	Compressor Parallelized?	Decompressor Parallelized?	Block Delimiter Pattern Exists?	Remarks
zlib (gzip) [15]	Data	✓	✓	✗	✗	Huffman coding
bzip2 [1]	Data	✓	✓	✗	✓ (48 bits)	Huffman coding
H.264 [3]	Video	✗	✓	✓	✓ (40 bits)	Arithmetic coding (CABAC)
jpeg [4]	Image	✗	✗	✗	✓ (16 bits)	Huffman coding
png [9]	Image	✓	✓	✗	✗	Huffman coding (zlib+wrapper)
Vorbis [13]	Audio	✗	✗	✗	✓ (24 bits)	Huffman coding (+vector quantization)

Table 1: Survey of variable-length compression algorithms

input or across different inputs to make it difficult to apply existing, domain-unaware value prediction algorithms [21, 23, 26, 28, 32].

This paper introduces novel high-confidence prediction algorithms to identify the block boundaries efficiently, and also proposes the SDM runtime system to effectively decompress multiple blocks in parallel using these algorithms. The execution model of SDM features speculative pipelining with three stages: Scanner, Decompressor and Merger. The scanner stage executes a prediction algorithm that finds block boundaries by *partial decompression* and *pattern matching*. This algorithm splits the input stream into multiple, well-aligned chunks of blocks that can be independently decompressed while taking only a fraction of total execution time. The parallel decompressor stage decompresses multiple chunks concurrently and passes the decompressed output to the merger, which in turn constructs the final output stream. To ensure the correctness of the final outcome, the SDM runtime implements misspeculation detection and recovery mechanisms, which are invoked when the prediction algorithm incorrectly predicts the starting point of a chunk. To make best use of a handful of cores in resource-constrained embedded platforms, SDM supports *distributed commit*, where merging is done by decompressor processes in a distributed manner.

Without modifying the compressor, we successfully parallelize three production-grade variable-length decompression algorithms using SDM: zlib (gzip) [15], bzip2 [1] and H.264 [3]. To demonstrate the practicality of SDM, we use two resource-constrained embedded platforms for evaluation, Samsung Exynos 4412 quad-core platform based on ARM's Cortex-A9 [10] (representing "fat" cores) and Tilera's 36-core platform [12] (representing "thin" cores). Compared with original program compiled with `gcc -O3`, the parallelized program achieves maximum speedups of 2.50× and 8.53× and geometric mean speedups of 1.96× and 4.04× on the ARM and Tilera platforms, respectively. Evaluation on these two platforms reveals interesting tradeoffs between the two commit modes that SDM supports.

In summary, this paper makes the following contributions:

- Introduction of efficient prediction algorithms to identify block boundaries for three widely-deployed variable-length decompression algorithms

- Design and implementation of the SDM runtime system to enable efficient speculative execution of parallel decompression on resource-constrained embedded platforms

- Detailed evaluation of the three variable-length decompression algorithms on ARM- and Tilera-based embedded platforms

2. Motivation

2.1 Variable-Length Decompression Algorithms

A compression algorithm adopting a variable-length coding (called *variable-length compression algorithm* for brevity) compresses input data by exploiting the probability distribution of the frequencies of input symbols. The most common symbol are usually assigned the shortest code word to maximize compression ratio. To adapt to phase behaviors of the input stream and improve error resilience,

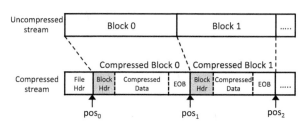

Figure 1: Variable-length compressed blocks created by compression algorithm (EOB stands for end-of-block and pos_n indicates the starting position of compressed block n)

the compressor often splits the input stream into multiple blocks and resets the *codebook* (i.e., code word assignment table) at the beginning of each block. Figure 1 illustrates such an example. Even if the block length in the input stream may be fixed, compressed blocks generally have variable lengths.

Table 1 surveys widely-used variable-length compression algorithms in various application domains. As the table illustrates, most of these algorithms are successfully parallelized at multiple granularities on the *compressor* side. However, parallel *decompressors* are much harder to find partly because it is difficult to extract efficient coarse-grain (e.g., block-level) parallelism. Although demanding less computations than the compressor, the decompressor is still an important target for parallelization as it often constitutes the critical path of a user application. This is particularly relevant on embedded/mobile platforms which cannot afford high-frequency cores due to cost and power constraints.

Figure 2 shows a simplified version of a variable-length decompression algorithm, which captures a common pattern across all the algorithms shown in Table 1. Every iteration of the loop decompresses one compressed block (Line 2). Position variable `pos` is updated to point to the starting position of the next compressed block, and decompressed data are stored into `out_buf`. Variables `eof` and `err` return end-of-file and error conditions, respectively. If no error occurred, the decompressed data are written to the output file (`out_stream`). This loop has three loop-carried dependences, as shown in Figure 2(b), which prevent parallel execution of multiple iterations. Line 1 creates a loop-carried control dependence through `eof`, Line 2 a loop-carried data dependence through `pos`, and Line 4 another loop-carried data dependence through `out_stream`.

Assuming high block count and very few erroneous blocks, the key challenge in parallelizing this decompressor loop is eliminating the loop-carried data dependence caused by the `pos` variable. Existing approaches address this by specializing the compressor to produce fixed-length compressed blocks by padding bits [8] and/or embedding hints from which the value of `pos` can be readily derived [18]. However, this approach has an obvious limitation of not working for a non-compliant input stream. Therefore, breaking this dependence without compressor-side support is crucial for practical block-level parallel decompression.

```
1: while (!eof)
   {
     // decompress one block
2:   len = decompress_block
            (&pos, out_buf, &eof, &err);
3:   if (!err && len>0)
4:      fwrite(out_buf, sizeof(char),
               len, out_stream);
   }
```

(a)

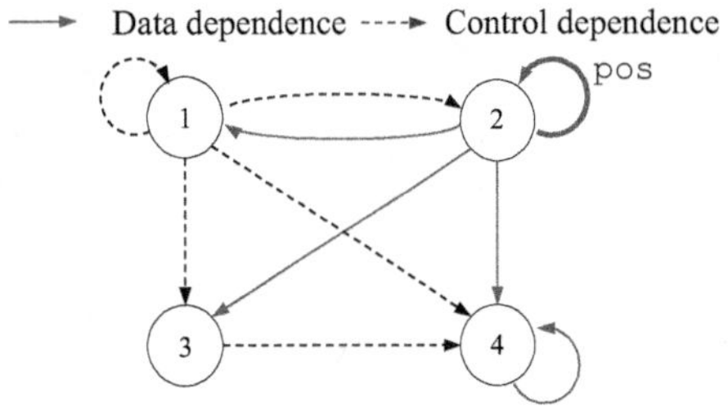

(b)

Figure 2: Example of variable-length decompression algorithm: (a) simple code; (b) program dependence graph.

2.2 Value Prediction-Based Speculative Parallelization

In general, it is difficult to find the block boundary (pointed to by pos in Figure 2) precisely without decompressing the preceding blocks. This makes speculative parallelization based on value prediction an attractive alternative. Instead of precisely calculating the block boundary, we may *predict* it at a much lower cost and decompress multiple blocks speculatively. Misspeculation detection can be performed by simply comparing the predicted starting position of a block with the ending position after decompressing the previous block. If they match, speculation is successful, and the program can continue execution; otherwise, it must rollback and re-execute the misspeculated block.

Some of exisiting speculative parallelization systems exploit value prediction to extract additional parallelism [21, 23, 26, 28, 32]. Most of the systems keep track of the value history of a variable of interest in the past to predict its value in the future. Common predictors include memoization predictor [21, 26], value stride predictor [28], and trace predictor [23]. However, the pos variable poses (nearly) zero correlations over time or across distinct inputs to make these predictors ineffective. Alternatively, a predictor function could be derived by *distilling* the original loop body down to an approximated version, which only computes the values of loop live-in variables [29, 32]. But, in most cases the complexity of calculating pos at the end of a block is comparable to that of decompressing the entire block since it requires the decoding of all code words within it. Moreover, complex dependence patterns and limited program analysis capabilities make it difficult for the automatic distiller to extract efficient, high-accuracy predictors in this domain.

Therefore, it would be highly valuable to provide a clean, easy-to-use API for a domain expert to implement a high-quality value predictor specific to a given variable-length decompression algorithm. This will allow the system to achieve much higher efficiency of parallel execution than domain-unaware speculative parallelization systems while minimizing programmer effort. This domain-specific framework based on value prediction is particularly attractive on resource-constrained embedded platforms. To realize this, three components are required:

- (Custom value predictors) Prediction algorithms to identify the starting point of each compressed block with high confidence and low overhead

- (Misspeculation detection and recovery mechanisms) Runtime support for misspeculation detection and recovery when speculation is incorrect

- (Parallelization API) Easy-to-use API to transform existing variable-length decompression algorithms into speculatively parallel codes based on value prediction

The remainder of this paper describes all of the above three components. Section 3 discusses prediction algorithms based on

partial decompression and pattern matching. Section 4 introduces the SDM runtime system with its speculative pipeline execution model and mechanisms for misspeculation detection and recovery. Section 5 describes the parallelizing API of SDM with a code transformation example.

3. Block Boundary Prediction Algorithms

The prediction algorithms we propose are classified into two categories: *partial decompression*-based and *pattern matching*-based. Some compression algorithms define a block delimiter string that indicates the beginning of a new compressed block. Table 1 summarizes the existence of a delimiter pattern and its length for each algorithm. If the delimiter pattern does not exist or is short (e.g., fewer than 40 bits), partial decompression-based algorithms may be used; otherwise, simpler pattern matching-based ones are used. The former is applied to zlib (Section 3.1), and the latter to bzip2 and H.264 (Section 3.2).

3.1 Prediction Algorithm based on Partial Decompression

We first describe how to predict the starting point of a block encoded with dynamic Huffman coding via partial decompression. Then we apply it to identify well-aligned chunks in a zlib-compressed stream, which can be decompressed in parallel.

3.1.1 Prediction Algorithm for Huffman Coded Blocks

Huffman coding is a lossless entropy coding algorithm. Taking the frequency of appearance of each input symbol into account, the most frequent symbols are coded with shortest code words, whereas the least frequent symbols with longest code words. This encoding information is compressed in a tree format, called Huffman tree (or codebook). Static Huffman coding uses a single fixed codebook for the entire input, while dynamic Huffman coding produces an optimal codebook for each block. Henceforth, we will assume dynamic Huffman coding since static Huffman coding is just a special case of it.

Figure 3 illustrates the block structure of a Huffman-coded compressed stream. A Huffman tree is placed at the beginning of each block, following an optional delimiter string specific to a compression standard. The decompressor first reconstructs the Huffman tree from the compression block. Using this information, the rest of the compression block is decompressed. The end of the compression block is marked by a special code called the *End Of Block (EOB)*. This code is assigned to the longest code word in the codebook because it appears only once within each block.

We propose a block boundary prediction algorithm for Huffman-coded streams exploiting the EOB code with the following steps. First, the prediction algorithm extracts the EOB code of the block by decompressing the Huffman tree. Then a potential starting point of the next block is obtained by pattern matching with the EOB code. Note that there is a non-zero probability of false positives since the search is done by simple pattern matching without actu-

57

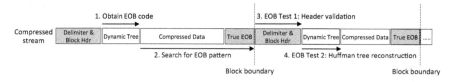

Figure 3: Identification of block boundaries from Huffman-coded compressed stream

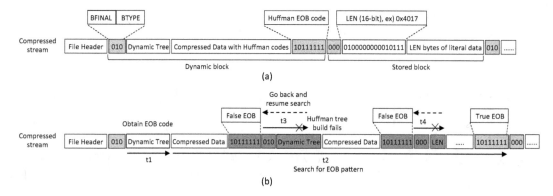

Figure 4: (a) Two interesting block types of zlib (DYNAMIC, STORED); (b) Operation of the prediction algorithm for DYNAMIC block

ally decompressing each code word. The probability increases for a shorter EOB code. To improve the accuracy of prediction, we employ two additional tests to validate an EOB:

- **Header validation**: By checking whether the header of the next block following the EOB code is well-formed or not, we can enhance the confidence of prediction. For example, if the compression algorithm of interest has a block delimiter string (as shown in Table 1), the predictor can make a comparison against the string. This can be applied to other header fields such as type, length, etc.

- **Huffman tree reconstruction**: Partial decompression of the next block also helps validating a true EOB. In most cases, a false-positive EOB causes an error while reconstructing a dynamic Huffman tree for the following block.

Although these additional tests significantly improve the accuracy, there is still a non-zero probability of false positives theoretically. Even so, program correctness is ensured by the misspeculation detection and recovery mechanisms discussed in Section 4.2.

3.1.2 Case Study: Zlib Decompression

Zlib (gzip) [15] implements the DEFLATE [15] compression algorithm, which is a combination of Huffman coding and the LZ77 algorithm [33]. Since it is based on Huffman coding, we can apply the prediction algorithm in Section 3.1.1 to identify block boundaries from a zlib-compressed stream. The rest of this section presents how we customize the prediction algorithm for zlib and augment it to break inter-block dependences caused by LZ77. Throughout this paper we use *minigzip* [15] as a reference implementation of gzip for its simplicity. However, the ideas introduced in this paper are generally transferable to other gzip implementations.

Figure 4(a) shows the file format of gzip. Each block starts with a 3-bit header containing two fields: BFINAL (1 bit) and BTYPE (2 bits). BFINAL indicates the end block. If BFINAL is set to "1", the block is considered as the last block of the compressed stream. BTYPE specifies the type of the block: (1) "00" indicates a *stored* block that directly copies the original data without compression. The following 16-bit LEN field contains the length of the uncom-

pressed data; (2) "01" indicates a static Huffman-coded block; (3) "10" indicates a dynamic Huffman-coded block, which is typically the most common block type; (4) "11" is not used (invalid).

Figure 4(b) illustrates how the prediction algorithm in Section 3.1.1 works for a dynamic Huffman block (BTYPE = "10"). The prediction algorithm first decompresses the dynamic Huffman tree to obtain the EOB code word for the block. Then it searches for the EOB code by pattern matching. If the next match is a true EOB, it will pass the EOB validation tests and the search time will be a sum of time for EOB extraction (t1) and time for pattern matching (t2). The validation time with Huffman tree reconstruction is overlapped with the EOB extraction time (t1) for the next block. To reduce the EOB search time (t2), the scanner exploits minimum block length speculation; the scanner skips the first min_blk_len bytes after the Huffman tree and start an EOB search from there. The value of min_blk_len is set to 14,000 by default.

The validation test time for a false positive case increases the scanning time. Once an EOB pattern is found, the prediction algorithm first checks the validity of BTYPE of the next block. The valid patterns are "10" (DYNAMIC) and "00" (STORED). Note that static ("01") and dynamic ("10") Huffman blocks are not allowed to co-exist in a single compressed stream, so all practically interesting cases use dynamic Huffman coding. If the block type is DYNAMIC, a Huffman tree reconstruction test is performed. The time t3 represents the overhead of this procedure. If the block type is STORED, the predictor tests the expected range of the LEN field. In minigzip [15], a stored block is emitted only when a 16 KB literal buffer is full and compression ratio with LZ77 is very small, hence the store block size is slightly greater than 16 KB in most cases. Therefore, the expected range is set to [16 KB, 16 KB+speculated_range] where speculated_range is 640 bytes by default. Note that, even if the value of LEN falls out of the range, correctness is preserved since it is handled as a misspeculation case.

The prediction algorithm described thus far enables us to efficiently obtain block boundaries predicted with high confidence. However, not all blocks in a zlib-compressed stream can be decompressed in parallel due to inter-block dependences created by the LZ77 algorithm, which employs a *dictionary-based* compression method. LZ77 compresses data by replacing repeated occurrences

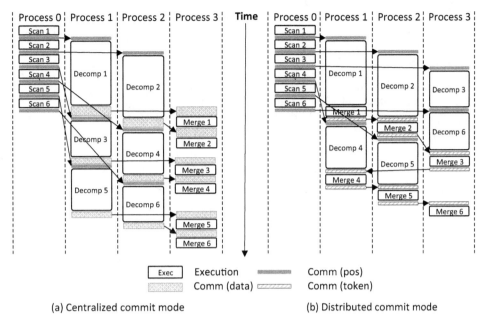

Figure 5: Two execution models of SDM : (a) Centralized commit; (b) Distributed commit

of a data pattern with a matching entry in the dictionary (referred to as a *sliding window*). The sliding window retains some of the recent, uncompressed input data already passed through the compressor. A match is encoded by a distance-length pair corresponding to the offset and length in the sliding window. Inter-block dependences may manifest through references to the sliding window to prevent parallel decompression of adjacent blocks. In minigzip, LZ77 uses a 32KB sliding window.

To put the decompressor into the right context (i.e., properly fill in the sliding window), we exploit stored blocks and overlapped chunk execution. Since a stored block is greater than 16 KB, two consecutive stored blocks will be large enough to fill in the 32 KB sliding window. This marks the beginning of an independently decompressible unit (IDU) spanning multiple blocks. One stored block fills only a half of the sliding window, so we need to redundantly decompress N extra blocks right before the stored block to fill in the remaining half. Since the N blocks are decompressed (using the INFLATE [15] algorithm) with an initially-empty sliding window, decompressed data do not yield correct results. This redundant decompression is performed only to fill in the sliding window; the correctly decompressed output will be gathered from execution of the previous chunk [2] which runs on a complete sliding window. According to our analysis using a number of gzipped files, the INFLATE algorithm works correctly if N is greater than 5.

We analyze the sensitivity of the prediction algorithm using 20 randomly picked packages from the list of Major Linux Application Programs compiled by the Linux Information Project [5]. The source code of each package is compressed using the *unmodified* minigzip with the default configuration parameters (Level 6). Those 20 packages are: abiword, dosemu, emacs, gftp, ghostscript, gqview, httpd, kaffeine, khexedit, lyx, mysql, perl, php, postgresql, python, samba, sql-ledger, tcl, xfig, xpdf, and zope. Our analysis indicates an average EOB length of 13.5 bits and 1.7 false-positive EOB matches per block. We find the two additional tests (header validation and Huffman tree reconstruction) to be essential to reduce the misspeculation rate, which effectively filter out *all* of these

false positives. However, we also identify the following limitations and room for improvement:

- 10 out of the 20 gzipped packages have no stored blocks. For these files, the current implementation of the scanner cannot break inter-block dependences caused by LZ77, and an alternative method needs to be devised. The distribution of stored blocks also affects load balancing of parallel execution, which is discussed in Section 6.1.

- Three parameters control tradeoffs between prediction accuracy and performance: `min_blk_len`, `speculated_range`, and N (number of blocks overlapped between adjacent chunks). Although the default values for these parameters work well for minigzip, optimal settings might vary on other implementations of gzip. However, note that the setting of these values affects only performance but not correctness.

3.2 Prediction Algorithm based on Pattern Matching

Some compression algorithms define block delimiter patterns to improve error resilience against network errors. If the length of the delimiter is long enough (e.g., 40 bits or longer), the prediction algorithm can predict the starting point of a compressed block with high confidence by simple pattern matching. This approach is applicable to bzip2 and H.264.

The bzip2 file format defines a 48-bit pattern called *magic header* (0x314159265359), which signals the beginning of a new compressed block. In this case high-confidence prediction of starting point of block can be implemented by simple pattern matching. Unlike gzip, inter-block dependences do not exist in bzip2 because it performs block-based compression. Therefore, block-level parallel execution can be implemented easily.

The H.264 video compression standard also defines a special video frame that breaks all inter-frame dependences crossing it, called *Instantaneous Decoding Refresh (IDR)* access unit, which can be easily identified by a 40-bit type field (0x0000000165) of Network Access Layer Unit (NALU). Since no inter-frame dependences exist across an IDR frame, a group of video frames beginning with an IDR frame forms a chunk that can be independently decoded.

---

[2] A *chunk* is the unit of work dispatched to a worker process and consists of one or more IDUs.

4. SDM Execution Model

This section introduces the execution model of the SDM parallelization framework. To make best use of hardware resources in embedded platforms, SDM supports two parallel execution models: *centralized commit* and *distributed commit*. The former is more suitable for a platform with many available cores and high communication bandwidth, whereas the latter with a small number of cores and low communication bandwidth. We also describe low-cost misspeculation detection and recovery mechanisms in SDM.

4.1 SDM Three-Stage Pipeline

SDM implements speculative pipeline execution with three stages: Scanner, Decompressor, and Merger. Figure 5(a) shows the execution model with centralized commit. The SDM runtime system uses processes rather than threads for parallel execution contexts. At program invocation, the main process creates and configures each stage. The scanner process executes a prediction algorithm introduced in Section 3 and sends chunk boundaries to the next stage. The parallel decompressor processes decompress multiple chunks concurrently and send the results to the merger stage. The main process itself becomes the merger stage to commit speculatively decompressed data to the output file if no error occurred. Since the decompressor stage is responsible for most of useful work, we create as many decompressor processes as the number of available cores by default.

For manycore embedded platforms with a plenty of available cores, the *centralized* commit model takes full advantage of three-stage pipelining by allocating a separate process for the merger stage. In this model the decompressor and merger stages are fully overlapped. This model entails efficient communication between processes since decompressor-merger communication may become a performance bottleneck.

However, platforms with only a handful of cores may not benefit from this additional process due to context switching and memory space overhead. Hence, SDM also supports the *distributed* commit model to better support such platforms as shown in Figure 5(b). This model fuses the decompressor and merger stages to enable in-process commit across the decompressor processes. To preserve write order, a commit token is communicated among decompressor processes in a sequential execution order. If a decompressor process has finished processing a chunk but received the token yet, it stores the decompressed chunk in a process-local buffer and continue to decompress the next assigned chunk. The buffered data will be committed when the token is passed to the process. The distributed commit model may outperform the centralized commit model on more resource-constrained platforms.

4.2 Misspeculation Detection and Recovery

In case of misspeculation of block boundary, a mechanism that kills misspeculated execution and re-execute the program from previously known correct state must be provided to ensure correctness. Taking the compressed stream in Figure 1 for example, if Block 0 and Block 1 are executed in parallel, the ending state (i.e., value of pos) after processing Block 0 must match the speculated initial state before processing Block 1 (i.e., predicted value of pos_1).

The merger process is responsible for misspeculation detection and recovery. It compares the predicted pos value received from the scanner process with the corresponding, non-speculative pos value received from a decompressor process. Since the first pos value (pos_0) is guaranteed to be correct, all the following pos values can be verified inductively.

If a misspeculation is detected, all speculative scanner and decompressor processes are squashed, and the rest of the program is sequentially executed. It is our design decision not to restart parallel execution since the prediction algorithms we propose in Section 3

yield very high accuracy so that there is no performance benefit from recovery of parallel execution. However, it could be a useful addition when the misspeculation rate is high. We leave this for future work.

5. SDM API

The SDM API functions are classified into two categories as summarized in Table 3. The first category includes functions already implemented by SDM to initiate and orchestrate pipeline execution. The second category defines interface functions that encapsulate algorithm-specific prediction and decompression codes and must be implemented by the programmer.

Parameter	Type	Default	Description
num_process	int	# of cores	Number of decompressor processes
chunk_size	int	1	Chunk size in independently decompressible units
commit_mode	enum	CENT	Commit mode: CENT (centralized), DIST (distributed)
in_file	char*	Input file	Name of input file
out_file	char*	Output file	Name of output file

Table 2: conf structure provided by SDM

Configuration parameters for SDM execution are defined in conf structure shown in Table 2. chunk_size specifies the amount of work dispatched to a decompressor process at a time in independently decompressible units (IDUs). The IDU of bzip2 is a compressed block; the IDU of gzip is a group of blocks beginning with a stored block; the IDU of H.264 is an IDR-frame group.

5.1 Using the API: An Example

Figure 6 illustrates how the sequential variable-length decompression algorithm in Figure 2 is transformed into a parallel code using the SDM API. We assume centralized commit, and the lines taken from the original loop are shaded. The main function (Figure 6(d)) first creates scanner and decompressor processes and then enters into the merge function (Line 8).

Figure 6(a) shows the scan function that constitutes the first stage. predict_boundary is a programmer-defined function implementing a block boundary prediction algorithm. This function returns the starting position of the next chunk, which is sent to both decompressor stage (for decompression) and merger stage (for misspeculation detection). Figure 6(b) shows the decompress function, which runs in the second stage. This function receives a predicted position value (pos) from the scanner and invokes decompress_chunk to start decompression from the position for the next chunk_size IDUs. Then it sends to the merger process the decompressed data and the pos value after processing this chunk (real_pos) for misspeculation detection in the merger stage. Figure 6(c) shows the merge function for the merger stage, which performs misspeculation detection and recovery if necessary and writes to the output file.

5.2 Programmer-provided Functions

The programmer must provide the following two functions that encapsulate prediction and decompression algorithms requiring domain-specific knowledge. Function predict_boundary implements a prediction algorithm as discussed in Section 3. It takes input file name, starting position for search, and chunk size as inputs and returns the starting position of the next chunk. Function decompress_chunk performs actual decompression of chunk_size IDUs starting from the position indicated by pos. It returns the length of the decompressed data in bytes and sets real_pos to be used for misspeculation detection.

Operation	Description
SDM System-provided Functions	
`init(conf)`	Read file size and create queue. If the commit mode is DIST, allocate some buffer.
`destroy(conf)`	Destroy the created queue and buffers.
`create_process(function, &pid, arg)`	Create a new process with process id that will execute the function with the arg
`join_process(conf)`	Wait for worker processes with the configured number of processes
`produce(dst, &val)`	Enqueue val in software queue that send it to dst;
`consume(src, &val)`	Dequeue val from src
`scan(conf)`	Execute scan process; Forward a predicted starting point of block to the targeted process
`decompress(decomp_pid)`	Execute decompress process; compute the compressed data with predicted starting point of block
`merge(conf)`	Execute merger process; write decompressed blocks on output file (Centralized)
`recover_misspec(real_pos)`	Handle recovery from misspeculation
`insert_merge_list(output_buf, len, merge_list)`	Insert decompressed chunk to linked list; the decompressed chunks are stored to merge list for each process (Distributed)
Programmer-provided Functions	
`next_pos = predict_boundary(conf.in_file, pos, conf.chunk_size, &eof)`	Find the starting point of block in compressed stream by using prediction algorithm
`decompress_chunk(conf.in_file, pos, &err, &real_pos)`	Decompress a given chunk and compute the end point of block (real_pos)

Table 3: SDM runtime system interface

```
1  void scan (conf){
2      decomp_pid = 0;
3      while(!eof){
4          next_pos = predict_boundary(conf.in_file, next_pos, conf.
               chunk_size, &eof);
5          produce(decomp_pid, &next_pos);
6          produce(merge, &next_pos);
7          decomp_pid++;
8          if(decomp_pid == conf.num_process)
9              decomp_pid = 0;
10     }
11     for(decomp_pid=0;decomp_pid<conf.num_process;)
12         produce(decomp_pid++, EOS);
13 }
```

(a) Scanner

```
1  void decompress (decomp_pid){
2      while(TRUE){
3          consume(scan, &pos);
4          if(pos == EOS) break;
5          len = decompress_chunk (pos, out_buf, &eof, &err, &real_pos);
6          if(!err && len > 0){
7              produce(merge, &len);
8              produce(merge, out_buf);
9              produce(merge, &real_pos);
10         }
11     }
12     produce(merge, EOD);
13 }
```

(b) Decompressor

```
1  void merge (scan_pid, total_decomp, conf){
2      decomp_pid = 0;
3      while(TRUE){
4          consume(decomp_pid, &len);
5          if(len == EOD) break;
6          consume(decomp_pid, &real_pos);
7          consume(merge, &pred_pos);
8          if(real_pos != pred_pos)
9              recover_misspec(real_pos, scan_pid, total_decomp, conf);
10         consume(decomp_pid, out_buf);
11         fwrite(out_buf, sizeof(char), len, conf.out_stream);
12         decomp_pid++;
13         if(decomp_pid == conf.num_process)
14             decomp_pid = 0;
15     }
16 }
```

(c) Merger

```
1  void main(conf){
2      pid_t scan_pid, *total_decomp;
3      total_decomp = malloc(sizeof(pid_t) * conf.num_process);
4      init(conf);
5      create_process(scan, &scan_pid, conf);
6      for(i=0; i<conf.num_process; i++)
7          create_process(decompress, &total_decomp[i], i);
8      merge(scan_pid, total_decomp, conf);
9      join_process(scan_pid, total_decomp, conf);
10     destroy(conf);
11 }
```

(d) Main Process

Figure 6: Parallelizing sequential code in Figure 2(a) using SDM (centralized commit). (a) Scanner function (Stage 1); (b) Decompressor function (Stage 2); (c) Merger function (Stage 3); (d) Main function.

6. Evaluation

SDM is evaluated on two resource-constrained embedded platforms: Samsung Exynos 4412 quad-core platform (representing "fat" cores) and Tilera TILE-Gx8036 36-core platform (representing "thin" manycores). Table 4 shows the detailed specifications of the two platforms. Using SDM the latest versions of three popular production-grade decompression programs are parallelized: minigzip (zlib 1.2.7) [2], bzip2 (libbzip2 1.0.6) [1], and H.264 (JM-software 18.0) [3]. Three inputs taken from public domains are used

for each program, as shown in Table 5. For H.264, an IDR-frame is inserted every 30 frames. The chunk size is set to one except for zlib (set to 5). Following the speedup measurement methodology of the SPEC CPU benchmark suite, we preload the input file into memory and write the decompressed output to a pre-allocated memory buffer without actually writing to the output file for both sequential and parallel codes.

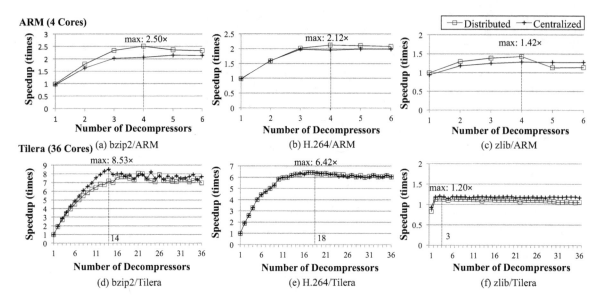

Figure 7: Whole program speedups calculated by taking geometric mean over three inputs for each data point on two platforms

	ODROID-X	NGSM-3600
Processor	Samsung Exynos 4412	Tilera Tile-Gx8036
# of cores	4 "fat" cores	36 "thin" cores
Core Speed	1.4 GHz	1.0 GHz
RAM	1GB, LP-DDR2	16GB, DDR3
OS	Linaro 12.10	Tilera Enterprise Linux 6.0
Compiler	gcc-4.4.6	gcc-4.6.3

Table 4: Detailed specifications for two embedded platforms

Decompression Utility	Input 1	Input 2	Input 3
bzip2 1.0.6 [1]	Firefox 1.7.13 [6]	Linux kernel 3.6.1 [11]	SPEC 2000 *ref* input [27]
zlib 1.2.7 [15]	Firefox 1.7.13 [6]	Linux kernel 3.6.1 [11]	SPEC 2000 *ref* input [27]
H.264-JM 18.0 [3]	Bridge 2000 frames [14]	Grandma 870 frames [14]	Akiyo 300 frames [14]

Table 5: Input files

6.1 Whole Program Speedups

Figure 7 shows the speedup results of the three algorithms on both platforms. The X-axis shows the number of decompressor processes, and the Y-axis speedups over the performance of the original sequential program compiled with `gcc -O3`. Each data point (for both sequential and parallel executions) is measured 10 times (excluding the time for input pre-loading and output buffer pre-allocation), and the minimum execution time is taken to isolate interferences from background processes. Then a geometric mean is calculated over the three inputs.

Figures 7(a)-(c) show whole program speedups for the three decompression programs on the fat quad-core platform. The maximum speedups are achieved with 4 decompressor processes: 2.50× for bzip2, 2.12× for H.264, and 1.42× for zlib. Beyond this point performance is saturated (or even goes down). Distributed commit performs consistently better than centralized commit for all three programs. We will discuss tradeoffs between the two commit modes in Section 6.2.

Figures 7(d)-(f) show the corresponding graphs on the thin manycore platform. The maximum speedups for the three programs

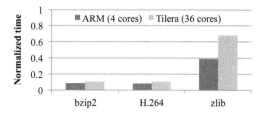

Figure 8: Scanner execution time normalized to execution time of the original sequential program

are achieved with different pipeline configurations: 8.53× with 14 decompressors for bzip2, 6.42× with 18 decompressors for H.264, and 1.20× with 3 decompressors for zlib. H.264 does not perform as well as bzip2 partly because two of the three input video clips have a relatively small size–Grandma has 870 frames (equal to 29 chunks), and Akiyo has only 300 frames (equal to only 10 chunks). Note that, unlike the quad-core platform, centralized commit performs comparably to or better than distributed commit.

On both platforms the performance of zlib is lower than the other two programs primarily due to two factors: higher scanner overhead and load imbalance. Figure 8 shows the first factor by comparing the scanner execution times of the three decompressors. As expected, the scanner stage of zlib employing partial decompression is heavier than pattern matching-based ones for bzip2 and H.264. According to Amdahl's Law, the maximum achievable speedup on the Tilera platform is upper bounded by 1.61×.

The second factor is load imbalance among parallel decompressor processes. As discusssed in Section 3.1, a new chunk can begin only on a stored block (i.e., BTYPE is STORED (00)). Since stored blocks are not uniformly distributed in general, load imbalance can occur. Table 6 evidences this. Table 6 tabulates speedups and load distributions across four decompressor processes for the three inputs. The third to sixth columns show how many bytes each process produces as a result of decompression. The most balanced input, `SPEC.gz`, has the smallest max/min ratio to achieve the best speedup of 1.80× on the quad-core platform. The most unbalanced input, `linux.gz`, has two big chunks decompressed by Processes 1 and 2; the other two processes are mostly idle to yield a much lower speedup of 1.24×. The third input, `firefox.gz`, falls somewhere between the other two inputs.

Input	Speedup	Process 1	Process 2	Process 3	Process 4
Firefox	1.29	87.26MB (40.7%)	41.80MB (19.5%)	19.41MB (9.1%)	65.66MB (30.7%)
Linux	1.24	302.49MB (64.8%)	163.35MB (35.1%)	0.32MB (0.1%)	0.15MB (0.0%)
SPEC 2000	1.80	14.16MB (22.0%)	14.77MB (23.0%)	24.88MB (38.9%)	10.19MB (15.9%)

Table 6: Speedups and load distributions for three gzipped inputs

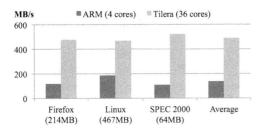

Figure 9: Communication bandwidth for two embedded platforms with centralized commit

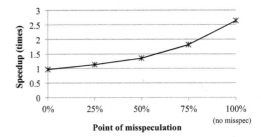

Figure 10: Misspeculation detection and recovery overhead

6.2 Centralized Commit versus Distributed Commit

On the fat quad-core platform distributed commit mode generally performs better than centralized commit mode as shown in Figures 7(a)–(c). In contrast, on the thin manycore platform centralized commit performs comparably (for H.264 and zlib) or even better (for bzip2) as shown in Figures 7(d)–(f). This is because the fat-core platform has fewer high-throughput cores and lower inter-core communication bandwidth than the manycore platform.

To better understand the tradeoffs between the two commit modes, we measure inter-core communication bandwidth with MCRingBuffer [20] used for decompressor-merger communication and the three input files of bzip2. The results are shown in Figure 9, where the manycore platform yields consistently higher throughput than the quad-core platform. Centralized commit favors a platform with higher communication throughput (possibly with weaker cores), and distributed commit a platform with relatively lower communication throughput.

6.3 Misspeculation Recovery Overhead

We evaluate the efficiency of the SDM runtime system in handling misspeculations in Figure 10. Note that the prediction algorithms we introduce in Section 3 have very high accuracy, causing zero mispredictions. Therefore, we inject a mispredicted value at 25%, 50%, 75% and 100% locations from the beginning of the input file, where 100% indicates the end of the input file (i.e., no misspeculation). As mentioned in the Section 4, SDM will fall back to sequential execution from the point of misspeculation. We use bzip2 with the reference input from the SPEC CPU 2000 benchmark suite.

The results indicate that, although the speedup varies depending on where a misspeculation occurs, the SDM-parallelized bzip2 provides robust performance in face of misspeculations. If a misspeculation occurs near the beginning of the input file, the program suffers slight performance degradation due to the overhead of misspeculation detection and recovery as well as program initialization. However, in most cases, SDM performs faster than sequential execution. This demonstrates the efficiency of the SDM runtime in handling misspeculation cases.

6.4 Programmer Effort

Table 7 shows estimated programmer effort required to port the original sequential program to the SDM API with the number of modified lines of code. A porting example is provided in Section 5.1. Columns 2 and 3 indicate the number of lines added for algorithm-specific prediction and decompression codes. As expected, the pattern matching-based boundary predictors for bzip2 and H.264 take fewer lines of code than the partial decompression-based predictor for zlib. Columns 4 through 6 measure the effort required to add to, modify and remove the existing code. Overall, it takes only modest effort to port to SDM since most changes happen within the two programmer-provided functions (`predict_boundary` and `decompress_chunk`) in an isolated manner.

7. Related Work

Parallel Huffman Decoding: Klein et al. [19] use the *self-synchronizing* property of Huffman coding to identify the boundaries of compressed blocks. Likewise, Zhao et al. [31] propose finite state machine (FSM) based speculative execution that performs the parallel decompression for multiple code words within a block. However, these techniques can be applied only to static Huffman coding, or within one block, where the codebook does not change. In theory, self-synchronization may never happen for particular inputs. Biskup et al. [17] introduce modifications to the original Huffman coding algorithm, which guarantees the occurrence of self-synchronization within a finite number of decompressed bits. This code word-level parallel decompression is complementary to SDM's block-level parallel decompression to exploit multi-level parallelism for a large block.

Parallelizing Variable-Length Video Decoders: Gurhanli et al. [18] parallelize the H.264 decoder in group-of-pictures (GOP) granularities, which has a similarity to this work. However, they embed hints for the starting point of GOP from the compression side. Thus, this approach has an obvious limitation of not working for a non-compliant input file. Nikara et al. [24] propose parallel variable-length decoding to decode multiple code words in parallel in MPEG-2 video streams. However, their technique is applicable to a single frame (block) and uses custom hardware based on FPGA. Bilas et al. [16] propose pipeline execution to implement real-time MPEG-2 video decoder, which exploits GOP-level parallelism via pattern matching. SDM is a more general framework that targets the domain of variable-length decompressors and uses a predictor based on partial decompression as well.

Speculative Parallelization Frameworks: Raman et al. [26] propose speculative parallel iteration chunk execution (Spice) parallelization model, which exploits a memoization predictor on hardware. Master/slave speculative parallelization (MSSP) [32] and the adaptive multiple value prediction scheme by Tian et al. [29] automatically extract one or more software value predictors for loop live-ins by taking backward data slices of the original loop. However, all of these hardware and software predictors have limited accuracies. On embedded platforms with limited resources the accuracy and efficiency of the predictor are crucially important to jus-

Program	Programmer-provided functions		Modification of existing code			Total lines modified	Total lines of original program
	predict_boundary()	decompress_chunk()	Added	Modified	Deleted		
bzip2-1.0.6	15	15	37	2	6	75	3147
H.264-JM 18.0 (decoder)	7	22	17	0	4	50	20718
zlib-1.2.7	142	76	26	0	10	254	4055

Table 7: Programs enhanced using SDM. Columns 2-7 indicate the programmer's effort required to port the original sequential program to the SDM API. Column 8 is the lines of the original source code.

tify the cost of custom predictors introduced in this paper. There are runtime support systems for speculative pipeline parallelization such as CorD [30] and SMTX [25], which might be used to implement a system similar to SDM. However, SDM elevates the abstraction level of the API, specifically targeting the domain of variable-length decompression to better separate the expertise of the algorithm from that of parallelization. Also, SDM is specialized to run more efficiently with a handful of cores via distributed commit, removal of memory version tracking, and so on. Mankin et al. propose a transactional memory system that runs efficiently on embedded systems [22]. But, this system is suitable only for speculative DOALL parallelization where iterations are mostly independent without frequently arising cross-iteration dependences.

8. Conclusion

This paper advocates value prediction-based speculative parallelization to effectively parallelize variable-length decompression algorithms, which would otherwise be difficult to parallelize. For this, we propose low-cost prediction algorithms based on partial decompression and pattern matching, to quickly identify block chunks that can be independently decompressed. Also, the SDM API and runtime system is designed and implemented to streamline parallel decompression of multiple chunks. The SDM API provides a clean, easy-to-use interface for an algorithm expert to implement a high-quality value predictor specific to a given variable-length decompression algorithm. The SDM runtime is specialized to execute this pipeline efficiently on resource-constrained embedded platforms while ensuring correctness by detecting and recovering from misspeculations. We have demonstrated the practicality of SDM by successfully parallelizing zlib, bzip2, and H.264 with only modest programmer effort. When evaluated on fat quad-core and thin 36-core embedded platforms, the SDM parallelized code achieves maximum speedups of $2.50\times$ and $8.53\times$ (and geometric mean speedups of $1.96\times$ and $4.04\times$), respectively.

Acknowledgments

We would like to thank the anonymous reviewers for their feedback and Albert Cohen for shepherding this paper. We also thank Hanjun Kim and Nick Johnson for reviewing an early draft of this paper, Jae Young Jang for providing an optimized communication queue, Kwang Hyun Won for his help with the H.264 decoder, and Narinet Inc. for their support with the Tilera machine. This work was supported in part by the IT R&D program of MKE/KEIT [KI001810041244, Smart TV 2.0 Software Platform] and a research grant from Samsung Electronics.

References

[1] bzip2 and libbzip2. http://bzip2.org/.

[2] gzip homepage. http://www.gzip.org/.

[3] H.264: Advanced video coding for generic audiovisual services. http://www.itu.int/rec/T-REC-H.264/.

[4] JPEG homepage. http://www.jpeg.org/jpeg/.

[5] The Linux Information Project. http://linfo.org/.

[6] Mozilla Developer Network. https://developer.mozilla.org/.

[7] Parallel bzip2. http://compression.ca/pbzip2/.

[8] A parallel implementation of gzip. http://zlib.net/pigz/.

[9] Portable Network Graphics. http://www.libpng.org/pub/png/.

[10] Samsung Exynos 4 Quad. http://www.samsung.com/exynos/.

[11] The Linux Kernel Archives. http://www.kernel.org/.

[12] Tilera TILE-Gx processor family. http://www.tilera.com/.

[13] Vorbis audio compression. http://xiph.org/vorbis/.

[14] YUV CIF reference videos. http://trace.eas.asu.edu/yuv/.

[15] zlib: A massively spiffy yet delicately unobtrusive compression library. http://zlib.net/.

[16] A. Bilas, J. Fritts, and J. P. Singh. Real-time parallel MPEG-2 decoding in software. In *Proc. of IPPS*, 1997.

[17] M. T. Biskup. Guaranteed synchronization of Huffman codes. In *Proc. of Data Compression Conference (DCC)*, 2008.

[18] A. Gurhanli, C. C.-P. Chen, and S.-H. Hung. Coarse grain parallelization of H.264 video decoder and memory bottleneck in multi-core architectures. *International Journal of Computer Theory and Engineering*, 2011.

[19] S. T. Klein and Y. Wiseman. Parallel Huffman decoding with applications to JPEG files. *Computer Journal*, 2003.

[20] P. P. C. Lee, T. Bu, and G. Chandranmenon. A lock-free, cache-efficient multi-core synchronization mechanism for line-rate network traffic monitoring. In *Proc. of IPDPS*, 2010.

[21] W. Liu, J. Tuck, L. Ceze, W. Ahn, K. Strauss, J. Renau, and J. Torrellas. POSH: a TLS compiler that exploits program structure. In *Proc. of PPoPP*, 2006.

[22] J. Mankin, D. Kaeli, and J. Ardini. Software transactional memory for multicore embedded systems. In *Proc. of LCTES*, 2009.

[23] P. Marcuello, J. Tubella, and A. Gonzalez. Value prediction for speculative multithreaded architectures. In *Proc. of ISCA*, 1999.

[24] J. Nikara, S. Vassiliadis, J. Takala, M. Sima, and P. Liuha. Parallel multiple-symbol variable-length decoding. In *Proc. of ICCD*, 2002.

[25] A. Raman, H. Kim, T. R. Mason, T. B. Jablin, and D. I. August. Speculative parallelization using software multi-threaded transactions. In *Proc. of ASPLOS*, 2010.

[26] E. Raman, N. Vachharajani, R. Rangan, and D. I. August. Spice: speculative parallel iteration chunk execution. In *Proc. of CGO*, 2008.

[27] Standard Performance Evaluation Corporation. http://www.spec.org/.

[28] J. G. Steffan, C. B. Colohan, A. Zhai, and T. C. Mowry. Improving value communication for thread-level speculation. In *HPCA*, 2002.

[29] C. Tian, M. Feng, and R. Gupta. Speculative parallelization using state separation and multiple value prediction. In *Proc. of ISMM*, 2010.

[30] C. Tian, M. Feng, V. Nagarajan, and R. Gupta. Copy or discard execution model for speculative parallelization on multicores. In *Proc. of MICRO*, 2008.

[31] Z. Zhao, B. Wu, and X. She. Speculative parallelization needs rigor: Probabilistic analysis for optimal speculation of finite state machine applications. In *Proc. of PACT*, 2012.

[32] C. Zilles and G. Sohi. Master/slave speculative parallelization. In *Proc. of MICRO*, 2002.

[33] J. Ziv and A. Lempel. A universal algorithm for sequential data compression. *IEEE Trans. Inf. Theor.*, 23(3):337–343, Sept. 2006.

Program Performance Spectrum

Sudipta Chattopadhyay   Lee Kee Chong   Abhik Roychoudhury

National University of Singapore
{sudiptac,cleekee,abhik}@comp.nus.edu.sg

Abstract

Real-time and embedded applications often need to satisfy several non-functional properties such as timing. Consequently, performance validation is a crucial stage before the deployment of real-time and embedded software. Cache memories are often used to bridge the performance gap between a processor and memory subsystems. As a result, the analysis of caches plays a key role in the performance validation of real-time, embedded software. In this paper, we propose a novel approach to compute the cache performance signature of an entire program. Our technique is based on exploring the input domain through different *path programs*. Two paths belong to the same path program if they follow the same set of control flow edges but may vary in the iterations of loops encountered. Our experiments with several subject programs show that the different paths grouped into a path program have very similar and often exactly same cache performance.

Our path program exploration can be viewed as partitioning the input domain of the program. Each partition is associated with its cache performance and a symbolic formula capturing the set of program inputs which constitutes the partition. We show that such a partitioning technique has wide spread usages in performance prediction, testing, debugging and design space exploration.

Categories and Subject Descriptors   C.3 [*Special-purpose and Application-based Systems*]: Real-time and embedded systems

General Terms   Design, Performance, Verification

Keywords   Cache Memories, Performance testing, Path Exploration, Symbolic Execution

1. Introduction

It is hard to build both *functionally correct* and *high performance* systems. For real-time and embedded software, it is often important to validate the system for certain non-functional properties, such as timing. Due to the huge amount of effort employed on the functionality validation of a software, the problem of performance validation is usually ignored. As a result, the deployed software may suffer from some serious performance bottlenecks. Such a loss of performance is often undesirable for real-time and embedded software, as most of such software are not just expected to produce a *correct* output, but also to produce a *correct* output within a *specified time bound*.

Memory subsystems, especially *caches*, have a significant impact on the performance of embedded software. In a typical memory subsystem, cache memory is several hundred times faster than the main memory. Therefore, a huge number of *cache misses* may lead to several magnitudes of performance degradation. Clearly, the performance of memory subsystem depends on the memory accesses made by the processor. On the other hand, the set of memory accesses made by the processor depends on the type of application it is running. As a result, the performance of an embedded system critically depends on the input provided to this specific application.

In this paper, we present a novel approach to partition the input domain of an application for validating performance. Such a partitioning strategy produces a performance spectrum of the entire program. Each partition in the spectrum is associated with a range of performance and a symbolic formula capturing the set of program inputs which constitutes the partition. In particular, we focus on the performance of the memory subsystem in this work, as cache misses are often the dominating factors for the performance degradation in embedded software. Although targeted towards embedded software, we believe that such a partitioning strategy could be useful for a variety of validation techniques.

To build a performance spectrum of the entire program, we face two significant challenges. The first problem appears due to the absence of any performance metric in a user program. Program behavior is usually captured by its input-output relationship. To overcome this problem, we instrument the program such that it computes a performance metric (in particular number of cache misses) when run on a particular input. Such an instrumentation is *entirely automatic* and it does not require any user annotations.

The second and more significant challenge appears in clustering the input domain with similar cache performance. It is clearly infeasible to execute a program for all possible inputs and measure the program performance for each of them. We therefore propose to *explore feasible path programs* (instead of *feasible program paths*) to partition the input domain of the program. A *path program* is a fragment of the original program where all the paths belonging to the same path program follow the same set of control flow edges, but may vary in the iterations of loops encountered. Therefore, a path program groups potentially *unbounded* number of paths together.

A crucial observation is that all the paths in a path program execute the same set of instructions (but may be in different number of times and in different order). It is possible that the ordering and frequency of different instructions may have a significant impact on the cache performance and therefore, the cache performance of different paths grouped into a path program may have a wide variation. However, we observed that a variation of this form mostly captures some serious cache performance issues, such as cache misses linearly increasing with the number of loop iterations due to *cache thrashing* (in the presence of small cache size or improper memory layout). As a result, path program creates a suitable abstraction for cache performance debugging. On the other hand, if the order-

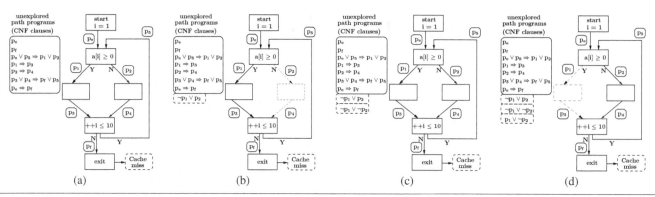

Figure 1. (a): Original program where array a is an input variable, (b)&(c)&(d): exploring different path programs, path program fragments are denoted by *thick and solid control flow edges*

ing and frequency of different instructions do not have a significant impact on cache misses, a path program can combine several paths having similar cache performance. Such a combination strategy is extremely useful for cache performance prediction and testing, as it partitions the input domain into a finite number of path programs. Each such path program corresponds to a set of inputs for which the program has very similar cache performance. As a result, instead of concentrating on the set of all inputs, we can only focus on the set of path programs produced by our framework. Moreover, the path program abstraction allows us to concentrate on a smaller part of the program at a time. Therefore, any analysis based on a path program is more *precise* and *scalable* than the same if applied on the entire program. We build a framework which dynamically explores path programs and each path program is analyzed only once during this exploration. Moreover, such analyses on path programs incrementally build the performance spectrum of the program. Therefore, at any time, the output from the set of already analyzed path programs captures a cache performance signature for a subset of the input domain (covered by the analyzed path programs).

The application of our framework can be summarized as follows. An immediate usage of our framework will be in *performance prediction*. For some *arbitrary input* provided to an application, we can locate the path program which captures the respective input and predict the performance of the application for the same input. The second significant usage is in *performance testing*. From the performance spectrum (*i.e.* the set of all path programs), we can generate concrete inputs which drive the execution of the program towards performance loss. Such critical test cases can often be missed by random testing. Thirdly, our framework can be used as a feedback to the compiler to perform *performance optimization*. Finally, as the application run on an embedded system is usually fixed, our framework can be used to decide an appropriate cache configuration for the system, as evidenced by our experiments.

We have evaluated our framework on several subject programs. Our experimental results show that we can achieve high accuracy in predicting performance as the different paths in a particular path program exhibit similar (and sometimes exactly same) cache behaviour. In addition, our experimental results also show that the different paths in a path program are similar in terms of overall execution time (and not just in terms of the number of cache misses). This is due to the reason that cache misses are often the key factors dominating the execution time of these programs.

2. Overview

In this Section, we shall give an outline of our overall technique using the example in Figure 1. The first problem in performance

analysis appears due to the absence of any performance metric in a user program. To solve this problem, we instrument the original program to measure performance. Such an instrumentation is *entirely automatic*. In this paper, we focus on the cache performance of a program and for the time being, we shall assume that our instrumented program computes the cache performance (*i.e* number of cache misses) of the original program when run with a particular input (as shown in Figure 1(b)-(d)). In this context, we must mention that the instrumented program may itself suffer more number of cache misses (compared to the original program) due to the additional instrumented code. However, the instrumented program manipulates a variable *miss* during execution. At the end of executing the instrumented program, the variable *miss exactly* captures the number of cache misses suffered by the original program.

To partition the input domain with respect to cache performance, we propose to explore *feasible path programs* (instead of *feasible program paths*). A path program is defined as follows:

DEFINITION 2.1. *Assume $G = (V, E)$ is the control flow graph (CFG) of the program. Given an execution trace π, a path program P_π captures a subgraph $G_\pi = (V_\pi, E_\pi)$ of the control flow graph G, such that V_π is the set of basic blocks and E_π is the set of control flow edges executed in π.*

Intuitively, a path program is a subset of the original program, where all the paths belonging to the path program follow exactly same set of control flow edges, but may vary in the iterations of loops encountered. Depending on the underlying cache configuration, path program creates a suitable abstraction for cache performance debugging or cache performance prediction/testing. For very small cache sizes, different paths grouped into a path program may show wide variation in cache performance – such as cache misses linearly increasing with the number of loop iterations due to cache thrashing. On the other hand, for an appropriate cache configuration (*i.e.* in the absence of heavy cache thrashing), different paths grouped into a path program may show very similar cache performance – making the path program a suitable abstraction for cache performance testing and prediction. Finally, it is still possible to have a wide variation in *unavoidable* (*i.e.* cold) data cache misses for a single path program. However, such effects can easily be distinguished by instrumenting the cold data cache misses separately (*i.e.* not counting the cold data cache misses within variable *miss*).

The example in Figure 1(a) has 2^{10} different paths, but it has only three path programs, as shown in Figures 1(b)-(d). The path programs can be summarized by the following three symbolic formulae on input array a:

- Figure 1(b): $\mathcal{S}_1 \equiv a[1] \geq 0 \wedge \ldots \wedge a[10] \geq 0$.
- Figure 1(d): $\mathcal{S}_2 \equiv a[1] < 0 \wedge \ldots \wedge a[10] < 0$.
- Figure 1(c): $\mathcal{S}_3 \equiv \neg \mathcal{S}_1 \wedge \neg \mathcal{S}_2$.

Before any exploration, we first produce a SAT encoding of all the unexplored path programs. The basic intuition behind the SAT encoding is to capture the structure of a program control flow graph (CFG). We associate an atomic proposition p_e for each control flow edge e. p_e is *true* if control flow edge e is executed and *false* otherwise. The entire encoding is captured by a propositional formula in conjunctive normal form (CNF). Figure 1(a) shows the set of CNF clauses which encodes all the available path programs (for a formal presentation of this encoding, refer to Section 4.1).

During exploration, we first execute the test program with a random input and collect the execution trace π. In example 1(a), assume that only the left leg of the branch conditional $a[i] \geq 0$ appears in the execution trace π. From this execution trace, we construct the respective path program. Such a path program also contains the *cache performance instrumentation*, where a single integer variable *miss* captures the number of cache misses suffered by the original program. As a result, bounding the value of variable *miss* bounds the number of cache misses suffered by any execution which might visit *exactly the same set of control flow edges as π*. The path program is statically analyzed to compute the bounds on variable *miss*. Therefore, the analysis of the path program produces a range of cache misses of the form $MIN \leq miss \leq MAX$, where MIN and MAX represent the minimum and maximum number of cache misses, respectively, over the path program being analyzed. The analysis also computes the weakest invariant on input variables satisfied by any path in the path program (i.e. the condition $\mathcal{S}_1 \equiv a[1] \geq 0 \wedge \ldots \wedge a[10] \geq 0$ for the path program shown in Figure 1(b)). Any standard invariant generation method can be used for such analysis.

After the analysis of a path program, we add additional CNF clauses to the SAT encoding, so that we can explore a *different path program in subsequent iterations*. As shown in Figure 1(b), we add the clause $\neg(p_1 \wedge \neg p_2) \equiv \neg p_1 \vee p_2$ in the existing SAT encoding. This additional clause symbolically captures the information that *the path program in Figure 1(b) will not be explored in future*.

We manipulate the path conditions obtained from previous executions and try to deviate towards a different path program. Manipulation of a path condition involves negating the different branches along the path condition. Assume that we negate the 10-th branch in the initial execution trace (which results the path program in Figure 1(b)). Therefore, we get a partial path condition $\theta \equiv a[1] \geq 0 \wedge a[2] \geq 0 \wedge \ldots \wedge a[9] \geq 0 \wedge \neg(a[10] \geq 0)$. θ is satisfiable, however, we additionally need to check whether θ belongs to some already analyzed path program. From the execution trace obtained for Figure 1(b), we can find that both the legs of the conditional $a[i] \geq 0$ must be executed to satisfy θ. Therefore, both p_1 and p_2 must be *true*. Given $p_1 = p_2 = true$, if we find a satisfying assignment of the CNF clauses in Figure 1(b), then θ may belong to some *unexplored path program*. It turns out that a satisfying assignment of the CNF clauses (reported in Figure 1(b)) is possible with $p_1 = p_2 = true$. As a result, we execute the program on some input satisfying θ and analyze the respective path program. This path program is shown in Figure 1(c), which also adds the clause $\neg(p_1 \wedge p_2) \equiv \neg p_1 \vee \neg p_2$ to the SAT encoding. Now consider a partial path condition $\theta' \equiv a[1] \geq 0 \wedge a[2] \geq 0 \wedge \ldots \wedge \neg(a[9] \geq 0)$, after we explore and analyze the path program in Figure 1(c). Even though θ' is satisfiable, we know that it must execute both the legs of the condition $a[i] \geq 0$. Therefore, both p_1 and p_2 must be *true* to satisfy θ'. However, there is no satisfying assignment for the CNF clauses reported in Figure 1(c) with $p_1 = p_2 = true$. As a result, we discard the partial path condition θ', since any path sat-

isfying θ' has already been analyzed via the path program in Figure 1(c). We eventually explore the path program in Figure 1(d), which adds the clause $\neg(\neg p_1 \wedge p_2) \equiv p_1 \vee \neg p_2$ to the SAT encoding.

After analyzing the path program in Figure 1(d), our SAT encoder *blocks* all the three path programs. Note that the three path programs are blocked by the CNF clauses $\neg(p_1 \wedge \neg p_2) \equiv \neg p_1 \vee p_2$, $\neg(p_1 \wedge p_2) \equiv \neg p_1 \vee \neg p_2$ and $\neg(\neg p_1 \wedge p_2) \equiv p_1 \vee \neg p_2$, as shown in Figure 1(d). All of the three clauses are *satisfiable* if and only if $p_1 = false$ and $p_2 = false$. However, due to the structure of the CFG, we encode the CNF clause $p_e \vee p_5 \Rightarrow p_1 \vee p_2$. Therefore, if both p_1 and p_2 are *false*, both p_e and p_5 are *false* as well. This leads to a contradiction to all the CNF clauses reported in Figure 1(d), as p_e (which captures the single program entry) must be *true* for any path program (as denoted by the CNF clause p_e separately in the encoding). As a result, our exploration loop terminates at this stage, since we do not have any more *unexplored* path program.

It is important to note that the path program in Figure 1(c) does not cover the path programs in Figure 1(b) and Figure 1(d). The path program in Figure 1(c) takes both legs of $a[i] \geq 0$ conditional *at least once*. Therefore, the path program in Figure 1(c) groups $2^{10} - 2$ different paths.

3. Cache performance instrumentation

Given a program $\mathcal{P}$, we annotate the program to compute the number of cache misses suffered by $\mathcal{P}$. Let us assume $\mathcal{P}_{miss}$ is the annotated program. $\mathcal{P}_{miss}$ depends on the underlying cache parameters, namely, *number of cache sets*, *cache line size*, *cache associativity* and the *cache replacement policy*. The main advantage of such a code instrumentation technique is that it can easily be changed to handle a variety of cache architectures. The primary goal of such instrumentation is to integrate a *light-weight cache model* inside the original program, rather than just measuring the cache performance for a particular execution. Such an integrated cache model is used to compute the bound on cache misses via static analysis.

The annotated program $\mathcal{P}_{miss}$ captures the number of cache misses suffered by $\mathcal{P}$ via a single global variable *miss*. It is important to note that the annotated program $\mathcal{P}_{miss}$ may itself suffer more number of cache misses than $\mathcal{P}$ due to the additional instrumented code. However, during execution, $\mathcal{P}_{miss}$ manipulates a global variable *miss* in such a fashion that the final value of *miss* exactly captures the number of cache misses suffered by $\mathcal{P}$. The relation between the original program $\mathcal{P}$ and the instrumented program $\mathcal{P}_{miss}$ can be formalized via the following property:

PROPERTY 3.1. *For a particular cache configuration $\mathcal{CF}$, let us assume that $\mathcal{CM}$ is the number of cache misses suffered by $\mathcal{P}$ for some input combination $\mathcal{I}$. For the same cache configuration $\mathcal{CF}$, assume that $\mathcal{P}_{miss}$ is the instrumented version of program $\mathcal{P}$. If $\mathcal{CM}'$ denotes the value of variable miss at the end of executing $\mathcal{P}_{miss}$ on input combination $\mathcal{I}$, then $\mathcal{CM} = \mathcal{CM}'$.*

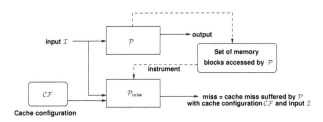

Figure 2. Cache performance instrumentation

Figure 2 shows the key relation (captured by Property 3.1) between $\mathcal{P}$ and $\mathcal{P}_{miss}$ in our proposed framework.

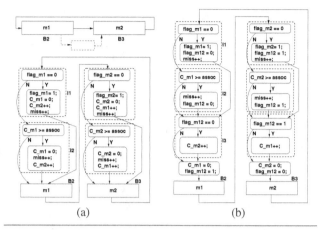

(a)   (b)

Figure 3. Instrumentation for (a) FIFO cache replacement policy, (b) LRU cache replacement policy.

In the following, we shall show the code annotation technique for two widely used cache replacement policies - *first-in-first-out* (FIFO) and *least recently used* (LRU).

Figure 3(a) shows the instrumentation for FIFO cache replacement policy. The original CFG is shown at the top of Figure 3(a). For the sake of simplicity, we shall illustrate the instrumentation of the path program which contains basic blocks $B2$ and $B3$. For the sake of illustration, let us assume that basic block $B2$ accesses memory block $m1$, basic block $B3$ accesses memory block $m2$ and $m1$ conflicts with $m2$ in the cache. In general, the cache conflict pattern of different memory blocks can be determined statically from the respective cache configuration (*i.e.* number of cache sets and cache line size). The sole purpose of the code instrumentation is to compute the number of cache misses faced by the original code. A cache miss can happen for the following reasons: i) *Cold cache miss* happens when a memory block is accessed for the first time, and ii) *Conflict miss and capacity miss* happen when the number of cache conflicts faced by a memory block exceeds the cache associativity. The total number of cache misses is captured by a variable $miss$ as shown in Figure 3(a). Block $I1$ captures the cold cache miss suffered by memory block $m1$ and block $I2$ updates the number of conflict and capacity misses suffered by $m1$. Variables C_m1 and C_m2 serve the purpose of counting cache conflicts to memory block $m1$ and $m2$, respectively and $assoc$ represents the associativity of the cache. $flag\_m1$ and $flag\_m2$ are used to distinguish the first accesses to $m1$ and $m2$, respectively.

Nevertheless, to update the number of conflict and capacity misses, we need to update the cache conflicts faced by each memory block at appropriate places. Updating such a cache conflict depends on the underlying cache replacement policy. In FIFO replacement policy, cache conflict to a memory block is increased whenever a new memory block enters the same cache set. In 3(a), since $m1$ and $m2$ conflict in the cache, the conflict count to $m2$ (*i.e.* C_m2) is increased whenever $m1$ makes a new entry to the cache (*i.e.* for all types of cache misses faced by $m1$). The annotated code for memory block $m2$ is entirely symmetric to the code inserted for memory block $m1$.

Assuming that the loop in Figure 3(a) executes 100 times, the value of $miss$ will be 200 for a direct mapped cache (*i.e.* $assoc$ is 1 in Figure 3(a)) at the end of execution. On the other hand, for a 2-way set-associative cache (*i.e.* $assoc$ is 2 in Figure 3(a)), value of $miss$ would be 2 at the end of execution. In both the cases, value of $miss$ capture the number of cache misses suffered by the original code (*i.e.* the path program containing basic blocks $B2$ and $B3$), hence satisfying Property 3.1.

Updating the cache conflict is slightly different in LRU compared to FIFO. In FIFO replacement policy, the state of the cache does not change on a *cache hit*. On the other hand, for LRU replacement policy, each memory block becomes the *most recently used* (*i.e.* its cache conflict is reset to zero) whenever it is accessed. Therefore, for any access of a memory block, we set its cache conflict count to zero (*e.g.* in Figure 3(b), C_m1 is set to zero before accessing $m1$). Moreover, accessing a memory block m increases the conflict to all the memory blocks which were *more recently used* than m before the access. In Figure 3(b), $flag\_m12$ tracks which memory block is *more recently used*, $m1$ or $m2$. $flag\_m12$ is set to *one* if $m1$ is more recently used than $m2$ and *zero* otherwise. Clearly, if $m1$ is not in the cache, we can always assume that $m1$ is the least recently used memory block. Therefore, for all types of cache misses of $m1$, we set $flag\_m12$ to zero. A symmetrical transformation is also applied before accessing $m2$. Finally, we increment the conflict to $m2$ (as shown by block $I3$ in Figure 3(b)) if and only if $m2$ was *more recently used* than $m1$ before the current access of $m1$ (*i.e.* $flag\_m12$ is set to zero).

In general, our code instrumentation technique traverses all the basic blocks of $\mathcal{P}$, computes the set of memory blocks accessed therein and it inserts additional code (as shown in Figures 3(a)-(b)) for each memory block at each *control flow edge* of $\mathcal{P}$. The essence of such a transformation is to integrate a cache model inside the original program $\mathcal{P}$. As shown in Figures 3(a)-(b), such a modeling of cache has been accomplished via the manipulation of a variable $miss$. Therefore, statically bounding the value of $miss$ directly gives a bound on the number of cache misses suffered by $\mathcal{P}$.

Challenges to handle data accesses For measuring data cache performance, the basic structure of the instrumentation is exactly the same as described in the preceding. However, it is worthwhile to note that statically estimating the set of memory blocks for a data access is very challenging. Existing research on address analysis [6] has looked at the problem of estimating an over-approximation of memory blocks accessed by each data reference. Since our instrumentation walks through the static control flow graph, it also needs to know the set of memory blocks accessed by each data reference. Once such an address analysis is performed, we can use the set of computed memory blocks by address analysis to instrument the code.

In our current implementation, however, we do not handle complex data memory accesses through pointers. Moreover, as our instrumentation statically needs to know the set of memory blocks, we currently do not handle dynamic memory allocations. Our framework currently handles accesses to scalar variables and static arrays. Array accesses inside a loop captures a special case. Note that different elements of an array can be accessed in different iterations of a loop. This is different from instruction memory block accesses, as every iterations of a loop access the same memory block for a specific instruction. As a result, we can add the instrumentation of an instruction memory block independent of loop iteration values (as shown in Figure 3).

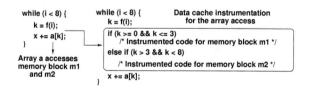

Figure 4. Instrumentation for array accesses

The minor change required for array accesses is shown in Figure 4. Assume that array elements $a[0\ldots3]$ accesses memory block

$m1$ and array elements $a[4 \ldots 7]$ accesses memory block $m2$. Such information can be computed from the base address of array a. The instrumentation for the array access is shown in Figure 4. Before the access, we check the bound of the array index. If the array index (*i.e.* k) is between 0 and 3, we add the instrumentation code for memory block $m1$ (exactly in the same fashion as shown in Figure 3). Similarly, if $k \in [4, 7]$, we add the instrumentation code for memory block $m2$. Note that the important difference is made by the conditional instrumentations. Such conditional checks are performed to compute the specific memory blocks being accessed from an array. The instrumentation is *entirely automatic*.

4. Analysis framework

Broadly, our input domain partitioning framework consists of two different steps: symbolic encoding of different path programs (Section 4.1) and systematic exploration of path programs to partition the input domain with respect to cache performance (Section 4.2). The symbolic encoding is used as an *oracle* to the path program exploration, so that it analyzes a path program only once.

4.1 SAT encoding

The SAT encoder symbolically encodes all the *unexplored path programs*. Due to the significant progress in SAT solver technologies, it is shown in [16] that such a symbolic encoding makes the path program enumeration feasible in practice. However in [16], all loops are treated in a *monolithic* fashion. More precisely, two path programs $P_\pi = (V_\pi, E_\pi)$ and $P'_\pi = (V'_\pi, E'_\pi)$ are distinguished in [16] if and only if there exists an edge e such that

- $e \in E_\pi$, $e \notin E'_\pi$ and e is a control edge outside of any loop, or
- $e \in E'_\pi$, $e \notin E_\pi$ and e is a control edge outside of any loop.

Therefore, to encode the notion of path program abstraction used in our framework, we extend the symbolic encoding used in [16] as follows. For each control flow edge e in the program, we introduce an atomic proposition p_e. The truth value of p_e captures the execution of control flow edge e. p_e is *true* if control flow edge e is executed, and *false* otherwise. We distinguish among the following two types of clauses: MSCC clauses and loop clauses.

MSCC clauses: These are the clauses proposed in [16]. MSCC clauses are created on *the maximal strongly connected decomposition* (MSCC) of the program control flow graph (CFG). In the MSCC decomposition of a CFG, a control flow is represented only across two different MSCCs. All other control flows inside an MSCC are hidden. Therefore, each control flow edge in the MSCC decomposition can be executed at most once. Assume E_D represents the set of control flow edges in the MSCC decomposition. Therefore, E_D includes only the set of control flow edges which do not appear inside any loop or recurrences. Without loss of generality, let us assume that n_e (n_f) represents the designated *entry* (*exit*) node of the program. We generate the following clauses:

$$onlyOne(out(n_e)), \; onlyOne(in(n_f)) \quad (1)$$

$$\bigwedge_{e \in E_D, src(e) \neq n_e} p_e \Rightarrow onlyOne(in(src(e))) \quad (2)$$

$$\bigwedge_{e \in E_D, end(e) \neq n_f} p_e \Rightarrow onlyOne(out(end(e))) \quad (3)$$

where $src(e)$ and $end(e)$ represent the source and target node of a directed control flow edge e. On the other hand, $in(n)$ and $out(n)$ represent the set of predecessors and successors of node n, respectively. $onlyOne(E)$ is a propositional formula which denotes that *exactly one* control flow edge in E can be executed.

Therefore, $onlyOne(E)$ is defined as follows:

$$onlyOne(E) \equiv \bigvee_{e \in E} p_e \wedge \bigwedge_{e, f \in E. e \neq f} p_e \Rightarrow \neg p_f \quad (4)$$

Loop clauses: Assume that b is a basic block appearing inside some loop. Since b is inside a loop, we can no longer say that *exactly one* predecessor or successor can appear in the execution. However, we can generate the following clause to distinguish the execution of b:

$$\bigvee_{e \in in(b)} p_e \Leftrightarrow \bigvee_{e' \in out(b)} p_{e'} \quad (5)$$

where $in(b)$ and $out(b)$ represent the set of predecessors and successors of node b, respectively. Intuitively, the above clauses ensure that some successor of b can be executed if and only if some predecessor of b is executed.

Similarly, for any loop l, we generate the following clauses:

$$\bigvee_{e \in in(l)} p_e \Leftrightarrow \bigvee_{e' \in out(l)} p_{e'} \quad (6)$$

where $in(l)$ and $out(l)$ represent the set of entry and exit control flow edges of loop l, respectively. The above clauses denote that if a loop l is entered, it will exit eventually. These clauses also capture the fact that every loop occurring in the program is *bounded*.

Clauses in Equation 5 and Equation 6 are introduced by us to distinguish the different control flow edges inside a loop.

4.2 Dynamic exploration of path programs

Our approach iteratively explores different *path programs*. In each iteration, a new test input is generated that may force the execution through an unexplored path program. This process continues until we explore all the *feasible path programs*.

The basic idea behind our exploration algorithm is as follows. We first run the program for a random test input and collect the execution trace. We then construct a *path program* from this execution trace. The path program is analyzed to produce a cache miss range - meaning the analysis computes the lower bound and the upper bound on the number of cache misses suffered by the path program. To continue with the exploration process, we need to generate an input that may deviate the execution towards a different path program. In a broader perspective, therefore, the path program exploration process needs to perform two different tasks: first, generation of different inputs through SMT-based constraint solvers. Such an input generation involves manipulating and solving path conditions from previous executions. Secondly, before generating an input from a path condition, we need to check whether the path condition belongs to some explored path program. Such a checking is performed by *satisfiability testing* via a propositional formula, which in turn encodes the set of *all unexplored path programs*.

Algorithm 1 captures the core of our dynamic path program exploration technique. As we mentioned in the preceding, we use the SMT-based constraint solvers to generate different inputs. Moreover, we use a propositional formula to track the set of unexplored path programs. At any point of time, Φ encodes the set of of all unexplored path programs. Assume that the executed path for a test input τ is π and the corresponding path condition is $\psi_1 \wedge \psi_2 \wedge \ldots \wedge \psi_k$. We want to find a test input τ' which deviates the execution from π and also walks through an *unexplored path program*. The deviation is made by negating any of the branch conditions appearing in π. If we want to deviate the execution at the r-th branch, the inputs to the program must satisfy the partial path condition $\theta \equiv \psi_1 \wedge \ldots \wedge \psi_{r-1} \wedge \neg \psi_r$. If θ is *unsatisfiable*, then θ resembles an *infeasible path* in the program and we discard it immediately. However, even if θ is *satisfiable*, it may walk through some previously explored path program. Therefore, we need to check whether

Algorithm 1 Dynamic exploration of path programs

1: **Input:**
2: $\mathcal{P}, \mathcal{P}_{miss}$: original and instrumented program
3: **Output:**
4: A set of *feasible* and *analyzed* path programs
5:
6: $AllPc = unexplored =$ empty
7: /* build a SAT encoding of the entire program $\mathcal{P}$ */
8: $\Phi \leftarrow \text{SATEncode}(\mathcal{P})$
9: select a random input τ
10: $\text{ExecuteAndAnalyze}(\mathcal{P}, \tau, \Phi)$
11: **while** $unexplored \neq$ empty $\wedge \Phi$ is satisfiable **do**
12:     select $\varphi \in unexplored$
13:     remove φ from $unexplored$
14:     let $\varphi \leftarrow \psi_1 \wedge \psi_2 \wedge \ldots \wedge \psi_{r-1} \wedge \psi_r$
15:     $\theta \leftarrow \psi_1 \wedge \psi_2 \wedge \ldots \wedge \psi_{r-1} \wedge \neg\psi_r$
16:     $\{b_1, \ldots, b_k\} \leftarrow$ set of control flow edges in $\mathcal{P}$ that are
17:     executed by any path satisfying θ
18:     $\eta \leftarrow \Phi \wedge p_{b_1} \wedge \ldots \wedge p_{b_k}$
19:     /* analyze only an unexplored path program */
20:     **if** η and θ are satisfiable **then**
21:         $t_\theta \leftarrow$ some concrete inputs satisfying θ
22:         $\text{ExecuteAndAnalyze}(\mathcal{P}, \mathcal{P}_{miss}, t_\theta, \Phi)$
23:     **end if**
24: **end while**
25:
26: **procedure** ExecuteAndAnalyze($\mathcal{P}, \mathcal{P}_{miss}, \tau, \Phi$)
27:     execute $\mathcal{P}$ on input τ
28:     let $\varphi \equiv \psi_1 \wedge \psi_2 \wedge \ldots \wedge \psi_k$ be the path condition
29:     /* build all partial path conditions */
30:     **for** $i \leftarrow 1, k$ **do**
31:         let $\varphi_i \leftarrow \psi_1 \wedge \psi_2 \wedge \ldots \wedge \psi_{i-1} \wedge \psi_i$
32:         **if** $\varphi_i \notin AllPc$ **then**
33:             $AllPc \bigcup = \varphi_i$
34:             $unexplored \bigcup = \varphi_i$
35:         **end if**
36:     **end for**
37:     let π be the executed path on input τ
38:     $\{b_1, \ldots, b_m\} \leftarrow$ set of branch edges that appears in π
39:     $\{b'_1, \ldots, b'_n\} \leftarrow$ set of branch edges in $\mathcal{P}$ that does not
40:     appear in π
41:     $\xi \leftarrow p_{b_1} \wedge \ldots \wedge p_{b_m} \wedge \neg p_{b'_1} \wedge \ldots \wedge \neg p_{b'_n}$
42:     /* analyze only an unexplored path program */
43:     **if** $\Phi \wedge \xi$ is satisfiable **then**
44:         /*construct path program from execution trace π
45:         and the instrumented program $\mathcal{P}_{miss}$ */
46:         $P_\pi \leftarrow \text{ConstructPathProgram}(\pi, \mathcal{P}_{miss})$
47:         /*analyze path program P_π */
48:         $\text{AnalyzePathProgram}(P_\pi)$
49:         /*block path program P_π for further exploration*/
50:         $\Phi \leftarrow \Phi \wedge \neg\xi$
51:     **end if**
52: **end procedure**

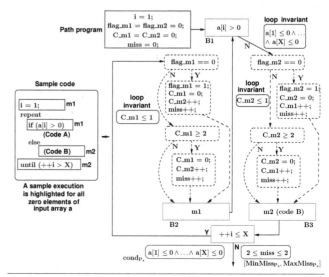

Figure 5. Analysis of a path program, array a is the input

been covered by an explored path program (recall that Φ encodes all the unexplored path programs). As a result, if η is unsatisfiable, we do not explore any path resulting from the partial path condition θ. In case, both θ and η are satisfiable, we generate a new test input from θ and try to deflect towards an *unexplored path program*.

Constructing a path program   A *path program* is constructed from a particular execution trace π of $\mathcal{P}$ and the instrumented program $\mathcal{P}_{miss}$. Assume that B_π denotes the set of executed basic blocks. A path program $P_\pi = (V_\pi, E_\pi)$ includes the set of basic blocks B_π and additionally, it includes the following basic blocks:

- If the control flow (B_i, B_j) appears in π, then $\mathcal{I}_{B_i \to B_j} \in V_\pi$, where $\mathcal{I}_{B_i \to B_j}$ is the set of all instrumented basic blocks (in $\mathcal{P}_{miss}$) inserted along the edge (B_i, B_j).

As an example, consider the instrumented program fragment of Figure 3(a). If $(B2, B3)$ and $(B3, B2)$ both appears in π, the constructed path program includes all the eight instrumented basic blocks inserted along the edges $(B2, B3)$ and $(B3, B2)$.

Checking an explored path program   Assume that we want to check whether a path π belongs to some *explored path program*. Further assume $\{b_1, \ldots, b_m\}$ is the set of branch edges that appears in the execution trace π and $\{b'_1, \ldots, b'_n\}$ is the set of branch edges that does not appear in the execution trace π. To check whether π has already been explored by a path program, we check the *satisfiability* of the following formula:

$$\Phi \wedge (p_{b_1} \wedge \ldots \wedge p_{b_m} \wedge \neg p_{b'_1} \wedge \ldots \wedge \neg p_{b'_n}) \qquad (7)$$

Recall that $p_{b_1}, \ldots, p_{b_m}, p_{b'_1}, \ldots, p_{b'_n}$ are the set of atomic propositions (used by the SAT encoder) introduced for the branch edges $b_1, \ldots, b_m, b'_1, \ldots, b'_n$, respectively. Since, Φ is used to keep track of all the *unexplored path programs*, the above formula must be *unsatisfiable* if π has already been covered by a *previously explored path program*.

Analysis of a path program   The main purpose of the instrumented program $\mathcal{P}_{miss}$ was to enable static analysis on *feasible path programs*, which are iteratively explored using Algorithm 1. The primary goal of the static analysis is to compute a sound lower bound and a sound upper bound on cache misses suffered by each path program. Additionally, the static analysis computes a symbolic formula on the input variables that must be satisfied by any

all the paths resulting from the partial path condition θ belong to some explored path program. Let us assume that $\{b_1, \ldots, b_k\}$ is a common set of control flow edges that must be executed by any path satisfying the partial path condition θ. This set of control flow edges can easily be computed from the execution trace π. Assume that $p_{b_1}, \ldots, p_{b_k}$ are the respective set of edge predicates used for the control flow edges $b_1, \ldots, b_k$ in the SAT encoding of $\mathcal{P}$. The formula $\eta \equiv \Phi \wedge p_{b_1} \wedge \ldots \wedge p_{b_k}$ is *unsatisfiable* only if each program path executing the set of control flow edges $\{b_1, \ldots, b_k\}$ has

path constituting the respective path program. It is worthwhile to note that a traditional profiler cannot guarantee any bound on cache misses. Moreover, a traditional profiler computes information only for a set of representative inputs. Unlike a traditional profiler, our framework systematically partitions the input domain of a program via the exploration of feasible path programs and guarantees the bound on cache misses for each path program via static analysis.

Recall that a path program P_π is constructed from the instrumented program $\mathcal{P}_{miss}$ and a feasible execution trace π. The static analysis on a path program P_π computes a triplet $\langle cond_{P_\pi}, MinMiss_{P_\pi}, MaxMiss_{P_\pi} \rangle$ which has the following interpretation:

- $cond_{P_\pi}$: a symbolic formula on the input variables, where any feasible path in P_π must satisfy $cond_{P_\pi}$.

- $MinMiss_{P_\pi}$: minimum number of cache misses suffered by any path in the path program P_π.

- $MaxMiss_{P_\pi}$: maximum number of cache misses suffered by any path in the path program P_π.

To compute the triplet $\langle cond_{P_\pi}, MinMiss_{P_\pi}, MaxMiss_{P_\pi} \rangle$, we use standard invariant generation methods (*e.g.* polyhedra [11], symbolic execution [1] etc.). Procedure `AnalyzePathProgram` (in Algorithm 1) captures the invariant generation.

Figure 5 demonstrates a sample code and the constructed path program P_π for an execution with all zero elements of input array a. In Figure 5, $m1$ and $m2$ capture the respective memory blocks accessed by the code. For the sake of simplicity in this example, we only show the path program with the instrumentation for instruction caches. However, as discussed in Section 3, our framework can be used for both instruction and data caches. The core of path program analysis is to reason about the value of variable *miss* (as shown in Figure 5), which derives $MinMiss_{P_\pi}$ and $MaxMiss_{P_\pi}$. This in turn requires generating *invariants* involving the variable *miss*. In the example shown in Figure 5, memory blocks $m1$ and $m2$ conflict in the cache. The two loop invariants $C\_m1 \leq 1$ and $C\_m2 \leq 1$ capture the fact that both the memory blocks $m1$ and $m2$ face at most one cache conflict within the loop. These two loop invariants ensure that the true leg of both the branches $C\_m1 \geq 2$ and $C\_m2 \geq 2$ can never be executed (since both the formulae $C\_m1 \geq 2 \wedge C\_m1 \leq 1$ and $C\_m2 \geq 2 \wedge C\_m2 \leq 1$ are *unsatisfiable*). As a consequence, the value of variable *miss* can be incremented exactly twice – once at the *true* branch of *flag_m1* $== 0$ and the other at the *true* branch of *flag_m2* $== 0$. Therefore, the value of variable *miss* is bounded by $2 \leq miss \leq 2$ at the exit of the loop (irrespective of the loop bound). Such an invariant on variable *miss* captures the fact that $m1$ and $m2$ only face *cold cache misses* for *any possible execution* of P_π. The analysis also generates an invariant (on input array a) $cond_{P_\pi} \equiv a[1] \leq 0 \wedge \ldots \wedge a[X] \leq 0$, which holds over path program P_π.

Currently, our framework requires a numeric upper-bound on the inputs which directly or indirectly (via a chain of data dependencies) affect loop bounds. As a consequence, the computed invariants on cache misses are always of the form $C_1 \leq miss \leq C_2$, where both C_1 and C_2 are constants. In the presence of parametric (or symbolic) loop bounds, the computed cache miss range might be parametric in terms of the input dependent loop bounds. For the example shown in Figure 5, if the cache is a direct-mapped cache and both m_1 and m_2 map to the same cache set, such a parametric cache miss range will be of the form $2X \leq miss \leq 2X$ (considering X as an input). Lifting the numeric performance range to a parametric range is a subject of our future work.

Termination Our exploration process terminates when the SAT encoder blocks all possible path programs (*i.e.* Φ becomes *unsatisfiable*). The exploration also terminates when Φ remains *satisfi-*

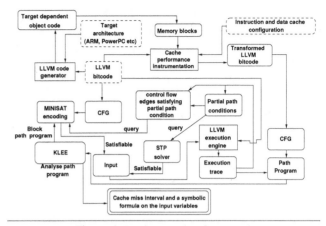

Figure 6. Implementation framework

able, but all *unexplored* path conditions are visited (*i.e. unexplored* becomes empty). Such a situation may arise in the presence of *infeasible path programs*, as we only explore *feasible path programs*.

5. Implementation

Figure 6 shows the outline of our implementation framework. We use the LLVM compiler infrastructure [2] as a baseline of our implementation. Individual benchmarks are compiled into LLVM bitcode format and their control flow graphs are extracted from the LLVM bitcode. This control flow graph is given as an input to our analysis framework. We first use the LLVM code generator to generate the object code for a specific target architecture (*e.g.* ARM, PowerPC). From the generated object code, the accessed memory blocks are extracted and they are mapped appropriately to the respective basic blocks at the LLVM bitcode level. The cache performance instrumentation is accomplished by augmenting the original control flow graph (CFG) with additional basic blocks (as explained in Section 3). Such an instrumentation accepts the set of memory blocks accessed in the target binary and a specific instruction and data cache configuration. As a result, our framework can be parameterized with respect to different target architectures and cache configurations. The execution of the test program is achieved through LLVM execution engine, from which we also collect the *basic block level execution trace* and the respective *path condition*. To manipulate and solve different path conditions, we use the *STP solver* [4]. We use the *minisat* satisfiability solver [3] to track the set of *unexplored path programs*. For analyzing a path program, any standard invariant generation method can be applied. In our current implementation, we modify LLVM-based *KLEE symbolic execution engine* [1] to generate invariants on the number of cache misses suffered by the original program (*i.e.* generating invariants on the variable *miss* as explained in Section 4.2). In general, KLEE performs a symbolic execution of the entire program. We modify the source code of KLEE to selectively analyze a path program, and thereby making a single invocation of KLEE much faster than usual. Each analysis by KLEE produces a cache miss interval and a symbolic formula on the input variables.

6. Evaluation

In this section, we shall evaluate our framework with different subject programs. Some salient features of these subject programs are listed in Table 1. Our proposed framework aims to partition the input domain with respect to cache performance. *Such a framework is mostly suitable for an application which exhibits varying*

Program	Lines of C code	Object code size (ARM)	Basic blocks
Papabench [14]	592	14240 bytes	311
Sha [15]	236	6104 bytes	77
Susan [15]	260	4172 bytes	82
JetBench [21]	766	33872 bytes	922
Nsichneu [5]	4255	49908 bytes	754

Table 1. Subject programs used for evaluation

cache performances for the same input size, but different input values. Therefore, we try to find subject programs which can potentially show varying performances for the fixed input size but different input values. Such a program should potentially have many input-dependent branches in the control flow graph. As a result, our framework will explore multiple path programs capturing the different outcomes of such input dependent branches. The characteristics of the subject programs can be summarized as follows:

- Papabench is an *unmanned aerial vehicle* (UAV) controller program which performs the navigation and stabilization tasks of an aircraft. We use the autonavigation component of Papabench due to the presence of many input dependent paths in the program. The autonavigation component goes through different control locations. The control flow for a typical execution depends on the starting position of navigation and several input signals. Therefore, the autonavigation component has the potential to exhibit varying performances with respect to different input values.

- Susan is an image processing kernel which manipulates an image matrix. The value of different image pixels are checked multiple times and the program has several control paths depending on the value of pixel.

- JetBench is a hard real-time, simulation of jet engines. Depending on the value of input flight profile data, this program performs different thermo-dynamic calculations. Therefore, we try to categorize the input flight profile data with respect to the performance of JetBench.

- Nsichneu is a petri-net simulator, which has a huge number of input dependent branches. The program simulates a petri-net along different control paths depending on the marked positions (given as an input).

- Finally, we show a program Sha which does not have any input dependent branch. The performance of Sha depends only on the input size. For such programs, we can use our framework to see the change in performance with respect to the input size.

We use our evaluation framework to answer the following crucial questions related to the performance validation of a program.

- *Performance prediction:* Given an arbitrary input, can we predict the program's cache performance with respect to the input? During the testing of an embedded software, the real execution platform may not be available. Therefore, tools and techniques to predict performance in the absence of real execution platform are crucial for embedded software.

- *Performance testing:* Can we synthesize inputs which may force the program to suffer heavy number of cache misses?

- *Performance debugging:* Can we replay some useful information to the user/compiler to pinpoint the reason of serious cache performance issues (*e.g.* cache thrashing)?

- *Design space exploration:* Can we decide the appropriate execution platform (*e.g.* cache configuration) for a particular application so that it meets certain timing guarantees?

Key result Table 2 reports a summary of our experiments. We use a 2-way associative, instruction and data cache with 16 bytes of cache line size and FIFO replacement policy. The results are reported for a 4 KB instruction and 4 KB data cache. The cache sizes are chosen in such a fashion so that they exhibit sufficient amount of conflicts in instruction and data caches. In Table 2, we also report the overall execution time of a path program. To compute the overall execution time, we add the total instruction and data cache miss penalty suffered by all the cache misses with the computation cost of all the executed instructions. Both instruction and data cache miss penalty is taken as 100 CPU cycles. We perform all experiments on an Intel i7-core processor having 8 GB of RAM and running Ubuntu 10.04 operating system. The computation time in Table 2 reports the total time taken by our framework for each subject program; including the cache performance instrumentation, path program exploration, execution of the program and path program analysis.

Due to space constraints, we cannot report the cache performance of all the path programs. However, Table 2 reports the cache miss range of maximum variation for each subject program. Four rightmost columns of Table 2 capture the *feasible path program* where the performance range (*i.e.* the interval for instruction cache miss, data cache miss and overall execution time) has maximum variation. The maximum variation in the execution time of a feasible path program is shown in the last column. For an interval $[min, max]$, the variation is computed as $\frac{max-min}{min} \times 100\%$. Note that the reported variation is reasonably short (maximum variation of 20% in Susan where the absolute numbers of cache misses have small values). As a result, we can observe that path program is a suitable abstraction to combine several paths having similar cache performances.

Currently, our framework only computes an absolute range of cache misses for all feasible path programs. It is, in general, possible that the value of cache miss depends on the bound k of some loop, where k is an input (*e.g.* input size). As a result, the computed cache miss range could be parametric in terms of such input variable k. In our current implementation, we do not handle such parametric cache miss expressions and our framework requires the bound on such input variables k.

For fixed input size, Sha does not have any input dependent program branches. Therefore, the performance of Sha is *independent* of input values and our framework produces exactly one path program for Sha (for an input size of 8 KB). Note that program Nsichneu reports *constant* cache performance for the explored (*i.e.* feasible) path programs. Similarly, Susan shows constant data cache performance for each *feasible path program*. Such constant cache performance can be generated when each explored (*i.e.* feasible) path program satisfies at least one of the following two conditions: i) the path program contains exactly one path, or ii) any path constituting the path program faces only *cold cache misses* (for all the subject programs in Table 2, cold cache miss is constant for a given path program and input size).

In the following discussion, unless otherwise stated, the reported cache miss corresponds to the *total number of cache misses*, including the number of *instruction cache misses* and *data cache misses* for the respective cache configurations.

Performance prediction Recall that the analysis of a path program p_i computes a triplet $\langle cond_{p_i}, MinMiss_{p_i}, MaxMiss_{p_i} \rangle$. $cond_{p_i}$ is a symbolic formula which captures the set of inputs along which path program p_i is reached and $MinMiss_{p_i}$ ($MaxMiss_{p_i}$) is the minimum (maximum) number of cache misses suffered by path program p_i. Assume that we have given an arbitrary input and we want to predict the performance of the program for this input. Given an arbitrary input, we can locate the path program p_i where the symbolic formula $cond_{p_i}$ is satisfied by the same input. Since we

Subject program	#partitions (#feasible path programs)	#infeasible path programs	Computation time (in seconds)	Instruction cache miss (maximum variation across any feasible path) program	Data cache miss (maximum variation across any feasible path) program	Execution time (CPU cycles) (maximum variation across any feasible path) program	Maximum variation in execution time
Papabench	20	4×10^8	158	[882,990]	[32,37]	[100851, 110279]	9.3%
Sha	1	15	20	[243,243]	[696,696]	[1130039,1130039]	0%
Susan	50	145622	163	[62,78]	[15,15]	[8109,9769]	20%
JetBench	7	2.7×10^9	250	[532,649]	[535,575]	[125003, 141213]	13%
Nsichneu	11	$> 2^{200}$	192	[9519,9519]	[196,196]	[1042732,1042732]	0%

Table 2. Path program partitioning of different subject programs. The reported cache miss range captures the *feasible path program* which exhibits *maximum variation* between the minimum and maximum number of suffered cache misses.

partition the input domain, there will be exactly one path program p_i for each such arbitrary input. The located path program p_i is also attached with its cache performance range. Therefore, our prediction will be the cache miss interval $[MinMiss_{p_i}, MaxMiss_{p_i}]$.

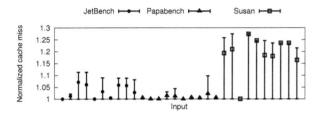

Figure 7. Cache performance prediction. The vertical bar captures the predicted cache miss interval and the point along each vertical bar captures the number of cache misses obtained by executing the program on the respective input

To check the correctness and accuracy of our prediction, we first run a subject program for a set of arbitrary inputs. For each input, we collect the number of cache misses actually suffered at the end of execution. Moreover, for each such arbitrary input, we locate the path program p_i where the symbolic formula $cond_{p_i}$ is satisfied by the same input. For each input i, we compare the three numbers – the minimum and maximum number of cache misses associated with the located path program p_i (i.e. $MinMiss_{p_i}$ and $MaxMiss_{p_i}$, respectively) and the actual number of cache misses (say $Cmiss_i$) obtained by executing the program on input i. Clearly, $MinMiss_{p_i} \leq Cmiss_i \leq MaxMiss_{p_i}$.

Figure 7 reports the result of cache performance prediction. For each input, the vertical bar captures the normalized cache miss interval $[1, \frac{MaxMiss_{p_i}}{MinMiss_{p_i}}]$ from our prediction and the point along each vertical bar captures the normalized number of cache misses $\frac{Cmiss_i}{MinMiss_{p_i}}$ after executing the program on the respective input. Figure 7 shows that we can obtain reasonably accurate prediction, as the length of the cache miss interval $[1, \frac{MaxMiss_{p_i}}{MinMiss_{p_i}}]$ is short. For Sha and Nsichneu, the cache miss range is *constant* for each path program and we always had *accurate* predictions. The results from Sha and Nsichneu are not reported in Figure 7.

Performance testing Our proposed framework has a significant usage in performance testing. Given the set of path programs produced by our framework, we can find the path program facing heavy cache misses or creating a severe performance bottleneck. Since such a path program is also associated with a symbolic formula on the input variables, we can use the SMT solver to generate a concrete input from this symbolic formula. Such performance stressing, concrete test inputs can be reported to the developer.

For Nsichneu, we found that two path programs experience cache misses several magnitudes (more than 10 times) higher than

the other path programs. Similarly, for Papabench, we found that the path program suffering from heaviest cache misses satisfies an input value 2. Using our framework, we can quickly locate such performance stressing path programs (as shown in Table 2, there are only 11 and 20 path programs for Nsichneu and Papabench, respectively) and generate a concrete test input from the respective symbolic formula on the input variables.

Different path programs of Susan also produce diverse cache performances (with the lowest performing path program having 10 magnitudes higher cache misses than the highest performing path program). Susan manipulates a character matrix of a fixed size. It is impossible to test Susan for all such matrices. However, from the set of explored path programs, we can observe the symbolic formulae on the input matrices which stress the execution of Susan towards performance loss. Such observation will greatly help in the performance testing of Susan, as we can pick up the set of appropriate test cases from a representative testing pool.

Performance debugging In the preceding, we have discussed the use of our framework to generate performance stressing test cases. Along with performance stressing test cases, it is also useful to report the root cause of performance loss. Since we focus on cache performance, such a reporting of root cause needs to highlight the specific program locations/data accesses which are suffering from heavy cache misses.

We can easily tune our basic framework to highlight the potential root causes of performance loss. Instead of generating bound on the overall cache miss count, we can generate bound on the cache misses suffered at each cache set. Let us assume $miss_i$ captures the range of cache misses suffered at cache set i. By checking the value of each $miss_i$, we can locate the memory blocks mapped to cache set i and subsequently, trace the memory blocks back to the source code level statements.

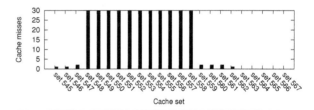

Figure 8. Cache performance debugging

Figure 8 captures a sample output for such modification. We have mentioned before that two path programs of Nsichneu suffer several magnitudes higher cache misses than the other path programs. Figure 8 shows a snapshot of the cache misses suffered by different cache sets. The snapshot is generated in such a fashion that it exhibits a few (but not all) cache sets suffering from relatively high cache misses. Since the total number of such cache sets (*i.e.* the cache sets suffering from relatively high cache misses) may be arbitrarily high, the total number of cache misses experienced by the program is several magnitudes higher than the number of cache misses suffered by a single cache set. It is worthwhile to note that a traditional profiler may not able to highlight the root causes of such cache performance issues. A traditional profiler relies on a few training runs of a program. If the training runs do not go through the performance stressing path programs, the root causes of such cache performance issues will remain unknown. The cache size for our experiments (*i.e.* to generate Figure 8) is chosen such that there are no *capacity* misses. We can observe that a few cache sets (set 548-558) suffer relatively high cache misses, whereas other cache sets suffer a small number of cache misses (*e.g.* set 559-562) or zero cache misses (*e.g.* set 563-567). This irregularity of cache misses often appear due to the improper code/data layout in the program. We observed that the number of memory blocks mapped to any cache set starting from 548 to 558 is more than the associativity of the cache. Such memory blocks are accessed inside a loop, introducing *cache thrashing*. The information generated by our framework can be replayed back to a compiler. The compiler can utilize such information for optimizations such as *cache locking* (to selectively lock memory blocks in the cache and avoid cache thrashing) and *code positioning* (changing the layout of code/data to avoid cache thrashing).

Design space exploration Finally we show the application of our framework to choose an appropriate execution platform, specifically, the right cache configuration. Figure 9 shows the sensitivity of cache misses (we plot the maximum cache miss suffered over all the path programs) for two of our subject programs with respect to different cache configurations and target architectures. Since our framework can be parameterized with respect to cache configuration, we can produce such sensitivity graph by running the cache performance spectrum module multiple times. Figure 9 shows that an 1-way, 16 KB (1-way, 8 KB) cache should be chosen for Papabench targeting PowerPC (ARM), as the cache miss stabilizes beyond the particular cache configuration. In a similar fashion, a 4-way, 64 KB cache is appropriate for program Nsichneu. Note that a traditional profiler may not be able to find a training input to stress the execution of the program towards maximum cache misses. As a result, we might end up choosing an inappropriate cache using a traditional profiler. This is due to the reason that the maximum number of cache misses may not stabilize using the cache configuration chosen by a traditional profiler.

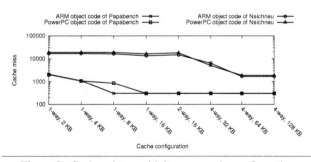

Figure 9. Cache miss sensitivity w.r.t. cache configuration

The performance of Sha only depends on the input size. Figure 10 shows the instruction and data cache miss sensitivity suffered by Sha for a direct-mapped, 1 KB cache. With respect to the input data size, we observe an exponential growth in the number of cache misses for a direct-mapped, 1 KB cache. Such an exponential growth in cache misses clearly captures a *cache thrashing*

behaviour. Therefore, we can conclude that 1 KB cache is inappropriate for Sha. The instruction cache thrashing entirely disappears when using a two-way, 8 KB cache (as also evidenced by Figure 10). The growth in data cache misses with respect to input data size does not disappear with a two-way, 8 KB cache. However, we investigated that such growths in data cache misses are merely due to the increased *cold data cache misses* for increased input size. Therefore, we can conclude that a two-way, 8 KB cache can be used for Sha without an appreciable loss of performance.

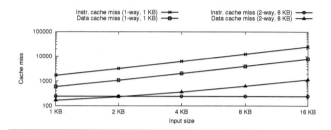

Figure 10. Cache miss sensitivity w.r.t. input size

7. Related work

Work on the performance validation of embedded software was started two decades ago. Previous approaches were mainly based on *static analysis*. Analysis of cache performance has been done, among others, in [23] via abstract interpretation. Recently, such abstract interpretation based cache analysis has been improved by a gradual and controlled used of model checking in [9]. Such analyses were performed on the entire program for computing its *worst case execution time* (WCET). On the other hand, our approach is orthogonal to these approaches. We partition the input domain of a program in terms of different path programs. Moreover, our partitioning strategy is dynamic in nature. We only explore a partition if there exists some feasible path inside it. A different work [20] uses an evolutionary algorithm to explore program paths for performance testing. However, [20] does not partition the input domain and it also does not guarantee to explore the entire input domain. The work in [12] employs the idea of pattern recognition to predict the whole program locality based on a few training runs of the program. Unlike our approach, the technique proposed in [12] does not guarantee to explore the entire input domain. Moreover, the technique proposed in [12] predicts program performance for a given input based on the past history/training-set (and the prediction may be wrong). On the other hand, as our approach is based on program analysis, we can always predict a *safe* lower bound and upper bound of performance for each of the explored partition.

Our idea is inspired by the recent advances in *program path exploration* and *satisfiability modulo theory* (SMT). *Directed* test generation [17] has made significant improvement over random testing in the past few years. Such test strategies attempt to cover *program paths* for testing. On the other hand, we are interested in building the performance footprint of the entire program. As there might be an unbounded number of paths in a program, a path-based search procedure is, in general, infeasible to build a performance footprint of the entire program. A recent work [22] has proposed to merge several paths for path-based testing. Two paths are merged if they have the same input-output relationship. However, our goal is *different* - we want to merge different paths having similar performance rather than merging paths with the same output expression.

In recent times, the idea of path program has been applied in [16] for path-sensitive functional verification. Our approach differs in two key aspects from this work: first, our goal is validating the performance and secondly, the path program in our framework is constructed from an execution trace rather than from the static control flow graph. Therefore, we only analyze a path program that has at least one feasible execution.

The work in [18] proposes to find the computational complexity of a program automatically. Similarly, [8] proposes a new approach to automatically find test inputs for the worst-case computational complexity. Our work differs from several aspects from these two previous works: first, our notion of performance is based on the execution time rather than computational complexity. Secondly, the primary goal of our framework is to build a performance signature of the entire program by partitioning its input domain. Of course, such a partitioning can also be used to generate test inputs for worst-case performance, as evidenced by our experiments.

Several techniques for program profiling have been studied in the past few decades (such as [7, 19], among others). Such traditional profiling techniques can be used to analyze (compressed) execution traces (*e.g.* in [19]) for deriving *program hotspots*. In contrast to our approach, profiling techniques do not guarantee to cover the entire input domain, instead such profiling techniques rely on training inputs. Moreover, our approach can act as a complementary to compute the set of relevant inputs for program profiling.

Recent works [10, 24] have proposed to extend the traditional profiling technique by determining an empirical cost function. Such a cost function is found automatically and it captures an approximate cost of the program with respect to different inputs (and in particular, with respect to different input sizes). Since the approaches in [10, 24] are based on a few training runs of the program, they can only capture an approximate cost of the program for a fixed input size. On the other hand, since our approach is based on program analysis, we can provide a *sound* lower and upper bound of cache performance. Moreover, the work of [10, 24] do not guarantee to capture the performance signature of the entire program. Our approach does the same by partitioning the input domain, in the form of representative path programs.

There has been some recent work on detecting performance bugs in distributed systems [13]. Such work systematically generates random simulations to detect performance bugs. However, as the testing is based on random simulations, this approach cannot guarantee to build any performance footprint of the *entire* program.

8. Discussion

Summary In this paper, we have proposed an approach to partition the input domain of a program based on cache performance. Our partitioning is based on exploring feasible path programs. As evidenced by our experimental results, the path program abstraction is suitable for a variety of purposes, such as performance debugging (*e.g.* to detect *cache thrashing*), performance prediction and performance testing. Moreover, we have shown that our proposed framework can be used to decide an appropriate cache configuration for an application.

Limitations Our technique is most suitable for the programs which exhibit varying cache performances on different input values. Since our approach computes a sound lower and upper bound of cache misses by statically analyzing each path program, it has the general limitations faced by any static analysis technique. Such limitations include the handling of dynamic memory allocations and complex pointer aliasing. Besides, in our current implementation, the static analysis of path programs accounts to majority of overhead. However, we believe that we can use several matured and efficient techniques for invariant generations to reduce such overhead in future.

Future work Our work can be extended in several directions. In this paper, we have focused on cache miss metric. For the set of subject programs used in our evaluation, the number of cache misses dominates the performance. In future, we plan to study other performance metrics apart from the cache miss metric. Besides, our framework currently builds the cache performance signature for the uninterrupted execution of a single program. In the presence of multi-tasking, a high priority task and external interrupts may affect the cache content, leading to additional cache misses. We plan to extend our framework for multi-tasking systems in future.

Acknowledgements

We thank the anonymous reviewers for their comments and feedback. This work was partially supported by A*STAR Public Sector Funding Project Number 1121202007 - "Scalable Timing Analysis Methods for Embedded Software".

References

[1] KLEE Symbolic Virtual Machine. http://klee.llvm.org/.

[2] LLVM compiler infrastructure. http://llvm.org/.

[3] MINISAT solver. http://minisat.se/Main.html.

[4] STP Constraint Solver. http://sites.google.com/site/stpfastprover/.

[5] WCET benchmarks. http://www.mrtc.mdh.se/projects/wcet/benchmarks.html.

[6] G. Balakrishnan and T. W. Reps. Analyzing memory accesses in x86 executables. In *CC*, 2004.

[7] T. Ball and J. R. Larus. Efficient path profiling. In *MICRO*, 1996.

[8] J. Burnim, S. Juvekar, and K. Sen. WISE: Automated test generation for worst-case complexity. In *ICSE*, 2009.

[9] S. Chattopadhyay and A. Roychoudhury. Scalable and precise refinement of cache timing analysis via model checking. In *RTSS*, 2011.

[10] E. Coppa, C. Demetrescu, and I. Finocchi. Input-sensitive profiling. In *PLDI*, 2012.

[11] P. Cousot and N. Halbwachs. Automatic discovery of linear restraints among variables of a program. In *POPL*, 1978.

[12] C. Ding and Y. Zhong. Predicting whole-program locality through reuse distance analysis. In *PLDI*, 2003.

[13] C. Killian et al. Finding latent performance bugs in systems implementations. In *FSE*, 2010.

[14] F. Nemer et al. Papabench: a free real-time benchmark. In *WCET Workshop*, 2006.

[15] M. R. Guthaus et al. Mibench: A free, commercially representative embedded benchmark suite. In *WWC-4. 2001 IEEE International Workshop*, 2001.

[16] W. R. Harris et al. Program analysis via satisfiability modulo path programs. In *POPL*, 2010.

[17] P. Godefroid, N. Klarlund, and K. Sen. DART: directed automated random testing. In *PLDI*, 2005.

[18] S. Gulwani, K. K. Mehra, and T. M. Chilimbi. SPEED: precise and efficient static estimation of program computational complexity. In *POPL*, 2009.

[19] J. R. Larus. Whole program paths. In *PLDI*, 1999.

[20] P. Puschner and R. Nossal. Testing the results of static worst-case execution-time analysis. In *RTSS*, 1998.

[21] M. Y. Qadri, D. Matichard, and K. D. McDonald-Maier. JetBench: An open source real-time multiprocessor benchmark. In *ARCS*, 2010.

[22] D. Qi, H. D. T. Nguyen, and A. Roychoudhury. Path exploration based on symbolic output. In *FSE*, 2011.

[23] H. Theiling, C. Ferdinand, and R. Wilhelm. Fast and precise WCET prediction by separated cache and path analyses. *Real-Time Systems*, 18(2/3), 2000.

[24] D. Zaparanuks and M. Hauswirth. Algorithmic profiling. In *PLDI*, 2012.

Non-Intrusive Program Tracing and Debugging of Deployed Embedded Systems Through Side-Channel Analysis

Carlos Moreno

University of Waterloo

cmoreno@uwaterloo.ca

Sebastian Fischmeister

University of Waterloo

sfischme@uwaterloo.ca

M. Anwar Hasan

University of Waterloo

ahasan@uwaterloo.ca

Abstract

One of the hardest aspects of embedded software development is that of debugging, especially when faulty behavior is observed at the production or deployment stage. Non-intrusive observation of the system's behavior is often insufficient to infer the cause of the problem and identify and fix the bug. In this work, we present a novel approach for non-intrusive program tracing aimed at assisting developers in the task of debugging embedded systems at deployment or production stage, where standard debugging tools are usually no longer available. The technique is rooted in cryptography, in particular the area of side-channel attacks. Our proposed technique expands the scope of these cryptographic techniques so that we recover the sequence of operations from power consumption observations (power traces). To this end, we use digital signal processing techniques (in particular, spectral analysis) combined with pattern recognition techniques to determine blocks of source code being executed given the observed power trace. One of the important highlights of our contribution is the fact that the system works on a standard PC, capturing the power traces through the recording input of the sound card. Experimental results are presented and confirm that the approach is viable.

Categories and Subject Descriptors D.2.5 [*Software Engineering*]: Testing and Debugging—Tracing

General Terms Theory, Algorithms, Experimentation

Keywords Embedded systems; debugging; tracing; side-channel analysis; simple power analysis

1. Introduction

Debugging is one of the hardest aspects of embedded software development. The task is especially hard when the faulty behavior is observed at the production or deployment stage, when the software no longer has any auxiliary components dedicated to assist in the debugging task [3]. For systems at this stage of the development cycle, non-intrusive observation of the system's behavior is likely the only available technique — developers are no longer allowed to modify the source code, or even re-compile to include or activate the debugging tools. Moreover, if we need to restart the device to enable any available debugging techniques, we may not be able to

reproduce the faulty behavior that the device was exhibiting. Without these debugging tools usually available in earlier phases of development, developers may be limited to non-intrusive observation, which often provides insufficient information to infer the cause of the problem and identify and fix the bug.

In this work, we present a novel approach for non-intrusive debugging of deployed embedded systems. The system can be observed and an output indicating the sequence of executed code is produced, without having to modify anything in the target system or even restart it. The technique is rooted in cryptography, in particular the area of side-channel attacks [11, 12]. These types of cryptographic attacks take advantage of the relationship between the instructions that a processor is executing and the data it is working with, and observable side-effects such as timing of computations (timing attacks), power consumption (power analysis), or electromagnetic emissions (EM analysis) to obtain the secret data (typically an encryption key). The techniques, as they exist, are not directly applicable to the debugging of embedded software, since they focus on obtaining specific pieces of secret data embedded in the device (and inaccessible through "legitimate" means), and they typically require interaction and direct control over what the target device is executing.

On the other hand, the goal when tracing and debugging a deployed embedded system is to analyze an operating device for which we have observed a faulty behavior, and obtain information allowing us to identify and fix the bug. It may be essential that we allow the device to continue its operation without restarting it or in any way exerting control over what the device is doing; otherwise, we could lead the device to a state where we may not be able to reproduce the faulty behavior.

As an additional aspect in terms of motivation, this tracing system could be used for monitoring as an *intrusion detection system* (IDS) [14]. In the wake of threats like Stuxnet [13], one should consider adapting tools like IDSs, classically viewed as applicable to servers and networks, to embedded systems as well. Unlike a software-based IDS embedded in the device, our approach could lead to a tamper-proof IDS, given that the monitoring system is physically independent of the device and the software running in it; thus, any malware that tampers with the functionality of the device will not be able to tamper with the IDS and as a consequence, any anomaly in the device's behavior will most likely be detected.

Our proposed technique focuses on power consumption (though the underlying techniques are in principle applicable to EM emissions). A current sensing shunt resistor is placed in series with the Power-In signal going to the Microcontroller Unit (MCU),[1] producing a voltage proportional to the current being consumed. The

---

[1] Though the technique is applicable to both CPUs and MCUs, we use MCU throughout the paper, to simplify the text, and also since it is the more likely target for our technique.

resistor is selected to produce a voltage in the range of a few millivolts, thus not affecting the operation of the device. Our technique expands the scope of the cryptographic techniques so that we recover the sequence of operations executed by a processor, as opposed to simply one piece of data accessed during a particular operation of the device. To this end, we use digital signal processing techniques (in particular, spectral analysis) to extract *features* of the signal (the power trace) that allow us to match sections of the power trace against fragments of the source code through the use of statistical pattern recognition techniques [21]. It is reasonably likely that this information would be valuable for the purpose of identifying and fixing the bug. We observe that in the context of embedded systems, this relationship between operations being executed and power consumption has been used for the purpose of estimating or minimizing power consumption, obtaining power consumption as a function of the executed instructions. Going in the other direction may be seen as a far bigger challenge, for at least two reasons: (1) the operation being executed is not uniquely determined as a function of the power consumption; thus, information about the progression of power consumption through an interval of time may be needed, combined with statistical processing; and (2) we need to get around the "polluting" effect of the data the processor is working with (i.e., the same operation with different data produces a different amount of power consumption) and the measurement noise.

One of the important highlights of our contribution is the fact that the system works on a standard personal computer (PC), capturing the power traces through the recording input of the sound card — side-channel analysis techniques usually rely on digital oscilloscopes or other expensive and bulky pieces of equipment. A standard, reasonably high-quality sound card (24-bits, 192kHz sampling rate, nowadays available at prices below $200) suffices to make the system work on a wide range of microprocessors and microcontroller units. Given the typical computing power of today's mainstream PCs, with this setup, we claim that on-the-fly processing is within reach for a wide range of target devices. Of course, the technique is suitable for use with a digital oscilloscope; indeed, for processors with high clock frequencies, higher sampling rates will be required for the system to work, most likely without on-the-fly processing, depending on the clock frequency and architectural aspects of the target device such as pipeline depth, memory management unit (MMU), and cache memory [9].

Experimental results confirm the validity of our technique and its practical aspects: we used an Atmel MCU, AVR Atmega2560 [1] as the target device (8-bit MCU running at 1MHz) and we included a subset of the MiBench suite [6] as a set of tasks representative of typical embedded software (at least typical for certain applications areas). The technique was implemented on a mainstream PC with an HT Omega Claro+ sound card [10], which at the time of purchase the cost was around $150, and as the results show, the setup is viable for on-the-fly processing obtaining accurate results.

The remaining of this paper is organized as follows: in Section 2 we briefly review the notions from side-channel analysis as well as the digital signal processing techniques and the statistical pattern recognition techniques used. Section 3 presents our proposed technique. Section 4 describes the experimental setup used to verify the validity and applicability of our approach, with Section 5 presenting the results. A brief discussion, future work and concluding remarks follow, in sections 6 and 7.

2. Background

Our work draws upon background from different areas: side-channel analysis, pattern recognition, and digital signal processing. We briefly review some of the basic notions and mathematical background from these areas.

2.1 Side-Channel Attacks and Simple Power Analysis

Side-channel analysis plays an important role in the area of embedded systems security. Mobile, hand-held, and many other types of embedded devices increasingly make use of cryptographic techniques, in particular public-key cryptography and elliptic-curve cryptography (ECC), where exponentiation with large *secret* exponents is one of the central operations on which the security of the system relies (we refer the reader to [16] or [8] for more details).

Paul Kocher pioneered the field of side-channel analysis, showing that even though the cryptographic algorithms are secure from a mathematical standpoint, *implementations* of such algorithms may be vulnerable to attacks that use side-effects of the computation — side-effects that can be observed by an attacker with physical access to the device [11, 12].

Of interest to us is power analysis, in particular simple power analysis (SPA), where the relationship between what the processor is executing at a given time and the power consumption at that time is exploited to recover the secret exponent with a single power trace during the execution of the exponentiation. Many countermeasures, as well as different encryption techniques and different attacks exist; we omit a more detailed description since this is beyond the scope of this work. The interested reader may consult [18] for a more in-depth description as well as several of the existing countermeasures.

We borrow and expand upon this idea of using the relationship between computation and power consumption to determine what the processor is doing given an observation of power consumption (a power trace). Our technique is more general (and thus, requires additional, novel approaches to processing the power trace) in that side-channel attacks focus on recovering specific pieces of data, and some of the more advanced side-channel attack techniques require that the attacker exert control over what the device is doing. In our case, however, it is essential that we observe what a faulty device is doing without disrupting it, to avoid the possibility of leading the device to a state where we are unable to reproduce the faulty behavior.

Though template attacks [2] use a technique that is somewhat closer to our approach, there is still a fundamental difference in that they use pattern matching for the noise characteristics, relying on the *diffusion* property of encryption techniques, making it a cryptography-specific approach.

2.2 Statistical Pattern Recognition

At the heart of our proposed technique are elements from the field of pattern recognition, since our goal is to *classify* a given segment of execution as an instance of one of the possible fragments of source code according to a database, given noisy observations that in principle provide enough statistical information to determine the most likely fragment of code that produced such observation [21]. We notice that the set of all possible fragments of code being executed under normal conditions is known with certainty — since we use our technique for tracing and debugging, we can safely assume that the source will be accessible.

Since we do not count on an analytic model for the probability distribution, we can resort to techniques based on databases of *training samples*, for which the classification is known with certainty. These training samples are in principle a set of values drawn from the probability distribution for the process in question. Thus, they should be representative of the probability distribution of the process. The task of the classification system is described as follows: Let $\mathbf{X}$ be a random variable corresponding to a *feature vector* with features from a given sample associated with an unknown class C from a set of Q possible classes $\mathcal{C} = \{C_1, C_2, \cdots, C_Q\}$. The task of the pattern recognition system is that of determining the class C to which the feature vector $\mathbf{X}$ corresponds with highest a posteriori probability:

$$C = \arg \max_{C_k \in \mathcal{C}} \{\Pr\{C \mid \mathbf{X}\}\} \qquad (1)$$

Among the common techniques used to achieve this goal are Linear Discriminant Functions (LDF) and Nearest Neighbors. With LDFs, the training phase of the system collects a database of S *labelled* samples $\{\mathbf{X}_1, \mathbf{X}_2, \cdots, \mathbf{X}_S\}$ of feature vectors (the label being the class C to which the sample is *known* to correspond). For each class C, we compute the sample average or centroid $\overline{\mathbf{C}}$ as

$$\overline{\mathbf{C}} = \frac{1}{S} \sum_{\mathbf{X}_i \in C_k} \mathbf{X}_i \qquad (2)$$

where S is the number of training samples labelled as C.

In the detection or classification phase, a given feature vector $\mathbf{X}$ is associated to the class C that corresponds to the nearest centroid (usually Euclidean distance in the multi-dimensional feature space is used):

$$C = \arg \min_{C_k \in \mathcal{C}} \{\| \mathbf{X} - \overline{\mathbf{C}} \|\} \qquad (3)$$

The LDF corresponds to a hyperplane orthogonal to the line between the two centroids and intersecting that line at the point equidistant from the centroids, providing an efficient implementation mechanism.

For the Nearest Neighbor (NN) rule, the classification phase associates a given feature vector $\mathbf{X}$ to the class of its nearest neighbor among all training samples:

$$C = C_I \text{ with } I = \arg \min_{1 \leqslant i \leqslant S} \{\| \mathbf{X} - \mathbf{X}_i \|\} \qquad (4)$$

The k-Nearest Neighbors (k-NN) rule [21] provides a higher level of robustness with respect to noise in the measured features. Given a feature vector $\mathbf{X}$, we obtain the k nearest neighbors among all training samples, and the classification is done by majority vote among the k labels of these nearest neighbors. That is, if the k nearest training samples have labels $\{C_{n_1}, C_{n_2}, \cdots, C_{n_k}\}$, then feature vector $\mathbf{X}$ is associated to class C given by

$$C = C_I \text{ with } I = \arg \max_n \left\{ \sum_{\substack{i=1 \\ n_i = n}} 1 \right\} \qquad (5)$$

2.3 Spectral Analysis of Digital Signals

One of the fundamental concepts when applying spectral analysis to digital signals is that of the Discrete Fourier Transform (DFT). Given a discrete-time signal $\mathbf{x}$ of finite duration, represented by a sequence of N real values $\mathbf{x} = \{x_0, x_1, \cdots, x_{N-1}\}$, its DFT $\mathcal{X}$ [19] is given by the sequence of N complex values $\mathcal{X} = \{\mathcal{X}_0, \mathcal{X}_1, \cdots, \mathcal{X}_{N-1}\}$, where each $\mathcal{X}$ is given by

$$\mathcal{X} = \sum_{n=0}^{N-1} x_n \, e^{-j \frac{2\pi k n}{N}} \qquad (6)$$

where j denotes the imaginary unit [2] (i.e., $j^2 = -1$)

A straightforward implementation clearly takes $O(N^2)$ time to compute the DFT of a sequence of N values. In practice, Fast Fourier Transform (FFT) is normally used, being an efficient algorithm to compute the DFT. FFT exploits the symmetry in the

---

[2] We use the standard "electrical engineering" notation j for the imaginary unit, to avoid the confusion of i with the standard symbol used to denote electrical current or intensity.

DFT to implement an in-place divide-and-conquer [4] algorithm and obtain the DFT in $O(N \log N)$ time.

For our system, we used the libfftw [5] implementation, as it is, to the best of our knowledge, a correct and very efficient FFT implementation.

3. Our Proposed Technique

As briefly described in Section 1, our proposed technique is centered around the idea of non-intrusively measuring power consumption as a function of time (i.e., capturing power traces), and use the relationship between what the processor is executing and the power consumption, combined with statistical processing to determine the sequence of instructions that were executed, thus assisting in the debugging process. To this end, a current-sensing shunt resistor is placed in series with the Power-In line going to the MCU, so that a voltage proportional to the power consumption is produced. This shunt resistor is selected to produce a voltage in the order of a few millivolts, thus not disrupting the functionality of the MCU. This voltage is then captured through the Line input of a sound card, as shown in Figure 1.

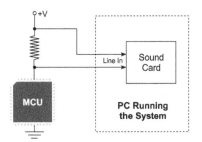

Figure 1. Simplified Diagram of our System.

The technique is centered around the idea of identifying fragments of code, corresponding to segments of the power trace. These fragments need to be sufficiently long so that: (1) there is a large enough amount of actions happening at the circuitry level to create a distinctive profile of power consumption. As an example, assigning a variable is unlikely to be distinguishable from any other operation involving memory, or even from a portion of some other action, such as fetching an instruction, or the additional memory access for instructions with immediate operands; and (2) so that the signal (in our setup, produced by an MCU running at 1MHz) can be sampled by a sound card at lower sampling frequency (in our setup, the sampling rate was 96kHz) and be able to extract meaningful information from it.

In this work, which is the initial phase of a longer project (we discuss future work in Section 6), we decided to use whole functions as the fragments of code to be considered (with only one exception, as will be discussed in Section 4 when describing our experimental setup). This decision was somewhat ad hoc, mainly related to simplifying the system in the context of a study of the feasibility of the technique. We do discuss an alternative approach and its potential benefits in Section 6.

The pattern recognition system then extracts features from these segments of the power trace, and uses one of the classification techniques described in Section 2.2. We tried and evaluated several classification techniques: nearest centroid techniques using LDFs and nearest neighbors techniques. We observed a much better classification performance when using the k-NN technique. We believe that the main factor is the fact that a function can do alternative things depending on the input data—and in general, a given fragment of code could do different things depending on the data it is working with. This leads to different execution times for different instances of the same function, and in general, it may lead to feature vectors that tend to be spread in the feature space, making the technique based on centroids less effective. For the k-NN rule, we tried values between 3 and 100 for k, obtaining best results with $k = 5$ for individual classification and $k = 21$ for continuous classification (we discuss this distinction in Section 4 as part of the description of our experimental setup). Notice that the use of techniques such as cross-validation [21] was not really necessary in our case, since additionally to the training set, we have the test set to evaluate the performance, and for that set the correct classification for each sample is known a priori.

One of the difficulties in our scenario is that the processing for the classification needs to be done in a continuous way, and it is the system's responsibility to achieve synchronization with the fragments of code to detect. That is, the system is not given a power trace with the assurance that it is the power trace for one of the fragments of code. Instead, the system is given a single power trace that extends indefinitely (in any case, as long as the system is running), and it has to apply the pattern recognition technique for variable starting position and length of the sequences to classify. As an example to illustrate the difficulties arising from this constraint, we can not use the length of the power trace as one of the features to extract — if we could, then this would provide a very relevant piece of information that even alone would give a very high probability of correct classification (since we could always select fragments of code that execute with distinct durations).

The starting point of the fragment is mainly a problem when the system starts up and has to synchronize to the execution; after that, then having recognized/classified a given section of the power trace provides information of where that fragment ends, so the starting point for the next item to be classified is then known, even though adjustments may be necessary to compensate for "noisy" or incorrect outcomes from the previous segments (e.g., a segment that was in reality L samples long may have been detected as being L' samples long). This will be discussed in more detail in Section 4. The system has to try various lengths and see which one gives the closest match with training samples from the database.

When deciding what parameters to use as features to be extracted from the entities (in our case, the power traces), there is often a bit of heuristics and intuition involved, especially when there is no analytic or otherwise simple description of a PDF with "nice" characteristics. To evaluate how good this feature set is, the rate of correct classifications does provide a quantitative measure. In particular, it does implicitly account for the distance between elements of different classes and how spread the PDF is. Misclassifications occur when elements are not far apart given the spread nature of the PDF; thus, the rate of correct classifications tells us how good this feature set is for the purpose of the classification process.

In our case, we decided to use spectral information — logarithmic magnitude and phase — as the feature vector. The intuition on why spectral information may give useful *and robust* information to identify the power trace as corresponding to one of the given fragments of code is based mainly on the following two aspects:

- Getting around issues of alignment — spectral contents are similar even when the signal or portions of the signal are shifted. Thus, for different instances of the same function, prominent portions of the code may still be common to all other traces, but located at different points in the trace (as the result of conditional execution affected by the input data).

- Variations due to "disrupting" factors in the system (such as noise or artefacts that occur due to the mechanism of leakage to the side-channel or the measurement) tend to produce higher deviations in the signal than in its spectrum, making the latter a more robust tool to identify a given power trace. In any case,

the deviations in the spectrum tend to have simpler patterns, making it easier to extract the identifying features from spectral information than directly from the signal.

One additional difficulty, for which we resorted to a heuristic approach as our adopted solution, comes from the fact that we use the DFT of the trace directly as the feature vector; that is, each of the N elements of the DFT (more precisely, its complex logarithm, which directly provides logarithmic magnitude and phase) corresponds to one of the coordinates (or one of the dimensions) in the N-dimensional feature space. However, since different traces have different lengths, then we do not have a fixed value of N. That is, computing and comparing Euclidean distances in the feature space poses a challenge. This was an additional issue that contributed to our decision to use k-NN instead of the nearest centroid classification technique, which is not directly suitable for variable-size fragments. We attempted to solve this by computing spectra at a fixed size through zero-padding to obtain an interpolated version of the spectrum at this higher resolution; this proved to be computationally expensive, in addition to exhibiting poor performance compared to the k-NN rule, as already mentioned.

Our heuristic includes two aspects: First, when given a trace and a starting point, we try all of the lengths present in the training database. That is, when looking for the nearest neighbors among the training samples, for each sample from the database, we take its length and consider the segment of the trace that matches that length, so that the distance can be evaluated. This is also consistent with the idea that we need to try different lengths, since we are only given the starting point, but the system needs to determine the length of the fragment as part of the task of identifying it.

The second aspect is that, given the detail mentioned above, it is clear that comparing distances for pairs of traces of one length with distances for pairs of traces of a different length becomes an issue. To get around this, we used the notion of a *normalized* distance, where we normalize with respect to the number of dimensions. As an example, if we have two tridimensional vectors, say

$$\mathbf{u_1} = (x_1, x_2, x_3)$$
$$\mathbf{u_2} = (x_1 + \delta, x_2 + \delta, x_3 + \delta)$$

then we get [3]

$$|\mathbf{u_2} - \mathbf{u_1}|^2 = 3\delta^2$$

Our intuition is that for two, say, 5-dimensional vectors

$$\mathbf{v_1} = (y_1, y_2, y_3, y_4, y_5)$$
$$\mathbf{v_2} = (y_1 + \delta, y_2 + \delta, y_3 + \delta, y_4 + \delta, y_5 + \delta)$$

the distance, in the context of comparing which of the two pairs are closer, should be the same, since each of the coordinates, corresponding to one descriptive feature, are equally apart. However, a direct Euclidean distance computation for this case gives us $|\mathbf{v_2} - \mathbf{v_1}|^2 = 5\,\delta^2$

Thus, to avoid the nearest neighbors selection to be biased towards the shorter traces, we need to normalize by computing the *square distance per dimension*. Also related to this issue of traces with different lengths: a longer trace may be at a disadvantage if sub-sections of it provide a sufficiently good match to other, shorter traces. We observed that this was the case for the set of MiBench functions that we used. Two different approaches were considered: (1) using an adjustment factor to favor longer traces when otherwise approximately equally close matches; and (2) using an adjustment factor to favor matches at the "nominal" position as determined by the classification at the previous iteration. We tried both approaches, and (2) had the severe adverse effect

---

[3] We use square distance since this is the common approach used when implementing NN rules.

of reducing the ability to maintain synchronization with the trace, especially resynchronizing after a misclassification.

Putting all the pieces together, we define our distance metric as follows: given a trace $\mathbf{x}$ of length N, with DFT $\mathcal{X}$, the associated feature vector is given by

$$\mathbf{X} = \{\mathrm{Log}\ \mathcal{X}_0, \mathrm{Log}\ \mathcal{X}_1, \cdots, \mathrm{Log}\ \mathcal{X}_{N-1}\} \tag{7}$$

where $\mathrm{Log}(\cdot)$ denotes the complex logarithm function. With this, the distance between N-dimensional feature vectors $\mathbf{X}$ and $\mathbf{Y}$ is given by

$$\|\mathbf{X} - \mathbf{Y}\| = \frac{1}{N} \sum_{=0}^{N-1} |X - Y|^2 \tag{8}$$

where X and Y are the entries in the feature vectors, corresponding to the complex log of the DFT entries.

4. Experimental Setup

This phase of our work consists of two experiments. In the first experiment we evaluate the effectiveness of the pattern recognition system by classifying power traces of known fragments of code and determining the success rate or *precision* (the fraction of power traces that were classified correctly). That is, we test detection of the various fragments of code in isolation, and evaluate the performance of the classification system. To isolate the trace corresponding to the exact time interval of execution, we use markers which are actions known to have high power consumption and thus produce a prominent pulse in the trace. This is one of many possible approaches, and we chose it for our experiments due to its simplicity. Given our STK600 setup, we used the LEDs for this purpose. Figure 2 illustrates these steps.[4]

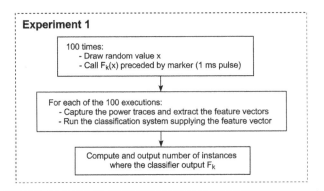

Figure 2. Experiment 1 – Classifier Performance.

In the second experiment, we execute a sequence of function calls (each function being one of the fragments of code for the pattern recognition system) and have the system determine the sequence of functions that was executed, with the power trace as its only input. Figure 3 shows the details. The first experiment tests the building blocks, the basic operations of the system, while the second experiment aims at modeling the operation of an eventual practical implementation of our proposed technique.

For the second experiment, the classification system tries adjusting the starting position to help resynchronizing in the cases where an incorrect classification occurs. That is, given a classification at iteration n, the starting position for the trace segment at iteration $n + 1$ is determined by the length of the classified trace. However, if the classification at iteration n was incorrect, the starting position for iteration $n + 1$ may be incorrect. Trying starting positions in an

interval around this "nominal" starting position allows the system to reestablish synchronization after a misclassification occurs. This will be shown in Section 5.2, where we show the experimental results. For more details, the reader can consult [17] (Chapter 7 and appendices, where source code for the classification programs is shown).

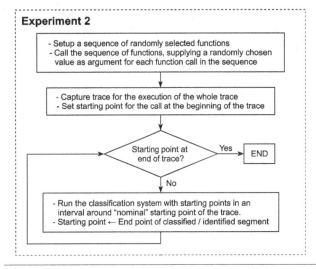

Figure 3. Experiment 2 – "Online" operation.

Notice that for continuous operation, the system could consider the fact that the sequence of fragments is not arbitrary, and classification at a certain point can be narrowed down according to the control-flow graph (CFG) obtained from the source code. In this initial phase of the project, we did not include this aspect, and we will discuss it more in detail in sections 5 and 6.

Both experiments rely on the training phase of the classification system — thus, in this initial step we execute each of the functions S_c times, where S_c corresponds to the number of training samples per class (per fragment of code to be detected); we decided to use $S_c = 1000$ as a reasonably large number to be used as a starting point (we present a more detailed discussion in the next section). The fragments of code, denoted F_k $(1 \leqslant k \leqslant |\mathcal{C}|)$, are either functions or fragments of a function, and for each call we supply a randomly selected value as input argument for the function, as illustrated in Figure 4. For Experiment 2, the training samples

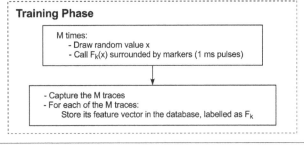

Figure 4. Training Phase.

were not marked by surrounding them with pulses, but rather, surrounding them with some other (randomly selected) function, since this is how they would appear in the classification phase when operating in continuous mode. We emphasize the detail that these traces used for the training database are different from those being identified/classified, since "fresh" random values are chosen at every instance as parameter values — the fragments of code are

---

[4] For some of the functions, the input is a graph or a tree. For these cases, we inserted random values in the data structure.

part of the same set of possible classes, but each instance of a trace being classified is different from every trace in the training database.

In a real-life application, this training step should consider, if available, the probability distribution for the arguments to each function. For example, if a given function receives as input parameter the measured temperature, we will draw values from a normal distribution with mean 25 °C and relatively small variance.[5] For our experiments, we used uniformly distributed random variables in a reasonable range (the ranges were consistent between the training phase and the classification phase). This does not take into account the possibility of a function being called with unreasonable parameters due to a defect in the software; however, one can easily compensate for this aspect by including a small fraction of training samples using parameter values outside the reasonable range.

The experiments required a target device and a host platform to compile the programs and "flash" the target device, capture and process the traces, and analyze the results. For the host platform, we used an Ubuntu Linux system, with avr-gcc 4.3.5 and avrdude 5.10. The target device was an Atmel AVR Atmega2560 MCU on an STK600 board [1], and we assembled a quick prototype card to facilitate the connections — a snap-in connector to place the shunt resistor so that different values can be easily tried (in our case, a 10 Ω resistor produced voltage in the correct range), pins to connect oscilloscope probes (for verification purposes, or for future experiments using a digital oscilloscope), and an RCA audio connector to easily connect to the input of the sound card. Figure 5 shows a photograph of this simple prototype card. The

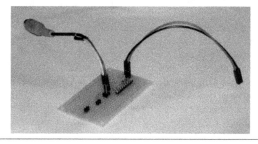

Figure 5. Prototype Card to Facilitate Connections.

red/black cable on the right, ending in a two-pin header connector goes to the VTARGET connector on the STK600 board (so that current to the MCU passes through), and the green connector on the left is the RCA audio connector.

The sound card was an HT Omega Claro+ [10], and we used Audacity [15] to record the power traces. Figure 6 shows a screenshot from one of the power traces in the training phase, showing the two surrounding pulses.

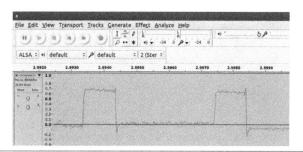

Figure 6. Screenshot – Power Trace in Audio Editor.

[5] Assuming a system intended to work at room temperature.

We used code from MiBench [6] as the source code for the target device in the experiments. That is, the set of fragments C includes fragments of code from MiBench; in particular, from the telecommunications, network, and security sections of it. We excluded code that required file access or intensive operations as well as code for which we required many modifications for it to compile with avr-gcc. We also excluded redundant items — for example, from the security section, there are several symmetric encryption algorithms and several hash functions; we used only AES (which is the one generally recommended for practical use) for a sample of symmetric encryption, and SHA as a sample of a cryptographic hash function. For simplicity reasons, our work currently operates at the granularity level of entire functions (that is, the fragments of code to be matched are entire functions), with the exception of the SHA algorithm. This exception is due to the fact that SHA executes a large number of rounds repeating the same procedure, thus taking a very long time to execute, making it more reasonable to choose that procedure as the fragment to consider. The exact set of functions used for our experiments is the following: ADPCM encode, ADPCM decode, CRC-32, FFT, SHA (fragment), AES (Rijndael) symmetric encryption, Dijkstra's shortest path algorithm, Patricia Trie (insertion), and pseudo-random number generation (C's `random()` function).

5. Results

We now present and discuss the results for both phases of the experimental setup.

5.1 Experiment 1 – Individual Classification

For Experiment 1, we evaluate and report the precision of the classifier. Since the classifier chooses one of the possible classes (one of the functions being considered), there are no false negatives; that is, there is always an output from the classifier, and it is either a true positive or a false positive. Thus, the precision fully describes the performance of the classifier. The precision P is given by

$$P \triangleq \frac{T_P}{T_P + F_P}$$

where T_P denotes the number of true positives (i.e., correct classifications) and F_P denotes the number of false positives (i.e., misclassifications, or incorrect classifications). For example, consider a scenario with ten candidate functions, $F_1, F_2, \cdots, F_{10}$, Experiment 1 is run and it executes 100 times function F_1. The classifier outputs 90 times F_1, 4 times F_2, 3 times F_5 and 3 times F_8. Then, the number of true positives is 90, and the number of false positives is $4 + 3 + 3 = 10$. The resulting precision for this example, P_{ex}, would be

$$P_{\text{ex}} = \frac{90}{90 + 10} = 0.9 \quad (90\%)$$

We first adjusted the system's parameters to obtain the best performance. For each of the functions, we initially captured 1000 training samples, but then varied the number of samples effectively used, to determine the optimal value (optimal within the range 1 to 1000, which is the maximum number of available samples). We first maintained the same number of samples for every function and varied the value to obtain the optimal. We then used this as the initial estimate in a simple optimization procedure to determine the optimal number of training samples *for each function*. We omit any additional details or figures, since there is nothing particularly relevant that they would show.

For some of the functions, more than 1000 samples were required for good performance, so we captured additional traces for those. In particular, functions like Dijkstra's shortest path required a larger set, possibly due to the variable nature of the algorithm — depending on the graph contents (weights, connections, etc.) there may be wide variations in execution time, requiring larger numbers of training samples to compensate for the spread nature of its PDF. For CRC32, we were obtaining a low precision when using 1000 training samples, so we increased the number of samples for this one as well.

With these parameters in place, we started measuring the performance for Experiment 1. Table 1 shows the results for each of the functions being tested. That is, it shows the precision obtained for the classifier when executing each different function.

Function	Precision
adpcm_encode	100%
adpcm_decode	97%
CRC32	92%
FFT	99%
SHA (Fragment)	100%
AES (Rijndael)	97%
Dijkstra's shortest path	98%
Patricia Trie (insertion)	100%
random()	99%
Overall (avg.)	**98.0%**

Table 1. Classifier Precision

The results clearly indicate an excellent performance for the classifier, with only one of the functions scoring a 92% precision and no other function scoring below 97% precision. The overall precision is given by the arithmetic mean — every function, being executed the same number of times, has the same overall weight, thus the arithmetic mean is the appropriate averaging mechanism. A figure of 98% for the overall precision is also a solid indication of the excellent performance that our classifier achieves.

5.2 Experiment 2 – Continuous Classification

For Experiment 2, we had to overcome several obstacles. For example, due to the limit of program memory of the MCU, we were unable to simultaneously include all sections of MiBench and make them execute correctly. In particular, Patricia trie insertion and Dijkstra's algorithm fail to run on the target due to insufficient resources. Excluding these two functions, we can run the experiment.

5.2.1 Description of the Experiment

To evaluate the performance of the classifier in continuous operation, we execute a long sequence of randomly chosen functions, with the only constraint being that we always call ADPCM encoding first, to then decode the data. We disregard the distinction between random and pseudo-random, and will refer to random values through the rest of the discussion. In that sense, we used the cryptographic-quality pseudo-random generator /dev/urandom, which is, for most practical purposes, "as close as it gets" to true random values [20]. Notice, however, that this random selection is done offline and the sequence is ultimately "hardcoded" in the source code to be compiled and run on the target. This restriction does not affect the random nature of the experiment, yet it is necessary: on-the-fly generation of random values by the target device itself between function calls would introduce artefacts that could skew or possibly even invalidate the results. In particular, the classifier identifies *contiguous* fragments of code; interleaving code to obtain random values for the selection of function and for the parameters would introduce non-negligible deviations from the sequence being tested.

We could not include arbitrarily long sequences of functions, since the entire sequence had to be hardcoded, and the target device

imposes a limit on the size of the executable — we observe that the randomly generated data *for each call to a function* had to be stored in a buffer, for the same reason explained above. The longest sequence that we could fit in the target was 500 calls long (close to 100 calls per function on average). Though this number could be considered large enough to claim that the experiment is valid, we repeated the process ten times and collected statistics over a total of 5000 function calls.

The offline program that generates this random sequence of calls, as well as the random data, produces two files to be included in the program to be run on the target. One file, buffer_sizes.h, defines (through #define directives) the sizes of the buffers that contain the parameter values. Below is an example of the contents of this file:

```
#define ADPCM_COUNT 50
#define FFT_COUNT 97
#define AES_COUNT 111
#define CRC_COUNT 101
```

The other file that this offline program generates is the file containing the actual function calls. Each function call receives input data obtained from one of the elements of the buffer, and while generating this sequence, the offline program goes over each element in sequence, hardcoding the value in this output program, as shown in the fragment below, taken from one of the generated files:

```
encrypt (plaintext + 0*AESSIZE, ciphertext, &ctx);
adpcm_coder(pcmdata + 0*PCMSIZE, adpcmdata, PCMSIZE,
            &coder_1_state);
rc = crc32buf (crcdata + 0*CRCSIZE, CRCSIZE);
fft_float (FFTSIZE, 0, real_in + 0*FFTSIZE, imag_in + 0*FFTSIZE,
            real_out, imag_out);
rc = crc32buf (crcdata + 1*CRCSIZE, CRCSIZE);
adpcm_decoder(adpcmdata, pcmdata_2, PCMSIZE, &decoder_state);
nothing = (random() ^ random()) & 0xFFFF;
adpcm_coder(pcmdata + 1*PCMSIZE, adpcmdata, PCMSIZE,
            &coder_1_state);
fft_float (FFTSIZE, 0, real_in + 1*FFTSIZE, imag_in + 1*FFTSIZE,
            real_out, imag_out);
nothing = (random() ^ random()) & 0xFFFF;
```

We can see, for example, for the first two calls to crc32buf, the input data coming from the first and second elements of buffer crcdata (offsets 0 and 1 hardcoded in the call). Same for adpcm_coder and fft_float. These hardcoded offsets continue to increase with each subsequent call to each function, until the XXX_COUNT value. Since we only show a short fragment of one of the files, the only offsets that we see are 0 and 1.

The declarations for these buffers (in the program that runs in the target device) are shown below:

```
#include "buffer_sizes.h"

short volatile pcmdata[ADPCM_COUNT*PCMSIZE];
char volatile  adpcmdata[PCMSIZE/2];   // Encoder output
short volatile pcmdata_2[PCMSIZE];     // Decoder output

volatile char plaintext[AES_COUNT*AESSIZE];
volatile char ciphertext[AESSIZE];

volatile float real_in[FFT_COUNT*FFTSIZE];
volatile float real_out[FFTSIZE];
volatile float imag_in[FFT_COUNT*FFTSIZE];
volatile float imag_out[FFTSIZE];

char crcdata[CRC_COUNT*CRCSIZE];
```

5.2.2 Performance Evaluation

We used a similar metric to that used for Experiment 1. Since we still have a classifier that always outputs one of the possible candidates, we only have true positives or false positives, which means that the precision still provides a complete picture of the classifier's performance.

However, an important distinction arises from the fact that in continuous classification, the sizes of the traces need to be determined and affect the performance of the process, as they affect the necessary resynchronization process in the cases of misclassifications. In that sense, a more sensible formula for the precision of the classifier in continuous mode, P_c, is given by the fraction of the time during which the output of the classifier corresponds to a true positive:

$$P_c \triangleq \frac{\sum |I_{T_P}|}{\sum |I_{T_P}| + \sum |I_{F_P}|}$$

where I_{T_P} denotes intervals during which the output of the classifier is a true positive, I_{F_P} denotes intervals during which the output is a false positive or a misclassification, and $|\cdot|$ denotes the length of its argument (the length of the interval). Furthermore, when obtaining the output from the classifier, we do not count on precise a priori knowledge of the lengths of the functions, since the values of the arguments may cause variation in the execution time. This means that we need to estimate these from the output. Section 5.2.4 discusses this aspect.

As an example, consider the scenario with three candidate functions, F_1, F_2, F_3, which take 10 ms, 20 ms, and 30 ms to execute, respectively. If the sequence $F_3 - F_1 - F_2$ is executed and the classifier outputs F_3 at time 0 ms, F_2 at time 20 ms, and F_2 at time 20 ms then, with all units implicitly ms, the intervals with true positive are $I_{T_1} = (0, 20)$ and $I_{T_2} = (40, 60)$, and the interval $I_F = (20, 40)$ is a false positive—the output is F_2, and during the sub-interval $(20, 30)$ the correct class is F_3 and during the sub-interval $(30, 40)$ the correct class is F_1. Thus, in this example, the precision P_{ex_2} would be approximately 67%:

$$P_{ex_2} = \frac{|I_{T_1}| + |I_{T_2}|}{|I_{T_1}| + |I_{T_2}| + |I_F|} = \frac{2}{3}$$

5.2.3 Results

As described in Section 5.2.1, ten sequences of 500 function calls each were executed, and traces were captured for each of them. Figure 7 shows a screenshot of the audio editor displaying the first few milliseconds of one of the traces; in particular, this trace fragment corresponds to the sequence of ten function calls shown in Section 5.2.1. The markers were manually added to the image for illustration purposes, indicating the boundaries between functions.

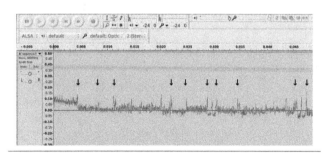

Figure 7. Power Trace for Sequence of Function Calls.

The complete traces were fed to the processing program implementing the classifier as described in the previous sections. An example of the output of this program is shown below (only a fragment, since each trace contains 500 function calls). The reported time uses the unit of audio samples, which is about $10.4\,\mu s$:

```
Executed aes at time 18
Executed adpcm-encode at time 428
Executed crc32 at time 810
Executed fft at time 1077
Executed crc32 at time 2127
Executed adpcm-encode at time 2394
Executed random at time 2786
Executed adpcm-encode at time 2942
Executed fft at time 3328
Executed random at time 4407
```

This example again corresponds to the same sequence of ten function calls shown in Section 5.2.1 and corresponding to the trace fragment shown in Figure 7. We observe that in this particular example, there was one misclassification (the sixth function call is reported as adpcm_encode when the actual function being executed is adpcm_decode).

To measure the performance (the precision) of the classifier in Experiment 2, the output for each of the ten traces was fed, along with the C source code corresponding to each of the ten sequences, to a custom-made program that compares the output and reports statistics allowing us to determine the precision and provide some additional potentially insightful information.

An important reason to use a custom-made program for the analysis of the experimental results was to allow for user intervention in the process of matching sequences that might be hard to properly identify and match algorithmically. Even more importantly, the matching includes timing that may need to be verified against the traces, for the less obvious cases (though only on two occasions we needed to resort to the traces in the audio editor to resolve a mismatch). The program does as much as possible in an automated way to minimize user intervention, and of course does as much validation as possible for the user input, to minimize the effect of human errors and oversights. We omit any additional details or screenshots; however, we do emphasize the aspect that this custom-made program requiring user assistance is necessary only for the purpose of analyzing the experimental results in the context of this study; an actual practical implementation of our system would not require this step.

5.2.4 Estimating the Precision

Measuring the exact value of the precision for the continuous classifier requires us to obtain more information than reasonably feasible given our setup. Computing the exact value of the precision requires that we determine the intervals where the output is correct, and this would require us to have exact timing information for the sequence being executed. However, the actual trace contains calls with random parameter values, so the duration is unknown, and instrumenting the program for the purpose of obtaining that information would affect the measurements, at least for the family of devices that we targeted in our work.

We can, however, obtain a good approximation of the precision if we use the timing that the classifier outputs. Specifically, the skipped elements from the classifier output (the right column in the above example of the processing software) are considered to be false positives and the rest is considered a true positive. As long as the sequences match, we assume that the timing for the matching items is correct and disregard any inaccuracies in the exact positions of the boundaries between functions.

Thus, the difference in the time indexes for the items that have to be skipped to reestablish synchronization reveal the length of the false positive intervals. The estimate is accurate provided that the misclassifications occur with a deviation that is balanced; that is, provided that some errors confuse a function with a longer (in duration) function and some confuse a function with a shorter function, without any imbalance on average. This is a reasonable assumption, and we did not observe any evidence suggesting that there would be any imbalance in the errors for the traces that we processed.

Table 2 summarizes the important parameters describing the performance of the classifier when operating in continuous mode. In addition to the precision, we also determined the average number of items that it took the system to recover from a misclassification. This was done based on the output of the custom-made analysis program mentioned in the previous section, which allows us to determine when the system is back in sync. For more details, the reader can consult [17]. This metric provides information about the robustness of the system in terms of ability to recover from a misclassification and reestablish synchronization with the trace. It also provides evidence to the quality of the classifier in general, in that short sequences of missed items are certainly easier to compensate for through auxiliary methods, such as doing additional validation of timings, validating feasible program sequences through static analysis, etc. Though we did not use any of these techniques in this initial phase of the project, it still makes sense to claim that smaller values for this parameter correspond to higher quality for the continuous classifier. Since all traces included the same number of fragments, we used arithmetic mean for the average values.

Sequence	Precision	Avg. Recovery
1	88.75%	1.29
2	89.78%	1.30
3	87.65%	1.27
4	88.63%	1.38
5	87.07%	1.34
6	89.03%	1.29
7	89.03%	1.32
8	86.97%	1.48
9	89.59%	1.19
10	87.84%	1.30
Overall (avg.)	**88.74%**	**1.32**

Table 2. Continuous Classifier Performance

For this second experiment we also obtained results indicating a good performance. This is encouraging, since this is clearly the more important of the two experiments, since it models the way an actual practical system would operate. The precision is not as good as that obtained for Experiment 1; this is expected, as this operating mode involves more parameters, more ambiguities and degrees of freedom, and the additional functionality of maintaining synchronization — with or without misclassifications. Also, the fact that traces are now in sequence one after another introduces the possibility that sub-fragments of a trace combined with sub-fragments of another trace could be a good match for some incorrect function. Experiment 1 does not face any of these difficulties. Thus, we believe that a figure of close to 90% precision for continuous classification is a very good result for this initial phase of the project, where the goal is to study the feasibility of our proposed approach.

Another important aspect revealed by these results is that of the robustness of the continuous classifier, in that the system never faced a situation where an error threw it irreversibly out of sync. In all cases, the system reestablished synchronization after a misclassification, and in most cases the misclassification involved just one function replaced with another, and then resynchronization immediately after, as suggested by an average of 1.32 functions skipped before resynchronization.

As suggested before, we can reasonably claim that individual incorrect classifications are essentially irrelevant, as the tool could be extended to make use of the CFG and consider possible execution sequences. Given this information, a match to an incorrect function may have been rejected with high probability, because the CFG would have given indication that it is impossible to reach that particular function within a short period of time after the preceding sequence.

5.2.5 Additional Insights

As additional observations and insights that we gained from the experimental results in this initial phase of the project, we could mention the following:

For some of the functions, long sequences of consecutive calls to the same function showed a higher likelihood of misclassification. For example, sequences of three consecutive calls to CRC32 showed up very often as a prompt for user assistance in the processing software, and in some cases required three or four skipped items from the trace to reestablish synchronization.

Also interestingly, we observed several instances where a sequence of three or more consecutive calls to random() either caused the function immediately following that sequence to be misclassified, or was misclassified as a smaller number of consecutive calls.

These two aspects suggest that it may be a good idea to restrict the fragments of code to sections of the source code with no control structures (conditionals and loops) such that every instance of a given fragment of code exhibits the same execution time. This not only has the potential to increase the precision, but also could play a role in dramatically increasing the computational performance of the system, in that a smaller training database could work well, and possibly the more efficient neareast centroid technique (using LDFs) could be applicable, since it was precisely this aspect of variable execution time within classes what put that approach at a disadvantage with respect to the k-NN technique.

5.3 Interrupts and Interrupt Service Routines

The current experiments were oblivious to interrupts and interrupt service routines (ISR) for two main reasons: (1) the approach to detect them differs due to their asynchronous and usually short-lived nature; and (2) from the evidence we collected and observed, we claim that their detection should be really easy.

We should expect an interrupt request (IRQ) to cause a "power-heavy" reaction by the processor, in that a lot of hardware components need to react and work on processing the IRQ correctly [7]. Consequently, we should see a prominent component in the power trace that would identify the exact moment at which the processor responds to an IRQ.

We collected some experimental evidence supporting this claim; Figure 8 shows a trace of a simple "do nothing" program that runs pointless tasks in the background and uses timer interrupts, with the IRQ firing approximately every 6.5 ms. We observe the prominent peaks that IRQs produce in the trace.

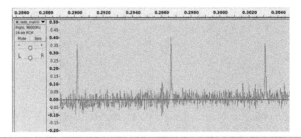

Figure 8. Power Trace Showing the Effect of IRQs.

For an actual practical implementation, however, we must consider interrupts for at least the following two reasons: (1) any fragment of code that the system is attempting to identify can be subject to another (small) fragment corresponding to the interrupt processing and the ISR to be inserted at any arbitrary and unpredictable position of the fragment to identify; and (2) many bugs arise from improper interactions between an ISR and the main/background processing, thus triggering the faulty behavior around the time that an interrupt occurs.

6. Discussion and Future Work

This initial phase of our project presents encouraging results; the effectiveness of the technique was confirmed by the experimental phase, at least in a preliminary way.

Further research is needed in several areas of the project; we focused on one target device, the Atmega2560, running at 1MHz. In general this is not an important limitation, in that we could extrapolate from the field of side-channel attacks, where SPA has been successfully applied on a wide variety of architectures and target devices. The important aspect for us to consider in this respect is the approach's ability to work with simple hardware, in particular with an off-the-shelf inexpensive sound card. With our Atmega2560 setup, we verified that a standard PC sound card sufficed for the system to run at the granularity level of function calls, producing traces in the order of 200 to 300 samples in length. However, to address either finer granularity, or higher clock speeds for the target device, we may need to investigate the relationship between these: for a given granularity, what is the maximum ratio between the device's clock speed and the sampling rate at which we capture the power trace? Equivalently, for a given clock speed and a given sampling rate, what is the finest granularity at which we can detect fragments of code?

Ideally, we would like our system to detect every possible code segment with fixed execution time (i.e., contiguous blocks of code without conditionals or loops). For example, instead of detecting execution of a loop (as a whole, with variable execution time), we would prefer to individually detect the evaluation of the condition and the body (assuming no nested loops or conditionals inside the body of the loop). This would be beneficial for at least the following three aspects:

- There is a potential increase of precision, since loops executing variable number of passes or other conditional executions can introduce wide variations within classes, potentially limiting the precision.

- There is additionally a potential increase in processing speed; the aspect mentioned in the item above also means that the database of training samples has to be larger to compensate for these variations (that is, to make sure that the training database is representative of the spread PDF when allowing variable length). Additionally, if we have fixed size segments, then the more efficient LDF technique could be suitable.

- The higher level of details in the output of our system will represent a significant improvement in terms of the system's ability to help developers go from program tracing to finding a bug.

We would like to emphasize the fact that these limitations in no way negate or compromise the validity or the value of the reported results. A large class of embedded systems run at low clock frequencies, and for those, the presented approach will be perfectly fine and valuable when assisting in the debugging task during advanced phases of the development cycle. Incidentally, this low-frequency aspect may be correlated with low transistor count MCUs, presumably with simple architectures that may lack any sophisticated debugging tools embedded in the hardware, making our technique particularly valid for this class of target device.

A positive aspect of the results derives from the fact that all of our tests and functions are CPU-bound. Practical systems typically use I/O, which makes a more prominent mark on the power trace and thus helps the classification process. The results of our experiments show a good level of performance even with this disadvantage.

The following are some of the important aspects that we intend to tackle through future research:

- Introduce the notion of *conditional* classification, possibly manually in an initial phase, but with the goal of using a CFG tool when it comes to a practical implementation. The idea is that by looking at the source code, we gain information about the possible fragments of code that could be executed at a particular time, given the previous fragment executed, or even better, the sequence of past fragments. Thus, the classifier can count on additional information, and thus its efficacy should improve.

  In this sense, the fact that our Experiment 1 used only nine fragments should not be seen at all as a number too low to produce valid results — in a practical setup that makes use of the CFG, for most classifications the system may need to consider no more than two or three possible candidate fragments following the most recent classified fragments.

- Reliable detection of a crash condition where the processor ends up executing random code. Detecting such condition, as well as the precise time at which it started, is clearly a valuable piece of information when assisting the developers in the debugging task. This may be related to the option of *reject* in the classifier [21], and would allow us to eliminate the assumption that the execution is restricted to a set of possible fragments of code — an assumption that is reasonable in the sense that the developers always can count on the source code, but less reasonable from the point of view of considering cases such as stack corruption, invalid pointer operations or other situations leading to "random" execution.

- Develop and test strategies to automate the training phase. Having to capture training samples of each fragment of code is perhaps the most severe limitation of our approach. We do believe, however, that this issue can be mitigated and possibly eliminated. One alternative could be instrumenting the program (during the development phase) to interact with an automated system to capture training samples. Another option could be using models of the target devices that would allow an external system to determine exact timings of the execution and thus capture training samples in an automated way by manipulating the data and signals connected to the device to control its execution.

- Considering different architectures; for example, processors with cache memory, deep pipeline or other forms of parallelism, etc. These in principle make our task harder, given that more information is combined together before leaking to the power trace. However, for some of these aspects, the additional complexity in the architecture may go hand-in-hand with additional information being leaked to the power trace, and those could end up making the task easier.

7. Conclusions

In this work, we have proposed a novel approach for non-intrusive debugging of embedded systems, especially useful for debugging faulty behavior observed at advanced phases of the development cycle, such as during production or even after deployment. The idea is based on exploiting the relationship between what a processor is executing and its power consumption to determine the sequence of code executed from observations of power consumption as a function of time (power traces). At the present stage, our approach is applicable to background/foreground programming (superloop structure), multitasking with run-to-completion semantics, and possibly also to co-operative multitasking, depending on whether we can easily identify the `yield` calls.

Our approach and our implementation feature the interesting highlight that the system runs on a standard PC, and the power traces are captured through the recording input of the sound card.

Techniques where power traces are required, such as Power Analysis cryptographic attacks, usually rely on digital oscilloscopes or other expensive or bulky pieces of equipment. Also worth noting, since our experiments produced good results even when using an inexpensive off-the-shelf sound card, we conclude that this technology is perfectly suitable for hobbyists as well as professional developers.

Experimental results confirmed the validity of our approach, showing very good performance when using part of the code base from the MiBench test suite. Several improvements and opportunities for future work were discussed, which we believe will lead to substantial improvements in the performance and the range of target devices for which our technique is suitable.

Acknowledgments

The authors would like to acknowledge the contribution of Summit Sehgal, who offered assistance with the setup and lab equipment for the preliminary tests and experimental phases of the project. The first author would like to thank Dr. Thomas Reidemeister as well, for his valuable assistance and discussions.

This work was supported in part through a grant from the Natural Sciences and Engineering Research Council of Canada, awarded to Dr. Hasan.

This research was supported in part by CFI 20314 and CMC, and the industrial partners associated with these projects.

References

[1] Atmel Corporation. AVR 8- and 32-bit Microcontrollers, 2012. URL http://www.atmel.com/products/microcontrollers/avr/.

[2] S. Chari, J. R. Rao, and P. Rohatgi. Template Attacks. *Cryptographic Hardware and Embedded Systems – CHES 2002*, pages 13–28, 2003.

[3] J. Cooling. *Software Engineering for Real-Time Systems*. Addison-Wesley, 2003.

[4] T. H. Cormen, C. E. Leiserson, R. L. Rivest, and C. Stein. *Introduction to Algorithms*. The MIT Press, Third edition, 2009.

[5] M. Frigo and S. G. Johnson. The design and implementation of FFTW3. *Proceedings of the IEEE*, 93(2):216–231, 2005. Special issue on "Program Generation, Optimization, and Platform Adaptation".

[6] M. R. Guthaus, J. S. Ringenberg, D. Ernst, T. M. Austin, T. Mudge, and R. B. Brown. Mibench: A free, commercially representative embedded benchmark suite. In *Proceedings of the Workload Characterization, 2001. WWC-4. 2001 IEEE International Workshop*, pages 3–14. IEEE Computer Society, 2001.

[7] C. Hamacher, Z. Vranesic, and S. Zaky. *Computer Organization*. McGraw-Hill, Fifth edition, 2002.

[8] D. Hankerson, A. Menezes, and S. Vanstone. *Guide to Elliptic Curve Cryptography*. Springer-Verlag, 2004.

[9] J. L. Hennessy and D. A. Patterson. *Computer Architecture: A Quantitative Approach*. Morgan Kaufmann Publishers, Fourth edition, 2007.

[10] HT Omega. Claro Plus – Online specifications. URL http://www.htomega.com/claroplus.html.

[11] P. Kocher. Timing Attacks on Implementations of Diffie-Hellman, RSA, DSS, and Other Systems. *Advances in Cryptology*, 1996.

[12] P. Kocher, J. Jaffe, and B. Jun. Differential Power Analysis. *Advances in Cryptology – CRYPTO' 99*, pages 388–397, 1999.

[13] R. Langner. Stuxnet: Dissecting a Cyberwarfare Weapon. *IEEE Security & Privacy*, 9(3):49–51, May-June 2011.

[14] Matt Bishop. *Computer Security: Art and Science*. Addison-Wesley, 2003.

[15] D. Mazzoni. Audacity: Free Audio Editor and Recorder. URL http://audacity.sourceforge.net.

[16] A. J. Menezes, P. C. van Oorschot, and S. A. Vanstone. *Handbook of Applied Cryptography*. CRC Press, 1996. URL http://www.cacr.math.uwaterloo.ca/hac/.

[17] C. Moreno. Side-Channel Analysis: Countermeasures and Application to Embedded Systems Debugging, 2013. PhD Thesis (Final version to be submitted May 2013).

[18] C. Moreno and M. A. Hasan. SPA-Resistant Binary Exponentiation with Optimal Execution Time. *Journal of Cryptographic Engineering*, pages 1–13, 2011.

[19] J. G. Proakis and D. G. Manolakis. *Digital Signal Processing: Principles, Algorithms, and Applications*. Prentice Hall, Fourth edition, 2006.

[20] J. Viega and G. McGraw. *Building Secure Software*. Addison-Wesley, 2002.

[21] A. R. Webb and K. D. Copsey. *Statistical Pattern Recognition*. Wiley, third edition, 2011.

The Role of C in the Dark Ages of Multi-Core

Marcel Beemster

ACE Associated Compiler Experts bv, The Netherlands
marcel@ace.nl

Abstract

Contrary to predictions of its demise, C remains a dominant programming language, especially in embedded systems. Speed and transparency dictate that it will be so for the next decade, despite its supposed unsuitability for programming parallel architectures. A flexible compiler development system is a unique vehicle to bend the C language and its implementation to the developers' will. Using hard-won experience in applying extended versions of C to diverse parallel architectures, C's potential in the dark ages of multi-core programming is examined.

Categories and Subject Descriptors D3.3 [*PROGRAMMING LANGUAGES*]: Language Constructs and Features - Concurrent programming structures

General Terms Languages, Performance

Keywords C programming language; multi-core; mapping; implementation efficiency

1. From High-Level Abstractions to the Dark-Ages

In the age of sequential programming beautiful abstractions were built to make the developer's life easy. These proved unsuitable when the world at large was finally confronted with multi-core processors in 2004. It was not that the research community had not seen this coming. The research into parallel architectures and its programming goes back a long way. This, however, has not resulted in programming languages that are suitable for the variety of multi-core architectures of today.

Successful application of parallelism does exist. In Supercomputing, applications have long been tuned to exploit the parallelism of millions of independent processors, connected by a high speed network. These applications are written in FORTRAN and C. In data-centers, for internet and cloud services, parallelism is inherently abundant through millions of independent queries with relatively few writes. In this application area, it is often more predictable and cost-effective to buy more hardware than to optimize the software. In computer graphics, parallelism is near infinite and homogeneous. OpenGL and DirectX are application development environments that actually provide some degree of portability of programs across graphics processor implementations without sacrificing efficiency. This is a rare phenomenon in parallel computing.

2. C: the Answer to Multi-Core Efficiency

The true measure of successful parallel programming is its use in embedded computing. This is because in embedded computing efficiency really counts. Two times more efficient means double the battery life-time, which is directly observable to the end-user. For that reason, the prevailing programming programming language in embedded is C.

There are many reasons why C is not a good choice for parallel computing, but they are all overruled by the efficiency argument. With C, developers have ultimate control over the mapping of the application to the architecture, and thus to achieve high efficiencies.

This also explains, despite more than fifty years of research into structured programming languages, the sudden popularity of OpenCL. OpenCL is an extension of C, partially by a few language extensions but mostly by a library that provides control over the mapping of the program and its data structures to processing elements and the memory hierarchy. OpenCL is popular because its mapping control promises tuning for maximal efficiency.

What it does not provide is portability. When a tuned OpenCL program is transferred from its dedicated architecture to another, one can expect it to run correctly (though even that is not guaranteed due to resource constraints), but one cannot expect it to run efficiently. The program needs to be re-tuned, perhaps completely restructured.

3. Parallel Programming Requirements

So here are the requirements, in order of priority, for a successful parallel programming language:

1. It needs to have a highly efficient implementation. For that reason, C will remain dominant until a new language arises that has comparable implementation efficiency.

2. It needs to separate the expression of parallelism in the program from the mapping of the parallelism to the architecture. This is what is wrong with OpenCL, where the mapping and the parallel program are intertwined.

3. It needs to have a good basis for software engineering because parallel programming is hard enough by itself. C clearly lacks in this area, but until the first two requirements are taken care of, software engineering will have to wait.

In the presentation, a number of extensions to C will be discussed that demonstrate how the objective of separating the expression and the mapping of parallelism can be achieved.

Acknowledgments

The work was supported by FP7-248976 REFLECT, FP7-247615 HEAP, FP7-288248 FlexTiles, ARTEMIS 100230 SMECY, ARTEMIS-100265 ASAM and CA104 COBRA.

FTL²: A Hybrid *Flash Translation Layer* with *Logging* for Write Reduction in Flash Memory

Tianzheng Wang[1] *

Duo Liu[2] †

Yi Wang[3]

Zili Shao[3]

[1] Department of Computer Science
University of Toronto
Toronto, ON, Canada
tzwang@cs.toronto.edu

[2] College of Computer Science
Chongqing University
Chongqing, P.R. China
liuduo@cqu.edu.cn

[3] Department of Computing
The Hong Kong Polytechnic University
Hung Hom, Kowloon, Hong Kong
{csywang, cszlshao}@comp.polyu.edu.hk

Abstract

NAND flash memory has been widely used to build embedded devices such as smartphones and solid state drives (SSD) because of its high performance, low power consumption, great shock resistance and small form factor. However, its lifetime and performance are greatly constrained by partial page updates, which will lead to early depletion of free pages and frequent garbage collections. On the one hand, partial page updates are prevalent as a large portion of I/O does not modify file contents drastically. On the other hand, general-purpose cache usually does not specifically consider and eliminate duplicated contents, despite its popularity.

In this paper, we propose a hybrid approach called *FTL²*, which employs both logging and mapping techniques in flash translation layer (FTL), to tackle the endurance problem and performance degradation caused by partial page updates in flash memory. FTL² logs the latest contents in a high-speed temporary storage, called *Content Cache* to handle partial page updates. Experimental results show that FTL² can greatly reduce page writes and postpone garbage collections with a small overhead.

Categories and Subject Descriptors D.4.2 [*Operating Systems*]: Storage Management–Secondary Storage

Keywords Flash memory; endurance; caching; logging; flash translation layer; solid state drives; partial page update.

1. Introduction

NAND flash memory is revolutionizing storage system design and has been adopted to build various embedded devices, including solid state drives (SSD) and smartphones [6, 7, 22]. Flash memory is fully electronic and has no moving parts, enabling high random read performance, low power consumption and good shock resistance. However, given the "erase-before-write" constraint and

---

* Work done while with The Hong Kong Polytechnic University.

† Duo Liu is the corresponding author.

Table 1: Access latency of NAND flash memory [32].

Operation	Latency (μs)
Read Time	25
Write Time	200
Erase Time	1,500

limited erase count per block [33], excessive *partial page updates* which modify only small portions of a page become a major cause of lifetime and performance degradation. In this paper, we focus on handling partial page updates and aim at prolonging the lifetime and improving write performance for flash memory. Particularly, we target at SSD, which is one of the most important and promising embedded devices in modern storage systems.

A Flash memory chip consists of blocks, each of which includes multiple pages (typically of 2KB or 4KB). A page is not rewritable until the whole block is erased. The unit of read/write for flash memory is a page, while that of erase is a block. For each block, the maximum number of erase is 10^4 to 10^5 [26, 33]. As shown in Table 1 [32], flash memory exhibits excellent read performance of 25μs latency. However, write and erase operations cause much longer latency of 200μs and $1,500\mu$s, respectively. Out-of-place update is therefore needed (i.e., new data are written to another free page, instead of the same page after erasing the block) to reduce write latency and avoid excessive block erase operations.

In order to provide backward compatibility and conceal the "erase-before-write" limitation, an intermediate software module called flash translation layer (FTL) is implemented to emulate a block device interface. It converts logical sector addresses to physical addresses in flash memory. When updating a page, even if only a tiny amount of data (e.g., several bytes) is changed, the whole page still has to be rewritten in the physical medium. We refer to this type of update as *partial page update* since only a portion of the page is modified.

Partial page updates are common in write-intensive workloads. For example, it is well known that typically each database transaction only touches a few bytes of a page [17]. In Figure 1, we show the cumulative distribution function graph for the percentage of bytes updated in page update operations of four write-intensive workloads. As shown, write requests which modify no more than 10% of data in a sector (x-axis) constitute more than 50% writes (y-axis) in the database transaction (denoted as "DB Running") and database creation (denoted as "DB Creation") workloads, and more than 20% in Email Server workload. A considerable amount

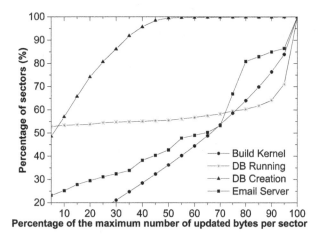

Figure 1: Characteristics of write-intensive workloads.

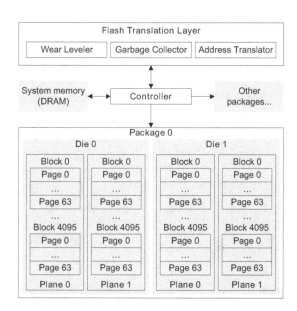

Figure 2: Architecture of NAND flash memory based SSD with multiple packages and dies. A die contains of two planes, each of which is formed by two 64-page blocks.

of write requests are partial page updates. Though supported by many flash chips, partial programming should be minimized because it accelerates disturbance and endangers data integrity [10]. Due to excessive partial page updates and the out-of-place update policy, free pages are consumed quickly. Time-consuming garbage collection may happen much earlier than with fewer or no partial page updates. More blocks are erased and the speed of serving write requests is slowed down. It becomes critical to avoid partial page updates for prolonging lifetime and improving write performance for flash memory.

To achieve this, we propose FTL^2, a hybrid **F**lash **T**ranslation **L**ayer with **L**ogging, which features both *mapping* and content-aware *logging* techniques to delay and avoid partial page updates. The basic idea is to *log* recently updated contents in a high-speed temporary storage called **Content Cache** before data reach flash memory. Content Cache can co-exist with or replace the general-purpose cache in SSD. For the former case, FTL^2 will submit I/O (on evictions from Content Cache) to flash memory chips through the general-purpose cache. Currently we propose to implement Content Cache in battery-backed DRAM such that when there is power failure, cache contents could be flushed to flash memory quickly. This work can also be extended to use non-volatile, byte addressable memories such as memristor and phase change memory (PCM) [12, 42] for better reliability.

FTL^2 identifies partial page updates by comparing the differences between the current and new page contents. New data which are part of a page are stored ("logged") in Content Cache. They are applied back to the original page for read requests on-the-fly. Therefore, time-consuming flash page writes are transformed into fast flash read and DRAM read/write operations. Both write performance and endurance of flash memory are enhanced. Experimental results show that our technique can reduce ~50% flash page writes and improve write performance with minuscule overheads.

This paper makes the following contributions:

- We present FTL^2, a hybrid **F**lash **T**ranslation **L**ayer with **L**ogging, to handle partial page updates in NAND flash memory based solid state drives.

- By transforming time-consuming flash page writes to fast flash read and DRAM read/write operations, FTL^2 enhances both write performance and endurance of flash memory.

- We demonstrate the effectiveness on write reduction of FTL^2 by comparing it with a baseline FTL using write-intensive I/O workloads, and show that FTL^2 is capable of reducing ~50% write activities for flash memory.

To the best of our knowledge, this is the first work to employ both mapping and logging at a finer granularity in FTL to tackle the partial page update problem and improve the lifetime and write performance of flash memory.

The rest of this paper is organized as follows. Section 2 provides background on flash memory and our motivation. Section 3 presents the design of FTL^2. Sections 4 and 5 present details on experimental setup and results, respectively. We discuss and compare FTL^2 with related work in Section 6. Finally, Section 7 concludes the paper and discusses future work.

2. Background and Motivation

In this section, we first revisit the system architecture of NAND flash memory based embedded systems, and then give a brief introduction of FTL. Finally, the motivation of this work is presented.

2.1 Flash Memory System Architecture

NAND flash memory is a type of non-volatile memory consisting of blocks. A block consists of multiple pages (usually 32 or 64). The size of a page is typically 2KB or 4KB. The unit of read/write operations is a page. Due to the *erase-before-write* limitation, the whole block must be erased to rewrite a page in it.

There are two types of NAND flash memory: single-level cell (SLC) and multi-level cell (MLC). Each SLC stores one bit, and each MLC can store two or more bits. SLC can sustain up to 10^5 erases per block, while the number for MLC is 10^4 [33]. FTL^2 is not designed specifically for SLC or MLC. Systems based on both types of flash memory can adopt FTL^2 for write reduction.

In this paper, we adopt a common SSD model [3, 20] shown in Figure 2. An SSD consists of an array of *packages*, each of which contains *dies*. There are multiple *planes* in each die. Inside a plane are blocks. Other components include a controller (an embedded processor), RAM, and FTL. For each package, there is a communication channel managed by the controller to schedule data transfer. FTL provides a block device interface for file systems and applications. RAM caches data and the mapping table needed by FTL. This model can also be generalized to cover other embedded systems (e.g., smartphones). In this paper, we only focus on SSD.

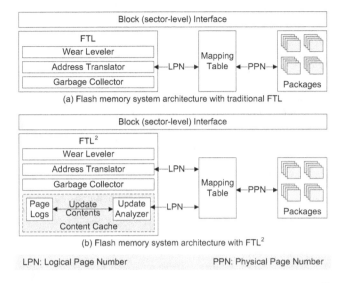

(a) Flash memory system architecture with traditional FTL

(b) Flash memory system architecture with FTL²

LPN: Logical Page Number   PPN: Physical Page Number

Figure 3: Comparison between architectures of traditional FTL and FTL².

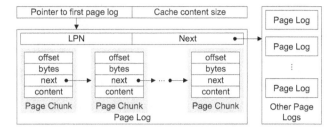

Figure 4: Overview structure of Content Cache in FTL².

2.2 Flash Translation Layer

In order to provide backward compatibility and hide the *erase-before-write* limitation, a flash translation layer is required. As shown in Figure 3(a), the FTL accepts I/O requests in sectors (typically of 512 bytes or 4KB) from the block device interface [3]. The sector level logical address is then translated into physical page address by *Address Translator* using the *Mapping Table* which is cached in RAM. If the write request updates existing page contents, the page is marked as "invalid" and a new page is allocated for writing new contents. In case the number of free pages is below a predefined threshold, *Garbage Collector* will reclaim invalid pages to make room for incoming requests. *Wear Leveler* is used for distributing write activities evenly across the whole flash memory chip to avoid worn-out of flash memory cells. There have been numerous studies on mapping schemes, wear leveling and garbage collection. Section 6 presents related work in these areas. In this paper, we focus on handling partial page updates.

2.3 Motivation

As mentioned in Section 1, partial page updates degrade write performance and reduce lifetime of flash memory. There have been numerous studies on improving endurance and performance, but most of them focused on proposing efficient mapping or general-purpose caching schemes. Though content-aware FTLs [8, 11, 21, 23, 36] can improve the endurance and performance of flash memory, they may still exhaust free pages and trigger garbage collection early. The effectiveness of these techniques is therefore limited.

General-purpose caching mechanisms usually cache at block or page level [9, 19, 41]. Most of them are not aware of partial page updates. It is possible that a page is evicted/pinned from/in memory due to limited cache capacity with only few modifications. As a result, general-purpose cache is not utilized to its full potential.

We therefore propose FTL², a hybrid FTL featuring both conventional mapping strategy and a new logging logic for handling partial page updates. Instead of writing the entire new page or differentials to flash memory, we try to retain and directly avoid partial page updates in high-speed temporary storage (e.g., battery-backed DRAM or memristor) before they reach the general-purpose cache or flash memory. Block erase and new page allocation operations are therefore delayed. When used with a general-purpose cache, data will reach it with multiple modifications (accumulated by

Content Cache) to the page, improving the utilization of general-purpose cache. FTL² aims at enhancing write performance and endurance of flash memory at the same time. Details on the design of FTL² are presented in Section 3.

3. FTL²: Flash Translation Layer with Logging

This section introduces detailed design of FTL². After an overview, the design of Content Cache, which is the major component of FTL² is illustrated. The rest of this section explains the new logic of handling read and write requests in FTL², and the management of Content Cache. In this paper, we assume page-level mapping.

3.1 Overview of FTL²

FTL² integrates logging logic in traditional mapping FTLs, such that expensive partial page writes and erase operations are transformed into fast flash random read and DRAM read/write operations. Figure 3(b) shows the structure of FTL². If an incoming page write request is a new write, traditional mapping is used. A new page will be allocated and written in flash memory. Otherwise, FTL² will try the logging logic. Compared to the traditional FTL design shown in Figure 3(a), FTL² features an additional **Content Cache** in high-speed temporary storage for storing the updated portion of the page (new contents). The number of updated bytes is obtained by the Update Analyzer. If it exceeds a predefined threshold, the request will be handled by the mapping mechanism. Otherwise, new contents are stored in Content Cache, avoiding one page write operation in flash memory.

3.2 FTL² Content Cache

Figure 4 depicts the internal structure of Content Cache. It maintains a list of *page log*, which is a list of *page chunks*. Update Analyzer extracts every physically continuous modified segment of a page and stores it as a page chunk, which includes the starting position of the segment ("offset"), update length ("bytes"), contents after update, and a pointer to the next page chunk. A page log keeps track of all the page chunks for a particular logical page.

To prevent data loss due to power failure, battery backed DRAM or a capacitor can be used for Content Cache. They can provide enough power to flush the cache content to flash memory. When the system is idle, cached data can be periodically flushed. Non-volatile memories such as PCM can also be considered to implement Content Cache for better reliability

3.3 Handling Write Operations

Upon receiving a write request in sectors from the block device interface, the address translator in FTL² first translates sector number (SN) to corresponding logical page number (LPN). After obtained the starting LPN and the number of pages to write, FTL² will start to handle write requests. For each page write, if it does not update existing page contents, the traditional mapping strategy is used. A new page is allocated and the request is served by writing the page

Algorithm 1 $FTL^2Write(LPN, newPage, threshold)$

Input:
    LPN: LPN of the write request.
    $newPage$: new contents to write.
    $threshold$: the maximum number of updated bytes for a page to be cached in Content Cache.
Output:
    $pageLog$: the latest page log for LPN
1: Let $currentPage = FTL^2Read(LPN)$.
2: **if** $currentPage == \emptyset$ **then**
3:    Do traditional mapping.
4:    **return** $\emptyset$.
5: **end if**
6: Let $pcs = getPageChunks(currentPage, newPage)$.
7: **if** $pcs.size > threshold$ **then**
8:    Do traditional mapping.
9:    **return** $\emptyset$.
10: **else**
11:    Let $pageLog =$ the page log for current LPN.
12:    **if** $pageLog == \emptyset$ **then**
13:        Let $pageLog =$ new page log
14:        Let $pageLog.LPN = LPN$.
15:        Let $pageLog.pcs = pcs$.
16:        **return** $pageLog$
17:    **end if**
18:    **for** each $pc \in pcs$ **do**
19:        Let $need\_insert = True$.
20:        **for** each $existing\_pc \in pageLog.pcs$ **do**
21:            **if** $existing\_pc \cap pc \neq \emptyset$ **then**
22:                Merge pc into $existing\_pc$.
23:                Let $need\_insert = False$ and break.
24:            **end if**
25:        **end for**
26:        **if** $need\_insert == True$ **then**
27:            Insert pc in $pageLog.pcs$ in ascending offset order.
28:        **end if**
29:    **end for**
30:    Clean up overlapped chunk pairs.
31:    Move $pageLog$ to the head of page log list.
32:    **return** $pageLog$
33: **end if**

Algorithm 2 $FTL^2Read(LPN)$

Input:
    LPN: LPN of the page to read.
Output:
    $page$: the target page.
1: Let $pageLog =$ the page log for current LPN.
2: **if** $pageLog == \emptyset$ **then**
3:    **return** page read from flash memory.
4: **else**
5:    **if** page chunk covers the whole page **then**
6:        $page =$ page chunk.
7:    **else**
8:        $page =$ original page read from flash.
9:        **for** each $pc \in pageLog.pcs$ **do**
10:            Apply portions of pc which was not applied to $page$.
11:        **end for**
12:    **end if**
13:    Move $pageLog$ to the head of page log list.
14:    **return** $page$.
15: **end if**

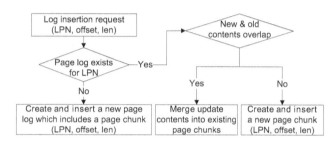

Figure 5: Work flow of log insertion in FTL^2.

If the head page chunk covers the whole page after a write operation (i.e., the page chunk is the latest page), then $FTL^2Read()$ can directly return the page from DRAM, avoiding one flash memory read operation. Note that for each write, we use a two-round merge scheme (as shown in lines 22 and 30 in Algorithm 1) to guarantee that there are no overlaps between any pair of page chunks in a page log (details in Sections 3.5 and 3.6). The head page chunk will then be the only one that could exist and cover the whole page.

The list of page logs is maintained in a "least recently used" (LRU) manner. The most recently accessed page log is moved to the head of the list. The least recently used page log gradually becomes the tail. If there is no enough space, the tail page log will be applied to the original page and evicted. In this case, a new page will be allocated to write the latest contents to flash memory.

3.4 Handling Read Operations

An additional step of applying page chunks is needed for every page read operation if the requested page is buffered in Content Cache. As shown in Algorithm 2, if the whole page is cached (i.e., it is covered by the head page chunk), the page chunk is returned directly. Otherwise, with the LPN of the requested page, FTL^2 finds the corresponding page log in Content Cache and applies all page chunks to the original page read from flash memory.

The search for the page log and the page chunk application operations will cause additional overheads. However, given that DRAM reads/writes at much faster speed than flash memory does, the overhead is minuscule. For the fully covered case, read performance is improved. The list of page logs can also be implemented in more search efficient data structures, such as Red-Black Tree and B+ Tree, to reduce search overhead.

content to flash memory. If the request is an update to existing contents, with traditional FTL which does mapping only (shown in Figure 3(a)), a free page for the new page contents will be allocated and written in flash memory. In FTL^2, the write operation is redefined as "*read-compare-write*", instead of "*write*". Algorithm 1 gives details of the redefined page write operation of FTL^2.

FTL^2 first invokes $FTL^2Read()$, which is the redefined read routine to obtain the up-to-date page (see Section 3.4). Page chunks are then generated by comparing the current and new page contents, if the write operation intends to update a page. The comparison is done by the "Update Analyzer" shown in Figure 3(b). It conducts exclusive-OR (XOR) operations against the current and new contents and then outputs a list of page chunks.

If the number of bytes updated (denoted by $pcs.size$ in Algorithm 1) is greater than a predefined threshold called "logging threshold" (e.g., 5% of the whole page, denoted as $threshold$ in Algorithm 1), FTL^2 will use the mapping approach to handle the request. Otherwise, page chunks will be inserted or merged into Content Cache (lines 18 – 30 in Algorithm 1). As shown in Figure 5, the corresponding page log is first located. If it does not exist, a new one will be created. New page chunks (denoted as pcs in Algorithm 1) are then merged with existing ones if there is any overlap. Otherwise, new page chunks are inserted into the page log in ascending offset order.

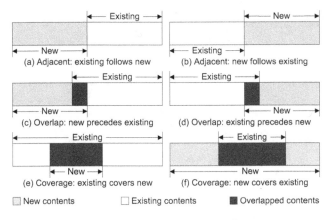

Figure 6: Merge patterns.

(a) Adjacent: existing follows new
(b) Adjacent: new follows existing
(c) Overlap: new precedes existing
(d) Overlap: existing precedes new
(e) Coverage: existing covers new
(f) Coverage: new covers existing

□ New contents   □ Existing contents   ■ Overlapped contents

3.5 Page Chunk Management

When inserting page chunks, FTL^2 examines if the new contents overlap with existing page chunks. New contents are merged into existing page chunks if overlap is detected (first round merge). The similar checking is also conducted after inserted all page chunks to avoid duplication in Content Cache (second round merge).

In the first round of merge operation, FTL^2 locates the first page chunk that overlaps with the new contents and then merge them as a new page chunk (line 22 of Algorithm 1). After the first round, the merged page chunk might overlap with other page chunks if the new contents overlap with multiple existing page chunks. Adjacent page chunks may also appear after page chunk insertions. Therefore, in the second round (line 30 of Algorithm 1), FTL^2 compares every adjacent pair of page chunks to avoid duplication and adjacency. It concatenates adjacent chunk pairs and removes invalid contents, thus ensures that there are no overlapping chunk pairs after each page write operation.

A pair of page chunks can be merged if they match one of the six patterns shown in Figure 6. Figures 6(a) and 6(b) depict the "adjacent" cases, in which the new and existing page chunks do not overlap, but can be concatenated to form a new page chunk. Figures 6(c) and 6(d) illustrate the "overlap" cases, in which the new content starts before and after the starting offset of the existing page chunk, respectively. Two "coverage" cases are shown in Figures 6(e) and 6(f), in which the new content is covered by an existing page chunk or vice versa, respectively. New contents are directly applied to existing page chunks in these two cases. For the other four cases, the starting offset and size of existing page chunk are adjusted accordingly. If necessary, the storage space is re-allocated to accommodate more data.

3.6 Performance Analysis

In this section, we model the read/write performance of FTL^2 and compare it with traditional FTL. The latency of conducting each operation is represented by T_{param}, where *param* is one of the parameters listed in Table 2.

3.6.1 Read

The read latency of traditional FTL is:

$$T_{FTL\ Read}(LPN) = T_{R\_MT} + T_{R\_F}, \quad (1)$$

which is dominated by T_{R_F}, the latency of reading a page from flash memory. For FTL^2, the read latency is:

$$T_{FTL^2\ Read}(LPN) = T_{F\_PL}(LPN) +$$

Table 2: Performance Parameters.

Parameter	Explanation
R_MT	Read LPN-PPN mapping table
R_F	Read one page from flash
F_PL	Locate the page log for LPN
WM	Write new contents to DRAM
A_pcs	Apply page chunks
N_page	Allocate a new page
W_MT	Write LPN-PPN in mapping table
W_F	Write one page in flash memory
XOR	Conduct an XOR operation against two pages
N_{mod}	Number of modified bytes in a page
N_{max}	The maximum number of modified bytes, calculated as *Page size* × *Logging threshold*
New_PL	Create and insert a page log
New_pcs	Create and insert page chunks
$M1$	Merge operation (round 1)
$M2$	Merge operation (round 2)
pl	The page log corresponding to LPN
fc	Page is fully covered by a page chunk. Possible values are T (True) and F (False).
$F1$	Find the first overlapped page chunk
B	Update the boundary of a page chunk
$Free$	Free unnecessary page chunk contents

$$\begin{cases} T_{R\_MT} + T_{R\_F} + T_{A\_pcs}, & if\ pl \neq \emptyset\ \&\ fc = F \quad (2a) \\ 0, & if\ pl \neq \emptyset\ \&\ fc = T \quad (2b) \\ T_{R\_MT} + T_{R\_F}, & if\ pl = \emptyset \quad (2c) \end{cases}$$

FTL^2 first searches the page log for *LPN*. According to whether the page log exists and whether the page is fully covered by page log, different latency will be incurred. For the second case in which the whole page is fully covered, the only latency is page log search (T_{F_PL}). Given that DRAM is orders of magnitude faster than flash page read, FTL^2 improves read performance for pages that are fully covered, while incurring a relatively small overhead for other cases.

3.6.2 Write

The write latency in traditional FTL is:

$$T_{FTL\ Write}(LPN) = T_{R\_MT} + T_{N\_page} + T_{W\_MT} + T_{W\_F}, \quad (3)$$

in which the FTL first searches mapping table to determine whether it is a new write or an update. Then a new page is allocated and written. The mapping table is updated with the new physical page address. Flash page write (T_{W_F}) dominates the write latency.

For FTL^2, the write latency differs in four cases:

$$T_{FTL^2\ Write}(LPN) = T_{FTL^2\ Read}(LPN) +$$

$$\begin{cases} T_{FTL\ Write}(LPN) + T_{XOR}, & if\ N_{mod} > N_{max} \quad (4a) \\ T_{FTL\ Write}(LPN), & if\ page = \emptyset \quad (4b) \\ T_{XOR} + T_{F\_PL} + T_{New\_PL} + T_{New\_pcs}, & if\ pl = \emptyset \quad (4c) \\ T_{XOR} + T_{F\_PL} + T_{M1} + T_{M2}, & if\ pl \neq \emptyset \quad (4d) \end{cases}$$

For all cases, the redefined read operation is invoked first to obtain the latest page content. If the request updates an existing logical page, an XOR operation will be executed (in Equation 4b) to obtain the number of modified bytes (N_{mod}). If N_{mod} exceeds the limit (N_{max}) or the request is a new write, the traditional mapping approach will be used with latency $T_{FTL\ Write}$.

If the new contents can be added to Content Cache, then FTL^2 will locate the corresponding page log. In case there is no existing page log for *LPN*, a new one together with the page chunks will be created and inserted into Content Cache. Otherwise, two rounds of merge operations (*M1* and *M2*) will be conducted to insert new page chunks, merge and avoid overlaps among page chunks. After merge operations, if the head page chunk covers the whole page, other page chunks are discarded. The page chunk can be returned directly in future read operations, without reading flash memory.

Equations 5a and 5b model the first round merge operation:

$$T_{M1} = T_{F1} + T_{WM} + \begin{cases} 0, & \text{if new content is covered (5a)} \\ T_B, & \text{otherwise (5b)} \end{cases}$$

For each new page chunk, FTL^2 tries to find the first overlap (if any) and writes the new content. If the new content boundaries are not covered by an existing page chunk, boundary adjustment (parameter "*B*") is required.

The second round merge is modeled as:

$$T_{M2} = \sum_{i=0}^{\#pcs-1} t_i, \qquad (6)$$

in which the value of each term

$$t_i = \begin{cases} 0, & \text{if } pcs[i] \cap pcs[i+1] = \emptyset \quad (7a) \\ T_B + T_{Free}, & \text{if } pcs[i] \cap pcs[i+1] \neq \emptyset \quad (7b) \end{cases}$$

In the second round of merge operation, FTL^2 will attempt to merge every adjacent pair of page chunks. Note that after the i-th and $(i+1)$-th page chunks are merged (if they overlap), the algorithm will use the page chunk resulted from merging as the $(i+1)$-th page chunk and continue to compare it with the $(i+2)$-th page chunk. The maximum number of merge is *the number of page chunks* -1 ("$\#pcs-1$" in Equation 6).

The above analysis shows that both read and write performances can be improved in best cases. In worst cases, write operations may incur an extra page read and multiple memory read/write operations. Except flash memory read/write operations, all other operations happen in DRAM. A single write in flash is transformed to multiple read/write operations in DRAM. The dominating factors affecting write latency now becomes page read and XOR (measured in Section 5). Given that the write speed of flash memory is orders of magnitude slower than DRAM, we can achieve great performance gain for write operations.

4. Experimental Setup

To evaluate the effectiveness of FTL^2, we conducted trace-driven experiments for four write-intensive applications: database running, database building, email server, and Linux kernel building. In the rest of this section, they are denoted as "DB Running", "DB Creation", "EMail Server", and "Build Kernel", respectively. FTL^2 is built based on and compared with a standard page-level FTL using FlashSim [20]. Figure 7 shows the experimental work flow. After pre-processing, traces are replayed in FlashSim for both designs. For simplicity, we selected the page-level FTL as our baseline. In future work, we plan to evaluate FTL^2 against FTLs with different mapping strategies, such as block-level mapping.

4.1 Trace Collection and Characteristics

To collect I/O traces with real data, we developed a trace collection tool called Content-Aware Block Device I/O Tracer (CA-Trace)[1] based on IOTRACE [31]. CA-Trace dumps both request information and real data in I/O requests, while IOTRACE only outputs request information such as starting sector and the number of sectors to read/write. To avoid interference by other requests, two separate disk partitions are dedicated to storing trace files and data generated by running applications, respectively. The raw data dumped by CA-Trace are then processed and fed to the simulator.

[1] Available at http://www.cs.toronto.edu/∼tzwang/catrace-130321.tar.gz.

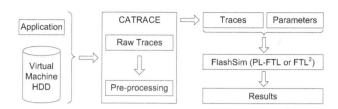

Figure 7: Experimental work flow.

Table 3: Trace characteristics.

Trace	Read Req.	Write Req.	Size
DB Creation	300,452	407,744	15.28 GB
DB Running	3,057	113,504	14.38 GB
EMail Server	119	29,170	15.28 GB
Build Kernel	2,704	12,443	897 MB

Both database traces are generated by Hammerora 2.8 [35] running MySQL [2] database for 30 minutes. Hammerora is an open source workload generation tool and provides the fair usage implementation of the TPC standards [37]. TPC-C is used for collecting DB Running traces. For DB Creation, we extracted the database *creation* phase of TPC-H workload[2]. The page size is set to 4KB. Postmark [27] is a file system benchmark which simulates read/write activities in an email server. We used it to collect traces for "EMail Server". Building the Linux kernel is a common practice for system developers and the period of trace collection includes file decompression, building configuration file, and building target kernel. We used the default configuration generated by "`make defconfig`" to build Linux kernel 3.7.0. All benchmarks/applications are run on Arch Linux [1] with Linux kernel 3.1.1 and ReiserFS version 3 file system [30] in a virtual machine to rule out disturbance from other applications. The I/O scheduler used for trace collection is *noop*, which inserts all I/O requests into a FIFO queue and is suitable for flash memory.

Table 3 summarizes basic trace characteristics. For each trace, the numbers of sector with 5%, 10%, until 100% contents updated are counted and converted to a cumulative distribution function (CDF) graph shown in Figure 1. More than 50% sector updates (y-axis) only modify no more than 5% of data (≈ 26 bytes) per section in database traces. The number for EMail Server is less than 20%. For Build Kernel, most requests updated at least 30% per sector, but the cumulative probability catches EMail Server quickly at 70% on x-axis. A significant number of updates only modify no more than half data in a sector. Partial page updates are common in write-intensive workloads, especially database ones.

4.2 Simulator

We implemented FTL^2 and the baseline page level FTL ("PL-FTL") based on FlashSim [20]. To make a fair comparison, the same garbage collection strategy is adopted for both FTLs. When the number of free pages is below a certain threshold, the garbage collector will identify a non-free block with the minimum number of valid pages and copy all valid pages in this block to a free block. The former block will be erased. Wear leveling is out of the scope of this paper and is left out for both designs. The configurations of SSD used to run traces are shown in Table 4.

Most embedded devices buffer data in a general-purpose cache (not modeled by FlashSim) and finish data transfer in background

[2] TPC-H is essentially a read-intensive workload, we therefore use its creation phase, which is write-intensive.

Table 4: SSD Configurations.

Parameter	Value
Pages per Block	64
Blocks per Plane	256
Planes per Die	8
Dies per Package	4
Packages per SSD	8
Total Capacity	16 GB
Provisioning Area	15% (2.4 GB)
Garbage Collection Threshold	40% (0.96 GB)

Table 5: FTL^2 Parameter settings.

Parameter	Candidate Values
Enable Merge	Yes / No
Logging Threshold	1%, 5%, 15%, 45%
Cache Size	128KB, 256KB, 512KB, 1MB

asynchronously [6, 8]. When Content Cache and a general-purpose cache co-exist, data to be written are intercepted before they reach the general-purpose cache. Content Cache can also replace general-purpose caches. In experiments, we ignore the general-purpose cache and assume that it is transparent to Content Cache.

4.3 FTL Schemes

Baseline FTL (PL-FTL) PL-FTL is a typical page-level mapping scheme [20]. Each logical page is mapped to a physical one. A pointer to the next free page is maintained. When a page write request is received, a new page is allocated and written. If the request is an update, the original page will be marked as invalid before writing new contents. The new page pointer is advanced after each page write. If the number of free pages is below a predefined threshold, the garbage collector is invoked to prepare free pages.

FTL^2 with Content Cache FTL^2 is built by augmenting PL-FTL with Content Cache. All other implementations are the same for both schemes. Note that FTL^2 intercepts incoming write requests before they reach the FTL mapping layer and tries to reduce write requests issued to flash memory. Therefore, with the same mapping strategy, we can observe the effectiveness of Content Cache. PL-FTL is adopted because of its easiness and simplicity in implementation. We use different parameter values to test FTL^2. The settings are summarized in Table 5.

4.4 Metrics

Number of Page Read/Write The number of total page writes is measured to show the effectiveness of FTL^2 in write reduction. As FTL^2 sacrifices read performance for reducing write activities and performance, we also collect the number of total page reads to observe overhead for read requests.

Speed of XOR Operation An XOR operation needs to be conducted for each page update request. Page chunk generation is the major overhead of FTL^2, as mentioned in Section 3.6.2. This metric indicates the number of CPU cycles and clock time for conducting an XOR operation against two 4 KB pages.

It is known that high speed embedded processors are widely adopted in embedded devices, especially in high-end smartphones and SSD [8]. To measure this metric, we adopt an ARM-based processor in our experiment. SimpleScalar-ARM [34] simulator is used to run our test program and gather timing information. The testing program is written in C language and takes two 4KB random strings which are generated to represent the original and new page contents, respectively. The clock time for conducting an XOR operation is then obtain by dividing the number of CPU cycles by the frequency of the embedded processor.

5. Experimental Results

5.1 Effectiveness of Write Reduction with FTL^2

In this section, we present the evaluation results of FTL^2 on write reduction and speed of XOR operations. Figure 8 presents the number of page read and write operations incurred with PL-FTL and FTL^2 using different parameter settings. From each figure, the number of page write operations is reduced by ~50% with FTL^2 when compared with PL-FTL. However, the number of page read operations is greatly increased, especially for database workloads. The reason is that in FTL^2, every page update operation incurs an extra page read operation. Though we experimented with multiple sets of parameters, we noticed that all the figures have very close numbers. For brevity, we give exact numbers in Table 6 for FTL^2 with a 128 KB Content Cache.

As shown in Table 6, for DB Running trace, the number of page writes decreases while the logging threshold increases from 1% to 45%. However, the number of writes is not sensitive to whether merge is enabled. The number of page write operations is slightly increased when merge is enabled. With larger logging thresholds, more updates could be cached into Content Cache, instead of being written to flash memory directly. For DB Creation, EMail Server, and Build Kernel traces, Table 6 shows the same trend. The number of page write is reduced by ~50% for each workload.

The above results are in line with the fact that FTL^2 essentially sacrifices read performance for write reduction and performance – each read operation is appended by several memory read operations. However, one expensive partial page write operation is converted to one page read and multiple memory write operations, or memory read/write operations only (if the whole page is cached). Given that the read performance for both memory and flash is much better than flash page write, the overall write performance is improved, with minor impacts on read performance.

5.2 Speed of XOR Operations

Using our experimental setup, the number of CPU cycles for an XOR operation against two 4KB pages we measured is 56,331. Note that FTL^2 performs XOR operations at byte level. Thus 56,311 actually includes 1024 individual XOR operations against two corresponding bytes in the original and new page contents. If we adopt an ARM Cortex-A9 [4] processor which runs at 2GHz frequency, $28.1655\mu s$ is needed to conduct the XOR operation for the new and existing page contents.

The overhead incurred by conducting XOR operations is between the read ($25\mu s$) and write ($200\mu s$) speeds. When the percentage of new contents is within the logging threshold, the write operation to flash memory will be avoided. The estimated latency of conducting a partial page write is $25\mu s + 28.1655\mu s = 53.1655\mu s$, which is much shorter than writing a page in flash memory directly. If the new contents cannot be cached in Content Cache, an extra overhead of $28.1655\mu s$ is added to the original $200\mu s$ latency of writing a page. With the continuously improved performance of embedded processors and the ever increasing popularity of using multi-core embedded processors such as ARM Cortex-A9 MP Core [4], we believe that overhead will continue to drop by utilizing the abundant processing power of the controller.

Table 6: Comparison on number of page read/write between PL-FTL and FTL^2 (with 128 KB Content Cache).

DB Running											
PL-FTL		FTL^2									
			Threshold = 1%		Threshold = 5%		Threshold = 25%		Threshold = 45%	
Page Reads	Page Writes	Merge	Page Reads	Page Writes	Page Reads	Page Writes	Page Reads	Page Writes	Page Reads	Page Writes
11,553	1,377,377	Enabled	640,767	680,034	666,749	669,677	671,913	648,253	672,528	632,876
		Disabled	642,813	682,080	666,848	669,776	672,015	648,355	672,605	632,953

DB Creation											
PL-FTL		FTL^2									
			Threshold = 1%		Threshold = 5%		Threshold = 25%		Threshold = 45%	
Page Reads	Page Writes	Merge	Page Reads	Page Writes	Page Reads	Page Writes	Page Reads	Page Writes	Page Reads	Page Writes
1,322	880,747	Enabled	311,280	437,550	325,742	437,249	357,363	439,981	360,425	440,050
		Disabled	311,525	437,795	326,300	437,807	357,386	440,004	360,432	440,057

EMail Server											
PL-FTL		FTL^2									
			Threshold = 1%		Threshold = 5%		Threshold = 25%		Threshold = 45%	
Page Reads	Page Writes	Merge	Page Reads	Page Writes	Page Reads	Page Writes	Page Reads	Page Writes	Page Reads	Page Writes
119	2,960,752	Enabled	21,957	1,468,855	23,068	1,468,264	27,195	1,469,735	28,973	1,469,912
		Disabled	21,957	1,468,855	23,104	1,468,300	27,204	1,469,744	28,974	1,469,913

Build Kernel											
PL-FTL		FTL^2									
			Threshold = 1%		Threshold = 5%		Threshold = 25%		Threshold = 45%	
Page Reads	Page Writes	Merge	Page Reads	Page Writes	Page Reads	Page Writes	Page Reads	Page Writes	Page Reads	Page Writes
22,204	484,883	Enabled	40,979	216,621	40,979	216,581	41,132	216,631	41,577	217,004
		Disabled	40,979	216,621	40,979	216,581	41,286	216,785	41,602	217,029

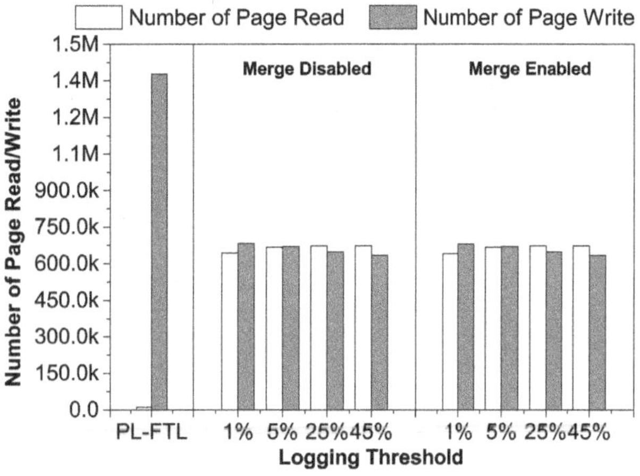

(a) DB Running

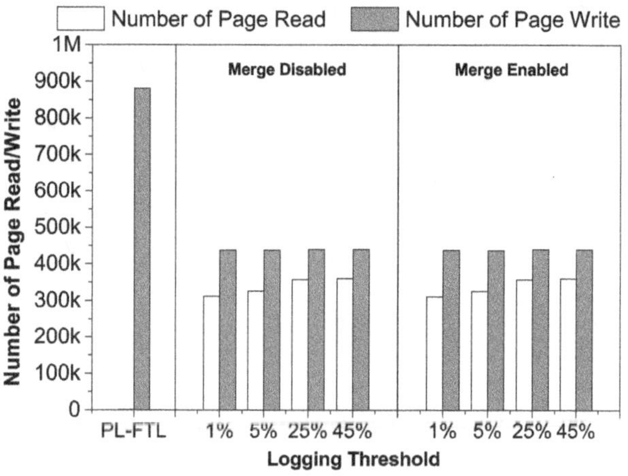

(b) DB Creation

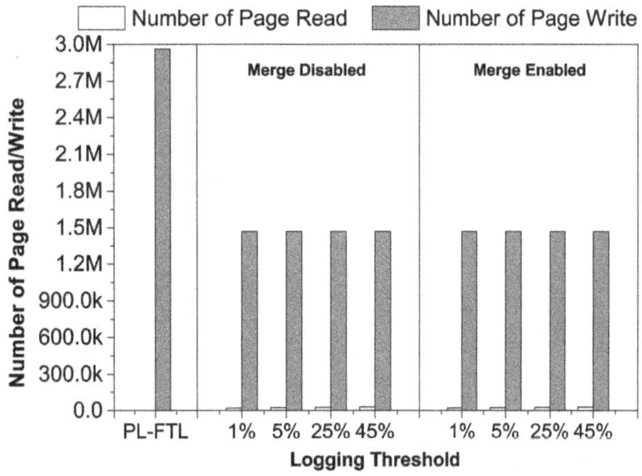

(c) EMail Server

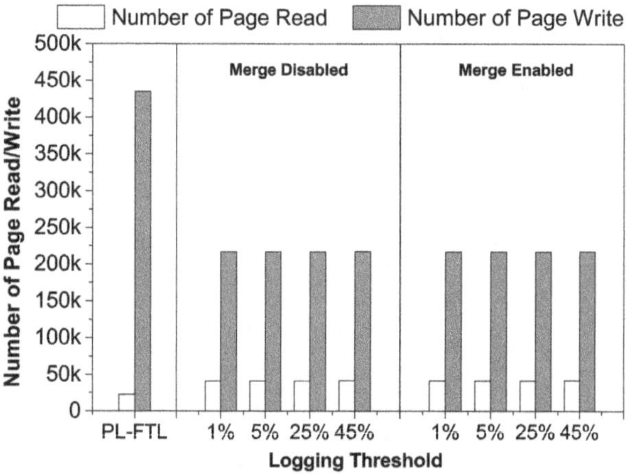

(d) Build Kernel

Figure 8: The number of page read/write operations with different logging thresholds for DB Running, DB Creation, EMail Server, and Build Kernel traces.

6. Related Work and Discussion

Workload-aware FTLs Data duplication has led to content-aware FTLs. Chen et al. [8] proposed a content-aware FTL to coalesce redundant contents. Gupta et al. [11] leveraged value locality to map one physical page to multiple logical pages. To improve random write performance, in-page logging [23] divides each block into data and log regions. ADAPT [38] observes access pattern and uses locality to handle random and sequential writes. Kim et al. [21] introduced a log-based approach which stores differentials between the new and original contents in dedicated pages.

Despite write activities are reduced, existing FTLs may exhaust free pages quickly and trigger garbage collection early. Instead of writing the entire new page or differentials to flash memory, FTL^2 tries to retain and directly avoid partial page updates in high-speed temporary storage to delay block erase operations and improve write performance and endurance.

Wear leveling and garbage collection Flash memory based storage systems are usually equipped with wear leveling algorithms to evenly distribute write activities among all flash cells. For example, observational wear leveling [39] considers the temporal locality of write activities and transfers data among blocks. RFTL [28] tries to guarantee the response time of garbage collection. Currently, wear leveling and garbage collection algorithms are transparent to FTL^2. Note that pages cached by Content Cache are actually invalid in flash memory. Therefore, in future work Content Cache could pass hints to notify the garbage collector or wear leveler, such that invalid pages and blocks can be reclaimed.

Utilizing byte-addressable NVMs NVMs such as PCM have been used to prevent metadata loss at power failure. PCM-FTL [24] and WAB-FTL [25] are two FTLs using PCM to store metadata for hybrid and block-level mappings, respectively. Sun et al. [36] proposed to store logs in PCM for in-page logging [23] to achieve log overwriting. Techniques for prolonging their lifetime are also proposed. Hu et al. [13] proposed to minimize write activities with scheduling and recomputation techniques. ER [15] utilizes data compression to prolong the lifetime of PCM. Jiang et al. [16] proposed write truncation with error correction code to improve endurance of MLC PCM. Low power techniques [14] are also proposed to improve PCM endurance.

In this paper, we suggest using battery-backed DRAM for storing Content Cache to rule out the complexity brought by limited endurance of NVMs. In the future, we will consider co-optimization of both Content Cache and NVMs.

Caches for flash memory General-purpose caching mechanisms have also been proposed to improve the performance and endurance of flash memory. Choudhuri et al. [9] suggested a lookup table and page cache to accelerate address translation. Kgil et al. [18] proposed to divide the cache as separate read/write regions. BPLRU [19] is a general-purpose buffer which utilizes block-level LRU to manage the buffer.

When used with general-purpose caches such as BPLRU, Content Cache intercepts I/O requests before data is buffered by the general purpose cache. By the time data reach the general purpose cache, usually multiple updates have been accumulated by Content Cache. Thus Content Cache can provide better utilization for general-purpose caches. This design also makes it easy to incorporate Content Cache in existing FTLs. Further studying the co-optimization of Content Cache and general-purpose cache is also an interesting future direction.

Logical-physical mapping designs in FTL Mapping schemes can be roughly categorized into page, block, and hybrid level designs. Hybrid FTLs have been widely adopted in flash memory storage systems, especially large-scale ones [5]. Demand-based block-level FTL [29] was proposed by Qin et al. RNFTL [40] prolongs the

lifetime of flash memory by preventing primary blocks with many free pages being recycled.

FTL^2 logs small partial page updates and sends requests which update large portions of the page directly to the mapping mechanism. By combining these two techniques together, FTL^2 reduces write activities and improves write performance with minuscule overheads. In future work, we will incorporate Content Cache with block-level and hybrid FTLs.

7. Conclusion and Future Work

In this paper, we have proposed FTL^2, which employs both logging and mapping approaches, to tackle the endurance problem and performance degradation caused by partial page updates in flash memory. Instead of being written to flash memory directly (mapping), the latest data are retained in Content Cache (logging). Experimental results show that by avoiding immediate mapping and logging the new contents, FTL^2 is able to reduce ~50% page write operations and delay partial page writes. Overall, FTL^2 can enhance the endurance and performance of flash memory at the same time.

In our future work, we will consider using Content Cache with block-level and hybrid mapping strategies, and making it aware of general-purpose cache, garbage collector, and wear leveler for better performance and reliability. Another direction is using NVMs to replace DRAM for Content Cache. Measuring the overheads of FTL^2 more thoroughly and accurately on real hardware is also an interesting future direction.

Acknowledgments

We would like to thank the anonymous reviewers for their valuable feedback and improvements to this paper. The work described in this paper is partially supported by the grants from the Innovation and Technology Support Programme of Innovation and Technology Fund of the Hong Kong Special Administrative Region, China (ITS/082/10), the Germany/Hong Kong Joint Research Scheme sponsored by the Research Grants Council of Hong Kong and the Germany Academic Exchange Service of Germany (G_HK021/12), National Natural Science Foundation of China (Project 61272103), National 863 Program (2013AA013202), Chongqing University 100 Youth Talent Program (2012T0006), Chongqing Sci&Tech Program (csct2012ggC40005), and the Hong Kong Polytechnic University (4-ZZD7, G-YK24 and G-YM10).

References

[1] Arch Linux - A simple, lightweight Linux distribution. *http://www.archlinux.org*.

[2] MySQL Database. *http://www.mysql.com/*.

[3] N. Agrawal, V. Prabhakaran, T. Wobber, J. D. Davis, M. Manasse, and R. Panigrahy. Design tradeoffs for SSD performance. In *USENIX 2008 Annual Technical Conference on Annual Technical Conference (ATC '08)*, pages 57–70, 2008.

[4] ARM Ltd. ARM Cortex-A9 Processor. *ARM Cortex-A9 Processors Whitepaper*, 2009.

[5] L.-P. Chang and T.-W. Kuo. An efficient management scheme for large-scale flash-memory storage systems. In *Proceedings of the 2004 ACM symposium on Applied computing (SAC '04)*, pages 862–868, 2004.

[6] F. Chen, D. A. Koufaty, and X. Zhang. Understanding intrinsic characteristics and system implications of flash memory based solid state drives. In *Proceedings of the eleventh international joint conference on Measurement and modeling of computer systems (SIGMETRICS '09)*, pages 181–192, 2009.

[7] F. Chen, D. A. Koufaty, and X. Zhang. Hystor: making the best use of solid state drives in high performance storage systems. In *Proceedings*

of the international conference on Supercomputing (ICS '11), pages 22–32, 2011.

[8] F. Chen, T. Luo, and X. Zhang. CAFTL: a content-aware flash translation layer enhancing the lifespan of flash memory based solid state drives. In *Proceedings of the 9th USENIX conference on File and stroage technologies (FAST '11)*, pages 6–6, 2011.

[9] S. Choudhuri and T. Givargis. Performance improvement of block based NAND flash translation layer. In *Proceedings of the 5th IEEE/ACM international conference on Hardware/software codesign and system synthesis (CODES+ISSS '07)*, pages 257–262, 2007.

[10] J. Cooke. The inconvenient truths of NAND flash memory. In *Flash Memory Summit*, 2007.

[11] A. Gupta, R. Pisolkar, B. Urgaonkar, and A. Sivasubramaniam. Leveraging value locality in optimizing NAND flash-based SSDs. In *Proceedings of the 9th USENIX conference on File and stroage technologies (FAST '11)*, pages 7–7, 2011.

[12] Y. Ho, G. M. Huang, and P. Li. Nonvolatile memristor memory: device characteristics and design implications. In *Proceedings of the 2009 International Conference on Computer-Aided Design (ICCAD '09)*, pages 485–490, New York, NY, USA, 2009. ACM.

[13] J. Hu, W.-C. Tseng, C. Xue, Q. Zhuge, Y. Zhao, and E.-M. Sha. Write activity minimization for nonvolatile main memory via scheduling and recomputation. *Computer-Aided Design of Integrated Circuits and Systems, IEEE Transactions on*, 30(4):584–592, 2011.

[14] L. Jiang, Y. Zhang, and J. Yang. Enhancing phase change memory lifetime through fine-grained current regulation and voltage upscaling. In *2011 International Symposium on Low Power Electronics and Design (ISLPED '11)*, pages 127–132, aug. 2011.

[15] L. Jiang, Y. Zhang, and J. Yang. ER: elastic RESET for low power and long endurance MLC based phase change memory. In *Proceedings of the 2012 ACM/IEEE international symposium on Low power electronics and design (ISLPED '12)*, pages 39–44, New York, NY, USA, 2012. ACM.

[16] L. Jiang, B. Zhao, Y. Zhang, J. Yang, and B. Childers. Improving write operations in MLC phase change memory. In *IEEE 18th International Symposium on High Performance Computer Architecture (HPCA '12)*, pages 1–10, Feb. 2012.

[17] R. Johnson, I. Pandis, N. Hardavellas, A. Ailamaki, and B. Falsafi. Shore-MT: a scalable storage manager for the multicore era. In *Proceedings of the 12th International Conference on Extending Database Technology: Advances in Database Technology (EDBT '09)*, pages 24–35, New York, NY, USA, 2009. ACM.

[18] T. Kgil, D. Roberts, and T. Mudge. Improving NAND flash based disk caches. In *Proceedings of the 35th International Symposium on Computer Architecture (ISCA '08)*, pages 327–338, Washington, DC, USA, 2008. IEEE Computer Society.

[19] H. Kim and S. Ahn. BPLRU: a buffer management scheme for improving random writes in flash storage. In *Proceedings of the 6th USENIX Conference on File and Storage Technologies (FAST'08)*, pages 16:1–16:14, Berkeley, CA, USA, 2008. USENIX Association.

[20] Y. Kim, B. Tauras, A. Gupta, and B. Urgaonkar. FlashSim: A simulator for NAND flash-based solid-state drives. In *Proceedings of the 2009 First International Conference on Advances in System Simulation (SIMUL '09)*, pages 125–131, 2009.

[21] Y.-R. Kim, K.-Y. Whang, and I.-Y. Song. Page-differential logging: an efficient and DBMS-independent approach for storing data into flash memory. In *Proceedings of the 2010 international conference on Management of data (SIGMOD '10)*, pages 363–374, 2010.

[22] T.-W. Kuo, Y.-H. Chang, P.-C. Huang, and C.-W. Chang. Special issues in flash. In *Proceedings of the IEEE/ACM International Conference on Computer-Aided Design (ICCAD '08)*, pages 821–826, November 2008.

[23] S.-W. Lee and B. Moon. Design of flash-based DBMS: an in-page logging approach. In *Proceedings of the 2007 ACM SIGMOD international conference on Management of data (SIGMOD '07)*, pages 55–66, 2007.

[24] D. Liu, T. Wang, Y. Wang, Z. Qin, and Z. Shao. PCM-FTL: a write-activity-aware NAND flash memory management scheme for PCM-based embedded systems. In *Proceedings of 2011 IEEE 32nd Real-Time Systems Symposium (RTSS '11)*, pages 357–366, Dec. 2011.

[25] D. Liu, T. Wang, Y. Wang, Z. Qin, and Z. Shao. A block-level flash memory management scheme for reducing write activities in PCM-based embedded systems. In *Proceedings of 15th IEEE/ACM Design, Automation Test in Europe Conference Exhibition (DATE '12)*, pages 1447–1450, march 2012.

[26] D. Liu, Y. Wang, Z. Qin, Z. Shao, and Y. Guan. A space reuse strategy for flash translation layers in SLC NAND flash memory storage systems. *IEEE Transactions on Very Large Scale Integration (VLSI) Systems*, 20(6):1094–1107, june 2012.

[27] NetApp. Postmark benchmark. *http://www.netapp.com/*, 2012.

[28] Z. Qin, Y. Wang, D. Liu, and Z. Shao. Real-time flash translation layer for NAND flash memory storage systems. In *Proceedings of the 2012 IEEE 18th Real Time and Embedded Technology and Applications Symposium*.

[29] Z. Qin, Y. Wang, D. Liu, and Z. Shao. Demand-based block-level address mapping in large-scale NAND flash storage systems. In *Proceedings of the eighth IEEE/ACM/IFIP international conference on Hardware/software codesign and system synthesis (CODES/ISSS '10)*, pages 173–182, New York, NY, USA, 2010. ACM.

[30] H. Reiser. Reiserfs. *http://rfsd.sourceforge.net*, 2013.

[31] Y. Saito. IOTRACE - Disk I/O Tracing Utility for Linux 2.6 Kernels.

[32] SAMSUNG Corporation. SAMSUNG 1G x 8 Bit / 2G x 8 Bit NAND Flash Memory. 2005.

[33] SAMSUNG Corporation. SAMSUNG NAND flash memory. *http://www.samsung.com/global/business/semiconductor*, 2009.

[34] SimpleScalar LLC. SimpleScalar (ARM Target) Version 4.0. *http://www.simplescalar.com/v4test.html*.

[35] Steve Shaw. Hammerora - the open source oracle load test tool. *http://hammerora.sourceforge.net*.

[36] G. Sun, Y. Joo, Y. Chen, D. Niu, Y. Xie, Y. Chen, and H. Li. A hybrid solid-state storage architecture for the performance, energy consumption, and lifetime improvement. In *2010 IEEE 16th International Symposium on High Performance Computer Architecture (HPCA '10)*, pages 1–12, Jan. 2010.

[37] Transaction Processing Performance Council. TPC Benchmarks. *http://www.tpc.org/*.

[38] C. Wang and W.-F. Wong. ADAPT: Efficient workload-sensitive flash management based on adaptation, prediction and aggregation. In *Proceedings of IEEE 28th Symposium on on Massive Data Storage (MSST '12)*, 2012.

[39] C. Wang and W.-F. Wong. Observational wear leveling: An efficient algorithm for flash memory management. In *Proceedings of 49th ACM/EDAC/IEEE Design Automation Conference (DAC '12)*, pages 235–242, june 2012.

[40] Y. Wang, D. Liu, M. Wang, Z. Qin, Z. Shao, and Y. Guan. RN-FTL: a reuse-aware NAND flash translation layer for flash memory. In *Proceedings of the ACM SIGPLAN/SIGBED 2010 conference on Languages, compilers, and tools for embedded systems (LCTES '10)*, pages 163–172, New York, NY, USA, 2010. ACM.

[41] C.-H. Wu, T.-W. Kuo, and C.-L. Yang. A space-efficient caching mechanism for flash-memory address translation. In *Proceedings of the Ninth IEEE International Symposium on Object and Component-Oriented Real-Time Distributed Computing (ISORC '06)*, pages 64–71, 2006.

[42] C. J. Xue, Y. Zhang, Y. Chen, G. Sun, J. J. Yang, and H. Li. Emerging non-volatile memories: opportunities and challenges. In *Proceedings of the seventh IEEE/ACM/IFIP international conference on Hardware/software codesign and system synthesis*, CODES+ISSS '11, pages 325–334, New York, NY, USA, 2011. ACM.

Compiler Directed Write-Mode Selection for High Performance Low Power Volatile PCM

Qingan Li

Computer School, Wuhan University
Department of Computer Science, City
University of Hong Kong
ww345ww@gmail.com

Lei Jiang   Youtao Zhang

Computer Science Department,
University of Pittsburgh
lej16@pitt.edu, zhangyt@cs.pitt.edu

Yanxiang He

Computer School, Wuhan University
yxhe@whu.edu.cn

Chun Jason Xue

Department of Computer Science, City University of Hong Kong
jasonxue@cityu.edu.hk

Abstract

Micro-Controller Units (MCUs) are widely adopted ubiquitous computing devices. Due to tight cost and energy constraints, MCUs often integrate very limited internal RAM memory on top of Flash storage, which exposes Flash to heavy write traffic and results in short system lifetime. Architecting emerging Phase Change Memory (PCM) is a promising approach for MCUs due to its fast read speed and long write endurance.

However, PCM, especially multi-level cell (MLC) PCM, has long write latency and requires large write energy, which diminishes the benefits of its replacement of traditional Flash. By studying MLC PCM write operations, we observe that writing MLC PCM can take advantages of two write modes — fast write leaves cells in volatile state, and slow write leaves cells in non-volatile state. In this paper, we propose a compiler directed dual-write (CDDW) scheme that selects the best write mode for each write operation to maximize the overall performance and energy efficiency. Our experimental results show that CDDW reduces dynamic energy by 32.4%(33.8%) and improves performance by 6.3%(35.9%) compared with an all fast(slow) write approach.

Categories and Subject Descriptors D.3.4 [*Programming Languages*]: Processors; C.3 [*Speical-Purpose and Application-based Systems*]: Real-time and embedded systems

Keywords phase change memory, multi-level cell, compiler, worst case execution time

1. Introduction

Due to increasing ubiquitous computing demands, Micro Controller Units (MCUs) have been widely adopted in everyday service devices, such as temperature sensors and MP3 players, to achieve better trade-offs among cost, performance, and energy consumption. MCUs usually integrate a very limited size of internal RAM

LCTES'13,   June 20–21, 2013, Seattle, Washington, USA.
Copyright © 2013 ACM 978-1-4503-2085-6/13/06. . . $15.00

(512B~512KB) on top of external Flash storage [9, 31], which exposes Flash to heavy write traffic. Given write operations of Flash consume high energy and Flash has limited write endurance, MCUs often suffer from low performance and short system lifetime. For example, 2-bit Multi-level cell (MLC) Flash only tolerates 10^3 programming cyclings [10].

Recent works have proposed to deploy emerging phase change memory (PCM) as an universal memory to replace internal RAM and external Flash [48]. PCM has better scalability than traditional DRAM. While the path to scale DRAM under $22nm$ is still unclear [39], PCM can reach $4F^2$ cell size at $20nm$ technology [7]. MLC PCM further reduces cost per bit [17, 37]. Through MLC PCM, MCUs obtain smaller chip size to achieve lower manufacture cost, which is a critical factor to embedded system industry. Compared to DRAM, PCM has comparable read latency and lower leakage power consumption [21, 35, 47]. Compared to Flash, PCM enjoys faster read/write access speed and much longer cell endurance [14].

However, write operations of PCM still suffer from long latency [36] and large write power [15, 16]. With a limited power budget, slow and high power PCM writes severely hurt system performance [11]. Recent work [48] proposed a sustainable wireless sensor design to strengthen PCM write power supply and prolong battery cycle life by absorbing solar energy. In high performance computing field, a fine-grained PCM write power management [15] was also presented to improve main memory write throughput.

Device level studies [5, 25] have shown that the non-volatility of MLC PCM can be traded for better performance and lower write energy. For MLC PCM, a small resistance range, referred to as guardband, is intentionally left between two resistance states to prevent the lower resistance state from drifting into the higher resistance state [5, 46]. There are two writing modes for MLC PCM. If the guardband is large while the resistance ranges for different resistance states are small, two resistance states have to spend a very long time to mingle together. MLC PCM cells, if written according to this setting, are considered as non-volatile. On the other hand, if the guardband is small while the resistance ranges for different resistance states are big, it takes shorter latency to write cells but the cells are volatile (as two resistance states may mess up after a short time). These two writing modes are referred to as slow write mode and fast write mode in this paper. To ensure data reliability, fast write mode needs periodical refresh, which not only involves hardware overhead, but also consumes additional energy and cycles. On the other hand, slow mode may lead to energy inefficient and longer write operations.

In this paper, we propose a **C**ompiler **D**irected **D**ual-**W**rite (CDDW) scheme to improve system performance while reducing write energy simultaneously. The followings summarize our contributions.

- We model the two MLC PCM write modes – slow write mode and fast write mode, and elaborate their trade-offs among write latency, write energy and retention time.

- We propose a Compiler Directed Dual-Write (CDDW) scheme for writing MLC PCM in MCUs. Based on static analysis of memory write instructions, CDDW estimates their Worst Case lifetime (WCLT), which guides the selection of the best write mode for each memory write instruction. CDDW achieves better trade-offs between high performance and low write energy.

- We conduct experiments to evaluate the proposed scheme. Our results show that compared to fast write mode baseline, CDDW improves the performance by 6.3% and reduces write energy by 32.4%. The cell endurance of MLC PCM can also be enhanced by nearly 5x.

The rest of this paper is organized as follows. The volatile PCM model, as well as a motivation example, is discussed in Section 2. The proposed Compiler Directed Dual-Write approach for PCM is shown in Section 3. Section 4 and Section 5 describe the experimental methodology and evaluation results respectively. Previous work is discussed in Section 6. At last, we conclude this paper in Section 7.

2. Volatile PCM Model and Motivation

In this section, we briefly introduce the background on phase change memory (PCM), multi-level cell (MLC), MLC PCM write operation and trade-off between MLC PCM write latency and its retention time. At the end of this section we will present a motivation example to illustrate how to improve system performance and reduce write energy with different writing modes.

2.1 MLC PCM and its Write

Phase Change Memory (PCM) utilizes the phase-change behaviour of chalcogenide glass (a.k.a GST, $Ge_2Sb_2Te_5$) to record data. By injecting electrical pulses to Joule Heater (Figure 1(a)), GST can be switched between large resistance state (amorphous state) and small resistance state (crystalline state). MLC PCM exploits intermediate resistance levels between these two states to store multiple logic bits per cell.

Due to process variations [45] and material composition fluctuation [17], different PCM cells in one memory line respond distinctively to programming pulses; and even the same cell responds differently at different times [28]. Therefore, PCM widely adopts an iteration-based programming and verifying (P&V) write scheme (Figure 1(b)) to precisely control the cell resistance. A *RESET* operation is always first conducted to put the cell in an initial state. A series of *SET* and verify (read) operations then follow until the target resistance level is reached.

2.2 Trade-off between Write Latency and Retention Time

As Figure 2 shows, PCM uses resistance ranges to represent the information stored in the cell. Four resistance ranges indicate four data value, from '00' to '10' (Gray Encoding). A small unused guardband is often left between two consecutive ranges to prevent resistance drift [18]. In PCM, due to the relaxation of the parameters of amorphous phase, the resistance of PCM spontaneously increases [5], this phenomenon is known as resistance drift. And the drifting speed is proportional to the volume fraction of amorphous

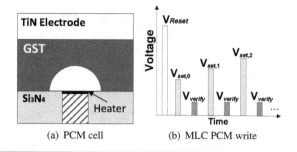

(a) PCM cell   (b) MLC PCM write

Figure 1. PCM cell and its write operation.

Figure 2. MLC PCM resistance distribution.

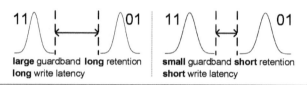

Figure 3. Trade-off on Volatile MLC PCM.

phase [5]. Drift affects the stability of the electrical behaviour of MLC PCM cell, and thus the reliability of MLC storage.

In [5], the guardband between '11' and '01' was identified as the most vulnerable one. So we use the guardband between '11' and '01' in Figure 3 as illustration. Longer retention time can be obtained by increasing guardband size, since larger guardband can tolerate larger resistance drifting. As Figure 3 shows, large guardband requires tight distribution of each neighborhood resistance state. To increase the programming accuracy and achieve tight resistance distribution, more write iterations and energy must be paid in each write operation. On the contrary, shorter write latency produces smaller guardband, which introduces smaller retention time.

2.3 Volatile Phase Change Memory Model

We modelled phase change memory with volatile characteristic as following. We generate the volatile memory model by current/resistance of PCM model in [19], process variation on PCM model [14] and resistance drifting model [5]. The current/resistance of PCM model calculates the resistance of PCM cell when applying a RESET or SET current on the cell for a given latency. Since PCM usually adopt iteration based programming method, we set the latency of an iteration as $1000ns$ in this paper. By applying different amplitudes of current on PCM cell for a $1000ns$ iteration, we can achieve different resistances. We produce a process variation distribution on the key parameters of PCM cell, such as heater radius, etc. And then, even with the same current, different cells achieve different resistances. We select the distances between worst case resistances (3σ in the process variation distribution) as our PCM resistance guardbands. Using the PCM resistance drifting model proposed in [5], we can get different retention times for different guardbands between PCM resistance states. The volatile PCM model can be summarized in Table 1. This MLC PCM model supports multi-level retention times and write latencies. Based on this model, we propose a Compiler Directed Dual Write (CDDW) ap-

Iteration(#)	Current(μA)	N. Energy	Retention(s)
10	310	1(baseline)	11158.84
8	320	0.85	4823.178
7	330	0.75	2084.719
6	340	0.72	713.7916
5	360	0.674	83.67949
4	380	0.6	20.67646
3	410	0.524	1.87

Table 1. The Volatile MLC PCM Model.

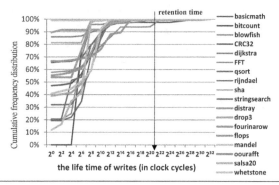

Figure 4. Lifetime distribution of memory writes.

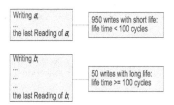

(a) A schematic sample program.

Scheme	Cost
fast	$time_{write} = (950 + 50) * 1 = 1000$ $time_{ref} = (wcet + time_{write}) * \frac{60}{99} \approx 3000$ $time_{total} = wcet + time_{write} + time_{ref} \approx 8000$
slow	$time_{write} = (950 + 50) * 3 = 3000$ $time_{ref} = 0$ $time_{total} = wcet + time_{write} + time_{ref} = 7000$
dual	$time_{write} = 950 * 1 + 50 * 3 = 1100$ $time_{ref} = 0$ $time_{total} = wcet + time_{write} + time_{ref} = 5100$

(b) Cost in different write modes.

Figure 5. A motivation example.

proach to exploit the trade-off between performance and retention time of PCM. Although the proposed CDDW approach only exploits the trade-off between MLC PCM retention and write latency in two modes, it can be easily extended to cover more modes.

2.4 Motivation Example

The performance of PCM can be improved by exploiting the trade-off between write latency and retention time of MLC PCM. We can select different write mode for different Memory Write Instructions (MWI) according to these instructions' lifetimes. The *lifetime of an MWI instance* is defined as the elapsed time from the time this MWI instance writes a value into a memory line to the time that the last read of this value occurs. Each MWI instance starts a new lifetime. If the lifetime of an MWI instance is shorter than the retention time of PCM cells, for this write no refresh is needed and the data correctness can be guaranteed. Based on this observation, we can employ a fast write mode for MWI instances with short lifetime so that the system performance can take advantage of the short write latency and low write energy while no refresh is needed.

A set of experiments are conducted to evaluate the lifetime of MWIs in a set of benchmarks. The experiment is set up as follows. We adopted a baseline MCU with no cache, no pipeline, and no Memory Management Unit (MMU). The MCU is operated at 1 MHz. In our evaluation, each instruction takes 1-clock cycle, each read takes 1-clock cycle, each fast-write takes 3-clock cycles, and each slow-write takes 10-clock cycles. The retention time of a fast write is set to be 1,870,000 clock cycles. The details of our volatile phase change memory model are discussed in Section 2.3.

Figure 4 shows the distribution of lifetime for MWIs. On average, about 99.5% memory writes have a lifetime shorter than 2^{20} clock cycles. As a result, ideally about 99.5% memory writes can be safely conducted in fast mode without refresh, since the retention time of a fast write is longer than 2^{20} clock cycles. From Figure 4, we also observe that a small group of memory writes have very long lifetime. If fast write mode is applied, these memory lines require refresh operations to maintain data correctness. Therefore, for these memory writes, slow write mode may work better than fast write mode which leads to refresh overhead. To boost system performance and reduce memory energy consumption, we can select fast write mode for MWI instances with short lifetime and slow write mode for those with long lifetime through analysing the lifetime of each MWI.

It is not practical to identify the exact lifetime of each MWI instance at runtime, since such kind of information is sensitive to program structure and program inputs. Alternatively, we can obtain the Worst Case lifetime (WCLT) of each MWI using static analysis techniques. If the WCLT of an MWI is less than the retention time of a fast write, an fast write mode can achieve better performance.

Figure 5 shows a motivation example to illustrate the benefits of selecting different write modes for different write operations. In this example, we assume a fast write takes 1 cycle, and a slow write takes 3 cycles. The retention time of a fast write is 10^2

cycles, and the retention time of a slow write is 10^5 cycles. The *wcet* of a program p is 4000 cylces, excluding the time consumed by write operations. To ensure correctness, the whole memory system is refreshed every 99 cycles in fast write mode. And each whole memory system refresh spends 60 cycles. In Figure 5 (a), a schematic sample program is shown. It is assumed that there are 950 short writes and 50 long writes. In Figure 5 (b), we can see that among three schemes, *dual-write* scheme achieves the best performance among the three options. This is because that in the *dual-write* scheme, short lifetime MWIs are conducted in fast mode and long lifetime MWIs are performed in slow mode, and thus the advantages of both write modes can be achieved. In this paper, we propose a compiler directed write mode selection scheme to choose the best write mode for each MWI via analysing its WCLT.

Figure 6 shows the number of successive writes with short lifetime. We can see that most writes of short lifetime occur sequentially, so in the *dual-write* scheme, we do not need to change write mode frequently.

3. Compiler Directed Dual-Write

To exploit the trade-off between write latency and retention time of MLC PCM, this section proposes a compiler directed dual-write (CDDW) approach to improve energy efficiency and performance.

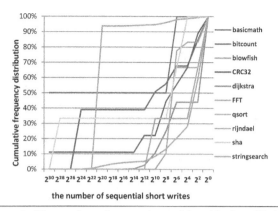

Figure 6. The number of successive writes with short lifetime. Here, a *short lifetime write* is a write with lifetime less than the retention time of a fast write.

This CDDW approach works on the binary code, and includes two parts: Worst Case lifetime (WCLT) analysis and code injection. The first part analyses the lifetime of each MWI in the worst case. The *lifetime of an MWI instance* is defined as the elapsed time from the time this MWI instance writes a value into a memory line to the time that the last read of this value occurs. One MWI may involve multiple instances and each instance has a distinct lifetime. The second part inserts Write-mode Selection Instructions (WSIs) into the binary file to select the best write mode for each MWI. As illustrated in Algorithm 3.1, the proposed approach consists of five steps. We will describe all steps in details in the following.

Algorithm 3.1 The proposed compiler directed dual-write (CDDW) algorithm.

1: **CFG construction.** The binary code is disassembled and the Control Flow Graph (CFG) is reconstructed.
2: **Memory address analysis.** An abstract interpretation is performed on disassembly code to identify the target memory address of each instruction.
3: **Reaching definition analysis.** The set of Memory Read Instructions (MRIs) for each Memory Write Instruction (MWI) is conservatively identified. After this step, a define-use chain is built to associate each MWI i_w with all MRIs reading the value written by i_w.
4: **WCLT analysis:** The WCLT of each MWI is analysed based on a modified worst-case execution time (WCET) analysis technique.
5: **Code injection:** WSIs are inserted to choose the best write mode for each MWI.

3.1 CFG construction

During this step, the binary code is disassembled first. Then, the CFG for each function can be constructed from disassembly code by tracking conditional/unconditional jump instructions and return instructions. During this step, the Inter-procedural Control Flow Graph (ICFG) is also constructed for the whole program by connecting CFGs at call sites. All following analysis and transformation techniques are conducted on the representation of the ICFG. A fraction of C sample code is shown in Figure 7 and the corresponding disassembly code[1] as well as CFG is shown in the first column in Figure 8.

---

[1] In Figure 8, the disassemble code uses MIPS instruction set, where register $28 is the global pointer register, register $29 is the stack pointer register, and register $31 is used to store the return address of caller function. The value of register $0 is always zero.

```
int x, y, z;
int main ()
{
    int a, b, c, *p;

    z = x * y;
    if ( z > 0 )
        p = &a;
    else
        p = &b;
    *p = x + y + z;
    a ++;
    b ++;
    *q = *p;
    return *q;
}
```

Figure 7. Sample C code

3.2 Memory address analysis

The abstract interpretation techniques proposed in [6, 40] can be employed for memory address analysis on the assembly code level ICFG. This technique uses *a-loc* abstraction to statically compute an accurate over-approximation to the set of values that each memory location or register may contain. The *a-loc* abstraction is based on the following observation: the data layout of the program is established before generating the executable. Each global object is accessed via global pointer register plus a constant offset. Each local object is accessed via stack pointer register plus a constant offset. A refined abstraction numerical domain is used to over-approximate the set of memory addresses that each *a-loc* holds at a particular program point. An abstract address in global area can be represented as (G, offset) and in local area of function f can be represented as (f, offset). A constant address or value c can be denoted as $(0, c)$. More details are presented in [6, 40].

The memory address analysis results of the C example code are shown in the third column in Figure 8. We assume that the stack base pointer at the entry of the *main* function is (*main*, 0). We use p_n to denote the program point immediately after the nth line code. At p_5, the content of *a-loc* $29 is (*main*, -24). At p_{10}, the content of (*main*,-16) is (*main*, -24). At p_{16}, it is uncertain that whether the content of (*main*, -16) is (*main*, -24) or (*main*, -20). As a result, at p_{17}, the content of $4 could be either value.

3.3 Reaching definition analysis

After calculating the set of possible memory addresses for each memory access instruction, a reaching definition analysis [2] can be conducted to construct the define-use chains for each MWI. A define-use chain $< w, \{r_1, r_2, \cdots, r_k\} >$ associates an MWI w with a set of MRIs r_i, if these MRIs read the content written by w.

Figure 8 shows the results of reaching definition analysis for the example in Figure 7. The memory addresses written by each MWI is shown in the fourth column, and the memory addresses read by each MRI is shown in the fifth column. It shows that both *i8* and *i11* write (*main*, -16) which is then read by *i17*. Since it is uncertain at compilation time which branch is taken, both *i8* and *i11* will be mapped to *i17*. Similarly, since *i18* may write either (*main*, -24) or (*main*, -20), *i19* reads (*main*, -24), and *i20* reads (*main*, -20), *i18* is mapped to both *i19* and *i20*. A simplified but possibly more illustrative version is shown in Figure 9.

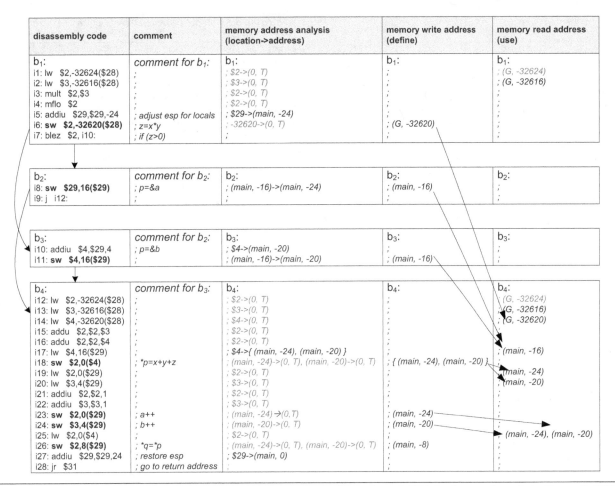

disassembly code	comment	memory address analysis (location->address)	memory write address (define)	memory read address (use)
b₁: i1: lw $2,-32624($28) i2: lw $3,-32616($28) i3: mult $2,$3 i4: mflo $2 i5: addiu $29,$29,-24 **i6: sw $2,-32620($28)** i7: blez $2, i10:	comment for b₁: ; ; ; ; ; adjust esp for locals ; z=x*y ; if (z>0)	b₁: ; $2->(0, T) ; $3->(0, T) ; $2->(0, T) ; $2->(0, T) ; $29->(main, -24) ; -32620->(0, T) ;	b₁: ; ; ; ; ; ; (G, -32620) ;	b₁: ; (G, -32624) ; (G, -32616) ; ; ; ; ;
b₂: i8: sw $29,16($29) i9: j i12:	comment for b₂: ; p=&a ;	b₂: ; (main, -16)->(main, -24) ;	b₂: ; (main, -16) ;	b₂: ; ;
b₃: i10: addiu $4,$29,4 i11: sw $4,16($29)	comment for b₂: ; p=&b ;	b₃: ; $4->(main, -20) ; (main, -16)->(main, -20)	b₃: ; ; (main, -16)	b₃: ; ;
b₄: i12: lw $2,-32624($28) i13: lw $3,-32616($28) i14: lw $4,-32620($28) i15: addu $2,$2,$3 i16: addu $2,$2,$4 i17: lw $4,16($29) **i18: sw $2,0($4)** i19: lw $2,0($29) i20: lw $3,4($29) i21: addiu $2,$2,1 i22: addiu $3,$3,1 **i23: sw $2,0($29)** **i24: sw $3,4($29)** i25: lw $2,0($4) **i26: sw $2,8($29)** i27: addiu $29,$29,24 i28: jr $31	comment for b₃: ; ; ; ; ; ; ; *p=x+y+z ; ; ; ; ; a++ ; b++ ; ; *q=*p ; restore esp ; go to return address	b₄: ; $2->(0, T) ; $3->(0, T) ; $4->(0, T) ; $2->(0, T) ; $2->(0, T) ; $4->{ (main, -24), (main, -20) } ; (main, -24)->(0, T), (main, -20)->(0, T) ; $2->(0, T) ; $3->(0, T) ; $2->(0, T) ; $3->(0, T) ; (main, -24) →(0,T) ; (main, -20)->(0, T) ; $2->(0, T) ; (main, -24)->(0, T), (main, -20)->(0, T) ; $29->(main, 0) ;	b₄: ; ; ; ; ; ; ; { (main, -24), (main, -20) } ; ; ; ; ; (main, -24) ; (main, -20) ; ; (main, -8) ; ;	b₄: ; (G, -32624) ; (G, -32616) ; (G, -32620) ; ; ; (main, -16) ; (main, -24) ; (main, -20) ; ; ; ; ; ; (main, -24), (main, -20) ; ;

Figure 8. A walk through example. The first column shows the disassembly code and CFG for the sample code in Figure 7. MWIs are highlighted in bold. The second column shows comments. The third column shows the results of memory address analysis in Section 3.2. This column shows the possible content for each register and memory address. For example, $29→(main,-24)$ indicates the content of register 29 is a memory address in local area of function *main* with the offset -24. When the content is about a pure numeric value rather than memory addresses, the corresponding results are shown in gray. $(0, \top)$ indicates an uncertain value. The fourth and fifth columns show the memory addresses written and read by each instruction, respectively. Additionally, an arrow from an instruction writing to an address to another instruction reading the same address indicates the define-use chain.

3.4 WCLT estimation

To analyze the WCLT of each MWI, the state-of-art Worst Case Execution Time (WCET) analysis techniques can be employed. The WCET analysis of a program usually involves two steps: micro-architectural modelling and program path analysis. Micro-architectural modelling captures micro-architectural features to over-approximate the WCET of each basic block. And then, program path analysis, including path enumeration and infeasible path elimination, is used to combine the WCET of individual basic blocks to obtain the WCET of the whole program. The state-of-art WCET analysis techniques commonly resort to Integer Linear Programming (ILP) formulation for program path analysis. The WCET of a program is given by the following objective function:

$$maximize \sum_{b \in B} N_b * c_b \qquad (1)$$

where B is the set of basic blocks of the program, N_b is an ILP variable denoting the execution count of basic block b, and c_b is a constant (computed during micro-architectural modelling) denoting the WCET of basic block b. Lots of constraints are provided to eliminate infeasible program paths, such as flow equation constraints, loop bound constraints and other constraints through additional infeasible path analysis.

The WCET analysis computing the WCET of a program cannot be applied directly for the WCLT analysis of an MWI. The WCLT computation cares about the worst case distance from the time an MWI writing a value to the last time that this value is read. So, WCLT computation only cares about instructions in paths from the MWI writing a value to the MRIs reading it. We need to extract the corresponding sub-graph from the ICFG. This can be done by the following steps:

1. For each basic block i, compute the set of blocks it can reach and store the information using a bit matrix $reach$. If i can reach basic block k, $reach[i][k]$ is set to be one. Otherwise, it is zero. The *reachability relationship* R is defined as: $(b_i, b_j) \in R$, if b_j is b_i or b_j is a successor of b_i or there is another block b_k satisfying $(b_i, b_k) \in R \land (b_k, b_j) \in R$. The reachability relationship can be computed as transition closure over the ICFG, as illustrated in Algorithm 3.2. Alternatively, a work-list algorithm can be utilized for better efficiency.

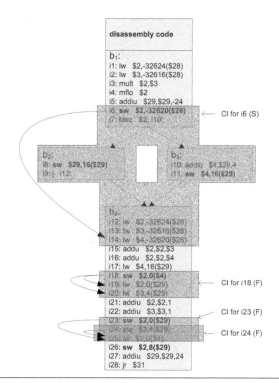

Figure 9. The define-use chains as well as CIs for some MWIs. In parentheses, 'S' indicates slow mode and 'F' indicates fast mode for the corresponding MWI.

Algorithm 3.2 Reachability computation.

Input:

    blocks: a list of basic blocks for the program
    N: the total number of basic blocks of the program
    $reach[N][N]$: a matrix representing the reachability relationship

Output:

    $reach[N][N]$: updated reachability relationship

1: // 1. initialize reach[N][N]
2: **for** each block b_i of *blocks* **do**
3:    **for** each block b_j of *blocks* **do**
4:      **if** b_j is a successor block of b_i or b_j is b_i **then**
5:        $reach[i][j] \leftarrow$ **true**;
6:      **else**
7:        $reach[i][j] \leftarrow$ **false**;
8:      **end if**
9:    **end for**
10: **end for**
11: // 2. computing the transition closure
12: **for** $k = 1$ to N **do**
13:   **for** $i = 1$ to N **do**
14:     **for** $j = 1$ to N **do**
15:      **if** $reach[i][k]$ && $reach[k][j]$ **then**
16:        $reach[i][j] \leftarrow$ **true**;
17:      **end if**
18:     **end for**
19:   **end for**
20: **end for**

---

2. Each MWI i, assuming that it belongs to block b_i, can reach all the blocks b_i reaches. Similarly, i is reached by all the blocks reaching b_i. For example, in Figure 9, MWI $i6$ can reach all blocks, while $i8$ can only reach block b_2 and b_4. Similarly, both MRI $i14$ and $i17$ can be reached by all blocks.

Algorithm 3.3 Computing covered instructions for each define-use chain.

Input:

    $< w, \{r_1, r_2, \cdots, r_k\} >$: a define-use chain, where w is the concerned MWI
    blocks: a list of basic blocks for the program
    $reach[N][N]$: a matrix representing the reachability relationship

Output:

    insts: the set of instructions covered by w

1: **for** each block b_i of *blocks* **do**
2:    **if** w belongs to b_i **then**
3:      add all instructions of b_i succeeding w into *insts*;
4:    **else if** any of r_i belongs to b_i **then**
5:      add all instructions of b_i preceding r_i into *insts*;
6:    **else if** $reach[w][b_i]$ && $(reach[b_i][r_1] \; || \; reach[b_i][r_2] \cdots read[b_i][r_k])$ **then**
7:      add all instructions of b_i into *insts*;
8:    **end if**
9: **end for**

---

3. For each define-use chain $< w, \{r_1, r_2, \cdots, r_k\} >$, it is easy to extract a vertex-induced sub-graph from the ICFG, including only the covered instructions (CI), as shown in Algorithm 3.3. This sub-graph can be view as a pseudo program which views w as the program entry and each r_i as a program exit. Then, we can obtain the WCLT of w by computing the WCET of the pseudo program.

For example, in Figure 9, according to define-use chain $< i6, \{i14\} >$, $i6$ reaches all blocks. We can calculate WCLT($i6$) by computing WCET of the sub-graph involving all blocks (from $i6$ to $i7$ of b_1, from $i12$ to $i14$ of b_4, all of b_2 and b_3). Assuming that each instruction takes one cycle, WCLT($i6$), WCLT($i8$), WCLT($i11$), and WCLT($i18$) need 9, 8, 7, and 3 cycles, respectively.

3.5 Code injection

With the WCLT analysis for each MWI, we can choose the best write mode for each MWI with the following steps:

1. *WSI insertion*: visit the CFG and scan each MWI w. If WCLT(w) is equal to or greater than the retention time of a fast write, insert a WSI immediately before w to select slow mode; otherwise, insert a WSI immediately before w to select fast mode.

2. *Optimization*: if consecutive MWIs require the same write mode, the intermediate WSIs can be safely eliminated.

We use an example to show how code injection works. We assume that the retention time of fast mode is 5 cycles. In Figure 9, the WCLTs of $i6$, $i8$ and $i11$ are greater than the retention time of fast mode. As a result, we choose slow mode for these three MWIs, and fast mode for the other MWIs. During the *WSI insertion* phase, we insert 3 WSIs to select slow mode for $i6$, $i8$ and $i11$, and 4 WSIs to select fast mode for the other MWIs. A total of 7 WSIs are inserted. During *Optimization* phase, since it can be determined at compilation time that after inserting a WSI for $i6$, the current write mode immediately before $i8$ and $i11$ is already slow mode, WSIs immediately before $i8$ and $i11$ can be safely eliminated. Similarly, the WSIs for fast mode immediately before $i18$, $i23$, $i24$ and $i26$ can be safely eliminated. The *Optimization* phase saves 5 WSIs.

4. Experimental Methodology

The experiment flow of this paper is shown in Figure 10. First, each benchmark's source code is compiled by GCC, and then the binary file can be generated. The Worst Case lifetime (WCLT) analysis is performed on the binary file to identify the WCLT of each write operation. With WCLT analysis results, the code

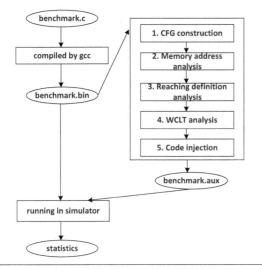

Figure 10. The experiment flow.

Table 3. Benchmark characteristics.

Benchmark	Total Instruction	Total Reads	Total Writes
basicmath	1.7E+09	6.1E+08	4.3E+08
bitcount	6.2E+08	9.0E+07	3.2E+07
blowfish	6.1E+08	3.1E+08	1.5E+08
CRC32	1.3E+09	8.3E+08	3.7E+08
dijkstra	2.0E+08	5.2E+07	2.3E+07
FFT	2.8E+08	1.2E+08	7.6E+07
qsort	3.4E+08	1.1E+08	7.5E+07
rijndael	2.3E+08	1.5E+08	2.4E+07
sha	1.2E+08	4.0E+07	1.2E+07
stringsearch	3.1E+06	9.4E+05	1.3E+06
distray	2.7E+10	1.2E+10	4.1E+09
drop3	2.1E+09	7.1E+07	2.0E+07
fourinarow	1.5E+09	7.0E+08	1.8E+08
flops	1.5E+09	2.2E+07	1.8E+04
mandel	3.0E+07	1.2E+07	9.1E+06
oourafft	1.1E+09	3.6E+08	2.9E+08
salsa20	4.6E+08	7.7E+07	6.6E+07
whetstone	1.3E+08	4.6E+07	1.5E+07

injection step is conducted by generating an auxiliary file, instead of actually revising the binary file. This auxiliary file provides a triple $< addr, mode, sel >$ for each MWI i, where $addr$ is the instruction address, $mode$ represents the write mode, and sel indicates whether a WSI is required or eliminated for i. Finally, the binary file runs in the simulator adapted with the auxiliary file.

The proposed WCLT analysis is implemented by following the practice of Chronos [24]. We adopted an energy efficient MCU, similar to megaAVR [3] and PIC [30], as our baseline. To enhance power efficiency, these MCUs have no cache or memory management unit (MMU). As a result, instructions access on-chip or off-chip memory directly. SimpleScalar [4] is modified for the performance and power evaluation. The baseline configuration is illustrated in Table 2. In the experiments, we choose the 10-iteration programmed mode as the slow mode, and the 3-iteration programmed mode as the fast mode. Since each current pulse has the same width, the write latency is determined by the number of iterations.

Table 2. Baseline configuration.

Components	Parameters
MCU core	single-issue, 1 MHz, no cache, no MMU
code memory	1-cycle per instruction without access to data memory 1-cycle per WSI execution
data memory	128 KB, 32-bit width, refresh cost: 2^{17} cycles[2] read cost: 1 μs and 48 pJ fast write cost: 3 μs and 955.2 pJ slow write cost: 10 μs and 1542.4 pJ fast write retention time: 1.87s slow write retention time: 11158.84s

To evaluate the proposed approach, a total of five schemes are evaluated, as depicted in Table 4. In *fast* scheme, all writes are in fast mode and a DRAM-style refresh method is employed. This refresh method refreshes the whole PCM periodically. In *slow* scheme, all writes are in slow mode. In *dual* scheme, write modes are statically selected for different MWIs based on the proposed approach. The *optimal* and *ideal* schemes are trace based. In *optimal* scheme, write modes are dynamically selected for each MWIs

---

[2] Assume that refreshing the whole memory consists of a read and a fast write of each 4-Byte block. So, about $(3 + 1) * \frac{2^{17}}{4} = 2^{17}$ μs are needed to refresh a PCM of 128 KB.

with the sample input. But each MWI can be conducted in only one mode. In *ideal* scheme, the best write mode is dynamically selected for each MWI instance independently. These trace based schemes are employed to evaluate the optimality of our program input insensitive CDDW method. The benchmarks, as well as the input, are selected from LLVM test suites [20]. Basic characteristics of the selected benchmarks are given in Table 3.

Table 4. Write schemes for experimental evaluation.

Name	Brief Description
fast	All writes are conducted in fast mode. Refresh required.
slow	All writes are conducted in slow mode. No refresh.
dual	An MWI is conducted in fast mode if and only if all its instances are conservatively estimated to have a short lifetime. No refresh. This is the proposed CDDW approach.
optimal	**An MWI** is conducted in fast mode if and only if all its instances has a short lifetime within the sample trace. No refresh.
ideal	**An MWI instance** is conducted in fast mode if and only if it has a short life time with the sample trace. No refresh.

5. Results and Analysis

In this section, the five schemes are compared first in measure of performance and energy consumption. Then, the MLC PCM memory system endurance improvement is presented. Further, the design overhead of the CDDW approach is discussed.

5.1 Performance improvement

Figure 11 shows the performance improvement achieved by the proposed CDDW. The results shown in Figure 11 are normalized to the *fast* scheme. As Figure 11 shows, for all benchmarks, *slow* scheme always achieves the worst performance, which is caused by the slow write operation. On averagely, the proposed CDDW improves the performance by 35.9% over *slow* scheme. Compared to the *fast* scheme, on average, the *dual*, *optimal* and *ideal* schemes improve performance by 6.3%, 6.5%, and 6.5%, respectively. It indicates the mandatory refresh blocks read operations and hurts system performance. Furthermore, the improvements from the latter three schemes are very close to each other. This is mainly due to the fact that, these three schemes can eliminate all refresh operations by introducing a small number of slow write operations, as will be discussed in Table 5.

We also observe that, for short running time or small memory space applications, the refresh overhead of *fast* scheme is small.

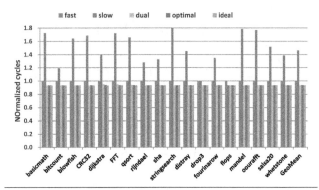

Figure 11. Performance improvement.

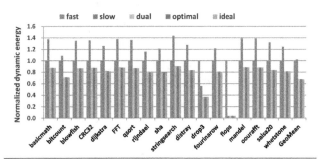

Figure 12. Write energy consumption.

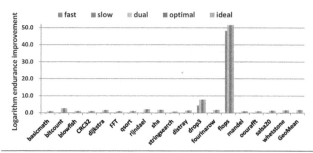

Figure 13. Logarithm of endurance under the scene with good wear leveling techniques. A larger value indicates better endurance.

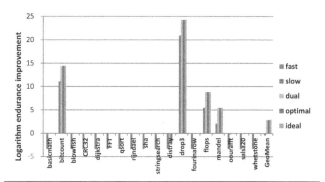

Figure 14. Logarithm of endurance under the scene without wear leveling techniques. A larger value indicates better endurance.

However, the performance of *slow* scheme is severely hindered by long latency write operations. On the contrary, for long lasting time or large memory space benchmarks, compared to *fast* scheme, *slow* scheme has better performance improvement, such as *drops* and *flops*. However, our *dual* scheme can always achieve better performance than both *fast* and *slow* schemes.

5.2 Write energy reduction

Figure 12 shows the write energy reduction of the proposed CDDW technique. We normalize all results to *fast* scheme. Without any surprise, *slow* scheme costs the most significant write energy in finishing all benchmarks. The proposed CDDW reduces write energy by 33.8% over *slow* scheme.

It also shows that, compared to the *fast* scheme, on average, the *dual*, *optimal* and *ideal* schemes can reduce the write energy consumption by 32.4%, 32.5%, and 32.5%, respectively. Again, the proposed CDDW approach is very close to the *ideal* scheme.

For *flops* and *drop3*, the improvement is extremely significant. The reason is that, for both benchmarks, the number of writes is relatively small compared to the number of refresh operations. Hence, the benefit from fast write is minimal, while the refresh overhead is significant. This also explains the phenomenon that the *slow* scheme works better than the *fast* scheme for both benchmarks.

5.3 Endurance evaluation

To evaluate the PCM endurance, we use the following equation which is proposed in [15, 16]:

$$\lg(lifetime) = -7 * \lg(NE_{write}) + 10 \qquad (2)$$

where NE_{write} is the write energy of the referred approach (normalized to optimal write energy). The PCM endurance is measured under two scenes respectively. In the first scene, it is assumed that a good PCM wear leveling technique, such as Start-Gap [34], is employed and thus the write operations on PCM are evenly distributed over all memory cells. As a result, the lifetime of the PCM is deter-

mined by the averaged write energy. In this scene, NE_{write} is the averaged write energy over all memory cells. In the second scene, it is assume that no PCM wear levelling technique is employ. As a result, the lifetime of the PCM is determined by the hottest memory cell which is written mostly. In this scene, NE_{write} is the write energy of the hottest memory cell.

The endurance evaluation under the first scene is shown in Figure 13. It shows that, the *dual*, *optimal* and *ideal* schemes can constantly improve the PCM endurance. And, the *slow* scheme works worst. This observation is consistent with the energy evaluation.

The endurance evaluation under the second scene is shown in Figure 14. It shows that, for most benchmarks, the *dual*, *optimal* and *ideal* schemes work exactly the same, and a little better than the *fast* scheme. This is because in this scene, the endurance is determined by the most worn cell. And, for most of the selected benchmarks, the most worn cell is always written in fast mode in all these four schemes, while the *fast* scheme involves additional refresh overhead.

It is also shown that for most benchmarks the *slow* scheme works worst. This observation is also consistent with the energy evaluation. However, for four benchmarks, even the *slow* scheme works better than the *fast* scheme. The reason is that for these benchmarks the number of writes are relatively small compared to the total number of refresh operations.

5.4 Discussion of overhead and effectiveness

In this section, we discuss the effectiveness and overhead of the proposed CDDW approach. As stated previously, the *dual* scheme is very close to the *optimal* and *ideal* schemes. This is due to the phenomenon that, although more writes are conducted using slow mode in the *dual* scheme than in the *optimal* scheme, the overhead from the additional slow writes are very small. This is because that the number of slow writes is very small relative to the total number of writes, as shown in Table 5.

Table 5. Comparison of *dual*, *optimal* and *ideal* schemes. *# of Slow MWIs* gives the number of slow MWIs. *# of Slow Writes* gives the number of writes conducted in the slow mode.

Benchmark	# of Slow MWIs			# of Slow Writes		
	dual	optimal	ideal	dual	optimal	ideal
	dual	optimal	ideal	dual	optimal	ideal
basicmath	2	2	2	2	2	2
bitcount	9	9	9	43	43	32
blowfish	8	3	3	1889	3	3
CRC32	7	6	6	6507	7	6
dijkstra	22	11	11	712145	151433	2417
FFT	19	13	13	1474712	65558	52866
qsort	11	10	10	300017	150012	10
rijndael	9	8	8	812	12	10
sha	10	7	7	810	10	7
stringsearch	2	2	2	2	2	
distray	6	5	5	1843212	1843205	5
drop3	4	1	1	12	1	1
fourinarow	48	48	48	1032772	1032769	1365
flops	8	7	7	47	49	25
mandel	0	0	0	0	0	0
oourafft	20	4	4	270077	19	7
salsa20	0	0	0	0	0	0
whetstone	13	8	8	82	34	23

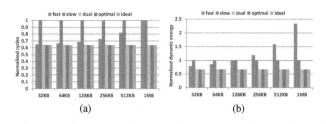

Figure 15. Impacts of PCM size. (a) Impacts on performance. (b) Impacts on energy consumption.

Since the code injection process inserts additional WSIs to control the write mode of each MWIs, it leads to code size overhead. The number of additional WSIs is less than or equal to the number of slow MWIs in the *dual* scheme. As shown in the second column of Table 5, the number of slow MWIs is negligible. The additional WSIs also consume clock cycles, the number of which is less than or equal to the number of writes conducted in slow mode in the *dual scheme*. As shown in the fifth column of Table 5, the number of writes conducted in slow mode is very small. Therefore, both code size and runtime overhead are very small.

5.5 More discussions

The additional cost of the *fast* scheme comes from the refresh operations. Figure 15 shows the impacts of PCM size on performance and energy consumption. It is found that, compared to other schemes, as the PCM space becomes larger, the *fast* scheme degrades sharply due to refresh overhead. This observation indicates that good refresh methods rather than the DRAM-style refresh method should be developed to exploit the *fast* scheme.

With respect to the hardware limitation in MCU system, we do not consider refresh schemes in this paper. The proposed CDDW approach can totally avoid the refresh operations. The slow mode is non-volatile and needs no refresh. The fast mode is applied to write instructions whose WCLT is shorter than the retention time, requiring no refresh. Therefore, we do not need dedicated refresh hardware support in our design.

With respect to interrupt mechanism, the WCLT analysis should take into account of the execution time of interrupt procedures. During the WCLT analysis, a conservative solution adds the WCET of the interrupt procedure to each interruptible program point. More techniques can be developed to choose different write modes for interrupt procedures, but these techniques depend on the detailed interrupt mechanism and are out of the scope of this paper.

6. Related Work

Non-volatile memory technologies, including NAND Flash [32, 33, 41], PCM [12, 13, 27], and STT-RAM [22, 23], have been widely researched recently for their high storage density and low leakage power. Micron has proposed a PCM chip demonstration [29] to target on embedded system market. Recent work [48] has im-

plemented PCM-based main memory for MCUs. MLC PCM has been widely deployed as main memory system in high performance computing systems [38]. In order to overcome the write latency of MLC PCM, recent works proposed many techniques to reduce the negative influence of slow writes or directly reduce long write latency. Qureshi *et al.* presented write cancellation to hide the read delay on critical path introduced by slow writes [36]. Jiang *et al.* proposed write truncation to reduce the redundant write iterations on MLC PCM cells, which are influenced more by material fluctuation [17]. However, these techniques need large hardware overhead. Write cancellation requires a large size write queue; while write truncation needs extra ECC storage overhead. These hardware overheads are too expensive for embedded MCUs.

During the development and validation process for reliable real-time systems, it is necessary to determine the upper bounds on execution times of a program, commonly called Worst-Case Execution Times (WCETs). Many academic as well as industrial WCET analysis tools has been proposed [44], such as aiT [1] and Chronos [24]. These works focus on developing techniques to obtain precise WCETs. More recently, WCETs aware compilation has been extensively studied. These works propose many optimization techniques to reduce the WCETs of a program, by allocating data and code [8, 42] in scratch pad memory (SPM), or locking data and instruction cache [26, 43]. Different from the WCET objective while borrowing techniques from WCET analysis, this paper proposes a WCLT analysis based approach to safely choose fast mode for instructions with short lifetime.

7. Conclusion

MLC PCM has been proposed to exploit the density potential of PCM. For MLC PCM, there is an explicit trade-off between retention time and performance. The PCM cell with a slow and energy consuming write can be viewed as non-volatile. The PCM cell with a fast and energy efficient write can be viewed as volatile PCM. In this paper, we propose a Compiler Directed Dual Write approach to choose the fast write / volatile mode for memory write instructions with short lifetime, and the slow write / non-volatile mode for memory write instructions with long lifetime. Evaluations show that the proposed approach can improve both performance and energy efficiency comparing to both full fast writes and full slow writes.

Acknowledgments

This work was partially supported by the Research Grants Council of the Hong Kong Special Administrative Region, China [Project No. CityU 123811], the National Natural Science Found of China [Project No. 61170022, 91118003], and Natural Science Foundation [Project No. US NSF CNS-1012070].

References

[1] AbsInt. ait worst-case execution time analyzers, 2013. URL http://www.absint.com/ait/index.htm.

[2] A. V. Aho, R. Sethi, and J. D. Ullman. *Compilers: principles, techniques, and tools*. Addison-Wesley Longman Publishing Co., Inc., Boston, MA, USA, 1986.

[3] Atmel. Avr 8-bit and 32-bit microcontroller, 2013. URL www.atmel.com/products/microcontrollers/avr/.

[4] T. Austin, E. Larson, and D. Ernst. Simplescalar: An infrastructure for computer system modeling. *Computer*, pages 59–67, 2002.

[5] M. Awasthi, M. Shevgoor, K. Sudan, B. Rajendran, R. Balasubramonian, and V. Srinivasan. Efficient scrub mechanisms for error-prone emerging memories. In *HPCA*, 2012.

[6] G. Balakrishnan and T. Reps. Analyzing memory accesses in x86 executables. In *CC*, 2004.

[7] Y. Choi, I. Song, and M.-H. Park. A 20nm 1.8v 8gb pram with 40mb/s program bandwidth. In *ISSCC*, 2012.

[8] H. Falk and J. Kleinsorge. Optimal static wcet-aware scratchpad allocation of program code. In *DAC*, 2009.

[9] Freescale. MC13224V Technical Data, 2012.

[10] L. M. Grupp, J. D. Davis, and S. Swanson. The bleak future of nand flash memory. In *FAST*, 2012.

[11] A. Hay, K. Strauss, T. Sherwood, G. Loh, and D. Burger. Preventing pcm banks from seizing too much power. In *MICRO*, 2011.

[12] J. Hu, C. Xue, W.-C. Tseng, Q. Zhuge, and E.-M. Sha. Minimizing write activities to non-volatile memory via scheduling and recomputation. In *SASP*, pages 101–106, 2010.

[13] J. Hu, W.-C. Tseng, C. Xue, Q. Zhuge, Y. Zhao, and E.-M. Sha. Write activity minimization for nonvolatile main memory via scheduling and recomputation. *Computer-Aided Design of Integrated Circuits and Systems, IEEE Transactions on*, 30(4):584–592, 2011. ISSN 0278-0070.

[14] L. Jiang, Y. Zhang, and J. Yang. Enhancing phase change memory lifetime through fine-grained current regulation and voltage upscaling. In *ISLPED*, 2011.

[15] L. Jiang, Y. Zhang, B. R. Childers, and J. Yang. Fpb: Fine-grained power budgeting to improve write throughput of multi-level cell phase change memory. In *MICRO*, 2012.

[16] L. Jiang, Y. Zhang, and J. Yang. Er: elastic reset for low power and long endurance mlc based phase change memory. In *ISLPED*, 2012.

[17] L. Jiang, B. Zhao, Y. Zhang, J. Yang, and B. R. Childers. Improving write operations in mlc phase change memory. In *HPCA*, 2012.

[18] M. Joshi, W. Zhang, and T. Li. Mercury: A fast and energy-efficient multi-level cell based phase change memory system. In *HPCA*, 2011.

[19] C.-M. Jung, E.-S. Lee, K.-S. Min, and S.-M. S. Kang. Compact verilog-a model of phase-change ram transient behaviors for multi-level applications. In *Semiconductor Science and Technology*, volume 25, 2011.

[20] C. e. Lattner. The llvm compiler infrastructure, 2012. URL http://llvm.org/.

[21] B. C. Lee, E. Ipek, O. Mutlu, and D. Burger. Architecting phase change memory as a scalable dram alternative. In *ISCA*, 2009.

[22] J. Li, L. Shi, C. Xue, C. Yang, and Y. Xu. Exploiting set-level write non-uniformity for energy-efficient nvm-based hybrid cache. In *Embedded Systems for Real-Time Multimedia (ESTIMedia), 2011 9th IEEE Symposium on*, pages 19–28, 2011.

[23] J. Li, C. Xue, and Y. Xu. Stt-ram based energy-efficiency hybrid cache for cmps. In *VLSI-SoC*, pages 31–36, 2011.

[24] X. Li, Y. Liang, T. Mitra, and A. Roychoudury. Chronos: A timing analyzer for embedded software. *Science of Computer Programming*, 69(1-3):56–67.

[25] J.-T. Lin, Y.-B. Liao, M.-H. Chiang, I.-H. Chiu, C.-L. Lin, W.-C. Hsu, P.-C. Chiang, S.-S. Sheu, Y.-Y. Hsu, W.-H. Liu, K.-L. Su, M.-J. Kao, and M.-J. Tsai. Design optimization in write speed of multi-level cell application for phase change memory. In *EDSSC*, 2009.

[26] T. Liu, M. Li, and C. Xue. Minimizing wcet for real-time embedded systems via static instruction cache locking. In *RTAS*, 2009.

[27] T. Liu, Y. Zhao, C. Xue, and M. Li. Power-aware variable partitioning for dsps with hybrid pram and dram main memory. In *DAC*, pages 405–410, 2011.

[28] D. Mantegazza, D. Ielmini, E. Varesi, A. Pirovano, and A. Lacaita. Statistical analysis and modeling of programming and retention in pcm arrays. In *IEDM*, 2007.

[29] Micro. PCM chip, 2012. URL http://www.micron.com/products/multichip-packages/pcm-based-mcp.

[30] Microchip. Pic microcontrollers, 2013. URL www.microchip.com/pagehandler/en-us/products/picmicrocontrollers.

[31] OracleLabs. SunSPOT, 2012. URL www.sunspotworld.com/.

[32] Z. Qin, Y. Wang, D. Liu, and Z. Shao. Demand-based block-level address mapping in large-scale nand flash storage systems. In *CODES/ISSS*, CODES/ISSS '10, pages 173–182, New York, NY, USA, 2010. ACM. ISBN 978-1-60558-905-3.

[33] Z. Qin, Y. Wang, D. Liu, Z. Shao, and Y. Guan. Mnftl: an efficient flash translation layer for mlc nand flash memory storage systems. In *DAC*, DAC '11, pages 17–22, New York, NY, USA, 2011. ACM. ISBN 978-1-4503-0636-2.

[34] M. K. Qureshi, J. Karidis, M. Franceschini, V. Srinivasan, L. Lastras, and B. Abali. Enhancing lifetime and security of pcm-based main memory with start-gap wear leveling. In *MICRO*, 2009.

[35] M. K. Qureshi, V. Srinivasan, and J. A. Rivers. Scalable high performance main memory system using phase-change memory technology. In *ISCA*, 2009.

[36] M. K. Qureshi, M. M. Franceschini, and L. A. Lastras-Montano. Improving read performance of phase change memories via write cancellation and write pausing. In *HPCA*, 2010.

[37] M. K. Qureshi, M. M. Franceschini, L. A. Lastras-Montano, and J. P. Karidis. Morphable memory system: A robust architecture for exploiting multi-level phase change memories. In *ISCA*, 2010.

[38] M. K. Qureshi, M. Franceschini, L. Lastras, and A. Jagmohan. Preset: Improving read write performance of phase change memories by exploiting asymmetry in write times. In *ISCA*, 2012.

[39] S. Raoux, G. W. Burr, M. J. Breitwisch, C. T. Rettner, Y.-C. Chen, R. M. Shelby, M. Salinga, D. Krebs, S.-H. Chen, H.-L. Lung, and C. H. Lam. Phase-change random access memory: A scalable technology. *IBM J. RES. & DEV.*, 2008.

[40] T. Reps and G. Balakrishnan. Improved memory-access analysis for x86 executables. In *CC*, 2008.

[41] L. Shi, C. J. Xue, J. Hu, W. C. Tseng, X. Zhou, and E. H. M. Sha. Write activity reduction on flash main memory via smart victim cache. In *GLSVLSI*, GLSVLSI '10, pages 91–94, New York, NY, USA, 2010. ACM. ISBN 978-1-4503-0012-4.

[42] V. Suhendra, T. Mitra, A. Roychoudhury, and T. Chen. Wcet centric data allocation to scratchpad memory. In *RTSS*, 2005.

[43] X. Vera, B. Lisper, and J. Xue. Data cache locking for tight timing calculations. *ACM Trans. Embed. Comput. Syst.*, 2007.

[44] R. e. Wilhelm. The worst-case execution-time problemoverview of methods and survey of tools. *ACM Trans. Embed. Comput. Syst.*, 2008.

[45] W. Zhang and T. Li. Characterizing and mitigating the impact of process variations on phase change based memory systems. In *MICRO*, 2009.

[46] W. Zhang and T. Li. Helmet: A resistance drift resilient architecture for multi-level cell phase change memory system. In *DSN*, 2011.

[47] P. Zhou, B. Zhao, J. Yang, and Y. Zhang. A durable and energy efficient main memory using phase change memory technology. In *ISCA*, 2009.

[48] P. Zhou, Y. Zhang, and J. Yang. The design of sustainable wireless sensor network node using solar energy and phase change memory. In *DATE*, 2013.

$BLog$: Block-level Log-block Management for NAND Flash Memory Storage Systems

Yong Guan, Guohui Wang

College of Information Engineering
Capital Normal University
Beijing, China
guanyxxxy@263.net, wgh_boy@hotmail.com

Yi Wang, Renhai Chen and Zili Shao

Department of Computing
The Hong Kong Polytechnic University
Hung Hom, Kowloon, Hong Kong
{csywang, csrchen,
cszlshao}@comp.polyu.edu.hk

Abstract

Log-block-based FTL (Flash Translation Layer) schemes have been widely used to manage NAND flash memory storage systems in industry. In log-block-based FTLs, a few physical blocks called log blocks are used to hold all page updates from a large amount of data blocks. Frequent page updates in log blocks introduce big overhead so log blocks become the system bottleneck.

To address this problem, this paper presents a block-level log-block management scheme called $BLog$ (Block- level Log-Block Management). In $BLog$, with the block-level management, the update pages of a data block can be collected together and put into the same log block as much as possible; therefore, we can effectively reduce the associativities of log blocks so as to reduce the garbage collection overhead. We also propose a novel partial merge operation called *reduced-order merge* by which we can effectively postpone the garbage collection of log blocks so as to maximally utilize valid pages and reduce unnecessary erase operations in log blocks. Based on $BLog$, we design an FTL called $BLogFTL$ for MLC NAND flash. We conduct experiments on a mixture of real-world and synthetic traces. The experimental results show that our scheme outperforms the previous log-block-based FTLs for MLC NAND flash.

Categories and Subject Descriptors   D.4.2 [*Operating Systems*]: Storage Management—Secondary storage

Keywords   NAND Flash memory, FTL (Flash Translation Layer), log block, garbage collection, response time

1. Introduction

NAND flash memory is widely adopted in various storage systems from USB drives, digital camera memory cards, to SSDs (Solid State Drivers) due to its non-volatility, low power consumption, high density and good shock resistance. However, NAND flash has some constraints that post challenges in its management. First, it suffers out-of-place updates, i.e., an update (re-write) to existing data on a given physical location (known as a page that is the basic unit for read and write operations) should be preceded by an erase operation on a larger region (known as a block that is the basic unit for erase operations). Second, a block becomes

worn-out if its erase count reaches a limited number. For example, one block in SAMSUNG K9F1G08U0C SLC (Single-Level Cell) NAND flash has 100K erase counts, while the one in SAMSUNG K9G4G08U0A MLC (Multi-Level Cell) NAND flash has only 5K erase counts. A block becomes worn-out if its erase counts reach the limit. To conceal these unfavorable characteristics and make NAND flash work like an ordinary block device, an intermediate software module called flash translation layer (FTL) is employed to serve inputted I/O requests and manage NAND flash correspondingly. Among various FTLs, log-block-based FTL schemes have been widely used in industry. This paper addresses the log-block management that is one of the most important problems in log-block-based FTLs.

In log-block-based FTLs, the physical space of NAND flash is divided into two parts: data blocks and log blocks. Data blocks are a large amount of physical blocks that are used to store the first written data, and managed with the block-level mapping. Log blocks are a few physical blocks that are used to hold updated data from all data blocks, and managed with the page-level mapping. Frequent page updates in log blocks introduce big overhead so log blocks become the system bottleneck. Various methods have been proposed to manage log blocks. In BAST [18], a log block can only be used by one data block. As there are only very few log blocks, they will be used up very quickly; then merge operations will be triggered, which causes big overhead with extra valid-page copies and erase operations. To solve this problem, in FAST [22], a fully-associative approach is proposed, in which all pages in a log blocks can be used by any data blocks. This can effectively postpone merge operations caused by log blocks. However, when log blocks are full and a merge operation is triggered, since one log block can be associated with many data blocks, a lot of valid-page copies and erase operations will be caused.

KAST [6] solves this problem by limiting the associativity of each log block, in which a log block is enforced to be used by at most K data blocks, so as to guarantee the worst-case log block merge time. Furthermore, log blocks are divided into two groups, sequential and random write log blocks. *Sequential-write log block* is used to store the sequential updated data, while *random-write log block* is used to store the updated data for random write operations. Compared with FAST, KAST can effectively improve the worst-case merge time. However, in KAST, merge operations may be triggered earlier when log blocks are not full. Moreover, its sequential-write requirement is very strict, which can cause extra merge operations. In Superblock FTL [17], log blocks are managed with an approach similar to KAST but without sequential-write log blocks. Basically, a superblock that is N adjacent logical blocks can use up to M log blocks. As N logical blocks in a superblock can fully utilize up to $N + M$ physical blocks, the merge cost can be reduced. However, hot superblocks may quickly use up log blocks

LCTES'13,   June 20–21, 2013, Seattle, Washington, USA.
Copyright © 2013 ACM 978-1-4503-2085-6/13/06...$15.00

allocated so as to trigger merge operations even when there are still free pages in log blocks allocated to cold superblocks.

In this paper, we propose a block-level log-block management scheme called **BLog** (**B**lock-level **Log**-Block Management). In *BLog*, we make the free space of all log blocks be freely used by all data blocks, and maintain a block-level mapping between a data block and the log blocks that contain its updated pages. Based on this mapping, the update pages of a data block can be collected together and put into the same log block as much as possible; therefore, we can effectively reduce the garbage collection overhead by downgrading the associativity of a log block, avoiding unnecessary merge operations, and decreasing valid-page copies in merge operations. Furthermore, we propose a novel partial merge operation called *reduced-order merge* by which we can do partial merge while simultaneously reducing the associativities of log blocks. Based on *reduced-order merge*, we propose two garbage collection policies considering the space and associativity of log blocks, respectively. Through these policies, the garbage collection of log blocks can be effectively postponed, and an erase operation to a log block occurs only when there are no free pages in log blocks. In this way, we can maximally utilize valid pages and reduce unnecessary erase operations in log blocks.

Our log-block management scheme can be applied to manage both SLC and MLC NAND flash. This paper focus on managing MLC NAND flash as it is the mainstream NAND flash product in the market. Based on BLog, we design an FTL called **BLogFTL** for MLC NAND flash. **BLogFTL** is built upon a hybrid address mapping mechanism: At the block level, a logical block is mapped to a data block or log block; at the page-level mapping, we propose an efficient fine-granularity page-level management method, in which a page mapping table of a logical block (stored in the spare areas of NAND flash) can be efficiently retrieved through a space-efficient page-mapping structure called Page-Mapping-Table-Directory in RAM. With this mechanism, pages can be written sequentially into a block and a page only needs to be written once, so the new constraints of MLC NAND flash can be satisfied. At the same time, via Page-Mapping-Table-Directory, we can directly access the page-level mapping table of a logical block so as to improve the system response time.

We conduct experiments on a set of traces downloaded from Storage Performance Council [1] (SPC) and collected from real workloads by DiskMon [4]. We compare our technique with several representative FTLs at different levels including the page-level FTL [5], DFTL [11], Superblock FTL [17], and GFTL [8]. The experimental results show that our scheme can effectively minimize valid-page copies and reduce the total number of erase operations so as to improve the system performance compared with DFTL, GFTL and Superblock FTL. Although the page-level FTL shows better average system response time than our scheme, it uses much more RAM space to store its page-level mapping table. For example, for a 4GB NAND flash shown in Table 1, our scheme only requires 129 KB RAM space while the page-level FTL requires 6MB RAM space. Thus, our scheme is more suitable in resource-constrained embedded systems.

The remainder of this paper is organized as follows. Section 2 introduces the background and the motivation. The log-block management scheme is presented in Section 3. BLogFTL, our FTL technique, is introduced in Section 4. The performance analysis of BLogFTL is presented in Section 5. Section 6 presents the experimental results. The related work is introduced in 7. The conclusion and future work are presented in Section 8.

2. Background

In this section, we introduce NAND flash and the implementation of a representative log-block FTL scheme. We first introduce the organization of NAND flash and summarize the system architecture of the NAND flash storage system in Sections 2.1 and 2.2, re-

spectively. Then we revisit the implementation of Superblock FTL in Section 2.3. Finally, we present the motivation of this paper in Section 2.4.

2.1 NAND Flash

A NAND flash memory chip consists of many blocks, and each block is divided into the fix number of pages. Block is the basic unit for erase operations while page is the basic unit for read/write operations. A page contains a data area and a spare area also known as *Out Of Band (OOB)* area. An OOB is mainly used to store the *Error Correction Code (ECC)* of the data of a page and other adhoc information. Table 1 shows the parameters of a 4GB MLC NAND flash from Samsung that has been used in our experiments.

Table 1. Samsung 4GB MLC NAND Flash (K9G4G08U0A [10]).

Page size	2KB
OOB size	64B
Block size	256KB(data) + 8KB(OOBs)
Pages per Block	128
Page read time (T_r)	$60\mu s$
OOB read time (T_{rs})	$20\mu s$
Page write time (T_w)	$800\mu s$
Block erase time (T_e)	$1500\mu s$
Endurance	5000 times
ECC coding	4 bits/512B

From Table 1, we can see that while we can efficiently read pages or OOBs ($60\mu s$ for one page; $20\mu s$ for one OOB), page write and block erase operations are more time consuming ($800\mu s$ for one page write; $1500\mu s$ for one block erase). Therefore, when designing FTLs, if we can **reduce unnecessary write and erase operations, the system performance can be effectively improved**.

MLC technology further increases the capacity of NAND flash memory by storing more than one bit data per cell. However, two new constraints are introduced in MLC NAND flash: (1) Pages within a block must be programmed in a consecutive manner [3, 25]; (2) Only one partial-page program operation is allowed in one page [2]. These new constraints post challenges for designing effective FTLs in MLC NAND flash memory storage systems. Considering the sequential-page-write constraint in MLC NAND flash, when a page is written into a block, it can only be written to an empty page whose block offset is bigger than that of an existing page written before. For many existing FTL schemes [19], block offsets are used to determine the location of a page in a block in write operations so pages are written in a block in a random manner. The one-partial-page-programming constraint also makes some previous FTL schemes inapplicable. In these FTL schemes, when a page is updated, a flag bit in the OOB of this physical page is set as "invalid"; later read/write/erase operations are dependent on this flag bit to proceed correspondingly. However, separately setting a flag bit after a page is written is no longer supported with the one-partial-page-programming constraint in MLC NAND flash. These influences should be considered in FTL designs for MLC NAND Flash.

2.2 NAND Flash Storage System

As shown in Figure 1, a typical NAND flash storage system usually includes two layers, the flash translation layer (FTL) and the memory technology device (MTD) layer. The MTD layer provides primitive functions such as read, write, and erase that directly operate on a flash memory system. The FTL emulates a flash memory system as a block device so that the file systems can access the flash memory transparently. The FTL usually provides three components: address translator, garbage collector, and wear-leveler. In FTL, the address translator translates addresses between logical page number (LPN) and physical page number (PPN); the garbage collector reclaims space by erasing obsolete blocks in which there exist invalidated data; the wear-leveler is an optional component that dis-

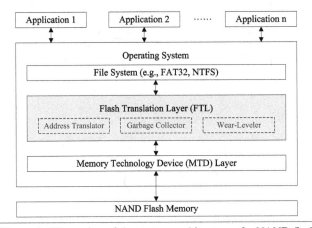

Figure 1. Illustration of the system architecture of a NAND flash storage system.

tributes write or erase operations evenly across all blocks, so the lifetime of a flash memory system can be improved.

2.3 The Implementation of Superblock FTL

In this section, we introduce the implementation of Superblock FTL that is one representative log-block-based FTL and can be applied to manage MLC NAND flash.

In Superblock FTL, N adjacent logical blocks consist of a superblock, and a superblock can contain up to $N + M$ physical blocks based on a block-level mapping table in RAM. A page in a superblock can be mapped to any location in up to $N + M$ physical blocks, which is achieved by maintaining a page mapping table for each logical block of a superblock. To avoid using a large amount of RAM space, this page mapping table is stored into the spare area of NAND flash memory and retrieved through a three-level structure considering the limited space of a spare area. In Superblock FTL, pages within a data block are written sequentially; therefore, it is suitable for MLC NAND flash. An example of Superblock FTL is shown in Figure 2.

Page update requests (Logical Page Numbers):   0, 4, 8, 1, 2, 0, 12, 27, 5, 9

Figure 2. Illustration of Superblock FTL.

In the example, there are nine data blocks and four log blocks, and each block has four pages. In the figure, the number inside a page in a block denotes the corresponding logical page number whose data is stored in the page. In Superblock FTL, one superblock contains three logical blocks ($N = 3$). As shown in Fig. 2, there are three superblocks, and each one contains three data blocks. For the simplification purpose, suppose some pages have been written into data blocks, and then a set of **page update requests** are coming. To serve these page update requests, log blocks are allocated. Finally, two log blocks (Blocks 9 and 10) are assigned to Superblock 1, and one is assigned to Superblocks 2 and 3, respectively. At this moment, a merge operation is triggered in Superblock 1 as there is no free space in the log blocks assigned to it. Although there are still free pages in other log blocks like Blocks 11 and 12,

they have been assigned to other superblocks and cannot be used by Superblock 1. If we can utilize all free pages in log blocks, this kind of unnecessary merge operations can be avoided.

To do the merge operation in Superblock 1, suppose Block 9 is picked up as the victim block (both Blocks 9 and 10 are associated with three data blocks, i.e., Blocks 0, 1, 2, but Block 9 has less valid pages). As it contains valid pages in three data blocks, we have to do the full merge. This means we need to copy valid pages from Blocks 0, 1, 2, and 9 to three new data blocks, and then erase Blocks 0, 1, 2, and 9. A lot of valid-page copies and erase operations are caused, because the page updates of the three data blocks in Superblock 1 are put into the two log blocks allocated *one by one following the order in the update requests*. Compared to other log-block-based FTLs, Superblock FTL has improved the associativity (i.e., the number of data blocks to share one log block) by limiting the associativity of a log block to N. However, we can reduce the associativity of the victim block by exploring the block-level information of page updates (which page updates belong to which data blocks). For example, by grouping all updates of a data block into the same log block, we can put Pages 0, 1, 2, 0 into Block 9 (as the updates of the data block 0) and Pages 4, 8, 5, 9 into Block 10; in this way, the associativity of Block 9 (the victim block) becomes one, and only Blocks 0 and 9 will be involved in the merge. In our scheme, the block-level information of page updates is utilized to reduce the associativity of a victim log block.

2.4 Motivation

From the above example, we can see that full merge operations should be avoided when log blocks are not full, as they introduce a lot of unnecessary valid-page copies and erase operations. Furthermore, if we can group all updates of a data block into the same log block, we can effectively reduce the associativities of log blocks so as to reduce the merge cost. Based on the above observations, we design our block-level log-block management scheme next.

3. Block-level Log-block Management

In this section, we present BLog, our block-level log-block management scheme. We first introduce the system architecture of BLog in Section 3.1. Then we present our log-block space allocation and garbage collection schemes in Sections 3.2 and 3.3, respectively.

3.1 System Architecture

BLog uses two tables to manage log blocks. The tables are *the Data-block to Log-block mapping Table* (DLT) and *the Log-block Management Table* (LMT). An example is shown in Fig. 3(b).

Page update request (Logical Page Numbers):   0

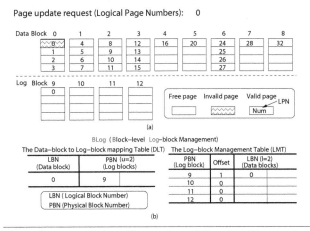

Figure 3. An example to illustrate how DLT and LMT are updated when one page update request (Page 0) is handled.

DLT is used to record the log blocks allocated to a data block. In the DLT, each row has the following items: LBN (the logical block number of a data block), and PBN (a set of log blocks allocated to this logical block, and the maximum number is u). u is used to control the maximum associativity of a data block (the maximum number of log blocks that can be allocated to a data block). Initially, the table is empty, and then it is updated based on the log-block management scheme.

LMT is used to record data blocks mapped to a log block. Each log block has one row in LMT. Each row in LMT has the following items: PBN (a log block), Offset (the block offset that represents the first free page of the log block), and LBN (a set of data blocks mapped to this log block, and the maximum number is l). Basically, each row contains a log block (the physical block number of the log block is recorded in Column PBN), its first free page (recorded in Column Offset), and all data blocks mapped to it (the logical block numbers of the data blocks are recorded in Columns LBN). l is used to control the maximum associativity of a log block (the maximum number of data blocks that can be mapped to a log block).

There should be a page-level mapping table so for a logical page, we can find its corresponding physical page in log blocks. When our scheme is applied to manage SLC NAND flash, we can have a page-level mapping table stored in RAM similar to other log-block FTLs like BAST, KAST and FAST. For MLC NAND flash, as discussed in Section 4, this is handled by a page-mapping structure stored in the spare areas of NAND flash in our FTL. The details will be given in Section 4.

3.2 Log-block Space Allocation

Compared with other log-block-based FTLs, one of the most important differences in $BLog$ is its log-block space allocation scheme. Our basic idea is to collect the updated pages of a data block together and put them into the same log block as much as possible. Log-block space allocation may trigger merge operations. In this section, we discuss the case in which no merge operation is triggered, and the case to trigger merge operations will be discussed in Section 3.3.

The case without triggering merge operations can be further divided into two situations based on whether or not a new log block is required to be allocated. Let us first consider **the situation in which a new log block is required**. This is the situation when either no any log block is allocated to a data block, or an allocated log block is full. In this situation, we will apply our **log-block space allocation policy** to allocate a new log block. The policy is to **find a log block in LMT whose associativity is the smallest among all log blocks with the maximum free pages**. In this way, a data block can fully utilize such an allocated log block that has the maximum free pages among all log blocks. Based on this policy, if there is such a log block in LMT, this log block and its first free page will be allocated to the requested data block. Correspondingly, in DLT, the logical block number of the data block and the physical block number of the allocated log block will be recorded; in LMT, Offset will be increased by one (to point to the next free page) in this log block. An example is shown in Fig. 3, in which the page update for the logical page number 0 is put into the first physical page in log block 9 (the first log block (PBN is 9) in LMT) where $u = 2$ in DLT and $l = 3$ in LMT.

The situation in which a new log block is not required occurs when a log block has been allocated to a data block and this log block has free space. In this situation, the logical block number obtained from the page update request will be used to check Column "LBN" in DLT, and then the log block allocated to this data block can be obtained from the corresponding row in DLT. In this row, there may be more than one log block recorded. However, only the last one is used as all the previous ones are full. Based on the last log block in DLT, we can find its corresponding row in LMT where we can find this log block and its first available page. The first free page of the log block will be used to serve the page update and offset of this log block in LMT will be increased by one. Note that for a data block, based on DLT, we will put all its updates into its last log block until the log block is full. In this way, we can group all the updates of a data block and put them into one log block as much as possible. Fig. 5 shows an example where several page update requests are processed and DLT and LMT are updated correspondingly.

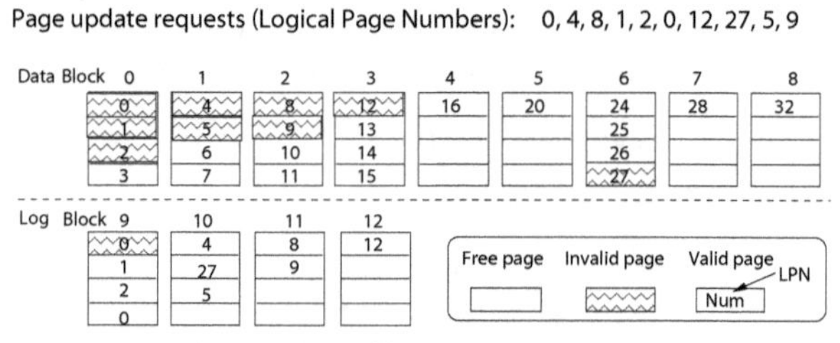

(a)

BLog (Block–level Log–block Management)

The Data–block to Log–block mapping Table(DLT)

LBN (Data block)	PBN (u=2) (Log blocks)	
0	9	
1	10	
2	11	
3	12	
6	10	

The Log–block Management Table (LMT)

PBN (Log block)	Offset	LBN (l=2) (Data blocks)	
9	4	0	
10	3	1	6
11	2	2	
12	1	3	

LBN (Logical Block Number)
PBN (Physical Block Number)

(b)

Figure 5. Process the same **page update requests** shown in Fig. 2 with $BLog$.

3.3 Garbage Collection

In this section, we discuss how to handle the case when merge operations are triggered. A merge operation will be triggered if one of the following three situations occurs:

- Situation 1: All spaces of u log blocks allocated to a data block have been used up (u is the maximum number of log block that can be allocated to a data block). This situation is handled by **reduced-order merge**.
- Situation 2: There is free space in log blocks but either the associativity of a log block has reached to l (l is the maximum number of data blocks that can be mapped to a log block) or a log block is full. This situation is handled by **Associativity-GC (Associativity-related Garbage Collection)**.
- Situation 3: No free space in log blocks. This situation is handled by **Space-GC (Space-related Garbage Collection)**.

In Situation 1, log blocks may contain free pages; however, they cannot be allocated to a data block as the maximum associativity of the data block has been achieved. We propose a new partial merge operation called **reduced-order merge** to handle this situation. Given the logical block number, LBN, of the corresponding data block, a *reduced-order merge* operation has two actions:

1. *Partial merge.* From its corresponding row in DLT, if a log block contains all valid pages of the data block, then it is swapped to be the data block, and the original data block is erased and used as the corresponding log block; otherwise, if we cannot swap any log blocks associated with this LBN in DLT, all valid pages of this LBN are copied to a new data block, and the old data block is erased.
2. *Reduce associativity.* Based on the corresponding row related to the LBN in DLT, we remove the LBN from each associated log block in LMT so as to reduce its associativity, and finally remove the row from DLT. We do this because all valid pages from both the data and log blocks will be moved to the new

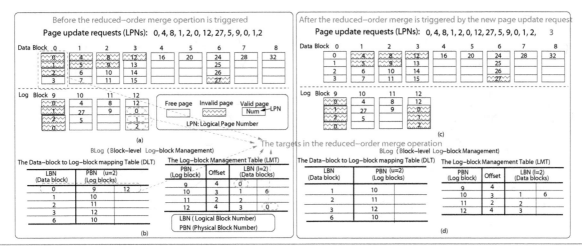

Figure 4. An example of the **reduced-order merge operation**. As shown in (a) and (b), when the page update request for Page 3 is processed, from DLT, we found that the last log block allocated to the data block (Block 0) is Block 12; from LMT, we found that Block 12 is full. As in DLT, Block 0 has achieved its maximum associativity ($u = 2$), we cannot allocate more log blocks to it. In this situation, the partial merge operation is triggered in which we copy all valid pages associated with Logical block 0 (Pages 0, 1, 2, 3) into a data block, erase the old data block (Block 0), and use the new data block to replace the old data block. Furthermore, we remove the corresponding row for this data block (the first row) in DLT, and the logical block number (0) from LMT. The results after performing the reduced-order merge operation are shown in (c) and (d).

data block; therefore, there is no need to record any previous log blocks associated with this data block.

Reduced-order merge can move valid pages to a new data block and simultaneously reduce the associativity of log blocks. Note that in a reduced-order merge, it will not erase any log block. Therefore, we can maximally utilize valid pages and reduce unnecessary erase operations in log blocks. An example for the reduced-order merge operation is shown in Fig. 4.

In Situation 2, either a log block is full or its associativity has achieved its maximum value. Therefore, our **Associativity-GC** policy targets at maximally reducing the associativities. In *Associativity-GC*, first, *a log block with the maximum free pages in LMT is selected; then for each LBN associated with this log block in LMT, its corresponding row in DLT is checked and the row with the maximum number of log blocks in DLT is selected.* Next, a *reduced-order merge* operation is performed on the selected row (the data block) in DLT. As the associativity becomes the major problem in Situation 2, this scheme can guarantee that at least a log block with the maximum free pages will be available after the garbage collection (by first selecting the log block with the maximum free pages), and at the same time it can maximally reduce the associativities of log blocks (by selecting the data block associated with the maximum number of log blocks). As a reduced-order merge will not erase any log block, in Situation 2, there is only one erase operation for the corresponding data block. An example for applying *Associativity-GC* is shown in Fig. 6.

In Situation 3, there is no free space in log blocks, so our **Space-GC** policy aims to reclaim space while introducing the minimum overhead. In *Space-GC, a log block with the minimum associativity in LMT is selected as the victim block.* Once the victim log block is selected, the corresponding LBNs (all the data blocks mapped to this log block) in LMT can be obtained. For each LBN related to this log block in LMT, a *reduced-order merge* is performed. Finally, the log block is erased, and its offset in LMT is updated. In this situation, we have to erase a log block to reclaim space so all data blocks associated with it need to be erased as well. This is why we pick up the log block with the minimum associativity. Our Space-GC is similar to full merge in other log-block-based FTLs but it will introduce the minimum overhead with its victim log-block selection policy. Note that Space-GC is only triggered when

all log blocks are full, while in other log-block-based FTLs, full merge can be triggered very early. Furthermore, by postponing the garbage collection of log blocks, when Space-GC is triggered, a victim log block selected may only contain invalid pages so we do not need to erase any data block. An example for applying *Space-GC* is shown in Fig. 7.

4. BLogFTL for MLC NAND FLASH

Based on $BLog$, we propose an FTL scheme called BLogFTL for MLC NAND flash. As mentioned in Section 2, in order to manage MLC NAND flash, we need to handle the two new constraints, the sequential-page-write constraint and the one-partial-page-programming constraint. In BLogFTL, pages are written in a block sequentially and in each page, we only write once including both the data and OOB. Therefore, these constraints can be satisfied. In this section, we first present the system overview in Section 4.1. Then we introduce the address translation and read/write operations in Section 4.2.

4.1 System Overview

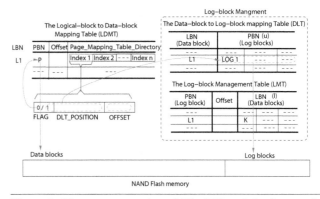

Figure 8. The system overview of *BLog*FTL and the format of a Page-Mapping-Table-Directory index.

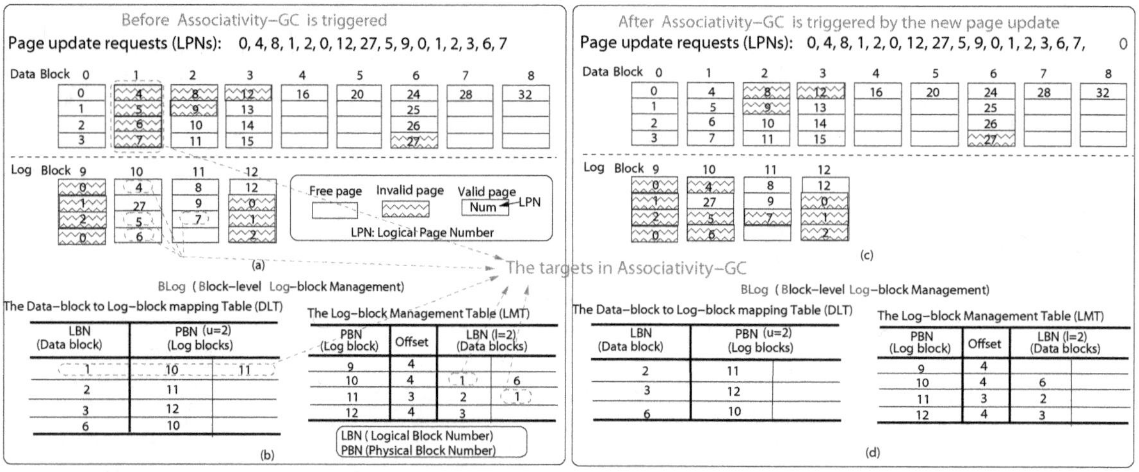

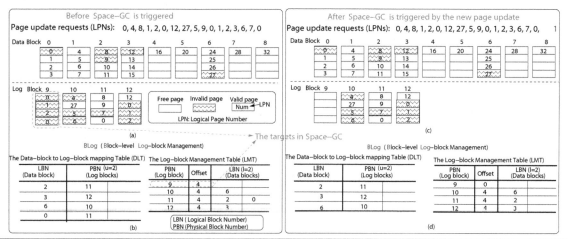

Figure 6. An example of **Associativity-GC**. As shown in (a) and (b), when the new page update for Page 0 is processed, in DLT, we cannot find any row associated with this data block. Thus, based on our log-block space allocation scheme, we need to allocated a new log block. However, in LMT, each log block is either full or has achieved its maximum associativity (Blocks 9, 10, 12 are full, and Block 11 achieves its maximum associativity). Therefore, Associativity-GC is triggered, by which we first select a log block with the maximum free pages in LMT (Block 11), check each data block (Blocks 2 and 1) associated with this log block (Block 11) in DLT, and pick up the data block with the maximum associativity (Block 1) as the victim data block for reduced-order merge. The results after the completion of Associativity-GC are shown in (c) and (d), in which a log block with the maximum free pages whose associativity is less than the maximum value (Block 11) is obtained. We can then use the free space of this log block to serve the new page request (Page 0) (the results are shown in Fig. 7(a) and (b)).

Figure 7. An example of **Space-GC**. As shown in (a) and (b), when the new page update for Page 1 is processed, in LMT, we found that all log blocks are full. Therefore, Space-GC is triggered, by which, in LMT, we select a log block with the minimum associativity (Block 9), perform reduced-order merge for each data block mapped to it (none), and finally erase the log block and update LMT and DLT correspondingly. In this case, Block 9 contains only invalid pages so we do not need to erase any data block. The results after the completion of Space-GC are shown in (c) and (d), in which an empty log block (Block 9) can be used to serve the new page update.

As shown in Fig. 8, in BLogFTL, one more table called LDMT (the Logical-block to Data-block Mapping Table) is added in additional to the two tables in BLog. Like other log-block-based FTLs, LDMT contains the mapping between logical blocks and physical blocks. Besides that, we add new information so we can efficiently retrieve the page-level mapping information of each logical block.

In LDMT, each logical block has one corresponding row, and each row contains three items, namely, PBN, Offset, and Page-Mapping-Table-Directory. PBN is used to record the data block (the physical block number) allocated to a logical block; Offset is used to record the current free page in the data block; Page-Mapping-Table-Directory is used to record the indexes of the page-level mapping table of a logical block. To satisfy the new constraints of MLC

NAND flash, in BLogFTL, pages are written in a physical block sequentially. Therefore, for each logical block, we need to record its page-level mapping information so we can find the physical page allocated to a logical page. To achieve this, we maintain a page-level mapping table for each logical block. In order to save RAM space, this table is stored in the OOB areas in NAND flash. To efficiently retrieve this table, we store its address information in Page-Mapping-Table-Directory in RAM.

The page-level mapping table of a logical block may be too big to be stored in one OOB. Therefore, the table may be divided into several parts and each part is stored in one OOB. Correspondingly, Page-Mapping-Table-Directory may contain several indexes, and each index refers to one OOB area in a page. To find an OOB, we need to know its physical block number and page offset. However, as we can find the data block and log blocks allocated to a logical block in LDMT and DLT, in Page-Mapping-Table-Directory, we do not directly store physical block numbers, and instead we store its relative location information in LDMT and DLT so as to save RAM space.

The format of a Page-Mapping-Table-Directory item is shown in Fig. 8. For each OOB that stores one part of the page-level mapping table of a logical block, it has one index in a Page-Mapping-Table-Directory. Each index contains FLAG, DLT_POSITION, and OFFSET. Here, FLAG is used to represent whether the OOB is in the data block or log blocks, DLT_POSITION is used to represent the position of the log block in DLT; OFFSET is used to represent the page offset. Based on FLAG, if one OOB is in the data block, we can find the physical block number in LDMT; otherwise, DLT_POSITION is used to find the physical block number of the log block in DLT. Then using OFFSET, we can get the physical address of an OOB. Note the maximum associativity of a logical block in DLT should be less than ten in practice (we have achieved very good results with 2 in our experiments). Therefore, the size of an index should be less than 2 bytes. For example, let $u = 8$ in DLT and each block contains 128 pages, then the size of an index is 11 bits (FLAG needs one bit, OFFSET needs seven bits for 128 pages per block, and DLT_POSITION needs three bits for the maxim associativity as 8).

In the page-mapping table of a logical block, we need to record physical page numbers that are mapped to logical pages. The same format in a Page-Mapping-Table-Directory index is used to represent a physical page number in a page-mapping table. Using this format, each physical page number can be represented by less than 2 bytes. Therefore, we can use very few OOB areas to store one page-level mapping table. For example, considering the MLC NAND flash shown in Table 1, with $u = 8$ in DLT (up to 8 log blocks can be allocated to one data block), we can use three OOBs to store one page mapping table.

In this flash memory, each block contains 128 pages and the size of an OOB is 64 bytes in which 2 bytes are for ECC coding (4 bits/512B). So a page mapping table contains 128 mapping items, and each mapping item contains one Page-Mapping-Table-Directory index that can be used to locate the corresponding physical page. With $u = 8$ in DLT, the size of a Page-Mapping-Table-Directory index is 11 bits (FLAG-1; OFFSET-7; DLT_POSITION-3); thus, each OOB can contain up to 45 page-level mapping items ([64 (OOB size) - 2 (ECC)]*8/11), and three OOBs are big enough for one page mapping table (128/45). As a result, each Page-Mapping-Table-Directory contains three indexes, and the size of one Page-Mapping-Table-Directory is less than 5 bytes (3*11=33 bits). Therefore, our method introduces small space overhead but achieves efficient address mapping as shown below.

4.2 Address Translation and Reads/Writes

In BLogFTL, the address translation is efficiently performed via Page-Mapping-Table-Directory in LDMT. Given a logical page number, we can obtain its LBN (Logical Block Number) and the page offset. With the LBN and the page offset, we can then find its corresponding row in LDMT (using the LBN) and its corresponding Page-Mapping-Table-Directory index (using the page offset). From the Page-Mapping-Table-Directory index, we can obtain the OOB address. From the OOB address, we can read the OOB and obtain the corresponding page-mapping table. Finally, from the table, based on the page offset, we can obtain the physical page corresponding to the logical page.

For read operations, after the above address translation, we can directly read the physical page. In write operations, we always write pages sequentially in a data or log block. As a page write changes the page-mapping table of a logical block, we need to write the updated page-mapping table into the OOB area together with the page write. So in a write operation, first, we still need to obtain the

corresponding part of a page mapping table based on the above the address translation. Then we obtain a free page from either the data block or the log block associated with the requested logical block, which can be done by checking "Offset" in LDMT and LMT. Next, we can update the part of the page mapping table, and write the data and the part of the page mapping information into the data and OOB area of the free page together. Finally, the corresponding Page-Mapping-Table-Directory index can be updated.

5. Performance Analysis

In this section, we analyze the system response time in BLogFTL and compare it with Superblock FTL. The system response time is an important metric to evaluate the performance of FTLs, and it is the time period from the point when an operation is issued to the point when the operation has been finished. For an FTL, its inputs are read and write operations. Thus, we conduct the analysis for the best-case and worst-case system response times of read and write operations in BLogFTL. The symbols we use are listed below.

T_{rd}	The time to read one page
T_{wr}	The time to write one page
T_{oob}	The time to read one OOB
T_{erase}	The time to erase a block
N_{age}	The number of pages in one block

For the best case, no garbage collection operations occur when a read/write is processed. In BLogFTL, as discussed in Section 4.2, for a read/write operation, we need to read one OOB that contains the page address information, and then we can read/write one page. So the system response time of a read or write operation in BLogFTL is $(T_{oob} + T_{rd})$ or $(T_{oob} + T_{wr})$. In Superblock FTL, a two-level page mapping scheme is used, so the system response time of a read or write operation is $(2 \times T_{oob} + T_{rd})$ or $(2 \times T_{oob} + T_{wr})$. Therefore, in the best case, for a read/write operation, BLogFTL can save one OOB read operation compared with Superblock FTL.

In the worst case, a garbage collection operation just occurs before a read/write operation is going to be processed. In BLogFTL, as shown in Section 3.3, when a garbage collection occurs, there are three situations. In both Situations 1 and 2, a reduced-order merge is caused. In a reduced-order merge, we need to copy all valid pages of a victim data block to a new block and then erase the victim block. The worst case is to copy all pages and the time is:

$$(T_{rd} + T_{wr}) \times N_{age} + T_{erase}.$$

In Situation 3, in the worst case, we need to perform l reduced-order merge operations before erasing a log block, where l is the maximum associativity of a log block allowed in LMT. Thus, the worst-case system response time in Situation 3 is:

$$l \times \{(T_{rd} + T_{wr}) \times N_{age} + T_{erase}\} + T_{erase}.$$

We can then obtain the worst-case system response time for read/write operations by adding the best-case read/write time into the above.

For Superblock FTL, considering $N + M$ mapping, in which a log block can be shared by N data blocks in the worst case, the worst-case system response time for garbage collection operations is:

$$N \times \{(T_{rd} + T_{wr}) \times N_{age} + T_{erase}\} + T_{erase}.$$

By choosing $l = N$, BLogFTL can have the same worst-case response time for garbage collection operations with Superblock FTL. However, compared with Superblock FTL, BLogFTL has better best-case system response times in read/write operations, and it shows better average system response time as well shown below.

117

6. Evaluation

To evaluate the performance of BLogFTL, we conduct a series of experiments. For comparison, we have also implemented other four FTL schemes which can be used for MLC NAND flash. They are Page-level FTL [5], DFTL [11], Superblock FTL [17], and GFTL [8]. The major performance metric to be evaluated is the average system response time, i.e., the average system response time for all requests. In this section, we first introduce the experimental environment and benchmarks. Then, we present the results collected from our simulation framework. Finally, we discuss the overhead of our technique.

6.1 Experimental Setup

In the experiment, we developed a simulator which simulates a 4GB Samsung MLC NAND flash with the specifications shown in Table 1. The framework of our simulation platform is shown in Figure 9. It consists of two modules: a NAND flash simulator module (nandsim) providing basic read, write and erase capabilities; a desired flash translation layer management scheme that can be executed on top of the NAND flash simulator. The traces along with various flash parameters, such as block size and page size, page read time and page write time etc., are fed into our simulation framework.

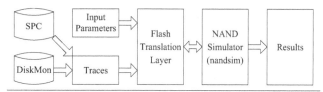

Figure 9. The framework of the simulation platform.

We use a mixture of real-world and synthetic traces to study the system performance for different FTL schemes. Two kinds of I/O workloads which reflect the representative storage access patterns for evaluation are used. Traces Financial1, Financial2 and Websearch1 are obtained from an OLTP application running at a financial institution [1] from Storage Performance Council (SPC). Second, Diskmon1, Diskmon2 and Diskmon3 are traces we obtained from a laptop by running DiskMon, a trace collection tool. Basically, Trace Websearch1 has very few writes, and others contain the mixture of read and write requests. The characteristics of the six traces are summarized in Table 2.

Table 2. The characteristics of the traces.

Benchmarks	Numbers of Request	Write (%)	Ave.Arr. Time (ms)	Avg.Req. Size (KB)
Financial1	5,334,987	76.83	8.19	3.17
Financial2	3,699,194	17.66	8.12	2.26
Websearch1	4,261,709	0.02	2.97	15.05
Diskmon1	1,312,942	58.1	196.9	48.03
Diskmon2	2,903,382	77.37	8.4	29.38
Diskmon3	5,049,182	28.95	38.3	49.87

6.2 Results and Discussion

Various experiments have been conducted. For *BLog*FTL, the average response time is influenced by u, l and the size of log blocks. Therefore, for BLogFTL, we first conduct experiments to show the results with various sizes of log blocks and with various u and l, respectively. Finally, we use one configuration to compare various FTLs.

6.2.1 BLogFTL with different sizes of log blocks

In this section, we show the results for how the size of log blocks influences the performance of BLogFTL. We fix $u = 2$ and $l = 4$ and let the number of log blocks vary from 64 to 1024.

Table 3. The average system response time from $BLog$FTL with various sizes of log blocks.

Traces	The number of log blocks ($u = 2$ and $l = 4$)				
	64	128	256	512	1024
Financial1	2,659	2,398	2,015	1,694	1,552
Financial2	262	257	251	244	234
Websearch1	96	96	96	96	96
Diskmon1	551	548	544	540	535
Diskmon2	787	776	763	749	740
Diskmon3	340	337	334	331	326

The experiments are shown in Table 3. It can be observed that the valid page copying and the erase counts under the six log-block number configurations are decreasing with the increase of log-block numbers. Due to the large numbers of write requests in the traces Financial1, Diskmon2 and Diskmon3, they introduce more valid page copying and more block erase counts. On the other hand, as a read-dominant trace, trace Websearch1 shows the lowest garbage collection overhead among the six traces. Furthermore, when the numbers of log-block is increased, the average system response time is decreased except for the trace Websearch1. This is because Websearch1 is a read-dominant trace, in which only very few garbage collection operations are triggered. From Table 3, we can see that BLogFTL can fully utilize the increased size of log blocks to improve the system performance.

6.2.2 BLogFTL with different u and l

We design a set of experiments to show the influence of parameters u and l on the system performance in BLogFTL. For each trace, we set the number of log blocks to be 512, and then apply different u and l.

Table 4. The average system response time (μs) from $BLog$FTL with different u and l.

Traces	($l=4$ and the number of log blocks is 512)				
	u=2	u=3	u=4	u=5	u=6
Financial1	1,694	1,618	1,590	1,579	1,572
Financial2	244	244	243	242	242
Websearch1	96	96	96	96	96
Diskmon1	540	539	539	538	538
Diskmon2	749	747	746	746	746
Diskmon3	331	330	329	328	328

Traces	($u=2$ and the number of log blocks is 512)				
	l=2	l=3	l=4	l=5	l=6
Financial1	2,388	1,803	1,694	1,779	1,879
Financial2	244	244	244	244	244
Websearch1	96	96	96	96	96
Diskmon1	540	540	540	540	540
Diskmon2	749	749	749	751	754
Diskmon3	330	330	331	331	331

The experimental results are shown in Table 4. It can be observed that Parameter u has no big impact in the system performance. We found that this is because log blocks have been full when most data blocks do not achieve their maximum associativity. On the other hand, Parameter l has more impact on the system performance. When l is increased from 2 to 4, the average response time decreases. However, when it is increased from 4 to 6, the average system response time increases. This is because when a log block is allowed to be utilized by too many data blocks, it may involve more erase operations in Space-GC.

6.2.3 Comparison with different FTLs

To compare with several FTLs that can support MLC NAND flash, we set $u = 2$ and $l = 4$ with 512 log blocks in BLogFTL. This configuration is selected because we want to make a fair comparison with Superblock FTL. In Superblock FTL, $N = 4$ and $M = 2$ with 512 log blocks, which is the major configuration used

Table 5. Performance Comparison of different FTL Schemes.

Traces	Metrics	FTL Schemes					BLogFTL over Superblock
		Page-level FTL	DFTL	GFTL	Superblock	BLogFTL	
Financial1	Valid-page copies	10,478,173	10,841,044	14,411,288	7,633,715	6,249,950	18.1%
	Erase counts	109,791	129,777	140,189	99,959	76,458	23.5%
	Average response time (μs)	2,349	2803	3,296	1,924	1,694	12.0%
Financial2	Valid-page copies	9,074	49,130	579,596	2,149,595	73,457	96.6%
	Erase counts	1,078	5,025	7,484	44,672	2,897	93.5%
	Average response time (μs)	194	376	1,418	745	244	67.3%
Websearch1	Valid-page copies	0	0	20	6	0	100%
	Erase counts	0	0	8	6	3	50%
	Average response time (μs)	61	173	1,490	96	96	0%
Diskmon1	Valid-page copies	1,799	35,877	56,852	2,884,012	17,568	99.4%
	Erase counts	1,878	5,978	4,047	66,023	2,914	95.6%
	Average response time (μs)	494	915	1,094	2,494	540	78.4%
Diskmon2	Valid-page copies	3,276	300,658	466,026	5,195,128	242,836	95.3%
	Erase counts	13,479	31,600	18,465	82,552	16,170	80.4%%
	Average response time (μs)	641	1,409	1,051	2,252	749	66.7%
Diskmon3	Valid-page copies	38,040	89,828	271,579	409,714	105,682	74.2%
	Erase counts	7,621	13,287	11,357	64,973	9,490	85.4%
	Average response time (μs)	283	484	1,144	1,028	331	67.8%

in the evaluation in [17]. No cache is applied for both the schemes. For DFTL, 64 KB RAM space is used as the cache so the total RAM spaces used by DFTL and BLogFTL are similar. For GFTL, the log block number is 512 as well. Table 5 shows the experimental results.

Table 5 shows the garbage collection overhead and average system response time for each FTL scheme. It can observed that BLogFTL can greatly reduce valid-page copies and erase operations so as to improve the average system response time compared with other FTL schemes except for Page-level FTL. Page-level FTL should get better performance at normally conditions; however, it is hardly used in low-end embedded systems because it uses too much RAM space. For trace Financial1, our scheme even outperforms the Page-level FTL. This trace contains a lot of separated sequential page updates across a few pages. As our scheme can group this kind of updates into one log block, we can greatly reduce garbage collection overhead. Compared with Superblock FTL, BLogFTL achieves a 48.7% reduction in the average system response time on average.

6.3 Overhead

BLogFTL uses more RAM space compared with Superblock FTL. In BLogFTL, at the block level, the sizes of DLT and LMT are small. Let Q be the number of log blocks. The size of LMT is bounded by $Q \times l$. For DLT, its maximum number of rows is $Q \times l$, which is the case when all logical block numbers in LMT are different. Therefore, the size of DLT is bounded by $Q \times l \times u$. In our experiments, we found that by setting u and l with small numbers (less than 10), we have already achieved very good results. Therefore, in practice, the sizes of the three block-level tables in $BLog$FTL are small.

Let us consider the configuration used to compare different FTLs. For the 4GB NAND flash, $u = 2$, $l = 4$ and 512 log blocks are used for BLogFTL. Based on the discussion in Section 4.1, with $u = 2$ in DLT, the size of a Page-Mapping-Table-Directory index is 9 bits (FLAG-1; OFFSET-7; DLT_POSITION-1). Thus, each OOB can contain up to 55 page-level mapping items (($64 - 2$) $* 8/9$); three OOBs are big enough to contain a page mapping table (128/55); one Page-Mapping-Table-Directory contains three indexes and 4 bytes can hold it (3*9=27 bits).

Based on the above, we can analyze the sizes of the three tables in BLogFTL. For LDMT, its size is up to 112 KB since the number of rows is $4 * 2^{30}/(2 * 2^{10} * 128)$, and the size of one row in LDMT is up to 7 bytes (2 bytes for PBN; 1 byte for Offset; 4 bytes for Page-Mapping-Table-Directory). The size of DLT is up to 12 KB (the maximum row number is 2048 (Q=512; l=4); the size of each

row is 6 bytes (2 bytes for one block and totally 3 block numbers (u=2)). The size of LMT is 5KB with 512 rows and 10 bytes each row (512 log blocks; 2 bytes for each block; l=4). So the total RAM space required by **BLogFTL is 129 KB**.

With the similar configuration of N=4, M=2 and 512 log blocks, the RAM space required by **Superblock FTL is 96 KB**. Superblock FTL needs to maintain a table with 2^{14} rows and 6 bytes for each row (2 bytes for one physical block number; 3 bytes for one physical page number as the page table index; one byte for each logical block (2 log block numbers needs to be recorded for every 4 data blocks so on average 1 byte for each block)).

In summary, for a 4GB NAND flash, *compared with Superblock FTL, BLogFTL achieves 48.7% improvement in the average response time while requiring more RAM space (96KB versus 128KB)*. Note that the RAM space requirement of BLogFTL is much less than that of the page-level FTL that requires 6 MB for storing its page-level mapping table.

7. Related Work

There have been many studies for FTLs in the previous work [9, 12, 16, 28]. They can be mainly categorized into three types, page-level, block-level and hybrid level. In page-level FTLs, a page-level mapping table is maintained so a logical page can be mapped to a physical page [5]. Page-level FTLs require big RAM space to hold the page-level mapping table; thus, they are not suitable for large-scale MLC NAND flash in embedded systems. In [11], DFTL is proposed in which the page mapping table is stored in flash memory and only on-demand address mapping information is cached in RAM. In [24], a two level caching mechanism is proposed for on-demand page mapping to improve the hit radio in RAM. On-demand page mapping can effectively reduce the RAM footprint. However, the page-level mapping table is still big in the flash memory; to manage it, more time and endurance overheads such as extra valid-page copies are introduced.

In block-level FTLs, a block-level mapping table is maintained so a logical block can be mapped to a physical block and much less mapping information needs to be stored in RAM [19]. Block-level FTLs use the block offset to locate the pages within a block, and pages can be programmed randomly within a block. In block-level FTLs, when merge operations occur, a victim block may contain many free pages.

In hybrid-level FTL schemes, physical blocks are logically partitioned into data blocks (primary blocks) and log blocks (replacement blocks) [6, 7, 18, 19, 21–23, 26, 27]. A block-level mapping table is maintained so a logical block can be mapped to a data block.

Log blocks are a few physical blocks to hold all page updates for all data blocks associated to logical blocks in the mapping table. Log blocks is managed with a page-level mapping table. In hybrid-level FTL schemes, the RAM space requirement is not big as the log-block region is usually small. So they has been widely used to manage NAND flash in embedded systems in industry.

8. Conclusion and future work

In this paper, we proposed a block-level log-block management scheme called $BLog$ by which the update pages of a data block can be collected together and put into the same log block as much as possible. We also proposed a novel partial merge operation called *reduced-order merge* by which we can effectively postpone the garbage collection of log blocks. Based on $BLog$, we designed an FTL called $BLogFTL$ for MLC NAND flash. We conducted experiments, and the results show that BLogFTL outperforms the previous log-block-based FTLs for MLC NAND flash.

How to extend BLog to other log-block-based FTLs should be an interesting problem. The reliability issue caused by power failure and the performance improvement with cache are not discussed in this paper, which will be studied in the future work. Emerging non-volatile memory techniques such as Phase Change Memory [13–15, 20, 29–31] shows excellent performance compared with NAND flash. How to combine our technique with them is an interesting problem to study.

9. Acknowledgements

The work described in this paper is partially supported by the grants from the Innovation and Technology Support Programme of Innovation and Technology Fund of the Hong Kong Special Administrative Region, China (ITS/082/10), the Germany/Hong Kong Joint Research Scheme sponsored by the Research Grants Council of Hong Kong and the Germany Academic Exchange Service of Germany (Reference No.G_HK021/12), National Natural Science Foundation of China (Project 61272103), National 863 Program 2013AA013202, and the Hong Kong Polytechnic University (4-ZZD7,G-YK24 and G-YM10).

References

[1] OLTP trace from umass trace repository. *http://traces.cs.umass.edu/index.php/Storage/Storage*.

[2] Samsung Electronics. K9LBG08U0M(v1.0)-32GB DDP MLC data sheet. *http://www.samsung.com*.

[3] Samsung Electronics. Page program addressing for MLC NAND application note. *http://www.samsung.com*, 2009.

[4] Diskmon for windows v2.01. *http://technet.microsoft.com /en-us/sysinternals/bb896646.aspx*, 2010.

[5] A. Birrell, M. Isard, C. Thacker, and T. Wobber. A design for high-performance flash disks. *ACM SIGOPS Operating Systems Review*, 41(2):88–93, April 2007.

[6] H. Cho, D. Shin, and Y. I. Eom. KAST: K-associative sector translation for NAND flash memory in real-time systems. In *DATE '09*, pages 507–512, April 2009.

[7] S. Choudhuri and T. Givargis. Performance improvement of block based NAND flash translation layer. In *CODES+ISSS '07*, pages 257–262, 2007.

[8] S. Choudhuri and T. Givargis. Deterministic service guarantees for NAND flash using partial block cleaning. In *CODES+ISSS '08*, pages 19–24, October 2008.

[9] Y.-S. Chu, J.-W. Hsieh, Y.-H. Chang, and T.-W. Kuo. A set-based mapping strategy for flash-memory reliability enhancement. In *DATE '09*, pages 405–410, 2009.

[10] S. Corporation. Samsung electronics. samsung K9G4G08U0A(v1.0)-4GB MLC NAND Flash data sheet. September 2006.

[11] A. Gupta, Y. Kim, and B. Urgaonkar. DFTL: A flash translation layer employing demand-based selective caching of page-level address mappings. In *ASPLOS '09*, pages 229–240, March 2009.

[12] J.-W. Hsieh, T.-W. Kuo, P.-L. Wu, and Y.-C. Huang. Energy-efficient and performance-enhanced disks using flash-memory cache. In *ISLPED '07*, pages 334–339, 2007.

[13] J. Hu, W.-C. Tseng, C. Xue, Q. Zhuge, Y. Zhao, and E.-M. Sha. Write activity minimization for nonvolatile main memory via scheduling and recomputation. *Computer-Aided Design of Integrated Circuits and Systems, IEEE Transactions on*, 30(4):584–592, 2011.

[14] J. Hu, C. J. Xue, W.-C. Tseng, Y. He, M. Qiu, and E. H.-M. Sha. Reducing write activities on non-volatile memories in embedded cmps via data migration and recomputation. In *DAC '10*, pages 350–355, New York, NY, USA, 2010. ACM.

[15] J. Hu, C. J. Xue, W.-C. Tseng, Q. Zhuge, and E. H.-M. Sha. Minimizing write activities to non-volatile memory via scheduling and recomputation. In *SASP '10*, pages 101–106. IEEE, 2010.

[16] P.-C. Huang, Y.-H. Chang, T.-W. Kuo, J.-W. Hsieh, and M. Lin. The behavior analysis of flash-memory storage systems. In *ISORC '08*, pages 529–534, 2008.

[17] J.-U. Kang, H. Jo, J.-S. Kim, and J. Lee. A superblock-based flash translation layer for NAND flash memory. In *EMSOFT '06*, pages 161–170, October 2006.

[18] J. Kim, J. M. Kim, S. H.Hoh, S. L. Min, and Y. Cho. A space-efficient flash translation layer for compactflash system. *IEEE Transactions on Consumer Electronics*, 48(2):366–375, May 2002.

[19] T.-W. Kuo, Y.-H. Chang, P.-C. Huang, and C.-W. Chang. Special issues in flash. In *ICCAD '08*, pages 821–826, Nov. 2008.

[20] B. Lee, P. Zhou, J. Yang, Y. Zhang, B. Zhao, E. Ipek, O. Mutlu, and D. Burger. Phase-change technology and the future of main memory. *Micro, IEEE*, 30(1):143 –143, Jan. 2010.

[21] S.-W. Lee, D.-J. Park, T.-S. Chung, D.-H. Lee, S. Park, and H.-J. Song. A log buffer-based flash translation layer using fully-associative sector translation. *ACM Transactions on Embedded Computing Systems*, 6(3):18, 2007.

[22] C. Park, W. Cheon, J. Kang, K. Roh, W. Cho, and J.-S. Kim. A reconfigurable FTL (flash translation layer) architecture for NAND flash-based applications. *ACM Transactions on Embedded Computing Systems*, 7(4):1–23, 2008.

[23] Z. Qin, Y. Wang, D. Liu, and Z. Shao. Demand-based block-level address mapping in large-scale NAND flash storage systems. In *CODES+ISSS'10*, pages 173–182, 2010.

[24] Z. Qin, Y. Wang, D. Liu, and Z. Shao. A two-level caching mechanism for demand-based page-level address mapping in NAND flash memory storage systems. In *RTAS '11*, 2011.

[25] Z. Qin, Y. Wang, D. Liu, Z. Shao, and Y. Guan. MNFTL: An efficient flash translation layer for MLC NAND flash memory storage systems. In *DAC '11*, pages 17 –22, 2011.

[26] Y. Wang, D. Liu, M. Wang, Z. Qin, Z. Shao, and Y. Guan. RNFTL: a reuse-aware NAND flash translation layer for flash memory. In *LCTES'10*, pages 163–172, 2010.

[27] C.-H. Wu and T.-W. Kuo. An adaptive two-level management for the flash translation layer in embedded systems. In *ICCAD '06*, pages 601–606, November 2006.

[28] P.-L. Wu, Y.-H. Chang, and T.-W. Kuo. A file-system-aware ftl design for flash-memory storage systems. In *DATE '09*, pages 393–398, 2009.

[29] C. J. Xue, Y. Zhang, Y. Chen, G. Sun, J. J. Yang, and H. Li. Emerging non-volatile memories: opportunities and challenges. In *CODES+ISSS '11*, pages 325–334, New York, NY, USA, 2011. ACM.

[30] P. Zhou, Y. Du, Y. Zhang, and J. Yang. Fine-grained QoS scheduling for pcm-based main memory systems. In *IPDPS '2010*, pages 1 –12, apr. 2010.

[31] P. Zhou, B. Zhao, J. Yang, and Y. Zhang. A durable and energy efficient main memory using phase change memory technology. In *ISCA '09*, pages 14–23, 2009.

A Two-step Optimization Technique for Functions Placement, Partitioning, and Priority Assignment in Distributed Systems

Asma Mehiaoui, Ernest Wozniak

CEA LIST DILS

{asma.mehiaoui, ernest.wozniak}@cea.fr

Sara Tucci-Piergiovanni, Chokri Mraidha

CEA LIST DILS

{sara.tucci, chokri.mraidha}@cea.fr

Marco Di Natale

Scuola Superiore Sant'Anna

marco@sssup.it

Haibo Zeng

McGill University

haibo.zeng@mcgill.ca

Jean-Philippe Babau, Laurent Lemarchand

Lab-STICC, University of Brest

{jean-philippe.babau,
laurent.lemarchand}@univ-brest.fr

Sbastien Gerard

CEA LIST DILS

sebastien.gerard@cea.fr

Abstract

Modern development methodologies from the industry and the academia for complex real-time systems define a stage in which application functions are deployed onto an execution platform. The deployment consists of the placement of functions on a distributed network of nodes, the partitioning of functions in tasks and the scheduling of tasks and messages. None of the existing optimization techniques deal with the three stages of the deployment problem at the same time. In this paper, we present a staged approach towards the efficient deployment of real-time functions based on genetic algorithms and mixed integer linear programming techniques. Application to case studies shows the applicability of the method to industry-size systems and the quality of the obtained solutions when compared to the true optimum for small size examples.

Categories and Subject Descriptors C.3 [*Real-time and embedded systems*]; G.1.6 [*Optimization*]: linear programming; stochastic programming

Keywords Distributed real-time applications, response-time analysis, optimization, linear programming, genetic algorithm, placement, partitioning, scheduling

1. Introduction

In the development of real-time cyber-physical systems, abstraction levels are used to manage complexity [17]. Industrial standards (like the automotive AUTOSAR [2] and the Model-Driven Architecture from the OMG [1]) and academic frameworks (including the Platform-Based Design [27]) recommend system development along the lines of the Y-chart approach [15]: a functional model representing the system functions and the signals exchanged among them is deployed onto an execution platform model consisting of nodes, buses, tasks and messages. End-to-end real-time constraints (deadlines) are specified on transactions, that is, chains of functions, activated by an external event (e.g. as detected by a sensor)

or a timer, and terminating with the execution of a sink function (e.g. sending a command to actuators) [2]. Classically as in AUTOSAR, two subsequent and separated activities (often carried out by different teams) are dedicated to functional deployment. First, the *placement* of functions on execution nodes is defined. Next, the *partitioning* of the set of functions and signals in tasks and messages and the *scheduling* of tasks and messages is computed. In fixed-priority scheduled systems, this includes the assignment of priorities. Once the functional level is arranged in tasks and messages, the worst-case timing behavior can be computed and compared against end-to-end deadlines. Ideally, the placement, partitioning, and scheduling problem should be automated by solving an optimization problem with respect to the metrics and real-time constraints, but because of its inherent complexity – placement, partitioning, and scheduling are NP-hard problems – suboptimal staged approaches and heuristics are used. The first stage (as in [17]) may be dedicated to placement in isolation, i.e. functions and signals are assigned to nodes and buses without the definition of the task and message model (including their priorities). As the deployment is only partial, worst-case latencies cannot be evaluated and the placement is evaluated by simple metrics and constraints, such as resource utilization. Other approaches lie in solving the placement and scheduling of tasks and messages with respect to latency-based constraints and metrics [8, 32]. In this case, the function-to-task and signal-to-message partitioning is previously solved in isolation with simple heuristics, such as grouping in one task all functions belonging to the same transaction and/or executing at the same rate or a one-to-one mapping between functions and signals to tasks and messages. Both approaches may lead to sub-optimal deployments.

In this paper we are intersted in tackling function placement, partitioning and scheduling exploring the use of Mixed Integer Linear Programming (MILP) and Genetic Algorithms (GA). MILP and GA algorithms are complementary and may derive mutual benefits from a joint application to the problem. An MILP formulation is easily extensible, re-targetable to a different optimization metric and can easily accommodate additional constraints or legacy components. An MILP formulation may benefit from the application of powerful commercial solvers. The method also *guarantees optimality in case the solver terminates* (when the problem size is manageable) and the distance of the current solution from the optimum can be bounded at any time (computed as the gap between the current best solution and the one of the relaxed linear problem), thus it is possible to evaluate the quality of the intermediate solutions generated by the solver. GA solutions typically scale much better. However, the quality of the solution provided by GA depends on many factors, for example, the appropriate choice of a crossover operator, and is very hard to evaluate. Using both techniques, the MILP solver can provide the true optimum for average size problems, helping in the tuning of the GA formulation and the assessment of its quality. For larger size problems, it can provide an upper bound to the optimum metric, helping in the evaluation of the quality obtained by the GA.

Our Contributions. In this paper we first present a MILP technique that solves the placement, partitioning and scheduling problem (from now on PPS) at the same time (unlike existing approaches). The MILP formulation of the problem can be solved and returns the optimal solution, but it is practically applicable only to small-size systems. In order to scale to industry-size systems we then propose a staged, divide-and-conquer approach with an iterative improvement optimization. Through divide-and-conquer the PPS is divided in two sub-problems of manageable size solved in cascade. Response-time optimization and latency constraints are considered for both sub-problems. This staged approach has been implemented using MILP and GA techniques. Of course, when a staged MILP solution is used, several benefits are lost, including the guarantee of optimality. However, the staged MILP solution provides a good tradeoff between scalability (a primary concern for industrial size systems) and the quality of solutions. Furthermore the MILP solution is useful to well-design the staged GA solution, which scales to even larger systems.

The paper is organized as follows. Section 2 presents the related work. Section 3 presents basic definitions and assumptions, then formally introduces the PPS problem. Section 4 presents the staged optimization strategy for the PPS problem and the two proposed formulations (MILP and GA) for the inner optimization stages. Section 5 shows the experimental results and Section 6 concludes the paper.

2. Related work

Most automotive controls are designed based on *run-time static priority scheduling* of tasks and messages. Examples of standards supporting this scheduling model are the AUTOSAR operating system [2], and the CAN bus [10] arbitration model.

Optimization techniques have been extensively used to find good solutions to deployment problems. [3] classifies 188 papers along many axes, i.e. design goals and constraints, degrees of freedom, problem solved. None of the surveyed papers, however, considers worst-case latency of the deployed transactions as either design constraint or goal.

End-to-end deadlines have been discussed in research work in single-processor and distributed architectures. In transaction-based activation models (such as the holistic and jitter propagation model in [24, 28] and the transaction model with offsets in [21]), messages are queued by sender tasks and the arrival of messages at the destination node triggers the activation of the receiver task. In such models, task and message schedulers have cross dependencies because of the propagation of the activation signals and real-time analysis can be performed using the holistic model [28] [23] based on the propagation of the release jitter along the computation path. When offsets can be enforced for tasks and messages to synchronize activations, the system can be analyzed as in [21].

Despite advances in timing analysis, the optimized deployment synthesis problem has not received comparable attention. In [24] the authors discuss the use of genetic algorithms for optimizing priority and period assignments to tasks with respect to an extensibility metric and a number of constraints, including end-to-end deadlines and jitter. In [9], the authors describe a procedure for period assignment on priority-scheduled single-processor systems. In [22, 23], a heuristics-based design optimization algorithm for

mixed time-triggered and event-triggered systems is proposed. The algorithm, however, assumes that nodes are synchronized. An integrated optimization framework is also proposed in [14] for systems with periodic tasks on a network of processor nodes connected by a time-triggered bus. The framework uses Simulated Annealing (SA) combined with geometric programming to hierarchically explore task allocation, task priority assignment, task period assignment and bus access configuration.

In [8], task allocation and priority assignment were defined with the purpose of optimizing the extensibility with respect to changes in task computation times. The proposed solution was based on simulated annealing. In [13], a generalized definition of extensibility on multiple dimensions (including changes in the execution times of tasks but also period speed-ups and possibly other metrics) was presented. Also, a randomized optimization procedure based on a genetic algorithm was proposed to solve the optimization problem. The focus is on the multi-parameter Pareto optimization, and how to discriminate the set of optimal solutions. Other works assume a communication-by-sampling model, in which tasks and messages are activated periodically and exchange information over shared variables. In this context, [32] provides an MILP formulation for the problem that considers the placement, scheduling and signal partitioning as degrees of freedom. The formulation is extended to consider extensibility in [30]. Azketa et al. used genetic algorithms to assign priorities to tasks and messages, then to map tasks and messages on the execution platform for event-triggered systems [6]. Finally, a mixed model in which information can be exchanged synchronously (with tasks and messages activating the successors, as in the transaction model) or by periodic sampling is considered in [29], where only the optimization of the activation modes is provided (task and message placement and priorities are fixed). A common characteristic of the above cited works is that function placement and partitioning is not considered.

Functions partitioning problem was considered in [7] [26] and [16] but only for a single-processor system, i.e., without the placement problem.

3. System model and the PPS problem

This section introduces the basic definitions and assumptions on the system model. Then, the PPS problem is defined and most significant parts of the MILP formulation are given.

3.1 System model

The considered system consists of a *physical* architecture (Network topology) and a *logical* architecture (Functional graph).

The network topology is represented by a graph ζ' of execution nodes $C = \{c_1, c_2, ..., c_c\}$ connected through buses $\beta = \{b_1, b_2,..., b_\beta\}$. Each node runs a real-time operating system with a preemptive fixed-priority scheduling (such as an AUTOSAR OS). Communication buses are assumed to be Controller Area Networks (CAN), arbitrated by priority (the identifier field of the message). The execution nodes and communication buses may have different processing and transmission speeds. Both execution nodes and communication buses have a maximal capacity utilization, respectively μ_c and μ_β, that must not be exceeded. Each execution node offers a set of tasks that perform the computation required by the system functions.. We denote the set of tasks offered by all the execution nodes as $T = \{t_1, t_2, \ldots, t_n\}$. Each task t_i is characterized by a set of functions that it executes and a priority level π_{t_i}. We denote as τ_{f_i} the task to which f_i belongs. In turn, communication buses offer a set of messages $\psi = \{m_1, m_2, ..., m_m\}$ that realize the transmission of signals between remote tasks. Each message m_i is defined by the set of signals that it transmits and a priority level π_{m_i}.

The functional graph depicts the operational process of the system, in which events generated by sensors or by users trigger the computation of a set of control functions or algorithms, which eventually define a system response. This behavior may be captured by a dataflow model, and described as a directed acyclic graph ζ composed by a set of concurrent linear transactions $\zeta = \{\Gamma_1, \Gamma_2, ..., \Gamma_\Gamma\}$. Each transaction is a 2-tuple, $\{F, \rho\}$, where $F = \{f_1, f_2, ..., f_f\}$ is the set of functions that represent the atomic operations and $\rho = \{l_1, l_2, ..., l_l\}$ is a set of links representing the interactions between functions. Functions exchange data through signals on these links. $\Phi = \{s_1, s_2, ..., s_s\}$ denotes the set of signals. A transaction Γ_i is triggered by an external event e_i that can be periodic or sporadic with, respectively, an activation period or a minimum inter-arrival time, denoted in both cases as P_i. Functions and signals within a transaction inherit their period (respectively P_{f_i} and P_{s_i}) from the activation period of the external event triggering this transaction. In addition, each transaction Γ_i has a deadline D_i that represents the maximum time value allowed for the associated transaction to be executed. Functions and signals are, respectively, characterized by a vector of worst-case execution times (WCETs) $\overrightarrow{\omega f_i} = (\omega_{f_i,c_1}, \omega_{f_i,c_2}, ..., \omega_{f_i,c_c})$ and worst-case transmission times (WCTTs) $\overrightarrow{\omega s_i} = (\omega_{s_i,b_1}, \omega_{s_i,b_2}, ..., \omega_{s_i,b_\beta})$, where ω_{f_i,c_c} and ω_{s_i,b_β} are respectively the WCET of f_i on node c_c and the WCTT of s_i on bus b_β.

The event-triggered activation model [28] is considered for functions and signals. In this model, the first function in each transaction Γ_i is triggered by an external event e_i. Subsequent functions are activated upon the completion of the predecessor function (if local) or the arrival of the message delivering the data values for its incoming signal (if remote). Messages are transmitted upon the completion of the sender functions. Figure 1 shows an example.

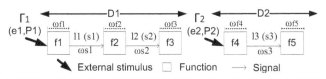

Figure 1. Example of a functional graph

3.2 PPS problem for system response-time optimization

The PPS problem consists in three sub-problems, namely *placement*, *partitioning* and *scheduling*. Placement consists in finding an execution node for each function and a bus for each signal. Partitioning decides which functions/signals to execute/transmit in each task or message. Scheduling is the problem of finding an execution or transmission order among tasks and messages in the same node/bus, this order is expressed by a priority order.

The WCET and WCTT of each function and signal is chosen from its WCETs and WCTTs vector, respectively. This choice depends on placement decisions. Then in the partitioning and scheduling stage, each task gets its set of functions as the group of functions with the same priority level and inherits this priority level. In the same way, a message is constructed such as it contains a set of signals with the same priority level.

Given a functional graph and a network topology, we are interested in finding a *valid* placement, partitioning and scheduling optimized with respect to the system response time. In this paper, we consider two metrics to express the optimization of system response time, the minimization of end-to-end transactions latencies and the maximization of the minimum transactional slack time, as detailed later in this section.

The constraints for the problem are detailed with their associated MILP formulation. For reasons of space availability, we do not report the full MILP formulation but only the most significant

or original parts (the full description is available from [18]). For what concerns the variables representing tasks and messages used in MILP formulation, since their number is unknown before optimization, we reserve one task and message slot for each function/signal on each node/bus. Empty slots are not considered in the formulation of the constraints and the metric function. In the following, when clear from the context, task slots and messages slots will be called tasks and messages.

Partitioning constraints include *harmonic rate* and *functional partitioning* constraints. Harmonic rate constraints prevent two functions/signals with non harmonic periods from being mapped into the same task/message. Functional partitioning constraints consists in mapping each function into exactly one task and each signal into at most one message. $A_{i,k}$ is a boolean variable set to 1 if function f_i (signal s_i) is placed on task t_k (message m_k). $X_{i,j,k}$ is also a boolean, and denotes whether both f_i and f_j are partitioned to t_k. The following constraints guarantee that each function is assigned to exactly one task and ensure the consistent definition of $X_{i,j,k}$. Constraints for signal and messages can be found in [18].

$$\sum_{t_k \in T} A_{i,k} = 1$$
$$X_{i,j,k} \le A_{i,k}, \quad X_{i,j,k} \le A_{j,k}, \quad X_{i,j,k} + 1 \ge A_{i,k} + A_{j,k}$$

Placement constraints are divided into two subsets. The first concerns *resource utilization* and consists in meeting the maximum capacity utilization of all execution nodes and communication buses. The second relates to *allocation*, and includes: (i) fixed allocation, when a function must be allocated to a specific node (e.g. a function responsible for collecting data from sensors has to be placed on the node linked to the sensor); (ii) exclusive allocation enforcing the placement of each function on exactly one node and each signal on one bus at most; and (iii) bus allocation enforcing the mapping of a signal on the bus connecting the nodes on which its sender and receiver functions are executed. This last constraint needs to take into account the topology of the communication network (e.g. if c_1 and c_2 are not connected then communicating functions f_1 and f_2 cannot be placed on c_1 and c_2, respectively). Function f_i is placed on node c_j if and only if it is placed on task t_k allocated to node c_j. The parameter $TN[j]$ represents the set of tasks slots for c_j. $An_{i,j}$ is a boolean variable which denotes whether f_i is placed on c_j. $X2_{i,j,k}$ is another boolean variable, with value 1 if f_i and f_j are placed on c_k and 0 otherwise. The following constraints ensure the consistency of the definitions of $X2_{i,j,k}$.

$$An_{i,j} = \sum_{t_k \in TN[j]} A_{i,k}$$
$$X2_{i,j,k} \le An_{i,k}, X2_{i,j,k} \le An_{j,k}, X2_{i,j,k} + 1 \ge An_{i,k} + An_{j,k}$$

Signal s_i is placed on bus b_j if and only if it is placed on the message slot m_k belonging to b_j. $MB[j]$ represents the set of messages slots belonging to b_j. $Ab_{i,j}$ is a boolean variable which denotes whether the signal s_i is transmitted over the bus b_j.

$$Ab_{i,j} = \sum_{m_k \in MB[j]} A_{i,k}$$

G_i is a boolean variable equal to 1 if s_i is transmitted on a bus and 0 if s_i is a local signal; $NB[j]$ is the set of nodes communicating through bus b_j. The following constraints enforce the conditions for s_i to be on b_j.

$$Ab_{i,j} \le G_i,$$
$$0 \le \sum_{c_k \in NB[j]} An_{rec_i,k} + G_i + \sum_{c_k \in NB[j]} An_{snd_i,k} - 3 \cdot Ab_{i,j} \le 2$$

where snd_i and rec_i are, respectively, the source and destination function of the signal s_i.

Execution order constraints are *local total order* and *functional order* constraints. The local total order constraints consist in a total priority order for tasks/messages belonging to the same node/bus. However, within each node and bus we assign a different priority order to task t_i and message m_j slots, which is denoted respectively as π_i and π_j. Functional order constraints represent partial orders of execution (such as t_j may not be executed before t_i when t_j depends on the output of t_i). Tasks dependencies are derived from the dependencies of the functions mapped in them. The (constant) parameter $dp_{i,j} = 1$ indicates that the execution of f_j depends on f_i in the functional graph. In this case, f_j cannot be placed on a task with priority higher than the task slot on which f_i is placed.

$$\forall f_i, f_j \ s.t. \ dp_{i,j} = 1 \ : \ \sum_{k \in T} A_{j,k} \cdot \pi_k \le \sum_{k \in T} A_{i,k} \cdot \pi_k$$

Response time constraints are common to the placement, partitioning and scheduling sub-problems. Each transaction $\Gamma_i \in \zeta$ has a latency L_i equal to the worst-case response time (WCRT) R_{f_k} of its last function f_k and the latency of each transaction should not exceeds its deadline ($L_i \le D_i$). To compute the WCRT of functions, we adapt the response time analysis with jitter propagation (as applied to tasks) given in [28] and [21].

The WCRT R_{f_i} of a function f_i is computed by considering all the q function instances (distinct executions of f_i after activation) in the busy period, as follows:

$$R_{f_i} = \max_{q=1,2,\dots} [W_{f_i}^{(q)} - (q-1)P_{f_i} + J_{f_i}] \tag{1}$$

Since f_i is executed by a task, its release jitter J_{f_i} is the task release jitter, that is, the largest among all the latest release times for the functions in the same task, which is zero if the function has no predecessor (or a predecessor within the same task), or the worst case response time of the signal it receives from a remote predecessor function (s_i is the signal received by f_i.)

$$J_{f_i} = \max_{\tau_{f_i} = \tau_{f_j}, \forall f_j \in F} \{0, R_{s_i}\} \tag{2}$$

$W_{f_i}^{(q)}$ is the completion time of the qth instance of function f_i

$$W_{f_i}^{(q)} = q \cdot (\omega_{f_i,c_k} + \sum_{f_j : \tau_{f_i} = \tau_{f_j}} \omega_{f_j,c_k}) + \sum_{f_j \in hp(f_i)} \left\lceil \frac{W_{f_i}^{(q)} + J_{f_j}}{P_{f_j}} \right\rceil \omega_{f_j,c_k} \tag{3}$$

where $hp(f_i)$ refers to the set of higher priority functions than f_i executing on the same node and within different tasks. The last term represents the preemption time from functions belonging to $hp(f_i)$. The completion time is computed for $q = 1, 2, \cdots$ until the busy period ends, that is, an instance completes at or before the activation of the next instance.

When a (higher priority) task contains functions with different periods, its interference is computed as the sum of the interferences of its functions, as shown in Figure 2, in which a task consists of two functions f_1, activated once every two task executions, and f_2 executed every time. The exact response time formula (3) is not suitable for an MILP formulation. It depends on the number of function activations q in the busy period, which is not known a-priori. Hence, we use a necessary-only (optimistic) conditions for feasibility that only considers the response time of the first instance ($q = 1$). The MILP formulation of (3) with $q = 1$ becomes (the integer variables $I_{j,i}$ represent the number of times f_j may interfere

Figure 2. Interference of a task with functions with different harmonic periods as the sum of the function interferences

with f_i in the worst case)

$$W_{f_i} = \omega_{f_i,c_k} + \sum_{f_j : \tau_i = \tau_j} \omega_{f_j,c_k} + \sum_{f_j \in hp(i)} I_{j,i} \cdot \omega_{f_j,c_k} \tag{4}$$
$$I_{j,i} \cdot P_{f_j} - P_{f_j} < W_{f_i} + J_{f_j} \le I_{j,i} \cdot P_{f_j}$$

The function response time is equal to its first instance (as computed by the above formula) in case of restricted deadline $L_i \le D_i \le P_i$. When end-to-end deadlines may be larger than the periods or the interarrival times of activation events, the formulation using the constraint (4) may compute an optimal solution that is not feasible. This is why all the solutions obtained from the MILP solver must be verified afterwards using the exact response time formula.

The WCRT R_{s_i} of a signal s_i is computed only for signals representing remote communications (otherwise it is equal to zero), using a similar formula as the WCRT of functions, except for an additional term B_{s_i} that represents the blocking time due to the impossibility of preempting messages. The release jitter of a remote signal is the worst-case response time of its sender function.

Constraint (5) represents the computation of B_{s_i} which is the largest WCTT of any message that shares the same communication bus [12] (or even simpler, the transmission time of the largest CAN message). Note that s_i, s_j and s_l are all transmitted on the bus b_k and m_{s_i} represents the message on which s_i is partitioned.

$$\forall s_j \in \Phi : m_{s_i} \ne m_{s_j}, B_{s_i} \ge \omega_{s_j,b_k} + \sum_{\substack{s_l : m_{s_l} = m_{s_j} \\ m_{s_l} \ne m_{s_i}}} \omega_{s_l,b_k} \tag{5}$$

Optimization metrics can be defined based on the system requirements. In this work we tried two formulations: (i) the minimization of the sum of all (or some) transactions latencies, which is a loose indication of the system performance, and (ii) the maximization of the minimum transactional slack time. A slack time for a given transaction is defined as the difference between the deadline and latency of the transaction. Maximizing the minimal transactional slack time (over all transactional slack times) means maximizing the minimum distance between the latency and deadline of the selected transaction (MinSlack $= \min_{\Gamma_i \in \zeta} [D_i - L_i]$). This latter metric can be easily related to the concept of robustness (or extensibility) of the system against changes in the time parameters of some functions.

4. Two-step optimization for PPS

The (one-step) MILP formulation of the PPS problem can only be solved for small systems. To handle industry-size systems, the problem is divided in two smaller (sub)problems and solved in cascade. Two MILP formulations are then provided, one for each sub-problem. A GA counterpart for each sub-problem is also given.

4.1 Overview

Our heuristic (algorithm in Figure 3) combines two classical optimization strategies: divide-and-conquer and iterative improvement.

Divide-and-conquer consists in dividing the PPS problem in two sub-problems solved in cascade, in which placement is solved first (placement problem or PP), and then partitioning and scheduling (PS).

Iterative improvement is used to move towards the optimum. Our algorithm considers an iterative improvement at two levels: inner and outer loops. The inner loop tries to find an optimal system configuration by applying iteratively an optimization sequence until convergence (two successive solutions are the same). The inner loop consists of the two stages of placement optimization (PP), followed by partitioning and scheduling optimization (PS). In both sub-problems, we aim at optimizing the latency- or slack-based metric. Each iteration starts from a PP step with an initial PS configuration. The PP step provides a new placement of functions/signals to nodes/buses. During this stage, tasks and messages are placed on nodes/buses and so are the functions mapped onto them. Next, the PS step tries to find a new partitioning and scheduling solution that improves the solution found in the PP stage. Depending on the selection of the initial configuration, the PP+PS solution may be a local optimum. To move away from local minima, the outer loop selects set of random initial configurations for partitioning and scheduling as possible starting points.

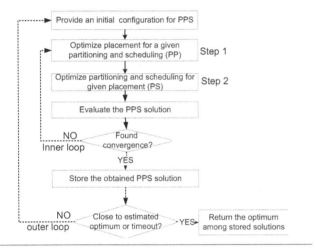

Figure 3. Overview of the Two-step optimization approach

4.2 The MILP formulation for the PP and PS stages

This section outlines the MILP formulation for each sub-problem in the two-step approach.

The two-step formulation uses the same optmization metric for the one-step formulation (Section 3.2).

4.2.1 MILP formulation of the Placement Problem

The objective of this step is optimizing the placement of either an initial configuration or the output of the previous iteration. The parameters are the partitioning of functions (signals) on tasks (messages) and the priorities assigned to tasks and messages. This objective is the optimal placement of tasks/messages and the function/signals in them.

Placement constraints: as mentioned before, they concern allocation and resource utilization constraints. $C[i]$ in (6) is the set of nodes on which t_i is allowed to execute (this includes the case of fixed allocation). $At_{i,c}$ is a binary variable set to 1 if a t_i is placed on node c. Each task must be placed on one node.

$$\Sigma_{c \in C[i]} At_{i,c} = 1 \tag{6}$$

The binary variable $H_{i,j,c}$ based on $At_{i,c}$. $H_{i,j,c}$ denotes whether t_i and t_j are placed on the same node.

$$0 \le At_{i,c} + At_{j,c} - 2 \cdot H_{i,j,c} \le 1 \tag{7}$$

Messages placement is based on the placement of tasks. A message can be placed on one bus or to no bus (in case of local communication). The binary variable g_i indicates if m_i is placed on a bus ($g_i = 1$) or is local ($g_i = 0$). The binary variable $Am_{i,j}$ is 1 if m_i is transmitted on bus b_j, 0 otherwise.

$$\Sigma_{b_j \in \beta} Am_{i,j} = g_i \tag{8}$$

m_i is placed on a bus ($g_i = 1$) iff its sender ($sen_{[i]}$) and receiver ($rec_{[i]}$) tasks are on different nodes.

$$\forall (t_i \in sen_{[i]}, t_j \in rec_{[i]}) : 1 - \Sigma_{c \in C} H_{i,j,c} = g_i \tag{9}$$

Since all communicating tasks residing on different nodes must have a connecting bus, the placement of messages must also take into account the network topology. The parameter $NB[j]$ is the set of nodes communicating through the bus b_j. A message m_i is placed on b_j iff the execution nodes of its sender and receiver tasks communicate through b_j.

$$\forall (t_i \in sen_{[i]}, t_j \in rec_{[i]}) :$$
$$0 \le g_i + \Sigma_{c \in NB[j]} At_{i,c} + \Sigma_{c \in NB[j]} At_{j,c} - 3 \cdot Am_{i,j} \le 2 \tag{10}$$

$H_{i,j,k}$ indicates if m_i and m_j are transmitted on the same bus b_k. The maximum utilization of nodes is enforced by constraint (11). The utilization of buses is constrained in a similar way.

$$\forall c_j \in C : \Sigma_i A_{i,j} \cdot \left(\omega_{i,c_j} / P_i \right) \le \mu_j \tag{11}$$

Latency constraints
The task WCRT is the sum of its completion time and jitter.

$$R_i = W_i + J_i \tag{12}$$

The Big M method is used in (15) and (16) to linearize the computation of $I_{i,j,c}$, the maximum number of times that t_j preempts t_i as $I_{i,j,c} = H_{i,j,c} * \sigma_{i,j}$, where $\sigma_{i,j} = \left\lceil \frac{W_i + J_j}{P_j} \right\rceil$. The binary parameter $gp_{i,j}$ denotes whether π_j is higher than π_i.

$$W_i = \sum_{c_p \in C} At_{i,p} \cdot \omega_{i,p} + \sum_{j \in T} \sum_{c_p \in C} I_{i,j,p} \cdot \omega_{j,p} \cdot gp_{i,j} \tag{13}$$

$$0 \le \sigma_{i,j} - \left(\frac{W_i + J_j}{P_j} \right) < 1 \tag{14}$$

$$\sigma_{i,j} - M * (1 - H_{i,j,c}) \le I_{i,j,c} \tag{15}$$

$$I_{i,j,c} \le \sigma_{i,j} \; ; \; I_{i,j,c} \le M * H_{i,j,c} \tag{16}$$

The jitter of a task is 0 if all its functions are initial and otherwise is equal to the largest WCRT of the received messages (17).

$$\forall m_i \in \psi \; s.t \; t_i \in rec_{[m_i]} : J_i \ge R_{m_i} \tag{17}$$

The constraints computing the WCRT of messages are similar to (12), (13), (14), (15), and (16) except for the addition of the blocking time B_{m_i} to the formula (13)

$$\forall m_j \in \psi : B_{m_i} \ge \Sigma_{b \in \beta} H_{m_i, m_j, b} \cdot \omega_{m_j, b} \tag{18}$$

Note that the WCRT of a message transmitted inside a node returns only its jitter as its completion time is zero. Thus the task jitter in this case is simply the WCRT of its predecessor.

The result of this MILP formulation consists in a placement of tasks and messages and the input for the next stage is the placement of functions and signals as partitioned in the tasks and messages.

4.2.2 MILP formulation for the Partitioning and Scheduling

At this stage, the placement of functions and signals is given and the following MILP formulation aims at improving (if possible) the partitioning and priority assignment. The MILP formulation assigns priorities to functions and signals within each node and bus, then tasks and messages are constructed based on priorities, i.e. a task (message) is the set of functions (signals) with the same priority order residing on the same node (bus).

Partitioning and scheduling constraints: most constraints are expressed in the same way for functions and signals. In the following, we address only functions and discuss the differences for signals. The binary variable $\chi_{i,j}$ indicates whether f_i has higher priority than f_j. If $\chi_{i,j} = 0$ and $\chi_{j,i} = 0$ then f_i and f_j have the same priority order, otherwise, either f_i has higher priority than f_j ($\chi_{i,j} = 1$) or f_j has higher priority than f_i ($\chi_{j,i} = 1$).

$$\chi_{i,j} + \chi_{j,i} \leq 1 \qquad (19)$$

A set of constraints is used to enforce the symmetric, transitive and inversion properties of the priority order relation and to ensure that each function is partitioned on exactly one task (omitted for space constraints).

A binary variable SP_{f_i,f_j} denotes whether f_i and f_j have the same priority order i.e. they are on the same task.

$$1 = SP_{f_i,f_j} + \chi_{j,i} + \chi_{i,j} \qquad (20)$$

Any pair of functions with non-harmonic rates must be assigned to different tasks (have different priorities).

$$\forall f_i, f_j \in F \ s.t. \ f_i \neq f_j : 1 = \chi_{i,j} + \chi_{j,i}$$
$$\text{if } P_{f_i} \geq P_{f_j} \text{ and } P_{f_i} \text{ modulo } P_{f_j} \neq 0 \qquad (21)$$

The second part of run-time constraints applies only to signals: s_i and s_j cannot be partitioned on the same task if they belong to the same transaction ($\Gamma_{[s_i]} = \Gamma_{[s_j]}$).

$$SP_{s_j,s_i} \neq 0 \text{ if } \Gamma_{[s_i]} = \Gamma_{[s_j]} \qquad (22)$$

In constraint (23) the parameter $dp_{f_i,f_j} = 1$ indicates that the execution of f_i depends on f_j in the functional graph. In this case, f_i cannot be placed on a task with priority higher than the task on which f_j is placed.

$$\chi_{i,j} = 0 \text{ if } dp_{f_i,f_j} = 1 \qquad (23)$$

Latency constraints: constraints on latency are similar to the previous ones, except that, since tasks are variables in this stage, we compute the WCRT on functions while considering their partitioning. The WCRT of a function f_i is the WCRT of the task containing f_i. Constraint (24) expresses the computation of functions WCRT. Signals WCRT are computed in the same way.

$$R_{f_i} = W_{f_i} + J_{f_i} \qquad (24)$$

The first term of the functions completion time (25) represents the WCET of the task containing f_i, as the sum of the WCET of its functions. The binary parameter SN_{f_i,f_j} indicates whether f_i and f_j are placed on the same node. The second term refers to the interferences from higher priority functions f_k that are on the same node as f_i. $I_{f_i,f_k} = \chi_{k,i} \cdot \sigma_{f_i,f_k}$ is a real variable representing the maximum number of times that f_k preempts f_i. σ_{f_i,f_k} is computed as in (14) and I_{f_i,f_k} is linearized using the Big M method.

$$W_{f_i} = \Sigma_{f_j \in F} SP_{f_i,f_j} \cdot \omega_{f_j,c} \cdot SN_{f_i,f_j}$$
$$+ \Sigma_{f_k \in F} I_{f_i,f_k} \cdot \omega_{f_k,c} \cdot SN_{f_i,f_k} \qquad (25)$$

The response time of signals is computed similarly, adding a term corresponding to the blocking time B_{s_i} as in (26), where SB_{s_i,s_j} is a binary parameter indicating whether s_i and s_j are transmitted over the same bus. W_{s_i} is 0 if s_i is local.

$$\forall s_j \in \Phi : B_{s_i} \geq \omega_{s_j,b} \cdot (1 - SP_{s_i,s_j}) \cdot SB_{s_i,s_j}$$
$$+ \Sigma_{s_k \in \Phi : k \neq j} \omega_{s_k,b} \cdot SP_{s_j,s_k} \cdot SB_{s_j,s_k} \qquad (26)$$

To compute functions jitter we need to define a real variable V_{f_i}, which is 0 if f_i is the first function in its transaction, otherwise, it

is the WCRT of the signal it receives.

$$V_{f_i} = \begin{cases} 0 & f_i \text{ is triggered by an external event} \\ R_{s_i} & s_i \text{ is the signal received by } f_i \end{cases} \qquad (27)$$

J_{f_i} is computed as the largest V_{f_j} value among all functions with the same priority and belonging to the same node. As above, the Big M method is used to linearize $V_{f_j} \cdot SP_{f_i,f_j}$.

$$\forall f_j \in F \ s.t \ SN_{f_i,f_j} = 1 : J_{f_i} \geq V_{f_j} \cdot SP_{f_i,f_j} \qquad (28)$$

Similarly, we use an auxiliary real variable (X_{s_i}) to compute the jitter of signals, which depends on the placement and partitioning of its sender and receiver functions. In (29), the real variables Y_{f_i,f_j} and Z_{f_i,f_j} are equal respectively to $J_{f_i} \cdot SP_{f_i,f_j}$ and $R_{f_i} \cdot (1 - SP_{f_i,f_j})$. These latter variables are also linearized using the Big M method. According to (29) and the above definition of Y_{f_i,f_j} and Z_{f_i,f_j}, X_{s_i} may have two values depending on the variable SP_{f_i,f_j} and the parameter SN_{f_i,f_j}. When the sender (sen_{s_i}) and receiver (rec_{s_i}) functions of s_i are on different nodes, or on the same node but different tasks, $X_{s_i} = R_{f_i}$. $X_{s_i} = J_{f_i}$ if the sender and receiver functions are on the same task.

$$X_{s_i} = (Y_{f_i,f_j} + Z_{f_i,f_j}) \cdot SN_{f_i,f_j} + R_{f_i} \cdot (1 - SN_{f_i,f_j})$$
$$s.t \ sen_{s_i} = f_i \text{ and } rec_{s_i} = f_j \qquad (29)$$

Since a message may transmit multiple signals, the jitter of a signal should take into account the jitter of all signals transmitted on the same message. Constraint (30) defines J_{s_i} as the largest value of X_{s_j} among all signals belonging to the same message. If s_i is local, then its jitter is simply equal to X_{s_i}.

$$\forall s_j \in \Phi \ s.t \ SB_{s_i,s_j} = 1 : J_{s_i} \geq X_{s_j} \cdot SP_{s_i,s_j} \qquad (30)$$

This MILP formulation returns as output a set of functions (signal) partitions as well as a priority order for each partition (task or message) on each node (bus). As priority orders are given locally to a node (bus), a post-processing, which consists in defining a global priority order, is required before the next iteration. The global priority order is simply defined based on the order considered as input in the previous step of the same iteration.

4.3 The GA formulation for the two-step approach

Genetic Algorithm (GA) is an optimization technique patterned after natural selection in biological evolution (Algorithm 4.3.1). In a GA, the space of all possible solutions (feasible and not feasible) to the optimization problem is encoded using a string of bits, called chromosome. Each bit or group of bits in the sequence typically encodes one parameter of the solution (such as the placement of a function or the priority of a task). Several solutions are generated at each round (population), starting from an initial set and then obtaining new solutions by a composition function (or *crossover*) that applies to two chromosomes and produces a new one or by a mutation operator that changes the bit string of a chromosome to generate a new one. Each new generation (or offspring) is evaluated. Some bit strings correspond to non-feasible solutions, or dead individuals and are discarded. A set of the most promising ones is retained and used for computing the next generation.

In the context of our problem, we implement two GA algorithms for the PP and PS stages respectively. GA is used because of its better scalability, in comparison to MILP. Let us note that the quality of the solutions obtained from GA is difficult to evaluate and guarantee, since it is based on many factors, such as the choice of the encoding, crossover and mutation operators, the fitness function and additional mechanisms that improve the search and guarantee constraints.

4.3.1 A GA Solution to the Placement Problem

The *Encoding* definition translates a solution configuration in a string of bits. In the placement problem, a specific solution, i.e.

single chromosome, represents the allocation of tasks onto the processing units, and messages on buses. We used the value encoding, in which each gene (subset of bits) in a chromosome contains a specific value. In our case, a gene relates either to a task or a message. The value held by a gene represents an execution node or a communication bus. Although formally PP stage refers to the functions and signals placement here we are encoding tasks and messages. This is due to the knowledge about the functions and signals partitioning during the PP stage. Therefore the placement of functions and signals can be directly inferred from the tasks/messages allocation. There are two advantages of this encoding. First, the number of tasks/messages is never greater than the number of functions/signals. Hence the size of a chromosome will not be greater if functions/signals were encoded. This can significantly save memory which is an issue especially if large initial populations are considered. Secondly, in case of functions/signals encoding, additional mechanism to preserve the correctness of the chromosome in regards to the allocation constraints would be required. Namely, all the functions/signals of the same task/message have to be allocated on the same processor/bus.

Algorithm 1 General form of a GA Algorithm

1: // Define encoding, crossover and mutation operator, fitness
2: // Specify the size of an initial population - P_{size}
3:
4: Generate initial population
5: **while** termination condition is not met **do**
6:     Evaluate each solution from the population P
7:     Generate new population P by applying the crossover and mutation operators
8: **end while**
9: **return** the best solution from P

Figure 4 shows an example of a chromosome that corresponds to the specific configuration for placement. Gene t_1 holds a value equal to 1, which is the index of the node on which t_1 and all its functions, i.e. f_1 and f_2 will run. The value of the gene m_1 is 0, indicating that message m_1 in this placement configuration is locally transmitted. The selection of the *Crossover* operator is very impor-

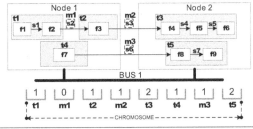

Figure 4. Chromosome for the specific placement configuration

tant for the quality of the GA solution. The operator combines information from two parent chromosomes to create a new child. The choice of the parent chromosomes can be done in many ways, but it is always highly dependent on a chromosome fitness rate. For our implementation we selected the OX3 crossover operator [11] with a tournament selector [19] (with size equal to 5). The OX3 creates two child chromosomes from two parents. It selects two random positions in a chromosome. The values between these points are copied from the first/second parent to the second/first child in the same absolute position. The remaining values are copied from the first/second parent to the first/second child. A simple result of the application of this operator on two chromosomes is shown on the Figure 5. The *Mutation* operator chooses a random point in a chromosome and changes the value of the gene at the selected point to a new random value. If the randomly selected gene corresponds to a task, the new value is chosen from the list of available execution

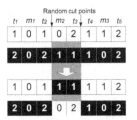

Figure 5. Example application of the crossover

nodes. If it relates to a message, the new value is chosen from the list of available buses.

The *Fitness function* defines how much the solution optimizes the performance criteria. Chromosomes are ranked according to this function and, the higher the rank, the higher the probability that the chromosome is selected as a parent for a crossover or the target of a mutation. Our fitness function corresponds to the optimization metrics, that is, in the case of the minimum transactional slack time, it computes $\min_{\Gamma_i \in \zeta}(D_i - L_i)$ where L_i is the latency of the transaction Γ_i and D_i its deadline.

The *Initial population* is generated randomly, i.e. for each task gene, a random number representing its execution node is assigned. However, the initial population does not contain solutions which violate the utilization constraints. Therefore if a generated chromosome leads to the violation of a utilization constraint, we call a correction procedure.

Correction mechanisms are used to avoid the generation of non-feasible solutions in the initial population or after the crossover and mutation. In the case of the violation of utilization constraint, the chromosome is modified by lowering the load of the node(s) with excessive utilization. The procedure randomly selects a task from one of these nodes and then moves it to a destination node, randomly selected among those that can accommodate the additional load. Tasks are moved until a feasible load distribution is found. Incorrect definitions of the communication are also fixed. If two communicating tasks are placed on different nodes, the gene in a chromosome that relates to the message exchanged between the tasks must have a number associated with one of the buses that connect the two nodes. Our correction mechanism checks all message values. Each time an incorrect bus is found, the procedure randomly generates a new bus identifier among those that are valid with respect to the tasks placement.

4.3.2 The GA Formulation for Partitioning and Scheduling

After the definition of the function and signal placement (implicitly by the placement of tasks and messages), the maximum number of new possible tasks and messages for each node and bus can be computed as the number of functions or signals allocated on the resource. Also, signals that result in local communications are not represented in chromosomes. For the PS stage, we only describe the encoding, the generation of the initial population, and the correction mechanism. The crossover mutation operators follow the same logic as in the placement stage. The fitness function is the same.

In the PS *Encoding* each gene represents a function or a signal exchanged among CPUs. The value of the gene is the index of the task or message executing the function or transmitting the signal. The index of a task or message also represents its priority, and its period is the gcd of the functions/signals mapped onto it. In the case of Figure 4, the system partitioning and scheduling is represented by the chromosome shown in Figure 6, where f_1 is executed by t_1 (with priority 1), together with function f_2.

The *Initial population* is randomly generated by assigning a task or message index to each function and signal.

Figure 6. Chromosome for the partitioning and scheduling configuration

The *Correction* function, called when a new chromosome is generated as part of the initial population or after the crossover and mutation enforces the order of execution constraints. The range of values for a gene is constrained by the values assigned to other genes. If function f_1 precedes f_2, and the gene representing f_1 is assigned to a task with priority π_i, then f_2 should be partitioned on the same task or a task with priority lower than π_i.

5. Experiments

The objective of the following experiments is to assess (i) the quality of solutions obtained with the two-step technique (MILP and GA) against optimal solutions given by the one-step MILP, (ii) comparison of the two-step MILP versus the two-step GA when applied to an industry-size system and (iii) scalability and runtime evaluation of all the techniques.

5.1 Quality evaluation of two-step techniques against one-step MILP

This section presents a first set of small-size tests with the same initial configuration. Results show the convergence of the inner loop and the impact of the initial configuration on the quality of results. The second experiment applies the two-step and the one-step techniques to an automotive case-study. For this case three different initial configurations are tested.

5.1.1 Small-size tests

To evaluate the quality of solutions given by the two-step techniques, we choose six randomly generated systems with functional graphs as in Figure 7). In all these systems, the WCETs of functions and the WCTTs of signals are the same for all nodes and buses, and the network topology consists of two nodes and a single bus. The maximal capacity utilization is set to 1 for the bus and both nodes. The initial configuration for partitioning and scheduling is as follows: (i) each function executes in one task and each signal is transmitted by one message; (ii) priorities are assigned to tasks as follows: (1) if they belong to the same transaction, if the function f_j depends on the function f_i then t_i is higher priority than t_j, (2) between transactions, we follow the deadline-monotonic (DM) approach [5]. Messages inherit the priority of the sending task. Figure 8 shows the comparison of the optimal solutions with the solutions provided by the two-step techniques (placement is represented by full lines, partitions are represented by dashed lines and the higher index of tasks represents the higher priority). For these tests the two-step techniques for both MILP and GA computed the same results. For tests 3, 4 and 5 the two-step techniques (MILP and GA) computes the optimal solution Figure 8(b). For tests 1, 2 and 6 they compute a local optimum Figure 8(a). In the three last cases, the selected initial configuration prevents finding the optimum. The two-step techniques return the solutions for which interferences between tasks are minimal. This results in splitting functions between nodes, which in next iterations prevents finding the solution in which all functions are on the same task and node. This situation does not occur for the test 3 where WCTTs are very large with respect to tasks interferences.

Table 1 shows partial results obtained at each step of the inner loop. For these tests, two-step MILP and GA computed the same results at each step of all iterations. The values in the cells represent the maximum of the minimum transactional slack time (O_s) and

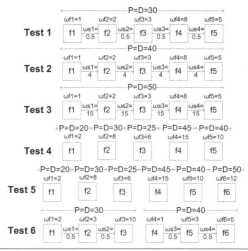

Figure 7. Tests for evaluating solutions quality

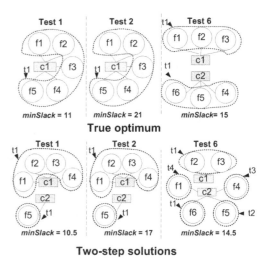

(a) Different solutions

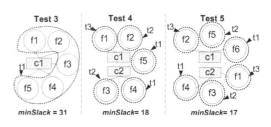

(b) Identical solutions

Figure 8. Comparison results between two-step and optimal solutions for tests 1-6

the minimum sum of latencies (O_l). At each step a better or equal solution is found. Convergence is obtained in the worst case at the third iteration.

Table 1. Intermediate results for two-step solutions

Test	Steps	Iter 1 O_s/O_l	Iter 2 O_s/O_l	Iter 3 O_s/O_l	Test	Steps	Iter 1 O_s/O_l	Iter 2 O_s/O_l
1	PP	1.5/28	7.5/22.5	10.5/19.5	4	PP	18/59	18/59
	PS	5.5/24	10.5/19.5	10.5/19.5		PS	18/59	18/59
2	PP	7/33	17/23	-/-	5	PP	17/91	17/91
	PS	17/23	17/23	-/-		PS	17/91	17/91
3	PP	7/43	31/19	-/-	6	PP	11.5/36	14.5/24
	PS	31/19	31/19	-/-		PS	14.5/24	14.5/24

Table 2. Intermediate results for each initial configuration

Initial configs	Steps	Metrics	Iter 1	Iter 2	Iter 3	Iter 4	Iter 5
1	PP	O_s	5.93	7.45	7.45	7.45	7.45
		O_l	112.69	96.67	78.85	72.75	71.82
	PS	O_s	7.45	7.45	7.45	7.45	7.45
		O_l	103.09	81.85	76.23	71.82	71.82
2	PP	O_s	7.45	7.45	7.45	7.45	-
		O_l	89.47	74.32	71.82	-	-
	PS	O_s	7.45	7.45	7.45	7.45	-
		O_l	78.32	71.82	71.82	-	-
3	PP	O_s	7.45	-	-	-	-
		O_l	68.27	-	-	-	-
	PS	O_s	7.45	-	-	-	-
		O_l	68.27	-	-	-	-

5.1.2 Automotive case study

We consider an automotive system composed of the CCS and ABS sub-systems [4][20]. Figure 9 represents the functional graph of this automotive system. Each function (signal) has the same WCET (WCTT) for all nodes (buses). The network topology for this test is composed of four nodes and a single bus. The maximal capacity utilization is 1 for the bus and all nodes. For this system, we de-

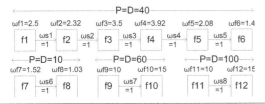

Figure 9. CCS and ABS sub-systems

fine three initial configurations for partitioning and scheduling as shown in Figure 10. Partitions are represented by dashed lines and the index of the partition defines its priority (higher index means higher priority). The optimal solution given by the one-step MILP

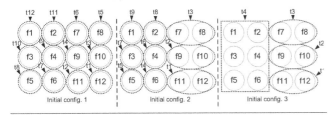

Figure 10. Initial configurations for partitioning and scheduling

is shown in Figure 11 (right-most solution). The values for the minimal slack and latency are respectively 7.45 and 68.27. Table 2 provides the results obtained with the two-step MILP at each iteration of the inner loop for the three selected initial configurations. Cell values refer to the maximum of the minimum transaction slack time (O_s) and the minimum sum of latencies (O_l). The obtained configurations are shown in Figure 11 for the MILP and in Figure 12 for the GA. GA computed different solutions with the same metric value and number of iterations for the first and second configurations. For the third configuration, the same solution was computed by MILP and GA. The optimal solution for this system is the one obtained with the two-step starting with the third configuration. Let us remark that considering different initial configurations in the outer loop allows moving towards better solutions. Other existing optimization heuristics [31] [22] consider only one random initial configuration.

5.2 Two-step techniques evaluation on an industrial-size system

The objective of the following experiment is to study the behavior of the two-step MILP and GA in the case of a large, distributed

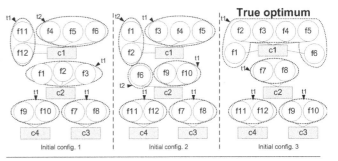

Figure 11. Solutions for all configurations - MILP

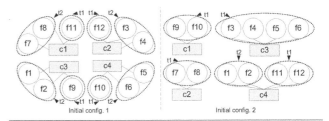

Figure 12. Solutions for configuration 1 and 2 - GA

industrial-size system as in [6], but where the partitioning is not fixed. Figure 14 shows the functional graph of the system. The system has 9 nodes communicating through a single bus. The maximum capacity utilization is 1 for the bus and nodes. Nodes are heterogeneous and have different computation speeds. The WCETs and nodes allocation constraints for this system are given in Table 3. The WCTT for all signals is 10. In the initial configuration each function is partitioned in one task and the task priority is inversely proportional to the index of the function in it (i.e. the highest priority task contains the function with the smallest index).

The solution obtained with the two-step MILP for the first iteration is shown in Figure 13. The minimal slack for the two-step MILP is 2396 for the PP step and 3269 after the PS step (for the first iteration). The two-step GA computes slightly worse results, i.e. a minimum slack of 2387 for the PP step and 3262 for the PS step. Latency (in the first iteration) is the same for both methods, 9981 for the PP, and 6251 for the PS step.

5.3 Runtime and scalability evaluation

In this section we show respectively (i) runtime evaluation of all the techniques, pointing out the limits of one-step MILP when the size of the system grows and (ii) runtime evaluation of the two-step techniques for large systems, showing their scalability.

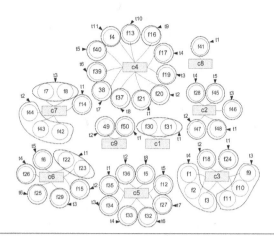

Figure 13. Deployment solution for the large case

P=D=4000
| f1 | s1 | f2 | s2 | f3 | s3 | f4 | s4 | f5 | s5 | f6 | s6 | f7 | s7 | f8 |

P=D=5000
| f9 | s8 | f10 | s9 | f11 | s10 | f12 | s11 | f13 | s12 | f14 | s13 | f15 | s14 | f16 |

P=D=7000
| f17 | s15 | f18 | s16 | f19 | s17 | f20 | s18 | f21 | s19 | f22 | s20 | f23 | s21 | f24 |

P=D=4500
| f25 | s22 | f26 | s23 | f27 | s24 | f28 | s25 | f29 | s26 | f30 | s27 | f31 | s28 | f32 |

P=D=5500
| f33 | s29 | f34 | s30 | f35 | s31 | f36 | s32 | f37 | s33 | f38 | s34 | f39 | s35 | f40 |

P=D=3500
| f41 | s36 | f42 | s37 | f43 | s38 | f44 | s39 | f45 |

P=D=5000
| f46 | s40 | f47 | s41 | f48 | s42 | f49 | s43 | f50 |

Figure 14. Functional graph of the large case

5.3.1 Runtime evaluation

In the first experiment, we are interested in showing the limits of the one-step MILP. We generate systems of 5,10,15 and 20 functions, by combining the transactions of Figure 7. The network topology is composed of four nodes communicating by two buses, the first bus connects nodes 1, 2 and 3 and the second nodes 3 and 4. The maximal capacity utilization is 1 for all nodes and buses. We run two outer loops for two-step techniques. We compare the quality of solutions returned by one-step and two-step techniques, then we study the time required to compute the solution.

The results of the runtime comparison are shown in Figure 15: the runtime of all techniques increases according to the number of functions. The runtime of the two-step techniques (for two outer loops) is very small compared to the one-step MILP runtime, and the one-step MILP runs out of memory (OOM) for systems with 20 functions, while the two-step MILP computes a solution in 1375 seconds. Let us note that in all the cases the one-step MILP returns without error, the obtained values of latency are the same for all algorithms.

5.3.2 Scalability evaluation of two-step techniques

To study the scalability of the two-step techniques, we generated systems of different sizes by combining the transactions shown in Figure 14. We consider only the inner loop iteration for two-step techniques (one initial configuration). The obtained results are

Table 3. Vectors of WCETs

	c1	c2	c3	c4	c5	c6	c7	c8	c9		c1	c2	c3	c4	c5	c6	c7	c8	c9
f_1	48	26	35	50	36	40	45	27	28	f_{26}						48	36		
f_2	36	52	59	34	26	43	50	48	49	f_{27}			26		50				
f_3			49							f_{28}		51		30					
f_4				50						f_{29}						32	39		
f_5					46					f_{30}	50	48	36	26	35	26	35	50	51
f_6						50				f_{31}	31	39		44					
f_7							51			f_{32}			52		27				
f_8	26	35	29	42	50	37	20	52	53	f_{33}	44	26	35	26	35	30	28	49	50
f_9	50	40	31	29	33	46	37	29	30	f_{34}				30	40	50			
f_{10}			52							f_{35}					49	39	29		
f_{11}	40	39	50	33	36	39	43	41	42	f_{36}					53	25	40		
f_{12}				50						f_{37}		32	40	48					
f_{13}			39							f_{38}		30	50	45					
f_{14}					38					f_{39}		54	28	36					
f_{15}					52					f_{40}	50	28	39	47	44	35	26	35	36
f_{16}	33	46	37	29	35	29	42	50	51	f_{41}	52	28	35	26	35	50	45	33	34
f_{17}		32		55		29				f_{42}					48	38	28		
f_{18}			51		26					f_{43}					30	50	40		
f_{19}	51	42	26	35	50	36	33	29	30	f_{44}					26	38	48		
f_{20}		50		28		36				f_{45}		51	30	42					
f_{21}	35	29	42	42	26	35	50	54	55	f_{46}		34	49	30					
f_{22}						29	50			f_{47}	28	39	47	50	26	35	50	51	52
f_{23}						48	32			f_{48}		36	29	53					
f_{24}		31		45						f_{49}	51	44	33	28	50	26	39	33	34
f_{25}	53	26	35	50	36	26	35	50	51	f_{50}	37	50	52	32	29	27	36	40	41

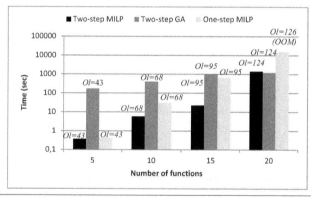

Figure 15. Performance of the two-step optimization technique vs the one-step approach

shown in Table 4, where n/a means that there is no solution from the MILP solver, (*) that the solver runs out of memory, (#) that the a solution is obtained after the PP stage, but the solver runs out of memory in the PS stage. The table shows that the two-step MILP (2-MILP) is more scalable (up to 80 functions) than the one-step MILP (1-MILP, up to 40 functions), but the 2-GA is the most scalable approach.

Please note that other approaches solving task placement and scheduling [6] [30] [25] do not deal with more than 50 tasks and 9 nodes.

6. Conclusions

We presented two approaches to optimize the deployment of (hard) real-time distributed systems w.r.t end-to-end latency metrics. We consider an event-triggered activation model and define the place-ment, partitioning and scheduling of functions and signals. We pro-

Table 4. Results on systems with different sizes

	Maximal MinSlack (O_s)			Runtime (seconds)		
Nb functions	1-MILP	2-MILP	2-GA	1-MILP	2-MILP	2-GA
32	3500	3430	3490	10278	65.07	553.12
40	3388*	3462	3490	21533*	81.5	830.52
50	n/a	3269	3262	n/a	1744	1345
60	n/a	2347#	3131	n/a	732#	1862
80	n/a	926#	3180	n/a	1260#	2667.95
100	n/a	n/a	3017	n/a	n/a	5316.11
200	n/a	n/a	2039	n/a	n/a	16705.21

vided an MILP integral formulation for the problem, which can compute the optimal solution for small size systems and a dual formulation, based on MILP and Genetic algorithm (GA) for a partitioned, two-stage iterative approach. We evaluated the performance of the two-step approach by comparing the results against the optima for some small systems and then applied to larger case studies, including an automotive system. Future work includes an improvement of the MILP formulation for application to larger systems, an extension to more complex functional graphs, in which transactions are non-linear, and finally, the consideration of other optimization metrics.

References

[1] http://www.omg.org/.

[2] Autosar 4.0 specifications. http://www.autosar.org/.

[3] A. Aleti, B. Buhnova, L. Grunske, A. Koziolek, and I. Meedeniya. Software architecture optimization methods: A systematic literature review. *IEEE Transactions on Software Engineering*, To appear.

[4] S. Anssi, S. Tucci-Piergiovanni, S. Kuntz, S. Gerard, and F. Terrier. Enabling scheduling analysis for autosar systems. *Object-Oriented Real-Time Distributed Computing, IEEE International Symposium on*, 0:152–159, 2011.

[5] N. Audsley, A. Burns, M. Richardson, and A. Wellings. Hard real-time scheduling: The deadline monotonic approach. In *Proceedings 8th IEEE Workshop on Real-Time Operating Systems and Software*, pages 127–132, 1991.

[6] E. Azketa, J. Uribe, J. Gutiérrez, M. Marcos, and L. Almeida. Permutational genetic algorithm for the optimized assignment of priorities to tasks and messages in distributed real-time systems. In *Proceedings of the 10th IEEE International Conference on Trust, Security and Privacy in Computing and Communications*, pages 958–965, 2011.

[7] C. Bartolini, G. Lipari, and M. Di Natale. From functional blocks to the synthesis of the architectural model in embedded real-time applications. In *Proc. 11th IEEE Real Time and Embedded Technology and Applications Symposium*, pages 458–467, 2005.

[8] I. Bate and P. Emberson. Incorporating scenarios and heuristics to improve flexibility in real-time embedded systems. In *Proceedings of the 12th IEEE Real-Time and Embedded Technology and Applications Symposium*, pages 221–230, 2006.

[9] E. Bini, M. D. Natale, and G. Buttazzo. Sensitivity analysis for fixed-priority real-time systems. In *Euromicro Conference on Real-Time Systems*, Dresden, Germany, June 2006.

[10] R. Bosch. CAN specification, version 2.0. Stuttgart, 1991.

[11] L. Davis, editor. *Handbook of Genetic Algorithms*. Van Nostrand Reinhold, 1991.

[12] R. Davis, A. Burns, R. Bril, and J. Lukkien. Controller area network (can) schedulability analysis: Refuted, revisited and revised. *Real-Time Systems*, 35(3):239–272, 2007.

[13] A. Hamann, R. Racu, and R. Ernst. Multi-dimensional robustness optimization in heterogeneous distributed embedded systems. In *Proceedings of the 13th IEEE Real Time and Embedded Technology and Applications Symposium*, April 2007.

[14] X. He, Z. Gu, and Y. Zhu. Task allocation and optimization of distributed embedded systems with simulated annealing and geometric programming. *The Computer Journal*, 53(7):1071–1091, 2010.

[15] B. Kienhuis, E. Deprettere, P. Van Der Wolf, and K. Vissers. A methodology to design programmable embedded systems. In *Embedded processor design challenges*, pages 321–324. Springer, 2002.

[16] S. Kodase, S. Wang, and K. Shin. Transforming structural model to runtime model of embedded software with real-time constraints. In *Proceedings of the conference on Design, Automation and Test in Europe*, pages 170–175, 2003.

[17] S. Kugele, W. Haberl, M. Tautschnig, and M. Wechs. Optimizing automatic deployment using non-functional requirement annotations. *Leveraging Applications of Formal Methods, Verification and Validation*, pages 400–414, 2009.

[18] A. Mehiaoui. A mixed integer linear programming formulations for optimizing timing performance during the deployment phase in real-time systems design. *Technical Report CEA, http://hal-cea.archives-ouvertes.fr/cea-00811359*, 2012.

[19] B. L. Miller, B. L. Miller, D. E. Goldberg, and D. E. Goldberg. Genetic algorithms, tournament selection, and the effects of noise. *Complex Systems*, 9:193–212, 1995.

[20] C. Mraidha, S. Tucci-Piergiovanni, and S. Gerard. Optimum: a marte-based methodology for schedulability analysis at early design stages. *ACM SIGSOFT Software Engineering Notes*, 36(1):1–8, 2011.

[21] J. C. Palencia and M. G. Harbour. Exploiting precedence relations in the schedulability analysis of distributed real-time systems. In *Proceedings of the 20th IEEE Real-Time Systems Symposium*, 1999.

[22] P. Pop, P. Eles, Z. Peng, and T. Pop. Analysis and optimization of distributed real-time embedded systems. *ACM Transactions on Design Automation of Electronic Systems*, 11(3):593–625, 2006.

[23] T. Pop, P. Eles, and Z. Peng. Design optimization of mixed time/event-triggered distributed embedded systems. In *Proc. of the First IEEE/ACM/IFIP International Conference on Hardware/Software Codesign and System Synthesis*, 2003.

[24] R. Racu, M. Jersak, and R. Ernst. Applying sensitivity analysis in real-time distributed systems. In *Proceedings of the 11th IEEE Real Time on Embedded Technology and Applications Symposium*, pages 160–169, 2005.

[25] M. Richard, P. Richard, and F. Cottet. Allocating and scheduling tasks in multiple fieldbus real-time systems. In *Proceedings of the IEEE Conference on Emerging Technologies and Factory Automation*, 2003.

[26] M. Saksena, P. Karvelas, and Y. Wang. Automatic synthesis of multi-tasking implementations from real-time object-oriented models. In *Proceedings of 3rd IEEE International Symposium on Object-Oriented Real-Time Distributed Computing*, pages 360–367, 2000.

[27] A. Sangiovanni-Vincentelli and G. Martin. Platform-based design and software design methodology for embedded systems. *IEEE Design and Test of Computers*, 18(6):23–33, 2001.

[28] K. Tindell and J. Clark. Holistic schedulability analysis for distributed hard real-time systems. *Microprocessing and microprogramming*, 40(2-3):117–134, 1994.

[29] W. Zheng, M. Di Natale, C. Pinello, P. Giusto, and A. Vincentelli. Synthesis of task and message activation models in real-time distributed automotive systems. In *Proceedings of the conference on Design, automation and test in Europe*, pages 93–98, 2007.

[30] Q. Zhu, Y. Yang, M. Di Natale, E. Scholte, and A. Sangiovanni-Vincentelli. Optimizing the software architecture for extensibility in hard real-time distributed systems. *IEEE Transactions on Industrial Informatics*, 6(4):621–636, 2010.

[31] Q. Zhu, Y. Yang, E. Scholte, M. Di Natale, and A. Sangiovanni-Vincentelli. Optimizing extensibility in hard real-time distributed systems. In *Proceedings of the 15th IEEE Real-Time and Embedded Technology and Applications Symposium*, pages 275–284, 2009.

[32] Q. Zhu, H. Zeng, W. Zheng, M. Di Natale, and A. Sangiovanni-Vincentelli. Optimization of task allocation and priority assignment in hard real-time distributed systems. *ACM Transactions on Embedded Computing Systems*, 11(4):85:1–85:30, 2012.

Buffer Minimization in Earliest-Deadline First Scheduling of Dataflow Graphs

Adnan Bouakaz

University of Rennes 1 / IRISA
adnan.bouakaz@irisa.fr

Jean-Pierre Talpin

INRIA / IRISA
jean-pierre.talpin@inria.fr

Abstract

Symbolic schedulability analysis of dataflow graphs is the process of synthesizing the timing parameters (i.e. periods, phases, and deadlines) of actors so that the task system is schedulable and achieves a high throughput when using a specific scheduling policy. Furthermore, the resulted schedule must ensure that communication buffers are underflow- and overflow-free. This paper describes a (partitioned) earliest-deadline first symbolic schedulability analysis of dataflow graphs that minimizes the buffering requirements.

Our scheduling analysis consists of three major steps. (1) The construction of an abstract affine schedule of the graph that excludes overflow and underflow exceptions and minimizes the buffering requirements assuming some precedences between jobs. (2) Symbolic deadlines adjustment that guarantees precedences without the need for lock-based synchronizations. (3) The concretization of the affine schedule using a symbolic, fast-converging, processor-demand analysis for both uniprocessor and multiprocessor systems. Experimental results show that our technique improves the buffering requirements in many cases.

Categories and Subject Descriptors C.3 [*Special-Purpose and Application-Based Systems*]: Real-Time and Embedded Systems; F.1.1 [*Theory of Computation*]: Models of Computation

General Terms Theory, Algorithms, Design

Keywords Dataflow graphs, Symbolic schedulability analysis, Buffer minimization, Affine relation, Earliest-deadline first scheduling

1. Introduction

Dataflow models of computation are commonly used in embedded system design to describe stream processing or control applications. Their simplicity allows waiving part of the difficult and error-prone tasks of programming real-time schedules for computations and communications from the engineering process by implementing automated code generation techniques.

Modern multicore architectures, as well as embedded real-time operating systems, such as RTEMS for aerospace, OSEK for automotive, or the SCJ virtual machine, enable multi-task implementations of dataflow specifications. Most of these operating systems implement a bunch of different priority-driven scheduling poli-

cies such as earliest-deadline first (EDF) policy. For that reason, we argue the need for automatic synthesis techniques that produce EDF schedules of dataflow specifications while guaranteeing functional determinism and EDF schedulability. Functional determinism means that, for a given sequence of inputs, the system will always produce the same sequence of outputs. This implies that neither overflow nor underflow exceptions over communication buffers may occur at runtime [8].

Unlike with the classical static-periodic scheduling of dataflow graphs, this paper considers a fixed-job-priority preemptive scheduling policy: the EDF policy. Real-time scheduling theory for both uniprocessor and multiprocessor systems has already provided a lot of algorithms to check whether a task system meets its timing requirements, even in the worst-case scenario [11,18]. However, most algorithms assume that timing parameters of tasks are known a priori. Our approach to the problem is rather to *synthesize* the timing parameters of actors in dataflow graphs so as to ensure functional determinism and uniprocessor/multiprocessor schedulability. For the multiprocessor case, we will consider the partitioned EDF policy on identical multiprocessors where each task is allocated to a processor and no migration is permitted [4]. The current state of the art favors the partitioned scheduling over the global one for reasons that concern the run-time cost of inter-processor migration and the optimality of schedulability tests.

In a dataflow model of computation, an application is usually specified as a set of actors that communicate through one-to-one FIFO channels (i.e. streams). When an actor fires, it consumes tokens from its input channels and produces tokens on its output channels. In this paper, we target the design of software applications where software tasks interact with each other via software buffers. Among dataflow models of computation, synchronous data-flow (SDF) [15] and cyclo-static dataflow (CSDF) [6] are popular in the embedded system community. An actor has constant production and consumption rates in SDF and periodic rates in CSDF. Figure 1(a) shows a cyclic dataflow graph with ultimately periodic production and consumption rates. Channels are annotated by production and consumption rates. Sequence 1(2,0) on the output channel of actor p_1 means that the first firing (i.e. job) of p_1 produces one token; and then, alternatively, even jobs produce two tokens and odd jobs produce nothing. A number inside a node represents the worst-case execution time of an actor.

In order to execute such a dataflow specification on a real-time operating system with an EDF scheduler, we map each actor to a periodic task that has appropriate timing parameters; i.e. period, phase (first start time), and deadline. Recently, techniques that schedule dataflow graphs as implicit-deadline periodic (IDP) task systems have been proposed with an aim of achieving a high processor utilization factor (i.e. throughput) [1,8]. An IDP task has a deadline equal to its period. Such scheduling approach gives the maximum achievable processor utilization for large set of dataflow

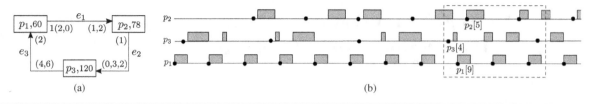

Figure 1. (a) A cyclic dataflow graph with ultimately periodic rates, and (b) its EDF scheduling on one processor.

graphs, called matched I/O rates graphs [1]. Furthermore, EDF symbolic schedulability of IDP task systems is quite simple with a polynomial time complexity [8]. However, the IDP model may increase the latency and the buffering requirements of the graphs. In [2], authors have shown that the IDP model increases the latency for a class of graphs called unbalanced graphs. In this paper, we will investigate the impact of the IDP model on the buffering requirements and we will propose a technique of deadlines adjustment that aims at reducing buffer sizes. Indeed, some embedded systems have strong memory constraints; therefore favoring buffer minimization over throughput maximization could be a legitimate choice. We will use a *constrained* task model where deadlines are less or equal to periods. Our technique is an extension of the affine dataflow approach [8] because, and unlike [1,2], that approach handles cyclic graphs.

1.1 Motivational example

Applying the scheduling technique proposed in [8] on the graph of Figure 1(a) results in the following timing parameters: periods $[\pi_1 = 160, \pi_2 = 240, \pi_3 = 400]$, phases $[r_1 = 0, r_2 = 360, r_3 = 40]$, and, of course, deadlines are equal to periods (i.e. implicit deadlines). For instance, based on the production and consumption rates of actors p_3 and p_1, actor p_1 must be exactly $\frac{5}{2}$ as fast as actor p_3 in order to implement channel e_3 as a bounded buffer. Figure 1(b) sketches the EDF scheduling of the graph on one processor where the jth job of an actor p is denoted by $p[j]$. Black dots represent release times of jobs. Now, we will investigate the impact of preemption on the computation of buffer sizes.

Actor p_3 is the producer of channel e_3, while actor p_1 is its consumer. As depicted in Figure 1(b), jobs $p_1[9]$ and $p_1[10]$ preempt job $p_3[4]$. Since the technique proposed in [8] does not assume any knowledge about the implementation code of actors (i.e. it is unknown when exactly the actor reads and writes tokens), it considers the worst-case scenarios when computing the minimum number of initial tokens on the channel that prevents underflow exceptions and the minimum buffer size that prevents overflow exceptions. As a safe approximation, the worst-case scenario for the underflow analysis is when the producer p_3 writes its results at the end of its execution; while the worst-case scenario for the overflow analysis is when p_3 writes at the beginning.

To get rid of the over-approximation, we may write the implementation code of actors so that they produce tokens only at the end of their firings. However, firstly, a job may complete before its *worst-case* execution time. Secondly, if jobs $p_1[8], p_1[9]$, and $p_1[10]$ consume many tokens before the producer writes something to channel e_3, this is likely to increase the minimum number of initial tokens on the channel and so the buffering requirements. Our solution is rather to keep total freedom on how to write the implementation code of actors and to adjust the deadline of actor p_3 instead. Indeed, if the deadline of job $p_3[4]$ is less or equal to the deadline of job $p_1[9]$, then this latter will not preempt job $p_3[4]$ according to the EDF policy. Hence, we enforce the precedence between jobs $p_3[4]$ and $p_1[9]$ without using lock-based mechanisms.

In a dual way, actor p_3 is the consumer of channel e_2; while actor p_2 is its producer. As depicted in Figure 1(b), job $p_2[5]$ also preempts job $p_3[4]$. If the deadline of job $p_3[4]$ is less or equal to that of $p_2[5]$, then this latter will not preempt job $p_3[4]$. This technique of deadlines adjustment can be used to play on priorities of jobs and enforce other kinds of precedences.

From the experimental results, the average improvement of the buffering requirements is up to 39% compared to the technique proposed in [8], and of 11% compared to the technique proposed in [1]. Furthermore, our technique may also reduce the context switching overhead since it results in fewer preemptions. However, in some cases, it is not possible to adjust deadlines without jeopardizing the throughput, as we will show in Section 5.

1.2 Paper contributions

The contributions of this paper are twofold.
- The IDP task model, used in [1,8], is too restrictive since deadlines can be constrained in realistic applications to values less than periods. While standard uniprocessor EDF schedulability analysis of IDP task systems has a polynomial time complexity, existing exact schedulability tests for constrained tasks systems have a pseudo-polynomial time complexity. The main contribution of this a paper is a pseudo-polynomial EDF *symbolic* schedulability analysis of dataflow graphs with constrained deadlines called "Symbolic Quick-convergence Processor-demand Analysis" (SQPA). It is based on the well-known QPA algorithm [24,25]. Instead of testing schedulability for all possible timing parameters, our algorithm does that *incrementally* and so maximizes the processor utilization factor. For partitioned EDF scheduling of dataflow graphs, the allocation problem is known to be NP-hard. We hence propose an allocation heuristic that aims at reducing the buffering requirements. The SQPA algorithm will be used to synthesize the timing parameters for which each partition fits on one processor. In the appendix, we will propose a global EDF symbolic schedulability analysis of dataflow graphs which is similar to the SQPA technique but based on (an improved version of) the speedup-optimal schedulability analysis presented in [3,5].
- Once we have a symbolic schedulability analysis for constrained task systems, the deadlines adjustment technique, as illustrated in the previous example, can be used to reduce the buffering requirements. The construction of the abstract affine schedule is similar to that of [8] (reviewed separately in Section 3) but also considers the deadlines adjustment as shown in Section 4. One benefit of adding precedence constraints is that the linear safe approximations used to solve the buffer minimization problem are less pessimistic than the ones obtained in [8].

The rest of the paper is organized as follows. Section 2 discusses additional related work. Section 3 introduces the background material on the affine model needed for understanding the contributions of this paper. Our deadlines adjustment technique is then presented in Sections 4 and 5. Sections 6 and 7 present our symbolic EDF schedulability analysis for both uniprocessor and multiprocessor systems. An empirical evaluation of the algorithms is presented in Section 8. Finally, Section 9 ends the paper with conclusions.

2. Related work

Schedules of (C)SDF graphs that minimize buffer sizes under throughput constraints have been investigated in many studies, for instance in [23]. Those works aim at creating static cyclic schedules of actors for which hard real-time scheduling theories are not applicable. It is well known that the buffer sizes influence the maximum throughput that can be achieved. Recently, a technique that computes the trade-offs between the throughput and buffer sizes for (C)SDF graphs was proposed in [20, 22]. Our approach rather aims at creating EDF schedules that achieve a high throughput while trying to reduce the total amount of buffer storage capacities. It also considers a more general model than CSDF where production and consumption rates can be ultimately periodic.

EDF scheduling of data-dependent tasks was tackled in [12] by adjusting deadlines and release times and without using lock-based synchronizations. That approach, implemented in the Prelude compiler [16], differs from the present one in three respects. 1) In Prelude, deadlines are adjusted so as to ensure data-dependencies w.r.t. multi-rate communication patterns; while precedences in the present mode may also impose an order of reads before writes. 2) Communications in the Prelude compiler are not flow-preserving: when the producer is faster than the consumer, an adapter is added allowing some produced tokens not be buffered; and when the consumer is faster, an adapter is added to allow for reading the same value several times. 3) Prelude adjusts deadlines and checks schedulability based on user-provided timing parameters while the present proposal performs symbolically both the deadlines adjustment and the schedulability analysis.

Few works had addressed the symbolic schedulability problem. Cimatti et al. [10] used parametric timed automata to symbolically compute the schedulability region (i.e. the region of the parameter space that corresponds to feasible designs) of a task system scheduled using *fixed* priorities. In [13], the Inverse method for parametric timed automata is used to synthesize zones of the timing parameter space where the system is schedulable. Our solution is tailored to a specific scheduling policy and to specific constraints; it has hence less complexity and implementation overhead.

Regarding affine relations, a subclass of affine relations between abstract clocks was used in [14] to address time requirements of streaming applications on multiprocessor systems on chip. The whole class of affine relations is used in this paper. The affine model is also used in [7] to compute fixed-priority schedules of dataflow graphs with constrained deadlines.

3. Background

This section outlines the generic approach for strictly (as opposite to static) periodic scheduling of dataflow graphs proposed in [8]. The method consists of two steps: construction of an abstract schedule of the graph (i.e. a set of scheduling constraints) and then the concretization of the schedule (i.e. computing the concrete timing parameters).

3.1 Affine dataflow graphs

A dataflow graph is a weakly connected directed graph $G = (P, E)$ which consists of a finite set of actors P, and a set of FIFO channels E. The worst-case execution time of each actor $p_i \in P$ is denoted by $C_i \in \mathbb{N}^*$ where $\mathbb{N}^*$ is the set of strictly positive integers. Each channel $e = (p_i, p_k, x, y)$ has exactly one producer p_i and one consumer p_k, and it is associated with two integer functions $x, y : \mathbb{N}^* \to \mathbb{N}$. The function x denotes the production rate; i.e. the producer writes $x(j)$ tokens on channel e during its jth firing. Similarly, the function y denotes the consumption rate; the consumer reads $y(j)$ tokens from channel e during its jth firing. Rate functions must be bounded since an actor cannot produce (or consume) an infinite number of tokens during a finite number of firings. Rate functions are constant in SDF, periodic in CSDF; but they can also be ultimately periodic as we will show in the sequel.

The number of initial tokens on channel $e \in E$ is denoted by $\theta(e)$ s.t. $\theta : E \to \mathbb{N}$, while its size is denoted by $\delta(e)$ s.t. $\delta : E \to \mathbb{N}^*$. Both the number of initial tokens and the size are assumed to be unknown at design time (but they can be user-imposed). Channels are implemented as separated storage spaces (i.e. empty space in one channel cannot be used to store tokens of other channels); as cyclic arrays for example. The buffering requirements of a dataflow graph is hence given by $\sum_{e \in E} F(e)\delta(e)$ where $F(e)$ is the size of a token communicated over channel e.

The cumulative function of a rate function x is a monotone function $X : \mathbb{N} \to \mathbb{N}$ such that $X(j) = \sum_{k=1}^{j} x(k)$. Hence, $X(j)$ denotes the total number of produced (or consumed) tokens until and including the jth firing. In the next section, we will use an ILP formalism; let us therefore take functions $X^l, X^u : \mathbb{N} \to Q$ to be the linear lower bound and the linear upper bound of the cumulative function X, respectively. In the dataflow model, we may allow any kind of rate functions as long as their cumulative functions are linearly bounded.

Example 1 (Ultimately periodic rates). A rate function x is ultimately periodic if and only if $\exists j_0, \pi \in \mathbb{N}^* : \forall j \geq j_0 : x(j + \pi) = x(j)$. The notation $x = u(v)$, for two finite integer sequences u and v, means that $x(j) = u[j]$ if $j \leq |u|$, and $x(j) = v[(j - |u| - 1) \mod |v| + 1]$ otherwise; such that $|u|$ denotes the length of a finite sequence u, $\|u\|$ denotes the sum of its elements, and $u[j]$ denotes its jth element. It is easy to compute the linear bounds of the cumulative function X which increases by $\|v\|$ every $|v|$ steps. So, we have that $\exists \lambda_x^l, \lambda_x^u \in \mathbb{Q} : \forall j \in \mathbb{N} : \frac{\|v\|}{|v|}j + \lambda_x^l \leq X(j) \leq \frac{\|v\|}{|v|}j + \lambda_x^u$.

In time-triggered scheduling of dataflow graphs, each actor p has an activation clock $\hat{p}$ (i.e. an infinite ordered set of ticks). An actor instance, or job, is released at each tick of $\hat{p}$ and its execution must complete before the next tick (i.e. auto-concurrency is disabled) and cannot self-suspend. The jth job of actor p is denoted by $p[j]$ for $j \in \mathbb{N}^*$.

Let $p_i, p_k \in P$ be two actors of the graph, and let us take the monotone function $\Delta_{i,k} : \mathbb{N}^* \to \mathbb{N}$ such that $\forall j \in \mathbb{N}^* : \Delta_{i,k}(j) = \max\{0, j' \in \mathbb{N}^* | \text{job } p_k[j'] \text{ is released strictly before job } p_i[j]\}$. The *relative positioning* of ticks of clocks $\hat{p}_i$ and $\hat{p}_k$ can be described entirely by the two functions $\Delta_{i,k}$ and $\Delta_{k,i}$. Those functions do not however describe the physical duration between clock ticks.

In the first step of the scheduling approach, activations clocks are regarded as abstract clocks in the sense that durations between ticks do not matter, and the most important thing is the *relative positioning* of ticks. Affine relations, defined below, between activation clocks are expressive enough to describe strictly periodic schedules of dataflow graphs. Affine transformations of abstract clocks were introduced in [19] and they enjoy a canonical form and other useful mathematical properties.

Definition 1 (Affine relation). A (n, φ, d)-affine relation between two clocks $\hat{p}_i$ and $\hat{p}_k$ has three parameters $n, d \in \mathbb{N}^*$ and $\varphi \in \mathbb{Z}$. In case φ is positive (resp. negative), clock $\hat{p}_i$ is obtained by counting each nth instant on a referential abstract clock $\hat{c}$ starting from the first (resp. $(-\varphi + 1)^{th}$) instant; while clock $\hat{p}_k$ is obtained by counting each dth instant on $\hat{c}$ starting from the $(\varphi + 1)^{th}$ (resp. first) instant.

Figure 2 depicts a $(3, -4, 5)$-affine relation between two actors. If actors p_i and p_k are (n, φ, d)-affine-related, then there is a

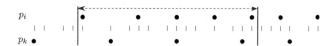

Figure 2. A $(3, -4, 5)-$affine relation. There is a positioning pattern which consists of 5 activations of p_i and 3 activations of p_k.

positioning pattern of ticks that will repeat infinitely so that for every $\frac{d}{\gcd(n,d)}$ activations of actor p_i, there are $\frac{n}{\gcd(n,d)}$ activations of actor p_k. The affine relation describes therefore the relation between the rates of activations of actors. Indeed, a $(1, \varphi, 2)$-affine relation means that the first actor is twice as fast as the second actor; while the difference between their phases is expressed by the parameter φ.

An affine relation can be also described by the two monotone functions $\Delta_{i,k}$ and $\Delta_{k,i}$ such that $\forall j \in \mathbb{N}^*$

$$\Delta_{i,k}(j) = \max\{0, \left\lceil \frac{n(j-1) - \varphi}{d} \right\rceil\}$$

$$\Delta_{k,i}(j) = \max\{0, \left\lceil \frac{d(j-1) + \varphi}{n} \right\rceil\}$$

The sign $\lceil x \rceil$ refers to the smallest integer not less than x. From these two equations, if p_i and p_k are (n, φ, d)-affine-related, then equivalently (1) p_k and p_i are $(d, -\varphi, n)$-affine related; and (2) p_i and p_k are $(cn, c\varphi, cd)$-affine-related for $c \in \mathbb{N}^*$.

3.2 Affine relation synthesis

An affine abstract schedule of the graph consists of all the affine relations between adjacent actors. In order to construct the abstract schedule, we need to find the appropriate affine relation between every two adjacent actors so that: (1) Overflow and underflow exceptions are *statically* excluded to ensure functional determinism. (2) The set of affine relations is consistent. (3) The buffering requirements are minimized.

3.2.1 Overflow and underflow analyses

An underflow exception occurs when an actor attempts to read from an empty channel; while an overflow exception occurs when an actor attempts to write into a full channel. Excluding overflow and underflow exceptions implies that the number of accumulated tokens on every channel and at each step of the execution is greater or equal to zero (i.e. no underflows) and less or equal to the buffer size (i.e. no overflows).

Let p_i be the producer and p_k be the consumer of channel $e = (p_i, p_k, x, y)$ such that actors p_i and p_k are $(n, \varphi, d)-$affine-related. When jobs $p_i[j]$ and $p_k[j']$ complete, the number of accumulated tokens on channel e is given by $\theta(e) + X(j) - Y(j')$. Of course, indices j and j' are affine-related as shown in details in Section 4.

• No overflow exception over channel e means that:

$$\forall(j, j'), \theta(e) + X(j) - Y(j') \leq \delta(e) \quad (2)$$

• No underflow exception over channel e means that:

$$\forall(j', j), \theta(e) + X(j) - Y(j') \geq 0 \quad (3)$$

3.2.2 Consistency

Consistency is an important property of (C)SDF graphs [6, 15]. A non-consistent graph requires unbounded memory to execute or it deadlocks during its execution. Consistency is related to cyclic graphs since bounded and deadlock-free schedules of acyclic graphs always exist.

Example 2. Let us take the cycle $\{p_1, p_2, p_3\}$ in the graph of Figure 1(a). Using Equations 2 and 3, we may compute three affine

relations $p_1 \xrightarrow{(n_1, \varphi_1, d_1)} p_2 \xrightarrow{(n_2, \varphi_2, d_2)} p_3 \xrightarrow{(n_3, \varphi_3, d_3)} p_1$ so that their parameters n and d are deduced from the rate functions. For every d_i activations of p_i, there are $n_{(i \bmod 3)+1}$ activations of $p_{(i \bmod 3)+1}$. Therefore, if $n_1 n_2 n_3 \neq d_1 d_2 d_3$, then the graph is non-consistent and cannot execute in a bounded memory.

A second condition for consistency considers the parameters φ (constrained by the number of initial tokens on the channels). Since the difference between phases of two successive actors in the cycle is encoded with the parameter φ, Equation 5 ensures that the difference between the phases of each actor and itself is null. The affine relations of the EDF schedule in Figure 1(b) are $p_1 \xrightarrow{(4,9,6)} p_2 \xrightarrow{(3,-4,5)} p_3 \xrightarrow{(10,-1,4)} p_1$ which satisfy both conditions.

The graph of affine relations is an undirected graph where nodes are actors and edges represent affine relations (recall that an affine relation can be reversed). Consistency of the affine abstract schedule is given by the following proposition.

Proposition 1 (from [8]). *The graph is consistent if for every fundamental cycle* $p_1 \xrightarrow{(n_1, \varphi_1, d_1)} p_2 \rightarrow \cdots \rightarrow p_m \xrightarrow{(n_m, \varphi_m, d_m)} p_1$ *in the graph of affine relations, we have that*

$$\prod_{i=1}^m n_i = \prod_{i=1}^m d_i \quad (4) \qquad \sum_{i=1}^m (\prod_{j=1}^{i-1} d_j)(\prod_{j=i+1}^m n_j)\varphi_i = 0 \quad (5)$$

If Proposition 1 is satisfied for fundamental cycles, then it will be also satisfied for any cycle in the graph since fundamental cycles are a cycle basis of the the cycle space. Fundamental cycles can be easily obtained from the spanning tree of the graph of affine relations. A cycle basis can be found in polynomial time.

Remark If the number of initial tokens on channels are imposed by the user, then underflow-free affine schedules may not exist in case of cyclic graphs. Therefore, it is better to let the scheduling algorithm decides the appropriate number of initial tokens.

3.3 EDF symbolic schedulability analysis

The computed affine schedule imposes some scheduling constraints on actors, but it does not indicate how actors will be concretely scheduled. We opt for an EDF scheduling of the dataflow graph, in which each actor p_i is mapped to a periodic task with a period π_i, a phase r_i, and a relative deadline d_i with $\pi_i, d_i \in \mathbb{N}^*$ and $r_i \in \mathbb{N}$ such that $C_i \leq d_i \leq \pi_i$. We also allow the user to impose lower and upper bounds on periods in response to some extra requirements so that $\pi_i^l \leq \pi_i \leq \pi_i^u$.

Symbolic schedulability analysis is the process of computing the timing parameters (π, r, d) of each actor so that

• They respect the affine abstract schedule, the bounds on periods, and other constraints if any.

• They ensure uniprocessor/multiprocessor EDF schedulability.

• They maximize the throughput, or equivalently they maximize the processor utilization factor $U = \sum_{p_i \in P} \frac{C_i}{\pi_i}$.

The first requirement implies that each $(n, \varphi, d)-$affine relation between actors p_i and p_k is concretized as follows.

• $n\pi_k = d\pi_i$.

• $r_k - r_i = \frac{\varphi}{n}\pi_i$.

In words, the concretization imposes constant time intervals between ticks of every activation clock. Indeed, at this stage of the scheduling, physical time does matter. For a weakly connected graph and from the first equation, the periods of all actors can be expressed in terms of the period of a fixed one. Therefore,

$\forall p_i \in P : \pi_i = \alpha_i T$ such that $\alpha_i \in \mathbb{Q}$ and $T^l \leq T \leq T^u$. The bounds on T, if any, are deduced from the bounds on periods imposed by the user. Since timing parameters are integers, T should be multiple of some integer B so that the previous equations may have a solution.

The second and third requirements of symbolic schedulability analysis depend on what approach is used for schedulability analysis: processor-demand approach, processor utilization approach, etc. In this paper, we will present a symbolic processor-demand analysis.

To sum up, this paper proposes a heuristic, that consists of two steps and favors buffer minimization over throughput maximization, to solve the following problem. Let $\theta_t(e)$ be the number of tokens in channel e at instant t and $f_i[j]$ be the finish time of job $p_i[j]$ during an EDF execution of the dataflow graph. The problem consists in finding for every actor $p_i \in P$ the timing parameters (π_i, r_i, d_i) and for every channel $e \in E$ the characteristics $(\theta(e), \delta(e))$ that maximizes the processor utilization U and minimizes $\sum_{e \in E} \Gamma(e)\delta(e)$ such that for every EDF execution of the graph we have that $\forall e \in E : \forall t : 0 \leq \theta_t(e) \leq \delta(e)$ and $\forall p_i \in P : \forall j \in \mathbb{N}^* : f_i[j] \leq r_i + (j-1)\pi_i + d_i$. The problem is further complicated in partitioned scheduling where every actor must be assigned to a processor.

4. Affine Schedules with deadlines adjustment

The first step of the approach consists in computing an affine relation between every two adjacent actors by means of an integer linear program (ILP). Therefore, we need to safely approximate Equations 2 and 3. If actors p_i and p_k are (n, φ, d)-affine-related and $e = (p_i, p_k, x = u_1(v_1), y = u_2(v_2))$ is a channel between them, then linear approximations are obtained as follows.

4.1 Overflow analysis

A linear upper bound of the number of accumulated tokens in the channel is given by $\theta(e) + X^u(j) - Y^l(j')$ which must be less or equal to the size $\delta(e)$. We have that (see Example 1) $X^u(j) = \frac{\|v_1\|}{|v_1|}j + \lambda_x^u$ and $Y^l(j') = \frac{\|v_2\|}{|v_2|}j' + \lambda_y^l$. It remains to compute the linear lower bound of j' in terms of j according to the affine relation and assuming that deadlines will be adjusted to enforce the needed precedences.

Let us suppose that p_i and p_k are allocated to the same processor. Figure 3 shows, for different cases, what job of p_k precedes immediately job $p_i[j]$. It shows hence what kind of precedences will be ensured by the deadlines adjustment. Case (c) corresponds to what has been explained in the introduction. In case (e), we have to look at the actors' ID to break the tie. According to these precedences, the lower bound of j' is equal to $\Delta_{i,k}(j)$. Thus, the linear lower bound of j' is $\frac{n}{d}j - \frac{n+\varphi}{d}$. By substituting all the linear bounds in Equation 2, we obtain the following linear constraint. $\forall j \in \mathbb{N}^* :$

$$\forall j \in \mathbb{N}^* : \theta(e) - \delta(e) + \frac{\|v_1\|}{|v_1|n}\varphi + \xi j \leq \lambda_y^l - \lambda_x^u - \frac{\|v_1\|}{|v_1|} \quad (6)$$

such that $\xi = \frac{\|v_1\|}{|v_1|} - \frac{\|v_2\|/n}{|v_2|d}$.

Since j tends to infinity, it is a requirement for an execution free of overflows and underflows that ξ equals zero. Consequently, the boundedness criterion is:

$$\frac{n}{d} = \frac{\|v_1\|}{|v_1|}\frac{|v_2|}{\|v_2\|} \quad (7)$$

This boundedness criterion is equivalent to the balance equation in static-periodic scheduling of (C)SDF graphs.

In case actors p_i and p_k are allocated to different processors, precedences will be more conservative since deadlines does not

ensure, for instance in case (c), that job $p_k[j']$ will complete before job $p_i[j]$ starts. Indeed, they can execute in parallel with each other.

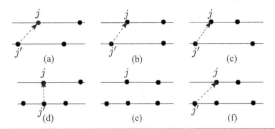

Figure 3. Precedences in the overflow analysis.

4.2 Underflow analysis

The underflow analysis is dual to the overflow analysis. A linear lower bound of the number of accumulated tokens on the channel is given by $\theta(e) + X^l(j) - Y^u(j')$ which must be greater or equal to zero. Again, we need to compute the linear lower bound of j in terms of j'. Without depicting the precedences, the lower bound of j is equal to $\Delta_{k,i}(j')$. Thus, the linear lower bound of j is $\frac{d}{n}j' + \frac{\varphi-d}{n}$. By substituting all the linear bounds in Equation 3, we obtain the following linear constraint.

$$\forall j' \in \mathbb{N}^* : \theta(e) + \frac{\|v_1\|}{|v_1|n}\varphi + \frac{d}{n}\xi j' \geq \lambda_y^u - \lambda_x^l + \frac{\|v_2\|}{|v_2|} \quad (8)$$

Equations 6 and 8 are less pessimistic than the ones obtained without imposing precedence constraints.

4.3 Algorithm

The input of this algorithm is a dataflow graph with ultimately periodic rates; while the output is the set of all affine relations. In the first place, the boundedness criterion (Equation 7) is used to compute the parameters n and d of all the affine relations. Then, Equation 4 is used to check the first requirement of the consistency of the graph. To compute the parameters φ, we construct an integer linear program by applying Equations 6, and 8 on channels; and Equation 5 on fundamental cycles. The objective function of the linear program is to minimize the buffering requirements. Integer linear programming is NP-hard; however solutions for real-life benchmarks, used in Section 8, can be computed in few seconds.

Sizes obtained by the solution of the linear program are a safe approximation of the actual sizes. Therefore, they may be recomputed after obtaining the affine relations.

5. Deadlines adjustment

This section shows how deadlines are adjusted to enforce the needed precedences so that if the task system is EDF-schedulable, then precedences are guaranteed without the need for locks. Let us denote by $R_i[j]$ the release time of job $p_i[j]$. We have that $R_i[j] = r_i + (j-1)\pi_i$. Let us also denote by $D_i[j]$ and $d_i[j]$ the absolute and relative deadlines of job $p_i[j]$, respectively, such that $D_i[j] = R_i[j] + d_i[j]$.

Let p_i and p_k be two (n, φ, d)-affine-related adjacent actors; and let us take $\Gamma_{i,k}(j) = \min\{j'|D_i[j]$ must be less or equal to $D_k[j']\}$. Figure 3 gives an intuition on how to compute $\Gamma_{i,k}(j)$. For instance, in case (c), $\Gamma_{i,k}(j) = j' + 1$ and $\Gamma_{k,i}(j') = j$.

The absolute deadline of job $p_i[j]$ of an actor p_i can be now computed as follows. Let us put $\mathcal{S}_i$ to be the set of neighbors of actor p_i. We have that

$$D_i[j] = \min_{p_k \in \mathcal{S}_i}\{R_i[j+1], D_k[j'] - 1|j' = \Gamma_{i,k}(j)\} \quad (9)$$

That is, the absolute deadline of a job $p_i[j]$ is less or equal to its implicit deadline (i.e. $R_i[j+1]$) and less than the absolute deadline $D_k[j']$ of any job $p_k[j']$ that must be preceded by $p_i[j]$. In Equation 9, $D_i[j]$ cannot depend on itself according to the way precedences are computed. If we consider relative deadlines, then Equation 9 can be written as

$$d_i[j] = \min_{p_k \in \mathcal{S}_i} \{\pi_i, d_k[j'] - 1 + R_k[j'] - R_i[j] | j' = \Gamma_{p_i, p_k}(j)\}$$

Recall that each affine relation contains a positioning pattern that repeats infinitely. Thus, relative deadlines of jobs of an actor will be ultimately periodic. From the concretization of affine relations, we know that periods and phases can be expressed in terms of the period of a fixed actor ($\forall p_i \in P : \pi_i = \alpha_i T$). Thus, the deadlines can be also expressed in terms of T.

5.1 Approximate deadlines

It is sometimes required, as in the schedulability analysis, that each actor has a single deadline. Thus, we may take $\forall p_i \in P : d_i = \min_j d_i[j]$. The deadlines computation will be much simpler as shown in the following.

$$
\begin{aligned}
d_i &= \min_j d_i[j] = \min_j \min_{p_k \in \mathcal{S}_i} \{\pi_i, d_k[j'] - 1 + R_k[j'] - R_i[j]\} \\
&= \min_{p_k \in \mathcal{S}_i} \{\pi_i, (\min_j d_k[j']) - 1 + \min_j(R_k[j'] - R_i[j])\} \\
&\geq \min_{p_k \in \mathcal{S}_i} \{\pi_i, d_k - 1 + \min_j(R_k[j'] - R_i[j])\} \\
&\quad \text{(because } \min_j d_k[j'] \geq \min_j d_k[j] = d_k)
\end{aligned}
$$

$\min_j(R_k[j'] - R_i[j])$ can be equal to zero as in case (f) of Figure 3 or can be equal to $\frac{\pi_i}{n}$ in other cases. If we put $X = (d_1, d_2, \ldots)^\top$, the deadlines computation can be written as $X = F(X)$. So, we need to compute the greatest fixed point of the function F. Since this latter is a monotone function, the fixed point, *if any*, can be found by computing the sequence $X^0, X^1 = F(X^0), X^2 = F(X^1), \ldots$ until stabilization such that X^0 is the vector where $\forall p_i \in P : d_i = \pi_i$.

Example 3. If we apply the affine relation synthesis described in Section 4 on the graph in Figure 1(a), we obtain the following affine relations: $p_1 \xrightarrow{(2,3,3)} p_2 \xrightarrow{(3,-3,5)} p_3 \xrightarrow{(5,0,2)} p_1$. So, we have that $p_1 = \frac{2}{3}T, p_2 = T$, and $p_3 = \frac{5}{3}T$. If we consider approximate deadlines, we obtain the following equations. $d_1 = \min\{\pi_1, d_2 - 1, d_3 - 1\}$, $d_2 = \min\{\pi_2, d_1 - 1 + \frac{\pi_2}{3}, d_3 - 1\}$, and $d_3 = \min\{\pi_3, d_1 - 1 + \frac{\pi_3}{5}, d_2 - 1 + \frac{\pi_3}{5}\}$. Hence, $d_1 = \pi_1, d_2 = \pi_2 - 2$, and $d_3 = \frac{3}{5}p_3 - 1$.

The new task system is schedulable for $T \geq 261$ as illustrated in Figure 4. As one can notice, no job is preempted by other jobs and all precedences as described above are satisfied. The safe buffering requirements of the schedule in Figure 1(b) equal 20; while they equal only 12 in the new schedule. This buffering improvement comes at the price of a processor utilization decrease from 1.0 to 0.92.

5.2 Impact on the processor utilization factor

The processor utilization factor is given by $U = \sum_{p_i \in P} \frac{C_i}{\alpha_i T} = \frac{\sigma}{T}$ with $\sigma = \sum_{p_i \in P} \frac{C_i}{\alpha_i}$. A necessary condition for EDF schedulability on m identical processors ($m \geq 1$) is that $U \leq m$; which implies that $T \geq \frac{\sigma}{m}$. For $T \simeq \frac{\sigma}{m}$, we obtain the maximum utilization factor when using an IDP model.

Suppose that after the deadlines computation, we have that $d_i[j] = \beta T - \beta'$ with $\beta \in \mathbb{Q}^+$ and $\beta' \in \mathbb{N}$. But $d_i[j] \geq C_i$

implies that $T \geq \frac{C_i + \beta'}{\beta}$. Therefore, if the bound $\frac{C_i + \beta'}{\beta}$ is much larger than $\frac{\sigma}{m}$, then the utilization factor will be definitely worse than the one obtained by the IDP model.

One solution is to exclude from the set $\mathcal{S}_i$ in Equation 9 each actor p_k for which imposing a precedence between a job $p_i[j]$ and a job $p_k[j']$ may jeopardize the utilization factor. When it comes to buffer sizes computation of channels between p_i and p_k, if a preemption occurs, then we will consider the worst-case scenarios as in [8].

Figure 4. EDF scheduling after deadlines adjustment.

6. Uniprocessor schedulability analysis

This section describes the symbolic uniprocessor EDF schedulability analysis of dataflow graphs. We have the following constraints that are deduced from the affine relation synthesis, deadlines adjustment, and concretization of affine relations.

- $\forall p_i \in P : \pi_i = \alpha_i T$ and $d_i = \beta_i T - \beta'_i$ (we take a single minimum deadline for each task).

- $T^l \leq T \leq T^u$ and T must be a multiple of some integer B since timing parameters must be integers. The bounds are obtained from the user-provided bounds on periods and from the constraint $C_i \leq d_i \leq \pi_i$.

- $U = \frac{\sigma}{T} < 1$.

The input of the symbolic schedulability analysis is the previous constraints while its output is the minimum value of T (which gives the maximum utilization factor) that guarantees uniprocessor EDF schedulability. All the timing parameters can be deduced once T is known. From the previous constraints, we have that $T \in \{T_k | \sigma' = \max\{T^l, \lfloor \sigma \rfloor + 1\} \leq T_k = kB \leq T^u \wedge k \in \mathbb{N}\}$. The sign $\lfloor x \rfloor$ refers to the largest integer not greater than x. Hence, $T_k = \lceil \frac{\sigma'}{B} \rceil B + kB$ for $k \geq 0$. If we want to bound the processor utilization factor to a value less than one (e.g. in case we want to add an aperiodic server that handles some aperiodic tasks in the system), we need just to change the lower bound on T.

The enumerative solution consists in checking the EDF schedulability of the task system for each T_k in an increasing order, staring from T_0 and until reaching an appropriate value or exceeding the upper bound T^u. However, this is a time-consuming approach. In the rest of this section, we present a faster solution based on the following observation. When T is increased, periods and deadlines are stretched while execution times remain constant. Hence, if a deadline is not missed for the previous value of T, then it will not be missed for the new one.

6.1 Standard schedulability analysis

The exact schedulability analysis of constrained periodic task systems is based on the processor-demand approach as given by the following lemma.

Lemma 1 (from [17]). *A synchronous periodic task set is schedulable if and only if $U < 1$ and $\forall l \leq L^* : h(l) \leq l$ where* $L^* = \frac{\sum_{p_i \in P} (\pi_i - d_i) U_i}{1 - U}$ *and* $U_i = \frac{C_i}{\pi_i}$.

L^* is called the feasibility bound. As proposed in [17], another feasibility bound consists in the the length of the synchronous busy period that can be computed by the following recurrence.

$$w^0 = \sum_{p_i \in P} C_i \qquad w^{m+1} = \sum_{p_i \in P} \left\lceil \frac{w^m}{\pi_i} \right\rceil$$

When the recurrence stops (i.e. $w^{m+1} = w^m$), then $L^* = w^m$.

The processor demand function $h(l)$ calculates the maximum processor demand of all jobs which have their arrival times and deadlines in a contiguous interval of length l. So, $h(l)$ is given by $h(l) = \sum_{p_i \in P} \max\{0, 1 + \left\lfloor \frac{l - d_i}{\pi_i} \right\rfloor\} C_i$. The value of the demand function does not change from one point l to another one l' unless there is at least one absolute deadline in $]l, l']$. Therefore, it is necessary to check condition $h(l) \leq l$ only for the set of absolute deadlines which are less than L^*. This set can be large and a technique like the Quick convergence Processor-demand analysis (QPA) [24] is needed. In the next paragraphs, d, d', d_m, and d^* denote some absolute deadlines.

Lemma 2 (from [24]). *For an unschedulable periodic task set, if $h(d_m) \leq d_m$, then $d^* < h(d^*) \leq d'$, where $d_m = \max\{d \mid d \leq L^*\}, d^* = \max\{d \mid 0 < d < L^* \wedge h(d) > d\}$, and $d' = \min\{d \mid d > d^*\}$.*

From Lemma 2, we can easily deduce that $\forall l \in [h(d^*), L^*]$, $h(l) \leq l$. Based on this result, Listing 1 represents the QPA algorithm (from [24]).

Algorithm 1: QPA algorithm

$l = d_m$;
while $h(l) \leq l \wedge h(l) > \min\{d\}$ **do**
  | **if** $h(l) < l$ **then** $l = h(l)$;   **else** $l = \max\{d \mid d < l\}$;
if $h(l) \leq \min\{d\}$ **then** the task set is schedulable;
else the task set is not schedulable;

6.2 Symbolic QPA

Our symbolic schedulability analysis of dataflow graphs consists in incorporating the search of the minimum T that ensures EDF schedulability into the QPA algorithm. Listing 2 represents the symbolic QPA algorithm. Let $L^*(T), U(T)$, and $h^T(t)$ denote respectively the values L^*, U, and $h(t)$ for a given T.

Starting from the minimum value of T (i.e. T_0), SQPA performs the QPA analysis in the interval $[0, L^*(T_0)]$. This first iteration leads either to $h^{T_0}(l) \leq \min\{d\}$ or to a deadline miss, i.e. $h^{T_0}(l) > l$ (Figure 5). In the first case, the task system is schedulable and the algorithm returns T_0.

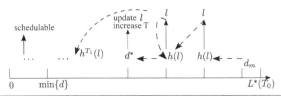

Figure 5. Illustration of SQPA.

In the second case, assume that the deadline miss occurs at d^* (i.e. $h^{T_0}(d^*) > d^*$). In this case, T must be increased to T_1 (instruction k++;). According to Lemma 3, $L^*(T_1) \leq L^*(T_0)$. Hence, the verification can restart from $L^*(T_1)$ instead of $L^*(T_0)$. But, according to Lemma 2, we have that $\forall l \in [h^{T_0}(d^*), L^*(T_0)]$: $h^{T_0}(l) \leq l$. Since Lemma 4 implies that $\forall l \in [h^{T_0}(d^*), L^*(T_0)]$: $h^{T_1}(l) \leq h^{T_0}(l) \leq l$, the verification process for T_1 can restart from $\min\{L^*(T_1), h^{T_0}(d^*)\}$. This process is repeated until the termination condition is reached or T exceeds the upper bound T^u.

Algorithm 2: SQPA algorithm

$k = 0$; $l = \max\{d \mid d \leq L^*(T_k)\}$;
while $h(l) > \min\{d\}$ **do**
  | **if** $h(l) < l$ **then** $l = h(l)$;
  | **else if** $l == h(l)$ **then** $l = \max\{d \mid d < l\}$;
  | **else**
  | | k++;
  | | **if** $T_k > T^u$ **then return** task set not schedulable;
  | | $l = \min\{h^{T_{k-1}}(l), \max\{d \mid d \leq L^*(T_k)\}\}$;

return T_k;

Lemma 3. *If $T \leq T'$, then $L^*(T) \geq L^*(T')$.*

Proof: The proof follows easily from the definition of the synchronous busy period. □

Lemma 4. *If $T \leq T'$, then $\forall l, h^T(l) \geq h^{T'}(l)$.*

Proof: We have that $h^T(l) = \sum_{p_i \in P} h_i^T(l)$ such that $h_i^T(l) = \sum_{D_i[j] \leq l} C_i$. Recall that any absolute deadline $D_i[j]$ can be written as $(\alpha_i(j-1) + \beta_i)T - \beta_i'$. But α_i and β_i are positive; which implies that a given absolute deadline occurs earlier for T than for T'. Therefore, $\forall l, h_i^T(l) \geq h_i^{T'}(l)$. □

SQPA algorithm has a pseudo-polynomial complexity since it checks in the worst-case scenario all the deadlines in interval $[0, L^*(T_0)]$ as a standard processor-demand analysis may do.

7. Multiprocessor schedulability analysis

One of the major advantages of using partitioned EDF over global EDF scheduling is that, once an allocation of actors to processors has been achieved, real-time symbolic schedulability analysis for uniprocessor systems (e.g. the SQPA technique) can be applied on each partition. The main objective of the allocation heuristic proposed in this section is to minimize the buffering requirements of dataflow graphs scheduled on an architecture that consists of m identical processors with a shared memory where channels are implemented as software buffers. The scheduling approach consists of the following steps.

1) Parameters n and d of every affine relation are computed using the boundedness criterion. So, we have that $\forall p_i \in P : \pi_i = \alpha_i T$.
2) Let $G = (V, E)$ be an undirected graph where nodes represent actors and edges represent affine relations. Each node v_i is associated with a weight that represents the utilization of actor p_i; i.e. $w(v_i) = \frac{C_i}{\alpha_i}$. The weight of edge $e_{i,j} = (v_i, v_j)$, denoted by $w(e_{i,j})$, is equal to zero if enforcing precedences between p_i and p_j may jeopardize the processor utilization factor, and equal to the approximate gain that comes from enforcing the precedences otherwise.
3) The graph G is partitioned into m balanced partitions $(V_i)_{i=1,m}$; that is, $\forall i, j : |w(V_i) - w(V_j)|$ is minimal such that $w(V_i) = \sum_{v \in V_i} w(v)$. The second objective of this partitioning is to minimize the total weight of edges connecting different partitions. The rational behind this requirement is that adjusting deadlines will not ensure precedences between actors allocated on different processors. This m-partitioning problem is well known in graph theory; for instance, we use the SCOTCH tool [9] to solve the problem.
4) Once each actor is assigned to a processor, overflow and overflow analysis can be performed to compute parameter φ of each affine relation such that the worst-case scenarios are considered for edges that have a weight equal to zero and edges connecting partitions.

5) Computation of symbolic deadlines of tasks in each partition.
6) The SQPA algorithm is then applied on each partition V_i. The algorithm will return the minimum value T_i that ensures EDF schedulability of the set V_i on a single processor. We need just to take $T = \max_{i=1,m} T_i$.

8. Experimental validation

We evaluate our scheduling technique w.r.t. buffering requirements, processor utilization factor, and performance by performing an experiment on a set of 18 real-life applications which come from different domains (see [1] for more details on the benchmarks) and some randomly generated SDF graphs and task sets.

8.1 Throughput and buffering requirements

Figures 6 and 7 present the results obtained by three tools on a single processor system: DARTS represents the results obtained by the DARTS tool [1, 2], ADF represents the results obtained by the ADF tool [8], and ADF2 represents the results obtained by the technique presented in this paper. Figure 6 shows the ratios of the buffering requirements to the minimum (regardless of the throughput) achievable buffering requirements. The minimum buffer sizes are obtained by the SDF³ tool [21] which computes static-periodic schedules of (C)SDF graphs (auto-concurrency disabled). Figure 7 shows the processor utilization factor obtained by each tool.

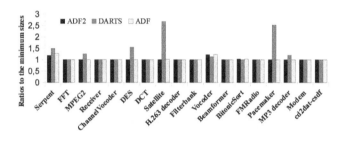

Figure 6. Buffering requirements comparison.

A channel $e = (p_i, p_k, u_1(v_1), u_2(v_2))$ is said to be a matched I/O channel if the values $\frac{\|v_1\|}{|v_1|}$ and $\frac{\|v_2\|}{|v_2|}$ are close to each other. It is said to be a perfectly matched I/O channel if $\frac{\|v_1\|}{|v_1|} = \frac{\|v_2\|}{|v_2|}$. The three tools seem to be able to achieve results close to the minimum buffering requirements for graphs that consist of perfectly matched I/O channels (e.g. FFT, DCT, FMRadio, Serpent). Our tool slightly outperforms the other tools, in terms of buffering requirements, for this kind of graphs (e.g. Serpent, DES, MPEG2). A $(1, \varphi, 1)$-affine relation is associated to each perfectly matched I/O channel. Hence, all the reads and writes are already ordered without the need for any deadlines adjustment. This is why, for graphs with perfectly matched I/O channels, the ADF2 tool gives similar throughput and buffer storage capacities to the ones obtained by the ADF tool.

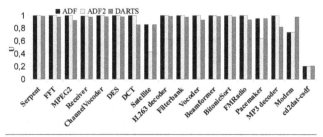

Figure 7. Throughput comparison.

For graphs with mis-matched I/O channels (e.g. Pacemaker, Satellite), the DARTS tool gives the worst buffering requirements. The average improvement obtained by our tool is of 11.43% compared to DARTS. The ADF2 tool slightly outperforms the ADF tool but at the price of a processor utilization decrease. Clearly, the IDP task model (i.e. ADF tool) results in the best throughput.

Most of the previous benchmarks consist of perfectly matched I/O channels; they unfortunately do not allow us to measure the benefit that comes from adjusting deadlines and using a constrained task model instead of the IDP model. We will use hence a set of randomly generated SDF graphs. The graphs are generated by the SDF³ tool with the following setting. Production and consumption rates follow a normal distribution with a mean equal to 5 and a variance equal to 4. Worst-case execution times follow a normal distribution with a mean equal to 1000 and a variance equal to 300. The graphs are generated with different number of nodes (from 6 to 80) such that the average degree of each node is 2. Figure 8 shows the obtained results where Imp denotes the improvement in buffering requirements obtained by the ADF2 tool compared to ADF; while Dec denotes the decrease in the processor utilization.

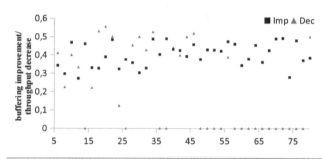

Figure 8. Impact of deadlines adjustment.

The average improvement is equal to 39.99% with a low standard deviation (0.05). This improvement comes at the price of a throughput decline with an average equal to 20.95%. In 50% of the graphs, the deadlines adjustment improves the buffering requirements without affecting the throughput. These are graphs with highly mis-matched I/O channels. Indeed, when factor B is too large (compared to σ), adjusting deadlines may not impact the achievable throughput. Compromised solutions can be obtained by excluding some precedences in the deadlines adjustment step.

8.2 Schedulability analysis

Since QPA algorithm outperforms the standard processor demand-analysis (see [25] for experiments), it is expected that SQPA algorithm also outperforms the enumerative solution. We will compare the number of checked points by both approaches on a huge set of randomly generated task sets. For each task p_i, we generate three parameters (C_i, α_i, β_i) such that $\pi_i = \alpha_i T$ and $d_i = \beta_i T$. The UUniFast algorithm is used to generate uniformly distributed $\frac{C_i}{\alpha_i}$ values. Worst-case execution times are uniformly distributed in the interval $[100, 1000]$. Parameters α_i and β_i are uniformly generated by fixing the value of B (T must be a multiple of B) and the value of an experimental parameter $D \in]0, 1]$ so that $\forall p_i : \beta_i \in [D\alpha_i, \alpha_i]$. Figure 9 shows the obtained results for different configurations of N, B, and D. Each point on the diagram is the average number of checked points by the enumerative solution for 2000 task sets divided by the average number of checked points by the SQPA algorithm. For each configuration, we denote by E the average number of checked points per task (obtained by the enumerative solution) to indicate the complexity of the problem.

The complexity of the symbolic schedulability problem increases inversely with the factor B. Indeed, if B has a small value, then the number of checked deadlines will be large since each time a deadline miss occurs, T is increased only by a small quantity. For dataflow graphs with matched I/O channels, factor B is generally small, and the schedulability problem is hence more complicated.

The SQPA algorithm outperforms the enumerative solution in all cases except cases with small N and cases with very small D. When deadlines are too constrained, deadline misses could be detected earlier by a forward search than by a backward search. Thus, for dataflow graphs with few actors or highly constrained deadlines, it is better to use the enumerative solution than the SQPA algorithm.

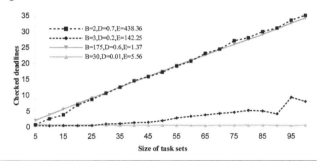

Figure 9. Performance of the SQPA algorithm.

9. Conclusion

We have presented a technique to reduce buffer sizes in uniprocessor/multiprocessor EDF scheduling of dataflow graphs. The technique consists in enforcing some precedences between jobs and encoding them by adjusting deadlines. After constructing an abstract affine schedule of the graph, our symbolic schedulability analysis computes all the necessary timing parameters so it maximizes the processor utilization factor. The technique has significantly improved the buffering requirements in many cases as shown by the experimental evaluation. Our ongoing work aims at further improving the processor utilization factor by looking to actors in a more fine-grained way. We are also investigating how to use deadlines adjustment to allow deterministic multi-producer/multi-consumer channels by imposing total order on writes and reads.

Acknowledgments

We would like to thank Mohamed Bamakhrama for his support with benchmarks and the DARTS tool. We would like also to thank the anonymous reviewers for their valuable comments.

References

[1] M. Bamakhrama and T. Stefanov. Hard-real-time scheduling of data-dependent tasks in embedded streaming applications. In *Proceedings of the 9th ACM International Conference on Embedded Software*, pages 195–204, 2011.

[2] M. A. Bamakhrama and T. Stefanov. Managing latency in embedded streaming applications under hard-real-time scheduling. In *Proceedings of the 8th IEEE/ACM/IFIP International Conference on Hardware/Software Codesign and System Synthesis*, pages 83–92, 2012.

[3] S. Baruah, V. Bonifaci, A. Marchetti-Spaccamela, and S. Stiller. Implementation of speedup-optimal global EDF schedulability test. In *Proceedings of the 21st Euromicro Conference on Real-Time Systems*, pages 259–268, 2009.

[4] S. K. Baruah and N. W. Fisher. The partitioned dynamic-priority scheduling of sporadic task systems. *Real-Time Syst.*, 36(3):199–226, 2007.

[5] M. Bertogna and S. Baruah. Tests for global EDF schedulability analysis. *J. Syst. Archit.*, 57(5):487–497, 2011.

[6] G. Bilsen, M. Engels, R. Lauwereins, and J. Peperstraete. Cyclestatic dataflow. *IEEE Transactions on Signal Processing*, 44:397–408, 1996.

[7] A. Bouakaz and J.-P. Talpin. Design of safety-critical Java Level 1 applications using affine abstract clocks. In *Proceedings of the 16th International Workshop on Software and Compilers for Embedded Systems*, 2013.

[8] A. Bouakaz, J.-P. Talpin, and J. Vitek. Affine data-flow graphs for the synthesis of hard real-time applications. In *Proceedings of the 12th International Conference on Application of Concurrency to System Design*, 2012.

[9] C. Chevalier and F. Pellegrini. PT-Scotch: a tool for efficient parallel graph ordering. *Parallel Comput.*, 34(6-8):318–331, 2008.

[10] A. Cimatti, L. Palopoli, and Y. Ramadian. Symbolic computation of schedulability regions using parametric automata. In *the 29th IEEE Real-Time Systems Symposium*, pages 80–89, 2008.

[11] R. I. Davis and A. Burns. A survey of hard real-time scheduling for multiprocessor systems. *ACM Comput. Surv.*, 43(4):35:1–35:44, 2001.

[12] J. Forget, F. Boniol, E. Grolleau, D. Lesens, and C. Pagetti. Scheduling dependent periodic tasks without synchronization mechanisms. In *Proceedings of the 16th IEEE Real-Time and Embedded Technology and Applications Symposium*, pages 301–310, 2010.

[13] L. Fribourg, R. Soulat, D. Lesens, and P. Moro. Robustness analysis for scheduling problems using the inverse method. In *19th International Symposium on Temporal Representation and Reasoning*, pages 73–80, 2012.

[14] A. Gamatié. Design of streaming applications on MPSoCs using abstract clocks. In *Design, Automation and Test in Europe Conference*, pages 763–768, 2012.

[15] E. A. Lee and D. G. Messerchmitt. Static scheduling of synchronous dataflow programs for digital signal processing. *IEEE Trans. Comput.*, 36:24–35, 1987.

[16] C. Pagetti, J. Forget, F. Boniol, M. Cordovilla, and D. Lesens. Multitask implementation of multi-periodic synchronous programs. *Discrete event dynamic systems*, 21(3):307–338, 2011.

[17] I. Ripoll, A. Crespo, and A. K. Mok. Improvement in feasibility testing for real-time tasks. *Real-Time Syst.*, 11(1):19–39, 1996.

[18] L. Sha, T. Abdelzaher, K.-E. Arzén, A. Cervin, T. Baker, A. Burns, G. Buttazzo, M. Caccamo, J. Lehoczky, and A. K. Mok. Real time scheduling theory: a historical perspective. *Real-Time Syst.*, 28(2-3):101–155, 2004.

[19] I. M. Smarandache, T. Gautier, and P. L. Guernic. Validation of mixed signal-alpha real-time systems through affine calculus on clock synchronisation constraints. In *Proceedings of the World Congress on Formal Methods in the Development of Computing Systems*, volume 2, pages 1364–1383, 1999.

[20] S. Stuijk, M. Geilen, and T. Basten. Exploring trade-offs in buffer requirements and throughput constraints for synchronous dataflow graphs. In *Proceedings of the 43rd annual Design Automation Conference*, pages 899–904, 2006.

[21] S. Stuijk, M. Geilen, and T. Basten. Sdf^3: Sdf for free. In *Proceedings of the 6th International Conference on Application of Concurrency to System Design*, pages 276–278, 2006.

[22] S. Stuijk, M. Geilen, and T. Basten. Throughput-buffering trade-off exploration for cyclo-static and synchronous dataflow graphs. *IEEE Trans. Comput.*, 57:1331–1345, 2008.

[23] M. H. Wiggers, M. J. G. Bekooij, and G. J. M. Smit. Efficient computation of buffer capacities for cyclo-static datatflow graphs. In *Proceedings of the 44th annual Design Automation Conference*, pages 658–663, 2007.

[24] F. Zhang and A. Burns. improvement to quick processor-demand analysis for EDF-scheduled real-time systems. In *Proceedings of the 21st Euromicro Conference on Real-Time Systems*, pages 76–86,

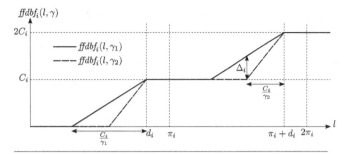

Figure 10. Illustration of *ffdbf*

2009.

[25] F. Zhang and A. Burns. Schedulability analysis for real-time systems with EDF scheduling. *IEEE Transactions on Computers*, 58:1250–1258, 2009.

A. Global EDF symbolic schedulability analysis

In this section, we will present a global EDF symbolic schedulability analysis of dataflow graphs where a single job can migrate to and execute on different processors. Interest in global EDF has been recently rekindled by the advancement in multiprocessor technology that reduces the migration penalties [5].

A.1 Standard schedulability analysis

Our symbolic schedulability analysis is based on the speedup-optimal schedulability analysis presented in [3, 5] which has a pseudo-polynomial complexity.

Lemma 5 (from [5]). *A task set is schedulable if* $\exists \gamma_{\min} \leq \gamma < \gamma_{\max} - \epsilon$ *(with an arbitrary small ϵ) such that* $\forall l \leq L^* : h(l, \gamma) \leq l$ *where*

$$L^* = \frac{\sum_{p_i \in P} (\pi_i - d_i) U_i}{m - (m-1)\gamma - U}, \gamma_{\min} = \max_{p_i \in P} \frac{C_i}{D_i}, \gamma_{\max} = \frac{m-U}{m-1}, h(l, \gamma) =$$

$\frac{ffdbf(l,\gamma)}{m-(m-1)\gamma}$, and $ffdbf(l, \gamma) = \sum_{p_i \in P} ffdbf_i(l, \gamma)$ *which is the forced-*

forward demand bound function. We have that: $q_i = \left\lfloor \frac{l}{\pi_i} \right\rfloor$, $r_i = (l \mod \pi_i)$, *and*

$$ffdbf_i(l, \gamma) = q_i C_i + \begin{cases} C_i & if\ r_i \geq d_i \\ C_i - (d_i - r_i)\gamma & if\ d_i > r_i \geq d_i - \frac{C_i}{\gamma} \\ 0 & otherwise \end{cases}$$

Figure 10 depicts the forced-forward demand bound function for two values γ_1 and γ_2 such that $\gamma_1 < \gamma_2$. It is sufficient to check condition of Lemma 5 for only absolute deadlines in the interval $[0, L^*]$. Furthermore, the technique of QPA can be used to reduce the number of points to be checked. Listing 3 represents the QPA-FFDBF algorithm proposed in [5].

Algorithm 3: QPA-FFDBF algorithm

$\gamma = \gamma_{\min}$;
while $\gamma < \gamma_{\max}$ **do**
    $l = L^*$;
    while $\min\{d\} < h(l, \gamma) \leq l$ **do**
        $l = \min\{h(l, \gamma), \max\{d | d < l\}\}$;
    if $h(l, \gamma) \leq \min\{d\}$ **then return** the task set is schedulable ;
    $\gamma = \gamma + \epsilon$;
return the task set is unschedulable;

A.2 Symbolic QPA-FFDBF

Firstly, we improve the QPA-FFDBF algorithm by exploiting the following lemma.

Lemma 6. *if* $\gamma_1 < \gamma_2$ *and* $ffdbf(l, \gamma_1) \geq \left(\frac{m - (m-1)\gamma_1}{(m-1)\gamma_2}\right) \sum_{p_i \in P} C_i$, *then* $h(l, \gamma_1) \leq h(l, \gamma_2)$.

Proof: As shown in Figure 10, we have clearly that $\forall l : 0 \leq \Delta_i(l) = ffdbf_i(l, \gamma_1) - ffdbf_i(l, \gamma_2) \leq \Delta_i$. Using basic geometry, we have that $\Delta_i = C_i(1 - \frac{\gamma_1}{\gamma_2})$. So,

$$h_i(l, \gamma_2) - h_i(l, \gamma_1) = \frac{ffdbf_i(l, \gamma_1) - \Delta_i(l)}{m - (m-1)\gamma_2} - \frac{ffdbf_i(l, \gamma_1)}{m - (m-1)\gamma_1}$$

Hence,

$$h(l, \gamma_2) - h(l, \gamma_1) = \frac{x}{(m - (m-1)\gamma_2)(m - (m-1)\gamma_1)}$$

s.t. $x = (m-1)(\gamma_2 - \gamma_1) ffdbf(l, \gamma_1) - (m - (m-1)\gamma_1) \sum_{p_i \in P} \Delta_i(l)$.

Therefore, if $x \geq 0$; i.e.

$$ffdbf(l, \gamma_1) \geq \frac{m - (m-1)\gamma_1}{(m-1)(\gamma_2 - \gamma_1)} \sum_{p_i \in P} \Delta_i(l)$$

then $h(l, \gamma_1) \leq h(l, \gamma_2)$. But, $\forall l : \sum_{p_i \in P} \Delta_i(l) \leq \sum_{p_i \in P} \Delta_i$.   □

Lemma 6 is used as follows. For a given γ_1, if $h(l, \gamma_1) > l$ and $ffdbf(l, \gamma_1) \geq F^* = \left(\frac{m - (m-1)\gamma_1}{(m-1)\gamma_1}\right) \sum_{p_i \in P} C_i$, then it does not matter if we increase γ_1 to γ_2 since $h(l, \gamma_2)$ will be also greater than l. Note that we used γ_1 in the dominator of F^* instead of γ_2.

Algorithm

Listing 4 represents the symbolic QPA-FFDBF algorithm. We have the same hypotheses as in SQPA; i.e. $\forall p_i \in P : \pi_i = \alpha_i T_k$ and $d_i = \beta_i T_k - \beta_i'$ such that $C_i \leq d_i \leq \pi_i$. In addition, $U = \frac{\sigma}{T_k}$ and $T_k = \left[\frac{\sigma'}{B}\right] B + kB \leq T^u$ such that $\sigma' = \max\{T^l, \lfloor \frac{\sigma}{m} \rfloor + 1\}$. Let $\gamma_{\min}(T), \gamma_{\max}(T)$, and $F^*(T)$ denote respectively $\gamma_{\min}, \gamma_{\max}$, and F^* for a given T.

If $h(l, \gamma) > l$, then we have to increase either γ or T according to Lemmas 6 and 5. As for SQPA, we note that
- If $T \leq T'$, then $\forall l : h^T(l, \gamma) \geq h^{T'}(l, \gamma)$. Hence, if d^* is the first deadline for which $h^T(d^*, \gamma) > d^*$, then we have that $\forall l \in [h^T(d^*, \gamma), L^*(T)] : h^{T'}(l, \gamma) \leq h^T(l, \gamma) \leq l$. For given values T_{k+1} and γ, we take $\text{Prev}(\gamma) = h^{T_k}(d^*, \gamma)$.
- If $T \leq T'$, then $L^*(T) \geq L^*(T')$.

Thanks to these observations, for a given value γ, it not necessary to recheck deadlines in the interval $[L^*(T'), \text{Prev}(\gamma)]$ when T is increased to T'.

Algorithm 4: SQPA-FFDBF algorithm

$k = 0$; $\gamma = \gamma_{\min}(T_k)$; $l = L^*(T_k)$;
while $h(l, \gamma) > \min\{d\}$ **do**
    if $h(l, \gamma) \leq l$ **then** $l = \min\{h(l, \gamma), \max\{d | d < l\}\}$;
    else
        if $ffdbf(l, \gamma) \geq F^*(T_k) \vee \gamma + \epsilon > \gamma_{\max}(T_k)$ **then**
            k++;
            if $T_k > T^u$ **then return** task set unschedulable;
            $\gamma = \gamma_{\min}(T_k)$;
        else $\gamma = \gamma + \epsilon$;
        $l = \min\{L^*(T_k), \text{Prev}(\gamma)\}$;
return T_k;

Automatic Dataflow Model Extraction from Modal Real-Time Stream Processing Applications

Stefan J. Geuns   Joost P.H.M. Hausmans

University of Twente

{stefan.geuns,joost.hausmans}@utwente.nl

Marco J.G. Bekooij

NXP Semiconductors/University of Twente

marco.bekooij@nxp.com

Abstract

Many real-time stream processing applications are initially described as a sequential application containing while-loops, which execute for an unknown number of iterations. These modal applications have to be executed in parallel on an MPSoC system in order to meet their real-time throughput constraints. However, no suitable approach exists that can automatically derive a temporal analysis model from a sequential specification containing while-loops with an unknown number of iterations.

This paper introduces an approach to the automatic generation of a Structured Variable-rate Phased Dataflow (SVPDF) model from a sequential specification of a modal application. The real-time requirements of an application can be analyzed despite the presence of while-loops with an unknown number of iterations. It is shown that an algorithm that has a polynomial time computational complexity can be applied on the generated SVPDF model to determine whether a throughput constraint can be met. The enabler for the automatic generation of an SVPDF model is the decoupling of synchronization between tasks that contain different while-loops. A DVB-T radio transceiver illustrates the derivation of the SVPDF model.

Categories and Subject Descriptors D.2.4 [*Software Engineering*]: Software/Program Verification

General Terms Design, Theory

Keywords Real-time; Dataflow; MPSoC; Automatic Parallelization

1. Introduction

Embedded stream processing applications, such as Software Defined Radio (SDR) transceivers, are often executed on Multiprocessor System-on-Chips (MPSoCs) to meet their real-time performance requirements. These requirements are a result of interaction with the environment. In order to analyze whether these real-time requirements are met by an application, an analysis model is required. For signal processing applications without modes the synchronous data flow (SDF) model [12] is often used. However, SDF models cannot model applications containing modes. Modal behavior can be found in modern SDR transceivers, making the SDF model unsuitable to model these SDR transceivers.

Various more expressive models have been proposed such that modes and mode transitions can be analyzed. Examples of such models are Scenario Aware Dataflow (SADF) [16] and Variable-rate Phased Dataflow (VPDF) [19]. Although these models are more expressive than SDF models, they suffer from a higher computational complexity or apply over-approximation to decrease the analysis time.

Even for the more expressive SADF and VPDF models, it remains a challenge to express an application such that it fits in the dataflow model. Another difficulty is that the dataflow model is often large, making it cumbersome to derive such a model manually. Furthermore, it is virtually impossible to show that a manually derived model is correct. Moreover, it is also hard to keep the model consistent with the application in case the application is modified during the design process.

This paper introduces the automatic generation of a Structured Variable-rate Phased Dataflow (SVPDF) analysis model, which is a temporal analysis model suitable to model applications containing if-statements and while-loops. The SVPDF model is similar to the VPDF model in the sense that both allow infinite iteration of actors, which is described by a parameterized consumption and production of the actors. By generating the model automatically, it is ensured that the model is correct by construction and it saves the programmer from having to rewrite the algorithm such that it can be modeled by an analysis model. The automatic generation of an SVPDF model from a sequential application is enabled by the exploitation of non-destructive read and destructive write semantics of variables inside a while-loop. This results in a decoupling of the synchronization of tasks that have statements in different while-loops. We limit the variables to scalars in this paper and exclude arrays. Our experience is that a variety of single-rate SDR applications only use scalars and this restriction increases the understandability of the concepts and proof. The extracted SVPDF model has a specific structure since it is extracted from a sequential specification. In this paper we show that this structure simplifies analysis significantly.

This paper is organized as follows. Section 2 outlines the different design approaches and motivates the approach proposed in this paper where a parallel implementation and a temporal analysis model are derived from a sequential specification. In Section 3 we describe the basic idea behind our approach. Section 4 highlights the important aspects of our sequential programming language and Section 5 explains the parallelization step in which synchronization statements are inserted such that an SVPDF temporal analysis model can be derived. This model is introduced in Section 6, and this section also explains the derivation of such a model from a task graph. In Section 7 we describe the analysis of SVPDF graphs. Section 8 illustrates the presented approach with a DVB-T application and Section 9 presents related work. Finally, Section 10 states the conclusions.

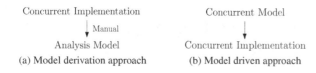

(a) Model derivation approach   (b) Model driven approach

Figure 1: Traditional design approaches for real-time applications

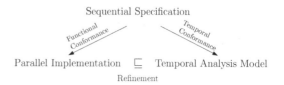

Figure 2: Proposed design approach

2. Design Approaches

Different design approaches can be applied to design concurrent stream processing applications. These approaches are outlined in this section, including a discussion and motivation of the approach taken in this paper.

Traditionally when software is designed, an application is written in a sequential or parallel programming language. When throughput constraints have to be taken into account, an analysis model is extracted by the programmer and this model is then analyzed. This traditional approach is illustrated in Figure 1a. A serious disadvantage of such an approach is that extracting an analysis model manually is very error prone and when the implementation changes, the programmer must manually update the model to keep it consistent. An even more serious drawback is that there are usually no guarantees that the model corresponds correctly with the implementation, thus any analysis results might not reflect the properties of the implementation.

Nowadays, model driven approaches are more often being used to implement applications with temporal constraints on MPSoCs. An example of such an approach is the PTIDES approach [6, 20]. An application is described as a concurrent model and from that model, a concurrent implementation is derived. Generating the implementation automatically ensures that the model and the implementation are consistent. This model driven approach is illustrated in Figure 1b. However, in a concurrent specification it is difficult to find a balance between expressiveness and analytical opportunities. For example deadlock can often be specified while analysis tools cannot always detect this. Reducing the expressiveness of a model might have as a consequence that practical applications can no longer be modeled.

To overcome the problems of the approaches mentioned in the previous paragraphs, the approach taken in this paper is based on the parallelization of sequential applications. An application is specified using a sequential language and a tool extracts a temporal analysis model from the sequential specification. This temporal analysis model abstracts from any functional behavior, except for the properties required for temporal analysis. At the same time, the tool also automatically extracts task-level parallelism from this specification such that the functional behavior of the parallel implementation and the sequential specification are equivalent. By deriving both the implementation and model from the same sequential specification, it is ensured that the implementation refines the temporal analysis model and thus satisfies the temporal requirements whenever the analysis model satisfies these requirements. This refinement relation $\sqsubseteq$ is the earlier-is-better refinement relation defined in [7]. The approach taken in this paper is illustrated in Figure 2.

This separation into a functional implementation and temporal analysis model allows for more flexibility in both the implementation and analysis. More flexibility in the implementation is exploited by separating synchronization and communication. For if-statements, synchronization statements are executed unconditionally, whereas communication statements are executed conditionally. In the temporal analysis model only synchronization statements are modeled, not communication statements. Modeling unconditional synchronization statements prevents that the analysis model must be a model with conditions, such as the Boolean Dataflow (BDF) model [4], in which detecting deadlock is undecid-

Figure 3: Decoupled synchronization

able in general. Our temporal model does contain the conditional repetition of while-loops. However, despite this conditional execution deadlock and buffer sizing remain decidable.

3. Basic Idea

The approach taken in this paper is based on three key ideas. To provide an intuitive idea of our approach, these key ideas are presented informally in this section. In the following sections, these key ideas are described in more detail.

The first idea behind our approach is that in the generated implementation, synchronization is decoupled between variables accessed by statements in and around each while-loop. In every task extracted from a function in the sequential application, synchronization has to be inserted to ensure correct communication of data. Previously, correct communication was ensured by inserting synchronization in all tasks accessing a shared variable. When variables were accessed by statements in- and outside of a while-loop, synchronization must be performed for all of these accesses. Therefore, synchronization was performed at the same rate, thus coupling tasks extracted from these statements. This paper introduces an approach were synchronization can be decoupled by making use of the fact that statements around a while-loop can only read or write shared variables once with respect to this loop. By renaming the names of shared variables accessed by statements in a while-loop and adding a selection code fragment which selects between this new and the existing variable, decoupling and therefore a rate conversion is achieved. This process is illustrated in Figure 3. A more detailed discussion on how decoupling is achieved can be found in Section 5.4.

When this synchronization decoupling method is applied, it must be shown how a valid temporal analysis model can be derived such that the real-time constraints can be verified. The decoupling method is in essence implementing non-destructive read and destructive write semantics for variables accessed in and outside of while-loops. Using the variable rates of the VPDF model, non-destructive read and destructive write semantics can be modeled. A parameter can be used to indicate how often a variable is read or written. The VPDF model which models this behavior is shown in Figure 4a. The model contains hierarchical blocks, shown as dashed rectangles, with port actors w_0, w_1, w_2 and w_3 on the edges. These port actors have a variable number of phases, given by the parameter p in the example, and thus model non-destructive read and destructive write semantics. The actual number of phases is not known at compile-time. In the figure, the second phase of the edge from w_1 to g is executed $p - 1$ times and the number of tokens produced is $(p - 1) \times 1 = p - 1$ while only a single token is consumed by w_1. If a VPDF model is structured with hierarchical blocks with port actors on the edges, we call it an SVPDF model. Since the structure of a block where all port actors share the

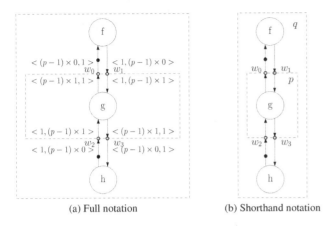

| (a) Full notation | (b) Shorthand notation |

Figure 4: SVPDF model with port actors w_0, w_1, w_2 and w_3, all sharing the parameter p

same parameter is always the same in an SVPDF model, we introduce the shorthand notation from Figure 4b where the parameter is shown in the top right corner of a block. This idea of modeling non-destructive read and destructive write semantics using variable phases is the second key idea of the presented approach.

The third key idea is that the structure in the generated SVPDF model can be exploited in such a way that a temporally equivalent static analysis model can be derived from this parameterized model. In the static model values of one can be chosen for all parameters, thus effectively removing all parameters from the model and simplifying analysis significantly. After showing in Section 7.1 that the throughput of an SVPDF model can be determined by assuming that all while-loops execute only once, sufficient buffer capacities can be derived for a given throughput.

4. Sequential Program Specification

The input of our parallelization tool Omphale is a sequential program specified in the Omphale Input Language (OIL) [9]. This section highlights the for this paper relevant aspects of this programming language. The OIL language is a single assignment language with support for if-statements and while-loops. These statements can have data-dependent behavior, thus the if-condition and while-loop termination conditions can be dependent on input data. Including these conditional statements allows for the description of modes, often present in stream processing applications.

The real-time throughput constraints of a stream processing application are imposed by a periodic communication with the environment. This communication is described in the OIL language with sources and sinks [9]. The environment is sampled periodically by a source, which passes its data to the application. After a sample is processed, data is periodically fed back to the environment via a sink. Sources and sinks are executed time triggered in our approach, while the algorithmic part executes event-driven [11]. Since the algorithmic does not communicate with the environment, no deadlines have to be determined for this part. The only requirement is that data is delivered in time at a sink.

A source and sink are specified in parallel to the algorithmic part of an application. Despite the parallel specification, a sequential semantics can be defined for sources and sinks. A source is assigned a new value by the environment at the beginning of a while-loop and a value is read from a sink by the environment at the end of a while-loop.

The most important reason to define the sequential semantics where every loop iteration a new value is processed, is that it can be verified at compile time whether an application will meet its throughput constraints. This also means that all values delivered

by a source are processed and all values delivered to a sink will be seen by the environment. Since a while-loop can have infinitely many iterations, it must be that all sources and sinks are accessed in every loop. Otherwise, there could be an infinite amount of time between accesses, which makes it impossible to guarantee a periodic execution of sources and sinks.

5. Automatic Parallelization

In our approach, a sequential OIL specification is automatically parallelized into a task graph. The parallelization step extracts function level parallelism such that a task is created for each function in the input specification. This is unlike methods where data parallelism is achieved by unrolling a while-loop. Every task communicates with its connected tasks via Circular Buffers (CBs). Synchronization statements are inserted into each task to ensure that the functional behavior from the sequential specification is preserved. From these synchronization statements, the SVPDF model will be derived in Section 6. Section 5.1 explains how the synchronization statements operating on these CBs work. The following sections show how synchronization statements are inserted into tasks for sources and sinks, if-statements and while-loops, such that the parallelized task graph has the same functional behavior as the sequential input specification.

A task graph is a directed graph which can contain cycles. Formally, a task graph is defined as $H = (T, B, \beta)$. Here T is a set of tasks. For convenience, we define T_S as the set of source or sink tasks, with $T_S \subseteq T$. The set of hyperedges $B \subseteq \mathcal{P}(T) \times \mathcal{P}(T)$ represents the CBs and $\beta : B \to \mathbb{N}$ specifies the sizes of these CBs. From every function f in the sequential OIL program a task t_f is extracted and added to T. For every variable x in the program, a hyperedge b_x is added to B. The incoming connections to b_x are all tasks in which the corresponding functions assign a value to x. In the example these are tasks t_f and t_g. The outgoing connections from b_x are all tasks in which the corresponding functions read from the variable x, tasks t_h and t_k in the figure.

5.1 Circular Buffers

The communication buffers to handle inter task communication are CBs with sliding windows [3]. These buffers can be accessed by multiple reading and writing tasks while preserving any possibility for pipelining. However, there can be only one task writing to a location in a buffer per iteration. An iteration ends when all reading tasks no longer require a location. This requirement, equivalent to single assignment in the sequential specification, ensures that no data races occur between writing tasks.

Every task reading from or writing to a buffer can access that buffer within a window. The head of a window of a writing task (a producer) is moved one place by calling the synchronization function $acqProd$. The tail of this window is moved one place when a producer calls $relProd$. For a task reading from a buffer (a consumer) the equivalent operations are called $acqCons$ and $relCons$ respectively.

Both $acqProd$ and $acqCons$ are blocking functions, meaning they wait until the location next to the current head of the window is empty or full respectively. The $relProd$ and $relCons$ functions are non-blocking. Every producer and every consumer must move its window an equal number of times. If one producer or consumer does not synchronize on a location, and thereby not move its window, all other windows will become blocked once they need to synchronize for this location the next time. Since a synchronization statement moves a window by one location and all windows must be moved the same number of times, every synchronization statement on a buffer must be called the same number of times in every task.

Figure 5 shows an example of the operations that can be performed on a buffer b_x. This buffer is connected to one producer, t_A, and one consumer, t_B. Every buffer location written by t_A is first

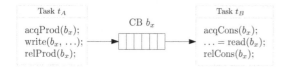

Figure 5: Operations on a CB with sliding windows.

```
source A = h();        do{                    do{
                          do{                   do{
loop{                       acqProd(b_A1);        acqCons(b_A1);
  loop{                     write(b_A1, h());     f(read(b_A1));
    f(A);                   relProd(b_A1);        relCons(b_A1);
  } while(C_1);          } while(C_1);         } while(C_1);
                                              } while(1);
  loop{                   do{
    g(A);                   acqProd(b_A2);        (c) Task t_f
  } while(C_2);            write(b_A2, h());
} while(1);                relProd(b_A2);
                        } while(C_2);         do{
  (a) Input program   } while(1);              do{
                                                 acqCons(b_A2);
                          (b) Task t_h           g(read(b_A2));
                                                 relCons(b_A2);
                                               } while(C_2);
                                             } while(1);

                                                 (d) Task t_g
```

Figure 6: Parallelization of an application with a source

Figure 7: Task graph transformation to decouple synchronization between reading tasks

acquired and released afterwards. The same holds for the consumer t_B. Writing to and reading from a CB is performed via *write* and *read* functions.

5.2 Sources and Sinks

Since sources and sinks are specified in parallel with the rest of the application, they do not have to be parallelized. However, also for the implementation of sources and sinks, synchronization statements have to be inserted in order to ensure correct functional behavior. The semantics of a source are such that the environment is sampled exactly once in every while-loop iteration. For a sink, a value is sent to the environment once in every while-loop iteration.

A source and a sink are specified by a variable and a function from which respectively a buffer and a task are created during parallelization [9]. However, a problem arises with synchronization. Consider the application from Figure 6a where a source A is read by two functions f and g. The task graph of this application is shown in Figure 7 on the left. Since the tasks t_f and t_g read from the same buffer, their synchronization rates must be coupled and thus both tasks have to synchronize, even if the task is not executing its corresponding function. In order to overcome this coupling of synchronization rates, we propose to transform the task graph such that a buffer is created for every consumer of a source and producer to a sink. The source then writes it data to, and the sink reads its data from the buffer connected to the task that is connected according to the input specification. This transformed task graph is shown in Figure 7 on the right.

Figure 6 shows how this transformation is applied in an example. When a task t_h is created for a source or sink, the structure from the input specification is copied to t_h. This process is shown for task t_h in Figure 6b. The figure shows that the three while-loops are copied and, as described in the previous paragraph, two buffers b_{A1} and b_{A2} are added to pass the source values to the functions requiring these values. The functions f and g now read from b_{A1} and b_{A2} respectively such that the functional behavior of the application remains the same. The tasks t_f and t_g created from these functions are shown in Figures 6c and 6d.

5.3 Parallelization of If-Statements

An if-statement makes assignments to and reading of variables conditional. After the parallelization to a task graph where communication between tasks is arranged via buffers with sliding windows, reading from and writing to the buffer is also conditional. Since the condition of an if-statement can be input-data dependent, it cannot be determined at compile-time whether and when a variable is accessed.

When synchronization is performed by a task on a CB, all tasks must eventually synchronize on this CB, thus all tasks must synchronize the same number of times on a CB. This would mean that if a task conditionally synchronizes on a CB, all tasks must conditionally synchronize. Therefore, all tasks should contain this if-statement. In order to prevent that all if-statements have to be included in all tasks, synchronization is made unconditional. Whenever synchronization statements are added to a branch of an if-statement, they are also added to the else-branch, thus resulting in unconditional synchronization. This approach for inserting synchronization for if-statements is detailed in [3].

5.4 Parallelization of While-Loops

In this section, we present a method for inserting synchronization in while-loops. The basic idea behind the presented method is that a value written by an assignment before a while-loop is only needed in the first iteration of a while-loop and only the last value written by an assignment in a while-loop is visible after the while-loop. Because of the limited lifetime of variables, values are lost every loop iteration independent of whether they are written in an iteration or not [8].

For a variable written in an assignment before and in a while-loop, two new variables are created to replace the variable accessed in the loop. One variable is used for writing and one variable for reading. It is known that a variable in the loop can be written only in the next iteration due to single assignment, all occurrences where the original variable is written are be replaced by the same variable. The newly created variable used for reading, is assigned either the value assigned to the existing variable written before the loop or the value of the new variable written in the loop.

This process is illustrated by the example in Figure 8. Here Figure 8a shows an OIL program with a while-loop and Figure 8b shows the result of the aforementioned transformation process. The assignment to x' means that the value made available for the next while-loop iteration. In the program the variable x is written by an assignment before and in the inner while-loop. Therefore, the access to x by the function h is replaced by a fresh variable z. The function g reads from x in the input program and therefore a selection is made whether to read from x or z. This choice is made by the if-statement in the transformed program. Note that it is guaranteed by construction that z is only read from the second loop iteration onwards, therefore no initial write to z is required.

After this translation process, there is no variable anymore written by assignments before and in a loop. Every variable read by a statement in a loop is no longer written in that loop. Therefore, synchronization can be added around the while-loop. This is demonstrated in Figure 9, which shows the parallelized application from

(a) Input program

(b) Transformed program

Figure 8: Example of a variable written by an assignment before and in the inner loop

(a) Task t_f

(c) Task t_h

(b) Task t_g

Figure 9: Parallelized task graph given the transformed program from Figure 8b

(a) Input program

(b) Transformed program

Figure 10: A variable is written by an assignment in the inner loop and read by a function after the inner loop

6. Structured Variable-rate Phased Dataflow

In this section we first define the SVPDF temporal analysis model and then explain the automatic derivation of such a model from a sequential OIL specification of an application.

Formally, an SVPDF model is a directed multigraph defined as $G = (V, E, P, \delta, \rho)$, where V is a finite set of actors and E is a finite set of edges with $(v_i, v_j) \in E$ and $v_i, v_j \in V$. An SVPDF model is structured into blocks with port actors, on the block boundaries. A block is characterized by a parameter $p \in P$, defining the number of consecutive iterations the actors in a block fire, after which the parameter value changes. A port actors perform the rate conversion between the rate of a block and its parent.

Actors in an SVPDF model are not auto-concurrent, meaning there is an implicit edge back from an actor to itself with one token on this edge. All actors, except port actors, consume one token from each input edge and produce one token on each output edge during every firing. The firing duration $\rho : V \to \mathbb{R}^+$ is the time between the start and finish of a firing. Actors consume tokens at the start of a firing and produce tokens at the moment the firing finishes. On an edge e are $\delta(e)$ initial tokens, with $\delta : E \to \mathbb{N}$.

Port actors are the actors that are used to consume from and produce tokens to actors outside of a block. These port actors are divided into two categories, upscale port actors and downscale port actors. An upscale port actor consumes one token and produces p tokens whereas a downscale port actor consumes p tokens and produces one token. Figure 4 shows an example of an upscale port actor, actor w_1, and a downscale port actor, actor w_0. The phases of a port actor are always structured the same, as shown in the figure.

An upscale port actor consumes one token from outside a block and enables the use (of a "copy") of this token multiple times in the block. This is modeled with an actor that has two phases. The first phase consumes and produces one token and the second phase consists of a parameter p. This parameter reflects the rate conversion such that one token is consumed and p tokens are produced.

A downscale port actor is used to produce tokens to actors outside a block. Every token produced by a downscale port actor is always produced in the last firing of the p consecutive firings of the block. This behavior is also modeled with two phases. The first phase consumes $(p-1)$ tokens from the block and produces 0 tokens to actors outside of the block whereas the second phase consumes and produces one token.

Thanks to the specific structure with port actors, only the first of p consecutive firings of a block depends on the consumption of tokens from outside the block. Next to that, only the last iteration of p consecutive firings of a block produces tokens to actors outside of the block. Note that a block does not act as a barrier because the moment at which different port actors consume/produce tokens from/to actors outside the component, does not have to be equal. Since a port actor is a modeling construct which has no corresponding object in a task graph, its firing duration is zero. Port actors are

the previous example. Since the variable x is only read in the inner while-loop from Figure 8b, synchronization for this variable is added around the loop, see Figure 9b.

When a function placed after a while-loop reads from a variable written by statements inside that while-loop, only the last written value is read. To store this value, a new variable is added to the program. This new variable is only assigned a value in the last loop iteration. Since it is now known by construction that this variable is assigned a value only once during the execution of all while-loop iterations, synchronization statements for this variable can be placed around the while-loop. All statements placed after the while-loop accessing the old variable are now changed to read from the new variable. Since the producing tasks synchronizes only once for this new variable, also the consuming tasks only have to synchronize once.

This process is illustrated in Figure 10. In the input program from Figure 10a a variable x is written by a function f in a while-loop and read by a function h after that loop. In the transformed program from Figure 10b a new variable y is created and in the last while-loop iteration this variable is assigned the last produced value of x. In the function h all accesses to x are now replaced by y. The parallelization and insertion of synchronization statements is analogue to the case described before and therefore not detailed in this paper.

left implicit in the formal description of the SVPDF model, which improves the readability of the proofs in Section 7.1.

6.1 Automatic Generation of an SVPDF Model

From every task graph extracted from a valid OIL program, a corresponding SVPDF model can be automatically generated. The dataflow model reflects the synchronization statements that are placed each task in the parallelized task graph. In a while-loop synchronization statements are executed conditionally, meaning that it is decided at run-time whether another loop iteration is executed or whether the statements after the while-loop are executed. The SVPDF model can be used to model this conditional synchronization. Synchronization statements for if-statements, functions and assignments are executed unconditionally, and thus a static dataflow model such as a Homogeneous Synchronous Dataflow (HSDF) model can be used to model these statements.

The translation of a task graph $H = (T, B, \beta)$ to an SVPDF model $G = (V, E, P, \delta, \rho)$ can be defined as follows. The function $\psi : \mathbb{N} \rightarrow \mathbb{N}$ returns the index $j = \psi(i)$-th of the block that is fired during the iteration i of the source. For every task $t_k \in T$ that is executed in block q, an actor v_k^q is added in the model, which is fired if $q = \psi(i) \% N$, where $\%$ is the modulo operation and N the number of while-loops. The firing duration of this actor, $\rho(v_k^q)$, is equal to the response time of t_k. In the case of budget-based run-time schedulers, the response time of tasks can be determined independent of the execution time and execution rate of other tasks [18].

For every source or sink task $t_s \in T_S$ there are N actors v_s^q added in the SVPDF model, with $q = \{0, 1, \ldots, N-1\}$. This is because a source or sink task contains multiple while-loops that execute at different rates, as can be seen in Figure 6b. These tasks thus belong to different blocks. The q-th block corresponds to the q-th while-loop in the OIL program. The port actors in the derived SVPDF model are left implicit.

For every actor v_i, corresponding with a task t_i in which CB b is written, and actor v_j, corresponding with a task t_j which reads from b, an edge (v_i, v_j) is added. When b corresponds with a variable representing a loop termination condition, a token is added on this edge. This token represents that a while-loop is always executed at least once. An edge $e = (v_j, v_i)$ is added to represent the empty locations in b. The number of initial tokens $\delta(e)$ on this edge is determined by the buffer capacity analysis. The sum of the initial tokens on the edges (v_i, v_j) and (v_j, v_i) is equal to the buffer capacity of the corresponding CB, $\beta(b)$. For a detailed discussion on how multiple tasks reading from and writing to the same buffer can be included in dataflow models, the reader is referred to [2].

A source or a sink places constraints on the throughput that an application must achieve. However, periodic execution constraints cannot be expressed in a dataflow graph. Therefore, separate constraints are added to the SVPDF model. Because multiple actors are derived for every source or sink task, the combined schedule of these actors must result in the periodic schedule of that task. As a transition between blocks can occur after any number of iterations of a block, a constraint is added to the SVPDF model for a repetitive firing of each source/sink actor and a constraint is also added for firings of successive actors corresponding with the same source or sink task.

For a repetitive firing of an actor in the same block it must hold that the time between firings is μ, where μ is the period of a source or sink, ie. one divided by the frequency of a source or sink. Therefore it must hold that $\sigma(v_s^q, i+1) = \sigma(v_s^q, i) + \mu$, where we define $\sigma(v, i)$ as the start time of an actor v in iteration $i \in \mathbb{N}$ if this actor fires in iteration i of a source or sink actor. For a transition between blocks a similar constraint exists. Take as the switching moment iteration i. Then it must hold that $\sigma(v_s^{(q+1) \% N}, i+1) = \sigma(v_s^q, i) + \mu$. If both constraints hold than it holds that the corresponding source or sink task t_s can execute

Figure 11: SVPDF model for Figure 6

every period μ, i.e.:

$$\forall_{t_s \in T_s, i \in \mathbb{N}} : \sigma'(t_s, i) = \sigma'(t_s, 0) + i \cdot \mu \tag{1}$$

Note that we define the start time of the first firing of the source and sink actors equal to their corresponding source or sink task. This is done irrespective of whether such an actor actually fires in iteration 0: $\forall_{v_s^q \in V_S} : \sigma(v_s^q, 0) = \sigma'(t_s, 0)$. Both of the constraints on the start times of actors corresponding to source and sink tasks can be verified using HSDF analysis techniques [14].

The first constraint (repetitive firing of the same actor) can be verified by analyzing each block in isolation. A block in isolation is obtained by removing all edges to port actors. The second constraint can be verified by analyzing a flattened version of the SVPDF model where only one iteration of each block is modeled. In the next section we prove that analyzing each block in isolation combined with analyzing the flattened graph, is sufficient to guarantee the periodicity constraint of the sources and sinks in the application.

The throughput of each block in isolation and of the flattened graph can be verified using an algorithm to find the maximum cycle mean (MCM) in HSDF graphs. A number of such algorithms exist that have a polynomial time computational complexity [5]. Because the complete SVPDF analysis method analyses N blocks, the computational complexity remains polynomial.

Figure 11 shows the SVPDF model corresponding to the example program from Figure 6. For the source defined by function h, two actors v_h^0 and v_h^1 are added in the model. Since there are two while-loops with a source access, the constraints in Equation 2 are added. These constraints state that the time between subsequent firings of every iteration of the source h fires is μ. These constraints are only valid when the same while-loop is repeatedly executed.

$$\begin{aligned} \sigma(v_h^0, i+1) &= \sigma(v_h^0, i) + \mu \\ \sigma(v_h^1, j+1) &= \sigma(v_h^1, j) + \mu \end{aligned} \tag{2}$$

The two instances of the source function h are executed sequentially in the source program because of the order of the while-loops. This results in the additional constraints that are shown in Equation 3. The first constraint states that when the first while-loop ends at iteration i_0, the source actor in the next while-loop must fire μ time later. The second constraint states that the transition back from the second to the first while-loop must also happen in μ time.

$$\begin{aligned} \sigma(v_h^0, i_0+1) &= \sigma(v_h^1, i_0) + \mu \\ \sigma(v_h^1, i_1+1) &= \sigma(v_h^0, i_1) + \mu \end{aligned} \tag{3}$$

7. Analysis of SVPDF Graphs

7.1 Throughput Analysis

This section discusses the throughput analysis of SVPDF graphs. The strictly periodic execution of sources and sinks imposes a throughput requirement on the application. Because sources and sinks are modeled by actors, this also places throughput constraints on the SVPDF graph. It is proven in this section that we can adhere to these temporal constraints by analyzing a flattened graph where only one iteration of each block is modeled and by analyzing each block in isolation. This is possible thanks to the specific structure of SVPDF graphs.

Source and sink tasks correspond with multiple mutual exclusive actors in the model, each actor belonging to one block. Every execution of a source or sink corresponds to the firing of exactly one such actor. The periodicity constraint of sources and sinks is thus spread over all blocks. For every block, the constraint is again split into two separate constraints. The first constraint (C1) specifies that as long as a block is repeated, the actors, corresponding to source or sink tasks, in that block can fire periodically. The second constraint (C2) specifies that when a block is finished, the actor in the next block fires one period after the last firing of the actor derived from the same source or sink but in the current block.

To prove that these two constraints hold, a parameterized schedule for the actors in the SVPDF graph is proposed. This is followed by the proof that this schedule is admissible. A schedule is admissible if sufficient tokens are present on the incoming queues in the model at the start of each firing of the actors in the schedule.

We prove that the proposed schedule is admissible by showing that the analysis results obtained by analyzing the flattened graph and every block in isolation are conservative when one or more blocks have consecutive iterations. From analyzing the flattened graph it is known whether this graph satisfies the periodicity constraint μ. For this proof we assume that this flattened graph satisfies the periodicity constraint and refer to this as Fact 1. We furthermore assume that the source and sink actors in every block in isolation can fire every μ, to which we will refer as Fact 2.

From the structure of the OIL language it is known that a block, which corresponds to a while-loop, is fired a number of times before the next block is fired. The function $\phi(j)$, with $\phi : \mathbb{N} \to \mathbb{N}^+$, returns the number of firings of block j before block $j + 1$ is fired. The function $\psi : \mathbb{N} \to \mathbb{N}$, as defined in Equation 4, returns the $j = \psi(i)$-th block that is fired during iteration i of the source, with $i \in \mathbb{N}$.

$$\psi(i) = \max\{x \mid \sum_{j=0}^{x-1} \phi(j) \leq i\} \tag{4}$$

The two constraints C1 and C2 can now be formalized in terms of these functions. The first constraint is that a successive firing of an actor derived from a source or sink starts μ time later. This constraint is formalized in Equation 5. This equation says that a firing of an actor v_s^q derived from a source or sink must occur every μ time, if the actors in the enclosing block are repeatedly fired.

$$\forall_{v_s^q \in V_S} : \psi(i+1) = \psi(i) \Rightarrow \\ \sigma(v_s^q, i+1) = \sigma(v_s^q, i) + \mu \tag{5}$$

The second constraint states that if a transition between blocks occurs, the time between the firings of actors derived from the same source or sink is μ. This constraint is formalized in Equation 6.

$$\forall_{v_s^q, v_s^{(q+1)\%N} \in V_S} : \psi(i+1) = \psi(i) + 1 \Rightarrow \\ \sigma(v_s^{(q+1)\%N}, i+1) = \sigma(v_s^q, i) + \mu \tag{6}$$

We define a parameterized schedule σ in Equation 7, where α is defined as $\alpha(i) = \sum_{j=0}^{\psi(i)-1} \phi(j)$. The value of $\alpha(i)$ corresponds with the number of iterations that are fired by the completely finished blocks, i.e. blocks that have executed $\phi(j)$ times.

$$\forall_{v^q \in V} : \sigma(v^q, i) = \sigma(v^q, 0) + \alpha(i) \cdot \mu + (i - \alpha(i)) \cdot \mu \\ \text{if } q = \psi(i) \% N \tag{7}$$

In the next two lemmas we show that the schedule σ is a schedule satisfying the periodicity constraint as defined by equations (5) and (6) for arbitrary parameters i.e. $\forall_j : \phi(j) \geq 1$. Then we show in Lemma 7.4 that the schedule σ is also an admissible schedule for arbitrary parameters.

Lemma 7.1. *The schedule defined by Equation 7 satisfies the constraint defined in Equation 5 for arbitrary parameter values, i.e.* $\forall_j : \phi(j) \geq 1$.

Proof. For two subsequent firing of an actor $v^q \in V_S$ for which it holds that $\psi(i) = \psi(i+1)$, we must prove that

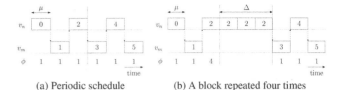

(a) Periodic schedule   (b) A block repeated four times

Figure 12: Periodic schedule for an SVPDF graph with two actors in different blocks. In the right schedule, the actor in block $\psi(i) = 2$ fires three additional iterations

$\sigma(v^q, i+1) = \sigma(v^q, i) + \mu$. Substituting (7) in this equation results in:

$$\alpha(i+1) \cdot \mu + (i+1 - \alpha(i+1)) \cdot \mu = \alpha(i) \cdot \mu + (i - \alpha(i)) \cdot \mu + \mu$$

which is true because $\alpha(i) = \alpha(i+1)$ if $\psi(i) = \psi(i+1)$ according to the definition of the function α. $\square$

Lemma 7.2. *The schedule defined by Equation 7 satisfies the constraint defined in Equation 6 for arbitrary parameter values, i.e.* $\forall_j : \phi(j) \geq 1$.

Proof. For two subsequent firing of actors $v_s^q, v_s^{(q+1)\%N} \in V_S$, for which it holds that $\psi(i+1) = \psi(i) + 1$, we must prove that $\sigma(v_s^{(q+1)\%N}, i+1) = \sigma(v_s^q, i) + \mu$. Because the start time of the first firing of both actors is equal, ie. $\sigma(v_s^q, 0) = \sigma(v_s^{(q+1)\%N}, 0)$, substituting (7) in this equation results in:

$$\alpha(i+1) \cdot \mu + (i+1 - \alpha(i+1)) \cdot \mu = \alpha(i) \cdot \mu + (i - \alpha(i)) \cdot \mu + \mu$$

Since it is known that $\psi(i+1) = \psi(i) + 1$ and using the definition of α we get $\phi(\psi(i)) \cdot \mu + (1 - \phi(\psi(i))) \cdot \mu = \mu$ which is true. $\square$

The next lemma shows that the self-timed execution of an SVPDF has a temporally linear behavior. This fact is used to prove Lemma 7.4.

Lemma 7.3. *The self-timed execution of an SVPDF graph has a temporally linear behavior.*

Proof. An SVPDF is a special case of a functionally deterministic data flow (FDDF) graph because all SVPDF actors have sequential firing rules [13]. Because an SVPDF is a special case of an FDDF graph it has a temporally linear behavior [19]. $\square$

In Lemma 7.4 we prove that the parameterized schedule σ as defined in Equation 7 is an admissible schedule for arbitrary parameters i.e. $\forall_j : \phi(j) \geq 1$. The intuition behind the proof is illustrated with the schedules shown in Figure 12. The numbers in the schedule of every actor indicate for a firing i the block number $\psi(i)$. The dotted arrows indicate dependencies between actors. All parameters $\phi(j)$ equal one in Figure 12a. In Figure 12b the block for which $j = \psi(i) = 2$ is fired three additional times. As a consequence the production of this block, which is indicated with an arrow, is delayed by Δ time. However the consumption by v_m is also delayed according to the parameterized schedule σ with Δ time. Therefore σ remains admissible for $\phi(j) \geq 1$ if σ is admissible for $\phi(j) = 1$. In the proof for Lemma 7.4 the parameterized schedule is split into three cases. In Figure 12b this case distinction is shown by two red lines.

Lemma 7.4. *The parameterized schedule in Equation 7 is an admissible schedule for arbitrary parameter values, i.e.* $\forall_j : \phi(j) \geq 1$.

Proof. This lemma is proven by induction. We define σ_K as $\sigma_K = \sigma$ with $\forall_{k<K} : \phi(k) \geq 1$ and $\forall_{k \geq K} : \phi(k) = 1$.

Base case: For $K = 0$ we have $\forall_{k \geq 0} : \phi(k) = 1$. We know that if $\forall_{k \geq 0} : \phi(k) = 1$ the schedule σ_K is admissible because this is given by Fact 1.

Induction step: We show that σ_{K+1} is an admissible schedule assuming that σ_K is an admissible schedule. This is shown in (8) by a case distinction in $\psi(i)$. To keep the notation compact we define $\Phi(K) = \phi(K) - 1$. Furthermore, without loss of generality, it is assumed that $\forall_{K, i \in \mathbb{N}} : \phi_K(i) = \phi(i)$.

$$\sigma_{K+1}(v, i) = \begin{cases} \sigma_K(v, i) & \text{if } \psi(i) < K \\ \sigma_K(v, \alpha(i)) + (i - \alpha(i)) \cdot \mu & \text{if } \psi(i) = K \\ \sigma_K(v, i - \Phi(K)) + \Phi(K) \cdot \mu & \text{if } \psi(i) > K \end{cases}$$
$$(8)$$

For the case that $\psi(i) < K$ it holds that $\sigma_{K+1}(v, i)$ is admissible because the induction hypothesis states that σ_K is admissible.

For the case that $\psi(i) = K$ we have that $\phi(K) = 1$ in $\sigma_K(v, i)$ but $\phi(K) \geq 1$ in $\sigma_{K+1}(v, i)$. By making use of Fact 2, which states that actors in a block can fire every μ, and that this block can fire $\Phi(K)$ times without consuming and producing any tokens from edges outside of that block, it follows that $\sigma_{K+1}(v, i)$ is admissible during the $\Phi(K)$ additional iterations of the block.

For the case that $\psi(i) > K$ we use the fact that only during the last iteration of a block tokens are produced via downscale port actors. Therefore, the $\Phi(K)$ additional iterations of the block delay the production of a token by at most $\Delta = \Phi(K) \cdot \mu$ time. From Lemma 7.3 we know that the self-timed execution of an SVPDF graph has a temporally linear behavior. Therefore, a production of an actor that is Δ time later will not delay the enabling of any actor firing later than that actor firing, by more than Δ. Thus is the delay of actor firings during the firing of the $\psi(i) > K$-th block, not more than Δ. In the parameterized schedule σ_{K+1} is is known that the firing of the actors during the firing of the $\psi(i) > K$-th block are delayed by $\Delta = \Phi(K) \cdot \mu$. From this it follows that $\sigma_{K+1}(v, i)$ is admissible because the actors are enabled before they are fired.

We can conclude that σ_K is an admissible schedule for every K by making use of the induction axiom because both the base case and the induction step hold. Because σ_K holds for every K, this schedule is equal to the parameterized schedule σ for arbitrary parameters $\phi(j) \geq 1$. $\qquad\square$

Theorem 7.5. *The existence of an admissible schedule σ of the SVPDF graph with period μ as defined in Equation 7 implies that the source and sink tasks can execute strictly periodically with period μ as defined in Equation 1.*

Proof. By making use of the earlier-is-better-refinement [7] we know that tasks will not produce data later than the corresponding actors produce tokens if the actors have firing durations that are larger or equal than the response times of the tasks. From this we conclude that (1) holds if (7) holds. $\qquad\square$

7.2 Buffer Sizing

Once it is determined using an SVPDF model whether an application can meet its throughput constraint, sufficient buffer capacities must be determined. This is because a pipelined execution of an application can require more than one value of a variable simultaneously. In the previous section it is shown that the throughput of an SVPDF model can be determined under two assumptions. To determine sufficient buffer capacities it must thus be shown that the required models meet these assumptions. To show that these models meet the throughput constraints, a sufficient number of tokens must be available on every edge. In [18] it is shown that the number of tokens relate directly to the buffer capacity of the buffer modeled by this edge.

When analyzing the flattened graph and the individual blocks, buffer capacities are computed twice if they are present in both the individual block and the flattened model. Therefore, to determine

```
source Symbol = dfe() @ 156 KHz;
loop{
    channel = selectChannel(474 MHz);
    loop{
        s = readInput(Symbol, channel);
        acquisition(s, out window');
    } while(!isValid(window'));
    loop{
        x = readInput(Symbol, channel);
        verifySync(x, out syncd, out window');
        fft(x, out y, window);
        z = equalization(y);
        demap(z);
    } while(syncd);
} while(1);
```

Figure 13: OIL specification of a simplified DVB-T receiver

sufficient tokens, and thus buffer capacities, we take the maximum number of tokens as determined by the analysis on these models. Taking the maximum ensures that sufficient tokens are available in both the individual blocks as well as in the flattened model.

Determining sufficient buffer sizes can be done using a linear program (LP) algorithm. Because the capacity of a buffer is always a discrete number, the capacity as determined by the LP algorithm can be rounded up [18]. An LP algorithm has a polynomial time computational complexity, thus also sizing buffers in an SVPDF model has a polynomial time computational complexity.

8. Case Study

In this case-study a simplified DVB-T transceiver illustrates the applicability of the introduced approach. In the DVB-T application, as shown in the OIL program from Figure 13, a periodic source dfe delivers symbols to the functions that belong to the acquisition and decoding mode. These two modes are specified by making use of two while-loops. First a channel is selected in the $selectChannel$ function by passing the frequency of the channel. Next, the first symbol can be read from the source by the $readInput$ function. The $acquisition$ function parses these symbols and tries to detect a reference symbol in the input stream. If this is successful, the stream of symbols is decoded by the functions in the second while-loop. A loss of synchronization is detected by the $verifySync$ function in the second while-loop. If this function detects that synchronization in the stream is lost, the outer while-loop is repeated.

Parallelization of this application results in a task for every assignment statement and function, including the while-loop termination condition in the OIL program. Therefore, 11 tasks are created for the DVB-T transceiver. The while-loop-structure of the application is copied inside the task derived from the source function dfe. This task communicate via two buffers, one buffer ($Symbol\_1$) for the communication with the tasks that correspond to functions in the first while-loop, the other buffer ($Symbol\_2$) for communication with the tasks that correspond to the functions in the second while-loop.

Figure 14 shows the SVPDF model of the DVB-T transceiver. This SVPDF model can be divided in three parts. On the left is the block modeling the tasks created from the functions in the first while-loop. The block created from tasks derived from functions in the second inner while-loop is depicted in the block on the right. Between these blocks is the actor for the $selectChannel$ function. The actors without a name are actors used to model buffers with multiple tasks reading from that buffer. Consequently, only a single edge models the buffer capacity. Note that the variable $window$ is written twice, but due to the renaming step explained in Section 5 two separate variables are automatically created in our approach. When the blocks in isolation are analyzed, only the edges shown in black are included for every block. This means that the edges modeling the $channel$ variable are not included when analyzing

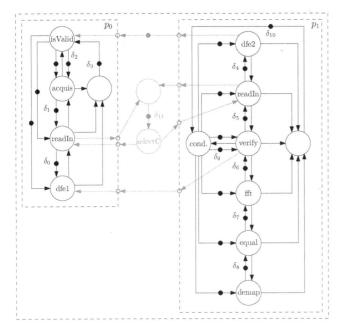

Figure 14: SVPDF graph derived from the DVB-T transceiver

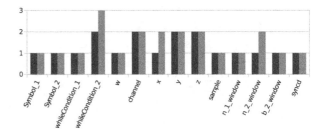

Figure 15: Buffer capacities as determined by the analysis tool

9. Related Work

In this section other parallelization approaches are discussed that generate an analysis model besides a parallel implementation. We also discuss temporal analysis models that allow dynamism to be expressed.

The *pn*-tools presented in [15] automatically parallelizes sequential applications. A polyhedral model is used to analyze the application behavior and to generate the parallel implementation. In [1] it is shown that the temporal behavior of an application generated by the *pn*-tools can be analyzed with a Cyclo-Static Dataflow (CSDF) model. Support for the parallelization of while-loops is added in [15], but without the generation of a temporal analysis model.

The structured dataflow approach [10], like this work, has additional structure in the form of blocks. Also in this approach blocks represent loops. However, unlike our approach blocks behave the same as actors and have firing rules. As a consequence a block acts as a barrier, prevent pipeline parallelism over loop boundaries.

This work extends the approach presented in [3] and [8]. The approach presented in [3] generates a CSDF analysis model from a sequential specification of an application to analyze the temporal behavior of applications. This sequential specification is parallelized using function level parallelism. However, the sequential specification does not allow for while-loops with an unknown number of iterations to be specified. Also the CSDF model does not allow for dynamic behavior to be expressed. This paper extends this approach by generating a dynamic SVPDF model which does allow for the expression of while-loops. In [8] the parallelization approach from [3] is extended by allowing while-loops in the input specification. Synchronization statements are inserted in the parallelized application such that in every task synchronizes the same number of times for every variable. However, synchronization statements can therefore also be executed repeatedly in tasks not having any repetition, thus potentially resulting in a large synchronization overhead. This paper decouples synchronization between tasks and then shows how a temporal analysis model can be generated from the application.

A dataflow model which allows for dynamic behavior is the Variable-rate Dataflow (VRDF) model [17]. In the VRDF model actors can have variable rates. However, an upper bound on the parameter values must be known at compile time. For while-loops there is no such upper bound definable. The VPDF model does allow for phases to be expressed and does not require upper bounds on the parameter values [19]. However, two problems exist with analysis for VPDF models. First, analysis techniques for this model can result in a false detection of deadlock when deriving the maximum throughput because a linearization step is applied which results in an over-approximation. Furthermore, determining the parameters in an VPDF model during analysis has an exponential computational complexity in the number of parameters P: $O(V2^P + E2^P)$. The analysis algorithms for the SVPDF model have a polynomial time computational complexity and a false detection of deadlock can not occur.

both blocks in isolation. The throughput constraint for both blocks in isolation is $\frac{1}{156\,\text{kHz}} = 6.4\mu s$, which corresponds to the period of the source *Symbol*.

Using these two models and the flattened SVPDF model, when p_0 and p_1 have a value of one, buffer capacities are determined. The throughput constraint for the flattened model is $2 \cdot 6.4\mu s = 12.8\mu s$ because the source *Symbol* is accessed at least once per inner while-loop. The computed buffer capacities are shown in the graph in Figure 15 with the bars on the left. When the execution time of the *fft* and *demap* functions are set to $6.4\mu s$, the buffer capacities shown on the right in the figure are obtained. It can be seen that for the buffer of the second while-loop condition three locations are now required and two locations for the buffers containing the values for x and n_2_window.

When the application is executed using these computed buffer capacities, the schedule as shown in Figure 16 is obtained. The tasks are executed as soon as they are enabled because in this example we assume that all task do not share a processor. The bars in the schedule containing the text "XXX" represent the time before a task fires for the first time. The numbers inside the bars represent the q-th execution of that task except for the source function *dfe* where the numbers represent $\psi(i)$.

The schedule shows that the execution of both inner while-loops overlaps. When the sixth execution of the source starts, also the tasks that corresponds with functions in the first inner while-loop start executing again while the tasks corresponding with functions in the second inner while-loop are not yet finished. In this example, the tasks derived from the functions *equalization* and *demap* need to finish their execution.

Furthermore, this schedule shows that the function *selectChannel* can have an execution time of $12.8\mu s$, which is indeed twice the period of the source. However, because the first value produced by this function is required by a function in the first while-loop, the source starts executing at a time greater than zero. If the source would start executing at time zero, a periodic execution cannot be guaranteed since the termination condition of the first while-loop determines whether the second value should be written to the source buffer for the first while-loop or the buffer for the second while-loop.

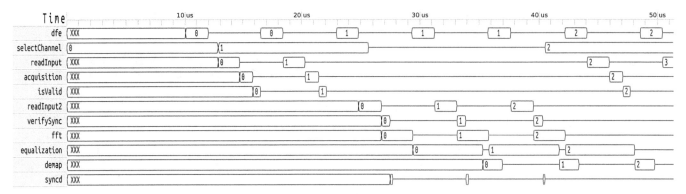

Figure 16: Fragment of a possible schedule for the DVB-T transceiver from Figure 13

The SADF model also allows for dynamic behavior to be expressed [16]. On top of an SDF model is a Finite State Machine (FSM) defined which specifies when mode transitions occur. Automatic derivation of the SDF model and the FSM has not been addressed. The SDF model is analyzed using model checking techniques which have a worst-case exponential complexity.

10. Conclusion

This paper introduced an approach in which a dataflow model is automatically derived from a sequential specification of a modal stream processing application. This derivation is enabled by a program transformation, which is introduced in this paper, where particular read operations in a while-loop are made non-destructive and particular write operations are made destructive. This results in a decoupling of the synchronization of tasks that correspond with functions in different while-loops.

The generated dataflow model is an SVPDF model which is used for the derivation of buffer capacities and the verification of temporal constraints. Because the model is generated from a sequential specification, it has a very specific structure. By making use of this structure we proved that we can verify whether the generated parallel application meets a throughput constraint using an algorithm that has a polynomial time computational complexity. The case-study shows the relevance and applicability of our approach. The generated schedule for a DVB-T application shows that the execution of tasks that belong to different modes can overlap and that the analysis using the SVPDF model takes this overlap into account.

We restricted variables in this paper to scalars for understandability of the methods and proofs. However, we consider it interesting future work to extend the presented approach to support arrays.

References

[1] M. Bamakhrama and T. Stefanov. Hard-real-time scheduling of data-dependent tasks in embedded streaming applications. In *Proc. of the ACM Int'l Conf. on Embedded Software (EMSOFT)*, pages 195–204. IEEE, 2011.

[2] T. Bijlsma. *Automatic parallelization of Nested Loop Programs - For non-manifest real-time stream processing applications.* PhD thesis, University of Twente, 2011.

[3] T. Bijlsma, M. Bekooij, P. Jansen, and G. Smit. Communication between nested loop programs via circular buffers in an embedded multiprocessor system. In *Proc. of the Int'l Workshop on Software & Compilers for Embedded Systems (SCOPES)*, pages 33–42. ACM, 2008.

[4] J. Buck and E. Lee. Scheduling dynamic dataflow graphs with bounded memory using the token flow model. In *IEEE Int'l Conf. on Acoustics, Speech, and Signal Processing (ICASSP)*, volume 1, pages 429–432. IEEE, 1993.

[5] A. Dasdan. Experimental analysis of the fastest optimum cycle ratio and mean algorithms. *ACM Transactions on Design Automation of Electronic Systems (TODAES)*, 9(4):385–418, 2004.

[6] P. Derler, T. Feng, E. Lee, S. Matic, H. Patel, Y. Zhao, and J. Zou. PTIDES: A programming model for distributed real-time embedded systems. *University of California, Berkeley, EECS Technical Report. EECS-2008-72*, 2008.

[7] M. Geilen, S. Tripakis, and M. Wiggers. The earlier the better: A theory of timed actor interfaces. In *Int'l Conf. on Hybrid Systems: Computation and Control*, April 2011.

[8] S. Geuns, M. Bekooij, T. Bijlsma, and H. Corporaal. Parallelization of while loops in nested loop programs for shared-memory multiprocessor systems. *Design, Automation and Test in Europe (DATE)*, 2011.

[9] S. Geuns, J. Hausmans, and M. Bekooij. Sequential specification of time-aware stream processing applications. *ACM Transactions on Embedded Computing Systems (TECS)*, 12(1s):35, 2013.

[10] J. Kodosky, J. MacCrisken, and G. Rymar. Visual programming using structured data flow. In *Proc' IEEE Workshop on Visual Languages*, pages 34–39. IEEE, 1991. ISBN 0818623306.

[11] H. Kopetz and G. Bauer. The time-triggered architecture. *Proc. of the IEEE*, 91(1):112–126, 2003.

[12] E. Lee and D. Messerschmitt. Synchronous data flow. *Proc. of the IEEE*, 75(9):1235–1245, 1987.

[13] E. Lee and T. Parks. Dataflow process networks. In *Proc. of the IEEE*, May 1995.

[14] O. Moreira and M. Bekooij. Self-timed scheduling analysis for real-time applications. *EURASIP Journal on Advances in Signal Processing*, 2007, 2007.

[15] D. Nadezhkin and T. Stefanov. Automatic derivation of polyhedral process networks from while-loop affine programs. In *IEEE Symposium on Embedded Systems for Real-Time Multimedia (ESTIMedia)*, pages 102–111. IEEE, 2011.

[16] S. Stuijk, M. Geilen, B. Theelen, and T. Basten. Scenario-aware dataflow: Modeling, analysis and implementation of dynamic applications. *Proc. Int'l Conf. on Embedded Computer Systems: Architectures, Modeling, and Simulation (SAMOS XI)*, 2011.

[17] M. Wiggers, M. Bekooij, and G. Smit. Buffer capacity computation for throughput constrained streaming applications with data-dependent inter-task communication. In *Real-Time and Embedded Technology and Applications Symposium (RTAS)*, pages 183–194. IEEE, 2008.

[18] M. Wiggers, M. Bekooij, and G. Smit. Monotonicity and run-time scheduling. In *Proc. of the ACM Int'l Conf. on Embedded Software (EMSOFT)*, pages 177–186. ACM, 2009.

[19] M. Wiggers, M. Bekooij, and G. Smit. Buffer capacity computation for throughput-constrained modal task graphs. *ACM Transactions on Embedded Computing Systems (TECS)*, 10(2):17, 2010. ISSN 1539-9087.

[20] J. Zou, J. Auerbach, D. Bacon, and E. Lee. PTIDES on flexible task graph: real-time embedded system building from theory to practice. In *ACM SIGPLAN Notices*, volume 44, pages 31–40. ACM, 2009.

Portable Mapping of OpenMP to Multicore Embedded Systems Using MCA APIs

Cheng Wang[‡]   Sunita Chandrasekaran[‡]   Peng Sun[‡]   Barbara Chapman[‡]   Jim Holt[†]

[‡]Department of Computer Science, University of Houston, Houston, TX, 77004, USA
[†]Freescale Semiconductor Inc., Austin, TX, 78735, USA
{cwang35, sunita, psun5, chapman}@cs.uh.edu, rwbl70@freescale.com

Abstract

Multicore embedded systems are being widely used in telecommunication systems, robotics, medical applications and more. While they offer a high-performance with low-power solution, programming in an efficient way is still a challenge. In order to exploit the capabilities that the hardware offers, software developers are expected to handle many of the low-level details of programming including utilizing DMA, ensuring cache coherency, and inserting synchronization primitives explicitly. The state-of-the-art involves solutions where the software toolchain is too vendor-specific thus tying the software to a particular hardware leaving no room for portability.

In this paper we present a runtime system to explore mapping a high-level programming model, OpenMP, on to multicore embedded systems. A key feature of our scheme is that unlike the existing approaches that largely rely on POSIX threads, our approach leverages the Multicore Association (MCA) APIs as an OpenMP translation layer. The MCA APIs is a set of low-level APIs handling resource management, inter-process communications and task scheduling for multicore embedded systems. By deploying the MCA APIs, our runtime is able to effectively capture the characteristics of multicore embedded systems compared with the POSIX threads. Furthermore, the MCA layer enables our runtime implementation to be portable across various architectures. Thus programmers only need to maintain a single OpenMP code base which is compatible by various compilers, while on the other hand, the code is portable across different possible types of platforms. We have evaluated our runtime system using several embedded benchmarks. The experiments demonstrate promising and competitive performance compared to the native approach for the platform.

Categories and Subject Descriptors D.3.4 [*Programming Languages*]: Processors—Compilers, Optimization

General Terms Languages, Performance, Standardization

Keywords OpenMP; MCA; Runtime optimizations; Embedded systems

1. Introduction

Multicore embedded systems usually consist of embedded CPUs, sensors and accelerators to provide high-performance but low-power solutions. Although these embedded systems offer great hardware capabilities, the limited availability of multicore software programming models and standards pose a challenge for their full adoption. Programmers typically have to write low-level codes, schedule task units and manage synchronization explicitly between cores. As the hardware complexity is rapidly growing, it is nearly impossible to expect programmers to manually handle all the low-level details. This is not only time-consuming but an error-prone approach.

Another major concern is the software portability. The state-of-the-art for programming embedded systems includes proprietary vendor-specific software development toolchains that are tightly coupled with specific platforms. As a result, software developers have to largely restructure the code if they want to port it to other platforms, while at the same time, ensure the performance. This leads to a less-productive and error-prone software development process that is unacceptable for ever growing complexity of embedded hardware. If the multicore embedded industry is to quickly adopt multicore embedded devices, one of the key factors to consider is to move from proprietary solutions to open standards.

The Multicore Association(MCA) APIs [4], an extensive industry standard founded by a group of vendors from semiconductor and embedded software industries. The road map of MCA consists of an extensive set of APIs that support multicore communication (MCAPI), resource management (MRAPI), and virtualization spanning cores on different chips. MCA also has an active working group to provide a set of APIs for task management (MTAPI) charged with creating an industry-standard specification that supports coordination of tasks on embedded parallel systems. We have been active members in this working group, participating in the design of MTAPI specification. In addition, the MCA APIs provide a standard interface for programmers which is independent of any operating systems and devices thus allowing it to be portable across various possible architectures. Standards take a long time to develop and establish. There are better chances of more and more programmers embracing such standards if OS, processor and tool vendors provide MCA API as part of their implementation. We see that there is a significant number of vendors that are supporting MCA APIs [5, 10].

However, a point to note is that the MCA APIs are low-level library-based protocols that could make programming still tedious. Programmers still have to explore the features of MCA APIs and largely restructure the code using MCA APIs. As a result, a high-level programming model is needed that could help to express concurrency in a given application easily, while on the other hand,

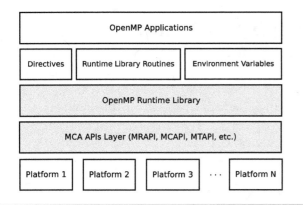

Figure 1. Overview of the embedded OpenMP solution stack.

provide sufficient features which are capable of capturing the low-level details of the underlying systems.

In this paper, we propose a compiler-runtime approach that offers a well-known high-level programming model, OpenMP to programmers, while the underlying OpenMP runtime library exploits the capabilities of MCA APIs to hide low-level details of the platform. OpenMP is a *de facto* standard for shared memory parallel programming. It provides a set of high-level directives, runtime library routines and environment variables that enable programmers to easily express data and task parallelism in an incremental programming style. The compiler handles the low-level details of thread management, loop scheduling and synchronization primitives. OpenMP code is portable across a number of compilers and architectures, which allows the programmer to focus on the application instead of low-level details of the platform. Embedded programmers could therefore benefit from such software portability and programmability.

As OpenMP was original designed for high performance computing systems, there are some challenges that prevent us from directly using OpenMP for multicore embedded systems. One of the hurdles is that embedded systems may lack some of the features which can be commonly found in general-purpose processors. For instance, a traditional OpenMP compiler translates non-executable pragmas (parallel, for, and so on) into multithreaded code with function calls to a customized runtime library, which typically relies on POSIX threads and SMP GNU/linux. However, when comes to embedded space, there are a large number of embedded platforms (e.g., Texas Instruments TMS320C6678 multi-core DSP [1]) do not come with such support. In certain scenarios, embedded applications may run on bare-metal processors, where operating systems and thread libraries do not even exist. Moreover, modern embedded systems usually consist of heterogeneous processors operating on different ISAs, OSes and non-cache coherent memory subsystems with separate memory space, where POSIX threads alone is incapable of capturing all these features of embedded systems. Although there are some recent proprietary implementations that support OpenMP for their platforms [24], this approach significantly sacrifices the portability property of OpenMP. In contrast, our approach utilizes the MCA APIs as the translation layer, thus the implementation is portable across various possible architectures. We will evaluate the portability and performance under different platforms in Section 6.

Figure 1 shows the overview of our embedded OpenMP solution stack. A typical OpenMP compiler transforms OpenMP directives into multi-threaded code with function calls to a customized runtime library. An efficient runtime library creates and schedules threads, manages shared memory and implements synchronization

primitives. In this paper, we designed and implemented an unified OpenMP runtime library, namely *libEOMP*, that utilizes the MCA APIs as a translation layer. The MCA APIs could help to bridge the gap between the existing OpenMP runtime implementations for general-purpose platforms and the unique challenges for multicore embedded systems. In addition, since our OpenMP runtime is built on top of the MCA layer and it is architecture independent, it is thus portable across various types of architectures. We evaluated our *libEOMP* using micro benchmark suite and real embedded applications on two state-of-the-art multicore embedded platforms. Experimental results showed that the *libEOMP* not only performs as well as vendor-specific approaches but also promises portability, programmability and productivity.

The rest of the paper is organized as follows. In Section 2, we discuss the state-of-the-art in programming multicore embedded systems. In Section 3 we briefly discuss the MCA APIs and how they can be used to implement OpenMP. We discuss in detail the design and implementation strategies of our novel approach in Section 4 and 5. Results of our evaluation are discussed in Section 6 and, finally, section 7 presents the conclusions and future work.

2. Related Work

In this section, we discuss the programming techniques for multicore embedded systems, which could be categorized as language extensions, parallel programming libraries and pragma-based approaches.

Language extensions: Assembly and C are the most commonly used programming languages for embedded systems. Assembly language is efficient but difficult to use. It also depends on specific architecture hence offers no portability. In the embedded market, compilers are not 100% ANSI C compliant, which is mainly because some of the C features are difficult to implement on embedded processors. Besides, vendors are usually required to extend C language due to the need to support special features on the chip. However, the major drawback of these vendor-specific SDKs is that the workload of managing limited on-chip resources has been shifted from hardware to programmers. Hence they can hardly exploit the underlying platform without the knowledge of the hardware details.

Some language extension-based approaches try to abstract the low-level details of the platform from the programmer. For instance, SoC-C [32] enables programmers to manage distributed memory and express pipeline parallelism. However SoC-C does not help explore data parallelism which is commonly available in embedded applications. Another effort is Offload [16] which provides extensions to C++, that offloads the code to Cell BE processor. However, this approach is unable to be ported to any other platforms other than the Cell processor. OpenCL [8] is a parallel programming language on heterogeneous systems, and Objective-C [7] is the primary language for developing the iPhone applications. Lime [11] is also a Java-based approach supporting heterogeneous processors. Other embedded systems such as FPGAs can also be programmed using similar language extension based approaches such as ImpulseC [31], Handel-C [28], Streams-C [19]. However, an important point to note is that these language extensions are still very low-level and do not quite express data and task parallelism easily. Programmers are required to manually restructure the source code and manage the barrier, loop scheduling, reduction, data sharing and synchronization, which leads to a nontrivial, less productive and error-prone technique.

Parallel programming libraries: Many programming languages also offer a set of customized runtime libraries (APIs) to ease programming to some extent. For instance, the IBM Data Communication and Synchronization (DaCS) [2] library also pro-

Table 1. Overview of the Resource Management API (MRAPI) feature set.

Features	Description
Domain and Nodes	Real execution entities,e.g., process, thread or accelerator
Memory primitives	Allocate and manage on-chip/off-chip shared/remote memory
Synchronization primitives	Mutexes, semaphore, and reader/writer locks
Metadata primitives	Retrieve hardware information

vides a set of data movement primitives that help programmers take advantage of the Cell processor's DMA engines, however it is not portable to other platforms other than Cell architectures. Several universal libraries such as MPI [35] and POSIX threads [17] do not require any specific compiler support. However the implementation of MPI is too heavyweight for embedded systems. As we have discussed before, the POSIX threads is yet insufficient to tackle all the characteristics for modern multiprocessor SoC. Apart from the MCA APIs, Phalanx [18] also provides an unified runtime system aiming to ease of programming on heterogeneous machines. By leveraging the GASNet runtime, Phalanx is also able to run across all the nodes of a distributed-memory machine.

Pragma-based approaches: Pragma-based approaches, such as OpenMP [9], are high-level, straightforward and easy to use. It allows the compiler and runtime system to exploit the hardware complexities thus abstracting these details from the programmers. Compared with language extension and library-based approaches, pragma-based approaches require only minimal modification to be done to parallelize a given code. There exists many efforts to implement OpenMP on some architectures other than general-purpose CPUs, including multicore DSP [24], Cell [30], and GPGPU [25, 26]. In addition, there also exists a large number of work trying to map a high-level programming model to heterogeneous platforms, such as CnC [34] and HiCUDA [21].

An initial experience of adapting OpenMP for multicore embedded systems is discussed in [14], in which OpenMP was implemented on Texas Instrument's multicore MPSoC platform by performing a source-to-source translation with the OpenUH compiler [27]. The Omni OpenMP compiler [33] which also adopted a source-to-source approach was implemented on three embedded SMP architectures in [22]. Texas Instrument's experience on porting the OpenMP to their TMSC6678 multicore DSP platform was also reported in [24]. However, the main limitation is none of these solutions can be ported to other platforms beyond the initial design. On the contrary, our *libEOMP* is built on top of the MCA APIs thus its implementation is seamlessly portable.

Extensions to OpenMP were also proposed in order to address the architectural challenges for embedded systems. OpenMDSP [23] proposed extensions for OpenMP to target multicore DSPs. In order to fill the gap between the OpenMP memory model and the memory hierarchy of multicore DSPs, three classes of directives were proposed: data placement, distributed array and stream access directives. Cao et al. [13] also proposed an extension for OpenMP tasks on the Cell BE. A major drawback of these existing approaches is that they are not standardized solutions which amortized the portability of OpenMP.

Our approach inherits the advantages of pragma-based approaches discussed above. Moreover, our approach neither requires the programmer to understand low-level details of the hardware nor requires the programmer to learn any new parallel programming language. The programmer simply needs to insert standard OpenMP directives wherever necessary to parallelize the code and allow the compiler and runtime to handle the low-level details.

To summarize, we see that there are various approaches to programming multicore systems, but most of these either involve significant manual intervention to explore parallelism or provide solutions that are heavily customized for a specific device. So if the program needs to be ported to other devices, there will involve significant efforts on code restructuring. Software developers are therefore not able to focus on the parallel solution of a problem but instead are busy dealing with hardware details of the platform. It is a challenge to resolve these issues while still be able to meet stringent time-to-market requirements which are an important factor in the world of embedded systems. An ideal solution is to provide a set of standard APIs for multicore applications, which must be fast, lightweight, scalable and portable across multiple target platforms and OSes.

3. Background

In this section, we introduce some background details to MCA APIs, in particular the resource management API (MRAPI) [6] that we have employed in this paper. The MRAPI provides essential feature sets required to manage shared resources in multicore embedded systems, including homogeneous/heterogeneous core on-chip, hardware accelerators and memory regions. Table 1 gives an overview of the MRAPI feature set.

Domain and Nodes: *Domain* and *nodes* define the overall granularity of the resources. An MCA *Domain* is a global entity which can consist of one or more MCA *nodes*. The major difference between MCA *nodes* and POSIX *threads* is that *nodes* offer a high-level semantics over *threads*, thus hiding real entities of the execution. Furthermore, the POSIX *threads* require that all threads in a team must be identical. However, this may not be the case for embedded systems where threads running on different cores can be heterogeneous as well. Therefore, the MRAPI *nodes* relaxes this condition and allows *nodes* in a team to be distinct with its own attributes and data structures. For instance, a team of *nodes* can consist of CPUs, DSPs and accelerators.

Memory Primitives: MRAPI supports two different types of memory, *shared memory* and *remote memory*. *Shared memory* provides the ability to allocate, access and delete on-chip and off-chip memory. But unlike the POSIX threads where we are not able to directly control the property of the shared memory, the MRAPI *shared memory*, on the other hand, allows programmers to specify attributes of shared memory as on-chip SRAM or off-chip DDR memory. In addition, modern embedded systems often consist of heterogeneous cores where they have separate memory address space that may not be directly accessible by other nodes. MRAPI also provides another memory primitives, `remote memory`, which enables the data movement between these memory space without involving CPU cycles but using DMA, serial rapidIO (SRIO) or software cache. MRAPI keeps the data movement operation hidden from the end-users.

Synchronization primitives: MRAPI *synchronization* inherits the essential feature sets from other thread libraries for shared memory programming, including that of *mutexes, semaphore* and *reader/writer locks*. But unlike the POSIX threads, the MRAPI synchronization primitives provide richer functionality to fulfill the characteristics for embedded systems. For example, MRAPI locks can be shared by all *nodes* as well as by only a group of *nodes*.

155

Metadata primitives: Using *metadata* primitives, we could gather information about hardware and application execution statistics that may be used for debugging and profiling purposes.

We see that OpenMP and MRAPI share common mapping relationships. The concept of *nodes* naturally maps on to OpenMP *threads* and *tasks*. We adopt the MRAPI *synchronization primitives* to implement the OpenMP synchronization directives, such as *barrier* and *critical*. We utilize the MRAPI *shared memory* and *remote memory* to address the OpenMP memory model that provides a relaxed-consistency, shared-memory model. We will discuss these in detail in Section 4.

4. Runtime Design and Key Optimizations

In this section, we focus on the runtime system and present the overall design choices for using MCA APIs. In our prior contribution [36], we presented an initial implementation of the *libEOMP*, the purpose was to only validate the functional correctness of each of the design phases. In our current paper we largely extend our prior work and perform a number of improvements to the design and implementation to achieve better results.

Typically an OpenMP compiler translates OpenMP directives into multithreaded code which consists of functions calls to a customized runtime library. Although the work division between an OpenMP compiler and an runtime library is implementation-defined, the essential functionality provided by a runtime includes:

- Efficient handling threads creation, synchronization and management.

- Parallel distributing loop iterations among threads when assisting the compiler to transform work sharing construct.

- Fulfilling the OpenMP memory model and managing the shared memory.

- Supporting runtime library routines and environment variables.

In addition, our runtime design inherits basic features from some of the commonly used open-source OpenMP implementations such as OpenUH [27], but since the features are not tailored for embedded systems, we had to adopt several strategies to customize the implementations for embedded systems. In the following subsections, we discuss the improvements made to the OpenMP implementation optimized for embedded systems.

4.1 Execution Model

OpenMP uses the fork-join model of parallel execution. An OpenMP program begins with a single sequential thread of execution, which is termed as *master* thread. When a parallel region is encountered, a team of *worker* threads will be created, and the program block enclosed in the parallel region will be executed concurrently among the *worker* threads. At the end of parallel region, all the *worker* threads will wait for each other until all the executions are finished allowing the *master* thread to run to completion. Several traditional approaches employ the POSIX threads or system functions to create and manage OpenMP threads. However this is not favorable to embedded systems as discussed in section 3. We map OpenMP threads to MCA *nodes* in our design. However, several optimization for efficient handling threads creation and management need to be performed before we adapt the existing techniques to embedded systems.

4.1.1 Optimizing the thread pool

The *thread pool* technique is commonly used for managing OpenMP threads. A team of *worker* threads is created only once during the runtime initialization. These *worker* threads wait until a parallel region is encountered, the *master* thread then assigns a microtask to them. A microtask consists of information about the entry function, data pointer and a wake-up message to wake-up the *worker* threads. Upon completion of the microtasks, the *worker* threads will wait in the pool until a new microtask is assigned. As a result, the *worker* threads are created only once but can be reused during the entire program execution time. This helps in reducing the thread creation overhead.

Although the concept of thread pool is straightforward, there are several issues that must be resolved before we adopt this approach to embedded systems. Conventionally a large number of threads (for example 256) are created in the thread pool for the need of nested parallelism. This may lead to thread oversubscription that typically high-performance computing systems can afford and sometimes oversubscription has the potential to improve performance with better load balancing and CPU utilization. Especially when executing applications that have control and data dependencies that requires threads to wait for each other. But with the dedicated environments (i.e., embedded systems) thread oversubscription degrades performance since the computational resources are relatively limited. Moreover, this approach is too heavyweight for embedded systems since memory in these systems is not available in abundance. Hence thread creation and usage in embedded systems requires careful management.

In our design, we adopt a simple heuristic to create an *elastic* thread pool. Primarily we obtain the number of *nodes* available on the platform, by using the MRAPI *metadata* primitive, then we only generate that many number of threads as required in the thread pool. As a result, thread oversubscription will not occur. At a later stage, if the programmer specifies the number of threads that is less than the size of the thread pool, the idle threads will stall freeing the CPU cycles by using our worker-initiated idle threads handling approach discussed below.

4.1.2 Worker-initiated idle threads handling

Here we discuss about managing the idle threads who are waiting in the pool to be assigned with microtasks. In the above discussion, we saw that once the thread pool has been created, there are idle threads in the pool waiting to be scheduled. Those idle threads must be well-handled as they should neither consume too much system resource nor have a long time delay when they receive a wake-up signal.

Traditionally, idle threads are handled by the master thread: i.e., if a worker thread finishes its execution, it simply declares itself as idle, by changing the status of the message queue. It then sleeps on a conditional wait until a wake-up signal with a new microtask is received. This is conventionally accomplished using the POSIX threads mutex lock and conditional variables. We call this *master-initiated* approach as it is the master thread's responsibility to wake up all the worker threads. The advantage of this approach is that CPU cycles will be released when worker threads are idle using conditional wait. Thus it is well-adopted in most of conventional OpenMP runtime implementation with a large thread pool, as it would be catastrophic if hundreds of idle threads are busy with polling new microtasks. However, the main drawback of the master-initiated approach is that all worker threads will compete for the mutex lock when they receive the wake-up signal. That is, worker threads have to acquire the lock before they can proceed to execute the new microtask. This will cause a large performance overhead when the system scales up.

In our runtime design, we introduce a *worker-initiated* idle threads handling mechanism. The key idea of our approach is to pass the duty of waking-up the idle threads to the worker threads, thus freeing the master thread of this responsibility and avoiding the need of using mutex locks. Specifically, each worker thread maintains a private message queue. When the master thread assigns a new microtask, it simply puts the new microtask into the queue. When a worker thread finishes its execution, it will check for a new microtask from its private queue. Therefore worker threads do not need to compete for the mutex lock and there is also no signaling overhead associated with inter-process communication.

It is still possible that this technique will increase the workload for the worker threads. However, such an overhead will not count into the critical path, as the communication is initialized by the idle worker threads instead of the busy master thread. In reality, costs with respect to this kind of polling operation is negligible since they perform a read operation from a local message queue and no inter-process communication takes place. Furthermore, we also introduce an interval, δ, between two polling attempts. The value of δ could be based on either randomness or the Poisson distribution. In our evaluation, we choose a heuristics value which equals to the average overhead of the runtime to finish a microtask. Therefore, the idle threads can sleep around until next microtask available. This approach outperformed the vendor-specific OpenMP implementation that will be discussed in section 6.

4.2 Memory Model

OpenMP specifies a shared memory, relaxed-consistency model [9]; i.e., threads access the same, global shared memory, while could have their own temporary view of private data until a synchronization point is reached where the private data is then written back to the global memory. The shared memory, relaxed-consistency model is trivial to achieve in general purpose CPUs where a large shared memory within a compute node with cache-coherent hardware modules always exist. However, the memory hierarchy for embedded systems is much more complicated. The cache coherency is not automatically supported by the embedded hardware. Moreover, they may also consist of on-chip and off-chip shared memory along with local memory with separate address space.

We use MRAPI memory primitives to manage the OpenMP memory. For the non-cache coherent embedded systems, shared data is stored into the MRAPI *shared memory*, which maps into the on-chip/off-chip shared memory. We configure the local cache as the scratchpad memory that is mapped into the MRAPI *remote memory* to store private data. Data transfers between *remote memory* is achieved through DMA, software cache or RapidIO, which will be handled by the *remote memory* implicitly.

4.3 Synchronization

In OpenMP, synchronization primitive consists of *barrier, critical, single* and *master*. *Barrier* synchronizes all threads in the team, while the *critical* region specifies only one thread that can execute at a time. The *single* construct that defines the region can only be executed by one thread, while *master* specifies that region be executed only by the master thread. As we discussed before, we utilize the MRAPI synchronization primitives to implement OpenMP synchronization directives.

4.3.1 Barrier Implementation

OpenMP heavily relies on barrier operations to synchronize threads. Implicit barriers are required at the end of the parallel region; they are also used implicitly at the end of the work-sharing construct. Explicit barriers are used by the OpenMP developers to synchronize the threads in the team. An efficient barrier implementation is therefore essential to achieve good performance and scalability.

In our runtime design, we employ the tournament algorithm [29] to implement the OpenMP barrier. Compared to the traditional centralized barrier and blocking barrier algorithms that require $O(n)$ operations on critical path, the tournament barrier only takes $log(n)$ operations, where n is the number of processes. As a result, it is

---

Algorithm 1: Tournament Barrier Algorithm

Data: round_t rounds[p][log P]
Initialization{...};
round_t round=current_thd→myround;
while *1* **do**
  if *round→role* & *LOSER* **then**
    round→opponent = current_thd→sense;
    while *champion_sense ≠ current_thd→sense* **do**
      ;
    break;
  else if *round→role* & *WINNER* **then**
    while *round→flag ≠ current_thd→sense* **do**
      ;
  else if *round→role* & *CHAMPION* **then**
    while *round_flag ≠ current_thd→sense* **do**
      ;
    champion_sense = current_thd→sense;
    break;

---

clear to see that the tournament barrier is able to offer better scalability.

Algorithm 1 shows the tournament barrier. The idea of the tournament algorithm comes from the tournament game. Two threads play against each other in each game. The role of each thread, i.e. the winner, loser or champion is predefined. The winners from each round play against each other until there is a champion, who will wake-up all threads and release the barrier. We will evaluate the scalability in section 6.

4.3.2 Critical, Single and Master Implementation

The *critical* construct defines a critical section of code that only one thread can access at a time. When the *critical* construct is encountered, the critical section will be outlined and two runtime library calls, _ompc_critical and ompc_end_critical respectively, will be inserted at the beginning and at the end of the critical section. The former is implemented as an MRAPI *mutex_lock*, and the latter as an MRAPI *mutex_unlock*.

The *single* construct specifies that the encapsulated code can only be executed by a single thread. Therefore, only the thread that encounters the *single* construct will execute the code within that region. The basic idea is that each thread tries to update a global counter, which is protected by MRAPI mutexes. Thus only the first thread that gains access to the mutex can update the global counter and return a flag. Only that thread having the flag can execute that *single* region.

The *master* construct specifies that only the master thread will execute the code. Since the *node_id* has been stored in the MRAPI resource tree, it is fairly easy to find the id of the master thread.

4.4 Work-sharing, Scheduling and Runtime library routines Implementation

OpenMP also has a *work-sharing* construct that defines a key component of data-parallelism that is widely needed in today's multicore embedded systems. The *loop* construct distributes the execution of the associated loop among the members of the thread team that encounters the loop. The schedule clause determines how the iterations of the loop, called chunks, are distributed among the threads. Each thread executes the chunk assigned to it.

In the default schedule type, i.e. static schedule, the loop iterations or chunks are divided among the threads almost equally. The

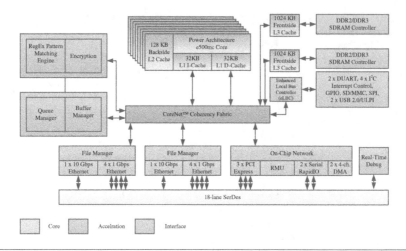

Figure 2. Block diagram of the Freescale QorIQ P4080 multicore platform.

implementation of the static scheduling in *libEOMP* maintains a global task queue which is filled with chunks. Then a scheduler dispatches the chunks in the queue to each thread in a round-robin fashion. When the scheduling type is dynamic, the runtime will assign chunks dynamically to the threads. In this case, although there is a global task queue, private task queues are maintained by each thread. Once the private queue is empty, it will request new tasks from the global queue, which is protected by an exclusive access provided by MRAPI mutex.

OpenMP also defines a group of ever-growing runtime library routines and environment variables that are easy to use. We have only implemented the most commonly used ones. For e.g. *omp_get_num_threads* to get the number of threads in a team, *omp_get_thread_num* to obtain the *thread_id*, the environment variable *OMP_NUM_THREADS* that sets the maximum number of threads to be used in parallel.

5. Implementation

In this section, we discuss the compilation strategies on two Freescale embedded platforms, the corresponding source-to-source translation and the code generation process.

5.1 Architecture Overview

We implemented the *libEOMP* on two Freescale state-of-the-art multicore platforms, one is Freescale P1022 Reference Design Kit (RDK), a dual-core Power Architecture^{TM} multicore platform, while the other one is Freescale QorIQ P4080 eight-core platform [3].

Figure 2 shows the block diagram of the Freescale P4080 platform, which is an eight-core Power Architecture^{TM} e500mc processors supporting dual-issue, out-of-order instructions with superscalar. It has three levels of cache hierarchy: 32KB I/D L1, with 128KB L2 private to each core, and 2M shared L3. It also has two 64-bit DDR2/DDR3 SDRAM memory controllers with ECC and interleaving support. Freescale P1022 RDK has similar configuration, except that it has a dual-core Freescale e500v2 processor with 32KB I/D L1 and 256KB shared L2.

5.2 Compilation Overview

Figure 3 shows the overview of the compilation process. We use the OpenUH compiler [27] as the front-end to perform a source-to-source translation. OpenUH is a branch of the open-source Open64 compiler suite for C, C++ and FORTRAN 95/2003. It

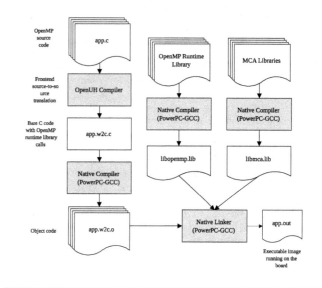

Figure 3. Overview of the cross-compilation process.

also supports OpenMP 3.0 and almost 3.1, Co-array FORTRAN and UPC. The OpenUH transforms OpenMP pragmas into an intermediate file, called *whirl*, mainly by two steps: *omp_prelower* and *lower_mp*. The former performs the preprocessing while the latter performs the major translations. It also has another translator, called *whirl2c and whirl2f*, that translates the IR to back-end compatible C and FORTRAN code. Then, the generated bare C code with the OpenMP runtime function calls will be fed into the back-end native compiler which generates the object files. For our evaluation, the back-end compiler is the Power Architecture GCC compiler toolchain for both Freescale e500v2 and e500mc processors. During the linking phase, the linker will link all the object codes together with the OpenMP runtime library and MCA libraries to generate the executable files for the target architecture.

6. Performance Evaluation

In this section, we evaluated the *libEOMP* for portability and performance on two Freescale platforms. For our experimental purposes, we use the MRAPI implementation provided by Freescale

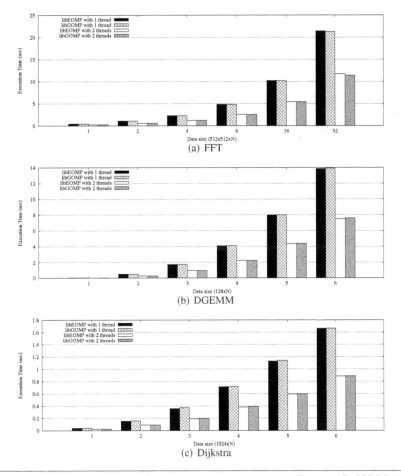

Figure 4. Execution time of FFT, DGEMM and Dijkstra on Freescale P1022 RDK.

Semiconductor Inc.. We have considered two benchmarks, ranging from micro benchmarks to real embedded applications, EPCC micro benchmarks [12] and MiBench [20]. To compare *libEOMP* with that of the currently available optimized library, we have also compiled the benchmarks and linked with a native vendor-specific runtime library *libGOMP* from Power Architecture GCC compiler toolchain for the Freescale platforms. We calculate the total execution time and the speedup achieved in both *libEOMP* and *libGOMP*.

The experiments include two phases. At the first step we evaluated the *libEOMP* on the Freescale P1022 Reference Design Kit (RDK). As the *libEOMP* is built on top of the MCA APIs, our initial focus has been to ensure the interface is functionally complete and correct to allow OpenMP runtime to target on.

As is shown in Figure 4, we initially compare the performance *libEOMP* over *libGOMP* on the Freescale P1022 RDK platform. Although our purpose in this stage is not to achieve the best performance, the results show that the additional MCA layer does not incur any significant performance penalty. The detail can be found in our prior work [36]. In this paper, we have performed extensive research and developed newer strategies in the runtime design. Specifically, as discussed in Section 4, we designed a new elastic thread pool and worker-initiated idle threads handling strategies. We explored and implemented a new tournament barrier algorithm to achieve better scalability. We evaluated the performance on the eight-core Freescale QorIQ P4080 platform.

Table 2. Relative overhead of libEOMP over libGOMP.

Directive	2 Threads	4 Threads	8 Threads
PARALLEL	0.97	0.96	0.93
FOR	1.01	1.01	1.01
PARALLEL FOR	0.98	0.97	0.94
BARRIER	1.00	1.00	0.97
SINGLE	0.07	0.15	0.46
CRITICAL	1.03	1.04	1.05
REDUCTION	1.01	1.04	1.09

6.1 Overhead Evaluation

We use EPCC micro benchmark [12] to evaluate the overheads associated with our runtime. EPCC is a set of low-level benchmarks that measures the overhead associated with OpenMP directives. Table 2 shows the percentage overhead of *libEOMP* over *libGOMP* while using different number of threads. Overall, we see that the performance of the two runtime systems is quite competitive. The absolute time difference is actually less than several microseconds but this is barely noticeable by programmers. For the *parallel* construct *libEOMP* even outperforms *libGOMP*. It is because our optimized thread pool approach along with the worker-initiated idle threads handling approach facilitates the *parallel* implementation to perform better. Moreover, better performance with increased number of threads also confirms that our approach scales well. With respect to the *barrier* construct, since we have used the scalable

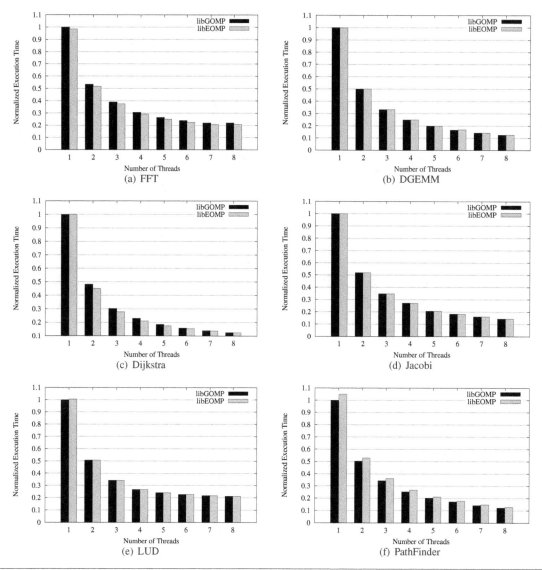

Figure 5. Comparison of execution time with *libEOMP* and *libGOMP* under different number of threads.

tournament barrier algorithm, we see that *libEOMP* scales better than *libGOMP*. We also notice that *single* directive in *libEOMP* performs much better than *libGOMP*. Although constructing the *libEOMP* framework is the central theme of this paper and we have not really concentrated on obtaining the optimum performance yet, it is encouraging to see from the table that our approach *libEOMP* can perform better than the vendor-specific approach *libGOMP*.

6.2 Benchmark Evaluation

We evaluated *libEOMP* using several real-world embedded applications chosen from Mibench [20] and Rodinia [15] benchmark suite. Figure 5 shows the normalized execution time of both *libEOMP* and *libGOMP* on the Freescale QorIQ P4080 platform. The results show that *libEOMP* performs competitively over *libGOMP*, which is consistent with the investigation illustrated in Table 2.

With respect to FFT and Dijkstra, *libEOMP* outperforms *libGOMP*. The reason is that these applications are embarrassingly parallel and we have mainly used the *parallel* constructs in the applications. Table 2 already showed that *libEOMP* outperforms *lib-*

GOMP for the *parallel* construct. For DGEMM, Jacobi and LUD, *libEOMP* performed similar to that of *libGOMP* since these applications consist of various dependencies within the program code. Therefore we had to use a combination of OpenMP constructs in order to parallelize the code including synchronization constructs. For the PathFinder we see that the *libEOMP* does not perform as well as the *libGOMP* at one thread, but is quite close to *libGOMP* as the number of threads increases, which shows good scalability.

To summarize, in this paper we have focused on demonstrating that OpenMP could be targeted for embedded systems using MCA APIs. We have also shown that our runtime *libEOMP* can perform as well as the native OpenMP runtime library customized for a specific platform, *libGOMP*. However, as our OpenMP runtime is built on top of MCA APIs, it is independent with any OS or architecture. Thus our runtime is highly portable, as is shown in the experiments. We believe that fine tuning our runtime system further could lead us to even better performance results.

7. Conclusion and Future Work

Programming model on multicore embedded systems is important yet challenging. In this paper, we have described the design and implementation details of a novel OpenMP runtime library, *libEOMP*. *libEOMP* utilizes an industry standard formulated by MCA underneath with high-level programming model, OpenMP atop. Using *libEOMP* the programmer gets enough control to write efficient code, especially when the hardware details are abstracted from the programmer. Evaluation results of *libEOMP* using several benchmarks demonstrate that *libEOMP* not only performs as good as the optimized vendor-specific approach but also offers adequate portability and productivity.

As a near future work, we plan to explore challenges posed by a heterogeneous platform to *libEOMP*. We plan to investigate minor language extensions to OpenMP that will facilitate usage of heterogeneous cores. This simple extension could be used to offload work from general purpose processors to a specialized processor. We also plan to explore task-based applications that are of interest to embedded developers.

Acknowledgments

The authors of this paper would like to express our sincere gratitude to the anonymous reviewers for their insightful comments. This research has been supported by grants from Freescale Semiconductor Inc. and Texas Instruments Inc. in association with Semiconductor Research Corporation(SRC).

References

[1] TMDXEVM6678L EVM Technical Reference Manual Version 1.0, Literature Number: SPRUH58. URL http://wfcache.advantech.com.

[2] Data Communication and Synchronization Library for Cell Broadband Engine Programmers Guide and API reference, Version 3.0. URL http://moss.csc.ncsu.edu/~mueller/cluster/ps3/SDK3.0/docs.

[3] Freescale Semiconductor Inc. URL http://www.freescale.com.

[4] The Multicore Association. URL http://www.multicore-association.org.

[5] A Case For MCAPI: CPU-to-CPU Communications in Multicore Designs. URL http://www.mentor.com/.

[6] Multicore Resource API (MRAPI) Specification, Version 1.0. URL http://www.multicore-association.org.

[7] The Objective-C Programming Languages. URL http://developer.apple.com.

[8] The OpenCL Specification, Version 1.0, . URL http://www.khronos.org.

[9] OpenMP Application Program Interface, Version 3.1, . URL http://www.openmp.org.

[10] Polycore MCAPI Offers ThreadX RTOS Support. URL http://www.eetasia.com.

[11] J. Auerbach, D. F. Bacon, I. Burcea, P. Cheng, S. J. Fink, R. Rabbah, and S. Shukla. A Compiler and Runtime for Heterogeneous Computing. In *Proceedings of DAC'12*, pages 271–276, NY, USA, 2012. ACM. ISBN 978-1-4503-1199-1. doi: 10.1145/2228360.2228411. URL http://doi.acm.org/10.1145/2228360.2228411.

[12] J. Bull. Measuring Synchronisation and Scheduling Overheads in OpenMP. In *Proceedings of the First European Workshop on OpenMP*, pages 99–105, 1999.

[13] Q. Cao, C. Hu, H. He, X. Huang, and S. Li. Support for OpenMP Tasks on Cell Architecture. In *Proc. of the 10th international conference on Algorithms and Architectures for Parallel Processing - Volume Part II*, ICA3PP'10, pages 308–317. Springer-Verlag, 2010.

[14] B. Chapman, L. Huang, E. Biscondi, E. Stotzer, A. Shrivastava, and A. Gatherer. Implementing OpenMP on a High Performance Embedded Multicore MPSoC. In *Parallel Distributed Processing, 2009. IPDPS 2009. IEEE International Symposium on*, pages 1–8, 2009. doi: 10.1109/IPDPS.2009.5161107.

[15] S. Che, M. Boyer, J. Meng, D. Tarjan, J. W. Sheaffer, S.-H. Lee, and K. Skadron. Rodinia: A Benchmark Suite for Heterogeneous Computing. In *Proceedings of IISWC'09*, pages 44–54, Washington, DC, USA, 2009. IEEE Computer Society. ISBN 978-1-4244-5156-2. doi: 10.1109/IISWC.2009.5306797. URL http://dx.doi.org/10.1109/IISWC.2009.5306797.

[16] P. Cooper, U. Dolinsky, A. F. Donaldson, A. Richards, C. Riley, and G. Russell. Offload: Automating Code Migration to Heterogeneous Multicore Systems. In *Proceedings of HiPEAC '10*, pages 337–352. Springer-Verlag, 2010.

[17] F. Garcia and J. Fernandez. POSIX Threads Libraries. *Linux J.*, 2000, 2000.

[18] M. Garland, M. Kudlur, and Y. Zheng. Designing a Unified Programming Model for Heterogeneous Machines. In *Proceedings of SC' 12*, pages 67:1–67:11, Los Alamitos, CA, USA, 2012. IEEE Computer Society Press. ISBN 978-1-4673-0804-5. URL http://dl.acm.org/citation.cfm?id=2388996.2389087.

[19] M. Gokhale, J. Stone, J. Arnold, and M. Kalinowski. Stream-oriented FPGA Computing in the Streams-C High Level Language. In *Field-Programmable Custom Computing Machines, 2000 IEEE Symposium on*, pages 49–56. IEEE, 2000.

[20] M. R. Guthaus, J. S. Ringenberg, D. Ernst, T. M. Austin, T. Mudge, and R. B. Brown. MiBench: A Free, Commercially Representative Embedded Benchmark Suite. In *Proc. of WWC-4, 2001.*, pages 3–14. IEEE Computer Society, 2001.

[21] T. D. Han and T. S. Abdelrahman. hiCUDA: High-Level GPGPU Programming. *IEEE Transactions on Parallel and Distributed Systems*, 22:78–90, 2011. ISSN 1045-9219. doi: http://doi.ieeecomputersociety.org/10.1109/TPDS.2010.62.

[22] T. Hanawa, M. Sato, J. Lee, T. Imada, H. Kimura, and T. Boku. Evaluation of Multicore Processors for Embedded Systems by Parallel Benchmark Program Using OpenMP. *Evolving OpenMP in an Age of Extreme Parallelism*, pages 15–27, 2009.

[23] J. He, W. Chen, G. Chen, W. Zheng, Z. Tang, and H. Ye. OpenMDSP: Extending OpenMP to Program Multi-Core DSP. In *Proceedings of PACT '11*, pages 288–297. IEEE, 2011.

[24] F. D. Igual, M. Ali, A. Friedmann, E. Stotzer, T. Wentz, and R. A. van de Geijn. Unleashing the High-Performance and Low-Power of Multi-core DSPs for General-Purpose HPC. In *Proceedings of SC ' 12*, SC '12, pages 26:1–26:11, Los Alamitos, CA, USA, 2012. IEEE Computer Society Press. ISBN 978-1-4673-0804-5. URL http://dl.acm.org/citation.cfm?id=2388996.2389032.

[25] S. Lee and R. Eigenmann. OpenMPC: Extended OpenMP Programming and Tuning for GPUs. In *Proceedings of SC '10*, pages 1–11. IEEE Computer Society, 2010.

[26] S. Lee, S.-J. Min, and R. Eigenmann. OpenMP to GPGPU: A Compiler Framework for Automatic Translation and Optimization. In *Proceedings of the 14th ACM SIGPLAN symposium on Principles and practice of parallel programming*, PPoPP '09, pages 101–110, New York, NY, USA, 2009. ACM. ISBN 978-1-60558-397-6. doi: 10.1145/1504176.1504194. URL http://doi.acm.org/10.1145/1504176.1504194.

[27] C. Liao, O. Hernandez, B. M. Chapman, W. Chen, and W. Zheng. OpenUH: an Optimizing, Portable OpenMP Compiler. *Concurrency and Computation: Practice and Experience*, 19(18):2317–2332, 2007.

[28] P. Martin. An Analysis of Random Number Generators for a Hardware Implementation of Genetic Programming using FPGAs and Handel-C. In *Proceedings of the genetic and evolutionary computation conference*, pages 837–844. Morgan Kaufmann Publishers Inc., 2002.

[29] J. M. Mellor-Crummey and M. L. Scott. Algorithms for Scalable Synchronization on Shared-memory Multiprocessors. *ACM Trans. Comput. Syst.*, 9(1):21–65, Feb. 1991. ISSN 0734-2071. doi: 10.1145/103727.103729. URL http://doi.acm.org/10.1145/103727.103729.

[30] K. O'Brien, K. O'Brien, Z. Sura, T. Chen, and T. Zhang. Supporting OpenMP on Cell. *Int. J. Parallel Program.*, 36(3):289–311, June 2008.

[31] D. Pellerin and S. Thibault. *Practical FPGA Programming in C*. Prentice Hall Press, 2005.

[32] A. Reid, K. Flautner, E. Grimley-Evans, and Y. Lin. SoC-C: Efficient Programming Abstractions for Heterogeneous Multicore Systems on Chip. In *Proceedings of CASES ' 08*, pages 95–104. ACM, 2008.

[33] M. Sato, M. S. Shigehisa, K. Kusano, and Y. Tanaka. Design of OpenMP Compiler for an SMP Cluster. In *In EWOMP 99*, pages 32–39, 1999.

[34] A. Sbîrlea, Y. Zou, Z. Budimlíc, J. Cong, and V. Sarkar. Mapping a Data-flow Programming Model onto Heterogeneous Platforms. In *Proceedings of the 13th ACM SIGPLAN/SIGBED International Conference on Languages, Compilers, Tools and Theory for Embedded Systems*, LCTES '12, pages 61–70, New York, NY, USA, 2012. ACM. ISBN 978-1-4503-1212-7. doi: 10.1145/2248418.2248428. URL http://doi.acm.org/10.1145/2248418.2248428.

[35] D. W. Walker, D. W. Walker, J. J. Dongarra, and J. J. Dongarra. MPI: A Standard Message Passing Interface. *Supercomputer*, 12:56–68, 1996.

[36] C. Wang, S. Chandrasekaran, B. Chapman, and J. Holt. libEOMP: A Portable OpenMP Runtime Library Based on MCA APIs for Embedded Systems. In *Proceedings of the 2013 International Workshop on Programming Models and Applications for Multicores and Manycores*, PMAM '13, pages 83–92, New York, NY, USA, 2013. ACM. ISBN 978-1-4503-1908-9. doi: 10.1145/2442992.2443001. URL http://doi.acm.org/10.1145/2442992.2443001.

Combined WCET Analysis of Bitcode and Machine Code using Control-Flow Relation Graphs

Benedikt Huber   Daniel Prokesch   Peter Puschner

Vienna University of Technology

{benedikt,daniel,peter}@vmars.tuwien.ac.at

Abstract

Static program analyses like stack usage analysis and worst-case execution time (WCET) analysis depend on the actual machine code generated by the compiler for the target system. As the analysis of binary code is costly, hard to diagnose and platform dependent, it is preferable to carry out parts of these analyses on a higher-level program representation. To this end, the higher-level code and the machine code need to be related, a difficult task due to the complexity of modern optimizing compilers.

In this article, we present a novel representation called control-flow relation graphs, which provide an accurate model of the control-flow relation between machine code and the compiler's intermediate representation. In order to facilitate the integration of our approach in existing compiler frameworks, we develop a construction algorithm that builds the control-flow relation graph from partial mappings provided by the compiler. The WCET calculation method for control-flow relation graphs processes flow information from both the intermediate representation and machine code. Furthermore, we demonstrate the transformation of flow information from the IR to the machine code level, in order to use existing industrial-strength WCET analysis tools operating on machine code. We implemented the construction algorithm within the LLVM compiler framework, along with an implementation of the combined WCET calculation method. The evaluation demonstrates that the approach is able to relate bitcode (LLVM's intermediate representation) and machine code in a precise way, with a WCET increase of at most 2% when using flow facts on the bitcode level, compared to equivalent ones on the machine-code level. As the methods presented in this article provide a cost-effective way to reuse platform independent flow information, they have the potential to simplify WCET analysis, and popularize its use in the development process of real-time systems.

Categories and Subject Descriptors   D.3.4 [*Programming Languages*]: Processors – Compilers

Keywords   Control-Flow Relation; WCET Analysis; Flow Facts Transformation; LLVM

LCTES'13,   June 20–21, 2013, Seattle, Washington, USA.
Copyright © 2013 ACM 978-1-4503-2085-6/13/06... $15.00

1. Introduction

Compilers transform one representation of a program into a different one, eventually generating code suitable for execution on a machine. Although compiler transformations do not change the semantics of the program (given the compiler is correct), the structure of the program does change, and metadata is lost or becomes hard to retrieve. This is problematic for program analyses like worst-case execution time (WCET) analysis, which depend on properties of the machine code, but would benefit from the availability of high-level information.

Contemporary compiler frameworks such as LLVM [10] construct a platform-independent intermediate representation (IR) first, and perform high-level optimizations on the IR. Subsequently, the compiler backend generates machine code for the target architecture, and runs low-level optimizations on the machine code. In order to relate source code and optimized IR code, previous work suggested to co-transform the source representation [3] and/or additional flow information [9] during optimizations.

The solution presented in this article primarily aims at providing fine-grained control mappings [22] that relate execution paths at the IR and the machine-code level, for static analysis. Our focus on this problem is motivated by the following considerations: (1) bitcode is both platform independent and appears to be well-suited to perform static program analyses [17, 23] (2) compiler backends differ for each architecture, and thus modifying every transformation to keep track of flow information is costly.

The present work demonstrates that it is feasible to directly relate the control-flow in the IR-level and machine-code–level representation. This is not a trivial problem, as transformations typically executed in the compiler backend also perform significant changes to the control-flow structure of the program. As the following example demonstrates, there is no one-to-one relation between execution paths in the IR and machine code, and not every machine block can be uniquely associated with one or more IR-level blocks.

Example 1 (Running Example). *Figure 2 illustrates a few relevant LLVM backend transformations on our running example. In Figure 1, the C source code for the function* count*, which counts the number of digits and whitespace in a string, is shown. Figure 2a illustrates the corresponding IR-level control-flow graph, using a C-like pseudo language. Figure 2b represents the same program after a few typical backend transformations have been performed (1) due to layout optimizations, a new basic block is introduced at the entry of the function (2) the switch instruction is replaced by two conditional branches; as a consequence, one outgoing edge of the switch block corresponds to two paths in the transformed program (3) the branch to the basic block* digit *is eliminated using a predicated instruction (if-conversion) (4) the tail of the loop body is duplicated, in order to reduce the number of branches.*

163

To the best of our knowledge, existing approaches that aim at directly relating execution paths associate each path on the IR or source level with exactly one matching machine code path, either to simulate machine code by instrumenting source code [18, 22], or to compare the semantics of related paths [12]. In contrast to these approaches, in our model one machine code execution path may correspond to several paths in the IR, and vice versa.

The contributions of this paper are the following:

- We present a hybrid control-flow representation called control-flow relation graphs (CFRGs), which model a useful class of relations between the execution paths of original and transformed programs.

- We demonstrate how to utilize CFRGs to carry out WCET analysis, and to transform flow information from one representation to the other.

- In order to apply our technique to existing compilers, we develop a construction algorithm to build control-flow relation graphs from information that is relatively easy to integrate into an existing compiler. We show its correctness and evaluate the practicability with respect to LLVM on a set of benchmarks for embedded systems.

The rest of the paper is structured as follows: Section 2 discusses related work. In Section 3, we introduce CFRGs and specify their semantics in terms of regular path relations. The construction algorithm, which builds control-flow relation graphs from partial mappings made available by the compiler, is presented in Section 4. In Section 5, we discuss how to carry out static WCET analysis on this representation and demonstrate the transformation of flow facts to the machine code level. Our implementation, based on the LLVM compiler framework, is presented in Section 6. The evaluation in Section 7 investigates the effectiveness of the control-flow relation graphs for WCET analysis. Section 8 concludes the paper.

2. Related Work

Different program representations need to be related in several research fields, including the well-known problem of providing source-level information for debugging machine code [10]. Two areas that need particularly precise relation models, and that need to deal with optimizing compilers, are WCET analysis and source-level simulation.

Source-level simulation aims at collecting information on machine code runs by instrumenting source code (or intermediate code), in order to simplify and speed up simulation [14]. For the purposes of this application area, exactly one machine-code path is simulated when executing one path at the source level. WCET analysis benefits from compiler support that allows users to specify annotations on the source code level, and provides additional information about the machine code supporting static analysis [9]. In contrast to simulations, it is not necessary to establish a one-to-one mapping for static analyses.

For both source-level simulations and WCET analysis using source-level flow information, it is necessary to deal with compiler optimizations. Early approaches simply disabled compiler optimizations and established a mapping using debugging information or markers inserted in the source code [11]. In order to support optimizing compilers, one solution is to transform external flow information and/or the intermediate representation in the compiler backend. In [3], accurate source-level simulation is achieved by "cross-transforming" the intermediate representation in the compiler backend, maintaining an isomorphism between the control-flow graphs of both representations. For WCET analysis, the situation is more complicated, as external flow information needs to be transformed as well. Engblom presents the concept of optimiza-

```
unsigned ws, digits;
void count(char *str) {
    while(*str) {
        switch(*str) {
            case ' ':
            case '\t':
                ws++;
                break;
            default:
                if(*str - '0' < 10)
                    digits++;
                break;
        }
        str++;
    }
}
```

Figure 1: C source code of the count example, which computes the number of digit and whitespace characters in a string.

tion traces, which are used to transform external flow information offline [5]. In [9], a framework to formally specify the effect of optimizations on flow information, and to transform flow information given optimization traces, is presented. For every optimization, update rules specify a transformation of the frequencies affected by the change. The WCET-aware C Compiler (WCC) [6] aims at reducing the WCET of programs. To keep flow information consistent throughout compiler optimizations that might invalidate it, the respective optimizations are extended by individual *flow-fact update* techniques.

In addition to transforming the intermediate representation, another strategy is to directly relate the control-flow between intermediate representation and machine code. In [22], both strategies are employed for source-level simulations: for high-level optimizations, the authors co-transform the source code, while for backend transformations, a direct relation is established. Their heuristic to establish an one-to-one correspondence in the backend uses debugging information to select matching basic blocks. In [18], the authors focus on a plausible association between blocks at the source and machine code level. They suggest that a plausible block mapping should respect dominator relations, and also consider paths when instrumenting the source code. In [19], source-level simulation was combined with machine-code analysis and abstract cache models to perform simulation-based analysis of data caches. The translation validation technique presented in [12] uses symbolic execution to verify that pairs of finite paths in the original and optimized code are equivalent. The necessary control-flow relation between the original and optimized IR code is obtained by associating every edge in the original program with either zero (branch was eliminated) or exactly one edge in the optimized code.

3. Control-Flow Relations

In order to relate the control-flow of IR-level and machine-code–level program representations, we investigate regular relations between control-flow graphs. Starting from this well-understood foundation, we develop the concept of CFRGs, a graph-theoretic model of control-flow relations.

3.1 Control Flow Representation

First, we briefly introduce standard notions concerning the representation of control-flow, which are used in the rest of the paper.

Definition 1. *A control flow graph (CFG) $\mathcal{G}$ is a 4-tuple $\langle V, E, s, t \rangle$; V is the set of control-flow nodes (or basic blocks), $E \subseteq V \times V$ the set of edges; $s \in V$ is the entry node, $t \in V$ the exit node.*

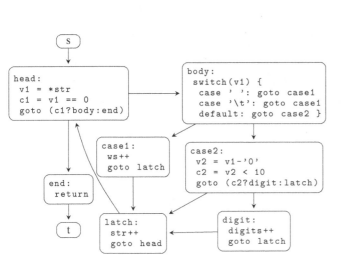

(a) IR-level CFG for the count function

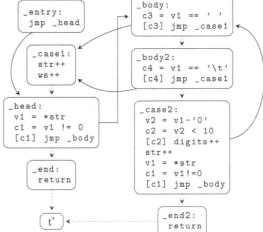

(b) Machine-code–level CFG after block layout; solid edges correspond to (conditional) jumps; predicates guarding the execution of an instruction are written in square brackets.

Figure 2: Running example demonstrating typical backend transformations

The purpose of the CFG abstraction is to model a superset of the possible paths through a function. Each node $v \in V$ corresponds to the execution of a sequence of instructions, and an edge $(v, v') \in E \subseteq V \times V$ to a possible transition of control from the last instruction of v to the first instruction of v'. For convenience, we introduce the distinguished entry node s and exit node t, which are the unique nodes without predecessors and successors, respectively.

Definition 2. *Given a set of nodes V and edges $E \subseteq V \times V$, a path $\pi \in P(v_1, v_n)$ from v_1 to v_n is a sequence $\langle e_1, e_2 \ldots, e_{n-1} \rangle$, such that $e_i = (v_i, v_{i+1}) \subseteq E$. The nodes v_1 and v_n are the first and the last node of π, and set $\{v_i \mid 1 < i < n\}$ contains the path's interior nodes.*

Given that $\mathcal{G}$ is a correct model of a function f, each execution of f (i.e., the sequence of instructions observed when executing the function in one particular environment) corresponds to one *execution path* from s to t. The set of all execution paths $P(s, t)$ thus characterizes the possible flow of control in $\mathcal{G}$, and is a superset of those paths corresponding to some execution of f.

The concatenation $\pi_1 \cdot \pi_2$ of two paths $\pi_1 = \langle e_1 \ldots e_{n-1} \rangle$ and $\pi_2 = \langle e_n \ldots e_{n+m} \rangle$ is defined *if* the last node of π_1 is equal to the first node of π_2 (i.e., $\pi_1 \in P(u, v)$ and $\pi_2 \in P(v, w)$). Then $\pi_1 \cdot \pi_2 \in P(u, w)$ is given by

$$\pi_1 \cdot \pi_2 = \langle e_1, \ldots, e_{n-1}, e_n, \ldots, e_{n+m} \rangle$$

The union of two path sets $P_1 \subseteq P(u, v)$ and $P_2 \subseteq P(u, v)$ is the usual set-theoretic union. For sets of paths $P_1 \subseteq P(u, v)$ and $P_2 \subseteq P(v, w)$, concatenation is defined as:

$$P_1 \cdot P_2 = \{\pi_1 \cdot \pi_2 \mid \pi_1 \in P_1, \pi_2 \in P_2\}$$

As a CFG can be interpreted as a finite-state automaton recognizing paths (i.e., sequences of adjacent edges), the set of all paths between two nodes is a regular expression over the alphabet of edges [20]. Therefore, the set of all structurally valid execution paths can be presented by a regular expression equivalent to $P(s, t)$.

3.2 Path Relations

In the following, we discuss relations between the flow of control in two CFGs. In our application context, $\mathcal{G}_b$ will be the CFG obtained from $\mathcal{G}_a$ by applying semantic-preserving compiler transformations. We consistently write $V_a, E_a, \ldots$ when we refer to elements of $\mathcal{G}_a$, and $V_b, E_b, \ldots$ to refer to constituents of $\mathcal{G}_b$. Objects which belong to the description of the control-flow relation, are decorated with a hat (e.g., $\hat{V}, \hat{E}$).

Definition 3. *Given two CFGs $\mathcal{G}_a$, $\mathcal{G}_b$, a path relation $\mathcal{R} \subseteq P(u_a, v_a) \times P(u_b, v_b)$ relates E_a-paths from u_a to v_a and E_b-paths from u_b to v_b.*

As the control flow modeled by a CFG is defined by the set of its execution paths $P(s, t)$, the relation between the flow of control in $\mathcal{G}_a$ and $\mathcal{G}_b$ is captured by a path relation $\mathcal{R} \subseteq P(s_a, t_a) \times P(s_b, t_b)$.

The composition of path relations relies on the usual definitions of concatenation and union on relations. However, similar to path sets, both concatenation and union are defined only if the resulting relation is again a path relation.

The union of two path relations $\mathcal{R}_1, \mathcal{R}_2 \subseteq P(u_a, v_a) \times P(u_b, v_b)$ is defined as the usual union operation on sets. Given two path relations $\mathcal{R}_1 \subseteq P(u_a, v_a) \times P(u_b, v_b)$ and $\mathcal{R}_2 \subseteq P(v_a, w_a) \times P(v_b, w_b)$, their concatenation is given by

$$\mathcal{R}_1 \cdot \mathcal{R}_2 = \{(\pi_a^1 \cdot \pi_a^2, \pi_b^1 \cdot \pi_b^2) \mid (\pi_a^1, \pi_b^1) \in \mathcal{R}_1, (\pi_a^2, \pi_b^2) \in \mathcal{R}_2\}$$

The class of path relations we focus on are *regular relations*, which include all finite relations between regular sets, and those relations built from regular relations using concatenation, union, and the Kleene closure [2].

A standard graph-theoretic model for regular relations are regular transducers. CFRGs, presented next, correspond to regular relations as well, but are closer to the usual CFG representation, ensure that the composition of relations is well-defined, and provide better opportunities for analyses operating on both representations. Furthermore, they are a well-suited representation to construct path relations from compiler information (see Section 4).

165

3.3 Control-Flow Relation Graphs

We now present CFRGs, which represent regular path relations (i.e., the subset of path relations which are regular relations) between CFGs.

Definition 4. *A control-flow relation graph $\hat{\mathcal{G}}$ that relates $\mathcal{G}_a$ and $\mathcal{G}_b$ is a 5-tuple $\langle \hat{V}, \hat{E}, \hat{s}, \hat{t}, \mathcal{L} \rangle$. The set of nodes $\hat{V} = \hat{V}_p \uplus \hat{V}_a \uplus \hat{V}_b$ is partitioned into a set of progress nodes $\hat{V}_p$, a set of source nodes $\hat{V}_a$ and a set of target nodes $\hat{V}_b$. The graph's edges $\hat{E} = \hat{E}_a \uplus \hat{E}_b$ consist of a set of source edges $\hat{E}_a \subseteq (\hat{V}_p \cup \hat{V}_a) \times (\hat{V}_p \cup \hat{V}_a)$, and a disjoint set of target edges $\hat{E}_b \subseteq (\hat{V}_p \cup \hat{V}_b) \times (\hat{V}_p \cup \hat{V}_b)$. The labeling function $\mathcal{L}$ is defined for progress nodes as an injective function $\hat{V}_p \to V_a \times V_b$ and for source and target nodes as (not necessarily injective) functions $\hat{V}_a \to V_a$ and $\hat{V}_b \to V_b$. The progress nodes $\hat{s} \in \hat{V}_p$ and $\hat{t} \in \hat{V}_p$ are the unique entry and exit nodes without predecessors and successors, respectively, with $\mathcal{L}(\hat{s}) = (s_a, s_b)$ and $\mathcal{L}(\hat{t}) = (t_a, t_b)$.*

Progress nodes, as their name indicates, ensure that progress in one representation is matched by progress in the other one, without forcing that the two representations proceed in a lock-step manner. Source and target nodes correspond to the execution of a basic block in $\mathcal{G}_a$ and $\mathcal{G}_b$ respectively, while progress nodes correspond to the execution of a basic block in both $\mathcal{G}_a$ and $\mathcal{G}_b$. Edges from $\hat{E}_a$ and $\hat{E}_b$ correspond to a change of control in the functions modeled by $\mathcal{G}_a$ and $\mathcal{G}_b$.

As $\hat{\mathcal{G}}$ models path relations, it also models execution paths from s_a to t_a (the first domain of the path relation) and paths from s_b to t_b (elements of the second domain). According to the definition of $\hat{\mathcal{G}}$, for every edge $\hat{e}_a = (\hat{v}_1, \hat{v}_2) \in \hat{E}_a$ there are two nodes $v_1, v_2 \in V_a$, such that $\hat{v}_1$ is labeled with v_1, and $\hat{v}_2$ is labeled with v_2. We write $\mathcal{L}(\hat{e}_a)$ for the corresponding edge $(v_1, v_2) \in E_a$, and symmetrically $\mathcal{L}(\hat{e}_b)$ for edges $e \in E_b$ corresponding to $\hat{e}_b$. The function $\mathcal{L}$ is extended to map $\hat{E}_a$-paths and $\hat{E}_b$-paths in the CFRG to E_a-paths and E_b-paths by

$$\mathcal{L}(\langle \hat{e}_1, \ldots, \hat{e}_n \rangle) = \langle \mathcal{L}(\hat{e}_1), \ldots, \mathcal{L}(\hat{e}_n) \rangle$$

The intuitive idea of the CFRG representation is the following: assume $\pi_a \in P(u_a, v_a)$ and $\pi_b \in P(u_b, v_b)$ are two related paths. The respective first and last node of π_a and π_b should be related as well, and thus need to correspond to progress nodes $\hat{u}$ and $\hat{v}$, with $\mathcal{L}(\hat{u}) = (u_a, u_b)$ and $\mathcal{L}(\hat{v}) = (v_a, v_b)$. In case there is no (modeled) relation between subpaths of π_a and π_b, there is a path of $\hat{E}_a$-edges $\hat{\pi}_a$ corresponding to π_a, and a path $\hat{\pi}_b$ corresponding to π_b, such that no interior node of $\hat{\pi}_a$ and $\hat{\pi}_b$ is a progress node. Conversely, if there are prefixes of π_a and π_b that are related, then there will be some progress node $\hat{w}$, such that the related prefixes of π_a and π_b have the first and second component of $\mathcal{L}(\hat{w})$ as their last nodes. Now the same considerations apply recursively to the related prefixes (from $\hat{u}$ to $\hat{w}$), and the related suffixes (from $\hat{w}$ to $\hat{v}$) of π_a and π_b.

Example 2. *Figure 3 visualizes the control-flow relation graph for the running example. There are eight progress nodes, each labeled with a pair of CFG nodes from Figure 2, four source nodes and two target nodes. One relation modeled by this CFRG is the one between the IR-level path $\pi_a = $ body $\to$ case1 $\to$ latch $\to$ head and the machine-code paths $\pi_b^1 = $ _body $\to$ _case1 $\to$ _head and $\pi_b^2 = $ _body $\to$ _body2 $\to$ _case1 $\to$ _head. Indeed, inspecting the respective CFGs, we see that every time the sequence π_a is executed at the IR-level, either π_b^1 or π_b^2 is executed on the machine-code level.*

The control-flow relation modeled by a CFRG is given in terms of (regular) path relations. To this end, we first define the *direct*

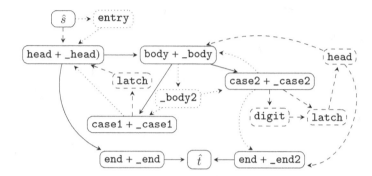

Figure 3: The control-flow relation graph for the running example. Progress nodes are drawn with solid shape, and labeled with with $v_a + v_b \in V_a \times V_b$. Source nodes are drawn with dashed, and target nodes with dotted shapes. Dashed lines correspond to source edges, dotted lines to target edges; we draw solid lines if there is both a source and target edge. Finally, $\hat{s}$ and $\hat{t}$ are the distinguished entry and exit node of the graph.

path relation $\mathcal{R}$ between two progress nodes $\hat{u}$ and $\hat{v}$. If $\hat{u}$ and $\hat{v}$ are labeled with (u_a, u_b) and (v_a, v_b), the direct path relation $\mathcal{R}(\hat{u}, \hat{v})$ is a regular path relation between $P(u_a, v_a)$ and $P(u_b, v_b)$. It includes every path pair (π_a, π_b) with the following properties: (1) there is a $\hat{E}_a$-path $\hat{\pi}_a$ and a $\hat{E}_b$-path $\hat{\pi}_b$ from $\hat{u}$ to $\hat{v}$ in the CFRG (2) no interior node of $\hat{\pi}_a$ and $\hat{\pi}_b$ is a progress node (3) $\mathcal{L}(\hat{\pi}_a) = \pi_a$ and $\mathcal{L}(\hat{\pi}_b) = \pi_b$.

Now the path relation $\mathcal{R}^*$ between any two progress nodes $\hat{v}_1$ and $\hat{v}_n$ is the union of

$$\langle \mathcal{R}(\hat{v}_1, \hat{v}_2) \cdot \ldots \cdot \mathcal{R}(\hat{v}_{n-1}, \hat{v}_n) \rangle$$

for all non-empty sequences of progress nodes $\langle \hat{v}_1, \ldots, \hat{v}_n \rangle$.

Note that $\mathcal{R}$ is the Cartesian product of two regular path sets, and is thus a regular path relation. As the set of all non-empty progress node sequences is regular as well, the path relation $\mathcal{R}^*$ modeled by $\hat{\mathcal{G}}$ is indeed regular.

In order to visualize the path relation, we use progress node graphs. They consist of all progress nodes of $\hat{\mathcal{G}}$, and edges labeled with regular path relations between them. Two progress nodes $\hat{v}_1$ and $\hat{v}_2$ are connected by an edge, if the corresponding direct path relation $\mathcal{R}(\hat{v}_1, \hat{v}_2)$ is non-empty.

Example 3. *In Figure 4, the progress node graph for the running example, and some of the path relations associated with its edges are displayed. In practice, the regular path relation between the execution paths of the IR-level and the machine-code level CFGs is calculated in two steps: First, the regular set describing the set of paths from the entry to the exit node in the progress graph is derived, in this case $A \cdot (B \cdot (E \cdot G)^* \cdot D \cdot F)^* \cdot (C \cdot J \cup B \cdot (E \cdot G)^* \cdot E \cdot H \cdot I)$. Second, each edge in this regular expression is substituted with the associated regular path relation (e.g., A by $\mathcal{R}(A)$), and $\cdot$ and $\cup$ are substituted with the corresponding operations on path relations. The resulting expression is an algebraic characterization of the path relation represented by the example's CFRG.*

As the CFRG representation is used to carry out conservative static analyses, it is obligatory to define when a CFRG is considered to be correct, that is, when it over-approximates the modeled implementations. Let $\mathcal{G}_a$ and $\mathcal{G}_b$ be control-flow models of two implementations of function f. A CFRG is a sound over-approximation, or simply correct, if it relates all pairs of execution paths $\pi_a \in P(s_a, t_a)$ and $\pi_b \in P(s_b, t_b)$ corresponding to one execution of f. In other words, to show that a CFRG $\hat{\mathcal{G}}$ is not correct,

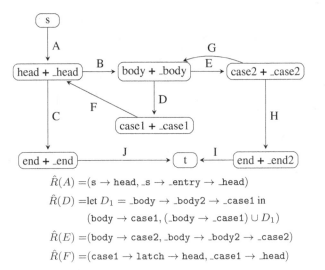

$$\hat{R}(A) = (\texttt{s} \to \texttt{head}, \texttt{\_s} \to \texttt{\_entry} \to \texttt{\_head})$$

$$\hat{R}(D) = \text{let } D_1 = \texttt{\_body} \to \texttt{\_body2} \to \texttt{\_case1} \text{ in}$$
$$(\texttt{body} \to \texttt{case1}, (\texttt{\_body} \to \texttt{\_case1}) \cup D_1)$$

$$\hat{R}(E) = (\texttt{body} \to \texttt{case2}, \texttt{\_body} \to \texttt{\_body2} \to \texttt{\_case2})$$

$$\hat{R}(F) = (\texttt{case1} \to \texttt{latch} \to \texttt{head}, \texttt{\_case1} \to \texttt{\_head})$$

Figure 4: Progress node graph for the CFRG of for the running example, and some of the regular relations associated with the graph's edges

one has to demonstrate an execution of f corresponding to π_a and π_b, such that π_a and π_b are not related by $\hat{\mathcal{G}}$.

By definition, if the execution paths π_a and π_b are related by $\hat{\mathcal{G}}$, then there is a non-empty sequence of progress nodes $\langle \hat{s}, \hat{v}_1, \ldots \hat{v}_{n-1}, \hat{t} \rangle$, such that

$$(\pi_a, \pi_b) \in \mathcal{R}(\hat{s}, \hat{v}_1) \cdot \ldots \cdot \mathcal{R}(\hat{v}_{n-1}, \hat{t})$$

Furthermore, if $(\pi_a, \pi_b) \in \mathcal{R}^*(\hat{s}, \hat{t})$, there is a $\hat{E}_a$-path $\hat{\pi}_a$ and a $\hat{E}_b$-path $\hat{\pi}_b$ from $\hat{s}$ to $\hat{t}$, such that $\mathcal{L}(\hat{\pi}_a) = \pi_a$, $\mathcal{L}(\hat{\pi}_b) = \pi_b$, and the subsequences of $\hat{\pi}_a$ and $\hat{\pi}_b$ obtained by deleting all non-progress nodes are equal.

4. Construction of Control-Flow Relation Graphs

The definition of a control-flow relation model is sufficient to discuss its theoretical properties, but in practice the hardest part concerns the integration with the rest of the compiler. The effort to keep a CFRG-based relation model up-to-date in the backend might be challenging even for compilers engineered with CFRG support in mind, and even more so for existing industrial-quality compiler frameworks such as LLVM.

Therefore, we develop an algorithm that allows to build CFRGs from partial event mappings, which need considerably less effort to be integrated into a compiler backend. Instead of assuming a CFRG is provided, we only require that the compiler provides a partial *mapping* function $\mathcal{M}$, from CFG nodes (both at the IR and machine-code level) to events.

The domain of the mapping function $\text{dom}(\mathcal{M}) \subseteq V_a \dot{\cup} V_b$ consists of all nodes in $V_a \cup V_b$ where $\mathcal{M}$ is defined, that is, those basic blocks which are associated with an event. The sequence of events associated with a path π_a is the sequence obtained from π_a by replacing (u_a, v_a) by the event e if $\mathcal{M}(v_a) = e$, and deleting (u_a, v_a) from π_a otherwise.

The mapping function $\mathcal{M}$ is correct, if for every pair of related execution paths (π_a, π_b), the same sequence of events is associated with π_a and π_b. Furthermore, we require that there are two distinguished events e_s and e_t, which are associated with the start nodes s_a and s_b and the end nodes t_a and t_b, respectively.

In our implementation (Section 6), the set of events is a subset of IR-level basic blocks. The correctness of the construction algorithm

---

Algorithm 1 CFRG Construction from a Partial Event Map

```
 1: procedure BUILDCFRG(𝒢ₐ,𝒢_b,ℳ)
 2:     ŝ, t̂ ← new progress node
 3:     V̂, Ê ← {ŝ,t̂}, {}
 4:     ℒ ← {ŝ ↦ (sₐ,s_b), t̂ ↦ (tₐ,t_b)}
 5:     while ∃v̂ ∈ V̂ₚ not yet expanded do
 6:         Expand(v̂,ℒ(v̂))
 7:     end while
 8:     return ⟨V̂, Ê, ŝ, t̂, ℒ⟩
 9: end procedure
```

present next, however, does not depend on this implementation choice, and is guaranteed to build a correct CFRG if $\mathcal{M}$ is correct.

4.1 Construction Algorithm

Let $\mathcal{G}_a$ and $\mathcal{G}_b$ be CFGs, and let $\mathcal{M}$ be a partial mapping from $V_a \cup V_b$ to events. To simplify notation, the variables pointing to components of the CFRG (i.e., $\hat{V}$, $\hat{E}$ and $\mathcal{L}$) are not passed as parameter to procedures explicitly, and should be considered as global variables.

The construction algorithm (Algorithm 1) starts with the entry node s_r, the unique progress node labeled with (s_a, s_b). It proceeds by expanding every progress node exactly once. As $\mathcal{L}$ is defined to be injective for progress nodes, there is at most one progress node for each pair of nodes in $V_a \times V_b$, and the loop in Line 5 terminates after at most $|V_a| |V_b|$ iterations.

The expansion step is given in Algorithm 2. It takes one progress node $\hat{v}$ labeled with (v_a, v_b), and expands the control-flow relation graph starting from this node.

First, the procedure ExpandUnmapped is called to process unmapped nodes reachable from v_a. It computes the set of nodes $S_a \subseteq V_a$, that includes v_a and all unmapped nodes u_a reachable from v_a in $\{v_a\} \cup (V_a \setminus \text{dom}(\mathcal{M}))$. Then ExpandUnmapped merges S_a into the CFRG: for every node $u_a \in (S_a \setminus \{v_a\})$, a corresponding source node $\hat{u}$ is added to $\hat{V}_a$, along with the label $\mathcal{L}(\hat{u}) = u_a$. For every edge $(u_a, w_a) \in S_a \times (S_a \setminus v_a)$, a source edge $(\hat{u}, \hat{w})$ between the corresponding CFRG nodes is inserted into $\hat{E}_a$. The procedure ExpandUnmapped is then called for v_b, which computes S_b and inserts nodes and edges in $\hat{V}_b$ and $\hat{E}_b$, respectively.

Second, SuccessorEvents groups the mapped successors of nodes in S_a by the associated event. Therefore, every node $w_a \in V_a \cap \text{dom}(\mathcal{M})$ that is a successor of some node in S_a is added to the list $W_a(\mathcal{M}(w_a))$. For $\mathcal{G}_b$, the call to SuccessorEvents groups the mapped successors of S_b.

Finally, for each event e in $W_a \cap W_b$, each pair of nodes in $w_a \in W_a(e)$ and $w_b \in W_b(e)$ is considered. The procedure GetProgressNode(w_a, w_b) checks whether there is a progress node $\hat{w} \in \hat{V}$ that is labeled with (w_a, w_b). If this is not the case, a new progress node $\hat{w}$ is created, with $\mathcal{L}(\hat{w}) = (w_a, w_b)$, otherwise the existing progress node is returned. Then, for each edge $(u_a, w_a) \in E_a$ and for each edge $(u_b, w_b) \in E_b$, corresponding edges are added to $\hat{E}_a$ and $\hat{E}_b$. Now that the progress node $\hat{v}$ has been expanded, it will not be considered again for expansion in Line 5 of Algorithm 1. Note that in this construction, progress nodes are always associated with exactly one event, namely $\mathcal{M}(w_a) = \mathcal{M}(w_b)$.

4.2 Correctness

In order to show the correctness of the construction algorithm, we need to show that if $\mathcal{M}$ is correct, $\hat{\mathcal{G}}$ is correct. This is established by the following theorem.

Algorithm 2 Expansion of a Progress Node

```
1:  procedure EXPANDPROGRESS(v̂,(vₐ,v_b))
2:      Sₐ ← ExpandUnmapped(vₐ,v̂)
3:      S_b ← ExpandUnmapped(v_b,v̂)
4:      Wₐ ← SuccessorEvents(Sₐ,v̂)
5:      W_b ← SuccessorEvents(S_b,v̂)
6:      for all Events e ∈ dom(Wₐ) ∩ dom(W_b) do
7:          for all (wₐ,w_b) ∈ Wₐ(e) × W_b(e) do
8:              ŵ ← GetProgressNode(wₐ,w_b)
9:              for all (uₐ,wₐ) ∈ Eₐ with uₐ ∈ Sₐ do
10:                  Êₐ ← Êₐ ∪ {(ûₐ,ŵ)}
11:             end for
12:             for all (u_b,w_b) ∈ E_b with u_b ∈ S_b do
13:                 Ê_b ← Ê_b ∪ {(û_b,ŵ)}
14:             end for
15:         end for
16:     end for
17: end procedure
```

Theorem 1. *The CFRG $\hat{\mathcal{G}}$ constructed by* BuildCFRG($\mathcal{M}$) *relates all pairs of execution paths (π_a, π_b) that are associated with the same sequence of events.*

Proof. First, we consider non-empty paths $\pi_a \in P(v_a^1, v_a^m)$ and $\pi_b \in P(v_b^1, v_b^n)$ where the first nodes of both paths are associated with event e_1, the last nodes with event e_2, and all interior nodes are not in the domain of $\mathcal{M}$. We show that if there is a progress node $\hat{v}$ with $\mathcal{L}(\hat{v}) = (v_a^1, v_b^1)$, then $\hat{\mathcal{G}}$ contains a progress node $\hat{w}$, with $\mathcal{L}(\hat{w}) = (v_a^m, v_b^n)$ and we have $(\pi_a, \pi_b) \in \mathcal{R}(\hat{v}, \hat{w})$.

As π_a is non-empty, it is of the form $\pi_a = \pi_a' \cdot (v_a^{m-1}, v_a^m)$. As the interior nodes of π_a are not in the domain of $\mathcal{M}$, $\forall 1 \leq i < m, v_a^i \in S_a$. Furthermore, all edges in π_a' are in $S_a \times (S_a \setminus \{v_a^1\})$. Consequently, the nodes and edges inserted by ExpandUnmapped($v_a^1, \hat{v}$) include a path of $\hat{E}_a$-edges corresponding to π_a'. The same argument applies to the path π_b and the call to ExpandUnmapped($v_b^1, \hat{v}$).

Because $v_a^{m-1} \in S_a$ and $v_b^{n-1} \in S_b$, SuccessorEvents adds v_a^m to $W_a(e_2)$ and v_b^n to $W_b(e_2)$. Therefore, $e_2 \in \text{dom}(W_a) \cap \text{dom}(W_b)$, and Line 8 in ExpandProgress ensures there is a progress node $\hat{w}$ with $\mathcal{L}(\hat{w}) = (v_a^m, v_b^n)$. Furthermore, edges corresponding to (v_a^{m-1}, v_a^m) and (v_b^{n-1}, v_b^n) are added to $\hat{E}_a$ and $\hat{E}_b$ in Line 10 and Line 13, respectively. At this point, there is an $\hat{E}_a$-path corresponding to π_a and an $\hat{E}_b$-path corresponding to π_b from $\hat{v}$ to $\hat{w}$ in $\hat{\mathcal{G}}$, and thus $(\pi_a, \pi_b) \in \mathcal{R}(\hat{v}, \hat{w})$.

Second, assume the two paths $\pi_a \in P(v_a^1, v_a^m)$ and $\pi_b \in P(v_b^1, v_b^n)$ generate the same sequence of events, and the first and last node are associated with events e_1 and e_n. We show that if there are progress nodes $\hat{v}$ labeled with v_a^1 and v_b^1 in $\hat{\mathcal{G}}$, then there is a progress node $\hat{w}$ such that $(\pi_a, \pi_b) \in \mathcal{R}^*(\hat{v}, \hat{w})$. We proceed by induction on the number of events associated with π_a and π_b. The base case with two events (there are at least two) was considered before. For the induction step, as there are at least three events associated with π_a and π_b, there are two minimal indices k and l such that the interior nodes v_a^k and v_b^l of π_a and π_b are associated with an event e_2. Let $\pi_a = \pi_a' \cdot \pi_a''$ and $\pi_b = \pi_b' \cdot \pi_b''$, with $\pi_a' \in P(v_a^1, v_a^k)$ and $\pi_b' \in P(v_b^1, v_b^l)$. As k and l are minimal, the interior nodes of π_a' and π_b' are not in $\text{dom}(\mathcal{M})$. Then, by the first part of the proof there is a progress node $\hat{u}$ with $\mathcal{L}(\hat{u}) = (v_a^k, v_b^l)$, such that $(\pi_a', \pi_b') \in \mathcal{R}(\hat{v}, \hat{u})$. For the path suffixes $\pi_a'' \in P(v_a^k, v_a^m)$ and $\pi_b'' \in P(v_b^l, v_b^n)$, the progress node $\hat{u}$ corresponds to the first nodes. As π_a'' and π_b'' are associated with one event less than π_a and π_b, the induction hypothesis applies. Consequently, $(\pi_a'', \pi_b'') \in \mathcal{R}^*(\hat{u}, \hat{w})$,

and thus

$$(\pi_a, \pi_b) \in \mathcal{R}(\hat{v}, \hat{u}) \cdot \mathcal{R}^*(\hat{u}, \hat{w}) = \mathcal{R}^*(\hat{v}, \hat{w})$$

Finally, given two execution paths π_a and π_b that are associated with the same sequence of events, the first and last nodes are associated with events corresponding to the CFRG's entry and exit node, respectively. Thus, by the second part of the proof, $(\pi_a, \pi_b) \in \mathcal{R}^*(\hat{s}, \hat{t})$, as required. □

4.3 Expressiveness

The least precise CFRG for $\mathcal{G}_a$ and $\mathcal{G}_b$ is obtained by the construction algorithm if the domain of the mapping $\mathcal{M}$ comprises the start and exit nodes only. The resulting CFRG relates all pairs of execution paths, and is always correct, albeit not very useful. At the other end of the spectrum, if there are isomorphisms $\mathcal{B}_1$ and $\mathcal{B}_2$ between the node sets V_a and V_b and the set of control-flow events, all of the corresponding CFRG's nodes are progress nodes, and the relation modeled by the CFRG is a isomorphism between execution paths.

We already demonstrated in the running example that CFRGs are able to deal with typical backend transformations found in contemporary compiler frameworks. The construction algorithm for CFRGs also supports several high-level loop optimizations, which are usually performed at the IR level. In Figure 5, we illustrate correct event mappings to relate program fragments transformed by loop peeling, loop unswitching and loop interchange.

The expressiveness of CFRGs is limited by the fact that they model regular relations, however. Regular relations are not capable of describing the global exchange of program fragments, which might result from the compiler reordering pure function calls, followed by inlining. Moreover, for some high-level optimizations such as loop interchange (see Figure 5), some precision is lost compared to flow fact transformation rules [9], as loop headers cannot be related precisely using regular relations.

Furthermore, there are compiler transformations which cannot be expressed by relating execution paths at all. For example, replacing a intermediate-representation instruction by a complex machine-code implementation (e.g., from a software floating-point library) cannot be captured in a control-flow relation.

In practice, the limitations concerning advanced optimizations are not an issue when relating IR-level code and machine code, as these optimizations are carried out on higher-level program representations. Dealing with program fragments which do not have a corresponding representation at the IR level (such as calls to a software floating-point library) is more challenging. At the moment, we do not use information from the IR-level for this code, and thus flow information has to be specified at the machine-code level for functions in the compiler's runtime library.

Finally, an aspect of interprocedural analyses not treated here is the relation between the possible targets of indirect calls. We consider this to be a separate problem, and require that the relation between call sites (of indirect calls) is provided by the compiler.

5. WCET Analysis on Control-Flow Relation Graphs

In this section, we present applications of CFRGs, focusing on WCET calculation and the transformation of flow facts. In general, CFRGs appear to be a suitable representation for those static analyses which depend on both IR and machine code properties. For example, dataflow analysis to classify instruction cache accesses [21] could use control-flow information available for IR code (e.g., that a certain transition is never taken in some context) to refine the results for machine code. WCET calculation depends on the maximal execution frequency of basic blocks (easier to derive at the IR level) and an upper bound on the the execution time needed for

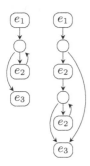 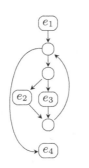 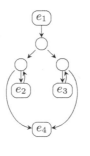 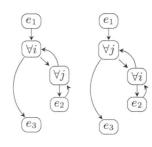

(a) Loop peeling duplicates the loop body associated with event e_2

(b) Loop unswitching moves a loop-invariant conditional branch outside the loop

(c) Loop interchange exchanges the inner and outer loop

Figure 5: Expressiveness of CFRGs: Modeling Loop Transformations using Events

each basic block (only available at the machine code level). CFRGs also permit to transform control-flow related information from one representation to the other. As an example, we will present a novel technique for transforming flow facts from the IR level to machine code, which is necessary if one wants to reuse existing analysis tools operating on the machine code level.

Obviously, the control-flow relation model needs to be correct in order to guarantee that the static analyses carried out on the hybrid control-flow model are sound. We thus will always assume that either a correct control-flow relation graph or a correct event mapping (as discussed in the previous section) is provided by the compiler.

5.1 WCET Calculation

Static Worst-Case Execution Time (WCET) analysis is concerned with calculating the maximum time it may take to execute a program. The corresponding formal problem for flow graphs asks for the maximum cost over all valid paths, given a set of flow constraints and a cost function for edges.

Flow constraints are predicates on the frequency of CFG edges, and provide additional control-flow information.

Given a CFG $\mathcal{G}$, a (linear) flow constraint is a linear inequality

$$\sum_{1 \le i \le n} a_i f(e_i) \le B$$

where $e_i \in E$, $f(e_i)$ is the execution frequency of edge e_i, and $a_i, B \in \mathbb{Z}$ are constants. Given a path π, $f(e_i)$ evaluates to the number of occurrences of e_i on π, and π satisfies the flow constraint if the linear inequality holds on π. Finally, a path π is said to be valid with respect to a set of flow constraints C if it satisfies all corresponding inequalities. A path that does not satisfy some flow constraint is infeasible, i.e., it does not correspond to any execution trace, according to the semantics of the program.

The IPET model for a WCET problem is an integer linear program (ILP) maximizing the total cost of all edges, with constraints corresponding to structural constraints (derived from the graph structure) and the given flow constraints [13]. The solution of an IPET problem is the optimal value of the corresponding ILP, which exists if (a) there is a feasible path through the graph and (b) the execution frequency of all edges is bounded above.

The ILP to calculate the WCET is constructed as follows: There is a variable $f(e) \ge 0$ for all edges $e \in E$. For all nodes $v \in V \setminus \{s, t\}$, there is one structural constraint $\sum_{e \in \text{In}(v)} f(e) = \sum_{e \in \text{Out}(v)} f(e)$, where $\text{In}(v)$ and $\text{Out}(v)$ are the ingoing and outgoing edges of v, respectively. For the entry and exit node, the structural constraint is $\sum_{e \in \text{Out}(s)} f(e) = \sum_{e \in \text{In}(t)} f(e) = 1$. The ILP's objective is to maximize $\sum_{e \in E} c_e f(e)$, where c_e

is the cost of executing edge e, subject to structural constraints and flow constraints. In practice, the calculation operates on an interprocedural callgraph, and needs to be context-sensitive to be precise. To simplify matters, we assume that the necessary virtual inlining and virtual unrolling [21] has already taken place, and leave out the formalization of the interprocedural problem. Our implementation (Section 6) does support interprocedural analysis, though.

5.2 WCET Analysis on Control-Flow Relation Graphs

In the following, we will assume that the CFRG $\hat{\mathcal{G}}$ relates the control flow of the IR-level CFG $\mathcal{G}_a$ and the machine-code level CFG $\mathcal{G}_b$. During static WCET analysis, one would preferably combine control-flow information available for the IR representation, and both control-flow and cost information (execution time) for the machine code representation. The combined WCET calculation problem considered here asks for the maximum execution time of a function, given two sets of flow constraints C_a and C_b (with respect to $\mathcal{G}_a$ and $\mathcal{G}_b$), and execution time bounds for each edge E_b.

The combined ILP model constructs the ILP problem for $\mathcal{G}_a$ and $\mathcal{G}_b$, and adds the respective constraints, and the costs $c(e)$ for edges in $\mathcal{G}_b$. The variables corresponding to edges in E_a and E_b are then related, using constraints derived from the CFRG:

- For each CFRG edge $\hat{e}$, there is one ILP variable $f(\hat{e}) \ge 0$

- As for every pair of execution paths π_a and π_b there is a corresponding $\hat{E}_a$-path and $\hat{E}_b$-path in the CFRG, the flow needs to be preserved for $\hat{E}_a$ and $\hat{E}_b$ edges. Therefore, for all CFRG nodes $\hat{v}$ it holds that

$$\sum_{\{\hat{e} \in \hat{E}_a | \hat{e} \in \text{In}(\hat{v})\}} f(\hat{e}) = \sum_{\{\hat{e} \in \hat{E}_a | \hat{e} \in \text{Out}(\hat{v})\}} f(\hat{e}) \quad (1)$$

$$\sum_{\{\hat{e} \in \hat{E}_b | \hat{e} \in \text{In}(\hat{v})\}} f(\hat{e}) = \sum_{\{\hat{e} \in \hat{E}_b | \hat{e} \in \text{Out}(\hat{v})\}} f(\hat{e}) \quad (2)$$

- The frequency of each edge $e_a \in E_a$ and $e_b \in E_b$ is equal to the sum of the corresponding CFRG edge's frequencies:

$$\sum_{\{\hat{e} \in \hat{E}_a | \mathcal{L}(\hat{e}) = e_a\}} f(\hat{e}) = f(e_a) \quad (3)$$

$$\sum_{\{\hat{e} \in \hat{E}_b | \mathcal{L}(\hat{e}) = e_b\}} f(\hat{e}) = f(e_b) \quad (4)$$

- As for every execution run there is a corresponding sequence of progress nodes, the sum of the outgoing source and target edges' frequencies have to match. So for each progress node

v_p, there is a constraint

$$\sum_{\{\hat{e}_a \in \hat{E}_a | \hat{e}_a \in \mathrm{Out}(v_p)\}} f(\hat{e}_a) = \sum_{\{\hat{e}_b \in \hat{E}_b | \hat{e}_b \in \mathrm{Out}(v_p)\}} f(\hat{e}_b) \quad (5)$$

As execution costs are provided for $\mathcal{G}_b$ only, the objective of the combined ILP is to maximize $\sum_{e \in E_b} c_e f(e)$. The solution of the combined ILP problem then provides a WCET bound for the function modeled by $\hat{\mathcal{G}}$.

In order to calculate a finite WCET bound for a non-recursive function modeled by $\mathcal{G}$, it is sufficient to provide a bound on the number of times each loop body is executed. Conversely, if all loop bounds are known, it is expected that the WCET calculation provides a WCET bound, that is, that the corresponding ILP is not unbounded. Thus the following question is of significant practical interest: What are sufficient conditions to obtain a finite WCET bound for a CFRG $\hat{\mathcal{G}}$, if the frequency of all edges in $\mathcal{G}_a$ is bounded above by the set of given flow constraints, but no constraints for $\mathcal{G}_b$ are known? The following theorem provides an answer:

Proposition 1. *Let $\mathcal{G}_a$ and $\mathcal{G}_b$ be the CFGs related by $\hat{\mathcal{G}}$, and let C be a set of flow constraints on $\mathcal{G}_a$. If there are no cycles in the CFRG that consist of $\hat{E}_b$-edges only, and the set of given flow constraints C on E_a implies that the maximum frequency of all edges in E_a is finite, then the solution of the combined IPET for $\hat{\mathcal{G}}$ is bounded.*

Proof. Suppose the solution assigns infinite frequency to some edge in E_b. Then by one of the equations in (4), it assigns infinite frequency to at least one edge in $\hat{E}_b$. By the flow preservation constraints for $\hat{E}_b$ edges in (2), the solution then assigns infinite frequency to at least one cycle of $\hat{E}_b$ edges in the CFRG. As this cycle contains at least one progress node by assumption, the frequency of at least one outgoing edge of a progress node is unbounded. By the equations in (5) the frequency of one of the edges in $\hat{E}_a$ is unbounded as well, and thus by (1) the frequency of one of the edges in E_a. But this contradicts the assumption that the frequency of all edges $\mathcal{G}_a$ is bounded above. □

5.3 Flow Fact Transformation

To leverage the strength of existing industrial WCET analysis tools, which necessarily carry out the WCET analysis directly on the machine code, flow facts have to be provided on machine code only. The set of constraints used in the previous section on WCET analysis contains edges from both the source representation $\mathcal{G}_a$ and the target representation $\mathcal{G}_b$, and therefore cannot be used directly in such tools.

However, when considering the ILP problem for the CFRG, edges $e \notin E_b$ can be eliminated using Fourier-Motzkin elimination [4]. An edge e is eliminated as follows: if e appears in an equation $e = T$, replace all occurrences of e by T. Otherwise, partition the set of constraints where e appears into a set of lower bounds C_L of the form $T_L \leq e$ and a set of upper bounds C_U of the form $e \leq T_U$. Then add the constraints $T_L \leq T_U$ for all $T_L, T_U \in C_L \times C_U$, and remove the original constraints and variable e from the problem.

This approach is most precise in the sense that the resulting problem is equivalent to the combined ILP – as the cost of all edges in E_a is zero, eliminating them from the set of constraints does not change the optimum value of the ILP.

Example 4. *Consider again the running example, and assume that the frequency $f(\mathtt{head})$ is bounded by N. In this case,*

$$\mathtt{head} \to \mathtt{body} \leq N - 1$$

holds in $\mathcal{G}_a$. By the equations in (3), the sum of the two incoming $\hat{E}_a$-edges of $(\mathtt{body+\_body})$ is bounded by $N - 1$. By the flow preservation constraints from (1), the frequency of the $\hat{E}_a$-edges

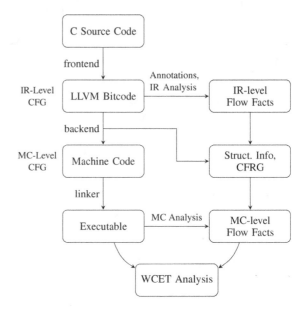

Figure 6: The compilation flow from the C source files to the WCET analysis.

outgoing from the progress node $(\mathtt{body} + \mathtt{\_body})$ is bounded by the same constant. Then, by the progress node constraints in (5), the frequency sum of outgoing $\hat{E}_b$-edges from this progress node is bounded by $N - 1$, and thus by (2) the frequency of the V_b-node $\mathtt{\_body}$:

$$\mathtt{\_body} \leq N - 1$$

It is then easy to verify that the combined ILP problem indeed has a solution.

6. Implementation

Figure 6 illustrates the compilation process using our tool chain, which is based on the LLVM compiler framework.[1]

First, the frontend translates each of the C source code files from the high-level program representation to *bitcode*, the intermediate representation of LLVM. At this level, the program is linked to a single bitcode module, containing both the user application as well as system and support libraries, and providing subsequent compiler passes a complete view of the program. After generic, target-independent optimizations on the bitcode level, the module is handed to our version of the compiler backend where it is translated to the specific machine code of the Patmos [16] architecture, performing further low-level transformations and code optimizations during the process.

At the end of the code-generation phase, in addition to the machine-code object file, we emit both the IR-level CFGs and the machine-code level CFGs, as well as the CFRGs, which we obtain using the construction algorithm of Section 4 and utilizing a mapping between basic blocks as described below. Finally, the object file is linked to obtain an executable with the final memory layout, and the actual addresses of machine basic blocks are extracted from the linked binary.

The final executable is subject to WCET analysis, in which flow constraints from both the bitcode level and the machine code level are considered. Our implementation prototype includes an interprocedural WCET calculation, using $\mathtt{lp\_solve}$ for solving the

---

[1] Our compilation tool chain is open source and available at https://github.com/t-crest/.

Table 1: Evaluation of CFRGs

Benchmark	$|V_a|$	$|V_b|$	$|u(V_b)|$	$|\hat{V}|$	T_b	$\frac{\hat{T}-T_b}{T_b}$
adpcm	18	20	20.0%	27	1489K	0%
base64	50	54	24.1%	139	45598	0%
bsort100	10	11	9.1%	12	111K	0%
compress	30	32	18.8%	39	5188	0%
cover	16	19	15.8%	20	1118	0%
edn	20	22	9.1%	23	82409	0%
fft1	12	11	18.2%	19	59094	0%
jumptable	15	17	35.3%	23	1435	2.0%
lcdnum	21	22	4.5%	23	139	0.0%
lift	62	62	14.5%	74	19383	0.23%
lms	42	36	13.9%	50	6757K	0.0%
ludcmp	37	39	12.8%	43	59642	0.05%
matmult	13	15	13.3%	16	62823	0%
minver	28	27	14.8%	34	11441	0%
ndes	37	26	15.4%	43	38578	0.04%
nsichneu	753	501	0.0%	754	7009	0%
qurt	14	9	11.1%	16	21840	0%
select	22	15	6.7%	24	4056	0%
statemate	18	17	17.6%	22	229	0%
other	≤ 10	≤ 10	$\leq 30\%$	≤ 11	-	0%

ILPs, and an implementation of Fourier-Motzkin elimination to transform flow facts. For the latter, it was necessary to normalize constraints and remove duplicates, in order to keep the number of generated constraints within reasonable limits.

LLVM provides facilities to maintain a partial mapping $\mathcal{B}$ from machine basic blocks to IR-level basic blocks. We use $\mathcal{B}$ to construct the control-flow event mapping $\mathcal{M}$ as follows: The node v_a^i in the IR-level CFG $\mathcal{G}_a$ is associated with a control-flow event e^i (i.e., $\mathcal{M}(v_a^i) = e^i$) if and only if v_a^i is in the range of $\mathcal{B}$. On the machine-code level, we set $\mathcal{M}(v_b^j) = e^i$ if $\mathcal{B}(v_b^j) = v_a^i$. Thus every machine-code block that is in the domain of $\mathcal{B}$ is associated with the same event as the corresponding bitcode-level block.

It was also necessary to carry out minor modifications to the compiler backend's construction of $\mathcal{B}$. In particular, the update of $\mathcal{B}$ during the *tail merging* optimization had to be modified. This optimization pass introduces a new machine basic block which corresponds to suffixes (tails) of two different blocks before the optimization. As $\mathcal{B}$ associates a machine basic block with at most one bitcode basic block, $\mathcal{B}$ has to be undefined for these newly introduced blocks.

7. Evaluation

The goal of the evaluation is to assess the preciseness of the CFRG models in practice, and to obtain insights on the size of CFRGs and the number of constraints generated by our flow-fact transformation technique. We calculate the WCET of standard benchmarks from the WCET community, using bitcode-level flow facts on the one hand, and machine-code–level flow facts on the other hand. In order to achieve meaningful results, we need to obtain comparable sets of flow facts on the bitcode and machine-code level. Furthermore, the flow facts used in the evaluation should reference the frequency of all blocks; if flow facts are limited to loop bounds and information on infeasible program fragments, we did not observe any differences. An effective way to obtain flow facts for evaluation purposes is to use flow-fact generation from execution traces. For deterministic benchmarks, there is exactly one feasible execution paths, and thus the flow facts extracted from bitcode traces and machine-code traces are both precise characterizations of the benchmark run.

The evaluation proceeds as follows: First, each benchmark is compiled following the procedure as described in Section 6, resulting in bitcode, the linked binary containing machine code, and an external file containing the information available in the compiler (including the CFRG).

For compilation, the default optimization level (-O2) is used, which enables the optimizations tail duplication, branch folding, tail merging and if-conversion, which modify the structure of the CFG. Besides optimizations, differences in the structure of the CFGs stem from the fact that some bitcode instructions require the compiler to introduce additional basic blocks. A notable example is the switch-statement, which is lowered in different ways, depending on the number of cases as well as the range and the density of the case label values [1].

In a second step, we generate flow facts for bitcode and machine code. For the former, the bitcode is translated to the input format of SWEET [7]. SWEET subsequently produces a large number of different types of flow facts, including loop bounds and bounds of block frequencies relative to the benchmark's entry function, which are used in the evaluation. For machine code, we generate a trace using the simulator for the Patmos architecture, and then analyze this trace. This analysis is a simpler form of the one SWEET provides, specialized for a single trace. In addition to loop bounds, the trace analysis extracts upper bounds for block frequencies, and possible targets of indirect calls.

The WCET calculation itself is carried out twice for each binary, once with machine-code flow facts, and once with bitcode flow facts and the CFRG constraints presented in Section 5. As the evaluation deals with WCET calculation, not low-level timing analysis, we settled for a simple timing model, assuming a cost of one cycle per instruction. Different low-level timing models would only change the cost model that is used for both WCET estimates. The ILP solver managed to solve every problem in less than half a second.

We investigated 30 out of 35 benchmarks from the MRTC benchmarks for WCET analysis [8], excluding those benchmarks that are not supported by the bitcode analysis toolchain. Additionally, we evaluated the C-port of the `Lift` benchmark from Jem-Bench [15], and a microbenchmark (`jumptable`), as they feature interesting switch statements not found in the MRTC suite.

Table 1 summarizes the results of the evaluation. $|V_a|$ and $|V_b|$ give the total number of basic blocks in the bitcode and machine code CFGs, respectively. The column $|u(V_b)|$ shows the percentage of unmapped machine-code basic blocks, that is, the percentage of blocks not in the domain of $\mathcal{B}$. $|\hat{V}|$ corresponds to the total number of relation graph nodes. In the column labeled with T_b, the WCET using machine-code flow facts is given. The column labeled $(\hat{T} - T_b)/T_b$ shows the increase of the calculated WCET bound when using bitcode flow facts and the CFRG equations, relative to T_b.

In order to assess the flow-fact transformation technique presented in Section 5.3, the constraints extracted from the machine-code traces are transformed to bitcode, and then back again to machine code. The number of constraints in the resulting ILP problem ranged from 0.8 to 1.2 times the size of the original problem. The results for WCET analysis using the resulting flow facts gave similar results as in the first evaluation, with an increase of at most 1.53% when using transformed flow facts instead of the original ones.

Discussion The percentage of unmapped machine-code basic blocks, that is, those blocks not in the domain of $\mathcal{B}$, is an indicator for the (local) uncertainty in the initial control-flow mapping provided by the compiler. Although in theory the size of a CFRG need not be linear in the number of basic blocks, in the evaluation it turned out to be at most twice as large.

Due to relying solely on a control-flow abstraction, using IR-level flow facts instead of flow facts on the machine code level potentially weakens the knowledge about the possible flow-of-control in the program, even if mapping information provided by the compiler is precise. In our evaluation, however, for most benchmarks investigated, bitcode flow-facts were as precise as machine-code flow facts. In those benchmarks where we found small differences (e.g., `lift`), this was due to the lowering of switch statements, in combination with control-flow optimizations.

8. Conclusion

In this article, we presented a solution to the fine-grained control-flow mapping problem suitable for static analyses, relating bitcode (LLVM's intermediate representation) and machine code. We introduced control-flow relation graphs (CFRGs) and presented a construction algorithm given a partial mapping between basic blocks. The combined WCET calculation algorithm takes flow information from both bitcode and machine code into account, and thus permits the reuse of flow information only available in higher-level representations. We implemented both the CFRG construction and the WCET calculation using the LLVM compiler framework, and evaluated the preciseness of the model using flow constraints obtained from bitcode analysis and an instruction set simulator, respectively.

The evaluation revealed that CFRGs are typically linear in the size of the corresponding bitcode and machine code CFGs. For most benchmarks, there was no relevant loss of information if bitcode instead of machine-code flow information was used to calculate the WCET. The maximum difference in the WCET observed was below 2%, for all benchmarks investigated.

In the future, we want to complement the method presented in this article with other techniques to support high-level optimizations not captured by our model. This will eventually allow to transform flow facts given at the source-code level to machine code. The ultimate goal is to eliminate the need for users to manually analyze machine code, which is essential to establish WCET analysis in the development process of embedded systems.

Acknowledgments

This work was partially funded under the European Union's 7th Framework Programme under grant agreement no. 288008: Time-predictable Multi-Core Architecture for Embedded Systems (T-CREST).

References

[1] R. L. Bernstein. Producing good code for the case statement. *Software: Practice and Experience*, 15(10):1021–1024, 1985.

[2] J. Berstel. *Transductions and context-free languages*, volume 4. Teubner Stuttgart, 1979.

[3] A. Bouchhima, P. Gerin, and F. Petrot. Automatic instrumentation of embedded software for high level hardware/software co-simulation. In *Design Automation Conference, 2009. ASP-DAC 2009. Asia and South Pacific*, pages 546–551, Jan. 2009.

[4] A. R. Bradley and Z. Manna. *The Calculus of Computation: Decision Procedures with Applications to Verification*. Springer-Verlag New York, Inc., Secaucus, NJ, USA, 2007.

[5] J. Engblom, A. Ermedahl, and P. Altenbernd. Facilitating worst-case execution times analysis for optimized code. In *Proceedings of the 10th Euromicro Workshop on Real-Time Systems*, pages 146–153, June 1998.

[6] H. Falk and P. Lokuciejewski. A compiler framework for the reduction of worst-case execution times. *Real-Time Systems*, pages 1–50, 2010.

[7] J. Gustafsson, A. Ermedahl, C. Sandberg, and B. Lisper. Automatic derivation of loop bounds and infeasible paths for wcet analysis using

abstract execution. In *Proceedings of the 27th IEEE International Real-Time Systems Symposium*, RTSS, pages 57–66, Washington, DC, USA, 2006. IEEE Computer Society.

[8] J. Gustafsson, A. Betts, A. Ermedahl, and B. Lisper. The Mälardalen WCET benchmarks – past, present and future. pages 137–147, Brussels, Belgium, July 2010. OCG.

[9] R. Kirner, P. Puschner, and A. Prantl. Transforming flow information during code optimization for timing analysis. *Real-Time Systems*, 45: 72–105, 2010. ISSN 0922-6443. 10.1007/s11241-010-9091-8.

[10] C. Lattner and V. Adve. LLVM: a compilation framework for lifelong program analysis transformation. In *Code Generation and Optimization, 2004. CGO 2004. International Symposium on*, pages 75–86, march 2004.

[11] A. Mok, P. Amerasinghe, M. Chen, and K. Tantisirivat. Evaluating tight execution time bounds of programs by annotations. *IEEE Real-Time Syst. Newsl.*, 5(2-3):81–86, May 1989.

[12] G. C. Necula. Translation validation for an optimizing compiler. In *Proceedings of the ACM SIGPLAN 2000 conference on Programming language design and implementation*, PLDI '00, pages 83–94, New York, NY, USA, 2000. ACM.

[13] P. P. Puschner and A. V. Schedl. Computing maximum task execution times - a graph-based approach. *Real-Time Systems*, 13(1):67–91, 1997.

[14] J. Schnerr, O. Bringmann, A. Viehl, and W. Rosenstiel. High-performance timing simulation of embedded software. In *Design Automation Conference, 2008. DAC 2008. 45th ACM/IEEE*, pages 290–295, june 2008.

[15] M. Schoeberl, T. B. Preußer, and S. Uhrig. The embedded Java benchmark suite JemBench. In *Proceedings of the 8th International Workshop on Java Technologies for Real-Time and Embedded Systems*, JTRES '10, pages 120–127, New York, NY, USA, 2010. ACM.

[16] M. Schoeberl, P. Schleuniger, W. Puffitsch, F. Brandner, C. W. Probst, S. Karlsson, and T. Thorn. Towards a time-predictable dual-issue microprocessor: The Patmos approach. In *First Workshop on Bringing Theory to Practice: Predictability and Performance in Embedded Systems (PPES 2011)*, pages 11–20, March 2011.

[17] C. Sinz, F. Merz, and S. Falke. LLBMC: A bounded model checker for LLVM's intermediate representation (competition contribution). In C. Flanagan and B. König, editors, *Proceedings of the 18th International Conference on Tools and Algorithms for the Construction and Analysis of Systems (TACAS '12)*, pages 542–544. Springer-Verlag, 2012.

[18] S. Stattelmann, O. Bringmann, and W. Rosenstiel. Dominator homomorphism based code matching for source-level simulation of embedded software. In *Proceedings of the seventh IEEE/ACM/IFIP international conference on Hardware/software codesign and system synthesis*, CODES+ISSS '11, pages 305–314, New York, NY, USA, 2011. ACM.

[19] S. Stattelmann, G. Gebhard, C. Cullmann, O. Bringmann, and W. Rosenstiel. Hybrid source-level simulation of data caches using abstract cache models. In *Design, Automation Test in Europe Conference Exhibition (DATE), 2012*, pages 376–381, Mar. 2012.

[20] R. E. Tarjan. A unified approach to path problems. *J. ACM*, 28(3): 577–593, July 1981.

[21] H. Theiling, C. Ferdinand, and R. Wilhelm. Fast and precise WCET prediction by separate cache and path analyses. *Real-Time Systems*, 18(2/3), 2000.

[22] Z. Wang and J. Henkel. Accurate source-level simulation of embedded software with respect to compiler optimizations. In *Design, Automation Test in Europe Conference Exhibition (DATE), 2012*, pages 382–387, Mar. 2012.

[23] F. Zuleger, S. Gulwani, M. Sinn, and H. Veith. Bound analysis of imperative programs with the size-change abstraction. In E. Yahav, editor, *Static Analysis*, volume 6887 of *Lecture Notes in Computer Science*, pages 280–297. Springer Berlin / Heidelberg, 2011.

Author Index